THE SECOND MISSISSIPPI INFANTRY REGIMENT

An Introduction to the Full Annotated Roster

MICHAEL R. BRASHER

Copyright © 1994-2021 by Michael R. Brasher. All rights reserved.

Version 2.0

No part of this book may be reproduced in any form or by any electronic or mechanical means, including information storage and retrieval systems, without written permission from the author, except for the use of brief quotations in a book review.

ISBN: 978-1-7342165-3-0

To Private Thomas Benton Weatherington, Company H, 2nd Mississippi Infantry Regiment (my great-grandfather), and his older brother Private George Washington Weatherington, Company H, 2nd Mississippi Infantry Regiment.

Table of Contents

Preface	viii
Background and Introduction	- 1 -
2nd Mississippi Alphabetical Roster	19
Adair, Oliver J.	19
Bachas, F. W.	30
Caldwell, Elijah B.	75
Dacus, David D.	104
Eaker, Moses J.	122
Falkner, James W.	130
Gailliard, William	145
Haggarty, W.	164
Inman, Henry A. J.	199
Jackson, Andrew	200
Kantenbuger, P.	211
Lafarge, Henry	220
Mabry, Thomas T.	240
Nance, John O.	284
O'Connell, James	294
Paden, William D.	298
Quillin, Henderson	317
Raby, James H.	317
Salmon, Richard T.	339
Tabler, John W. H.	379
Usher, John D.	394
Vairin, Augustus L. P.	394
Wade, James L.	397
Yancey, Robert L.	428
The 2nd Mississippi Roll of Honor Introduction	431
2nd Mississippi Roll of Honor Listing	433
Bibliography	437

About the Author 443

Also by Michael R. Brasher 445

THE SECOND MISSISSIPPI INFANTRY REGIMENT

An Introduction to the Full Annotated Roster

"The Fight for the Colors" Corporal Frank Waller of the Sixth Wisconsin and Corporal William Murphy of the Second Mississippi struggle for possession of the Confederate colors at the Railroad Cut at Gettysburg on July 1, 1863. (Don Troiani Historical Art Prints. Used by permission.)

Preface

There have been many regimental histories written since the end of our terrible Civil War. Many deserving regiments, Union and Confederate, and perhaps some less deserving, have been immortalized by various authors. Most, if not all, at least have had several paragraph-length narratives summarizing their activities in various Union and Confederate unit compilations. The latter, unfortunately, is all that exists for the hard-fighting 2nd Mississippi Infantry Volunteers, which is surprising. By all accounts the regiment was one of General Lee's "go-to" units whenever the action got the hottest. Its sister regiment from Mississippi, the 11th Mississippi Infantry Volunteers, has had a well-researched and well-written history in existence for the last 20 years or so – a tome of almost 1,000 pages (*Duty-Honor-Valor: The Story of the Eleventh Mississippi Infantry Regiment*). It is an excellent history. I bought one of the first copies when it was first published. I would never disparage the 11th Mississippi, but the 2nd Mississippi's combat record was just as impressive, if not as well documented.

I have been researching the 2nd Mississippi Infantry Regiment for over 25 years now. I have gathered tons of material and have compiled portions into various essays, an old (now archived) web site, and blog posts. However, this is my first attempt at putting the information into book form and publishing it.

I finally "bit the bullet" and decided I was probably never going to create a regimental history like that of the 11th Mississippi's. A thousand pages is just too much for me to bite off all at once. To use an old expression, I have to "eat the elephant one bite at a time." So, the first "bite" of the elephant is this publication. I thought the first piece should be the introduction and annotated roster of the 2nd Mississippi. More of the regimental history will follow, but this is the first piece. I hope this will give those readers, especially those with ancestors that served in the regiment, useful information from a genealogical standpoint.

I also decided to self-publish this first part of the regimental history as a free PDF e-book, and not go my usual Amazon self-publishing route and charge for it. The regimental history of the 2nd Mississippi is truly a labor of love for me. No amount of money could ever compensate for the number of hours of "blood, sweat, and tears" that went into the research. And, had I charged for the roster information contained herein, it may have prevented some descendants of members of the 2nd Mississippi and other interested individuals from purchasing because of the price.

Having said that however, I have included as part of the back matter of the book, links to my Amazon page and a listing of my other publications. If you do have an interest in any of these other topics, please do browse through the descriptions and pick up a copy through Amazon. I would be most appreciative for your monetary support also.

Background and Introduction

> An Army is not merely a large aggregation of men with guns in their hands. To make an army, you must have men and you must have guns, but there is an additional, intangible ingredient which is the deciding factor in its success or failure. An army has a personality. It has a character of its own, totally aside from the character of the individuals who compose it. – Stanley F. Horn, *The Army of Tennessee*[1]

Representing a microcosm of the army of which it is the basic building block, the Civil War regiment also epitomizes these words of Stanley Horn. Although there existed, of course, famous brigades, divisions, and even corps, the individual Confederate fighting man always identified most closely with his regiment. This is an introduction to the story of one such regiment, the 2nd Mississippi Infantry Volunteers, that served in the Army of Northern Virginia. It fought in most of the Virginia army's major battles, being detached and absent only at Fredericksburg and Chancellorsville. The 2nd Mississippi met its final demise a week before Lee's surrender at Appomattox when it was overwhelmed by the Federal breakthrough of the Petersburg defenses on April 2, 1865 along the banks of a stream called Hatcher's Run (see Figure 1).

Although the regiment has a character of its own, apart from the individuals who comprise its ranks, the characteristics of those individuals are important to gain a full understanding of its history. Just who were the individuals who flocked to the banner of the 2nd Mississippi? Unfortunately for historians, the men of the regiment were apparently of the belief that "actions speak louder than words." Primary source material is scarce. For a variety of reasons, not even one regimental "after action" report is included in the *Official Records*,[2] and references to the regiment in other regimental, brigade and divisional reports, Confederate or Federal, are few and scattered. Unlike its "sister" regiment, the Eleventh Mississippi, the Second did not include a

---

[1] Stanley F. Horn, *The Army of Tennessee* (Norman, OK, 1993), p. XI.
[2] U.S. War Department, *War of the Rebellion: The Official Records of the Union and Confederate Armies*, 128 vols. (Washington, D.C., 1880-1901), Series I, vol. 2, p. 868-869, hereinafter cited as *O.R.* All cites are to Series I unless otherwise noted.

company composed mainly of college students like the University Greys.[3] Had such been the case, more written source material might now be available to help reconstruct the regiment's historical record.

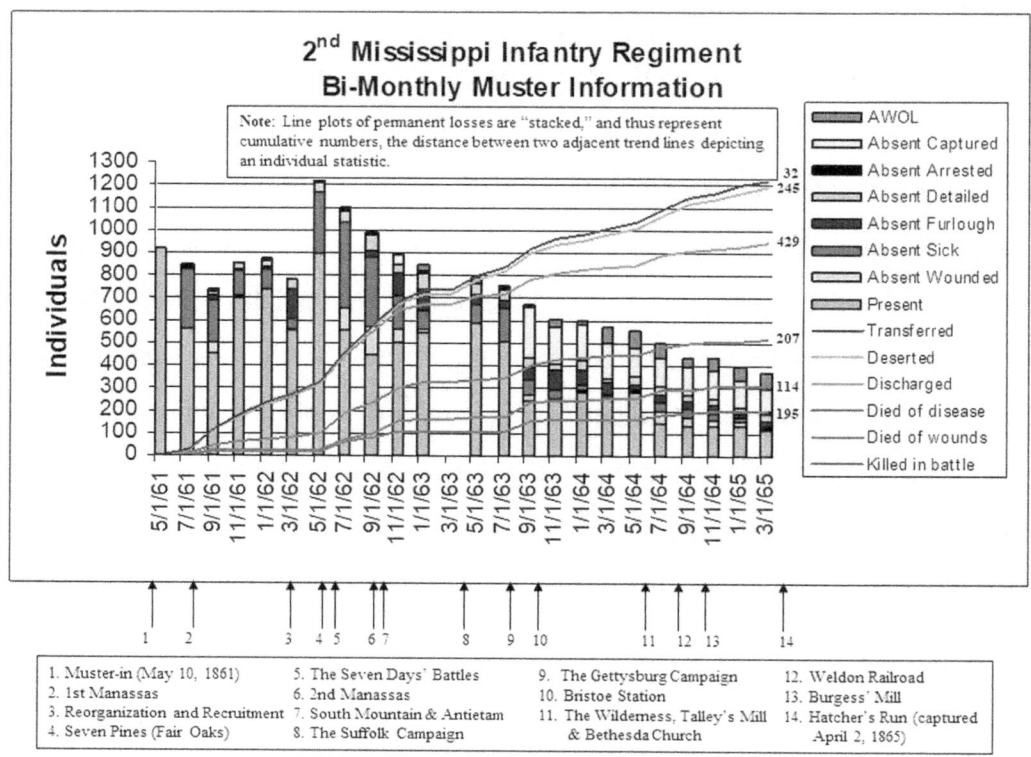

A Graphic Illustration of the Life and Death of the 2nd Mississippi Infantry Regiment (May 3, 1861 - April 2, 1865)

Figure 1: The Life and Death of the 2nd Mississippi Infantry

Within these limitations then, the principal materials utilized in this roster introduction in an attempt to gain some insight into the makeup of the regiment consisted, to a large extent, of the surviving individual Compiled Military Service Records (CMSRs) obtained on microfilm from the

---

[3] Steven R. Davis, "'...Like Leaves in an Autumn Wind': The 11th Mississippi Infantry in the Army of Northern Virginia," *Civil War Regiments: A Journal of the American Civil War* 2, no. 4 (1992), p. 270.

National Archives.[4] From these thirteen rolls of microfilm, more than 2,800 names were obtained. Of these names, however, only 1,888 individuals were identified (the rest of the names were aliases for these same individuals). Some individuals were identified only by Federal prisoner of war records, and it became obvious that several of these are misidentified. For example, there was also a 2nd Mississippi Cavalry Regiment, a 2nd Mississippi Infantry Battalion, and a 2nd Missouri Infantry Regiment, all of which were sometimes incorrectly identified in the Federal records because of identical abbreviations in the record "headers." As a result, some of these incorrectly ended up in the 2nd Mississippi Infantry Regiment records. Where possible, these mistakes were noted in the "comments" section of the complete roster summaries. However, these types of errors were relatively few so a good estimate for the total number of men who served in the regiment (or its precursor state companies) at some point in time probably lies between 1,750-1,800 individuals.[5] After Mississippi seceded from the Union and began to raise companies of state troops, the men from the then four counties of northeast Mississippi – Tishomingo, Tippah, Itawamba and Pontotoc – began enrolling in February and March of 1861 (see Figure 2. **Note:** old county lines are approximate only. Towns close to a boundary line could have existed slightly to either side of the lines shown).[6] These companies would initially be assigned to the Second Regiment, Mott's Brigade, State Army of Mississippi.

---

[4] Compiled Military Service Records of Confederate Soldiers who served in the 2nd Mississippi, National Archives Microfilm Pub. M268, rolls 111-123. Washington, DC: National Archives and Record Service, 1959, hereinafter cited as CMSR.
[5] CMSR.
[6] Following the Civil War, the four original northeastern counties were partitioned into several additional ones.

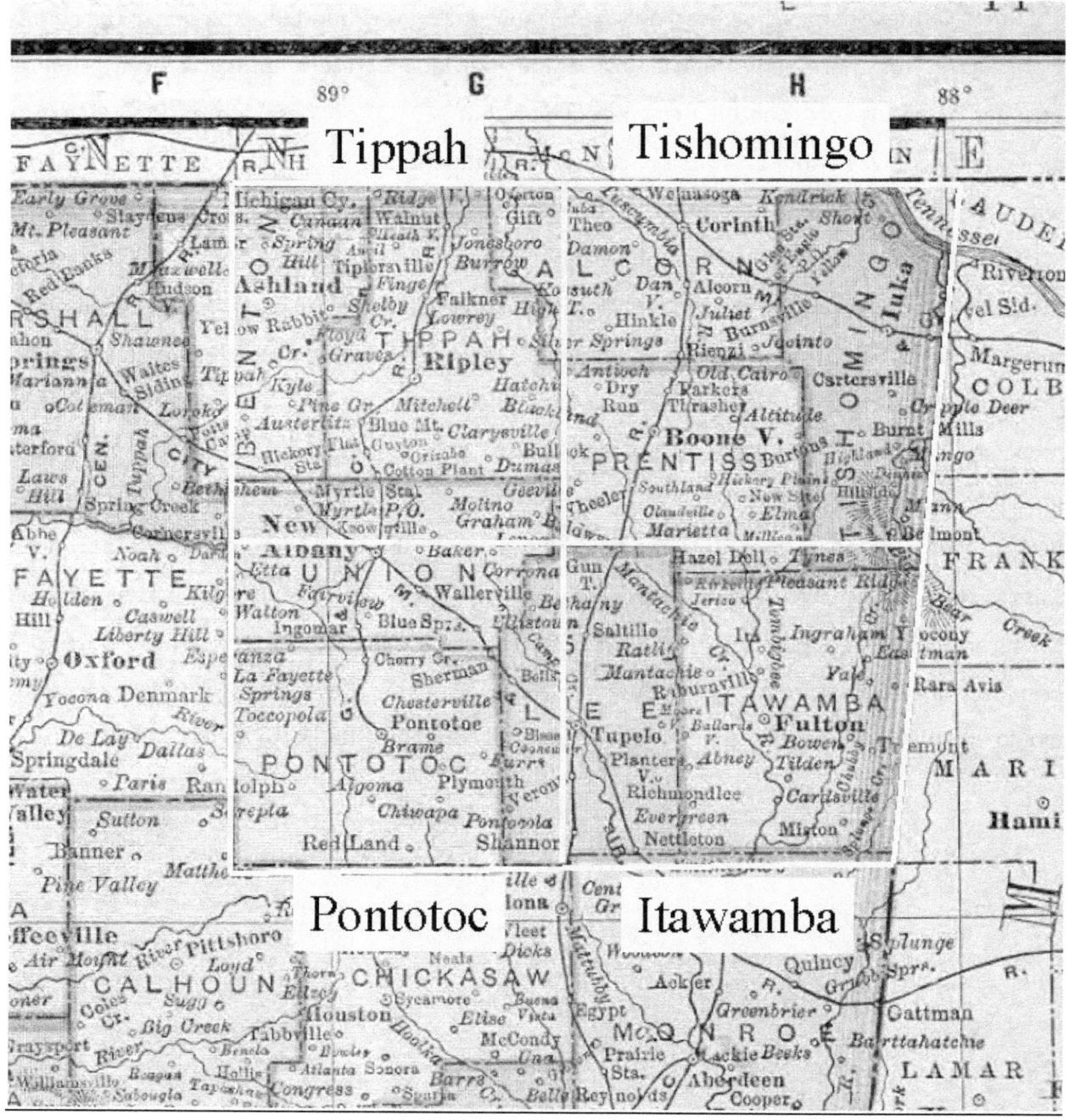

Figure 2: The Original Four Counties of Northeast Mississippi (reproduced from 1864 map)

Once they became part of the 2nd Mississippi Infantry Volunteers, the independent companies were assigned letters as follows:

> A – Tishomingo Riflemen, Tishomingo County
>
> B – O'Connor Rifles, Tippah County
>
> C – Town Creek Riflemen, Itawamba County
>
> D – Joe Matthews Rifles (or Beck Rifles), Tippah County
>
> E – Calhoun Rifles, Itawamba County
>
> F – Magnolia Rifles, Tippah County
>
> G – Pontotoc Minute Men, Pontotoc County
>
> H – Coonewah Rifles, Pontotoc County
>
> I – Cherry Creek Rifles, Pontotoc County
>
> K – Iuka Rifles, Tishomingo County
>
> L – Liberty Guards, Tippah County[7]

---

[7] Dunbar Rowland, *Military History of Mississippi* (Spartanburg, 1978), pp. 40-43. It should be noted that Company L, the eleventh company, was not organized until March 5, 1862 and did not join the regiment, then at Fredericksburg, until April 6, 1862. In trying to analyze specific regimental actions, an eleventh company complicates matters somewhat. The "standard" formation for the companies of a regiment when forming a battle line is a two-rank arrangement for each company with the companies deployed in the following manner (as viewed from the rear of the regiment, left to right): B, G, K, E, H, C, I, D, F, A. With the addition of Company L, by following the preceding deployment logic, the arrangement should be B, G, K, E, H, C, I, D, L, F, A. Thus, it is assumed that Company L is normally deployed with the right wing of the regiment between Companies D and F. This protocol was not always followed in practice however and could depend upon the seniority of the captains commanding. One or more companies might be deployed as skirmishers and companies could be held in reserve. Thus, one should take care in assuming that the entire regiment was deployed in "textbook" line of battle during each engagement.

It should come as no great surprise that the compiled service records show that most of the men identified themselves as farmers or planters.[8] Unfortunately, this categorization does not necessarily allow this occupation to be classified under the "skilled," more or less "semiskilled," or "unskilled" breakdown as has been done in some other recent regimental studies.[9] In order to successfully do this, the service records would need to be correlated with census data (especially property value and slave ownership) since the term "farmer" could encompass several social classes ranging from farm laborer all the way to plantation owner.

Of the 1,888 individual records, occupations were identified for 1,422 (75.3%) of them. Of these, almost 64% identified themselves as farmers. If "planters" are included in the same category – which should probably be the case – nearly 70% of the records would be included in this occupational group. The next most numerous categories included "clerk" at 4.4%, "student" at 3.5%, "carpenter" at 3.2%, "laborer" at 3.0%, "mechanic" (sometimes used interchangeably with carpenter) at 2.6%, "merchant" at 2.1%, "teacher" at 1.8%, "blacksmith" at 1.1%, and "physician" at 1.1% (See Figure 3).

---

[8] CMSR. Upon closer examination, it was found that there was no real distinction between the two terms as used in the compiled service records.
[9] Edward J. Hagerty, *Collis' Zouaves: The 114th Pennsylvania Volunteers in the Civil War* (Baton Rouge, 1997), pp. 78-79.

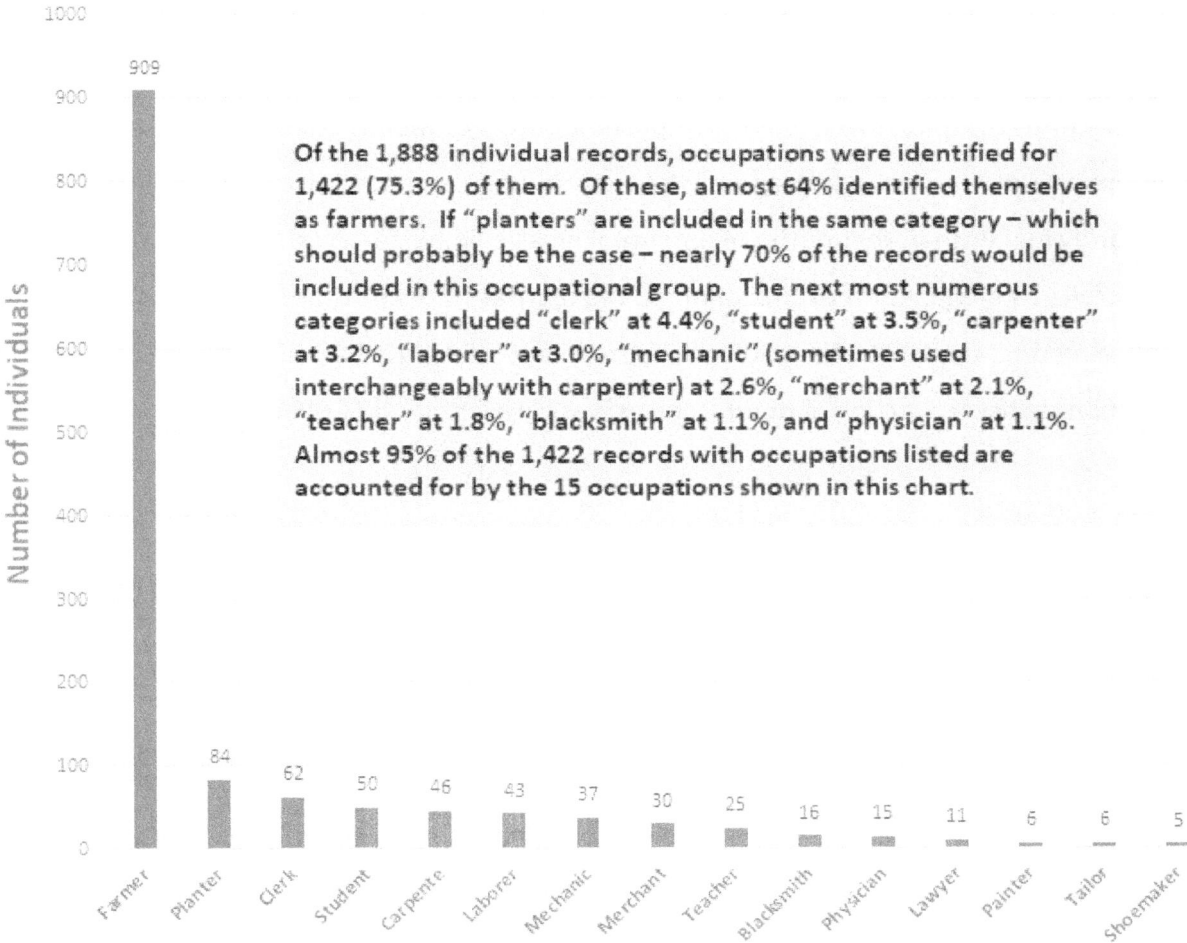

Figure 3: Occupations of the Members of the 2nd Mississippi

The mean (average) and median[10] ages were obtained from an analysis of 1,511 (80%) of the 1,888 individual records. The mean age was found to be 24.8 while the median age was 23. It should be noted that these numbers include both the "early" volunteers, and those recruits who signed up in the spring of 1862 under the implicit threat of the recently enacted Confederate Conscription Act. If these groups are taken separately, the one-year volunteers' mean age was

---

[10] Where the spread in the data can be large, the median is statistically a more "robust" measure of central tendency than is the mean, which can be skewed by one or more "outlier" data points.

24.6 (1,043 valid cases) while the median was 23. The later three-year recruits' mean age was somewhat older at 25.2 (452 valid cases), but the median age remained at 23 (see Figure 4).

Of interest is the plot of mean age versus company shown in Figure 5. Note especially Company L (the eleventh company) which was composed entirely of men recruited in the spring of 1862 from Tippah County. The mean age of the men in this company, at almost 27.5 years old, is significantly higher than that of the regiment taken as a whole, or even the group of later three-year recruits as a whole. An examination of the marital status of these groups also shows that the later recruits tended to have a higher percentage of married men, and this was especially true of Company L (reporting of marital status was rare within the CMSRs).

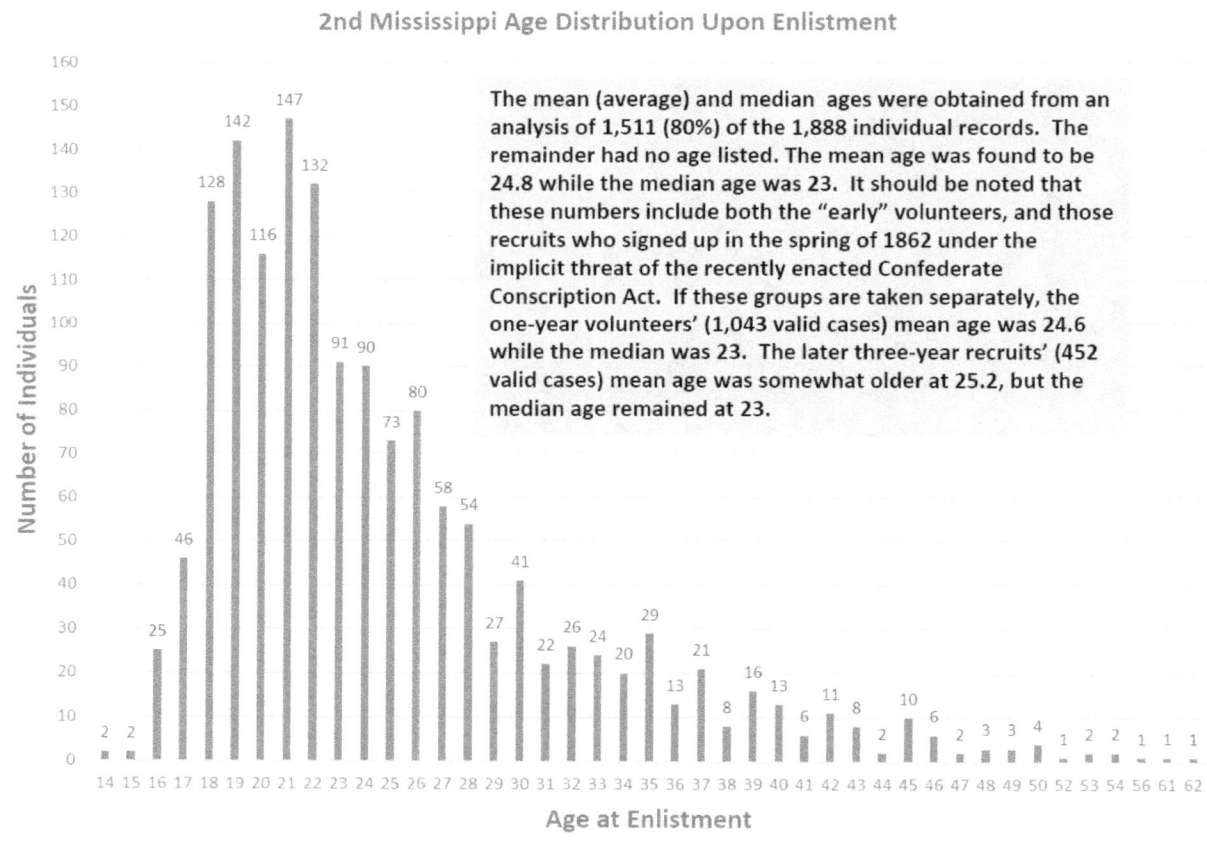

Figure 4: Age Distribution at Enlistment of Members of the 2nd Mississippi

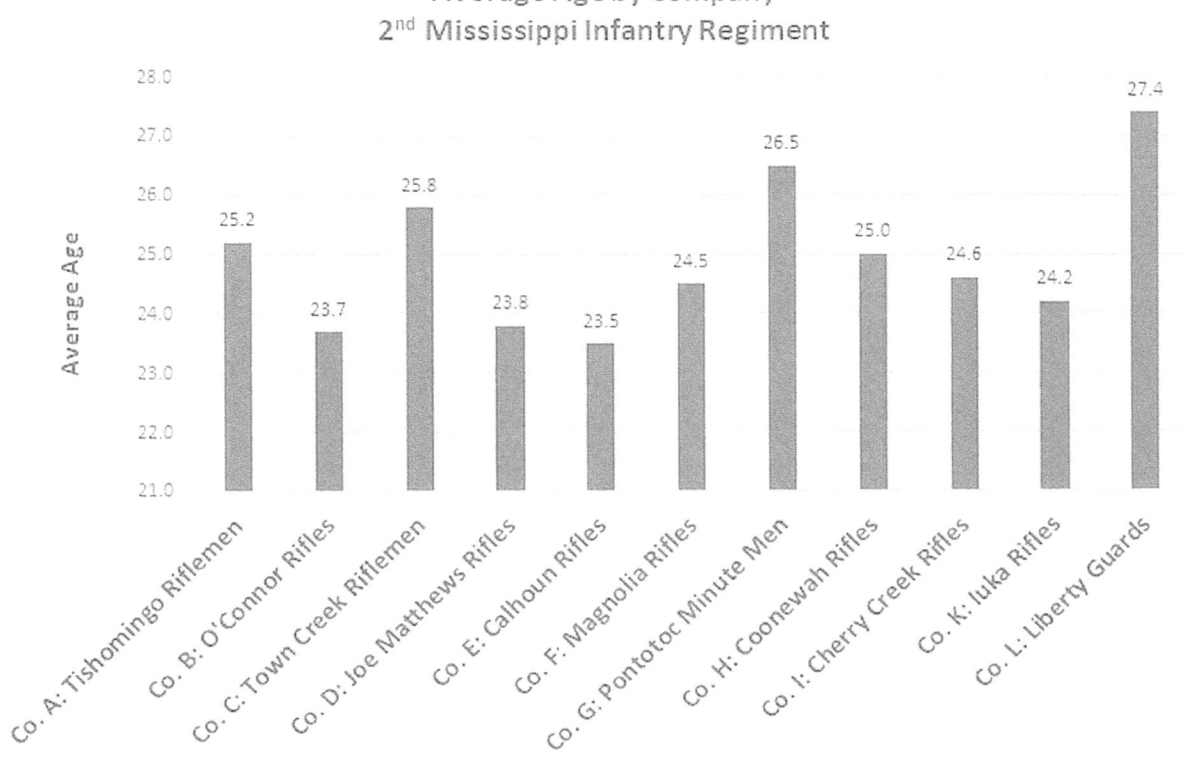

Figure 5: Average Age by Company Variations in the 2nd Mississippi

In discussing potential differences in the group of early volunteers versus the later three-year recruits, refer to Figure 6. It becomes quite apparent that there were only two significant time periods of heavy enrollment. The first was during the late April and early May 1861 period, just prior to the regiment being mustered into Confederate service (May 10, 1861). The second period was the mid-February to mid-March 1862 time frame. It was during this time that Company L was added and most of the regiment's original ten companies also recruited heavily. In fact, based on the available service records (1,690 valid records of 1,888 individuals), fully 60.7% of the regiment's cumulative strength was enrolled prior to muster into Confederate service at Lynchburg, Virginia. By the end of November 1861, the total enrollment had reached 69.6% of its final tally. During the spring 1862 recruiting period (February 20-March 24, 1862), the number jumped to 97.9% of the final total. Only a handful of new recruits were added after this date, the last joining the regiment on September 1, 1864.

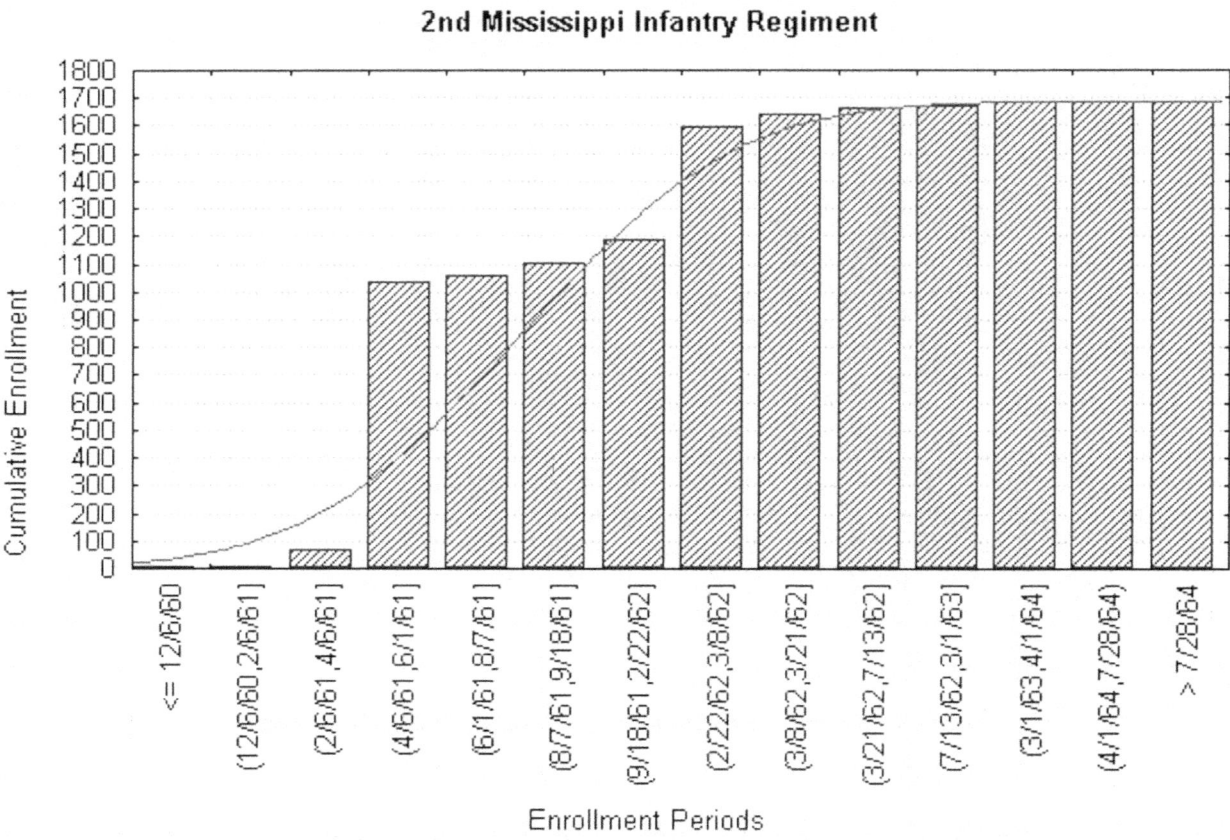

Figure 6: Enrollment Histogram for Total Enrollment in the 2nd Mississippi

Another interesting aspect of the makeup of the 2nd Mississippi is the place of birth of its members. Surprisingly, of the 983 records (52.2%) that provided place of birth information, only 25.3% listed Mississippi. 22.3% gave Alabama; 19.5% listed Tennessee; 13.8% South Carolina; 7.6% Georgia; 4.5% North Carolina; 2.0% Virginia; and 1.5% Ireland. These numbers are illustrated in the histogram below (Figure 7).

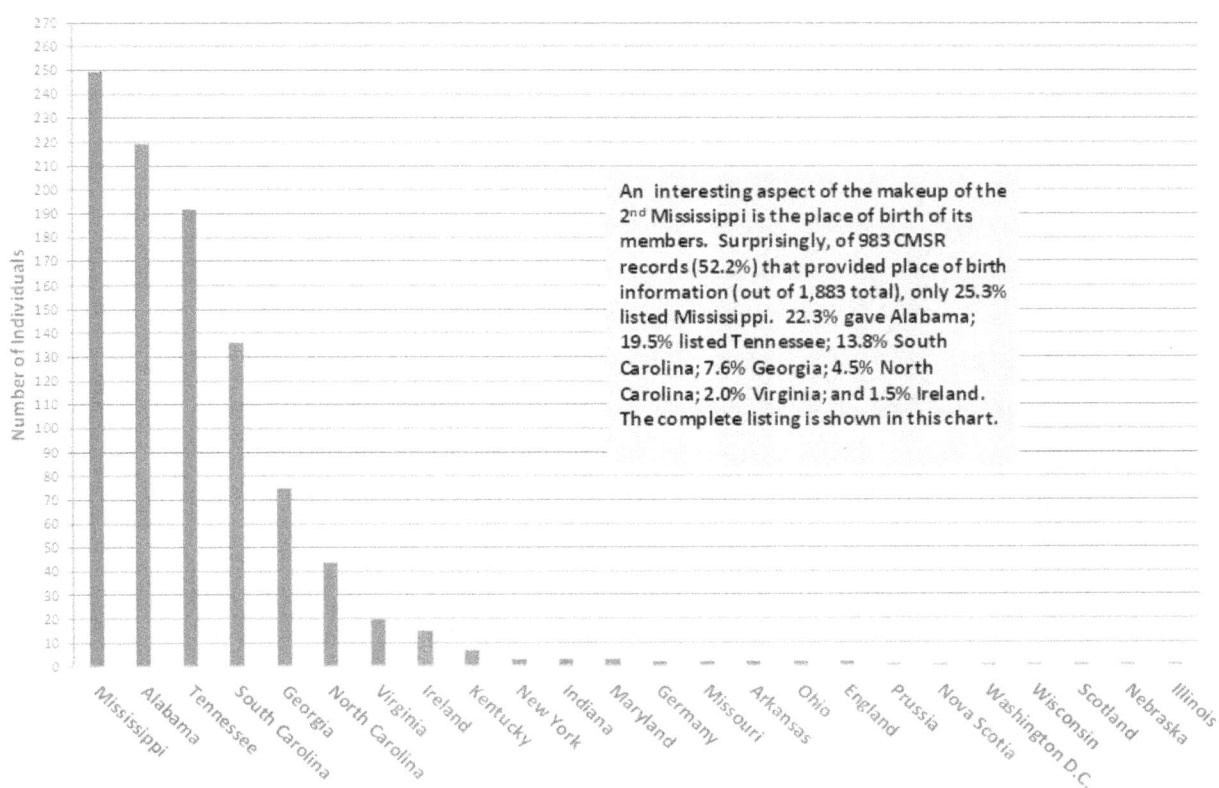

Figure 7: Place of Birth for Members of the 2nd Mississippi

An intriguing question is raised from an examination of the average and median age of members of the regiment, grouped by place of birth. On performing the basic statistical analysis, the plot (Figure 8) is obtained.

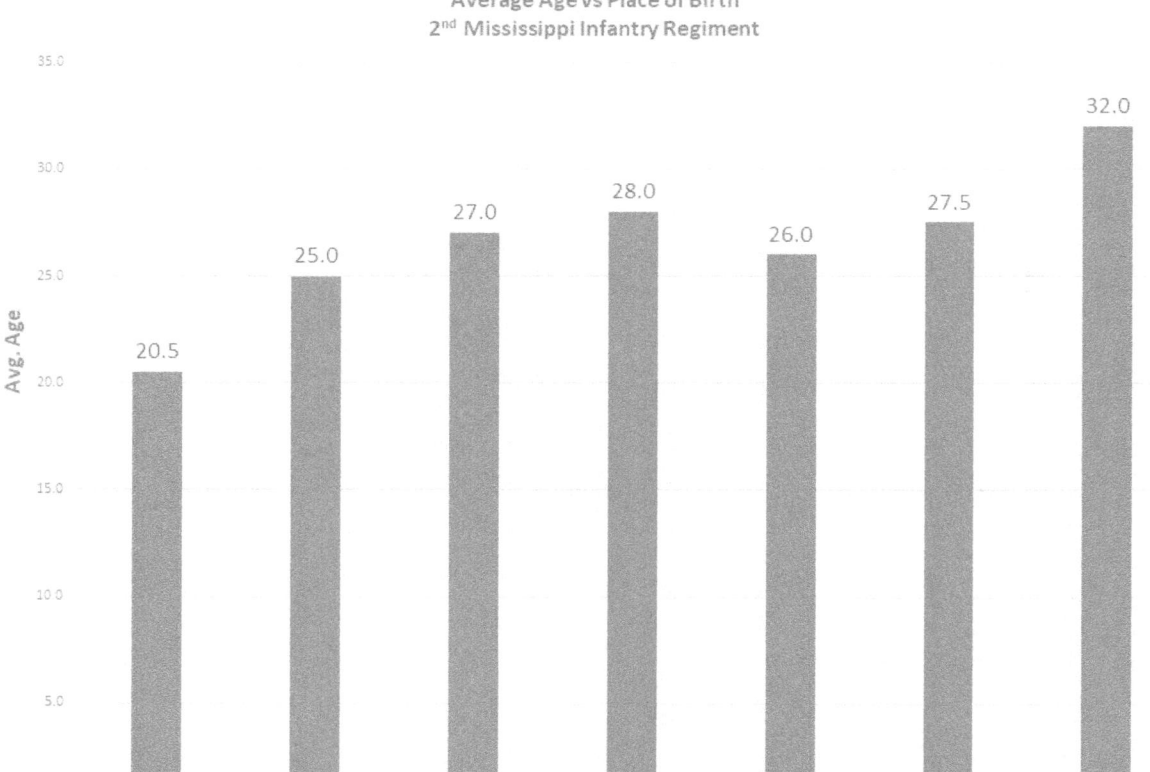

Figure 8: Average Age versus Place of Birth for Members of the 2nd Mississippi

Please note that most of the regiment came from the six states of Mississippi, Alabama, Tennessee, North and South Carolina, and Georgia. The remainder of the locations supplied only a tiny fraction of the regiment's members. Of particular interest, however, is the mean age for the members of the regiment born in Mississippi. At only 20.5 years of age, it is far below the overall mean of 24.6. Also, the median age for this group is only 20 years of age! As a matter of fact, if the native-born Mississippians are excluded from the age statistics, the mean age for the remainder of the regiment jumps to 26.7 and the median to 25 years of age. At first, this appeared to be some sort of mistake in the analysis or an anomaly in the data from the compiled service records. However, with some additional research into the early history of northeastern Mississippi, a plausible explanation was found.

Prior to 1832, the northeastern part of the state belonged to the Chickasaw Nation. On October 20, 1832, the Chickasaws signed the Treaty of Pontotoc which ceded their territory to the state of Mississippi and provided for Chickasaw relocation in the West. However, it was 1837 before tribal leaders made a final decision on where to relocate. Throughout this period, white settlers had been unlawfully settling on Chickasaw lands. By the early 1840's, most of the Chickasaws had been relocated, and the influx of new settlers increased with the organization of nine counties from the former Indian lands. Thus, it could be said that most of the military aged residents who were native born within Tishomingo, Tippah, Pontotoc, and Itawamba counties, would have been born no earlier than the late 1830's to early 1840's. This would explain the age variation when compared with the older "pioneer settlers" from Tennessee, Alabama, the Carolinas, and Georgia.[11]

Although a much more exhaustive statistical analysis could be carried out on compiled service record data, for the purposes of this narrative, a presentation of some of the more important descriptive statistics was felt to be sufficient for the roster introduction. Additional analysis is planned for a full version of the regimental history of the 2nd Mississippi in the future.

A final example of a descriptive statistic that might be of interest is a plot of the average age versus the enrollment rank of the individual. Of course, individuals were promoted throughout the existence of the regiment, but the age of selected officers and non-commissioned officers (NCOs) at the regiment's formation might provide some useful insights (see Figure 9).

The average age of the regiment's members, overall, has previously been discussed. As might be expected, the large number of privates tends to drive the average age of the entire regiment downward. Corporals, however, averaged more than 27 years of age, and sergeants (5th through 1st Sergeant ranks, inclusive), 29. For 3rd Lieutenants, we find the average age again drops to 26. 2nd Lieutenants are older at almost 30. 1st Lieutenants push the scales a bit higher to almost 31.

---

[11] *A Concise History of Early Itawamba County*, Itawamba County GenWeb Internet site, 1998.

Interestingly, the Captains averaged more than 37 years of age, while the field grade officers again drop lower in age and averaged only 31.5.

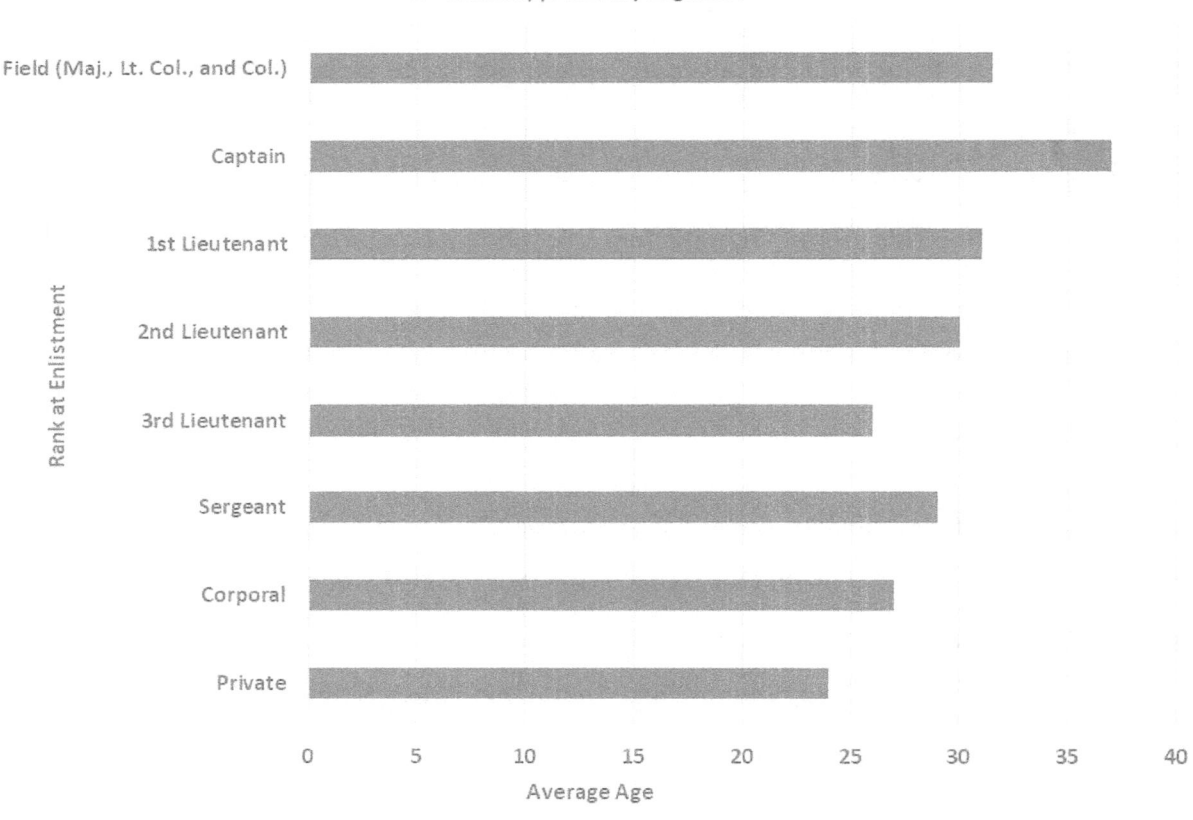

Figure 9: Average Age versus Rank of the Members of the 2nd Mississippi

This brief introduction with some statistical information from the compiled service records probably provides no "earth-shattering" insights into the makeup of the regiment or the motivating factors of the individuals who joined the 2nd Mississippi. However, hopefully it will help provide, even to a small degree, a somewhat better understanding of their regiment from its creation to its ultimate destruction almost four years later.

The companies that comprised the 2nd Mississippi were raised in the then four counties that made up the northeastern corner of the state - Tishomingo, Itawamba, Tippah, and Pontotoc. Following the Civil War, these counties were partitioned into several new ones that, in addition to the four "old" counties above, include all or parts of these "new" counties: Alcorn, Prentiss, Lee, Union and Benton. (**Note:** Old county lines are approximate only. Towns close to a line could have existed slightly to either side of the lines shown. See Figure 10).

Figure 10: Counties of Northeast Mississippi where the 2nd Mississippi Companies were Recruited

With the addition of Company L in April 1862, the 2nd Mississippi contained eleven companies instead of the usual complement of ten per regiment. You will note that there is no "lettered" Company J. Although there are several arguments as to why this long-standing tradition exists within the military, just rest assured that my compiled roster does not, in fact, skip a company! In addition to the eleven lettered company rosters, there is a separate roster for the Field and Staff of the regiment and a roster for individuals for which a company could not be identified.

Notes regarding the military record summaries: The information obtained on the members of the 2nd Mississippi in almost all cases comes only from their Compiled Military Service Records

(CMSRs) as recorded on microfilm in the National Archives. The information provided was generally transcribed "as is." However, it became clear as the research was continuing that the company commanders and regimental staff in some circumstances were often uninformed as to the true status of members of the regiment, particularly those who were furloughed home to recover from wounds, for instance. It must be recalled that for a large part of the war, northern Mississippi was essentially under occupation by Federal forces. Even though Federal soldiers were not always in evidence in all communities at all times, periodic "sweeps" by cavalry and infantry would be conducted to round up Confederate soldiers.

Thus, recuperating members of the regiment often would be seized by these sweeps and sent to northern prison camps. Because of the poor communications from within Federally occupied parts of the Confederacy back to the Confederate authorities, the regiment often never received word as to the true status of these men. The company commanders, therefore, had no choice but to record the men as "absent without leave" (AWOL) or to presume in some cases that they had actually deserted. In fact, during the Civil War, the term "AWOL" did not seem to carry the stigma that we tend to associate with the term today. Many officers and men were listed as AWOL at one time or another. And, although there were of course, many genuine deserters from the 2nd Mississippi (and the reasons were many and varied), please keep in mind that some of these men were not actually deserters at all, but simply caught up in circumstances similar to those discussed above. Thus, individuals researching ancestors who were members of the regiment should not jump to conclusions if they happen to see the terms "AWOL" or "deserter" within the CMSR summaries unless it is made quite apparent from additional information that these were truly deliberate acts by the soldiers in question and not simply an unfortunate misclassification in their records.

Most of the field titles in the listings should be self-explanatory. "ROH" stands for Roll of Honor, a Confederate award for bravery in battle. There were generally two "terms of service" for the men who mustered into the regiment. The early volunteers were for the most part enrolled for a 12-month term of service. Most re-enlisted for "three years or the war" when the regiment reorganized in April 1862. Those who became members of the regiment in 1862 and later, generally enlisted for 3-years or the war. If the soldier served in more than one company, it is noted in the roster and his full listing may be found in either company.

The individual companies that were to become the regiment were assembled at Corinth in early May 1861, assigned letters and were organized into the 2nd Mississippi Infantry Regiment on 3 May 1861 with the election of regimental officers. These companies are identified below:

Field and Staff: Identified from their original company.

Company A - Tishomingo Riflemen - Tishomingo County: Mustered into State service at Corinth on 20 February 1861. Its officers were commissioned on 30 April 1861.

Company B - O'Connor Rifles - Tippah County: Mustered into State service at Ripley on 4 March 1861. The Governor commissioned its officers on 4 February 1861. The company was presented a flag by Mrs. Judge Green; it marched to Saulsbury, Tennessee and took the train to Corinth.

Company C - Town Creek Riflemen - Itawamba County: Mustered into State service at Verona on 27 February 1861.

Company D - Joe Matthews Rifles (also called the Beck Rifles) - Tippah County: Mustered into State service at Toombs' Store on 9 March 1861.

Company E - Calhoun Rifles - Itawamba County: Mustered into State service on 18 February 1861.

Company F - Magnolia Rifles - Tippah County: Mustered into State service on 4 March 1861 at Ripley. Presented a flag by Mrs. W. R. Cole on 30 April 1861.

Company G - Pontotoc Minute Men - Pontotoc County: Mustered into State service at Pontotoc on 2 March 1861. For additional information on individual members of this company, please see Bob Thompson's roster of Company G.

Company H – Coonewah (often misspelled as 'Conewah') Rifles - Pontotoc County: Mustered into State service at Chesterville on 1 March 1861.

Company I - Cherry Creek Rifles - Pontotoc County: Officers commissioned by the Governor on 1 April 1861.

Company K - Iuka Rifles - Tishomingo County: Mustered into State service at Iuka on 6 April 1861.

Company L - Liberty Guards - Tippah County: Enrolled on 5 March 1862 at Ripley for three years. This company joined the regiment at Fredericksburg, Virginia on 6 April 1862.

Company Unknown: Company to which the individual belonged could not be found in his records.

2nd Mississippi Alphabetical Roster

Adair, Oliver J.
CO: A, L **Initial Rank:** Private
Joined: Saturday, March 1, 1862 **Term (yrs):** 3 **Occupation:** Farmer **Age** 35
Enrolled at: Jacinto, MS **Enrolled By:** Lt. Clayton **Promoted:** No **ROH:** No
Born: Tennessee **Marital Status:** M **Residence** Silver Springs, MS

Transferred from Company A to Company L on 4/30/1862. Wounded at battle of 2nd Manassas on 8/28/1862. Sent to hospital at Warrenton, VA. Furloughed. Transferred back to Company A on 11/1/1862. Returned to duty. Wounded at Gettysburg (date not given). Furloughed. Did not return. Listed as AWOL during last company muster (Jan/Feb 1865).

Adair, Robert W.
CO: A, L **Initial Rank:** Private
Joined: Saturday, March 1, 1862 **Term (yrs):** 3 **Occupation:** Farmer **Age** 26
Enrolled at: Jacinto, MS **Enrolled By:** Lt. Clayton **Promoted:** No **ROH:** No
Born: Tennessee **Marital Status:** M **Residence** Dry Run, MS

Also see Ham's Regiment Mississippi Cavalry. Transferred from Company A to Company L on 4/30/1862. Transferred back to Company A on 11/1/1862. Wounded (date or engagement not listed in company records, but hospital records show him admitted at Richmond on 7/16/1863 with gunshot wound to right thigh) and furloughed for 35-days from 8/15/1863 to Mississippi. Listed as AWOL since 2/1/1864. Deserter who joined Harris' Battalion of Cavalry (Miss. State Troops) as Lieutenant without regular transfer or discharge from his company.

Adams, Jefferson
CO: A **Initial Rank:** Private
Joined: Saturday, March 1, 1862 **Term (yrs):** 3 **Occupation:** Farmer **Age** 32
Enrolled at: Jacinto, MS **Enrolled By:** Lt. Clayton **Promoted:** No **ROH:** No
Born: North Carolina **Marital Status:** M **Residence** Jacinto, MS

Killed in battle at Gaines Mill on 6/27/1862.

Adams, John J.
CO: I **Initial Rank:** Private
Joined: Wednesday, May 1, 1861 **Term (yrs):** 1 **Occupation:** Farmer **Age** 27
Enrolled at: Cherry Creek, MS **Enrolled By:** Capt. Herring **Promoted:** No **ROH:** No
Born: South Carolina **Marital Status:** **Residence** Pontotoc, MS

Killed in battle at Gettysburg on 7/1/1863.

2nd Mississippi Alphabetical Roster (Annotated)

Adams, John L.
CO: A **Initial Rank:** Private
Joined: Tuesday, April 30, 1861 **Term (yrs):** 1 **Occupation:** Farmer **Age** 30
Enrolled at: Corinth, MS **Enrolled By:** Capt. Leeth **Promoted:** No **ROH:** No
Born: Tennessee **Marital Status:** M **Residence** Jacinto, MS

Discharged on 1/8/1862 for disability at Camp Fisher, VA.

Adams, Samuel C.
CO: B **Initial Rank:** Private
Joined: Wednesday, May 1, 1861 **Term (yrs):** 1 **Occupation:** Overseer **Age** 25
Enrolled at: Tippah Co., MS **Enrolled By:** Capt. Buchanan **Promoted:** No **ROH:** No
Born: **Marital Status:** **Residence**

Captured at battle of South Mountain, MD on 9/14/1862. Taken to Fort Delaware. Exchanged on 11/10/1862 at Aikens Landing, VA. Returned to duty. Captured at Gettysburg on 7/3/1863. Taken to Fort Delaware. Released on oath on 6/11/1865.

Adams, Washington C.
CO: K **Initial Rank:** Private
Joined: Wednesday, May 1, 1861 **Term (yrs):** 1 **Occupation:** Merchant **Age** 24
Enrolled at: Tishomingo Co., MS **Enrolled By:** Capt. Stone **Promoted:** Yes **ROH:** No
Born: **Marital Status:** **Residence**

Appointed 2nd Sergeant on 2/1/1862 (according to remarks in company records), however listed as 1st Sergeant in records from that date. Discharged on 6/11/1862 by reason of providing a substitute.

Adkins, Charles B.
CO: G **Initial Rank:** Private
Joined: Tuesday, April 30, 1861 **Term (yrs):** 1 **Occupation:** Tailor **Age** 28
Enrolled at: Pontotoc, MS **Enrolled By:** Capt. Kilpatrick **Promoted:** No **ROH:** No
Born: **Marital Status:** **Residence**

Died of disease (typhoid fever) at Charlottesville, VA on 8/12/1861 (other records say 8/11/1861 or 8/25/1861). [Same person as J.B. Adkins?].

Adkins, J. B.
CO: G **Initial Rank:** Private
Joined: Tuesday, April 30, 1861 **Term (yrs):** 1 **Occupation:** Tailor **Age** 30
Enrolled at: Lynchburg, VA **Enrolled By:** **Promoted:** No **ROH:** No
Born: Virginia **Marital Status:** S **Residence** Lynchburg, VA

Died August 1861. No other record. [Same person as Charles B. Adkins?].

2nd Mississippi Alphabetical Roster (Annotated)

Adkins, John W.
CO: A **Initial Rank:** Private
Joined: Saturday, March 1, 1862 **Term (yrs):** 3 **Occupation:** Farmer **Age** 19
Enrolled at: Jacinto, MS **Enrolled By:** Lt. Clayton **Promoted:** No **ROH:** No
Born: Tennessee **Marital Status:** S **Residence** Jacinto, MS

Wounded at battle of Gaines Mill on 6/27/1862. Sent to hospital in Richmond, VA. Returned to duty. Wounded and captured at Gettysburg on 7/3/1863. Sent to Fort Delaware. Died at Fort Delaware of disease on 10/12/1863 (other records show 11/8/1863).

Aingell, Elijah L.
CO: G **Initial Rank:** Private
Joined: Wednesday, May 1, 1861 **Term (yrs):** 1 **Occupation:** Tailor **Age** 33
Enrolled at: Pontotoc, MS **Enrolled By:** Capt. Miller **Promoted:** No **ROH:** No
Born: Kentucky **Marital Status:** S **Residence** Pontotoc, MS

Discharged for disability on 1/3/1862 at Camp Fisher, VA.

Akers, James L.
CO: K **Initial Rank:** Private
Joined: Tuesday, July 1, 1862 **Term (yrs):** 3 **Occupation:** Student **Age** 17
Enrolled at: Richmond, VA **Enrolled By:** Capt. Latham **Promoted:** No **ROH:** Yes
Born: Mississippi **Marital Status:** **Residence**

Also see John J. Akers. Substitute for John J. Ackers, his brother. Killed in battle at Gettysburg on 7/3/1863 (other records say 7/1/1863). ROH for South Mountain and Gettysburg, July 3rd (means most likely killed on 7/3).

Akers, John J.
CO: K **Initial Rank:** Private
Joined: Tuesday, April 30, 1861 **Term (yrs):** 1 **Occupation:** Student **Age** 20
Enrolled at: Iuka, MS **Enrolled By:** Capt. Stone **Promoted:** No **ROH:** No
Born: **Marital Status:** **Residence**

Also see James L. Akers (substitute). Discharged on 7/1/1862. His brother, James L. Akers, substituted in his place.

Albritton, Washington
CO: H **Initial Rank:** Private
Joined: Monday, April 29, 1861 **Term (yrs):** 1 **Occupation:** Farmer **Age** 24
Enrolled at: Pontotoc Co., MS **Enrolled By:** Capt. Taylor **Promoted:** No **ROH:** No
Born: Alabama **Marital Status:** S **Residence** Chesterville, MS

Discharged on account of disability 7/16/1861 at Camp Bee, VA (near Manassas).

2nd Mississippi Alphabetical Roster (Annotated)

Aldridge, Isaac N.

CO: K *Initial Rank:* Private

Joined: Wednesday, May 1, 1861 *Term (yrs):* 1 *Occupation:* Farmer *Age* 21

Enrolled at: Tishomingo Co., MS *Enrolled By:* Capt. Stone *Promoted:* No *ROH:* Yes

Born: Alabama *Marital Status:* *Residence*

Wounded at Sharpsburg on 9/17/1862. Subsequently died as a result of wounds at Winchester, VA on 3/8/1863 (other records show his death at the Mount Jackson General Hospital on 12/3/1862). ROH for Second Manassas, 8/28/1862.

Aldridge, William P.

CO: A *Initial Rank:* Private

Joined: Wednesday, May 1, 1861 *Term (yrs):* 1 *Occupation:* Farmer *Age* 26

Enrolled at: Tishomingo Co., MS *Enrolled By:* Capt. Leeth *Promoted:* No *ROH:* No

Born: *Marital Status:* S *Residence* Burnsville, MS

Discharged on 9/20/1861 due to disability at Camp Fisher, VA.

Alexander, Daniel H.

CO: F *Initial Rank:* Private

Joined: Wednesday, May 1, 1861 *Term (yrs):* 1 *Occupation:* Carpenter *Age* 22

Enrolled at: Tippah Co., MS *Enrolled By:* Capt. Davis *Promoted:* No *ROH:* No

Born: Tennessee *Marital Status:* *Residence*

Discharged on 8/6/1861 due to disability at Camp Jones, VA.

Alexander, James W.

CO: G *Initial Rank:* Private

Joined: Wednesday, May 1, 1861 *Term (yrs):* 1 *Occupation:* Cabinet maker *Age* 22

Enrolled at: Pontotoc, MS *Enrolled By:* Capt. Miller *Promoted:* No *ROH:* No

Born: Mississippi *Marital Status:* S *Residence* Pontotoc, MS

Severely wounded (in hip) in battle at 1st Manassas on 7/21/1861. Sent to hospital at Charlottesville, VA. Discharged due to disability caused by wound on 8/21/1861.

Alford, S. D.

CO: *Initial Rank:* Private

Joined: *Term (yrs):* 0 *Occupation:* *Age*

Enrolled at: *Enrolled By:* *Promoted:* No *ROH:* No

Born: *Marital Status:* *Residence*

Appears on a Federal list of prisoners of war delivered at Vicksburg, MS for exchange on 12/14/1862. No other record.

2nd Mississippi Alphabetical Roster (Annotated)

Allen, A. W. B.
CO: K **Initial Rank:** Private
Joined: *Term (yrs):* 0 *Occupation:*   *Age*
Enrolled at: *Enrolled By:*   *Promoted:* No *ROH:* No
Born: *Marital Status:*   *Residence*

Appears on a hospital record at Camp Douglas dated 8/9/1862. No other record.

Allen, Aden W.
CO: K **Initial Rank:** Private
Joined: Saturday, March 1, 1862 *Term (yrs):* 3 *Occupation:*   *Age* 35
Enrolled at: Iuka, MS *Enrolled By:* Lt. Latham *Promoted:* No *ROH:* No
Born: *Marital Status:*   *Residence*

Listed as "absent wounded" during May/Jun 1864 muster roll (date of wound or engagement not given in company records. Returned to duty. Captured at Petersburg (Hatcher's Run?) on 4/2/1865. Taken to Fort Delaware. Released on oath on 6/11/1865.

Allen, Ezekiel N.
CO: D **Initial Rank:** 2nd Corporal
Joined: Wednesday, May 1, 1861 *Term (yrs):* 1 *Occupation:* Mechanic *Age*
Enrolled at: Tippah Co., MS *Enrolled By:* Capt. Beck *Promoted:* Yes *ROH:* No
Born: *Marital Status:* M *Residence* Snow Creek, MS

Promoted to 3rd Sergeant on 4/23/1862. Detailed as ward master in hospital at Richmond from Sept/Oct 1863. Listed as AWOL in Mississippi since 10/1/1864. Deserted, dropped from rolls by order of Colonel Stone on 12/31/1864. Surrendered to Federal forces on 4/9/1865 and paroled at Holly Springs, MS on 6/3/1865.

Allen, John
CO: E **Initial Rank:** Private
Joined: Wednesday, May 1, 1861 *Term (yrs):* 1 *Occupation:* Farmer *Age* 18
Enrolled at: Itawamba Co., MS *Enrolled By:* Capt. Booth *Promoted:* No *ROH:* No
Born: Mississippi *Marital Status:* S *Residence*

Discharged for disability on 8/22/1861 at Camp Jones, VA by order of General Johnston.

Allen, John H.
CO: B **Initial Rank:** Private
Joined: Saturday, March 1, 1862 *Term (yrs):* 3 *Occupation:* Carpenter *Age* 28
Enrolled at: Ripley, MS *Enrolled By:* Capt. Buchanan *Promoted:* No *ROH:* No
Born: North Carolina *Marital Status:* M *Residence*

Shot himself in hand on 6/6/1862. Discharged on 7/28/1862 due to gunshot wound to hand resulting in amputation of left arm.

2nd Mississippi Alphabetical Roster (Annotated)

Allen, Joseph H.
CO: H **Initial Rank:** Private
Joined: Monday, April 29, 1861   **Term (yrs):** 1 **Occupation:** Farmer   **Age** 23
Enrolled at: Pontotoc Co., MS   **Enrolled By:** Capt. Taylor   **Promoted:** No   **ROH:** No
Born: Alabama   **Marital Status:**   **Residence**

Discharged on 8/13/1862 due to disability.

Allen, R. H.
CO: H **Initial Rank:** Private
Joined: **Term (yrs):** 0 **Occupation:**   **Age**
Enrolled at: **Enrolled By:**   **Promoted:** No   **ROH:** No
Born: **Marital Status:**   **Residence**

Appears on a Confederate report. Discharged on 8/18/1861 due to disability at Camp Jones, VA. No other record. [same man as Richard Allen of Company H?].

Allen, Richard
CO: H **Initial Rank:** Private
Joined: Friday, May 10, 1861   **Term (yrs):** 1 **Occupation:** Farmer   **Age** 23
Enrolled at: Lynchburg, VA   **Enrolled By:**   **Promoted:** No   **ROH:** No
Born: Alabama   **Marital Status:** S   **Residence** Chesterville, MS

Appears on a Confederate "record" dated Petersburg, VA on 3/15/1865. Discharged on account of disability on 9/22/1861. No other record. [same man as R. H. Allen?].

Allen, Richard A.
CO: D **Initial Rank:** Private
Joined: Wednesday, May 1, 1861   **Term (yrs):** 1 **Occupation:** Mechanic   **Age** 33
Enrolled at: Tippah Co., MS   **Enrolled By:** Capt. Beck   **Promoted:** No   **ROH:** No
Born: Alabama   **Marital Status:** M   **Residence** Snow Creek, MS

Wounded at battle of 1st Manassas on 7/21/1861. Discharged due to disability on 12/22/1861 by order of General Whiting at Camp Fisher, VA.

2nd Mississippi Alphabetical Roster (Annotated)

Allen, Robert
CO: A, L **Initial Rank:** Private
Joined: Wednesday, May 1, 1861 **Term (yrs):** 1 **Occupation:** Farmer **Age** 19
Enrolled at: Tishomingo Co., MS **Enrolled By:** Capt. Leeth **Promoted:** No **ROH:** No
Born: Mississippi **Marital Status:** S **Residence** Jacinto, MS

Transferred to Company L from Company A on 4/30/1862 [must have immediately been transferred back, because he is still carried on rolls of Company A]. Wounded at battle of 2nd Manassas on 8/29/1862. Furloughed. Listed as AWOL and deserted as of 12/1/1862. Captured by Federal forces near Corinth, MS on 10/22/1863. Sent to Alton, IL. On list of prisoners who object to being exchanged. Note says he wishes to be released on oath and bond. Escaped from Alton on 9/24/1864.

Allen, William S.
CO: E **Initial Rank:** Private
Joined: Wednesday, May 1, 1861 **Term (yrs):** 1 **Occupation:** Farmer **Age** 23
Enrolled at: Itawamba Co., MS **Enrolled By:** Capt. Booth **Promoted:** Yes **ROH:** No
Born: Virginia **Marital Status:** S **Residence** Baldwyn, MS

Promoted to 4th Sergeant on 8/21/1861 to fill vacancy caused by [George W.] Monk's discharge on 8/21/1861. Promoted to 1st Lieutenant 4/17/1862. Severely wounded at Sharpsburg on 9/17/1862 (requiring amputation of left leg at thigh). Sent to hospital in Richmond, VA. Furloughed to Lagrange, GA. Appointed Captain on 11/1/1862. Retired to Invalid Corps, P.A.C.S. on account of wound on 5/19/1864. Paroled at Meridian, MS on 5/15/1865.

Alsbrook, Joseph
CO: B **Initial Rank:** Private
Joined: Wednesday, May 1, 1861 **Term (yrs):** 1 **Occupation:** Wagon maker **Age** 43
Enrolled at: Tippah Co., MS **Enrolled By:** Capt. Buchanan **Promoted:** No **ROH:** No
Born: North Carolina **Marital Status:** **Residence**

Discharged due to disability on 8/18/1861 by order of General Johnston at Camp Jones, VA.

Anderson, Ben
CO: K **Initial Rank:** Private
Joined: **Term (yrs):** 0 **Occupation:** **Age**
Enrolled at: **Enrolled By:** **Promoted:** No **ROH:** No
Born: **Marital Status:** **Residence**

Appears on a Federal register of prisoners of war in custody of provost marshal in Memphis, TN dated 11/10/1863. Note says prisoner released on oath and sent north on 11/11/1863. No other record.

2nd Mississippi Alphabetical Roster (Annotated)

Anderson, James L.

	CO: C	**Initial Rank:** Private
Joined: Wednesday, May 1, 1861	**Term (yrs):** 1 **Occupation:** Farmer	**Age** 19
Enrolled at: Itawamba Co., MS	**Enrolled By:** Capt. Bromley	**Promoted:** No **ROH:** Yes
Born:	**Marital Status:**	**Residence**

Wounded battle of Sharpsburg on 9/17/1862. Furloughed. Returned to duty. Admitted to hospital in Richmond with wound on 6/13/1864 (company records provide no details on date of wound or engagement). Furloughed 60-days from 7/2/1864. Returned to duty. Killed in action at battle of Weldon Railroad on 8/19/1864. ROH for Weldon Railroad, 8/19/1864.

Andrews, Henry

	CO: I	**Initial Rank:** Private
Joined: Wednesday, May 1, 1861	**Term (yrs):** 1 **Occupation:** Farmer	**Age** 26
Enrolled at: Pontotoc Co., MS	**Enrolled By:** Capt. Herring	**Promoted:** No **ROH:** Yes
Born: South Carolina	**Marital Status:** S	**Residence**

Killed in battle at Falling Waters, MD on 7/14/1863. ROH for Malvern Hill, 7/1/1862. [Same individual as Hillery Andrews, below].

Andrews, Hillery

	CO: I	**Initial Rank:** Private
Joined:	**Term (yrs):** 0 **Occupation:**	**Age**
Enrolled at:	**Enrolled By:**	**Promoted:** No **ROH:** Yes
Born:	**Marital Status:**	**Residence**

Appears on a Confederate listing of Roll of Honor selectees for the battle of Malvern Hill. No other records. [Duplicate Record. Misspelled first name. See Henry Andrews. Same individual].

Andrews, Martin W.

	CO: I	**Initial Rank:** Private
Joined: Wednesday, May 1, 1861	**Term (yrs):** 1 **Occupation:** Farmer	**Age** 20
Enrolled at: Pontotoc Co., MS	**Enrolled By:** Capt. Herring	**Promoted:** No **ROH:** No
Born:	**Marital Status:**	**Residence**

Wounded at battle of The Wilderness on 5/5/1864. Sent to hospital in Lynchburg, VA. Detailed to go with Colonel Stone to Mississippi after absentees and deserters on 1/9/1865.

Andrews, Samuel Y.

	CO: I	**Initial Rank:** Private
Joined: Wednesday, May 1, 1861	**Term (yrs):** 1 **Occupation:** Farmer	**Age** 24
Enrolled at: Pontotoc Co., MS	**Enrolled By:** Capt. Herring	**Promoted:** No **ROH:** No
Born:	**Marital Status:**	**Residence**

Died of disease near Manassas on 8/9/1861.

2nd Mississippi Alphabetical Roster (Annotated)

Argus, J. M.

		CO: B	*Initial Rank:* Private
Joined:	*Term (yrs):* 0	*Occupation:*	*Age*
Enrolled at:	*Enrolled By:*	*Promoted:* No	*ROH:* No
Born:	*Marital Status:*	*Residence*	

Appears on a Federal roll of prisoners of war sent for exchange from Fort Delaware to Aikens Landing, VA. Declared exchanged on 11/10/1862. Captured on 9/14/1862 at battle of South Mountain. No other record.

Armstrong, Kade A.

		CO: C	*Initial Rank:* Private
Joined: Wednesday, May 1, 1861	*Term (yrs):* 1	*Occupation:* Farmer	*Age* 35
Enrolled at: Itawamba Co., MS	*Enrolled By:* Capt. Bromley	*Promoted:* No	*ROH:* No
Born: Alabama	*Marital Status:*	*Residence*	

Discharged on plea of military exemption on 5/16/1862 (over 35 years old).

Armstrong, Weldon P.

		CO: I	*Initial Rank:* Private
Joined: Tuesday, September 10, 1861	*Term (yrs):* 1	*Occupation:*	*Age*
Enrolled at: Guntown, MS	*Enrolled By:* Lt. Davenport	*Promoted:* No	*ROH:* No
Born:	*Marital Status:*	*Residence*	

Listed as "present" during most of the company musters. Captured at Petersburg (Hatcher's Run?) on 4/2/1865. Taken to Point Lookout, MD. Released on oath on 6/9/1865.

Arnold, Thomas N.

		CO: A	*Initial Rank:* Private
Joined: Wednesday, May 1, 1861	*Term (yrs):* 1	*Occupation:* Farmer	*Age* 21
Enrolled at: Corinth, MS	*Enrolled By:* Capt. Leeth	*Promoted:* No	*ROH:* No
Born: South Carolina	*Marital Status:* S	*Residence* Booneville, MS	

Wounded at Gettysburg on 7/1/1863. Returned to duty. Detailed scout for General [Joseph R.] Davis in April 1864. Detailed to accompany Colonel Stone to arrest deserters and absentees in Mississippi on 1/9/1865.

Asbury, James D.

		CO: B	*Initial Rank:* Private
Joined: Wednesday, May 1, 1861	*Term (yrs):* 1	*Occupation:* Farmer	*Age* 19
Enrolled at: Tippah Co., MS	*Enrolled By:* Capt. Buchanan	*Promoted:* No	*ROH:* No
Born:	*Marital Status:*	*Residence*	

Wounded at battle of Gaines Mill on 6/27/1862. Furloughed. Returned to duty. Died near Culpeper Court House, VA on 11/16/1862 of disease (smallpox).

2nd Mississippi Alphabetical Roster (Annotated)

Ashford, William T.
CO: C **Initial Rank:** Private
Joined: Wednesday, May 1, 1861 **Term (yrs):** 1 **Occupation:** Farmer **Age** 16
Enrolled at: Itawamba Co., MS **Enrolled By:** Capt. Bromley **Promoted:** No **ROH:** No
Born: **Marital Status:** **Residence**

Listed as AWOL as of 2/8/1865.

Atkins, James A.
CO: C **Initial Rank:** Private
Joined: Wednesday, May 1, 1861 **Term (yrs):** 1 **Occupation:** Farmer **Age** 19
Enrolled at: Itawamba Co., MS **Enrolled By:** Capt. Bromley **Promoted:** Yes **ROH:** Yes
Born: **Marital Status:** **Residence**

Listed as 4th Sergeant for Sep/Oct 1862 muster. Listed as 2nd Sergeant for Mar/Apr 1863 muster. Wounded in action at Suffolk, VA (date unknown). Subsequently died of wounds at Jerusalem, VA on 4/22/1863. ROH for Malvern Hill, 7/1/1862.

Atkins, John T.
CO: K **Initial Rank:** Private
Joined: Saturday, March 1, 1862 **Term (yrs):** 3 **Occupation:** Farmer **Age** 18
Enrolled at: Iuka, MS **Enrolled By:** Lt. Latham **Promoted:** No **ROH:** No
Born: South Carolina **Marital Status:** **Residence**

Died of disease on 5/21/1862 at Ashland, VA.

Atkins, Joseph
CO: K **Initial Rank:** Private
Joined: Saturday, March 1, 1862 **Term (yrs):** 3 **Occupation:** Farmer **Age** 45
Enrolled at: Iuka, MS **Enrolled By:** Lt. Latham **Promoted:** No **ROH:** No
Born: South Carolina **Marital Status:** **Residence**

Died of disease on 5/6/1862 at Ashland, VA.

Atkins, William M.
CO: K **Initial Rank:** Private
Joined: Saturday, March 1, 1862 **Term (yrs):** 3 **Occupation:** **Age** 24
Enrolled at: Iuka, MS **Enrolled By:** Lt. Latham **Promoted:** No **ROH:** No
Born: **Marital Status:** **Residence**

Wounded at battle of Seven Pines (not dated). Returned to duty. Listed as absent wounded since 10/1/1864. Name appears on a Federal list of paroled prisoners dated 5/12/1865.

2nd Mississippi Alphabetical Roster (Annotated)

Atwood, Toliver W.
CO: E, A **Initial Rank:** Private
Joined: Wednesday, May 1, 1861 **Term (yrs):** 1 **Occupation:** Farmer **Age** 17
Enrolled at: Itawamba Co., MS **Enrolled By:** Capt. Booth **Promoted:** No **ROH:** No
Born: South Carolina **Marital Status:** S **Residence** Guntown, MS

Transferred from Company E to Company A on 3/1/1863. Wounded (right arm) and captured at Gettysburg on 7/3/1863. Paroled from U. S. Army General Hospital in Chester, PA to City Point, VA for exchange on 9/17/1863. Furloughed from hospital at Williamsburg, VA on 9/28/1863. Returned to duty. Admitted to hospital in Richmond with wound on 1/8/1864 (company records provide no details as to date of wound or engagement). Furloughed 30-days from 1/91864.

Austin, Calvin H.
CO: A **Initial Rank:** Private
Joined: Wednesday, May 1, 1861 **Term (yrs):** 1 **Occupation:** Mechanic **Age** 21
Enrolled at: Tishomingo Co., MS **Enrolled By:** Capt. Leeth **Promoted:** No **ROH:** No
Born: **Marital Status:** S **Residence** Rienzi, MS

Died at Harpers Ferry, VA on 6/8/1861 (cause not stated).

Austin, Isaac
CO: K **Initial Rank:** Private
Joined: Saturday, March 1, 1862 **Term (yrs):** 3 **Occupation:** Farmer **Age** 53
Enrolled at: Iuka, MS **Enrolled By:** Lt. Latham **Promoted:** No **ROH:** No
Born: Georgia **Marital Status:** **Residence**

Discharged (wound of arm – no details – admitted to hospital on 8/26/1862) on 9/19/1862 due to disability.

Ayers, John M.
CO: B **Initial Rank:** Private
Joined: Monday, March 3, 1862 **Term (yrs):** 3 **Occupation:** Farmer **Age** 18
Enrolled at: Ripley, MS **Enrolled By:** Capt. Buchanan **Promoted:** No **ROH:** No
Born: Mississippi **Marital Status:** S **Residence**

Captured at Sharpsburg on 9/17/1862. Paroled and exchanged. Furloughed 30-days from 11/11/1862. Did not return to company. Listed as AWOL and deserted in Mar/Apr 1863 muster roll.

2nd Mississippi Alphabetical Roster (Annotated)

Ayers, William T.
CO: H, F **Initial Rank:** Private
Joined: Tuesday, April 30, 1861 **Term (yrs):** 1 **Occupation:** Carpenter **Age** 23
Enrolled at: Tupelo, MS **Enrolled By:** Capt. Taylor **Promoted:** No **ROH:** Yes
Born: Tennessee **Marital Status:** M **Residence** Chesterville, MS

According to accompanying list of engagements, was wounded at battle of 1st Manassas on 7/21/1861 (not mentioned in company records). Wounded at battle of Gaines Mill on 6/27/1862. Killed in battle at Cold Harbor (Shady Grove Church) on 6/3/1864. ROH for Malvern Hill, 7/1/1862 and Bethesda Church, 6/3/1864.

Bachas, F. W.
CO: **Initial Rank:** Private
Joined: **Term (yrs):** 0 **Occupation:** **Age**
Enrolled at: **Enrolled By:** **Promoted:** No **ROH:** No
Born: **Marital Status:** **Residence**

Appears on a Federal receipt for exchanged prisoners of war near Vicksburg, MS, dated 11/15/1862. No other record.

Bailey, A.
CO: E **Initial Rank:** Private
Joined: **Term (yrs):** 0 **Occupation:** **Age**
Enrolled at: **Enrolled By:** **Promoted:** No **ROH:** No
Born: **Marital Status:** **Residence** Itawamba Co., MS

Appears on a Federal roll of prisoners of war, surrendered and paroled, dated Columbus, Mississippi 5/17/1865. No other record. [Same individual as J. W. Bailey?]

Bailey, Absolom W.
CO: K **Initial Rank:** Private
Joined: Wednesday, May 1, 1861 **Term (yrs):** 1 **Occupation:** Farmer **Age** 20
Enrolled at: Tishomingo Co., MS **Enrolled By:** Capt. Stone **Promoted:** No **ROH:** No
Born: **Marital Status:** **Residence** Tishomingo Co.

Captured at Petersburg (Hatcher's Run?) on 4/2/1865. Taken to Fort Delaware. Released on oath on 6/11/1865.

Bailey, J. W.
CO: E **Initial Rank:** Private
Joined: **Term (yrs):** 0 **Occupation:** **Age**
Enrolled at: **Enrolled By:** **Promoted:** No **ROH:** No
Born: **Marital Status:** **Residence** Itawamba Co., MS

Appears on a Federal roll of prisoners of war, surrendered and paroled, dated Columbus, Mississippi 5/17/1865. No other record. [Same individual as A. Bailey?]

2nd Mississippi Alphabetical Roster (Annotated)

Bailey, Peyton R.
CO: E **Initial Rank:** Private
Joined: Wednesday, August 7, 1861 **Term (yrs):** 1 **Occupation:** Mechanic **Age** 21
Enrolled at: Camp Jones, VA **Enrolled By:** Col. Falkner **Promoted:** Yes **ROH:** No
Born: Alabama **Marital Status:** S **Residence** Guntown, MS

Appointed 2nd Lieutenant on 6/27/1862. Appointed 1st Lieutenant on 7/14/1862. Captured at Gettysburg on 7/1/1863. Sent first to Point Lookout, MD, then to Fort Delaware and thence to Johnson's Island, OH. Paroled and sent to City Point, VA for exchange on 3/7/1865. Subsequently paroled at Columbus, MS on 5/17/1865.

Baily, Charles M.
CO: E **Initial Rank:** Private
Joined: Saturday, March 8, 1862 **Term (yrs):** 3 **Occupation:** Farmer **Age** 14
Enrolled at: Guntown, MS **Enrolled By:** Capt. Bates **Promoted:** No **ROH:** No
Born: Mississippi **Marital Status:** S **Residence** Marietta, MS

Discharged on 10/23/1862 – underage. Surrendered and paroled at Columbus, MS on 5/17/1865.

Baker, Thomas D.
CO: E **Initial Rank:** Private
Joined: Monday, March 3, 1862 **Term (yrs):** 3 **Occupation:**   **Age** 48
Enrolled at: Guntown, MS **Enrolled By:** Capt. Bates **Promoted:** No **ROH:** No
Born: **Marital Status:**   **Residence**

Detailed to brigade teamster duties, 6/4/1862. Discharged for disability on 12/10/1862 by order of General A. P. Hill.

Ball, Franklin
CO: I **Initial Rank:** Private
Joined: Wednesday, May 1, 1861 **Term (yrs):** 1 **Occupation:** Farmer **Age** 19
Enrolled at: Pontotoc Co., MS **Enrolled By:** Capt. Herring **Promoted:** No **ROH:** No
Born: South Carolina **Marital Status:**   **Residence**

Killed in battle at Gettysburg on 7/1/1863.

Ball, Washington
CO: I **Initial Rank:** Private
Joined: Tuesday, September 17, 1861 **Term (yrs):** 1 **Occupation:**   **Age**
Enrolled at: Cherry Creek, MS **Enrolled By:** Lt. Davenport **Promoted:** No **ROH:** No
Born: **Marital Status:**   **Residence**

Captured at Falling Waters, MD on 7/14/1863. Exchanged on 11/1/1864. Captured at Hatcher's Run on 4/2/1865. Sent to Point Lookout, MD. Released on oath on 6/9/1865.

2nd Mississippi Alphabetical Roster (Annotated)

Ball, William M.
CO: I   **Initial Rank:** Private
Joined: Wednesday, May 1, 1861   **Term (yrs):** 1   **Occupation:** Farmer   **Age** 26
Enrolled at: Pontotoc Co., MS   **Enrolled By:** Capt. Herring   **Promoted:** No   **ROH:** No
Born: **Marital Status:**   **Residence**

Captured at Gettysburg on 7/1/1863. Sent to Fort Delaware where he died of disease on 2/27/1865 (inflammation of the lungs). Location of grave: "Jersey Shore."

Ball, Willis
CO: I   **Initial Rank:** Private
Joined: Wednesday, May 1, 1861   **Term (yrs):** 1   **Occupation:** Farmer   **Age** 24
Enrolled at: Pontotoc Co., MS   **Enrolled By:** Capt. Herring   **Promoted:** No   **ROH:** No
Born: **Marital Status:**   **Residence**

Listed as deserted on 7/10/1863. Taken into Federal custody at some point in time. Released from Point Lookout, MD on 6/23/1865.

Barcley, L. M.
CO: E   **Initial Rank:**
Joined: **Term (yrs):** 0   **Occupation:**   **Age**
Enrolled at: **Enrolled By:**   **Promoted:** No   **ROH:** No
Born: **Marital Status:**   **Residence**

Appears on a list for the Calhoun Rifles dated 2/11/1861. No other record.

Barkley, Anderson
CO: L   **Initial Rank:** Private
Joined: Monday, March 3, 1862   **Term (yrs):** 3   **Occupation:** Farmer   **Age** 21
Enrolled at: Ripley, MS   **Enrolled By:** Col. Falkner   **Promoted:** No   **ROH:** No
Born: Tennessee   **Marital Status:** S   **Residence** Ripley, MS

Discharged for disability on 9/28/1862 (amputated fingers of right hand – cause not stated).

Barkley, George G.
CO: F   **Initial Rank:** Private
Joined: Wednesday, May 1, 1861   **Term (yrs):** 1   **Occupation:** Carpenter   **Age** 30
Enrolled at: Tippah Co., MS   **Enrolled By:** Capt. Davis   **Promoted:** Yes   **ROH:** No
Born: North Carolina   **Marital Status:**   **Residence**

Appointed Corporal on 12/5/1861. Discharged on 7/31/1862 for disability.

2nd Mississippi Alphabetical Roster (Annotated)

Barksdale, James M.   CO: G   Initial Rank: Private
Joined: Wednesday, May 1, 1861   **Term (yrs):** 1   **Occupation:** Planter   **Age** 45
Enrolled at: Pontotoc, MS   **Enrolled By:** Capt. Miller   **Promoted:** Yes   **ROH:** No
Born: South Carolina   **Marital Status:** M   **Residence** Pontotoc, MS

Appointed Corporal on 8/1/1861. Appointed to 5th Sergeant on 1/1/1862. Wounded in battle of Seven Pines on 5/31/1862. Discharged on 8/2/1862 due to over age.

Barksdale, Rowdy M.   CO: G   Initial Rank: Private
Joined: Monday, September 16, 1861   **Term (yrs):** 1   **Occupation:** Farmer   **Age** 17
Enrolled at: Pontotoc, MS   **Enrolled By:** Lt. Davenport   **Promoted:** No   **ROH:** No
Born: Mississippi   **Marital Status:** S   **Residence** Pontotoc, MS

Killed in battle at Seven Pines on 5/31/1862.

Barnet, H. B.   CO: E   Initial Rank:
Joined: **Term (yrs):** 0   **Occupation:**   **Age**
Enrolled at: **Enrolled By:**   **Promoted:** No   **ROH:** No
Born: **Marital Status:**   **Residence**

Appears on a list for the Calhoun Rifles dated 2/11/1861. No other record.

Barnet, L. J.   CO: B   Initial Rank: Private
Joined: **Term (yrs):** 0   **Occupation:**   **Age**
Enrolled at: **Enrolled By:**   **Promoted:** No   **ROH:** No
Born: **Marital Status:**   **Residence**

Appears on a Federal register of prisoners of war, captured near Ripley, Mississippi on 1/22/1864 and sent to Fort Delaware. No other record.

Barnett, James T.   CO: B   Initial Rank: Private
Joined: Wednesday, May 1, 1861   **Term (yrs):** 1   **Occupation:** Farmer   **Age** 23
Enrolled at: Tippah Co., MS   **Enrolled By:** Capt. Buchanan   **Promoted:** No   **ROH:** No
Born: **Marital Status:**   **Residence** Hickory Flat, MS

Wounded at Gaines Mill on 6/27/1862. Taken to hospital at Richmond, VA. Returned to duty. Hospital records show him admitted for wound on 7/9/1863 (company records provide no details as to date of wound or engagement). Returned to duty on 7/29/1863. Listed as deserter, AWOL since 3/12/1864. Surrendered on 4/23/1865 and paroled near Holly Springs, Mississippi on 6/5/1865.

2nd Mississippi Alphabetical Roster (Annotated)

Barnett, Joseph S.
CO: K **Initial Rank:** Private
Joined: Saturday, March 1, 1862 **Term (yrs):** 3 **Occupation:** **Age** 18
Enrolled at: Iuka, MS **Enrolled By:** Lt. Latham **Promoted:** No **ROH:** No
Born: **Marital Status:** **Residence**

Wounded at Gaines Mill on 6/27/1862. Returned to duty. Captured at Falling Waters, MD on 7/14/1863. Sent to Point Lookout, MD. Exchanged on 3/14/1865.

Barnett, William J.
CO: K **Initial Rank:** Private
Joined: Saturday, March 1, 1862 **Term (yrs):** 3 **Occupation:** **Age** 35
Enrolled at: Iuka, MS **Enrolled By:** Lt. Latham **Promoted:** No **ROH:** No
Born: **Marital Status:** **Residence**

Captured at Gettysburg on 7/4/1863. Sent to Fort Delaware and transferred to Point Lookout, MD on 9/20/1863. Took oath of allegiance and released on 4/11/1864. Note indicates that W. J. Barnett appears to have assumed the name of J. W. McCracken of the 3rd Tennessee Infantry (who was captured at Raymond, MS on 5/12/1863 and died at Fort Delaware on 8/9/1863) for the purpose of getting exchanged.

Barr, William
CO: G **Initial Rank:** Private
Joined: Wednesday, May 1, 1861 **Term (yrs):** 1 **Occupation:** Farmer **Age** 39
Enrolled at: Pontotoc, MS **Enrolled By:** Capt. Miller **Promoted:** No **ROH:** No
Born: South Carolina **Marital Status:** S **Residence** Pontotoc, MS

Discharged at Camp Fisher, VA on 11/6/1861 for disability by order of General Smith.

Barron, Josiah W.
CO: D, F **Initial Rank:** Private
Joined: Wednesday, May 1, 1861 **Term (yrs):** 1 **Occupation:** Blacksmith **Age** 33
Enrolled at: Tippah Co., MS **Enrolled By:** Capt. Beck **Promoted:** No **ROH:** No
Born: **Marital Status:** M **Residence** Jonesboro, TN

Also see the 79th Tennessee Infantry Regiment. Detailed blacksmith from 6/30/1861. Transferred to Company F on 4/30/1862. "On daily duty as blacksmith." Transferred to Co. E of 79th Tennessee due as a citizen of the state of Tennessee.

2nd Mississippi Alphabetical Roster (Annotated)

Bartlett, James
CO: L *Initial Rank:* Private
Joined: Monday, March 3, 1862 *Term (yrs):* 3 *Occupation:* Farmer *Age* 25
Enrolled at: Ripley, MS *Enrolled By:* Col. Falkner *Promoted:* No *ROH:* No
Born: Tennessee *Marital Status:* M *Residence* Dumas, MS

Captured at Gettysburg on 7/1/1863. Sent to Fort Delaware. Released on oath on 6/11/1865.

Bartlett, Joshua
CO: L *Initial Rank:* Private
Joined: Monday, March 3, 1862 *Term (yrs):* 3 *Occupation:* Farmer *Age* 24
Enrolled at: Ripley, MS *Enrolled By:* Col. Falkner *Promoted:* No *ROH:* No
Born: Tennessee *Marital Status:* M *Residence* Dumas, MS

Died of disease (typhoid fever) on 6/19/1862 in Chimborazo Hospital #5, Richmond, VA.

Barton, C. G.
CO: A *Initial Rank:* Private
Joined: Saturday, March 1, 1862 *Term (yrs):* 3 *Occupation:* Clerk *Age* 18
Enrolled at: Jacinto, MS *Enrolled By:* Lt. Clayton *Promoted:* No *ROH:* No
Born: Alabama *Marital Status:* S *Residence* Jacinto, MS

Also see 26th Mississippi Infantry Regiment. Wounded (in arm) at Gaines Mill on 6/27/1862. Sent to hospital at Lynchburg, VA. Discharged January 1863 as result of wounds received.

Barton, Elias
CO: G *Initial Rank:*
Joined: Saturday, March 2, 1861 *Term (yrs):* 0 *Occupation:* *Age*
Enrolled at: Pontotoc Co., MS *Enrolled By:* Capt. Kilpatrick *Promoted:* No *ROH:* No
Born: *Marital Status:* *Residence*

Appears on company muster roll. No other record.

Barton, William L.
CO: H *Initial Rank:* Private
Joined: Monday, April 29, 1861 *Term (yrs):* 1 *Occupation:* Clerk *Age* 26
Enrolled at: Pontotoc, MS *Enrolled By:* Capt. Taylor *Promoted:* Yes *ROH:* No
Born: Alabama *Marital Status:* M *Residence* Tupelo, MS

Appointed 1st Corporal on 9/10/1861. Appointed Jr. 2nd Lieutenant on 7/14/1862. Wounded at battle of 2nd Manassas on 8/29/1862. Furloughed. Resigned on 4/24/1863 due to disability from wound. Captured on 5/4/1863 near Tupelo by Federal forces. Sent to Alton, IL. Sent to Point Lookout, MD, Johnson's Island, OH, and then to Fort Delaware. Paroled at Charleston Harbor, SC on 12/15/1864.

2nd Mississippi Alphabetical Roster (Annotated)

Bates, James T.
CO: E **Initial Rank:** Private
Joined: Wednesday, May 1, 1861 **Term (yrs):** 1 **Occupation:** Farmer **Age** 17
Enrolled at: Itawamba Co., MS **Enrolled By:** Capt. Booth **Promoted:** No **ROH:** No
Born: **Marital Status:** **Residence**

Discharged for underage in July 1862.

Bates, Robert P.
CO: E **Initial Rank:** 1st Lieutenant
Joined: Wednesday, May 1, 1861 **Term (yrs):** 1 **Occupation:** Merchant **Age** 27
Enrolled at: Itawamba Co., MS **Enrolled By:** **Promoted:** Yes **ROH:** No
Born: Mississippi **Marital Status:** S **Residence** Guntown, MS

Elected Captain to take the place of Booth [John F.] who resigned on 8/20/1861. Resigned on 11/15/1862 due to expiration of term of service.

Bates, Thomas P.
CO: E **Initial Rank:** Private
Joined: Monday, February 18, 1861 **Term (yrs):** 1 **Occupation:** Farmer **Age** 16
Enrolled at: Guntown, MS **Enrolled By:** **Promoted:** No **ROH:** No
Born: Mississippi **Marital Status:** S **Residence** Guntown, MS

Discharged on 7/23/1863 – underage.

Bazemore, John G.
CO: C **Initial Rank:** Private
Joined: Wednesday, May 1, 1861 **Term (yrs):** 1 **Occupation:** Farmer **Age** 19
Enrolled at: Itawamba Co., MS **Enrolled By:** Capt. Bromley **Promoted:** No **ROH:** No
Born: **Marital Status:** **Residence**

Hospital records show he was admitted for a wound on 7/12/1863 at Richmond, VA (company records provide no details as to date of wound or engagement). Returned to duty on 8/7/1863. Deserted on 3/31/1865. Taken into Federal custody. Oath taken and transportation furnished to Nashville, TN on 4/4/1865.

Bazemore, William D.
CO: C **Initial Rank:** Private
Joined: Wednesday, May 1, 1861 **Term (yrs):** 1 **Occupation:** Farmer **Age** 22
Enrolled at: Itawamba Co., MS **Enrolled By:** Capt. Bromley **Promoted:** No **ROH:** Yes
Born: Georgia **Marital Status:** **Residence**

Killed in battle at Gettysburg on 7/1/1863. ROH for Gettysburg, 7/3/1863. (obviously means he was most likely killed on 7/3 instead of 7/1).

2nd Mississippi Alphabetical Roster (Annotated)

Beachum, H. L.   CO: C   Initial Rank: Private
Joined: Saturday, March 1, 1862   **Term (yrs):** 3   **Occupation:** Farmer   **Age** 22
Enrolled at: Verona, MS   **Enrolled By:** Lt. Pounds   **Promoted:** No   **ROH:** No
Born: **Marital Status:**   **Residence**

Wounded at Malvern Hill on 7/1/1862. Sent to hospital at Richmond, VA. Returned to duty. Wounded at Gettysburg (right leg) on 7/1/1863. Sent to hospital at Williamsburg, VA (admitted on 7/27/1863). Listed as deserter from 8/2/1863.

Beachum, James M.   CO: C   Initial Rank: Private
Joined: Wednesday, May 1, 1861   **Term (yrs):** 1   **Occupation:** Farmer   **Age** 18
Enrolled at: Itawamba Co., MS   **Enrolled By:** Capt. Bromley   **Promoted:** Yes   **ROH:** No
Born: **Marital Status:**   **Residence**

Wounded battle of Gaines Mill on 6/27/1862. Returned to duty. Listed as 2nd Corporal during Sep/Oct 1862 muster roll. Captured at Gettysburg on 7/1/1863. Sent to Fort Delaware. Released on oath on 6/11/1865.

Beam, George   CO: C   Initial Rank: Private
Joined: **Term (yrs):** 0   **Occupation:**   **Age**
Enrolled at: **Enrolled By:**   **Promoted:** No   **ROH:** No
Born: **Marital Status:**   **Residence** Itawamba Co., MS

Appears on a Federal roll of prisoners of war at Harrisburg, PA. Dated 7/7/1863. Appears on prisoner of war register from Gettysburg, captured 7/3/1863. Sent to Fort Delaware. Released on oath on 6/11/1865.

Beam, J. H.   CO: H   Initial Rank:
Joined: **Term (yrs):** 0   **Occupation:**   **Age**
Enrolled at: **Enrolled By:**   **Promoted:** No   **ROH:** No
Born: **Marital Status:**   **Residence**

Appears on a Federal list of sick and wounded Confederates in and about Gettysburg, PA after the battle and lists of prisoners. No other records.

2nd Mississippi Alphabetical Roster (Annotated)

Beam, John A. *CO:* C   *Initial Rank:* Private

Joined: Tuesday, October 1, 1861   *Term (yrs):* 1   *Occupation:*   *Age*

Enrolled at: Richmond, MS   *Enrolled By:* Lt. Davenport   *Promoted:* Yes   *ROH:* No

Born: *Marital Status:*   *Residence* Itawamba Co., MS

Promoted to Sergeant. Hospital records show admitted at Richmond for wound on 7/12/1863 (company records provide no details as to date of wound or engagement). Furloughed on 9/28/1863 for 30-days. Returned to duty. Captured at Petersburg (Hatcher's Run?) on 4/2/1865. Sent to Fort Delaware. Released on oath on 6/11/1865.

Beard, Jacob S. *CO:* F   *Initial Rank:* Private

Joined: Tuesday, March 11, 1862   *Term (yrs):* 3   *Occupation:* Farmer   *Age* 24

Enrolled at: Ripley, MS   *Enrolled By:* Capt. Powers   *Promoted:* No   *ROH:* No

Born: Indiana   *Marital Status:* M   *Residence*

Wounded (left foot) at battle of Gaines Mill on 6/27/1862. Sent to hospital at Richmond, VA. Furloughed 30-days from 7/28/1862. Furlough extended to 11/1/1862. Did not return to company. Listed as deserted as of 11/1/1862. Oath of allegiance taken at Memphis, TN on 3/27/1865.

Beard, N. C. *CO:* A   *Initial Rank:* Private

Joined: Saturday, March 1, 1862   *Term (yrs):* 3   *Occupation:* Farmer   *Age* 17

Enrolled at: Jacinto, MS   *Enrolled By:* Lt. Clayton   *Promoted:* No   *ROH:* No

Born: Mississippi   *Marital Status:* S   *Residence* Jacinto, MS

Wounded(?) and captured at Gettysburg on 7/5/1863. Paroled at DeCamp General Hospital, Davids Island, NY Harbor to City Point, VA on 9/8/1863 for exchange. AWOL since 3/1/1864. Listed as deserter.

Beard, R. L. *CO:* A   *Initial Rank:*

Joined: *Term (yrs):* 0   *Occupation:*   *Age*

Enrolled at: *Enrolled By:*   *Promoted:* No   *ROH:* No

Born: *Marital Status:*   *Residence*

Appears on a Federal register of sick and wounded Confederates in the hospitals in and about Gettysburg, PA and on the rolls of prisoners of war. No other records.

2nd Mississippi Alphabetical Roster (Annotated)

Bearden, John G.

	CO: F	*Initial Rank:* Private
Joined: Wednesday, May 1, 1861	*Term (yrs):* 1 *Occupation:* Planter	*Age* 23
Enrolled at: Tippah Co., MS	*Enrolled By:* Capt. Davis	*Promoted:* Yes *ROH:* No
Born:	*Marital Status:*	*Residence*

Elected 2nd Lieutenant on 4/11/1862 and took command on 4/22/1862. Wounded at Gaines Mill on 6/27/1862. Returned to duty. Wounded (right leg) at Sharpsburg on 9/17/1862. Furloughed 30-days from 10/11/1862. Returned to duty. Resigned on 11/24/1863 due to disability from wounds.

Bearwald, Edward

	CO: A	*Initial Rank:* Private
Joined: Wednesday, May 1, 1861	*Term (yrs):* 1 *Occupation:* Merchant	*Age* 26
Enrolled at: Tishomingo Co., MS	*Enrolled By:* Capt. Leeth	*Promoted:* No *ROH:* No
Born: Prussia	*Marital Status:* S	*Residence* Jacinto, MS

Discharged due to disability on 7/18/1862.

Beaseley, Isaiah

	CO: L	*Initial Rank:* Private
Joined: Monday, March 3, 1862	*Term (yrs):* 3 *Occupation:* Farmer	*Age* 19
Enrolled at: Ripley, MS	*Enrolled By:* Col. Falkner	*Promoted:* No *ROH:* No
Born: South Carolina	*Marital Status:* S	*Residence* Dumas, MS

Captured at Sharpsburg on 9/17/1862. Paroled and exchanged (? – no details in records). Returned to duty. Wounded and captured at Gettysburg on 7/1/1863. Sent to Fort Delaware. Released on oath on 6/11/1865.

Beaty, David

	CO: A	*Initial Rank:* Private
Joined: Saturday, March 1, 1862	*Term (yrs):* 3 *Occupation:*	*Age* 22
Enrolled at: Jacinto, MS	*Enrolled By:* Lt. Clayton	*Promoted:* No *ROH:* No
Born:	*Marital Status:*	*Residence*

Wounded (across forehead) and captured at Gettysburg on 7/1/1863. Paroled at DeCamp General Hospital, NY Harbor to City Point, VA on 9/16/1863 to await exchange. Sent home on wounded furlough on 9/20/1863. Subsequently died in Tishomingo Co., MS. Date unknown.

2nd Mississippi Alphabetical Roster (Annotated)

Beaty, J. L.
CO: A **Initial Rank:** Private
Joined: Saturday, March 1, 1862 **Term (yrs):** 3 **Occupation:** Farmer **Age** 19
Enrolled at: Jacinto, MS **Enrolled By:** Lt. Clayton **Promoted:** No **ROH:** No
Born: Georgia **Marital Status:** S **Residence** Jacinto, MS

Wounded at Malvern Hill (according to company muster records). However, he appears on a Confederate list of casualties wounded on 6/27/1862. [This would mean he was wounded at Gaines Mill, not Malvern Hill]. Furloughed. Returned to duty. Wounded at Gettysburg (date not given). Subsequently died from wounds on Nov. 25, 1863.

Beck, James O.
CO: D **Initial Rank:** 2nd Sergeant
Joined: Wednesday, May 1, 1861 **Term (yrs):** 1 **Occupation:** Farmer **Age** 17
Enrolled at: Tippah Co., MS **Enrolled By:** Capt. Beck **Promoted:** No **ROH:** No
Born: Mississippi **Marital Status:** S **Residence** Salem, MS

Discharged 7/27/1862 – under 18 years of age.

Beck, Orrin A.
CO: D **Initial Rank:** 3rd Lieutenant
Joined: Saturday, April 27, 1861 **Term (yrs):** 1 **Occupation:** Farmer **Age**
Enrolled at: Pine Grove, MS **Enrolled By:** Capt. Beck **Promoted:** Yes **ROH:** No
Born: Mississippi **Marital Status:** M **Residence** Pine Grove, MS

Also see 18th Mississippi Cavalry (?). Listed as 2nd Lieutenant from circa 4/27/1861 to 6/30/1861 time period. Discharged 4/23/1862 due to reorganization of Company.

Beck, William D.
CO: D **Initial Rank:** Captain
Joined: Wednesday, May 1, 1861 **Term (yrs):** 1 **Occupation:** Farmer **Age**
Enrolled at: Tippah Co., MS **Enrolled By:** Capt. Beck **Promoted:** No **ROH:** No
Born: **Marital Status:** S **Residence** Salem, MS

Wounded at 1st Manassas on 7/21/1861. Returned to duty. Discharged 4/23/1862 due to reorganization of Company.

2nd Mississippi Alphabetical Roster (Annotated)

Belcher, Arthur M. *CO:* A *Initial Rank:* 2nd Sergeant

Joined: Wednesday, May 1, 1861   *Term (yrs):* 1 *Occupation:* Teacher   *Age* 27
Enrolled at: Tishomingo Co., MS   *Enrolled By:* Capt. Leeth   *Promoted:* Yes   *ROH:* No
Born: Tennessee   *Marital Status:* S   *Residence* Baldwin, MS

Promoted to 1st Sergeant on 4/22/1862. Elected 2nd Lt on 3/21/1863. Wounded 7/1/1863 at Gettysburg and captured (at Greencastle). Sent to Johnson's Island, OH. Transferred to Point Lookout, MD thence to Fort Delaware on 6/23/1864. Paroled to James River, VA on and exchanged 10/11/1864. Returned to duty. Captured at Hatcher's Run on 4/2/1865 and taken to Johnson's Island, OH. Released on oath on 6/18/1865.

Bell, James T.   *CO:* H   *Initial Rank:* Private

Joined: Monday, April 29, 1861   *Term (yrs):* 1 *Occupation:* Farmer (Student?)   *Age* 21
Enrolled at: Pontotoc Co., MS   *Enrolled By:* Capt. Taylor   *Promoted:* No   *ROH:* No
Born: Alabama   *Marital Status:* S   *Residence* Tupelo, MS

Wounded (right thigh) 7/1/1863 at Gettysburg and captured (at Greencastle on 7/5/1863). Paroled from Hammond U. S. General Hospital, Point Lookout, MD to City Point, VA on 3/20/1864 for exchange. Furloughed 30-days from hospital in Richmond on 3/26/1864. Listed as AWOL since 8/10/1864. However, records note: "Has authority to appear before a medical examining board for retirement."

Bell, John G.   *CO:* C   *Initial Rank:* Private

Joined: Saturday, June 29, 1861   *Term (yrs):* 1 *Occupation:* Carpenter   *Age* 31
Enrolled at: Winchester, VA   *Enrolled By:* Capt. Bromley   *Promoted:* Yes   *ROH:* No
Born: *Marital Status:*   *Residence*

Appointed 3rd Corporal on 8/1/1861. Reduced to ranks on 4/23/1862. Listed as 3rd Sergeant during Mar/Apr, 1863 muster. Captured 7/1/1863 at Gettysburg. No record following last company muster (Jan/Feb 1865).

Bell, John R.   *CO:* C   *Initial Rank:* Private

Joined: Tuesday, October 1, 1861   *Term (yrs):* 1 *Occupation:*   *Age*
Enrolled at: Richmond, MS   *Enrolled By:* Lt. Davenport   *Promoted:* No   *ROH:* No
Born: *Marital Status:*   *Residence*

Wounded (right thigh) at 2nd Manassas on 8/29/1862 and furloughed from hospital for 30-days from 10/8/1862. Returned to duty. Hospital records show he was admitted to the hospital in Richmond for a wound on 7/9/1863 (company records provide no details on date of wound or engagement). Furloughed 60-days from 8/26/1863. Last company record (Sep/Oct 1864) remarks: "Sick in hospital in North Carolina." No further record.

2nd Mississippi Alphabetical Roster (Annotated)

Bell, Leroy *CO:* B *Initial Rank:* Private
Joined: Thursday, February 27, 1862 *Term (yrs):* 3 *Occupation:* Farmer *Age* 18
Enrolled at: Ripley, MS *Enrolled By:* Capt. Buchanan *Promoted:* No *ROH:* No
Born: Tennessee *Marital Status:* S *Residence*

Died 8/30/1862 of wounds received in battle at 2nd Manassas on 8/29/1862 (other records list death as 9/12/1862 at Warrenton, VA).

Bell, William *CO:* C *Initial Rank:* Private
Joined: Saturday, June 29, 1861 *Term (yrs):* 1 *Occupation:* Farmer *Age* 23
Enrolled at: Winchester, VA *Enrolled By:* Capt. Bromley *Promoted:* No *ROH:* Yes
Born: Alabama *Marital Status:* S *Residence*

Killed at battle of Gaines Mill on 6/27/1862. ROH for Gaines Mill, 6/27/1862.

Bellew, Wiley *CO:* C *Initial Rank:* Private
Joined: Saturday, March 1, 1862 *Term (yrs):* 3 *Occupation:* *Age*
Enrolled at: Verona, MS *Enrolled By:* Lt. Pounds *Promoted:* No *ROH:* No
Born: South Carolina *Marital Status:* *Residence*

Died of disease (dysentery), 5/17/1862 at Richmond, VA, Chimborazo Hospital #5.

Belsher, Wylie *CO:* D *Initial Rank:* Private
Joined: *Term (yrs):* 0 *Occupation:* *Age*
Enrolled at: *Enrolled By:* *Promoted:* No *ROH:* No
Born: *Marital Status:* *Residence*

See Wiley M. Belsher of Ham's Regt. Mississippi Cavalry. No other record.

Bennett, Edward D. *CO:* H *Initial Rank:* Private
Joined: Saturday, March 15, 1862 *Term (yrs):* 3 *Occupation:* *Age* 18
Enrolled at: Chesterville, MS *Enrolled By:* Lt. Porter *Promoted:* No *ROH:* No
Born: *Marital Status:* *Residence*

Listed as deserted on 1/7/1865. Oath of allegiance taken while in Federal custody on 1/11/1865. Transportation furnished to Cincinnati, OH.

2nd Mississippi Alphabetical Roster (Annotated)

Bennett, Henry H.
CO: K, E **Initial Rank:** Private
Joined: Saturday, March 1, 1862 **Term (yrs):** 3 **Occupation:** **Age** 21
Enrolled at: Iuka, MS **Enrolled By:** Lt. Latham **Promoted:** No **ROH:** No
Born: **Marital Status:** **Residence**

Transferred to Co. E from Company K on 4/28/1862. Discharged on 5/7/1862 for disability.

Bennett, James
CO: B **Initial Rank:** Private
Joined: Wednesday, May 1, 1861 **Term (yrs):** 1 **Occupation:** **Age** 24
Enrolled at: Tippah Co., MS **Enrolled By:** Capt. Buchanan **Promoted:** No **ROH:** No
Born: **Marital Status:** **Residence**

Appears on a company muster-in roll. No record after muster-in roll.

Bennett, Levi M.
CO: E **Initial Rank:** Private
Joined: Wednesday, May 1, 1861 **Term (yrs):** 1 **Occupation:** Carpenter **Age** 21
Enrolled at: Itawamba Co., MS **Enrolled By:** Capt. Booth **Promoted:** Yes **ROH:** No
Born: Alabama **Marital Status:** M **Residence** Guntown, MS

Promoted to Orderly Sergeant on 6/15/61. Killed in battle on 6/27/1862 at Gaines Mill.

Bennett, Miles J.
CO: B **Initial Rank:** Private
Joined: Wednesday, May 1, 1861 **Term (yrs):** 1 **Occupation:** Farmer **Age** 21
Enrolled at: Tippah Co., MS **Enrolled By:** Capt. Buchanan **Promoted:** Yes **ROH:** Yes
Born: **Marital Status:** **Residence**

Listed as 5th Sergeant during Jul/Aug 1862 muster; 4th Sergeant during Sep/Oct 1862 muster. Admitted to hospital in Richmond with wound on 7/13/1863 (date of wound or engagement not noted in company records). Returned to duty. Promoted to 3rd Sergeant circa May/Jun 1864. Promoted to 1st Sergeant during Sep/Oct, 1864 time period. Captured at Petersburg (Hatcher's Run?) on 4/2/1865. Taken to Fort Delaware. Released on oath on 6/11/1865. ROH for Gettysburg, 7/1/1863.

Bennett, Richard
CO: H **Initial Rank:** Private
Joined: Sunday, March 23, 1862 **Term (yrs):** 3 **Occupation:** Farmer **Age** 21
Enrolled at: Corinth, MS **Enrolled By:** Lt. Porter **Promoted:** No **ROH:** No
Born: Alabama **Marital Status:** S **Residence** Richmond, MS

Wounded at South Mountain on 9/14/1862. Deserted to the enemy on 1/7/1865.

2nd Mississippi Alphabetical Roster (Annotated)

Bennett, Richard G.
CO: B   *Initial Rank:* Private
Joined: Tuesday, February 25, 1862   *Term (yrs):* 3   *Occupation:* Farmer   *Age* 25
Enrolled at: Ripley, MS   *Enrolled By:* Capt. Buchanan   *Promoted:* No   *ROH:* Yes
Born: South Carolina   *Marital Status:* S   *Residence*

Captured 4/2/1865 at Hatcher's Run. Released on oath on 6/9/1865. ROH for The Wilderness, 5/6/1864.

Bennett, Walter J.
CO: B   *Initial Rank:* Private
Joined: Tuesday, April 30, 1861   *Term (yrs):* 1   *Occupation:* Merchant   *Age* 25
Enrolled at: Ripley, MS   *Enrolled By:* Capt. Buchanan   *Promoted:* No   *ROH:* No
Born: *Marital Status:*   *Residence*

Detached service as brigade clerk – with General Whiting's staff. Captured in Ripley, Miss on 1/22/1864. Sent to Alton, IL. Transferred to Fort Delaware on 2/29/1864. Released on oath on 6/11/1865.

Benson, George W.
CO: E   *Initial Rank:* Private
Joined: Wednesday, May 1, 1861   *Term (yrs):* 1   *Occupation:* Teacher (Farmer?)   *Age* 19
Enrolled at: Itawamba Co., MS   *Enrolled By:* Capt. Booth   *Promoted:* No   *ROH:* No
Born: Mississippi   *Marital Status:* S   *Residence* Baldwyn, MS

Deserted. "Left the company in front of the enemy at Manassas" (8/1862) and AWOL.

Benson, Joseph P.
CO: G   *Initial Rank:* Private
Joined: Wednesday, May 1, 1861   *Term (yrs):* 1   *Occupation:* Student (Farmer?)   *Age* 18
Enrolled at: Pontotoc Co., MS   *Enrolled By:* Capt. Miller   *Promoted:* No   *ROH:* No
Born: Mississippi   *Marital Status:* S   *Residence* Pontotoc, MS

Discharged by order of General Whiting on 12/31/1861 for disability at Camp Fisher, VA.

Benson, William C.
CO: E   *Initial Rank:* Private
Joined: Saturday, February 22, 1862   *Term (yrs):* 3   *Occupation:*   *Age* 17
Enrolled at: Guntown, MS   *Enrolled By:* Capt. Bates   *Promoted:* No   *ROH:* No
Born: *Marital Status:*   *Residence*

Died of pneumonia, 7/15/1862 (one record says 7/8/1862) at General Hospital #1, Lynchburg, VA.

2nd Mississippi Alphabetical Roster (Annotated)

Benson, William O.
CO: E *Initial Rank:* Private
Joined: Saturday, March 1, 1862 *Term (yrs):* 3 *Occupation:* Farmer *Age* 18
Enrolled at: Guntown, MS *Enrolled By:* *Promoted:* No *ROH:* No
Born: Mississippi *Marital Status:* S *Residence* Baldwyn, MS

Discharged in May 1862 on account of disability.

Benton, Mordica E.
CO: H *Initial Rank:* Private
Joined: Monday, September 30, 1861 *Term (yrs):* 1 *Occupation:* Laborer *Age* 30
Enrolled at: Iuka, MS *Enrolled By:* Lt. Davenport *Promoted:* No *ROH:* No
Born: Maryland *Marital Status:* S *Residence* Maryland

Deserted 6/13/1862.

Bessonette, William C.
CO: C *Initial Rank:* Private
Joined: Wednesday, May 1, 1861 *Term (yrs):* 1 *Occupation:* B. Mason *Age* 23
Enrolled at: Itawamba Co., MS *Enrolled By:* Capt. Bromley *Promoted:* Yes *ROH:* No
Born: *Marital Status:* *Residence*

Appointed 2nd Corporal on 8/1/1861. Appointed 4th Sergeant on 8/15/1862. Listed as 3rd Sergeant for Sep/Oct 1862 muster. Listed as 2nd Lieutenant for May/Jun 1863 muster roll. Admitted to hospital in Richmond on 7/14/1863 (cause not given). Wounded 8/19/1864 at the Weldon Railroad. Furloughed 50-days from 9/9/1864. Returned to duty. Severely wounded (right leg) and captured at Hatcher's Run on 4/2/1865. Released on oath on 6/9/1865.

Bieber, John H.
CO: L *Initial Rank:* Private
Joined: Monday, March 3, 1862 *Term (yrs):* 3 *Occupation:* Farmer *Age* 27
Enrolled at: Ripley, MS *Enrolled By:* Col. Falkner *Promoted:* No *ROH:* No
Born: Tennessee *Marital Status:* M *Residence* Dumas, MS

Accidentally wounded on 6/10/1862 in hand. Sent to hospital in Richmond. Arm amputated and sent home on wounded furlough. Did not return to company. Listed as deserted and dropped from rolls on 8/31/1863. Captured by 5th Regiment Ohio Cavalry near Corinth on 10/6/63, took oath of allegiance at Memphis, TN and was released on 11/14/1863. Served as a guide for Federal forces.

2nd Mississippi Alphabetical Roster (Annotated)

Biggs, William F.   CO: K   Initial Rank: Private

Joined: Wednesday, May 1, 1861   **Term (yrs):** 1   **Occupation:** Farmer   **Age** 30

Enrolled at: Tishomingo Co., MS   **Enrolled By:** Capt. Stone   **Promoted:** No   **ROH:** No

Born: Tennessee   **Marital Status:**   **Residence**

Wounded (chest) at Sharpsburg on 9/17/1862 and captured. Died from wounds in U. S. Army hospital on 10/13/1862 at Frederick, MD.

Bigham, Finis M.   CO: I   Initial Rank: Private

Joined: Wednesday, May 1, 1861   **Term (yrs):** 1   **Occupation:** Farmer   **Age** 23

Enrolled at: Pontotoc Co., MS   **Enrolled By:** Capt. Herring   **Promoted:** No   **ROH:** No

Born: Mississippi   **Marital Status:**   **Residence**

Wounded (left ankle joint) at Sharpsburg on 9/17/1862. Furloughed from hospital 60-days from 10/10/1862. Discharged from effects of wound on 9/12/1863.

Billingsley, Thomas W.   CO: I   Initial Rank: Private

Joined: Tuesday, September 10, 1861   **Term (yrs):** 1   **Occupation:** Farmer   **Age** 20

Enrolled at: Guntown, MS   **Enrolled By:** Lt. Davenport   **Promoted:** No   **ROH:** Yes

Born: Alabama   **Marital Status:**   **Residence**

Killed in battle at Weldon Railroad, VA on 8/18/1864. ROH for The Wilderness, 5/6/1864 and Weldon Railroad, 8/18/1864.

Birmingham, Joshua M.   CO: C   Initial Rank: Private

Joined: Saturday, September 20, 1862   **Term (yrs):** 3   **Occupation:**   **Age**

Enrolled at: Enterprise, MS   **Enrolled By:** Lt. Byrn   **Promoted:** No   **ROH:** No

Born: **Marital Status:**   **Residence**

Captured at Gettysburg on 7/1/1863. Sent to Fort Delaware. Transferred to Point Lookout, MD (Hammond General Hospital) on 10/20/1863. Died at Point Lookout of disease on 12/22/1863.

Bishop, James M.   CO: K   Initial Rank: Private

Joined: Saturday, March 1, 1862   **Term (yrs):** 3   **Occupation:** Farmer   **Age** 22

Enrolled at: Iuka, MS   **Enrolled By:** Lt. Latham   **Promoted:** No   **ROH:** No

Born: Mississippi   **Marital Status:** M   **Residence**

Also see J. M. Bishop, 26th Mississippi Cav [? – maybe 26th Infantry, there is no history for the 26th Miss. Cavalry Regiment]. Killed in battle at Gaines Farm on 6/27/1862.

2nd Mississippi Alphabetical Roster (Annotated)

Black, James P.
CO: F *Initial Rank:* Private
Joined: Wednesday, May 1, 1861 *Term (yrs):* 1 *Occupation:* Planter *Age* 21
Enrolled at: Tippah Co., MS *Enrolled By:* Capt. Davis *Promoted:* Yes *ROH:* Yes
Born: Tennessee *Marital Status:* S *Residence*

Appointed 4th Corporal on 7/26/1861. Appointed 5th Sergeant on 4/24/1862. Killed in battle at Sharpsburg on 9/17/1862. ROH for Sharpsburg, 9/17/1862.

Blackburne, Joseph
CO: D *Initial Rank:* Private
Joined: Wednesday, May 1, 1861 *Term (yrs):* 1 *Occupation:* Mechanic *Age* 34
Enrolled at: Tippah Co., MS *Enrolled By:* Capt. Beck *Promoted:* No *ROH:* No
Born: Ohio *Marital Status:* S *Residence* Salem, MS

Discharged on 7/27/1862 – over 35 years of age.

Blackwell, Michael A. P.
CO: B *Initial Rank:* Private
Joined: Wednesday, May 1, 1861 *Term (yrs):* 1 *Occupation:* Farmer *Age* 22
Enrolled at: Tippah Co., MS *Enrolled By:* Capt. Buchanan *Promoted:* No *ROH:* No
Born: *Marital Status:* *Residence*

Killed in action at Gettysburg on 7/1/1863 [may have been mortally wounded and captured, according to Federal records. However, date of death not given. (some confusion may exist with prisoner records between William and Michael Blackwell). Records indicate one or the other may have been mortally wounded and captured but died shortly afterward].

Blackwell, William T.
CO: B *Initial Rank:* Private
Joined: Wednesday, September 18, 1861 *Term (yrs):* 1 *Occupation:* *Age*
Enrolled at: Ripley, MS *Enrolled By:* Lt. Davenport *Promoted:* No *ROH:* No
Born: *Marital Status:* *Residence*

Killed in action at Gettysburg on 7/1/1863 [some confusion may exist with prisoner records between William and Michael Blackwell). Records indicate one or the other may have been mortally wounded and captured but died shortly afterward].

2nd Mississippi Alphabetical Roster (Annotated)

Blair, John A.

CO: K, S *Initial Rank:* Private

Joined: Wednesday, May 1, 1861 *Term (yrs):* 1 *Occupation:* Lawyer *Age* 25

Enrolled at: Tishomingo Co., MS *Enrolled By:* Capt. Stone *Promoted:* Yes *ROH:* No

Born: *Marital Status:* *Residence*

Appointed Sergeant Major on 5/1/1861. Slightly wounded at 1st Manassas on 7/21/1861. Elected Major from 4/22/1862. Wounded at Sharpsburg on 9/17/1862. Captured at Gettysburg on 7/1/1863. Sent to Johnson's Island, OH. Exchanged on 3/1/1864. Appointed Lieutenant Colonel on 7/3/1863. Wounded (right leg) on 8/18/1864 at the Weldon Railroad. Furloughed 60-days from 10/5/1864. Commanding Regiment on 1/30/1865. [Incorrectly reported in some sources as having been captured at Hatcher's Run during the fighting on 2/5/1865-2/7/1865. Actually, was commanding Regiment and captured with the rest of the Regiment at Hatcher's Run on 4/2/1865]. Sent to Johnson's Island, OH. Released on oath on 6/18/1865.

Bland, Allen P.

CO: H *Initial Rank:* Private

Joined: Tuesday, April 30, 1861 *Term (yrs):* 1 *Occupation:* Carpenter *Age* 29

Enrolled at: Corinth, MS *Enrolled By:* Capt. Taylor *Promoted:* No *ROH:* No

Born: North Carolina *Marital Status:* S *Residence* Tupelo, MS

Reported missing in action at Seven Pines on 5/31/1862. Was captured, taken to Fort Delaware and exchanged on 8/5/1862. Present with company in Sept/Oct 1862 muster. Wounded and captured at Gettysburg on 7/3/1863. Taken to Fort Delaware. Released on oath on 6/11/1865.

Blythe, Irvin J.

CO: D *Initial Rank:* Private

Joined: Saturday, April 27, 1861 *Term (yrs):* 1 *Occupation:* Farmer *Age*

Enrolled at: Pine Grove, MS *Enrolled By:* Capt. Beck *Promoted:* No *ROH:* No

Born: *Marital Status:* M *Residence* Pine Grove, MS

Discharged on 8/15/1861 for disability.

Blythe, J. H.

CO: D *Initial Rank:* Private

Joined: *Term (yrs):* 0 *Occupation:* *Age*

Enrolled at: *Enrolled By:* *Promoted:* No *ROH:* No

Born: *Marital Status:* *Residence*

Appears on a Confederate report of sick and wounded for August 1861. Discharged 8/20/1861 for disability at Camp Jones, VA. No other records. [same person as James J. Blythe?]

2nd Mississippi Alphabetical Roster (Annotated)

Blythe, James J.
CO: D   *Initial Rank:* Private
Joined: Wednesday, May 1, 1861   *Term (yrs):* 1   *Occupation:*   *Age* 25
Enrolled at: Tippah Co., MS   *Enrolled By:* Capt. Beck   *Promoted:* No   *ROH:* No
Born: *Marital Status:*   *Residence*

Discharged 8/5/1861 [Same person as J. H. Blythe?].

Blythe, John W.
CO: D   *Initial Rank:* Private
Joined: Saturday, March 9, 1861   *Term (yrs):* 0   *Occupation:*   *Age*
Enrolled at: Toombs Store, MS   *Enrolled By:* John McGuirk   *Promoted:* No   *ROH:* No
Born: *Marital Status:*   *Residence*

Appears on a company muster roll. No other records. [Same person as previous entries?]

Blythe, Lewis J.
CO: F   *Initial Rank:* Private
Joined: Saturday, March 1, 1862   *Term (yrs):* 3   *Occupation:* Farmer   *Age* 24
Enrolled at: Ripley, MS   *Enrolled By:* Col. Falkner   *Promoted:* No   *ROH:* Yes
Born: Mississippi   *Marital Status:* S   *Residence*

Killed in battle at Gettysburg on 7/3/1863 (other records say 7/1/1863). ROH for Gettysburg, 7/3/1863 (so most likely killed 7/3, not 7/1).

Blythe, Newton J.
CO: D   *Initial Rank:* 1st Lieutenant
Joined: Saturday, April 27, 1861   *Term (yrs):* 1   *Occupation:* Farmer   *Age* 22
Enrolled at: Pine Grove, MS   *Enrolled By:* Capt. Beck   *Promoted:* No   *ROH:* No
Born: Alabama   *Marital Status:* S   *Residence* Pine Grove, MS

Demoted to private on 5/10/1861. Discharged on 10/22/1861 for disability at Camp Fisher, VA.

Bolen, Brantley
CO: H   *Initial Rank:* Private
Joined: Monday, April 29, 1861   *Term (yrs):* 1   *Occupation:* Farmer   *Age* 50
Enrolled at: Pontotoc Co., MS   *Enrolled By:* Capt. Taylor   *Promoted:* No   *ROH:* No
Born: Alabama   *Marital Status:* M   *Residence* Chesterville, MS

Discharged on 8/13/1861 on account of disability.

2nd Mississippi Alphabetical Roster (Annotated)

Bolen, James R.
CO: H **Initial Rank:** Private
Joined: Monday, April 29, 1861 **Term (yrs):** 1 **Occupation:** Farmer **Age** 21
Enrolled at: Pontotoc Co., MS **Enrolled By:** Capt. Taylor **Promoted:** No **ROH:** No
Born: Alabama **Marital Status:** S **Residence** Chesterville, MS

Wounded at Gaines Mill on 6/27/1862. Taken to hospital in Richmond, VA. Furloughed. Returned to duty. Furloughed from hospital sick for 60-days from 2/25/1865.

Bond, William
CO: C **Initial Rank:** Private
Joined: Saturday, March 1, 1862 **Term (yrs):** 3 **Occupation:** Farmer **Age** 17
Enrolled at: Verona, MS **Enrolled By:** Lt. Pounds **Promoted:** No **ROH:** No
Born: Georgia **Marital Status:** **Residence**

Discharged on account of disability on 10/13/1862.

Bonds, James W.
CO: A **Initial Rank:** Private
Joined: Saturday, March 1, 1862 **Term (yrs):** 3 **Occupation:** Clerk **Age** 23
Enrolled at: Jacinto, MS **Enrolled By:** Lt. Clayton **Promoted:** No **ROH:** No
Born: Alabama **Marital Status:** M **Residence** Jacinto, MS

Killed in battle at Gettysburg on 7/1/1863.

Bonds, Robert A.
CO: K **Initial Rank:** Private
Joined: Saturday, March 1, 1862 **Term (yrs):** 3 **Occupation:** Farmer **Age** 20
Enrolled at: Iuka, MS **Enrolled By:** Lt. Latham **Promoted:** No **ROH:** No
Born: Mississippi **Marital Status:** **Residence**

Died of disease on 5/11/1862.

Booker, John B.
CO: F **Initial Rank:** Private
Joined: Saturday, February 22, 1862 **Term (yrs):** 3 **Occupation:** Farmer **Age** 22
Enrolled at: Ripley, MS **Enrolled By:** Capt. Powers **Promoted:** No **ROH:** No
Born: Mississippi **Marital Status:** M **Residence**

Wounded at Gettysburg on 7/1/1863. Captured at Hatcher's Run on 4/2/1865. Released on oath on 6/9/1865.

2nd Mississippi Alphabetical Roster (Annotated)

Booker, Joseph M.
CO: F *Initial Rank:* Private
Joined: Saturday, February 22, 1862 *Term (yrs):* 3 *Occupation:* Farmer *Age* 25
Enrolled at: Ripley, MS *Enrolled By:* Capt. Powers *Promoted:* No *ROH:* No
Born: Mississippi *Marital Status:* S *Residence*

Deserted in June 1863.

Bookout, William G.
CO: B *Initial Rank:* Private
Joined: Saturday, March 8, 1862 *Term (yrs):* 3 *Occupation:* Farmer *Age* 27
Enrolled at: Ripley, MS *Enrolled By:* Capt. Buchanan *Promoted:* No *ROH:* No
Born: Tennessee *Marital Status:* M *Residence*

Wounded at 2nd Manassas on 8/29/1862; subsequently died of wounds on 9/16/1862.

Boone, Bartley B.
CO: A, S *Initial Rank:* Captain
Joined: Wednesday, February 20, 1861 *Term (yrs):* 1 *Occupation:* Lawyer *Age* 28
Enrolled at: Corinth, MS *Enrolled By:* R. Griffith *Promoted:* Yes *ROH:* No
Born: Tennessee *Marital Status:* M *Residence* Jacinto, MS

Promoted by election to Lieutenant Colonel on 5/10/1861. Captured at 1st Manassas on 7/21/1861. Resigned on 1/31/1862.

Boone, Benjamin F.
CO: A *Initial Rank:* 4th Sergeant
Joined: Wednesday, May 1, 1861 *Term (yrs):* 1 *Occupation:* Farmer *Age* 29
Enrolled at: Tishomingo Co., MS *Enrolled By:* Capt. Leeth *Promoted:* Yes *ROH:* No
Born: Tennessee *Marital Status:* M *Residence* Rienzi, MS

Died on 7/22/1861 from wounds received at battle of 1st Manassas on 7/21/1861.

Boone, Francis M.
CO: A *Initial Rank:* Private
Joined: Wednesday, May 1, 1861 *Term (yrs):* 1 *Occupation:* *Age* 40
Enrolled at: Tishomingo Co., MS *Enrolled By:* Capt. Leeth *Promoted:* No *ROH:* No
Born: *Marital Status:* *Residence*

Appears on a company muster-in roll and a State service company muster roll. No other records.

2nd Mississippi Alphabetical Roster (Annotated)

Boone, R. B.
CO: **Initial Rank:**
Joined: *Term (yrs):* 0   *Occupation:*   **Age**
Enrolled at: *Enrolled By:*   *Promoted:* No   *ROH:* No
Born: *Marital Status:*   *Residence*

Appears on a Federal list of prisoners received on 11/12/1861 at Fort McHenry, MD to be sent to Fortress Monroe. No other record.

Boone, Reuben L.
CO: A   **Initial Rank:** Private
Joined: Wednesday, May 1, 1861   *Term (yrs):* 1   *Occupation:* Farmer   **Age** 18
Enrolled at: Tishomingo Co., MS   *Enrolled By:* Capt. Leeth   *Promoted:* No   *ROH:* Yes
Born: Mississippi   *Marital Status:* S   *Residence* Rienzi, MS

Wounded at Sharpsburg on 9/17/1862. Sent home on wounded furlough. Wounded at Gettysburg. Sent to Mississippi on furlough. Captured in Tishomingo Co. while on furlough. ROH for South Mountain (Boonesboro), 9/14/1862.

Boone, William H. H.
CO: A   **Initial Rank:** Private
Joined: Wednesday, May 1, 1861   *Term (yrs):* 1   *Occupation:* Farmer   **Age** 41
Enrolled at: Tishomingo Co., MS   *Enrolled By:* Capt. Leeth   *Promoted:* No   *ROH:* No
Born: Tennessee   *Marital Status:* S   *Residence* Rienzi, MS

Detailed on wagon master duty from 7/14/1861 and discharged on 5/20/1862 (overage).

Booth, Joel W.
CO: A   **Initial Rank:** Private
Joined: Wednesday, May 1, 1861   *Term (yrs):* 1   *Occupation:* Teacher   **Age** 18
Enrolled at: Tishomingo Co., MS   *Enrolled By:* Capt. Leeth   *Promoted:* No   *ROH:* No
Born: Tennessee   *Marital Status:* S   *Residence* Rienzi, MS

Wounded at Malvern Hill on 7/1/1862. Never returned from furlough. Listed as deserter from 10/1/1862.

Booth, John F.
CO: E   **Initial Rank:** Captain
Joined: Wednesday, May 1, 1861   *Term (yrs):* 1   *Occupation:* Physician   **Age** 37
Enrolled at: Itawamba Co., MS   *Enrolled By:* R. Griffith   *Promoted:* No   *ROH:* No
Born: Alabama   *Marital Status:* M   *Residence* Guntown, MS

Resigned on 8/16/1861.

2nd Mississippi Alphabetical Roster (Annotated)

Boren, William C.
CO: E *Initial Rank:* Private
Joined: Wednesday, May 1, 1861 *Term (yrs):* 1 *Occupation:* Farmer *Age* 23
Enrolled at: Itawamba Co., MS *Enrolled By:* Capt. Booth *Promoted:* No *ROH:* No
Born: *Marital Status:* M *Residence* Baldwyn, MS

Dropped from rolls – AWOL since late 1862 from furlough.

Borum, William C.
CO: C *Initial Rank:* Private
Joined: Wednesday, May 1, 1861 *Term (yrs):* 1 *Occupation:* Farmer *Age* 20
Enrolled at: Itawamba Co., MS *Enrolled By:* Capt. Bromley *Promoted:* Yes *ROH:* No
Born: *Marital Status:* *Residence*

Killed in battle at 2nd Manassas on 8/29/1862.

Boshers, John H.
CO: A *Initial Rank:* Private
Joined: Wednesday, May 1, 1861 *Term (yrs):* 1 *Occupation:* Farmer *Age* 24
Enrolled at: Tishomingo Co., MS *Enrolled By:* Capt. Leeth *Promoted:* No *ROH:* No
Born: *Marital Status:* *Residence*

Captured while on sick furlough in Tishomingo Co., MS on 11/13/1863. Died on 4/7/1864 at Alton Military Prison.

Bostwick, Mark R.
CO: B *Initial Rank:* Private
Joined: Wednesday, March 19, 1862 *Term (yrs):* 3 *Occupation:* Farmer *Age* 34
Enrolled at: Ripley, MS *Enrolled By:* Capt. Buchanan *Promoted:* No *ROH:* No
Born: North Carolina *Marital Status:* S *Residence*

Wounded at 2nd Manassas on 8/30/1862. Died of wounds on 9/6/1862.

Bounds, Thomas B.
CO: L *Initial Rank:* 3rd Corporal
Joined: Monday, March 3, 1862 *Term (yrs):* 3 *Occupation:* Farmer *Age* 38
Enrolled at: Ripley, MS *Enrolled By:* Capt. Powers *Promoted:* Yes *ROH:* No
Born: Tennessee *Marital Status:* M *Residence* Dumas, MS

Reduced to ranks on 9/1/1862. Discharged on account of disability on 4/7/1863.

2nd Mississippi Alphabetical Roster (Annotated)

Bounds, William
CO: L **Initial Rank:** Private
Joined: Friday, March 13, 1863 **Term (yrs):** 3 **Occupation:** Farmer **Age**
Enrolled at: Tippah Co., MS **Enrolled By:** Lt. Bearden **Promoted:** No **ROH:** No
Born: Mississippi **Marital Status:** S **Residence** Dumas, MS

AWOL from 9/20/1863. Dropped from rolls as deserter on 8/31/1864.

Bowen, Daniel W.
CO: H **Initial Rank:** Private
Joined: Saturday, March 15, 1862 **Term (yrs):** 3 **Occupation:** Farmer **Age** 19
Enrolled at: Chesterville, MS **Enrolled By:** Lt. Porter **Promoted:** No **ROH:** No
Born: South Carolina **Marital Status:** **Residence**

Wounded at 2nd Manassas on 8/29/1862. Died on 9/2/1862 of wounds received.

Bowen, J. H.
CO: H **Initial Rank:** Private
Joined: Saturday, March 15, 1862 **Term (yrs):** 3 **Occupation:** Farmer **Age** 23
Enrolled at: Chesterville, MS **Enrolled By:** Lt. Porter **Promoted:** No **ROH:** No
Born: South Carolina **Marital Status:** M **Residence** Chesterville, MS

Wounded at Gettysburg on 7/1/1863 and captured. Listed as deserter for failing to report back to unit when exchanged upon expiration of furlough on 2/25/1864.

Bowen, William R.
CO: C, H **Initial Rank:** Private
Joined: Saturday, March 1, 1862 **Term (yrs):** 3 **Occupation:** Farmer **Age** 35
Enrolled at: Verona, MS **Enrolled By:** Lt. Pounds **Promoted:** No **ROH:** No
Born: Georgia **Marital Status:** M **Residence** Richmond, MS

Transferred from Company C to Company H about 5/1/1862. Killed at battle of The Wilderness on 5/5/1864.

Bowhit, M.
CO: **Initial Rank:** Private
Joined: **Term (yrs):** 0 **Occupation:** **Age**
Enrolled at: **Enrolled By:** **Promoted:** No **ROH:** No
Born: **Marital Status:** **Residence**

Federal records listed as captured at Gettysburg. No other record.

2nd Mississippi Alphabetical Roster (Annotated)

Box, A. M.　　　　　　　　　　　　　　　　　*CO:* G　　*Initial Rank:* Private

Joined: Thursday, March 20, 1862　　*Term (yrs):* 3　*Occupation:* Farmer　　　　*Age* 18

Enrolled at: Pontotoc, MS　　*Enrolled By:* G. B. Mears　　*Promoted:* No　*ROH:* No

Born: Mississippi　　*Marital Status:* S　　*Residence* Pontotoc, MS

Listed as AWOL since 8/28/1863. Listed as deserted, Sept. 1863.

Box, Henry M.　　　　　　　　　　　　　　　*CO:* D　　*Initial Rank:* Private

Joined: Wednesday, May 1, 1861　　*Term (yrs):* 1　*Occupation:*　　　　　　*Age* 30

Enrolled at: Tippah Co., MS　　*Enrolled By:* Capt. Beck　　*Promoted:* Yes　*ROH:* No

Born:　　*Marital Status:*　　*Residence*

Captured at South Mountain, MD on 9/14/1862. Paroled. Captured at Gettysburg on 7/3/1863. In parole camps at Petersburg, VA. Declared AWOL from 2/1/1864. Dropped from rolls and declared deserter by order of Colonel Stone on 12/31/1864.

Box, William R.　　　　　　　　　　　　　　*CO:* B　　*Initial Rank:* Private

Joined: Wednesday, March 19, 1862　　*Term (yrs):* 3　*Occupation:* Farmer　　*Age* 17

Enrolled at: Ripley, MS　　*Enrolled By:* Capt. Buchanan　　*Promoted:* No　*ROH:* No

Born: Mississippi　　*Marital Status:* S　　*Residence*

Deserted 7/15/1863.

Boyce, David　　　　　　　　　　　　　　　*CO:* G　　*Initial Rank:* Private

Joined: Wednesday, May 1, 1861　　*Term (yrs):* 1　*Occupation:* Tinner　　　*Age* 27

Enrolled at: Pontotoc, MS　　*Enrolled By:* Capt. Miller　　*Promoted:* No　*ROH:* No

Born: Virginia　　*Marital Status:* S　　*Residence* Pontotoc, MS

Wounded 1st Manassas 7/21/1861. Discharged for disability on 2/25/1862.

Boyd, Joseph L.　　　　　　　　　　　　　　*CO:* B　　*Initial Rank:* Private

Joined: Wednesday, May 1, 1861　　*Term (yrs):* 1　*Occupation:* Farmer　　　*Age* 18

Enrolled at: Tippah Co., MS　　*Enrolled By:* Capt. Buchanan　　*Promoted:* No　*ROH:* No

Born:　　*Marital Status:*　　*Residence*

Wounded at battle of Seven Pines on 5/31/1862. Died from wounds on 6/13/1862. [*Buried at Hollywood Cemetery, Richmond, VA. Soldiers Section P Lot: 214].

2nd Mississippi Alphabetical Roster (Annotated)

Boyd, Nathaniel P.
CO: B **Initial Rank:** Private
Joined: Wednesday, March 19, 1862 **Term (yrs):** 3 **Occupation:** **Age** 17
Enrolled at: Ripley, MS **Enrolled By:** Capt. Buchanan **Promoted:** No **ROH:** No
Born: Virginia **Marital Status:** S **Residence**
Killed at Gettysburg on 7/1/1863.

Braddock, Perry G.
CO: B **Initial Rank:** Private
Joined: Wednesday, May 1, 1861 **Term (yrs):** 1 **Occupation:** Farmer **Age** 18
Enrolled at: Tippah Co., MS **Enrolled By:** Capt. Buchanan **Promoted:** Yes **ROH:** Yes
Born: **Marital Status:** **Residence**
Wounded at battle of Seven Pines on 5/31/1862. Wounded at battle of The Wilderness on 5/6/1864. Returned from wounded furlough on 8/29/1864. Detailed to engineer corps on 2/9/1865. Paroled at Appomattox Court House on 4/9/1865. ROH for Falling Waters, 7/14/1863.

Braddock, Stephen B.
CO: B **Initial Rank:** Private
Joined: Wednesday, May 1, 1861 **Term (yrs):** 1 **Occupation:** Farmer **Age** 21
Enrolled at: Tippah Co., MS **Enrolled By:** Capt. Buchanan **Promoted:** No **ROH:** No
Born: **Marital Status:** **Residence**
Killed at battle of Bristoe Station on 10/14/1863.

Braden, Wilie F.
CO: H **Initial Rank:** Private
Joined: Monday, April 29, 1861 **Term (yrs):** 1 **Occupation:** Farmer **Age** 18
Enrolled at: Pontotoc Co., MS **Enrolled By:** Capt. Taylor **Promoted:** No **ROH:** No
Born: Alabama **Marital Status:** S **Residence** Tupelo, MS
Captured at Gettysburg on 7/1/1863. Exchanged on 10/30/1864. No further record.

Bradford, George W.
CO: D **Initial Rank:** Private
Joined: Saturday, March 9, 1861 **Term (yrs):** 0 **Occupation:** **Age**
Enrolled at: Toombs Store, MS **Enrolled By:** John M. McGuirk **Promoted:** No **ROH:** No
Born: **Marital Status:** **Residence**
Appears on a company muster roll. No other record.

2nd Mississippi Alphabetical Roster (Annotated)

Bradford, James
CO: D *Initial Rank:* Private
Joined: Saturday, March 9, 1861 *Term (yrs):* 0 *Occupation:* *Age*
Enrolled at: Toombs Store, MS *Enrolled By:* John M. McGuirk *Promoted:* No *ROH:* No
Born: *Marital Status:* *Residence*

Appears on a company muster roll. [Same as George W.?] No other record.

Bradley, John W.
CO: E *Initial Rank:* Private
Joined: Friday, February 8, 1861 *Term (yrs):* 0 *Occupation:* *Age*
Enrolled at: Saltillo, MS *Enrolled By:* R. Griffith *Promoted:* No *ROH:* No
Born: *Marital Status:* *Residence*

Appears on a company muster roll and a list of the Calhoun Rifles dated 2/11/1861. No other records.

Bradley, William C.
CO: L *Initial Rank:* Private
Joined: Monday, March 3, 1862 *Term (yrs):* 3 *Occupation:* Farmer *Age* 29
Enrolled at: Ripley, MS *Enrolled By:* Col. Falkner *Promoted:* No *ROH:* No
Born: Georgia *Marital Status:* M *Residence* Ripley, MS

Died of disease at Fredericksburg on 4/6/1862.

Bradley, Williamson
CO: E *Initial Rank:* Private
Joined: Wednesday, May 1, 1861 *Term (yrs):* 1 *Occupation:* Farmer *Age* 17
Enrolled at: Itawamba Co., MS *Enrolled By:* Capt. Booth *Promoted:* No *ROH:* No
Born: Mississippi *Marital Status:* S *Residence* Baldwyn, MS

Discharged on 12/8/1861.

Bradon, William M.
CO: E *Initial Rank:* Private
Joined: Monday, March 3, 1862 *Term (yrs):* 3 *Occupation:* *Age* 31
Enrolled at: Guntown, MS *Enrolled By:* Capt. Bates *Promoted:* No *ROH:* No
Born: *Marital Status:* *Residence*

Appears on a company muster-in roll. No other record.

2nd Mississippi Alphabetical Roster (Annotated)

Brandon, Philip F.
CO: F, H **Initial Rank:** Private
Joined: Saturday, March 22, 1862 **Term (yrs):** 3 **Occupation:** Farmer **Age** 25
Enrolled at: Corinth, MS **Enrolled By:** Capt. Powers **Promoted:** No **ROH:** No
Born: Alabama **Marital Status:** S **Residence** Tupelo, MS

Transferred to Company H from Company F on 4/1/1862. Wounded at The Wilderness on 5/5/1864. Furloughed from hospital. Did not return to company. Surrendered to Federal forces and paroled at La Grange, TN on 5/26/1865.

Brandon, Robert M.
CO: D **Initial Rank:** Private
Joined: Wednesday, May 1, 1861 **Term (yrs):** 1 **Occupation:** Farmer **Age** 22
Enrolled at: Tippah Co., MS **Enrolled By:** Capt. Beck **Promoted:** Yes **ROH:** No
Born: Mississippi **Marital Status:** S **Residence** Snow Creek, MS

Promoted to Captain. Wounded at Gaines Mill on 6/27/62. Wounded and captured at Gettysburg on 7/3/1863. Subsequently died of wounds on 7/15/1863 at Chester, PA. [*Buried at Hollywood Cemetery, Richmond, VA. Gettysburg Section Lot: 1].

Brandon, Samuel J.
CO: H **Initial Rank:** Private
Joined: Saturday, August 10, 1861 **Term (yrs):** 1 **Occupation:** Farmer **Age** 26
Enrolled at: Camp Jones, VA **Enrolled By:** Lt. Stone **Promoted:** No **ROH:** No
Born: Alabama **Marital Status:** S **Residence** Tupelo, MS

Wounded battle of The Wilderness on 5/5/1864. Listed as AWOL since 10/31/1864.

Brannon, John M.
CO: K **Initial Rank:** Private
Joined: Saturday, April 6, 1861 **Term (yrs):** 0 **Occupation:** **Age**
Enrolled at: Iuka, MS **Enrolled By:** W. M. Inge **Promoted:** No **ROH:** No
Born: **Marital Status:** **Residence**

Appears on a company muster roll. No other record.

Braselman, Nathan T.
CO: F **Initial Rank:** 2nd Lieutenant
Joined: Wednesday, May 1, 1861 **Term (yrs):** 1 **Occupation:** Planter **Age** 28
Enrolled at: Tippah Co., MS **Enrolled By:** Capt. Davis **Promoted:** No **ROH:** No
Born: **Marital Status:** **Residence**

Killed in battle at 1st Manassas 7/21/1861.

2nd Mississippi Alphabetical Roster (Annotated)

Bratten, Joseph M.
CO: B *Initial Rank:* Private
Joined: Wednesday, May 1, 1861 *Term (yrs):* 1 *Occupation:* Farmer *Age* 21
Enrolled at: Tippah Co., MS *Enrolled By:* Capt. Buchanan *Promoted:* No *ROH:* No
Born: *Marital Status:* *Residence*

Wounded and captured at Gettysburg on 7/1/1863. Paroled to City Point, VA on 8/24/1863. AWOL since 9/20/1863. Notes say he joined another command (deserted).

Brawner, Jesse W.
CO: E *Initial Rank:* Private
Joined: Saturday, March 8, 1862 *Term (yrs):* 3 *Occupation:* Farmer *Age* 36
Enrolled at: Guntown, MS *Enrolled By:* Capt. Bates *Promoted:* No *ROH:* No
Born: Georgia *Marital Status:* M *Residence* Guntown, MS

Died in hospital of disease (typhoid fever) on 6/25/1862 (date of death also noted as 7/8/1862 or 6/26/1862 in other records).

Brawner, John M.
CO: E *Initial Rank:* Private
Joined: Saturday, March 8, 1862 *Term (yrs):* 3 *Occupation:* Farmer *Age* 33
Enrolled at: Guntown, MS *Enrolled By:* Capt. Bates *Promoted:* No *ROH:* No
Born: Georgia *Marital Status:* M *Residence* Guntown, MS

Captured at Gettysburg on 7/1/1863. Taken to Fort Delaware. Released on oath on 6/11/1865.

Brazeal, John H.
CO: C *Initial Rank:* Private
Joined: Wednesday, May 1, 1861 *Term (yrs):* 1 *Occupation:* Farmer *Age* 19
Enrolled at: Itawamba Co., MS *Enrolled By:* Capt. Bromley *Promoted:* No *ROH:* No
Born: *Marital Status:* *Residence*

Captured at Gettysburg on 7/1/1863. Taken to Fort Delaware. Released on oath on 6/11/1865.

Bremer, P.
CO: *Initial Rank:*
Joined: *Term (yrs):* 0 *Occupation:* *Age*
Enrolled at: *Enrolled By:* *Promoted:* No *ROH:* No
Born: *Marital Status:* *Residence*

Appears on a Federal record of sick and wounded prisoners captured at Gettysburg. Listed as "nurse." No other record.

2nd Mississippi Alphabetical Roster (Annotated)

Brewer, James H.
CO: A **Initial Rank:** Private
Joined: Wednesday, May 1, 1861 *Term (yrs):* 1 *Occupation:* Farmer *Age* 19
Enrolled at: Tishomingo Co., MS *Enrolled By:* Capt. Leeth *Promoted:* No *ROH:* No
Born: Alabama *Marital Status:* S *Residence* Hickory Plains, MS

Captured 7/3/1863 at Gettysburg. Taken to Fort Delaware. Released on oath 6/11/1865.

Brewer, Noah
CO: F **Initial Rank:** Private
Joined: *Term (yrs):* 0 *Occupation:* *Age*
Enrolled at: *Enrolled By:* *Promoted:* No *ROH:* No
Born: *Marital Status:* *Residence*

Galvanized Yankee. Enlisted in Federal service at Camp Morton, IN sometime in August 1863. Captured at Jackson, MS. Date unknown. No further record. Deserted.

Bridgeman, W. A.
CO: E **Initial Rank:** Private
Joined: *Term (yrs):* 0 *Occupation:* *Age*
Enrolled at: *Enrolled By:* *Promoted:* No *ROH:* No
Born: *Marital Status:* *Residence*

Note on jacket says to check same name, 2nd Missouri Cavalry. No other records.

Bright, Isaiah
CO: F, D **Initial Rank:** Private
Joined: Tuesday, February 25, 1862 *Term (yrs):* 3 *Occupation:* Farmer *Age* 26
Enrolled at: Ripley, MS *Enrolled By:* Capt. Powers *Promoted:* No *ROH:* No
Born: Mississippi *Marital Status:* S *Residence* Salem, MS

Transferred to Company D from Company F on 5/1/1862. Listed as deserted on 8/30/1863.

Bright, Samuel
CO: E **Initial Rank:** Private
Joined: Wednesday, May 1, 1861 *Term (yrs):* 1 *Occupation:* *Age*
Enrolled at: Itawamba Co., MS *Enrolled By:* Capt. Booth *Promoted:* No *ROH:* No
Born: *Marital Status:* *Residence*

Appears on a company muster-in roll and on a list of the Calhoun Rifles dated 2/11/1861. No further record.

2nd Mississippi Alphabetical Roster (Annotated)

Brinton, J. W.　　　　　　　　　　　CO: F　　Initial Rank: Private
Joined:　　　　　　　　　　*Term (yrs):* 0　*Occupation:*　　　　　　　　　　*Age*
Enrolled at:　　　　　　　*Enrolled By:*　　　　　　　　*Promoted:* No　*ROH:* No
Born:　　　　　　*Marital Status:*　　　　　*Residence*

Listed on Federal roll of Prisoners of War, captured at Petersburg, VA (Hatcher's Run?) on 4/2/1865 and sent to Fort Delaware. No other record.

Broadfoot, W. G.　　　　　　　　　　CO: E　　Initial Rank: Private
Joined:　　　　　　　　　　*Term (yrs):* 0　*Occupation:*　　　　　　　　　　*Age*
Enrolled at:　　　　　　　*Enrolled By:*　　　　　　　　*Promoted:* No　*ROH:* No
Born:　　　　　　*Marital Status:*　　　　　*Residence*

Note on jacket says to see William G. Broadfoot of the 11th Miss. Inf. Rgt. No other record.

Bromley, John W.　　　　　　　　　　CO: C　　Initial Rank: Sergeant
Joined: Wednesday, May 1, 1861　*Term (yrs):* 1　*Occupation:* Farmer　　*Age* 30
Enrolled at: Itawamba Co., MS　*Enrolled By:* Capt. Bromley　*Promoted:* No　*ROH:* No
Born:　　　　　　*Marital Status:* S　　　　*Residence*

Died of disease (typhoid fever) on 7/28/1861.

Bromley, William C.　　　　　　　　　CO: C　　Initial Rank: Captain
Joined: Wednesday, May 1, 1861　*Term (yrs):* 1　*Occupation:* Member of　*Age* 34
Enrolled at: Itawamba Co., MS　*Enrolled By:* Col. Falkner　*Promoted:* No　*ROH:* No
Born:　　　　　　*Marital Status:*　　　　　*Residence*

No record after February 1862.

Brookshire, Franklin R.　　　　　　　CO: H　　Initial Rank: Corporal
Joined: Monday, April 29, 1861　*Term (yrs):* 1　*Occupation:* Clerk　　*Age* 23
Enrolled at: Pontotoc Co., MS　*Enrolled By:* Capt. Taylor　*Promoted:* Yes　*ROH:* No
Born: Alabama　*Marital Status:* S　　*Residence* Chesterville, MS

Re-enlisted on 4/6/1862 and elected 2nd Lieutenant. On 4/14/1862. Assigned to duty on 4/23/1862. Killed in battle at Gaines Mill on 6/27/1862.

2nd Mississippi Alphabetical Roster (Annotated)

Brookshire, James B.
CO: H **Initial Rank:** Private
Joined: Friday, May 10, 1861 **Term (yrs):** 1 **Occupation:** Student **Age** 20
Enrolled at: Lynchburg, VA **Enrolled By:** Maj. Clay **Promoted:** No **ROH:** No
Born: Alabama **Marital Status:** S **Residence** Chesterville, MS

Re-enlisted for the war on 4/6/1862. Wounded at Sharpsburg on 9/17/1862. Ordered to report to BGen. Gardner at Richmond for light duty, 12/22/1864. Retired from field service.

Brown, David M.
CO: F, D **Initial Rank:** Private
Joined: Monday, February 24, 1862 **Term (yrs):** 3 **Occupation:** Farmer **Age**
Enrolled at: Ripley, MS **Enrolled By:** Capt. Powers **Promoted:** No **ROH:** No
Born: Mississippi **Marital Status:** M **Residence** Shelby Creek, MS

Transferred from Company F to Company D on 5/5/1862. Dropped from rolls on 12/31/1863 as deserter for prolonged absence without leave.

Brown, George
CO: C **Initial Rank:** Private
Joined: Wednesday, May 1, 1861 **Term (yrs):** 1 **Occupation:** Farmer **Age** 20
Enrolled at: Itawamba Co., MS **Enrolled By:** Capt. Bromley **Promoted:** No **ROH:** No
Born: **Marital Status:** **Residence**

Discharged (cause not given) on 8/22/1861.

Brown, George W.
CO: D **Initial Rank:** Private
Joined: **Term (yrs):** 0 **Occupation:** **Age**
Enrolled at: **Enrolled By:** **Promoted:** No **ROH:** No
Born: **Marital Status:** **Residence**

Appears on Federal prisoner of war records. Date of capture or location not given. Sent to Camp Douglas, IL and received on 9/23/1863. Notes – Brigade: Chalmer; Division: Bragg. Record headings list unit variously as Co. D 2 Regt Miss; Co. D. 2. Miss. Battery; and Co. D, 2 Miss. Batt. [Misidentified. This man belongs to a cavalry unit under Chalmers, not the 2nd Mississippi Infantry.] No other records.

Brown, Isaac M.
CO: A **Initial Rank:** Private
Joined: Saturday, March 1, 1862 **Term (yrs):** 3 **Occupation:** Farmer **Age** 37
Enrolled at: Jacinto, MS **Enrolled By:** Lt. Clayton **Promoted:** No **ROH:** No
Born: Alabama **Marital Status:** **Residence** Jacinto, MS

Died of disease at Liberty, VA on 7/7/1862.

2nd Mississippi Alphabetical Roster (Annotated)

Brown, James W.

CO: C **Initial Rank:** Private

Joined: Tuesday, October 1, 1861 **Term (yrs):** 1 **Occupation:** **Age**

Enrolled at: Richmond, MS **Enrolled By:** Lt. Davenport **Promoted:** Yes **ROH:** No

Born: **Marital Status:** **Residence**

Promoted to 2nd Lieutenant. Resigned on 12/7/1864 on account of disease.

Brown, John J.

CO: F **Initial Rank:** Private

Joined: Wednesday, May 1, 1861 **Term (yrs):** 1 **Occupation:** Planter **Age** 21

Enrolled at: Tippah Co., MS **Enrolled By:** Capt. Davis **Promoted:** No **ROH:** Yes

Born: **Marital Status:** **Residence**

Wounded at battle of Spotsylvania on 5/12/1864. Furloughed from 6/7/1864 for 60-days. Did not return to company. Listed as AWOL since. ROH for The Wilderness, 5/6/1864.

Brown, Joseph

CO: B **Initial Rank:** Private

Joined: Wednesday, May 1, 1861 **Term (yrs):** 1 **Occupation:** Clerk **Age** 22

Enrolled at: Tippah Co., MS **Enrolled By:** Capt. Buchanan **Promoted:** No **ROH:** No

Born: **Marital Status:** **Residence**

Died of disease (typhoid fever) at Strasburg, VA on 8/22/1861.

Brown, Joseph H.

CO: F **Initial Rank:** Private

Joined: Wednesday, May 1, 1861 **Term (yrs):** 1 **Occupation:** Farmer **Age** 20

Enrolled at: Tippah Co., MS **Enrolled By:** Capt. Davis **Promoted:** No **ROH:** No

Born: Mississippi **Marital Status:** **Residence**

Discharged for disability on 3/1/1862.

Brown, William M.

CO: K **Initial Rank:** Private

Joined: Saturday, March 1, 1862 **Term (yrs):** 3 **Occupation:** **Age** 18

Enrolled at: Iuka, MS **Enrolled By:** Lt. Latham **Promoted:** No **ROH:** No

Born: **Marital Status:** **Residence**

Captured at Gettysburg on 7/1/1863. Held at Fort Delaware. Released on oath on 6/11/1865.

2nd Mississippi Alphabetical Roster (Annotated)

Browning, Elijah
CO: I *Initial Rank:* Private
Joined: Wednesday, May 1, 1861   *Term (yrs):* 1 *Occupation:* Farmer   *Age* 23
Enrolled at: Pontotoc Co., MS   *Enrolled By:* Capt. Herring   *Promoted:* No   *ROH:* Yes
Born: South Carolina   *Marital Status:*   *Residence*

Killed in battle at Sharpsburg on 9/17/1862. ROH for South Mountain (Boonsboro), 9/14/1862.

Broyles, Lafayette G.
CO: A *Initial Rank:* Private
Joined: Saturday, March 1, 1862   *Term (yrs):* 3 *Occupation:* Carpenter   *Age* 28
Enrolled at: Jacinto, MS   *Enrolled By:* Lt. Clayton   *Promoted:* No   *ROH:* No
Born: Tennessee   *Marital Status:* M   *Residence* Jacinto, MS

Listed as deserted as of 9/20/1862. However, also shown in Federal records as captured in northern Mississippi circa October 1862. Paroled at Corinth, MS on 10/13/1862. Exchanged on 11/8/1862 at Vicksburg,

Bruton, Albury
CO: D *Initial Rank:* Private
Joined: Wednesday, May 1, 1861   *Term (yrs):* 1 *Occupation:*   *Age* 19
Enrolled at: Tippah Co., MS   *Enrolled By:* Capt. Beck   *Promoted:* No   *ROH:* No
Born: *Marital Status:*   *Residence*

Captured at Gettysburg on 7/1/1863. Held at Fort Delaware. Released on oath 6/11/1865.

Bryan, Sulathia P.
CO: L *Initial Rank:* Private
Joined: Monday, March 3, 1862   *Term (yrs):* 3 *Occupation:* Farmer   *Age* 29
Enrolled at: Ripley, MS   *Enrolled By:* Col. Falkner   *Promoted:* No   *ROH:* No
Born: Mississippi   *Marital Status:* S   *Residence* Ripley, MS

Wounded at Gettysburg. Sent home on wounded furlough. Captured on 11/28/1863 while on furlough in Mississippi. Held at Fort Delaware. Released on oath on 6/11/1865.

Bryan, William H.
CO: L *Initial Rank:* Private
Joined: Monday, March 3, 1862   *Term (yrs):* 3 *Occupation:* Farmer   *Age* 32
Enrolled at: Ripley, MS   *Enrolled By:* Col. Falkner   *Promoted:* No   *ROH:* Yes
Born: Mississippi   *Marital Status:* M   *Residence* Ripley, MS

Wounded at Sharpsburg on 9/17/1862. Died of wounds on 9/20/1862. ROH for Gaines Mill, 6/27/1862.

2nd Mississippi Alphabetical Roster (Annotated)

Bryant, Benjamin R.
CO: E **Initial Rank:** Private
Joined: Monday, March 17, 1862 **Term (yrs):** 3 **Occupation:** Farmer **Age** 17
Enrolled at: Guntown, MS **Enrolled By:** Capt. Bates **Promoted:** No **ROH:** No
Born: Georgia **Marital Status:** S **Residence** Birmingham, MS

Admitted to hospital in Richmond with gunshot wound to left hand on 7/21/1863 (company records provide no details on date of wound or engagement). Sent home on wounded furlough for 20-days from 9/17/1863. Returned to duty. Deserted on 2/12/1864 from camp near Orange Court House, VA. Taken into custody by Federal forces on 2/12/1864 and disposed of by the Provost Marshal General, Army of the Potomac.

Bryant, John B.
CO: E **Initial Rank:** Private
Joined: Monday, March 17, 1862 **Term (yrs):** 3 **Occupation:** Farmer **Age** 25
Enrolled at: Guntown, MS **Enrolled By:** Capt. Bates **Promoted:** No **ROH:** No
Born: Georgia **Marital Status:** S **Residence** Birmingham, MS

Died of disease on 7/8/1862 at Richmond, VA.

Bryant, Joseph S.
CO: E **Initial Rank:** Private
Joined: Monday, September 30, 1861 **Term (yrs):** 1 **Occupation:** Farmer **Age** 19
Enrolled at: Corinth, MS **Enrolled By:** Lt. Davenport **Promoted:** No **ROH:** Yes
Born: Georgia **Marital Status:** S **Residence** Birmingham, MS

Wounded at the battle of the Wilderness on 5/5/1864. Subsequently died of wounds on 5/8/1864. ROH for The Wilderness, 5/5/1864.

Bryant, William
CO: E **Initial Rank:** Private
Joined: Wednesday, May 1, 1861 **Term (yrs):** 1 **Occupation:** Farmer **Age** 21
Enrolled at: Itawamba Co., MS **Enrolled By:** Capt. Booth **Promoted:** No **ROH:** No
Born: Georgia **Marital Status:** S **Residence** Birmingham, MS

Captured at Gettysburg on 7/1/1863. Taken to Fort Delaware. Released on oath on 6/11/1865.

Bryson, William D.
CO: E **Initial Rank:** Corporal
Joined: Wednesday, May 1, 1861 **Term (yrs):** 1 **Occupation:** Farmer **Age** 22
Enrolled at: Itawamba Co., MS **Enrolled By:** Capt. Booth **Promoted:** Yes **ROH:** No
Born: South Carolina **Marital Status:** S **Residence** Guntown, MS

Reduced to ranks during Jul/Aug 1861 time period. Wounded at battle of The Wilderness on 5/5/1864. Furloughed 60-days from 5/28/1864. Returned to duty. Captured at Hatcher's Run on 4/2/1865. Taken to Point Lookout, MD. Released on oath on 6/10/1865.

2nd Mississippi Alphabetical Roster (Annotated)

Buchanan, John H.
CO: B, S **Initial Rank:** Captain
Joined: Wednesday, May 1, 1861 **Term (yrs):** 1 **Occupation:** Blacksmith **Age** 41
Enrolled at: Tippah Co., MS **Enrolled By:** Col. Falkner **Promoted:** Yes **ROH:** No
Born: **Marital Status:** **Residence**

Wounded (right leg) and captured at Gettysburg on 7/3/1863. Sent to Johnson's Island, OH. Exchanged on 3/3/1864. Promoted Major on 7/12/1864 to date from 7/3/1863. Wounded on 8/18/1864 resulting in amputation of little finger and injury to metacarpal bone. Furloughed 30-days. Resigned on 1/14/1865.

Buchanan, John T.
CO: B **Initial Rank:** Private
Joined: Wednesday, May 1, 1861 **Term (yrs):** 1 **Occupation:** Physician **Age** 20
Enrolled at: Tippah Co., MS **Enrolled By:** Capt. Buchanan **Promoted:** No **ROH:** No
Born: **Marital Status:** **Residence**

Detailed as Hospital Steward and Ward Master through most of the war in Virginia and at Goldsboro, NC. Paroled at Greensboro, NC on 5/1/1865.

Buchanan, Joseph M.
CO: G **Initial Rank:** Private
Joined: Wednesday, May 1, 1861 **Term (yrs):** 1 **Occupation:** Merchant **Age** 22
Enrolled at: Pontotoc, MS **Enrolled By:** Capt. Kilpatrick **Promoted:** No **ROH:** No
Born: Mississippi **Marital Status:** S **Residence** Pontotoc, MS

Discharged for disability on 12/28/1861 at Camp Fisher, VA.

Buchanan, Robert W.
CO: K **Initial Rank:** Private
Joined: Wednesday, May 1, 1861 **Term (yrs):** 1 **Occupation:** Farmer **Age** 28
Enrolled at: Tishomingo Co., MS **Enrolled By:** Capt. Stone **Promoted:** No **ROH:** No
Born: **Marital Status:** **Residence**

Deserted before Richmond about end of July 1862. Appears on a Federal register of prisoners of war as paroled and "Deserter from CSA."

Buchanan, Samuel A.
CO: K **Initial Rank:** Private
Joined: Wednesday, May 1, 1861 **Term (yrs):** 1 **Occupation:** **Age** 21
Enrolled at: Tishomingo Co., MS **Enrolled By:** Capt. Stone **Promoted:** No **ROH:** No
Born: **Marital Status:** **Residence**

Deserted at Lynchburg, VA on 5/14/1861.

2nd Mississippi Alphabetical Roster (Annotated)

Buchanan, Seaborn P.
CO: I **Initial Rank:** Private
Joined: Wednesday, May 1, 1861 **Term (yrs):** 1 **Occupation:** Farmer **Age** 19
Enrolled at: Pontotoc Co., MS **Enrolled By:** Capt. Herring **Promoted:** No **ROH:** No
Born: **Marital Status:** **Residence**

Discharged on 10/22/1861 for disability at Camp Fisher, VA.

Buchanan, William R.
CO: B **Initial Rank:** Private
Joined: Monday, March 4, 1861 **Term (yrs):** 0 **Occupation:** **Age** 23
Enrolled at: Ripley, MS **Enrolled By:** J. R. Chalmers **Promoted:** No **ROH:** No
Born: **Marital Status:** **Residence**

Appears on company muster roll for state service and a Federal register of prisoners of war dated 3/5/1865, at Memphis, TN deserters from rebel army. Place of residence Tuscumbia, AL and physical description and age. No other records.

Buford, Theodore W.
CO: D, E **Initial Rank:** Private
Joined: Wednesday, May 1, 1861 **Term (yrs):** 1 **Occupation:** Farmer **Age** 23
Enrolled at: Tippah Co., MS **Enrolled By:** Capt. Beck **Promoted:** No **ROH:** No
Born: **Marital Status:** S **Residence** Corinth, MS

Transferred to Company E from Company D on 4/25/1862. Wounded at battle of Sharpsburg on 9/17/1862. Discharged on 4/25/1863 due to disability from wound received at Sharpsburg.

Bugg, James M.
CO: H **Initial Rank:** Private
Joined: Saturday, August 10, 1861 **Term (yrs):** 1 **Occupation:** Farmer **Age** 30
Enrolled at: Camp Jones, VA **Enrolled By:**   **Promoted:** No **ROH:** No
Born: Alabama **Marital Status:** S **Residence** Tupelo, MS

Died of disease on 9/14/1861 at Camp Fisher, VA.

Burcham, John M.
CO: A **Initial Rank:** Private
Joined: Saturday, March 1, 1862 **Term (yrs):** 3 **Occupation:** Farmer **Age** 22
Enrolled at: Jacinto, MS **Enrolled By:** Lt. Clayton **Promoted:** No **ROH:** No
Born: Tennessee **Marital Status:** S **Residence** Jacinto, MS

Captured on 7/1/1863 at Gettysburg. Sent to Fort Delaware. Released on oath on 6/11/1865.

2nd Mississippi Alphabetical Roster (Annotated)

Burge, John
CO: D **Initial Rank:** Private
Joined: Wednesday, May 1, 1861 **Term (yrs):** 1 **Occupation:** Farmer **Age** 41
Enrolled at: Tippah Co., MS **Enrolled By:** Capt. Beck **Promoted:** No **ROH:** No
Born: Missouri **Marital Status:** M **Residence** Pine Grove, MS

Discharged at Camp Fisher, VA on 10/22/1861 for disability.

Burge, John P.
CO: A **Initial Rank:** Private
Joined: Wednesday, May 1, 1861 **Term (yrs):** 1 **Occupation:** Farmer **Age** 21
Enrolled at: Tishomingo Co., MS **Enrolled By:** Capt. Leeth **Promoted:** No **ROH:** No
Born: North Carolina **Marital Status:** **Residence**

Wounded at 1st Manassas on 7/21/1861. Discharged on 12/25/1861 from disability due to wounds.

Burnett, Daniel A.
CO: B **Initial Rank:** Private
Joined: Wednesday, May 1, 1861 **Term (yrs):** 1 **Occupation:** Carpenter **Age** 37
Enrolled at: Tippah Co., MS **Enrolled By:** Capt. Buchanan **Promoted:** Yes **ROH:** No
Born: Tennessee **Marital Status:** **Residence**

Appointed 5th Sergeant on 8/27/1861. Discharged on 5/25/1862 for being over age.

Burns, Giles M.
CO: A **Initial Rank:** Private
Joined: Saturday, March 1, 1862 **Term (yrs):** 3 **Occupation:** Farmer **Age** 27
Enrolled at: Jacinto, MS **Enrolled By:** Lt. Clayton **Promoted:** No **ROH:** No
Born: **Marital Status:** **Residence** Corinth, MS

Captured at South Mountain on 9/15/1862. Exchanged on 11/10/1862. Wounded battle of The Wilderness on 5/5/1864. Captured on 10/1/1864 near Petersburg. Sent to Elmira, NY. Released on oath on 6/14/1865.

Burns, John S.
CO: A **Initial Rank:** Private
Joined: Tuesday, August 20, 1861 **Term (yrs):** 3 **Occupation:** Farmer **Age** 28
Enrolled at: Iuka, MS **Enrolled By:** Capt. Stogden **Promoted:** No **ROH:** No
Born: Alabama **Marital Status:** S **Residence** Jacinto, MS

Transferred from 26th Mississippi on 10/1/1861 (? Maybe 10/1/1864? – no records until Sep/Oct 1864). Wounded in battle on 10/1/1864 at Fort Bratton. Captured at Petersburg (Hatcher's Run?) on 4/2/1865. Taken to Point Lookout, MD. Released on oath on 6/9/1865.

2nd Mississippi Alphabetical Roster (Annotated)

Burns, Ralph A.
CO: A **Initial Rank:** Private
Joined: Saturday, March 1, 1862 **Term (yrs):** 3 **Occupation:** Farmer **Age** 26
Enrolled at: Jacinto, MS **Enrolled By:** Lt. Clayton **Promoted:** No **ROH:** No
Born: Alabama **Marital Status:** M **Residence** Jacinto, MS

Admitted to hospital in Richmond with wound (to foot) on 9/19/1862, 7/9/1863, and 1/21/1864 (initial date of wound or engagement not detailed in company records). Captured on 4/3/1865 (probably at brigade hospital) at Richmond. Paroled on 5/3/1865.

Burns, S.
CO: **Initial Rank:** Private
Joined: **Term (yrs):** 0 **Occupation:**   **Age**
Enrolled at: **Enrolled By:**   **Promoted:** No **ROH:** No
Born: **Marital Status:**   **Residence**

Appears on a Federal list of prisoners taken and paroled during the march to the Mobile and Ohio Railroad. List dated Holly Springs, MS on 12/25/1862. No other record.

Burns, William
CO: F **Initial Rank:** Private
Joined: Wednesday, May 1, 1861 **Term (yrs):** 1 **Occupation:** Planter **Age** 21
Enrolled at: Tippah Co., MS **Enrolled By:** Capt. Davis **Promoted:** No **ROH:** No
Born: **Marital Status:**   **Residence**

Died in camp at Camp Fisher, VA on 1/6/1862.

Burnside, Emmitt W. L.
CO: A **Initial Rank:** Private
Joined: Thursday, September 1, 1864 **Term (yrs):** 3 **Occupation:** Farmer **Age** 18
Enrolled at: Petersburg, VA **Enrolled By:** Capt. Walker **Promoted:** No **ROH:** No
Born: Mississippi **Marital Status:** S **Residence** Jacinto, MS

Listed as AWOL since 12/31/1864.

Burton, James
CO: H **Initial Rank:** Private
Joined: **Term (yrs):** 0 **Occupation:**   **Age**
Enrolled at: **Enrolled By:**   **Promoted:** No **ROH:** No
Born: **Marital Status:**   **Residence**

Appears on a Federal register of prisoners of war at Fort Delaware received from Petersburg, VA on 4/4/1865 (probably captured at Hatcher's Run on 4/2/1865).

2nd Mississippi Alphabetical Roster (Annotated)

Burton, James W.
CO: L, F   **Initial Rank:** Private
Joined: Monday, March 3, 1862   **Term (yrs):** 3   **Occupation:** Farmer   **Age** 28
Enrolled at: Ripley, MS   **Enrolled By:** Col. Falkner   **Promoted:** No   **ROH:** No
Born: Tennessee   **Marital Status:**   **Residence**

Wounded (right thigh and left leg) and captured at Gettysburg on 7/3/1863. Paroled and exchanged on 9/27/1863. Furloughed from hospital for 20-days from 10/12/1863. Transferred to Company F from Company L on 1/1/1865.

Burton, Robert M.
CO: L   **Initial Rank:** Private
Joined: Monday, March 3, 1862   **Term (yrs):** 3   **Occupation:** Farmer   **Age** 27
Enrolled at: Ripley, MS   **Enrolled By:** Col. Falkner   **Promoted:** No   **ROH:** No
Born: Tennessee   **Marital Status:**   **Residence**

Died of measles at Chimborazo Hospital in Richmond, VA on 5/7/1862.

Buse, Benjamin T.
CO: E   **Initial Rank:** Private
Joined: Wednesday, May 1, 1861   **Term (yrs):** 1   **Occupation:** Farmer   **Age** 16
Enrolled at: Itawamba Co., MS   **Enrolled By:** Capt. Booth   **Promoted:** No   **ROH:** No
Born: Mississippi   **Marital Status:** S   **Residence** Guntown, MS

Discharged on 7/23/1862 on account of being underage. (Records also show name as Thomas W. Buse).

Buse, John W.
CO: E   **Initial Rank:** Private
Joined: Wednesday, May 1, 1861   **Term (yrs):** 1   **Occupation:** Farmer   **Age** 23
Enrolled at: Itawamba Co., MS   **Enrolled By:** Capt. Booth   **Promoted:** No   **ROH:** No
Born: Mississippi   **Marital Status:** S   **Residence**

Died on 7/2/1861 of disease.

Butler, Armistead M.
CO: F   **Initial Rank:** Private
Joined: Wednesday, May 1, 1861   **Term (yrs):** 1   **Occupation:** Planter (Farmer)   **Age** 19
Enrolled at: Tippah Co., MS   **Enrolled By:** Capt. Davis   **Promoted:** No   **ROH:** Yes
Born: **Marital Status:**   **Residence**

Wounded (in shoulder) at the battle of The Wilderness on 5/6/1864. Surrendered to Federal forces in Mississippi at Holly Springs on 4/9/1865. Released on oath on 6/2/1865. ROH for Bristoe Station, 10/14/1863.

2nd Mississippi Alphabetical Roster (Annotated)

Butler, Elliott L.
CO: A   **Initial Rank:** Private
Joined: Wednesday, May 1, 1861   **Term (yrs):** 1   **Occupation:** Carpenter   **Age** 31
Enrolled at: Tishomingo Co., MS   **Enrolled By:** Capt. Leeth   **Promoted:** No   **ROH:** No
Born: Alabama   **Marital Status:** M   **Residence** Rienzi, MS
Discharged on 4/7/1863 for disability.

Butler, George W.
CO: F   **Initial Rank:** Private
Joined: **Term (yrs):** 0   **Occupation:**   **Age**
Enrolled at: **Enrolled By:**   **Promoted:** No   **ROH:** No
Born: **Marital Status:**   **Residence**
Appears on a Federal report of prisoners of war paroled at Memphis, TN circa 5/20/1865. No other record.

Butler, James C.
CO: D   **Initial Rank:** 2nd Lieutenant
Joined: Saturday, April 27, 1861   **Term (yrs):** 1   **Occupation:** Farmer   **Age**
Enrolled at: Pine Grove, MS   **Enrolled By:** Capt. Beck   **Promoted:** No   **ROH:** No
Born: **Marital Status:** S   **Residence** Pine Grove, MS
Killed on 7/21/1861 at 1st Manassas.

Butler, John H.
CO: D   **Initial Rank:** Private
Joined: Wednesday, May 1, 1861   **Term (yrs):** 1   **Occupation:** Farmer   **Age** 19
Enrolled at: Tippah Co., MS   **Enrolled By:** Capt. Beck   **Promoted:** No   **ROH:** No
Born: **Marital Status:** S   **Residence** Pine Grove, MS
Deserted on 5/28/1862 ("carried away musket and accoutrements complete, $21.45").

Butler, Mercer D.
CO: A   **Initial Rank:** Private
Joined: Saturday, March 1, 1862   **Term (yrs):** 3   **Occupation:** Farmer   **Age** 29
Enrolled at: Jacinto, MS   **Enrolled By:** Lt. Clayton   **Promoted:** No   **ROH:** No
Born: Tennessee   **Marital Status:** M   **Residence** Rienzi, MS
Died of disease at Glade Springs, VA on 4/11/1862.

2nd Mississippi Alphabetical Roster (Annotated)

Butler, Robert R.
CO: A *Initial Rank:* Private
Joined: Wednesday, May 1, 1861   *Term (yrs):* 1 *Occupation:* Farmer   *Age* 24
Enrolled at: Tishomingo Co., MS   *Enrolled By:* Capt. Leeth   *Promoted:* No   *ROH:* No
Born: Tennessee   *Marital Status:* S   *Residence*

Died at Camp Fisher, VA of disease on 10/7/1861.

Butler, Thomas N.
CO: A *Initial Rank:* Private
Joined: Wednesday, May 1, 1861   *Term (yrs):* 1 *Occupation:* Farmer   *Age* 19
Enrolled at: Tishomingo Co., MS   *Enrolled By:* Capt. Leeth   *Promoted:* No   *ROH:* No
Born: Mississippi   *Marital Status:* S   *Residence* Rienzi, MS

Wounded at battle of Seven Pines on 5/31/1862. Returned to duty. Admitted to hospital in Richmond with wound on 10/1/1864 (company records provide no details as to exact date of wound or engagement). Furloughed from 10/7/1864 for 40-days to Mississippi. Reported AWOL since 12/31/1864.

Bynum, George W.
CO: A *Initial Rank:* Private
Joined: Wednesday, May 1, 1861   *Term (yrs):* 1 *Occupation:* Student   *Age* 21
Enrolled at: Tishomingo Co., MS   *Enrolled By:* Capt. Leeth   *Promoted:* Yes   *ROH:* No
Born: North Carolina   *Marital Status:* S   *Residence* Rienzi, MS

Also see Ham's Regiment of Mississippi Cavalry and the 11th Consolidated Mississippi Cavalry. Promoted to 4th Corporal on 4/22/1862. Apparently captured near Shepherdstown, VA and paroled on 9/25/1862. Promoted to 3rd Corporal on 10/16/1862. Promoted to 2nd Sergeant on 7/1/1863. Listed as AWOL since 2/1/1864 and deserted. Appointed Adjutant in Harris' Battalion of Cavalry (Miss State Troops) while on furlough without a regular transfer or discharge from his company.

Bynum, Joseph N.
CO: A *Initial Rank:* Private
Joined: Saturday, September 21, 1861   *Term (yrs):* 1 *Occupation:* Student   *Age* 19
Enrolled at: Rienzi, MS   *Enrolled By:* Lt. Davenport   *Promoted:* No   *ROH:* No
Born: North Carolina   *Marital Status:* S   *Residence* Rienzi, MS

Wounded on 6/27/1862 at battle of Gaines Mill. Discharged on 4/3/1863 on surgeon's certificate of disability due to wounds received at Gaines Mill.

2nd Mississippi Alphabetical Roster (Annotated)

Bynum, Marcus W.   CO: A   Initial Rank: Private
Joined: Monday, September 30, 1861   *Term (yrs):* 1   *Occupation:* Physician   *Age* 25
Enrolled at: Iuka, MS   *Enrolled By:* Lt. Davenport   *Promoted:* No   *ROH:* No
Born: North Carolina   *Marital Status:* M   *Residence* Rienzi, MS

Discharged on 7/17/1862 – substitute provided.

Bynum, Nathaniel M.   CO: A   Initial Rank: Private
Joined: Saturday, March 1, 1862   *Term (yrs):* 3   *Occupation:* Student   *Age* 17
Enrolled at: Jacinto, MS   *Enrolled By:* Lt. Clayton   *Promoted:* No   *ROH:* No
Born: North Carolina   *Marital Status:* S   *Residence* Rienzi, MS

Captured at Petersburg (Hatcher's Run) on 4/2/1865. Released from Fort Delaware on oath on 6/11/1865.

Bynum, Turner   CO: A   Initial Rank: 1st Corporal
Joined: Wednesday, May 1, 1861   *Term (yrs):* 1   *Occupation:* Clerk   *Age* 19
Enrolled at: Tishomingo Co., MS   *Enrolled By:* Capt. Leeth   *Promoted:* Yes   *ROH:* No
Born: North Carolina   *Marital Status:* S   *Residence* Rienzi, MS

Promoted to 5th Sergeant circa Nov/Dec 1861. Promoted to 3rd Sergeant about Mar/Apr 1862. Promoted to 2nd Sergeant about May/Jun 1862. Wounded at Gaines Mill on 6/27/1862. Promoted to 1st Sergeant in Sep/Oct 1864 time period (while a POW). Captured at Gettysburg on 7/3/1863. Taken to Fort Delaware. Released on oath on 6/11/1865.

Bynum, William L. D.   CO: A   Initial Rank: Private
Joined: Saturday, September 21, 1861   *Term (yrs):* 1   *Occupation:* Farmer   *Age* 27
Enrolled at: Rienzi, MS   *Enrolled By:* Lt. Davenport   *Promoted:* No   *ROH:* No
Born: North Carolina   *Marital Status:* M   *Residence* Rienzi, MS

Note on jacket says to also see 7th Miss Cavalry Regiment (Partisan Rangers). Wounded on 6/27/1862 at battle of Gaines Mill. Transferred to 7th Mississippi Cavalry Regiment (elected 2nd Lt.) on 11/5/1862.

2nd Mississippi Alphabetical Roster (Annotated)

Byrn, Hugh L.

CO: B *Initial Rank:* Private
Joined: Wednesday, May 1, 1861 *Term (yrs):* 1 *Occupation:* Clerk *Age* 21
Enrolled at: Tippah Co., MS *Enrolled By:* Capt. Buchanan *Promoted:* Yes *ROH:* No
Born: *Marital Status:* *Residence*

Bvt. 2nd Lieutenant. On 4/21/1862. Assigned to duty on 4/23/1862. Promoted to Senior 2nd Lieutenant vice [William C.] Moody. Wounded and captured at Gettysburg on 7/3/1863. Sent to Johnson's Island, OH. Exchanged on 3/17/1864. Returned to duty from hospital on 8/28/1864. Listed as AWOL since 12/17/1864. Furloughed by medical examining board. Surrendered at La Grange, TN on 5/31/1865 and paroled on oath.

Byrn, Lucas H.

CO: B *Initial Rank:* Private
Joined: Wednesday, May 1, 1861 *Term (yrs):* 1 *Occupation:* Clerk *Age* 23
Enrolled at: Tippah Co., MS *Enrolled By:* Capt. Buchanan *Promoted:* No *ROH:* No
Born: *Marital Status:* *Residence* Ripley, MS

Acting Sergeant Major from 9/29/1862. Detail duty as acting Assistant Quartermaster since 12/21/1862. Detailed as ambulance sergeant since 4/25/1864 by medical examining board. AWOL since 2/15/1865. Paroled at Memphis, TN on 5/25/1865.

Byrn, Rose K.

CO: B *Initial Rank:* Private
Joined: Wednesday, May 1, 1861 *Term (yrs):* 1 *Occupation:* Farmer *Age* 20
Enrolled at: Tippah Co., MS *Enrolled By:* Capt. Buchanan *Promoted:* No *ROH:* No
Born: *Marital Status:* *Residence*

Slightly wounded at battle of 1st Manassas on 7/21/1861. "Stunned by a shell" during Jul/Aug 1862 muster period.

Byrn, William H.

CO: B *Initial Rank:* Private
Joined: Wednesday, April 15, 1863 *Term (yrs):* 3 *Occupation:* *Age*
Enrolled at: Ripley, MS *Enrolled By:* Capt. Storey *Promoted:* No *ROH:* Yes
Born: *Marital Status:* *Residence*

Captured at Petersburg (Hatcher's Run?) on 4/2/1865 [Last regimental color bearer]. Sent to Fort Delaware. Released on oath on 6/11/1865. ROH for Talley's Mill, 5/10/1864.

2nd Mississippi Alphabetical Roster (Annotated)

Caldwell, Elijah B.

	CO: I	**Initial Rank:** Private
Joined: Wednesday, May 1, 1861	**Term (yrs):** 1 **Occupation:** Farmer	**Age** 21
Enrolled at: Pontotoc Co., MS	**Enrolled By:** Capt. Herring	**Promoted:** No **ROH:** No
Born:	**Marital Status:**	**Residence**

Captured at Gettysburg on 7/1/1863. Sent to Fort Delaware. Exchanged at Aiken's Landing, VA on 9/30/1864. On parole furlough.

Campbell, Samuel A.

	CO: I	**Initial Rank:** 1st Lieutenant
Joined: Wednesday, May 1, 1861	**Term (yrs):** 1 **Occupation:** Farmer	**Age** 24
Enrolled at: Pontotoc Co., MS	**Enrolled By:** Capt. Herring	**Promoted:** No **ROH:** No
Born:	**Marital Status:**	**Residence**

Retired from service on expiration of term of enlistment (Mar/Apr 1862 time frame). [Later may have been associated with Wirt Adam's cavalry brigade (circa Feb 1864)].

Canes, Henry

	CO: D	**Initial Rank:** Private
Joined:	**Term (yrs):** 0 **Occupation:**	**Age**
Enrolled at:	**Enrolled By:**	**Promoted:** No **ROH:** No
Born:	**Marital Status:**	**Residence**

Also see Henry Craves of 2nd Missouri Infantry. No other record.

Cantrill, Calaway H.

	CO: A	**Initial Rank:** Private
Joined: Wednesday, May 1, 1861	**Term (yrs):** 1 **Occupation:** Mechanic	**Age** 27
Enrolled at: Tishomingo Co., MS	**Enrolled By:** Capt. Leeth	**Promoted:** No **ROH:** No
Born:	**Marital Status:**	**Residence**

Captured at battle of Sharpsburg on 9/17/1862. Paroled on 9/21/1862. Captured at Gettysburg on 7/1/1863. Died of scurvy at Fort Delaware on 5/29/1865.

Caraway, James P.

	CO: A, S	**Initial Rank:** Private
Joined: Wednesday, May 1, 1861	**Term (yrs):** 1 **Occupation:** Farmer	**Age** 21
Enrolled at: Tishomingo Co., MS	**Enrolled By:** Capt. Leeth	**Promoted:** Yes **ROH:** No
Born: Tennessee	**Marital Status:** S	**Residence** Rienzi, MS

Appointed 3rd Corporal on 11/29/1861. Promoted to Ordnance Sergeant on 5/17/1862 (Field & Staff).

2nd Mississippi Alphabetical Roster (Annotated)

Carhorn, L. B. | CO: H | Initial Rank: Private

Joined: **Term (yrs):** 0 *Occupation:* **Age**
Enrolled at: *Enrolled By:* **Promoted:** No **ROH:** No
Born: *Marital Status:* *Residence*

Appears on a Federal record of sick and wounded Confederates in the hospitals in and around Gettysburg after the battle. Captured at Gettysburg (date not given). No other record.

Carmack, Edward W. | CO: A | Initial Rank:

Joined: Wednesday, February 20, 1861 **Term (yrs):** 0 *Occupation:* **Age**
Enrolled at: Corinth, MS *Enrolled By:* R. Griffith **Promoted:** No **ROH:** No
Born: *Marital Status:* *Residence*

Appears on a company muster roll for Company A. No other record.

Carmack, Joshua Y. | CO: A | Initial Rank: Private

Joined: Wednesday, May 1, 1861 **Term (yrs):** 1 *Occupation:* Lawyer **Age** 25
Enrolled at: Tishomingo Co., MS *Enrolled By:* Capt. Leeth **Promoted:** No **ROH:** No
Born: *Marital Status:* S *Residence* Jacinto, MS

Transferred to Chickasaw Rangers (cavalry) on 10/21/1861.

Carpenter, Owen F. | CO: L | Initial Rank: Private

Joined: Monday, March 3, 1862 **Term (yrs):** 3 *Occupation:* Farmer **Age** 25
Enrolled at: Ripley, MS *Enrolled By:* Col. Falkner **Promoted:** No **ROH:** Yes
Born: Mississippi *Marital Status:* M *Residence* Ripley, MS

Records say killed at Gettysburg on 7/1/1863. However, ROH lists Gettysburg, 7/3/1863 (so more likely he was killed on 7/3, not 7/1).

Carr, John W. | CO: H | Initial Rank: Private

Joined: Monday, April 29, 1861 **Term (yrs):** 1 *Occupation:* Carpenter **Age** 31
Enrolled at: Pontotoc Co., MS *Enrolled By:* Capt. Taylor **Promoted:** No **ROH:** Yes
Born: Georgia *Marital Status:* S *Residence* Chesterville, MS

Muster record indicates he was transferred to Company C from Company H on 5/31/1862 [however, he is still carried on Company H's muster roll for next and subsequent periods]. Captured at Hatcher's Run on 4/2/1865. Taken to Point Lookout, MD. Released on oath on 6/10/1865. ROH for Bethesda Church, 5/31/1864.

2nd Mississippi Alphabetical Roster (Annotated)

Carr, Oliver C.   CO: G   Initial Rank: 4th Corporal

Joined: Wednesday, May 1, 1861   **Term (yrs):** 1   **Occupation:** Law Student   **Age** 22

Enrolled at: Pontotoc Co., MS   **Enrolled By:** Capt. Kilpatrick   **Promoted:** Yes   **ROH:** No

Born: Mississippi   **Marital Status:** S   **Residence** Pontotoc, MS

Elected 3rd Lieutenant. on 10/29/1861 to fill vacancy caused by resignation of Charles D. Fontaine. Discharged by reason of election on 4/23/1862.

Carroll, James H.   CO: C   Initial Rank: Private

Joined: Tuesday, April 7, 1863   **Term (yrs):** 3   **Occupation:**   **Age**

Enrolled at: Suffolk, VA   **Enrolled By:** Lt. Sargent   **Promoted:** No   **ROH:** No

Born: **Marital Status:**   **Residence**

Captured at Petersburg (Hatcher's Run?) on 4/2/1865. Taken to Fort Delaware. Released on oath on 6/11/1865.

Carter, Charles H.   CO: A   Initial Rank:

Joined: Wednesday, February 20, 1861   **Term (yrs):** 0   **Occupation:**   **Age**

Enrolled at: Corinth, MS   **Enrolled By:** R. Griffith   **Promoted:** No   **ROH:** No

Born: **Marital Status:**   **Residence**

Appears on a Company A muster roll for state service. No other record.

Carter, John C.   CO: A   Initial Rank: Private

Joined: Wednesday, May 1, 1861   **Term (yrs):** 1   **Occupation:** Farmer   **Age** 33

Enrolled at: Tishomingo Co., MS   **Enrolled By:** Capt. Leeth   **Promoted:** No   **ROH:** No

Born: Virginia   **Marital Status:** M   **Residence** Jacinto, MS

Discharged due to disability on 8/12/1861.

Carter, Thomas S.   CO: A   Initial Rank: Private

Joined: Wednesday, May 1, 1861   **Term (yrs):** 1   **Occupation:** Farmer   **Age** 22

Enrolled at: Tishomingo Co., MS   **Enrolled By:** Capt. Leeth   **Promoted:** Yes   **ROH:** Yes

Born: Mississippi   **Marital Status:** S   **Residence** Jacinto, MS

Appointed to 4th Corporal on 10/16/1862. Wounded and captured at Gettysburg on 7/1/1863. Paroled from DeCamp General Hospital, Davids Island, NY Harbor to City Point, VA to await exchange on 8/38/1863. Returned to duty. Listed as 3rd Corporal during Jan/Feb 1864 muster roll. Listed as 2nd Corporal during Mar/Apr 1864 muster roll. Killed at battle of The Wilderness on 5/5/1864. ROH for The Wilderness, 5/5/1864.

2nd Mississippi Alphabetical Roster (Annotated)

Carter, William E. D.
CO: A **Initial Rank:** Private
Joined: Wednesday, May 1, 1861 **Term (yrs):** 1 **Occupation:** Farmer **Age** 32
Enrolled at: Tishomingo Co., MS **Enrolled By:** Capt. Leeth **Promoted:** No **ROH:** No
Born: Tennessee **Marital Status:** M **Residence** Rienzi, MS

Detailed as regimental teamster. Surrendered and paroled on 4/?/1865 at Lynchburg, VA.

Carter, William R. C.
CO: B, F **Initial Rank:** Private
Joined: Monday, March 3, 1862 **Term (yrs):** 3 **Occupation:** Farmer **Age** 20
Enrolled at: Ripley, MS **Enrolled By:** Capt. Buchanan **Promoted:** No **ROH:** No
Born: **Marital Status:** M **Residence**

Transferred to Company F from Company B on 4/30/1862. Deserted on 5/3/1863.

Cartwright, James H.
CO: L **Initial Rank:** Private
Joined: Monday, March 3, 1862 **Term (yrs):** 3 **Occupation:** Farmer **Age** 18
Enrolled at: Ripley, MS **Enrolled By:** Col. Falkner **Promoted:** No **ROH:** No
Born: Mississippi **Marital Status:** S **Residence** Silver Springs, MS

Died at Ashland, VA of pneumonia on 4/23/1862.

Caruthers, Gilbert G.
CO: E **Initial Rank:** Private
Joined: Wednesday, May 1, 1861 **Term (yrs):** 1 **Occupation:** Clerk (merchant) **Age** 22
Enrolled at: Itawamba Co., MS **Enrolled By:** Capt. Booth **Promoted:** Yes **ROH:** No
Born: Alabama **Marital Status:** S **Residence** Guntown, MS

Promoted to 3rd Corporal on 9/25/1861. Promoted to 2nd Lieutenant on 4/17/1862. Wounded at Gaines Mill on 6/27/1862. Subsequently died of wounds on 6/29/1862 (some records list as killed in battle).

Cary, Miles
CO: G **Initial Rank:** Private
Joined: Sunday, July 13, 1862 **Term (yrs):** 2 **Occupation:** Clerk **Age** 46
Enrolled at: Richmond, VA **Enrolled By:** Capt. Crawford **Promoted:** No **ROH:** No
Born: Virginia **Marital Status:** M **Residence** Virginia

Listed as AWOL since 12/5/1863 and deserter. He was a substitute for Isaac A. Mooser [Moozer].

2nd Mississippi Alphabetical Roster (Annotated)

Casey, William A.
Joined: Wednesday, May 1, 1861 *CO:* D *Initial Rank:* Private
Enrolled at: Pine Grove, MS *Term (yrs):* 1 *Occupation:* Farmer *Age* 21
Born: Georgia *Enrolled By:* Capt. Beck *Promoted:* No *ROH:* No
Marital Status: S *Residence* Snow Creek, MS

Deserted on 5/28/1862.

Cason, John H.
Joined: Wednesday, May 1, 1861 *CO:* C *Initial Rank:* Private
Enrolled at: Itawamba Co., MS *Term (yrs):* 1 *Occupation:* Farmer *Age* 24
Born: *Enrolled By:* Capt. Bromley *Promoted:* No *ROH:* No
Marital Status: *Residence*

Killed in battle at 2nd Manassas on 8/29/1862 (other records say he died on 8/30/1862).

Castleberry, Winchester D.
Joined: Wednesday, May 1, 1861 *CO:* K *Initial Rank:* Private
Enrolled at: Tishomingo Co., MS *Term (yrs):* 1 *Occupation:* Lumber *Age* 23
Born: *Enrolled By:* Capt. Stone *Promoted:* Yes *ROH:* No
Marital Status: *Residence*

Appointed 2nd Sergeant on 2/1/1862. Appointed 1st Sergeant on 6/11/1862. Wounded at 2nd Manassas (?), [probably on 8/29/1862 (based on hospital admission records)]. Listed as 2nd Lieutenant. in Mar/Apr 1862 muster. Detached service since 11/3/1863 to round up deserters and conscripts. Listed as company commander of Company L in July/Aug 1864 muster. Listed as 1st Lieutenant. during Sept/Oct 1864 muster. Died on 10/13/1864 of wounds received in battle (what action?) on 10/1/1864. [*Buried at Hollywood Cemetery, Richmond, VA. Soldiers Section V Lot: 227. Note says he died on 10/14/1864.]

Cathey, Gilbreath A.
Joined: Wednesday, May 1, 1861 *CO:* D *Initial Rank:* Private
Enrolled at: Tippah Co., MS *Term (yrs):* 1 *Occupation:* Farmer *Age* 20
Born: Mississippi *Enrolled By:* Capt. Beck *Promoted:* No *ROH:* No
Marital Status: S *Residence* Snow Creek, MS

Wounded in battle at 1st Manassas on 7/21/1861. Wounded in battle at Gaines Mill on 6/27/1862. Captured at Gettysburg on 7/1/1863. Sent to Fort Delaware. Released on oath on 6/11/1865.

2nd Mississippi Alphabetical Roster (Annotated)

Caveness, William A.   *CO:* A   *Initial Rank:* Private
Joined: Wednesday, May 1, 1861   *Term (yrs):* 1   *Occupation:* Clerk   *Age* 19
Enrolled at: Tishomingo Co., MS   *Enrolled By:* Capt. Leeth   *Promoted:* No   *ROH:* No
Born: Mississippi   *Marital Status:* S   *Residence* Burnsville, MS

Discharged on 10/22/1861 due to disability.

Cayce, James M.   *CO:* E   *Initial Rank:* Private
Joined: Monday, February 24, 1862   *Term (yrs):* 3   *Occupation:* Merchant   *Age* 24
Enrolled at: Guntown, MS   *Enrolled By:* Capt. Bates   *Promoted:* Yes   *ROH:* No
Born: Tennessee   *Marital Status:* M   *Residence* Guntown, MS

Promoted to Quartermaster Sergeant on 7/10/1862. Captured at Gettysburg on 7/5/1863. Taken to Fort Delaware. Paroled to Aiken's Landing, VA for exchange on 9/30/1864. Surrendered and paroled at Appomattox Court House on 4/9/1865.

Cayce, Shadrick N.   *CO:* K   *Initial Rank:* Private
Joined: Wednesday, May 1, 1861   *Term (yrs):* 1   *Occupation:* Student   *Age* 17
Enrolled at: Tishomingo Co., MS   *Enrolled By:* Capt. Stone   *Promoted:* Yes   *ROH:* No
Born: Mississippi   *Marital Status:*   *Residence*

Discharged on 5/27/1862 – underage.

Chamberlain, Thomas   *CO:* K   *Initial Rank:*
Joined: *Term (yrs):* 0   *Occupation:*   *Age* 26
Enrolled at: *Enrolled By:*   *Promoted:* No   *ROH:* No
Born: *Marital Status:*   *Residence*

Appears on a Federal register of prisoners of war surrendered at Appomattox Court House on 4/10/1865 and paroled on 7/14/1865 at Mobile, AL. Residence of Tishomingo Co., MS. No other record.

Chambers, Claiborne C.   *CO:* K   *Initial Rank:* Private
Joined: Saturday, March 1, 1862   *Term (yrs):* 3   *Occupation:*   *Age* 18
Enrolled at: Iuka, MS   *Enrolled By:* Lt. Latham   *Promoted:* No   *ROH:* No
Born: Alabama   *Marital Status:*   *Residence*

Died of disease on 8/30/1862 at Lynchburg, VA.

2nd Mississippi Alphabetical Roster (Annotated)

Chambers, Thomas F.
CO: K **Initial Rank:** Private
Joined: Saturday, March 1, 1862 **Term (yrs):** 3 **Occupation:** **Age** 22
Enrolled at: Iuka, MS **Enrolled By:** Lt. Latham **Promoted:** No **ROH:** No
Born: Illinois **Marital Status:** **Residence**

Listed as deserted on 6/27/1863. Federal records report captured at Emmitsburg, PA on 6/28/1863. "Remarks" say 'volunteered Miss. Where born: Ill. Also see listings under Thomas F. Champers [same person].

Chambliss, William
CO: A **Initial Rank:** Private
Joined: Saturday, March 1, 1862 **Term (yrs):** 3 **Occupation:** **Age** 27
Enrolled at: Jacinto, MS **Enrolled By:** Lt. Clayton **Promoted:** No **ROH:** No
Born: **Marital Status:** **Residence**

Appears on list of engagements as mortally wounded at Sharpsburg on 9/17/1862 (?). However, company muster roll indicates he "died about the last of April at Ashland" VA.

Champion, George W.
CO: C **Initial Rank:** Private
Joined: Wednesday, February 6, 1861 **Term (yrs):** 1 **Occupation:** Farmer **Age** 20
Enrolled at: Richmond, MS **Enrolled By:** Capt. Bromley **Promoted:** No **ROH:** Yes
Born: **Marital Status:** **Residence**

Wounded at battle of The Wilderness on 5/6/1864. Died of wounds on 6/25/1864. ROH for The Wilderness, 5/6/1864.

Champion, Jacob M.
CO: C **Initial Rank:** Private
Joined: Wednesday, February 6, 1861 **Term (yrs):** 1 **Occupation:** **Age**
Enrolled at: Richmond, MS **Enrolled By:** Capt. Bromley **Promoted:** No **ROH:** No
Born: **Marital Status:** **Residence**

Captured at Gettysburg on 7/3/1863 (?). [Probably wounded (appears on a list of sick and wounded Confederates)]. Paroled to City Point, VA on 9/27/1863 from DeCamp General Hospital, Davids Island, NY Harbor. Retired from service on account of wounds received in battle [at Gettysburg?], 2/24/1865.

2nd Mississippi Alphabetical Roster (Annotated)

Champion, Leander M.

CO: D **Initial Rank:** Private

Joined: Tuesday, October 1, 1861 **Term (yrs):** 1 **Occupation:** Farmer **Age** 19

Enrolled at: Iuka, MS **Enrolled By:** Lt. Davenport **Promoted:** No **ROH:** No

Born: Mississippi **Marital Status:** S **Residence** Salem, MS

Wounded at Gaines Mill on 6/27/1862. Captured near Hatcher's Run on 4/2/1865. Released on oath on 6/11/1865. Admitted to U.S.A. Post Hospital at Jackson, MS on 7/13/1865 complaining of gunshot wound to leg. Discharged on 7/17/1865.

Chaney, John H.

CO: A, L **Initial Rank:** Private

Joined: Saturday, March 1, 1862 **Term (yrs):** 3 **Occupation:** Mechanic **Age** 38

Enrolled at: Jacinto, MS **Enrolled By:** Lt. Clayton **Promoted:** No **ROH:** No

Born: South Carolina **Marital Status:** M **Residence** Rienzi, MS

Transferred to Company L from Company A on 4/30/1862. Captured at South Mountain, MD on 9/15/1862. Exchanged on 11/10/1862. Listed as "deserted to the enemy in Miss." However, Federal records list him as a POW captured at Danville, MS on 4/25/1863. Sent to Alton, IL on 5/22/1863.

Chapman, Benjamin F.

CO: H **Initial Rank:** Private

Joined: Monday, April 29, 1861 **Term (yrs):** 1 **Occupation:** Farmer **Age** 38

Enrolled at: Pontotoc Co., MS **Enrolled By:** Capt. Taylor **Promoted:** No **ROH:** No

Born: South Carolina **Marital Status:** S **Residence** Chesterville, MS

Discharged on account of over age on 7/29/1862.

Charles, James T.

CO: H **Initial Rank:** Private

Joined: Sunday, March 23, 1862 **Term (yrs):** 3 **Occupation:**   **Age**

Enrolled at: Shannon, MS **Enrolled By:** Lt. Porter **Promoted:** No **ROH:** No

Born: **Marital Status:**   **Residence**

Also see 1st Mississippi Infantry Regiment. Wounded [Gettysburg Campaign] (admitted to hospital in Richmond with wound on 7/12/1863 (date of wound or engagement not noted in company records). Wounded at The Wilderness on 5/5/1864 and captured. Exchanged (date?). Transferred to Company C of the 1st Regiment Mississippi Volunteers by S.O. 217/13 dated 8/13/1864.

2nd Mississippi Alphabetical Roster (Annotated)

Charlton, George T.

CO: K **Initial Rank:** Private

Joined: Saturday, March 1, 1862 **Term (yrs):** 3 **Occupation:** Laborer **Age** 21

Enrolled at: Iuka, MS **Enrolled By:** Lt. Latham **Promoted:** No **ROH:** No

Born: **Marital Status:** **Residence**

Wounded at Gettysburg on 7/1/1863. Captured on 7/5/1863 and paroled from DeCamp General Hospital, Davids Island, NY Harbor to City Point, VA for exchange on 8/24/1863. Dropped from rolls as deserter circa August 1864.

Cherry, Joel T.

CO: D **Initial Rank:** Private

Joined: Wednesday, May 1, 1861 **Term (yrs):** 1 **Occupation:** Farmer **Age** 29

Enrolled at: Tippah Co., MS **Enrolled By:** Capt. Beck **Promoted:** No **ROH:** No

Born: Tennessee **Marital Status:** M **Residence** Snow Creek, MS

Perfect attendance record as "Present" through the entire period of the war! Captured at Petersburg (Hatcher's Run?) on 4/2/1865. Taken to Fort Delaware and released on oath on 6/11/1865.

Childers, James

CO: F **Initial Rank:** Private

Joined: Wednesday, May 1, 1861 **Term (yrs):** 1 **Occupation:** Planter **Age** 19

Enrolled at: Tippah Co., MS **Enrolled By:** Capt. Davis **Promoted:** No **ROH:** No

Born: **Marital Status:** **Residence**

Also see 2nd Mississippi State Cavalry. Listed as deserted during July/Aug 1864 muster roll.

Childers, John

CO: E **Initial Rank:** Private

Joined: Saturday, March 1, 1862 **Term (yrs):** 3 **Occupation:** Farmer **Age** 16

Enrolled at: Guntown, MS **Enrolled By:** Capt. Bates **Promoted:** No **ROH:** No

Born: Mississippi **Marital Status:** S **Residence** Guntown, MS

According to accompanying list of engagements, captured at Gettysburg on 7/3/1863 (not so noted in company muster records). Paroled 9/25/1863 and exchanged. Listed as deserted during Mar/Apr 1864 muster roll. Took oath of allegiance on 5/23/1864.

Childers, Landon D.

CO: F **Initial Rank:** Private

Joined: Wednesday, May 1, 1861 **Term (yrs):** 1 **Occupation:** Planter **Age** 20

Enrolled at: Tippah Co., MS **Enrolled By:** Capt. Davis **Promoted:** No **ROH:** No

Born: **Marital Status:** **Residence**

Deserted on 5/3/1863.

2nd Mississippi Alphabetical Roster (Annotated)

Childers, Levi A.   CO: D, G   Initial Rank: Private

Joined: Thursday, September 19, 1861   **Term (yrs):** 1   **Occupation:** Farmer   **Age** 23

Enrolled at: Salem, MS   **Enrolled By:** Lt. Davenport   **Promoted:** No   **ROH:** No

Born: Mississippi   **Marital Status:** S   **Residence** Snow Creek, MS

Transferred from Company D to Company G in on 2/1/1863. Wounded at The Wilderness on 5/5/1864. Returned to duty on 5/17/1864. Listed as AWOL since 2/28/1865.

Childers, W. C.   CO: G   Initial Rank: Private

Joined: Thursday, March 20, 1862   **Term (yrs):** 3   **Occupation:** Farmer   **Age** 30

Enrolled at: Pontotoc, MS   **Enrolled By:** G. B. Mears   **Promoted:** No   **ROH:** No

Born: Tennessee   **Marital Status:** M   **Residence** Pontotoc, MS

Wounded at Gettysburg on 7/1/1863. Furloughed for 40 days from 8/12/1863. Listed as AWOL from furlough and deserter in Oct. 1863. On a Federal list of prisoners of war reporting at Memphis and received paroles circa 5/20/1865.

Chisholm, Edward S.   CO: D   Initial Rank: Private

Joined: **Term (yrs):** 0   **Occupation:** Dentist   **Age** 22

Enrolled at: **Enrolled By:**   **Promoted:** No   **ROH:** No

Born: **Marital Status:**   **Residence**

Probably misidentified. Listed on a roll of prisoners of war from Camp Douglas, IL dated 9/29/1862 for exchange at Vicksburg, MS. Other listed headed "2nd Miss. Battery" and "2 Miss. Battn." Identified brigade: Chalmers; Division: Bragg [Misidentified. Belongs to a cavalry command, not the 2nd Mississippi Infantry].

Chisholm, James   CO: K   Initial Rank: Private

Joined: Wednesday, May 1, 1861   **Term (yrs):** 1   **Occupation:**   **Age** 22

Enrolled at: Tishomingo Co., MS   **Enrolled By:** Capt. Stone   **Promoted:** No   **ROH:** No

Born: **Marital Status:**   **Residence**

Appears on a muster-in roll dated Lynchburg, VA 5/10/1861. No other record.

2nd Mississippi Alphabetical Roster (Annotated)

Chism, David G.
CO: K **Initial Rank:** Private
Joined: Saturday, March 1, 1862 **Term (yrs):** 3 **Occupation:** **Age** 26
Enrolled at: Iuka, MS **Enrolled By:** Lt. Latham **Promoted:** No **ROH:** Yes
Born: **Marital Status:** **Residence**

Apparently deserted to the enemy about 3/29/1865. Federal records indicate he took oath of allegiance and transportation furnished to Paducah, KY. ROH for Bethesda Church, 5/31/1864.

Choate, William P.
CO: E **Initial Rank:** Private
Joined: Wednesday, May 1, 1861 **Term (yrs):** 1 **Occupation:** Farmer **Age** 25
Enrolled at: Guntown, MS **Enrolled By:** Gen. Barksdale **Promoted:** No **ROH:** No
Born: Tennessee **Marital Status:** S **Residence** Guntown, MS

Missing at 1st Manassas. Returned to regiment on 10/15/1861. Died 11/9/1861 of disease.

Chrestter, John
CO: A **Initial Rank:** Private
Joined: **Term (yrs):** 0 **Occupation:** **Age**
Enrolled at: **Enrolled By:** **Promoted:** No **ROH:** No
Born: **Marital Status:** **Residence**

Appears on a Federal register of prisoners of war in custody of Provost Marshall in Memphis, TN and released on oath of allegiance. Dated 8/18 (year not given). No other record.

Chrisman, Isaac
CO: D **Initial Rank:** Private
Joined: Wednesday, May 1, 1861 **Term (yrs):** 0 **Occupation:** Farmer **Age** 20
Enrolled at: Tippah Co., MS **Enrolled By:** Capt. Beck **Promoted:** No **ROH:** No
Born: Mississippi **Marital Status:** S **Residence** Shelby Creek, MS

Discharged on 6/27/1861 due to disability.

Christman, John C.
CO: A **Initial Rank:** Private
Joined: Wednesday, May 1, 1861 **Term (yrs):** 1 **Occupation:** Mechanic **Age** 47
Enrolled at: Tishomingo Co., MS **Enrolled By:** Capt. Leeth **Promoted:** No **ROH:** Yes
Born: Germany **Marital Status:** S **Residence** Jacinto, MS

Wounded at 2nd Manassas on 8/29/1862. Died of wounds on 9/25/1862.

2nd Mississippi Alphabetical Roster (Annotated)

Clark, Archibald
CO: H **Initial Rank:** 3rd Corporal
Joined: Monday, April 29, 1861   **Term (yrs):** 1 **Occupation:** Farmer   **Age** 44
Enrolled at: Pontotoc Co., MS   **Enrolled By:** Capt. Taylor   **Promoted:** No   **ROH:** No
Born: South Carolina   **Marital Status:** M   **Residence** Chesterville, MS

Mortally wounded at 1st Manassas on 7/21/1861. Died on 7/23/1861.

Clark, Hosea L.
CO: F **Initial Rank:** Private
Joined: Saturday, March 1, 1862   **Term (yrs):** 3 **Occupation:** Farmer   **Age** 18
Enrolled at: Ripley, MS   **Enrolled By:** Capt. Powers   **Promoted:** No   **ROH:** No
Born: Alabama   **Marital Status:** S   **Residence**

Died of disease at Scottsville, VA on 7/15/1862.

Clark, James M.
CO: F **Initial Rank:** Private
Joined: Monday, March 4, 1861   **Term (yrs):** 1 **Occupation:**   **Age**
Enrolled at: Ripley, MS   **Enrolled By:** J. R. Chalmers   **Promoted:** No   **ROH:** No
Born: **Marital Status:**   **Residence**

Captured at Petersburg (Hatcher's Run?) on 4/2/1865. Sent to Fort Delaware. Released on oath on 6/7/1865.

Clark, Joseph C.
CO: F **Initial Rank:** Private
Joined: Wednesday, May 1, 1861   **Term (yrs):** 1 **Occupation:** Planter   **Age** 21
Enrolled at: Tippah Co., MS   **Enrolled By:** Capt. Davis   **Promoted:** No   **ROH:** No
Born: Mississippi   **Marital Status:**   **Residence**

Wounded (right leg and side) at battle of Falling Waters, MD on 7/14/1863. Furloughed for 40-days from 8/1/1863. AWOL upon expiration of furlough. Listed as deserted during Jul/Aug 1864 muster roll.

Clark, Joseph F. M.
CO: F **Initial Rank:** Private
Joined: Wednesday, May 1, 1861   **Term (yrs):** 1 **Occupation:** Planter   **Age** 19
Enrolled at: Tippah Co., MS   **Enrolled By:** Capt. Davis   **Promoted:** No   **ROH:** No
Born: Tennessee   **Marital Status:**   **Residence**

Some records show him discharged for disability on 12/18/1861. However, other records indicate he was with the regiment until captured at Petersburg (Hatcher's Run?) on 4/2/1865 [he may have re-enlisted].

2nd Mississippi Alphabetical Roster (Annotated)

Clark, Micagah L., Jr.   CO: L   Initial Rank: Private

Joined: Monday, March 3, 1862   *Term (yrs):* 3   *Occupation:* Farmer   *Age* 19

Enrolled at: Ripley, MS   *Enrolled By:* Col. Falkner   *Promoted:* No   *ROH:* Yes

Born: Mississippi   *Marital Status:* S   *Residence* Ripley, MS

Hospital records show admission for wound at Richmond on 6/14/1863 (date of wound or engagement not listed in company records). Records indicate AWOL since 5/5/1864 and in arrest since 12/26/1864 at Petersburg. ROH for Bethesda Church, 6/2/1864 (records inconsistent...he couldn't have been AWOL and fought at Bethesda Church during the same time period).

Clark, Micagah L., Sr.   CO: L   Initial Rank: 3rd Corporal

Joined: Monday, March 3, 1862   *Term (yrs):* 3   *Occupation:* Farmer   *Age* 39

Enrolled at: Ripley, MS   *Enrolled By:* Col. Falkner   *Promoted:* Yes   *ROH:* No

Born: Tennessee   *Marital Status:* M   *Residence* Ripley, MS

Promoted to 2nd Corporal on 3/23/1862. Reduced to ranks on 9/1/1862. Listed as AWOL from 10/31/1864.

Clark, Pleasant   CO: H   Initial Rank: Private

Joined: Monday, April 29, 1861   *Term (yrs):* 1   *Occupation:* Farmer   *Age* 33

Enrolled at: Pontotoc Co., MS   *Enrolled By:* Capt. Taylor   *Promoted:* Yes   *ROH:* Yes

Born: Alabama   *Marital Status:* M   *Residence* Chesterville, MS

Promoted to 3rd Corporal on 12/13/1861. Reduced to ranks circa May/June 1863. Killed in the battle of The Wilderness on 5/5/1864. ROH for The Wilderness, 5/5/1864.

Claybrooks, William L.   CO: K   Initial Rank: Private

Joined: Wednesday, May 1, 1861   *Term (yrs):* 1   *Occupation:* Student   *Age* 19

Enrolled at: Tishomingo Co., MS   *Enrolled By:* Capt. Stone   *Promoted:* No   *ROH:* No

Born: *Marital Status:*   *Residence*

Absent on furlough from 11/6/1864. AWOL since.

Clayton, A. S.   CO: C   Initial Rank: Private

Joined: Tuesday, October 1, 1861   *Term (yrs):* 1   *Occupation:*   *Age*

Enrolled at: Verona, MS   *Enrolled By:* Lt. Davenport   *Promoted:* No   *ROH:* No

Born: *Marital Status:*   *Residence*

Killed in battle of Sharpsburg on 9/17/1862.

2nd Mississippi Alphabetical Roster (Annotated)

Clayton, Charles C.
CO: C **Initial Rank:** Private
Joined: Wednesday, May 1, 1861 *Term (yrs):* 1 *Occupation:* Farmer **Age** 27
Enrolled at: Itawamba Co., MS *Enrolled By:* Capt. Bromley *Promoted:* No *ROH:* No
Born: Alabama *Marital Status:* *Residence*

Captured at Gettysburg on 7/1/1863. Sent to Fort Delaware. According to Federal records, became "Galvanized Yankee" and joined the 3rd Maryland Cavalry (U.S.). Company records list him as deserted to the enemy at Fort Delaware.

Clayton, Joshua S.
CO: C **Initial Rank:** Private
Joined: Wednesday, May 1, 1861 *Term (yrs):* 1 *Occupation:* Farmer **Age** 31
Enrolled at: Itawamba Co., MS *Enrolled By:* Capt. Bromley *Promoted:* No *ROH:* No
Born: *Marital Status:* *Residence*

Wounded at Gaines Mill on 6/27/1862. Captured at Gettysburg on 7/1/1863. Taken to Fort Delaware where he died of disease on 10/2/1863.

Clayton, Newton
CO: H **Initial Rank:** Private
Joined: Monday, April 29, 1861 *Term (yrs):* 1 *Occupation:* Farmer **Age** 25
Enrolled at: Pontotoc Co., MS *Enrolled By:* Capt. Taylor *Promoted:* Yes *ROH:* No
Born: *Marital Status:* *Residence*

Appointed 4th Corporal on 4/22/1862. Appointed 4th Sergeant on 8/1/1862. Wounded at Sharpsburg on 9/17/1862. Wounded at battle of The Wilderness on 5/5/1864 and died of wounds on 5/7/1864.

Clayton, Richard E.
CO: A **Initial Rank:** Jr. 2nd Lieutenant
Joined: Wednesday, May 1, 1861 *Term (yrs):* 1 *Occupation:* Clerk **Age** 24
Enrolled at: Tishomingo Co., MS *Enrolled By:* Capt. Leeth *Promoted:* Yes *ROH:* No
Born: Alabama *Marital Status:* S *Residence* Jacinto, MS

Appointed Adjutant on 11/1/1861. Elected Captain on 4/22/1862. Wounded at battle of Sharpsburg on 9/17/1862 and died of wounds on 9/30/1862.

Clemens, P. C.
CO: D **Initial Rank:** Private
Joined: *Term (yrs):* 0 *Occupation:* **Age**
Enrolled at: *Enrolled By:* *Promoted:* No *ROH:* No
Born: *Marital Status:* *Residence*

See Payton Clemmons of the 32nd Mississippi Infantry. No other record.

2nd Mississippi Alphabetical Roster (Annotated)

Clements, Andrew J.
CO: G *Initial Rank:* Private
Joined: Wednesday, May 1, 1861   *Term (yrs):* 1 *Occupation:* Farmer   *Age* 30
Enrolled at: Pontotoc Co., MS   *Enrolled By:* Capt. Miller   *Promoted:* No   *ROH:* No
Born: *Marital Status:* M   *Residence* Pontotoc, MS

Severely wounded (throat, jaw) at 1st Manassas on 7/21/1861 and died of wounds on 8/15/1861 at Charlottesville, VA.

Clements, Gabriel A.
CO: G *Initial Rank:* Private
Joined: Wednesday, May 1, 1861   *Term (yrs):* 1 *Occupation:* Farmer   *Age* 27
Enrolled at: Pontotoc Co., MS   *Enrolled By:* Capt. Miller   *Promoted:* Yes   *ROH:* No
Born: South Carolina   *Marital Status:* S   *Residence* Pontotoc, MS

Listed as Corporal circa Nov/Dec 1861. Promoted to 5th Sergeant on 8/1/1862. Wounded at 2nd Manassas on 8/29/1862. Died from wounds on 12/31/1862 at Howards Grove, VA.

Cobb, Greenberry
CO: H *Initial Rank:* Private
Joined: Monday, April 29, 1861   *Term (yrs):* 1 *Occupation:* Farmer   *Age* 23
Enrolled at: Pontotoc Co., MS   *Enrolled By:* Capt. Taylor   *Promoted:* Yes   *ROH:* Yes
Born: South Carolina   *Marital Status:* S   *Residence* Chesterville, MS

Promoted to 2nd Corporal on 10/1/1862. Wounded at battle of The Wilderness on 5/6/1864. Died of wounds about 5/24/1864 at Lynchburg, VA. ROH for The Wilderness, 5/6/1864.

Cobb, William D.
CO: I *Initial Rank:* Private
Joined: Wednesday, May 1, 1861   *Term (yrs):* 1 *Occupation:* Farmer   *Age* 21
Enrolled at: Pontotoc Co., MS   *Enrolled By:* Capt. Herring   *Promoted:* No   *ROH:* Yes
Born: Alabama   *Marital Status:*   *Residence*

Mortally wounded at Gettysburg on 7/1/1863 and died on 7/2/1863. ROH for Gettysburg, 7/1/1863.

Cochran, James J.
CO: B *Initial Rank:* Private
Joined: Sunday, March 1, 1863   *Term (yrs):* 3 *Occupation:*   *Age*
Enrolled at: Blackwater, VA   *Enrolled By:* Capt. Buchanan   *Promoted:* No   *ROH:* No
Born: *Marital Status:*   *Residence*

Furloughed from hospital for 40-days on 7/25/1864 and listed as AWOL from 12/1/1864.

2nd Mississippi Alphabetical Roster (Annotated)

Cochran, Levi T.

CO: H **Initial Rank:** Private

Joined: Saturday, March 15, 1862   **Term (yrs):** 3   **Occupation:** Farmer   **Age** 18

Enrolled at: Chesterville, MS   **Enrolled By:** Lt. Porter   **Promoted:** No   **ROH:** No

Born: Mississippi   **Marital Status:** S   **Residence** Chesterville, MS

Wounded and captured at Gettysburg on 7/3/1863. Paroled from DeCamp General Hospital, Davids Island, NY Harbor to City Point, VA on 9/16/1863 for exchange. Retired to "Invalid Corps, P.A.C.S. on 5/2/1864 at Okolona, MS.

Cochran, Stephen T.

CO: H **Initial Rank:** Private

Joined: Monday, April 29, 1861   **Term (yrs):** 1   **Occupation:** Farmer   **Age** 19

Enrolled at: Pontotoc Co., MS   **Enrolled By:** Capt. Taylor   **Promoted:** No   **ROH:** No

Born: Mississippi   **Marital Status:** S   **Residence** Chesterville, MS

Severely wounded (arm) in battle at Bethesda Church on 6/2/1864. 60-day furlough from 7/16/1864. AWOL since 10/31/1864 (has authority to appear before a medical examining board for retirement – arm amputated).

Cochran, William G.

CO: H **Initial Rank:** Private

Joined: Monday, April 29, 1861   **Term (yrs):** 1   **Occupation:** Farmer   **Age** 18

Enrolled at: Pontotoc Co., MS   **Enrolled By:** Capt. Taylor   **Promoted:** No   **ROH:** No

Born: Alabama   **Marital Status:** S   **Residence** Chesterville, MS

Severely wounded in battle at Sharpsburg on 9/17/1862. Furloughed. Circa Nov/Dec 1863 listed as absent on detached service arresting deserters in MS. Discharged at Rapidan, VA on 3/16/1864 due to disability.

Cochran, William M.

CO: B **Initial Rank:** Private

Joined: Wednesday, May 1, 1861   **Term (yrs):** 1   **Occupation:** Farmer   **Age** 20

Enrolled at: Tippah Co., MS   **Enrolled By:** Capt. Buchanan   **Promoted:** No   **ROH:** Yes

Born: **Marital Status:**   **Residence**

Paroled at Appomattox Court House on 4/9/1865. ROH for Bethesda Church, 5/31/1864.

Cochran, William McDuff

CO: B **Initial Rank:** Private

Joined: Wednesday, May 1, 1861   **Term (yrs):** 1   **Occupation:** Farmer   **Age** 28

Enrolled at: Tippah Co., MS   **Enrolled By:** Capt. Buchanan   **Promoted:** Yes   **ROH:** No

Born: **Marital Status:**   **Residence**

Promoted to 3rd Corporal circa May/June 1864. Captured at Petersburg (Hatcher's Run?) on 4/2/1865. Taken to Fort Delaware. Released on oath on 6/11/1865.

2nd Mississippi Alphabetical Roster (Annotated)

Coggins, Jerry   *CO:* E   *Initial Rank:* Private
Joined: Saturday, March 8, 1862   *Term (yrs):* 3   *Occupation:*   *Age* 28
Enrolled at: Guntown, MS   *Enrolled By:* Capt. Bates   *Promoted:* No   *ROH:* No
Born: *Marital Status:*   *Residence*
Died of typhoid fever at Chimborazo Hospital #1 at Richmond on 9/11/1862.

Coker, W. T.   *CO:* C   *Initial Rank:* Private
Joined: Saturday, March 1, 1862   *Term (yrs):* 3   *Occupation:*   *Age*
Enrolled at: Verona, MS   *Enrolled By:* Lt. Pounds   *Promoted:* No   *ROH:* No
Born: *Marital Status:*   *Residence*
Hospital records indicate he was admitted for a wound at Richmond on 7/3/1863 (company records provide no details as to date of wound or engagement). Furloughed 60-days from 10/29/1863. AWOL since 12/29/1863. Listed as deserted at home during May/Jun 1864 muster roll.

Coker, William K.   *CO:* H   *Initial Rank:* Private
Joined: Saturday, March 1, 1862   *Term (yrs):* 3   *Occupation:* Farmer   *Age* 28
Enrolled at: Chesterville, MS   *Enrolled By:* Lt. Porter   *Promoted:* No   *ROH:* No
Born: Alabama   *Marital Status:* M   *Residence* Tupelo, MS
Wounded at battle of The Wilderness on 5/6/1864 and died of wounds on 5/11/1864 at Gordonsville, VA.

Cole, John W.   *CO:* E   *Initial Rank:* Private
Joined: Saturday, March 1, 1862   *Term (yrs):* 3   *Occupation:* Farmer   *Age* 20
Enrolled at: Guntown, MS   *Enrolled By:* Capt. Bates   *Promoted:* No   *ROH:* No
Born: Alabama   *Marital Status:* S   *Residence* Guntown, MS
Died of disease (pneumonia) at Chimborazo Hospital #4 at Richmond on 6/3/1862.

Cole, Stephen   *CO:* A   *Initial Rank:* Private
Joined: Saturday, March 1, 1862   *Term (yrs):* 3   *Occupation:* Farmer   *Age* 23
Enrolled at: Jacinto, MS   *Enrolled By:* Lt. Clayton   *Promoted:* No   *ROH:* No
Born: Mississippi   *Marital Status:*   *Residence* Burnsville, MS
Killed in battle at Gaines Mill on 6/27/1862.

2nd Mississippi Alphabetical Roster (Annotated)

Cole, Wesley
CO: E **Initial Rank:** Private
Joined: Saturday, March 1, 1862 **Term (yrs):** 3 **Occupation:** Farmer **Age** 21
Enrolled at: Guntown, MS **Enrolled By:** Capt. Bates **Promoted:** No **ROH:** No
Born: Alabama **Marital Status:** M **Residence** Guntown, MS

Listed as AWOL since 2/15/1864. Deserted from camp near Orange Court House, VA. Federal records indicate he was taken into custody on 2/12/1864.

Cole, William R.
CO: B **Initial Rank:** Private
Joined: Wednesday, September 18, 1861 **Term (yrs):** 1 **Occupation:** **Age**
Enrolled at: Ripley, MS **Enrolled By:** Lt. Davenport **Promoted:** No **ROH:** No
Born: **Marital Status:** **Residence**

Died of disease at Camp Fisher, VA on 11/7/1861.

Coleman, Henry L.
CO: L **Initial Rank:** Private
Joined: Monday, March 3, 1862 **Term (yrs):** 3 **Occupation:** Farmer **Age** 29
Enrolled at: Ripley, MS **Enrolled By:** Col. Falkner **Promoted:** Yes **ROH:** No
Born: South Carolina **Marital Status:** M **Residence**

Promoted to 1st Corporal on 7/2/1862. Killed in battle at Gettysburg on 7/1/1863.

Coleman, John
CO: B **Initial Rank:** Private
Joined: Friday, July 18, 1862 **Term (yrs):** 3 **Occupation:** **Age**
Enrolled at: Near Richmond, VA **Enrolled By:** Capt. Buchanan **Promoted:** No **ROH:** No
Born: **Marital Status:** **Residence**

Substitute for Byrd B. Smith. Wounded at Sharpsburg on 9/17/1862. Returned to duty. Listed as deserted from hospital on 1/14/1864.

Collins, James W.
CO: I **Initial Rank:** Private
Joined: Wednesday, May 1, 1861 **Term (yrs):** 1 **Occupation:** Farmer **Age** 29
Enrolled at: Pontotoc Co., MS **Enrolled By:** Capt. Herring **Promoted:** No **ROH:** No
Born: **Marital Status:** **Residence**

See also 3rd Tennessee Infantry Regiment. Transferred to 3rd Tennessee on 10/6/1862.

2nd Mississippi Alphabetical Roster (Annotated)

Coltharp, Brantley K.   CO: B   Initial Rank: Private

Joined: Wednesday, May 1, 1861   **Term (yrs):** 1   **Occupation:** Farmer   **Age** 23
Enrolled at: Tippah Co., MS   **Enrolled By:** Capt. Buchanan   **Promoted:** Yes   **ROH:** No
Born: South Carolina   **Marital Status:**   **Residence**

Promoted to 1st Corporal circa May 1861; 3rd Sergeant on 4/30/1862. Wounded at 2nd Manassas on 8/29/1862. Died on 9/18/1862 of wounds at Warrenton, VA.

Coltharp, John C.   CO: B   Initial Rank: Private

Joined: Saturday, March 1, 1862   **Term (yrs):** 3   **Occupation:** Farmer   **Age** 35
Enrolled at: Ripley, MS   **Enrolled By:** Capt. Buchanan   **Promoted:** No   **ROH:** No
Born: South Carolina   **Marital Status:** M   **Residence**

Captured at Gettysburg on 7/3/1863. Taken to Fort Delaware. Transferred to Aiken's Landing, VA on 9/30/1864 for exchange. Exchanged on 12/5/1864. Listed as AWOL since 12/5/1864. Paroled at Holly Springs, MS on 5/31/1865.

Coltharp, Mathew N.   CO: B   Initial Rank: Private

Joined: Wednesday, May 1, 1861   **Term (yrs):** 1   **Occupation:** Farmer   **Age** 31
Enrolled at: Tippah Co., MS   **Enrolled By:** Capt. Buchanan   **Promoted:** No   **ROH:** No
Born: Tennessee   **Marital Status:**   **Residence**

Discharged due to disability on 10/7/1861.

Colwell, James M.   CO: H   Initial Rank: Private

Joined: Monday, April 29, 1861   **Term (yrs):** 1   **Occupation:** Farmer   **Age** 18
Enrolled at: Pontotoc Co., MS   **Enrolled By:** Capt. Taylor   **Promoted:** No   **ROH:** No
Born: Alabama   **Marital Status:** S   **Residence** Chesterville, MS

Killed in battle at Sharpsburg on 9/17/1862.

Combs, James W.   CO: G   Initial Rank: Private

Joined: Wednesday, May 1, 1861   **Term (yrs):** 1   **Occupation:** Student (Farmer)   **Age** 33
Enrolled at: Pontotoc Co., MS   **Enrolled By:** Capt. Miller   **Promoted:** Yes   **ROH:** No
Born: Alabama   **Marital Status:** S   **Residence** Pontotoc, MS

Wounded at 1st Manassas on 7/21/1861. Elected 2nd Lieutenant. on 4/21/1862. Wounded at 2nd Manassas on 8/29/1862. Returned to duty on 11/20/1862. Wounded at Gettysburg on 7/3/1863. Returned to duty on 8/2/1863. On "furlough of indulgence" during last company muster roll (Jan/Feb 1865).

2nd Mississippi Alphabetical Roster (Annotated)

Combs, William M.   CO: G   Initial Rank: Private
Joined: Wednesday, May 1, 1861   *Term (yrs):* 1   *Occupation:* Student   *Age* 19
Enrolled at: Pontotoc Co., MS   *Enrolled By:* Capt. Miller   *Promoted:* No   *ROH:* No
Born: Alabama   *Marital Status:* S   *Residence* Pontotoc, MS

Wounded at battle of Seven Pines on 5/31/1862. Wounded at Sharpsburg on 9/16/1862. Furloughed. Returned to duty on 4/20/1863. Captured at Falling Waters, MD on 7/14/1863. Taken to Point Lookout, MD. Exchanged on 2/10/1865.

Commander, James L.   CO: L   Initial Rank: Private
Joined: Thursday, February 12, 1863   *Term (yrs):* 3   *Occupation:* Farmer   *Age* 22
Enrolled at: Moorsville, MS   *Enrolled By:* Lt. Bearden   *Promoted:* No   *ROH:* No
Born: Mississippi   *Marital Status:*   *Residence*

Captured at Gettysburg on 7/1/1863. Died at Fort Delaware on 9/12/1863 of typhoid fever.

Compson, J. M.   CO: C   Initial Rank: Private
Joined: *Term (yrs):* 0   *Occupation:*   *Age*
Enrolled at: *Enrolled By:*   *Promoted:* No   *ROH:* No
Born: *Marital Status:*   *Residence*

Appears on a Federal roll of sick and wounded prisoners of war at the hospitals in and about Gettysburg. No other record.

Compton, Joseph E.   CO: E   Initial Rank: Private
Joined: Saturday, March 22, 1862   *Term (yrs):* 3   *Occupation:* Farmer   *Age* 21
Enrolled at: Guntown, MS   *Enrolled By:* Capt. Bates   *Promoted:* No   *ROH:* Yes
Born: Alabama   *Marital Status:* S   *Residence* Guntown, MS

Killed in battle at Gaines Mill on 6/27/1862. ROH for Gaines Mill, 6/27/1862.

Condrey, William J.   CO: K   Initial Rank: Private
Joined: Tuesday, September 24, 1861   *Term (yrs):* 1   *Occupation:* Farmer   *Age* 19
Enrolled at: Iuka, MS   *Enrolled By:* Lt. Davenport   *Promoted:* No   *ROH:* Yes
Born: Mississippi   *Marital Status:*   *Residence*

Killed in battle at Gettysburg on 7/1/1863. ROH for Gettysburg, 7/1/1863.

2nd Mississippi Alphabetical Roster (Annotated)

Condry, Thomas R.

CO: A **Initial Rank:**

Joined: Wednesday, February 20, 1861 **Term (yrs):** 0 **Occupation:** **Age**

Enrolled at: Corinth, MS **Enrolled By:** R. Griffith **Promoted:** No **ROH:** No

Born: **Marital Status:** **Residence**

Appears on a company muster roll for state service (not dated). No other record.

Conner, James J.

CO: C **Initial Rank:** Private

Joined: Wednesday, May 1, 1861 **Term (yrs):** 1 **Occupation:** Farmer **Age** 21

Enrolled at: Itawamba Co., MS **Enrolled By:** Capt. Bromley **Promoted:** No **ROH:** No

Born: **Marital Status:** **Residence**

Detailed as regimental teamster. Wounded (left thigh) at The Wilderness on 5/5/1864. Furloughed from hospital for 50-days from 7/20/1864. Returned to duty. Captured at Hatcher's Run on 4/2/1865. Taken to Point Lookout, MD. Released on oath on 6/10/1865.

Conway, Michael

CO: F **Initial Rank:** Private

Joined: Wednesday, May 1, 1861 **Term (yrs):** 1 **Occupation:** Planter **Age** 24

Enrolled at: Tippah Co., MS **Enrolled By:** Capt. Davis **Promoted:** No **ROH:** No

Born: Ireland **Marital Status:** **Residence**

Discharged on 10/5/1862 as a foreign national not subject to conscription.

Cook, ?

CO: D **Initial Rank:**

Joined: **Term (yrs):** 0 **Occupation:** **Age**

Enrolled at: **Enrolled By:** **Promoted:** No **ROH:** No

Born: **Marital Status:** **Residence**

Appears on a Federal roll of prisoners of war at the hospitals in and about Gettysburg. No other record.

Cook, Jesse A.

CO: K **Initial Rank:** Private

Joined: Wednesday, May 1, 1861 **Term (yrs):** 1 **Occupation:** Trader **Age** 21

Enrolled at: Tishomingo Co., MS **Enrolled By:** Capt. Stone **Promoted:** Yes **ROH:** No

Born: **Marital Status:** **Residence**

Appointed to 4th Corporal on 9/1/1861. Elected 1st Lieutenant. on 4/8/1862. Assigned to duty on 4/23/1862. Promoted to Captain on 8/30/1862. Wounded and captured at Sharpsburg on 9/17/1862 (left thigh and both ankles). Died on 9/25/1862.

2nd Mississippi Alphabetical Roster (Annotated)

Cook, John
CO: F **Initial Rank:** Private
Joined: Wednesday, May 1, 1861 **Term (yrs):** 1 **Occupation:** Laborer **Age** 27
Enrolled at: Tippah Co., MS **Enrolled By:** Capt. Davis **Promoted:** No **ROH:** No
Born: **Marital Status:** **Residence**

Wounded (shin) at battle of Seven Pines on 5/31/1862. Discharged from hospital on 8/5/1862. Never returned to his company (AWOL). Listed as deserted from Nov/Dec 1862 muster roll.

Cooley, Thomas J.
CO: A **Initial Rank:** Private
Joined: Wednesday, May 1, 1861 **Term (yrs):** 1 **Occupation:** Farmer **Age** 24
Enrolled at: Tishomingo Co., MS **Enrolled By:** Capt. Leeth **Promoted:** No **ROH:** No
Born: South Carolina **Marital Status:** **Residence**

Wounded at 1st Manassas on 7/21/1861. Furloughed. Discharged 1/23/1863 of disability due to wounds.

Coombs, William W.
CO: B **Initial Rank:** Private
Joined: Tuesday, April 30, 1861 **Term (yrs):** 1 **Occupation:** Farmer **Age** 23
Enrolled at: Ripley, MS **Enrolled By:** Capt. Buchanan **Promoted:** No **ROH:** No
Born: South Carolina **Marital Status:** **Residence**

Died of disease at Camp Fisher, VA on 12/14/1861.

Coon, John
CO: K **Initial Rank:** Private
Joined: Wednesday, May 1, 1861 **Term (yrs):** 1 **Occupation:** Laborer **Age** 18
Enrolled at: Tishomingo Co., MS **Enrolled By:** Capt. Stone **Promoted:** No **ROH:** No
Born: South Carolina **Marital Status:** **Residence**

Discharged on 7/18/1862 due to expiration of term of service.

Coon, John A.
CO: I **Initial Rank:** Private
Joined: Wednesday, May 1, 1861 **Term (yrs):** 1 **Occupation:** Shoemaker **Age** 28
Enrolled at: Pontotoc Co., MS **Enrolled By:** Capt. Herring **Promoted:** No **ROH:** No
Born: **Marital Status:** **Residence**

See also J. A. Coon, 2nd Battalion Virginia Infantry, Local Defense Troops. Detailed as shoemaker in Richmond government shoe shop on 1/7/1862.

2nd Mississippi Alphabetical Roster (Annotated)

Cooper, Christopher C.
CO: D *Initial Rank:* Private
Joined: Wednesday, May 1, 1861   *Term (yrs):* 1 *Occupation:* Farmer   *Age* 20
Enrolled at: Tippah Co., MS   *Enrolled By:* Capt. Beck   *Promoted:* No   *ROH:* No
Born: Mississippi   *Marital Status:*   *Residence*

Died of disease at Camp Jones, VA on 9/9/1861.

Cooper, James M.
CO: B   *Initial Rank:* Private
Joined: Wednesday, May 1, 1861   *Term (yrs):* 1   *Occupation:* Farmer   *Age* 19
Enrolled at: Tippah Co., MS   *Enrolled By:* Capt. Buchanan   *Promoted:* No   *ROH:* No
Born: *Marital Status:*   *Residence*

Almost perfect muster attendance record. Captured at Petersburg (Hatcher's Run?) on 4/2/1865. Taken to Point Lookout, MD. Released on oath on 6/10/1865.

Cooper, Marion M.
CO: K, D   *Initial Rank:* Private
Joined: Wednesday, May 1, 1861   *Term (yrs):* 1   *Occupation:* Farmer   *Age* 18
Enrolled at: Tishomingo Co., MS   *Enrolled By:* Capt. Stone   *Promoted:* No   *ROH:* No
Born: *Marital Status:*   *Residence*

Wounded at Gaines Mill on 6/27/1862. Transferred to Company D from Company K on 6/27/1863. Captured (various dates ranging from 7/1/1863 to 7/7/1863) during Gettysburg Campaign. Taken to Fort Delaware. Released on oath on 5/11/1865.

Cooper, Robert T.
CO: B   *Initial Rank:* Private
Joined: Wednesday, May 1, 1861   *Term (yrs):* 1   *Occupation:* Farmer   *Age* 21
Enrolled at: Tippah Co., MS   *Enrolled By:* Capt. Buchanan   *Promoted:* No   *ROH:* No
Born: *Marital Status:*   *Residence*

Wounded at Gaines Mill on 6/27/1862. Furloughed in March 1863. Detailed to detached duty with the Pioneer Corps from 6/12/1863. Paroled at Appomattox Court House on 4/9/1865.

Cooper, Solon L.
CO: B   *Initial Rank:* Private
Joined: Wednesday, September 18, 1861   *Term (yrs):* 1   *Occupation:*   *Age*
Enrolled at: Ripley, MS   *Enrolled By:* Lt. Davenport   *Promoted:* No   *ROH:* No
Born: *Marital Status:*   *Residence*

Killed at 2nd Manassas on 8/30/1862.

2nd Mississippi Alphabetical Roster (Annotated)

Cooper, Thomas J. S.   CO: G   Initial Rank: Private

Joined: Tuesday, April 30, 1861   **Term (yrs):** 1   **Occupation:** Farmer   **Age** 18

Enrolled at: Pontotoc Co., MS   **Enrolled By:** Capt. Kilpatrick   **Promoted:** Yes   **ROH:** Yes

Born: Alabama   **Marital Status:** S   **Residence** Pontotoc, MS

Promoted 1st Corporal on 3/1/1862. Wounded at Malvern Hill on 7/1/1862. Wounded (fractured rib) at battle of The Wilderness on 5/5/1864. Furloughed 60-days from 5/20/1864. Returned to duty 9/27/1864. Captured at Petersburg (Hatcher's Run?) on 4/2/1865. Taken to Fort Delaware. Released on oath on 6/11/1865. ROH for Malvern Hill, 7/1/1862.

Cooper, William S.   CO: D   Initial Rank: Private

Joined: Wednesday, May 1, 1861   **Term (yrs):** 1   **Occupation:** Farmer   **Age** 18

Enrolled at: Tippah Co., MS   **Enrolled By:** Capt. Beck   **Promoted:** Yes   **ROH:** No

Born: Mississippi   **Marital Status:** S   **Residence**

Wounded at 1st Manassas on 7/21/1861. Promoted to 1st Corporal on 4/23/1862. Wounded battle of The Wilderness on 5/6/1864. Furloughed 60-days from hospital on 5/19/1864. Wounded 8/19/1864 at the Weldon Railroad. Listed as AWOL since 2/20/1865. Paroled at Holly Springs, MS on 5/29/1865.

Coper, George A.   CO: C   Initial Rank: Private

Joined: Wednesday, May 1, 1861   **Term (yrs):** 1   **Occupation:** Carpenter   **Age** 40

Enrolled at: Itawamba Co., MS   **Enrolled By:** Capt. Bromley   **Promoted:** No   **ROH:** No

Born: Tennessee   **Marital Status:**   **Residence**

Discharged on plea of military exemption (over age) on 5/25/1862.

Cottingim, M. M.   CO: A   Initial Rank: Private

Joined: Saturday, March 1, 1862   **Term (yrs):** 3   **Occupation:** Overseer   **Age** 24

Enrolled at: Jacinto, MS   **Enrolled By:** Lt. Clayton   **Promoted:** No   **ROH:** No

Born: Tennessee   **Marital Status:** S   **Residence** Rienzi, MS

Wounded and captured at Sharpsburg on 9/17/1862. Died of wounds on 11/18/1862 (leg amputated).

Cotton, John H.   CO: B   Initial Rank: Private

Joined: Wednesday, May 1, 1861   **Term (yrs):** 1   **Occupation:** Farmer   **Age** 19

Enrolled at: Tippah Co., MS   **Enrolled By:** Capt. Buchanan   **Promoted:** No   **ROH:** Yes

Born: **Marital Status:**   **Residence**

Wounded at battle of Seven Pines on 5/31/1862 and died of wounds on 6/3/1862 (shot in abdomen). ROH for Seven Pines, 5/31/1862.

2nd Mississippi Alphabetical Roster (Annotated)

Counseille, Henry T.
CO: B **Initial Rank:** 2nd Sergeant
Joined: Tuesday, April 30, 1861   **Term (yrs):** 1 **Occupation:** Farmer   **Age** 24
Enrolled at: Tippah Co., MS   **Enrolled By:** Col. Falkner   **Promoted:** Yes   **ROH:** No
Born: **Marital Status:**   **Residence**

Also see 7th Mississippi Cavalry. Appointed 2nd Lieutenant. circa 5/10/1861. Relieved from duty upon reorganization of regiment on 4/23/1862. Discharged.

Counts, Calvin H.
CO: A **Initial Rank:** Private
Joined: Wednesday, May 1, 1861   **Term (yrs):** 1 **Occupation:** Mechanic   **Age** 22
Enrolled at: Tishomingo Co., MS   **Enrolled By:** Capt. Leeth   **Promoted:** No   **ROH:** No
Born: Alabama   **Marital Status:**   **Residence** Baldwyn, MS

Discharged due to disability on 12/24/1861.

Counts, James K.
CO: K **Initial Rank:** Private
Joined: Saturday, April 6, 1861   **Term (yrs):** 0 **Occupation:**   **Age**
Enrolled at: Iuka, MS   **Enrolled By:** W. M. Inge   **Promoted:** No   **ROH:** No
Born: **Marital Status:**   **Residence**

Appears on a company muster roll for state service. No other record.

Cowan, William H.
CO: B **Initial Rank:** Private
Joined: Friday, March 7, 1862   **Term (yrs):** 3 **Occupation:** Student   **Age** 17
Enrolled at: Ripley, MS   **Enrolled By:** Capt. Buchanan   **Promoted:** No   **ROH:** No
Born: South Carolina   **Marital Status:** S   **Residence**

Captured at Petersburg (Hatcher's Run?) on 4/2/1865. Taken to Point Lookout, MD. Released on oath on 6/10/1865.

Cox, James M.
CO: B **Initial Rank:** Musician
Joined: Wednesday, May 1, 1861   **Term (yrs):** 1 **Occupation:** Clerk   **Age**
Enrolled at: Tippah Co., MS   **Enrolled By:** Capt. Buchanan   **Promoted:** No   **ROH:** No
Born: **Marital Status:**   **Residence**

Detailed to hospital duties. Paroled at Appomattox Court House on 4/9/1865.

2nd Mississippi Alphabetical Roster (Annotated)

Cox, Joseph J.

CO: D	**Initial Rank:** Private	
Joined: Wednesday, May 1, 1861	**Term (yrs):** 1 **Occupation:** Farmer	**Age** 19
Enrolled at: Tippah Co., MS	**Enrolled By:** Capt. Beck	**Promoted:** Yes **ROH:** No
Born: Mississippi	**Marital Status:** S	**Residence** Snow Creek, MS

Wounded at 1st Manassas on 7/21/1861. Furloughed 30-days from 8/16/1861. Appointed 4th Corporal on 12/1/1862. Killed in battle at Gettysburg on 7/1/1863.

Cox, Robert H.

CO: F	**Initial Rank:** Private	
Joined: Wednesday, May 1, 1861	**Term (yrs):** 1 **Occupation:** Planter	**Age** 26
Enrolled at: Tippah Co., MS	**Enrolled By:** Capt. Davis	**Promoted:** No **ROH:** No
Born:	**Marital Status:**	**Residence**

Slightly wounded at Sharpsburg on 9/17/1862. Reported deserted during retreat from Shepherdstown to Winchester.

Cox, William

CO: F, H	**Initial Rank:** Private	
Joined: Saturday, March 22, 1862	**Term (yrs):** 3 **Occupation:** Farmer	**Age** 18
Enrolled at: Corinth, MS	**Enrolled By:** Capt. Powers	**Promoted:** No **ROH:** No
Born: Georgia	**Marital Status:** S	**Residence** Chesterville, MS

Transferred to Company H from Company F about 4/1/1862. Reported as deserted on 8/19/1863. Appears on a Federal register of prisoners of war in custody in Memphis, TN. Captured at Middleton (TN?) on 12/19/1863. Sent to Alton, IL. Transferred to Camp Douglas on 8/23/1864. Galvanized Yankee – enlisted in Co. F of 6th U.S. Volunteers on 3/26/1865.

Cox, William F.

CO: D	**Initial Rank:** Private	
Joined: Tuesday, October 1, 1861	**Term (yrs):** 1 **Occupation:** Farmer	**Age** 18
Enrolled at: Iuka, MS	**Enrolled By:** Lt. Davenport	**Promoted:** No **ROH:** No
Born: Mississippi	**Marital Status:** S	**Residence** Snow Creek, MS

Killed in battle at Gaines Mill on 6/27/1862.

Cranford, William

CO: K	**Initial Rank:** Private	
Joined: Saturday, March 1, 1862	**Term (yrs):** 3 **Occupation:** Farmer	**Age** 24
Enrolled at: Iuka, MS	**Enrolled By:** Lt. Latham	**Promoted:** No **ROH:** No
Born: Mississippi	**Marital Status:**	**Residence**

Died of disease at Ashland, VA on 5/31/1862.

2nd Mississippi Alphabetical Roster (Annotated)

Crase, William A.
CO: B **Initial Rank:** Private
Joined: *Term (yrs):* 0 *Occupation:*   *Age*
Enrolled at: *Enrolled By:*   *Promoted:* No *ROH:* No
Born: *Marital Status:*   *Residence*

Appears on a Federal roll of sick and wounded prisoners of war at the hospitals in and about Gettysburg. No other record.

Crawford, Benjamin
CO: H **Initial Rank:** Private
Joined: Tuesday, April 30, 1861 *Term (yrs):* 1 *Occupation:* Carpenter *Age* 23
Enrolled at: Pontotoc Co., MS *Enrolled By:* Capt. Taylor *Promoted:* No *ROH:* No
Born: South Carolina *Marital Status:* S *Residence* Tupelo, MS

See also 13th and 5th South Carolina Infantry. Was transferred to a South Carolina Regiment (13th South Carolina Infantry) on 9/3/1861.

Crawford, Thomas J.
CO: G **Initial Rank:** 1st Sergeant
Joined: Tuesday, April 30, 1861 *Term (yrs):* 1 *Occupation:* Clerk *Age* 27
Enrolled at: Pontotoc Co., MS *Enrolled By:* Capt. Kilpatrick *Promoted:* Yes *ROH:* No
Born: South Carolina *Marital Status:* S *Residence* Pontotoc, MS

Promoted to 1st Lieutenant. by election on 7/21/1861 to fill vacancy caused by death of Lieutenant [Richard A.] Palmer, and to Captain on 4/23/1862. Wounded on 10/1/1864 (gunshot flesh wound). Furloughed to Okolona, MS for 40-days. AWOL since 12/31/1864. Paroled on 5/19/1865.

Crayton, William W.
CO: C **Initial Rank:** Private
Joined: Tuesday, October 1, 1861 *Term (yrs):* 1 *Occupation:*   *Age*
Enrolled at: Verona, MS *Enrolled By:* Lt. Davenport *Promoted:* No *ROH:* No
Born: *Marital Status:*   *Residence*

Wounded battle of The Wilderness on 5/5/1864. Listed as AWOL since 10/22/1864.

Crockett, David C. W.
CO: D **Initial Rank:** Private
Joined: Wednesday, May 1, 1861 *Term (yrs):* 1 *Occupation:* Farmer *Age* 22
Enrolled at: Tippah Co., MS *Enrolled By:* Capt. Beck *Promoted:* No *ROH:* No
Born: *Marital Status:* M *Residence* Snow Creek, MS

Listed as deserted to the enemy on 5/23/1863 near Winsor [Windsor], VA "while in a skirmish fight with the enemy." Appears on a Federal report of prisoners of war paroled on 5/20/1865 at Memphis TN.

2nd Mississippi Alphabetical Roster (Annotated)

Crosby, J. *CO:* D *Initial Rank:* Private

Joined: *Term (yrs):* 0 *Occupation:* *Age*

Enrolled at: *Enrolled By:* *Promoted:* No *ROH:* No

Born: *Marital Status:* *Residence*

Appears on a Federal list of prisoners of war captured and paroled by U.S. forces in the battles of Iuka (9/19/1862), of Corinth on the 3rd and 4th of Oct, and of Hatchie on the 5th and 6th of Oct 1862. List dated Corinth, MS 10/13/1862. No other record. [Misidentified. 2nd Mississippi not involved in this fight].

Crum, Benjamin L. *CO:* B *Initial Rank:* Private

Joined: Monday, March 17, 1862 *Term (yrs):* 3 *Occupation:* Farmer *Age* 22

Enrolled at: Ripley, MS *Enrolled By:* Capt. Buchanan *Promoted:* No *ROH:* No

Born: Alabama *Marital Status:* S *Residence*

Wounded at Gettysburg (date not given) and furloughed for 40-days from 7/28/1863. Returned to duty. Wounded at battle of The Wilderness on 5/5/1864. In hospital. Returned to duty on 2/7/1865. Paroled on 4/9/1865 at Appomattox Court House.

Crum, James G. *CO:* B *Initial Rank:* Private

Joined: Saturday, March 8, 1862 *Term (yrs):* 3 *Occupation:* Farmer *Age* 19

Enrolled at: Ripley, MS *Enrolled By:* Capt. Buchanan *Promoted:* No *ROH:* No

Born: Tennessee *Marital Status:* S *Residence*

Mortally wounded at 2nd Manassas on 8/29/1862. Died on 9/12/1862 in hospital at Warrenton.

Culp, Thomas J. *CO:* B *Initial Rank:* Private

Joined: Tuesday, March 11, 1862 *Term (yrs):* 3 *Occupation:* Farmer *Age* 18

Enrolled at: Ripley, MS *Enrolled By:* Capt. Buchanan *Promoted:* No *ROH:* No

Born: Mississippi *Marital Status:* S *Residence*

Discharged on 7/24/1862 due to disability.

Cunningham, Anthony *CO:* K *Initial Rank:* Private

Joined: Saturday, March 1, 1862 *Term (yrs):* 3 *Occupation:* *Age* 39

Enrolled at: Iuka, MS *Enrolled By:* Lt. Latham *Promoted:* No *ROH:* No

Born: *Marital Status:* *Residence*

Detached service detailed as hospital nurse from July 1862.

2nd Mississippi Alphabetical Roster (Annotated)

Cunningham, S. E.
CO: K **Initial Rank:** Private
Joined: Saturday, March 1, 1862 **Term (yrs):** 3 **Occupation:** Laborer **Age** 52
Enrolled at: Iuka, MS **Enrolled By:** Lt. Latham **Promoted:** No **ROH:** No
Born: Ireland **Marital Status:** **Residence**

Appears on a Confederate Certificate of Disability dated 2/8/1865 due to loss of right eye (cause not given). Discharged. No other records.

Cunningham, William M.
CO: H **Initial Rank:** 1st Sergeant
Joined: Monday, April 29, 1861 **Term (yrs):** 1 **Occupation:** **Age** 31
Enrolled at: Pontotoc Co., MS **Enrolled By:** Capt. Taylor **Promoted:** Yes **ROH:** No
Born: **Marital Status:** **Residence**

Promoted to Jr. 2nd Lieutenant in June 1861 and 2nd Lieutenant. in July 1861. Elected 1st Lieutenant. 3/1/1862 and Captain on 4/14/1862. Assigned to duty on 4/22/1862. Wounded at Gettysburg (right arm and left hip) and captured on 7/1/1863. Taken to Johnson's Island, OH on 10/4/1863, then to Fort Delaware for parole. Exchanged at Aiken's Landing, VA on 9/30/1864. Retired to Invalid Corps on 2/23/1865.

Curlee, Cullen B.
CO: A **Initial Rank:** Private
Joined: Wednesday, May 1, 1861 **Term (yrs):** 1 **Occupation:** Farmer **Age** 22
Enrolled at: Tishomingo Co., MS **Enrolled By:** Capt. Leeth **Promoted:** No **ROH:** No
Born: **Marital Status:** **Residence**

Also see 26th North Carolina Infantry Regiment. Transferred on 8/11/1862 to 26th North Carolina [other notes say the 26th Mississippi Infantry Regiment].

Curtis, James F.
CO: K **Initial Rank:** Private
Joined: Saturday, March 1, 1862 **Term (yrs):** 3 **Occupation:** **Age** 21
Enrolled at: Iuka, MS **Enrolled By:** Lt. Latham **Promoted:** No **ROH:** No
Born: **Marital Status:** **Residence**

Wounded (upper part of right arm) and captured at Gettysburg on 7/3/1863. Taken to DeCamp General Hospital, Davids Island, NY Harbor and paroled to City Point, VA on 8/28/1863 to await exchange. Died of wounds during Jan/Feb 1864 time frame.

2nd Mississippi Alphabetical Roster (Annotated)

Cutberth, Christopher C.　　　　CO: F　　Initial Rank: Private
Joined: Monday, September 30, 1861　　**Term (yrs):** 1　**Occupation:**　　**Age**
Enrolled at: Ripley, MS　　**Enrolled By:** Lt. Davenport　　**Promoted:** No　**ROH:** No
Born:　　**Marital Status:**　　**Residence**

Assigned to detached service with the Pioneer Corps on 6/10/1863. Paroled at Appomattox Court House on 4/9/1865.

Cutbirth, Daniel B.　　　　CO: F　　Initial Rank: Private
Joined: Saturday, March 1, 1862　　**Term (yrs):** 3　**Occupation:** Farmer　　**Age** 25
Enrolled at: Ripley, MS　　**Enrolled By:** Capt. Powers　　**Promoted:** No　**ROH:** Yes
Born: Mississippi　　**Marital Status:** M　　**Residence**

Mortally wounded in battle of The Wilderness on 5/5/1864. Died on 5/7/1864. ROH for The Wilderness, 5/5/1864.

Cutbirth, Francis M.　　　　CO: F　　Initial Rank: Private
Joined: Wednesday, May 1, 1861　　**Term (yrs):** 1　**Occupation:** Planter　　**Age** 39
Enrolled at: Tippah Co., MS　　**Enrolled By:** Capt. Davis　　**Promoted:** No　**ROH:** No
Born: Tennessee　　**Marital Status:**　　**Residence**

Discharged on 7/31/1862 due to over age and expiration of term of service.

Cutbirth, Robert　　　　CO: F　　Initial Rank: Private
Joined: Saturday, March 1, 1862　　**Term (yrs):** 3　**Occupation:** Farmer　　**Age** 22
Enrolled at: Ripley, MS　　**Enrolled By:** Capt. Powers　　**Promoted:** No　**ROH:** No
Born: Mississippi　　**Marital Status:** M　　**Residence**

Killed in battle at Gaines Mill on 6/27/1862.

Dacus, David D.　　　　CO: B　　Initial Rank: Private
Joined: Monday, March 3, 1862　　**Term (yrs):** 3　**Occupation:** Farmer　　**Age** 25
Enrolled at: Ripley, MS　　**Enrolled By:** Capt. Buchanan　　**Promoted:** No　**ROH:** No
Born: Tennessee　　**Marital Status:** M　　**Residence**

Captured at Gettysburg on 7/1/1863. Sent to Fort Delaware. Released on oath on 6/11/1865.

2nd Mississippi Alphabetical Roster (Annotated)

Daggett, Frederick H.
CO: G   **Initial Rank:** Private
Joined: Wednesday, May 1, 1861   **Term (yrs):** 1   **Occupation:** Student (Clerk)   **Age** 17
Enrolled at: Pontotoc Co., MS   **Enrolled By:** Capt. Miller   **Promoted:** Yes   **ROH:** Yes
Born: Ohio   **Marital Status:** S   **Residence** Pontotoc, MS

Promoted to 3rd Sergeant on 12/1/1862. 2nd Sergeant circa Mar/Apr 1863. Captured at Gettysburg on 7/1/1863. Taken to Fort Delaware. Released on oath on 6/11/1865. ROH for Sharpsburg, 9/17/1862.

Dale, James M.
CO: H   **Initial Rank:** Private
Joined: Saturday, March 1, 1862   **Term (yrs):** 3   **Occupation:** Farmer   **Age** 18
Enrolled at: Chesterville, MS   **Enrolled By:** Lt. Porter   **Promoted:** No   **ROH:** No
Born: South Carolina   **Marital Status:** S   **Residence** Chesterville, MS

Detached with Colonel Stone on 1/9/1865 to Mississippi to arrest absentees and deserters.

Dale, John H.
CO: D   **Initial Rank:** Private
Joined: **Term (yrs):** 0   **Occupation:**   **Age**
Enrolled at: **Enrolled By:**   **Promoted:** No   **ROH:** No
Born: **Marital Status:**   **Residence**

Appears on a Federal roll of prisoners of war dated Louisville, KY on 1/16/1865. Captured at Nashville on 12/16/1864. No other record [Misidentified. Not likely a member of the 2nd Mississippi, the unit was not at the battle of Nashville – probably a member of the 2nd/6th Missouri Infantry Consolidated which the Federals sometimes abbreviated 2 Regt. Miss. Inft].

Dale, William
CO: D   **Initial Rank:** Private
Joined: **Term (yrs):** 0   **Occupation:**   **Age**
Enrolled at: **Enrolled By:**   **Promoted:** No   **ROH:** No
Born: **Marital Status:**   **Residence**

Appears on a Federal roll of prisoners of war – [Misidentified. With residence listed as "St. Louis, MO and heading reading "Co D 2&6 Regt Miss Inf." means he belonged to the 2nd & 6th Missouri Infantry Regiment Consolidated – not the 2nd Mississippi].

2nd Mississippi Alphabetical Roster (Annotated)

DaLieutenanton, Nicholas
CO: C   **Initial Rank:** Private
Joined: Saturday, March 1, 1862   **Term (yrs):** 3   **Occupation:** Carpenter   **Age** 19
Enrolled at: Verona, MS   **Enrolled By:** Lt. Pounds   **Promoted:** No   **ROH:** No
Born: North Carolina   **Marital Status:**   **Residence**

Wounded in battle at Gaines Mill on 6/27/1862. Wounded in battle at Sharpsburg on 9/17/1862 and furloughed. Discharged as result of wounds on 1/14/1863.

Dalton, James H.
CO: F   **Initial Rank:** Private
Joined: Wednesday, May 1, 1861   **Term (yrs):** 1   **Occupation:** Planter   **Age** 19
Enrolled at: Tippah Co., MS   **Enrolled By:** Capt. Davis   **Promoted:** Yes   **ROH:** No
Born: **Marital Status:**   **Residence**

Wounded at Gettysburg on 7/1/1863. Furloughed 40-days from 7/24/1863. Appointed 2nd Sergeant on 3/31/1864 to replace S. B. Liddell. [Records indicate that he may have been captured and paroled by the 10th Michigan Cavalry near Newton, NC about 4/19/1865].

Dalton, Joseph
CO: L   **Initial Rank:** Private
Joined: Monday, March 3, 1862   **Term (yrs):** 3   **Occupation:** Farmer   **Age** 31
Enrolled at: Ripley, MS   **Enrolled By:** Capt. Powers   **Promoted:** Yes   **ROH:** No
Born: Tennessee   **Marital Status:** S   **Residence** Dumas, MS

Promoted to Corporal on 9/1/1862. Promoted to 4th Sergeant on 10/1/1862. Captured at Gettysburg on 7/1/1863. Taken to Fort Delaware. Released on oath on 3/22/1865.

Dancer, Henry
CO: A   **Initial Rank:** Private
Joined: Monday, September 30, 1861   **Term (yrs):** 1   **Occupation:** Farmer   **Age** 43
Enrolled at: Iuka, MS   **Enrolled By:** Lt. Davenport   **Promoted:** No   **ROH:** No
Born: Tennessee   **Marital Status:** M   **Residence**

Discharged at Camp Fisher, VA on 1/28/1862 due to disability.

Dancer, Stephen P.
CO: A   **Initial Rank:** Private
Joined: Monday, September 30, 1861   **Term (yrs):** 1   **Occupation:** Farmer   **Age** 19
Enrolled at: Iuka, MS   **Enrolled By:** Lt. Davenport   **Promoted:** No   **ROH:** No
Born: Tennessee   **Marital Status:** S   **Residence**

Wounded (left shoulder) at Gaines Mill on 6/27/1862. Furloughed. Discharged on 9/25/1862 due to disability due to wounds.

2nd Mississippi Alphabetical Roster (Annotated)

Dancer, William M.   CO: A   Initial Rank: Private
Joined: Monday, September 30, 1861   *Term (yrs):* 1   *Occupation:* Farmer   *Age*
Enrolled at: Iuka, MS   *Enrolled By:* Lt. Davenport   *Promoted:* No   *ROH:* No
Born: *Marital Status:* S   *Residence*

Died of disease (pneumonia) on 1/1/1862 at Camp Fisher, VA.

Dandridge, Spottswood B.   CO: G   Initial Rank: Private
Joined: Wednesday, May 1, 1861   *Term (yrs):* 1   *Occupation:* Student (Farmer)   *Age* 18
Enrolled at: Pontotoc Co., MS   *Enrolled By:* Capt. Miller   *Promoted:* No   *ROH:* No
Born: Mississippi   *Marital Status:* S   *Residence* Pontotoc, MS

Wounded (fracture of left thigh) at 1st Manassas on 7/21/1861. Discharged on 11/15/1861 for disability due to wounds.

Daniel, John M.   CO: D   Initial Rank: Private
Joined: Wednesday, May 1, 1861   *Term (yrs):* 1   *Occupation:*   *Age* 20
Enrolled at: Tippah Co., MS   *Enrolled By:* Capt. Beck   *Promoted:* No   *ROH:* No
Born: *Marital Status:*   *Residence*

Wounded at 1st Manassas on 7/21/1861. Furloughed from hospital. Detailed as regimental teamster. Listed as AWOL from 6/9/1864. Listed as deserted and dropped from rolls by order of Colonel Stone on 12/31/1864.

Darby, Ransom S.   CO: D   Initial Rank: Private
Joined: *Term (yrs):* 0   *Occupation:* Farmer   *Age* 19
Enrolled at: *Enrolled By:*   *Promoted:* No   *ROH:* No
Born: *Marital Status:*   *Residence*

Appears on a Federal list of prisoners of war received at Camp Douglas, IL also recorded variously as belonging to the 2nd Mississippi Battery and the 2nd Mississippi Battalion. Brigade: Chalmers; Division: Bragg [Misidentified. This man belongs to a cavalry unit, not the 2nd Mississippi Infantry Regiment]. No other record.

Davenport, Henry   CO: A   Initial Rank: 1st Sergeant
Joined: Wednesday, May 1, 1861   *Term (yrs):* 1   *Occupation:* Clerk (Student)   *Age* 25
Enrolled at: Tishomingo Co., MS   *Enrolled By:* Capt. Leeth   *Promoted:* Yes   *ROH:* No
Born: *Marital Status:* S   *Residence* Jacinto, MS

Promoted to 1st Sergeant on 5/10/1861. Elected 2nd Lieutenant. on 7/15/1861. Resigned on 4/23/1862 due to reorganization of company and regiment.

2nd Mississippi Alphabetical Roster (Annotated)

Davenport, John W.
CO: F **Initial Rank:** Private
Joined: Wednesday, May 1, 1861 **Term (yrs):** 1 **Occupation:** Laborer **Age** 19
Enrolled at: Tippah Co., MS **Enrolled By:** Capt. Davis **Promoted:** No **ROH:** No
Born: **Marital Status:** **Residence**

Wounded at Sharpsburg on 9/17/1862. Furloughed on 10/11/1862 for 90-days. Did not return upon expiration of furlough. Listed as deserted. "supposed to have joined some other command" during Nov/Dec 1863 muster roll.

Davis, A. W.
CO: **Initial Rank:**
Joined: **Term (yrs):** 0 **Occupation:** **Age**
Enrolled at: **Enrolled By:** **Promoted:** No **ROH:** No
Born: **Marital Status:** **Residence**

Name appears on a Federal parole of prisoners of war dated Office of the Provost Marshal General, Army of the Potomac, 9/27/1862. Remarks indicate wounded in arm and shoulder (engagement not noted). No other record.

Davis, Christopher C.
CO: D, S **Initial Rank:** Private
Joined: Wednesday, May 1, 1861 **Term (yrs):** 1 **Occupation:** Farmer **Age** 21
Enrolled at: Tippah Co., MS **Enrolled By:** Capt. Beck **Promoted:** Yes **ROH:** Yes
Born: Alabama **Marital Status:** S **Residence** Pine Grove, MS

Wounded at Sharpsburg on 9/17/1862 (left on the field and captured). Exchanged in December 1862. Promoted to 4th Sergeant on 2/16/1863. Wounded (both legs) and captured at Gettysburg on 7/3/1863. Taken to Point Lookout, MD. Became a "Galvanized Yankee" and joined Union army on 2/26/1864. Apparently deserted the Union Army (escaped) in June 1864 and rejoined the regiment. Promoted to Ensign and 1st Lieutenant P.A.C.S. on 8/25/1864. [Color bearer during Pickett's Charge, July 3rd at Gettysburg]. ROH for Second Manassas, 8/28/1862.

Davis, Cyrus
CO: B **Initial Rank:** Private
Joined: Monday, March 4, 1861 **Term (yrs):** 0 **Occupation:** **Age**
Enrolled at: Ripley, MS **Enrolled By:** J. R. Chalmers **Promoted:** No **ROH:** No
Born: **Marital Status:** **Residence**

Appears on a company muster roll for state service. No other record.

2nd Mississippi Alphabetical Roster (Annotated)

Davis, Emanuel W.
CO: E **Initial Rank:** Private
Joined: Wednesday, May 1, 1861 **Term (yrs):** 1 **Occupation:** Farmer **Age** 40
Enrolled at: Itawamba Co., MS **Enrolled By:** Capt. Booth **Promoted:** No **ROH:** No
Born: **Marital Status:** M **Residence** Guntown, MS

Died of disease at Camp Jones, VA on 8/7/1861.

Davis, James E. M.
CO: C **Initial Rank:** Private
Joined: Wednesday, May 1, 1861 **Term (yrs):** 1 **Occupation:** Farmer **Age** 28
Enrolled at: Itawamba Co., MS **Enrolled By:** Capt. Bromley **Promoted:** No **ROH:** No
Born: **Marital Status:** **Residence**

Detailed as forage master from May through August 1862. Apparently admitted to hospital on 7/13/1863 due to wound (date of wound or engagement not detailed in company records). Furloughed 40-days from 7/28/1863. Discharged to Invalid Corps on 11/12/1864.

Davis, Jefferson J.
CO: F **Initial Rank:** Private
Joined: Wednesday, May 1, 1861 **Term (yrs):** 1 **Occupation:** Planter **Age** 24
Enrolled at: Tippah Co., MS **Enrolled By:** Capt. Davis **Promoted:** Yes **ROH:** No
Born: **Marital Status:** **Residence**

Elected Jr. 2nd Lieutenant. on 7/26/1861. Discharged for expiration of term of service on 4/25/1862.

Davis, John R.
CO: K **Initial Rank:** Private
Joined: Saturday, March 1, 1862 **Term (yrs):** 3 **Occupation:** Farmer **Age** 32
Enrolled at: Iuka, MS **Enrolled By:** Lt. Latham **Promoted:** No **ROH:** No
Born: Tennessee **Marital Status:** **Residence**

Died of disease on 6/2/1862 at Richmond, VA. [*Buried at Hollywood Cemetery, Richmond, VA. Soldiers Section P Lot: Unknown. Note says he died on 6/5/1862.]

Davis, John T.
CO: C **Initial Rank:** Private
Joined: Wednesday, May 1, 1861 **Term (yrs):** 1 **Occupation:** Teacher **Age** 27
Enrolled at: Itawamba Co., MS **Enrolled By:** Capt. Bromley **Promoted:** No **ROH:** No
Born: Alabama **Marital Status:** **Residence**

Discharged at Camp Fisher, VA due to disability on 2/26/1862.

2nd Mississippi Alphabetical Roster (Annotated)

Davis, Lindsey L.
CO: C **Initial Rank:** Private
Joined: Wednesday, May 1, 1861 *Term (yrs):* 1 *Occupation:* Clerk **Age** 27
Enrolled at: Itawamba Co., MS *Enrolled By:* Capt. Bromley *Promoted:* Yes *ROH:* No
Born: *Marital Status:* *Residence*

Appointed 5th Sergeant on 10/1/1861. Appointed 1st Sergeant on 4/23/1862. Elected 3rd Lieutenant. on 8/15/1862. Killed in battle at Sharpsburg on 9/17/1862.

Davis, William
CO: C **Initial Rank:** Private
Joined: Wednesday, May 1, 1861 *Term (yrs):* 1 *Occupation:* Carpenter (Farmer) **Age** 43
Enrolled at: Itawamba Co., MS *Enrolled By:* Capt. Bromley *Promoted:* Yes *ROH:* No
Born: New York *Marital Status:* *Residence*

Appointed 5th Sergeant on 4/22/1862. Discharged on 5/1/1864 due to over age.

Davis, William H.
CO: B **Initial Rank:** Private
Joined: Wednesday, May 1, 1861 *Term (yrs):* 1 *Occupation:* Farmer **Age** 19
Enrolled at: Tippah Co., MS *Enrolled By:* Capt. Buchanan *Promoted:* No *ROH:* Yes
Born: *Marital Status:* *Residence*

Killed at 2nd Manassas on 8/29/1862. ROH for Second Manassas, 8/28/1862.

Davis, William J.
CO: K **Initial Rank:** Private
Joined: Saturday, March 1, 1862 *Term (yrs):* 3 *Occupation:* **Age** 27
Enrolled at: Iuka, MS *Enrolled By:* Lt. Latham *Promoted:* No *ROH:* No
Born: *Marital Status:* *Residence*

Admitted to hospital from gunshot wound (left hand – amputation of middle finger) on 5/11/1864 (date of wound and engagement not given in company records). Furloughed for 60-days from 5/14/1864. Listed as deserted during Nov/Dec 1864 muster. Dropped from rolls.

Davis, William L.
CO: F **Initial Rank:** Captain
Joined: Wednesday, May 1, 1861 *Term (yrs):* 1 *Occupation:* **Age** 32
Enrolled at: Tippah Co., MS *Enrolled By:* Col. Falkner *Promoted:* No *ROH:* No
Born: *Marital Status:* *Residence*

Resigned due to health on 11/28/1861.

2nd Mississippi Alphabetical Roster (Annotated)

Dawkins, Henry M.
CO: F *Initial Rank:* Private
Joined: Wednesday, May 1, 1861 *Term (yrs):* 1 *Occupation:* Planter *Age* 24
Enrolled at: Tippah Co., MS *Enrolled By:* Capt. Davis *Promoted:* No *ROH:* No
Born: Mississippi *Marital Status:* *Residence*

Died of wounds (date of wound or engagement not noted in company records) on 10/6/1863 at Staunton, VA.

Dawson, John
CO: I *Initial Rank:* Private
Joined: *Term (yrs):* 0 *Occupation:* *Age*
Enrolled at: *Enrolled By:* *Promoted:* No *ROH:* No
Born: *Marital Status:* *Residence*

Appears on a Federal record of paroled prisoners of war reported by the Provost Marshal, District of West Tennessee. Dated 6/18/1865 and "paroled at Memphis, Tenn." No other record.

Dean, Andrew
CO: B *Initial Rank:* Private
Joined: *Term (yrs):* 0 *Occupation:* *Age*
Enrolled at: *Enrolled By:* *Promoted:* No *ROH:* No
Born: *Marital Status:* *Residence*

Appears on a Federal roll of prisoners of war received at and discharged from Gratiot Street Prison, St. Louis, MO. dated St. Louis 4/13/1863. Captured in Tippah Co., Miss on 3/23/1863. [Probably misidentified member of the 2nd Miss Cav.].

Dean, Robert M.
CO: K *Initial Rank:* Private
Joined: Wednesday, May 1, 1861 *Term (yrs):* 1 *Occupation:* Student *Age* 20
Enrolled at: Tishomingo Co., MS *Enrolled By:* Capt. Stone *Promoted:* No *ROH:* No
Born: *Marital Status:* *Residence*

Discharged at Camp Fisher, VA for disability on 10/19/1861.

Deaton, James A.
CO: C *Initial Rank:* Private
Joined: Wednesday, May 1, 1861 *Term (yrs):* 1 *Occupation:* Farmer *Age* 26
Enrolled at: Itawamba Co., MS *Enrolled By:* Capt. Bromley *Promoted:* No *ROH:* No
Born: Tennessee *Marital Status:* *Residence*

Discharged for disability on 3/11/1863.

2nd Mississippi Alphabetical Roster (Annotated)

Deaton, Thomas
CO: C **Initial Rank:** 2nd Sergeant
Joined: Wednesday, May 1, 1861 *Term (yrs):* 1 *Occupation:* Farmer **Age** 56
Enrolled at: Itawamba Co., MS *Enrolled By:* Capt. Bromley *Promoted:* No *ROH:* No
Born: North Carolina *Marital Status:* *Residence*

Discharged at Camp Jones, VA on 8/8/1861 — over age.

Deaton, Thomas J.
CO: C **Initial Rank:** Private
Joined: Wednesday, May 1, 1861 *Term (yrs):* 1 *Occupation:* Farmer **Age** 26
Enrolled at: Itawamba Co., MS *Enrolled By:* Capt. Bromley *Promoted:* No *ROH:* No
Born: *Marital Status:* M *Residence*

Killed at 1st Manassas on 7/21/1861.

Delaney, Robert E.
CO: B **Initial Rank:** Private
Joined: Wednesday, May 1, 1861 *Term (yrs):* 1 *Occupation:* Painter **Age** 28
Enrolled at: Tippah Co., MS *Enrolled By:* Capt. Buchanan *Promoted:* No *ROH:* No
Born: Alabama *Marital Status:* *Residence*

Slightly wounded at 1st Manassas on 7/21/1861. Discharged at Camp Fisher, VA for disability on 10/14/1861. Took oath of allegiance dated Memphis, TN, 9/14/1864.

Demnam, N. A.
CO: D **Initial Rank:** Private
Joined: *Term (yrs):* 0 *Occupation:* **Age**
Enrolled at: *Enrolled By:* *Promoted:* No *ROH:* No
Born: *Marital Status:* *Residence*

Appears on a Federal register of prisoners of war surrendered at Citronelle, AL dated 6/1/1865 and paroled at Mobile. (Misidentified. Probably a member of the 2nd/6th Missouri Infantry — not the 2nd Mississippi).

Dennis, Joe
CO: K **Initial Rank:** Private
Joined: *Term (yrs):* 0 *Occupation:* **Age**
Enrolled at: *Enrolled By:* *Promoted:* No *ROH:* No
Born: *Marital Status:* *Residence*

Paroled at Appomattox Court House on 4/9/1865. No other record.

2nd Mississippi Alphabetical Roster (Annotated)

Depper, Charles
Joined: *CO:*   *Initial Rank:*
Joined: *Term (yrs):* 0   *Occupation:*   *Age*
Enrolled at: *Enrolled By:*   *Promoted:* No   *ROH:* No
Born: *Marital Status:*   *Residence*

Appears on a Federal record of prisoners of war at Old Capitol Prison in Washington, D.C. Arrested as a "Confederate soldier and deserter" on 2/2/1863. No other record.

Deval, Joseph A. M.
CO: C   *Initial Rank:* 3rd Sergeant
Joined: Wednesday, May 1, 1861   *Term (yrs):* 1   *Occupation:* Farmer   *Age* 61
Enrolled at: Itawamba Co., MS   *Enrolled By:* Capt. Bromley   *Promoted:* No   *ROH:* No
Born: South Carolina   *Marital Status:*   *Residence*

Reduced to ranks on 8/1/1861. Discharged on 9/8/1861.

Devall, Francis M
CO: C   *Initial Rank:* Private
Joined: Wednesday, May 1, 1861   *Term (yrs):* 1   *Occupation:* Farmer   *Age* 19
Enrolled at: Itawamba Co., MS   *Enrolled By:* Capt. Bromley   *Promoted:* No   *ROH:* No
Born: Mississippi   *Marital Status:*   *Residence*

Apparently discharged due to disability on 9/6/1861, but re-enlisted in March 1862 for 3-years. Wounded (left leg) and captured at Gettysburg on 7/3/1863. Paroled from DeCamp General Hospital, Davids Island, NY Harbor on 9/8/1863 for exchange at City Point, VA. Returned to duty. Captured at Hatcher's Run on 4/2/1865. Taken to Point Lookout, MD. Released on oath on 6/10/1865.

Dewoody, Samuel N
CO: K   *Initial Rank:* Private
Joined: Wednesday, May 1, 1861   *Term (yrs):* 1   *Occupation:* Postmaster   *Age* 19
Enrolled at: Tishomingo Co., MS   *Enrolled By:* Capt. Stone   *Promoted:* No   *ROH:* No
Born: *Marital Status:*   *Residence*

Captured at Gettysburg on 7/1/1863. Sent to Fort Delaware. Released on oath on 6/7/1865.

2nd Mississippi Alphabetical Roster (Annotated)

Dial, Jesse P. *CO:* L *Initial Rank:* Private

Joined: Monday, March 3, 1862   *Term (yrs):* 3 *Occupation:* Farmer   *Age* 24

Enrolled at: Ripley, MS   *Enrolled By:* Capt. Powers   *Promoted:* No   *ROH:* No

Born: Tennessee   *Marital Status:* M   *Residence* Silver Springs, MS

Wounded (in arm) at Seven Pines on 5/31/1862. Wounded and captured at Gettysburg on 7/1/1863. Paroled from DeCamp General Hospital, Davids Island, NY Harbor to City Point, VA on 9/16/1863 for exchange. Listed as deserter from furlough during Mar/Apr 1864 muster.

Dickson, George A. *CO:* G *Initial Rank:* Private

Joined: Wednesday, May 1, 1861   *Term (yrs):* 1 *Occupation:* Farmer   *Age* 46

Enrolled at: Pontotoc Co., MS   *Enrolled By:* Capt. Miller   *Promoted:* No   *ROH:* No

Born: Tennessee   *Marital Status:*   *Residence*

Discharged 8/2/1862 — over age.

Dickson, McA. *CO:* G *Initial Rank:* Private

Joined: Thursday, March 20, 1862   *Term (yrs):* 3 *Occupation:* Farmer   *Age* 18

Enrolled at: Pontotoc Co., MS   *Enrolled By:* G. B. Mears   *Promoted:* No   *ROH:* No

Born: Mississippi   *Marital Status:* S   *Residence*

Died of disease on 5/15/1862 at Richmond, VA. (other records say 5/13/1862).

Dickson, Robert B *CO:* G *Initial Rank:* Private

Joined: Thursday, March 20, 1862   *Term (yrs):* 3 *Occupation:* Farmer   *Age* 20

Enrolled at: Pontotoc Co., MS   *Enrolled By:* G. B. Mears   *Promoted:* No   *ROH:* No

Born: Mississippi   *Marital Status:* S   *Residence*

Died of disease at Staunton, VA on 12/15/1862 (other records indicate 12/01/1862 or 12/02/1862 — probably more likely one of the latter two dates).

2nd Mississippi Alphabetical Roster (Annotated)

Dillard, James M.
CO: G **Initial Rank:** Private
Joined: Wednesday, May 1, 1861 **Term (yrs):** 1 **Occupation:** Student **Age** 20
Enrolled at: Pontotoc Co., MS **Enrolled By:** Capt. Miller **Promoted:** Yes **ROH:** No
Born: Georgia **Marital Status:** S **Residence** Pontotoc, MS

Promoted to 4th Sergeant on 1/1/1863. 3rd Sergeant circa Mar/Apr 1863. Wounded (left leg) and captured at Gettysburg on 7/1/1863 (wounded 7/1/1863; captured on 7/5/1863). Paroled at Hammond U.S. General Hospital, Point Lookout, MD to City Point, VA on 4/30/1864 for exchange. Admitted to hospital in Richmond on 5/1/1864. Furloughed for 30-days from 5/21/1864 and AWOL since 10/31/1864. Listed on a Federal roll of prisoners of war paroled dated Columbus, MS on 5/17/1865.

Dillard, James T.
CO: G **Initial Rank:** Private
Joined: Thursday, March 20, 1862 **Term (yrs):** 3 **Occupation:** Farmer **Age** 18
Enrolled at: Pontotoc Co., MS **Enrolled By:** G. B. Mears **Promoted:** No **ROH:** Yes
Born: Tennessee **Marital Status:** S **Residence** Pontotoc, MS

Detailed to hospital guard duty from September 1862 through June 1863. Paroled at Appomattox Court House on 4/9/1865. ROH for Tally's Mill, 5/10/1864 and Bethesda Church, 6/3/1864.

Dillard, John W.
CO: G **Initial Rank:** 4th Sergeant
Joined: Wednesday, May 1, 1861 **Term (yrs):** 1 **Occupation:** Merchant **Age** 23
Enrolled at: Pontotoc Co., MS **Enrolled By:** Capt. Kilpatrick **Promoted:** Yes **ROH:** No
Born: Georgia **Marital Status:** S **Residence** Pontotoc, MS

Promoted by election on 7/26/1861 to 2nd Lieutenant. Promoted to 1st Lieutenant. on 4/23/1862. Wounded and captured at Gettysburg on 7/3/1863 (actually wounded on 7/3/1863 and taken prisoner at Green Castle, PA on 7/5/1863). Sent to Johnson Island. Paroled and forwarded for exchange to City Point, VA on 2/24/1865. Promoted while a POW to Captain on 7/8/1863.

Dixon, Andrew M.
CO: A, F **Initial Rank:** Private
Joined: Wednesday, May 1, 1861 **Term (yrs):** 1 **Occupation:** Farmer **Age** 25
Enrolled at: Tishomingo Co., MS **Enrolled By:** Capt. Leeth **Promoted:** No **ROH:** No
Born: Mississippi **Marital Status:** **Residence**

Transferred to Company F from Company A on 1/1/1863. Killed at The Wilderness on 5/5/1864.

2nd Mississippi Alphabetical Roster (Annotated)

Dodd, Daniel
CO: G **Initial Rank:** Private
Joined: Wednesday, May 1, 1861   **Term (yrs):** 1 **Occupation:** Farmer   **Age** 21
Enrolled at: Pontotoc Co., MS   **Enrolled By:** Capt. Miller   **Promoted:** No   **ROH:** No
Born: Mississippi   **Marital Status:** S   **Residence** Pontotoc, MS

Killed at 2nd Manassas on 8/29/1862.

Donald, Rufus O.
CO: **Initial Rank:**
Joined: **Term (yrs):** 0 **Occupation:**   **Age**
Enrolled at: **Enrolled By:**   **Promoted:** No   **ROH:** No
Born: **Marital Status:**   **Residence**

Appears on a Federal register of prisoners of war at Old Capitol Prison, Washington, D.C. Captured at Madison Court House, VA on 9/22/1863 (remarks say "entered by mistake"). No other record.

Donaldson, Joel J.
CO: G **Initial Rank:** Private
Joined: Wednesday, May 1, 1861   **Term (yrs):** 1 **Occupation:** Farmer   **Age** 30
Enrolled at: Pontotoc Co., MS   **Enrolled By:** Capt. Miller   **Promoted:** Yes   **ROH:** Yes
Born: **Marital Status:**   **Residence**

Promoted to Corporal on 8/1/1862 and wounded at battle of 2nd Manassas on 8/29/1862. Promoted to 4th Sergeant in Jan 1863. Wounded (both legs) and captured at Gettysburg on 7/3/1863. Paroled from DeCamp General Hospital, Davids Island, NY Harbor to City Point, VA on 8/28/1863 for exchange. Exchanged and returned to duty on 10/25/1863. Captured at Petersburg (Hatcher's Run?) on 4/2/1865. Taken to Point Lookout, MD. Released on oath on 6/11/1865. ROH for Gettysburg, 7/3/1863.

Donaldson, John B.
CO: G **Initial Rank:** Private
Joined: Monday, September 16, 1861   **Term (yrs):** 1 **Occupation:** Farmer   **Age** 26
Enrolled at: Pontotoc Co., MS   **Enrolled By:** Lt. Davenport   **Promoted:** Yes   **ROH:** No
Born: Alabama   **Marital Status:** S   **Residence** Pontotoc, MS

Wounded at 2nd Manassas on 8/29/1862. Returned to duty on 11/20/1862. Listed as 4th Corporal during Sept/Oct 1864 muster. Severely wounded in battle near Fort McRae on 10/1/1864. Retired by order of medical examining board on 2/1/1865.

2nd Mississippi Alphabetical Roster (Annotated)

Donaldson, William
CO: G *Initial Rank:* Private
Joined: Wednesday, May 1, 1861 *Term (yrs):* 1 *Occupation:* Farmer *Age* 33
Enrolled at: Pontotoc Co., MS *Enrolled By:* Capt. Miller *Promoted:* No *ROH:* No
Born: Tennessee *Marital Status:* S *Residence* Pontotoc, MS

Discharged for disability (asthma) on 9/8/1861 by order of General Johnston.

Donohue, Rody
CO: K *Initial Rank:* Private
Joined: *Term (yrs):* 0 *Occupation:* *Age*
Enrolled at: *Enrolled By:* *Promoted:* No *ROH:* No
Born: *Marital Status:* *Residence*

Appears on a Federal roll of prisoners of war at Fort Delaware discharged and joined U.S. Service to 8/1/1863. Captured at Gettysburg on 7/4/1863. Became "Galvanized Yankee" and joined Capt. Mlotskowski's Battery A, Pennsylvania Volunteers. Deserted. No other record.

Dorset, John A.
CO: L *Initial Rank:* Private
Joined: Monday, March 3, 1862 *Term (yrs):* 3 *Occupation:* Farmer *Age* 26
Enrolled at: Ripley, MS *Enrolled By:* Col. Falkner *Promoted:* No *ROH:* No
Born: Mississippi *Marital Status:* M *Residence* Ripley, MS

Captured at Sharpsburg on 9/17/1862. Listed as deserter during Nov/Dec 1862 muster roll. Took oath of allegiance to the United States while a POW.

Drake, Richard
CO: G *Initial Rank:* 3rd Sergeant
Joined: Wednesday, May 1, 1861 *Term (yrs):* 1 *Occupation:* Clerk (Student) *Age* 20
Enrolled at: Pontotoc Co., MS *Enrolled By:* Capt. Kilpatrick *Promoted:* Yes *ROH:* Yes
Born: Mississippi *Marital Status:* S *Residence* Pontotoc, MS

Also see general & staff officers. Appointed Orderly Sergeant on 6/15/1862. Wounded at Gaines Mill on 6/27/1862. Furloughed. Returned to duty 9/28/1862. Acting Chief of Ordnance for General Law's Brigade since 10/29/1862. ROH for Gaines Mill, 6/27/1862.

Driscoll, Timothy
CO: I *Initial Rank:* Private
Joined: Wednesday, May 1, 1861 *Term (yrs):* 1 *Occupation:* Laborer *Age* 33
Enrolled at: Pontotoc Co., MS *Enrolled By:* Capt. Herring *Promoted:* No *ROH:* No
Born: Ireland *Marital Status:* *Residence*

Killed in battle at 2nd Manassas on 8/30/1862.

2nd Mississippi Alphabetical Roster (Annotated)

Dry, Charles F.
CO: B **Initial Rank:** Private
Joined: Wednesday, May 1, 1861 **Term (yrs):** 1 **Occupation:** Farmer **Age** 21
Enrolled at: Tippah Co., MS **Enrolled By:** Capt. Buchanan **Promoted:** No **ROH:** No
Born: North Carolina **Marital Status:** S **Residence**

Discharged for disability on 7/28/1861, but apparently re-enlisted in March 1862 for 3-years. Wounded at Gaines Mill on 6/27/1862. Leg amputated below right knee. Furloughed for 60-days from 8/28/1862. Furloughs extended. Retired from service and assigned to the Invalid Corps, P.A.C.S on 8/29/1864 due to disability from wounds.

Duff, John L.
CO: G **Initial Rank:** Private
Joined: Wednesday, May 1, 1861 **Term (yrs):** 1 **Occupation:** Farmer **Age** 24
Enrolled at: Pontotoc Co., MS **Enrolled By:** Capt. Miller **Promoted:** No **ROH:** No
Born: **Marital Status:** S **Residence**

Died in February 1862 (cause not stated).

Duke, James
CO: H **Initial Rank:**
Joined: Friday, March 1, 1861 **Term (yrs):** 1 **Occupation:** **Age**
Enrolled at: Chesterville, MS **Enrolled By:** Capt. Kilpatrick **Promoted:** No **ROH:** No
Born: **Marital Status:** **Residence**

Appears on a company muster roll. Also appears on a hospital record from Winder, No. 2, dated 10/29/1862 and relocated to Danville, VA on 12/29/1862. No other records. [Probably the same person as John D. Duke of Company H].

Duke, John D.
CO: H **Initial Rank:** Private
Joined: Monday, April 29, 1861 **Term (yrs):** 1 **Occupation:** Farmer **Age** 21
Enrolled at: Pontotoc Co., MS **Enrolled By:** Capt. Taylor **Promoted:** No **ROH:** No
Born: Alabama **Marital Status:** S **Residence** Chesterville, MS

Wounded at Weldon Railroad on 10/19/1864. Returned to duty. Captured at Hatcher's Run on 4/2/1865 and taken to Point Lookout, MD. Released on oath on 6/11/1865. [Probably same individual as James Duke].

2nd Mississippi Alphabetical Roster (Annotated)

Dulany, W. H.
CO: E *Initial Rank:* Private
Joined: *Term (yrs):* 0 *Occupation:* *Age*
Enrolled at: *Enrolled By:* *Promoted:* No *ROH:* No
Born: *Marital Status:* *Residence*

Appears on a Federal roll of prisoners of war paroled dated Talladega, AL on 6/20/1865. Paroled 5/24/1865. No other record.

Dunaway, Andrew M.
CO: A *Initial Rank:* Private
Joined: Saturday, March 1, 1862 *Term (yrs):* 3 *Occupation:* Farmer *Age* 32
Enrolled at: Jacinto, MS *Enrolled By:* Lt. Clayton *Promoted:* No *ROH:* No
Born: Tennessee *Marital Status:* *Residence*

Listed as deserter for prolonged AWOL during Mar/Apr 1864 muster roll.

Dunbar, Pat P.
CO: F *Initial Rank:*
Joined: Monday, March 4, 1861 *Term (yrs):* 1 *Occupation:* *Age*
Enrolled at: Ripley, MS *Enrolled By:* J. R. Chalmers *Promoted:* No *ROH:* No
Born: *Marital Status:* *Residence*

Appears on a company muster roll for state service. No other record.

Duncan, Charles P.
CO: A *Initial Rank:* Private
Joined: Saturday, March 1, 1862 *Term (yrs):* 3 *Occupation:* Farmer *Age* 18
Enrolled at: Jacinto, MS *Enrolled By:* Lt. Clayton *Promoted:* No *ROH:* No
Born: Georgia *Marital Status:* S *Residence* Jacinto, MS

Captured at Falling Waters, MD on 7/14/1863. Exchanged 4/27/1864. Rejoined Company on 6/30/1864. Captured at Petersburg (Hatcher's Run?) on 4/2/1865. Taken to Point Lookout, MD. Released on oath on 6/10/1865.

Duncan, Edwin R.
CO: D *Initial Rank:* Private
Joined: Tuesday, October 1, 1861 *Term (yrs):* 1 *Occupation:* Farmer *Age* 22
Enrolled at: Iuka, MS *Enrolled By:* Lt. Davenport *Promoted:* No *ROH:* No
Born: Mississippi *Marital Status:* S *Residence* Hickory Flat, MS

Discharged at Camp Fisher, VA due to disability on 1/1/1862.

2nd Mississippi Alphabetical Roster (Annotated)

Duncan, Henry W. CO: D Initial Rank: Private
Joined: Wednesday, May 1, 1861   **Term (yrs):** 1   **Occupation:** Farmer   **Age** 25
Enrolled at: Tippah Co., MS   **Enrolled By:** Capt. Beck   **Promoted:** No   **ROH:** No
Born: **Marital Status:** S   **Residence** Hickory Flat, MS

Listed as deserted to the enemy on 5/23/1863 near Winsor, VA while engaged in a skirmish fight with the enemy.

Duncan, Thomas CO: D Initial Rank: Private
Joined: Wednesday, May 1, 1861   **Term (yrs):** 1   **Occupation:** Farmer   **Age** 24
Enrolled at: Tippah Co., MS   **Enrolled By:** Capt. Beck   **Promoted:** No   **ROH:** No
Born: **Marital Status:** M   **Residence** Pine Grove, MS

Discharged on 7/1/1861 due to disability.

Duncan, Thomas J. CO: B Initial Rank: 3rd Sergeant
Joined: Wednesday, May 1, 1861   **Term (yrs):** 1   **Occupation:** Cabinet Maker   **Age** 28
Enrolled at: Tippah Co., MS   **Enrolled By:** Capt. Buchanan   **Promoted:** No   **ROH:** No
Born: **Marital Status:**   **Residence**

Reduced to ranks, circa March/April 1862 muster. Wounded and captured at Gettysburg on 7/1/1863. Escaped from Point Lookout, MD on 12/8/1863. Furloughed 30-days from 12/13/1863. Died of wounds on 9/23/1864 (date of wound or engagement information not available in company records, except hospital records note the wound was inflicted "near Petersburg, VA."

Dunn, George W. CO: E Initial Rank: Private
Joined: Friday, April 1, 1864   **Term (yrs):** 3   **Occupation:**   **Age** 19
Enrolled at: Rapidan, VA   **Enrolled By:** Lt. Long   **Promoted:** No   **ROH:** No
Born: Mississippi   **Marital Status:** S   **Residence**

See also Jeff Davis Legion Mississippi Cavalry as G. W. Dunn. Transferred from Co. B Jeff Davis Legion to Co. E, 2nd Mississippi Infantry Regiment on 4/26/1864. Listed as AWOL from 5/5/1864 and deserted during Nov/Dec 1864 muster roll. However, hospital records show him admitted on 5/9/1864 due to wound. No other record.

2nd Mississippi Alphabetical Roster (Annotated)

Dunn, Jesse N.   *CO:* E   *Initial Rank:* Private
Joined: Monday, March 10, 1862   *Term (yrs):* 3   *Occupation:* Mechanic   *Age* 22
Enrolled at: Guntown, MS   *Enrolled By:* Capt. Bates   *Promoted:* No   *ROH:* No
Born: Mississippi   *Marital Status:* M   *Residence* Guntown, MS

Listed as deserted 6/2/1863 or 6/6/1863.

Dunn, Joseph F.   *CO:* F   *Initial Rank:* Private
Joined: Wednesday, May 1, 1861   *Term (yrs):* 1   *Occupation:* Clerk   *Age* 25
Enrolled at: Tippah Co., MS   *Enrolled By:* Capt. Davis   *Promoted:* No   *ROH:* No
Born: *Marital Status:*   *Residence*

Detailed as regimental teamster. Furloughed 30-days from 8/23/1862. Remarks in Mar/Apr 1863 muster roll say "died." Did not report back from expiration of furlough. Presumed dead.

Dunn, Joseph N.   *CO:* E   *Initial Rank:* Private
Joined: Friday, April 1, 1864   *Term (yrs):* 3   *Occupation:*   *Age* 40
Enrolled at: Rapidan, VA   *Enrolled By:* Lt. Long   *Promoted:* No   *ROH:* No
Born: *Marital Status:* M   *Residence*

Also see Jeff Davis Legion, Mississippi Cavalry. Transferred from Co. B Jeff Davis Legion to Co. E., 2nd Mississippi Infantry on 4/26/1864. Listed as never reported, AWOL since 5/5/1864. Deserted as of Nov/Dec, 1864 muster roll.

Dye, James A.   *CO:* G   *Initial Rank:* Private
Joined: *Term (yrs):* 0   *Occupation:*   *Age*
Enrolled at: *Enrolled By:*   *Promoted:* No   *ROH:* No
Born: *Marital Status:*   *Residence*

Appears on a Federal roll of prisoners of war dated 1/15/1865. Captured at Franklin, TN on 12/17/1864. No other record. [Almost certainly, confusion in records. Misidentified. This person probably belongs to the 2nd/6th Missouri Infantry Regiment Consolidated — not the 2nd Mississippi].

Dyer, John T.   *CO:* D   *Initial Rank:* Private
Joined: Wednesday, May 1, 1861   *Term (yrs):* 1   *Occupation:* Farmer   *Age* 19
Enrolled at: Tippah Co., MS   *Enrolled By:* Capt. Beck   *Promoted:* No   *ROH:* No
Born: Mississippi   *Marital Status:* S   *Residence* Salem, MS

Killed in battle at Gaines Mill on 6/27/1862.

2nd Mississippi Alphabetical Roster (Annotated)

Eaker, Moses J.
CO: D **Initial Rank:** Private
Joined: Wednesday, May 1, 1861 **Term (yrs):** 1 **Occupation:** Blacksmith **Age** 22
Enrolled at: Tippah Co., MS **Enrolled By:** Capt. Beck **Promoted:** No **ROH:** No
Born: North Carolina **Marital Status:** S **Residence** Snow Creek, MS

Killed at 1st Manassas on 7/21/1861.

Earle, Charles W.
CO: G **Initial Rank:** Private
Joined: Wednesday, May 1, 1861 **Term (yrs):** 1 **Occupation:** Farmer **Age** 17
Enrolled at: Pontotoc Co., MS **Enrolled By:** Capt. Miller **Promoted:** No **ROH:** No
Born: Mississippi **Marital Status:** S **Residence** Pontotoc, MS

Listed in Sept/Oct 1862 muster as captured by the enemy in hospital at Warrenton. Paroled and exchanged, returned to duty on 1/1/1863. Captured at Gettysburg on 7/1/1863. Sent to Fort Delaware. Released on oath on 6/11/1865.

Earle, Ezias L.
CO: G **Initial Rank:** Private
Joined: Wednesday, May 1, 1861 **Term (yrs):** 1 **Occupation:** Clerk (Student of **Age** 25
Enrolled at: Pontotoc Co., MS **Enrolled By:** Capt. Miller **Promoted:** Yes **ROH:** Yes
Born: Kentucky **Marital Status:** S **Residence** Pontotoc, MS

Served on detached service in hospital. Appointed 2nd Corporal on 8/28/1863. Wounded in battle on 6/2/1864 (Cold Harbor?) and furloughed from hospital on 6/17/1863 for 60-days. Paroled from hospital, CSA on 5/12/1865. Roll dated Meridian, MS on 5/12/1865. Listed residence as Union City, TN. ROH for Spotsylvania Court House, 5/12/1864.

Early, Levi
CO: G **Initial Rank:** Private
Joined: Thursday, March 20, 1862 **Term (yrs):** 3 **Occupation:** Farmer **Age** 35
Enrolled at: Pontotoc, MS **Enrolled By:** G. B. Mears **Promoted:** No **ROH:** No
Born: Mississippi **Marital Status:** M **Residence** Pontotoc, MS

Died of disease in camp near Richmond on 11/15/1862.

2nd Mississippi Alphabetical Roster (Annotated)

Earnest, James C.
CO: K **Initial Rank:** Private
Joined: Saturday, March 1, 1862 **Term (yrs):** 3 **Occupation:** **Age** 21
Enrolled at: Iuka, MS **Enrolled By:** Lt. Latham **Promoted:** No **ROH:** No
Born: **Marital Status:** **Residence**

Also see 26th Mississippi Infantry. Listed as deserted on 6/5/1863 and appears on a Federal roll of rebel deserters received from Washington, D.C. 6/21/1863 — remarks: "Suffolk, VA June 9, 1863. Had oath of allegiance administered on 6/24/1863."

Earwood, Isaac L.
CO: E **Initial Rank:** Private
Joined: Friday, February 28, 1862 **Term (yrs):** 3 **Occupation:** Farmer **Age** 20
Enrolled at: Guntown, MS **Enrolled By:** Capt. Bates **Promoted:** No **ROH:** No
Born: Mississippi **Marital Status:** S **Residence** Saltillo, MS

Died on 5/1/1862 from disease at Richmond, VA.

Easley, Pleasant L.
CO: E **Initial Rank:** Private
Joined: Saturday, March 1, 1862 **Term (yrs):** 3 **Occupation:** Farmer **Age** 21
Enrolled at: Guntown, MS **Enrolled By:** Capt. Bates **Promoted:** No **ROH:** No
Born: **Marital Status:** S **Residence** Guntown, MS

Captured at Gettysburg on 7/1/1863. Taken to Fort Delaware. Died of disease at Fort Delaware on 8/26/1864. Note says grave located at "Jersey Shore".

Easterwood, George M.
CO: G **Initial Rank:** Private
Joined: Wednesday, May 1, 1861 **Term (yrs):** 1 **Occupation:** Planter **Age** 24
Enrolled at: Pontotoc Co., MS **Enrolled By:** Capt. Miller **Promoted:** Yes **ROH:** Yes
Born: Alabama **Marital Status:** M **Residence** Pontotoc, MS

Appointed 1st Corporal on 2/14/1862. Wounded (left side) at Falling Waters, MD on 7/13/1863. In hospital at Richmond. Furloughed to 11/1/1863. Returned to duty on 11/10/1863. Wounded in battle on 6/2/1864. Furloughed from hospital on 6/17/1864 for 40-days. Promoted to 5th Sergeant on in July 1864. Detailed for detached duty in division commissary (Quartermaster Department) on 10/24/1864 by special order. ROH for Falling Waters, 7/14/1863.

2nd Mississippi Alphabetical Roster (Annotated)

Eastham, James A. S.
CO: K *Initial Rank:* Private
Joined: Saturday, March 1, 1862 *Term (yrs):* 3 *Occupation:* Farmer *Age* 18
Enrolled at: Iuka, MS *Enrolled By:* Lt. Latham *Promoted:* No *ROH:* No
Born: *Marital Status:* *Residence*
Killed in action at Spotsylvania on 5/10/1864.

Echols, B. F.
CO: G *Initial Rank:* Private
Joined: Thursday, March 20, 1862 *Term (yrs):* 3 *Occupation:* Farmer *Age* 18
Enrolled at: Pontotoc, MS *Enrolled By:* G. B. Mears *Promoted:* No *ROH:* No
Born: Mississippi *Marital Status:* S *Residence* Pontotoc, MS
Killed in action at Sharpsburg on 9/17/1862.

Eddings, Paschal C.
CO: B *Initial Rank:* Private
Joined: Wednesday, May 1, 1861 *Term (yrs):* 1 *Occupation:* Farmer *Age* 26
Enrolled at: Tippah Co., MS *Enrolled By:* Capt. Buchanan *Promoted:* Yes *ROH:* Yes
Born: *Marital Status:* *Residence*
Wounded at Sharpsburg on 9/17/1862. Sent to hospital. Furloughed for 30-days on 10/10/1862. Appears on a Federal list of prisoners taken and paroled during the march to the Mobile and Ohio Railroad, dated Holly Springs, MS on 12/25/1862. Listed as 5th Sergeant on May/June 1864 muster. Wounded in battle on 8/18/1864 at the Weldon Railroad and in hospital. Furloughed on 9/15/1864 for 60-days. Appears on a Federal report of prisoners of war paroled at Holly Springs, MS during May 1865, dated 5/31/1865. ROH for Bristoe Station, 10/14/1863.

Eddington, Robert S.
CO: G *Initial Rank:* Private
Joined: Wednesday, May 1, 1861 *Term (yrs):* 1 *Occupation:* Farmer *Age* 31
Enrolled at: Pontotoc Co., MS *Enrolled By:* Capt. Miller *Promoted:* No *ROH:* No
Born: South Carolina *Marital Status:* S *Residence* Pontotoc, MS
Wounded (right lung) in battle at Gettysburg on 7/1/1863. Sent to hospital at Richmond. Returned to duty on 1/15/1864. Captured at Hatcher's Run on 4/2/1865. Taken to Point Lookout, MD. Released on oath on 6/11/1865.

Edge, David M.
CO: E *Initial Rank:* Private
Joined: Wednesday, February 26, 1862 *Term (yrs):* 3 *Occupation:* *Age* 26
Enrolled at: Guntown, MS *Enrolled By:* Capt. Bates *Promoted:* No *ROH:* No
Born: *Marital Status:* M *Residence* Guntown, MS
Captured at Gettysburg on 7/1/1863. Sent to Fort Delaware. Released on oath on 6/11/1865.

2nd Mississippi Alphabetical Roster (Annotated)

Edge, Elijah
CO: E *Initial Rank:* Private
Joined: Wednesday, May 1, 1861 *Term (yrs):* 1 *Occupation:* Carpenter *Age* 38
Enrolled at: Itawamba Co., MS *Enrolled By:* Capt. Booth *Promoted:* No *ROH:* No
Born: *Marital Status:* M *Residence* Guntown, MS
Discharged on 12/25/1861 due to disability.

Edington, John M.
CO: G *Initial Rank:* Private
Joined: Sunday, February 15, 1863 *Term (yrs):* 3 *Occupation:* Farmer *Age* 40
Enrolled at: Okolona, MS *Enrolled By:* Capt. Ingate *Promoted:* No *ROH:* No
Born: South Carolina *Marital Status:* M *Residence* Pontotoc, MS
Captured at Gettysburg on 7/5/1863 (detailed as hospital nurse for Confederate wounded). Taken to Point Lookout, MD. Died in prison on 9/28/1863.

Edwards, George W.
CO: A *Initial Rank:* Private
Joined: Wednesday, May 1, 1861 *Term (yrs):* 1 *Occupation:* Farmer *Age* 24
Enrolled at: Tishomingo Co., MS *Enrolled By:* Capt. Leeth *Promoted:* No *ROH:* No
Born: Alabama *Marital Status:* *Residence* Booneville, MS
Discharged on 2/10/1863 due to disability.

Edwards, James W.
CO: G *Initial Rank:* Private
Joined: Wednesday, May 1, 1861 *Term (yrs):* 1 *Occupation:* Farmer *Age* 20
Enrolled at: Pontotoc Co., MS *Enrolled By:* Capt. Miller *Promoted:* No *ROH:* No
Born: Mississippi *Marital Status:* S *Residence* Pontotoc, MS
Wounded at Gettysburg on 7/1/1863. In hospital at Charlottesville, VA. Returned to duty on 9/15/1863. Listed as AWOL from 2/6/1864. Deserted from Jul/Aug 1864 muster roll.

Edwards, John A.
CO: C *Initial Rank:* Private
Joined: Saturday, March 1, 1862 *Term (yrs):* 3 *Occupation:* *Age*
Enrolled at: Verona, MS *Enrolled By:* Lt. Pounds *Promoted:* No *ROH:* No
Born: South Carolina *Marital Status:* *Residence*
Died of disease on 5/5/1862 at Richmond, VA.

2nd Mississippi Alphabetical Roster (Annotated)

Edwards, William A.
CO: G **Initial Rank:** Private
Joined: Wednesday, May 1, 1861 **Term (yrs):** 1 **Occupation:** Farmer **Age** 22
Enrolled at: Pontotoc Co., MS **Enrolled By:** Capt. Miller **Promoted:** No **ROH:** Yes
Born: **Marital Status:** **Residence**

Wounded in battle at Sharpsburg on 9/17/1862. Sent to hospital. Furloughed to Mississippi. Returned to duty on 9/2/1863. Wounded at The Wilderness on 5/5/1864. Returned to duty. Listed as "deserted to the enemy" on various dates: 2/4/1865, 3/2/1865, and 3/5/1865. Federal rolls say he was received as a rebel deserter on 3/2/1865. ROH for The Wilderness, 5/5/1864.

Elliott, George M.
CO: D **Initial Rank:** Private
Joined: Wednesday, May 1, 1861 **Term (yrs):** 1 **Occupation:** Farmer **Age** 20
Enrolled at: Tippah Co., MS **Enrolled By:** Capt. Beck **Promoted:** No **ROH:** No
Born: Tennessee **Marital Status:** S **Residence** Pine Grove, MS

Discharged on 2/15/1862 due to disability.

Elliott, James J.
CO: D **Initial Rank:** Jr. 2nd Lieutenant
Joined: Wednesday, May 1, 1861 **Term (yrs):** 1 **Occupation:** Merchant **Age**
Enrolled at: Tippah Co., MS **Enrolled By:** Capt. Beck **Promoted:** No **ROH:** No
Born: **Marital Status:** S **Residence** Snow Creek, MS

Discharged on 6/26/1861 due to disability. Appears on a Federal roll of prisoners of war who died at Alton Military Prison. Captured on 12/8/1862 in Tippah Co., MS and died on 3/23/1863 of pneumonia.

Elliott, John B.
CO: D **Initial Rank:** Private
Joined: Thursday, September 19, 1861 **Term (yrs):** 1 **Occupation:** Farmer **Age** 19
Enrolled at: Salem, MS **Enrolled By:** Lt. Davenport **Promoted:** No **ROH:** Yes
Born: Tennessee **Marital Status:** S **Residence** Pine Grove, MS

Severely wounded (gunshot wound of left leg) and captured at Gettysburg on 7/3/1863. Paroled from Point Lookout, MD 3/6/1864 to City Point, VA for exchange. Sent to hospital in Richmond and back to Mississippi on 12/5/1864. Appears on a Federal roll of prisoners of war paroled at La Grange, TN dated 5/24/1865. Remarks say he surrendered at that point on 5/24/1865 and note says "wounded at Gettysburg, PA July 3, 1863." ROH for Sharpsburg, 9/17/1862.

2nd Mississippi Alphabetical Roster (Annotated)

Elliott, John S.
CO: K **Initial Rank:** Private
Joined: Wednesday, May 1, 1861 **Term (yrs):** 1 **Occupation:** Farmer **Age** 18
Enrolled at: Tishomingo Co., MS **Enrolled By:** Capt. Stone **Promoted:** No **ROH:** No
Born: **Marital Status:** **Residence**

Listed as wounded in May/June 1862 muster roll (date of wound or engagement not noted in company records). Furloughed. Listed as AWOL during Nov/Dec 1862 muster and deserted in the Mar/Apr 1863 muster roll.

Ellis, John R.
CO: G **Initial Rank:** Private
Joined: Wednesday, May 1, 1861 **Term (yrs):** 1 **Occupation:** Merchant **Age** 48
Enrolled at: Pontotoc Co., MS **Enrolled By:** Capt. Miller **Promoted:** No **ROH:** No
Born: **Marital Status:** S **Residence** Pontotoc, MS

Discharged for disability on 5/27/1862.

Ellis, William P.
CO: E **Initial Rank:** Private
Joined: Wednesday, May 1, 1861 **Term (yrs):** 1 **Occupation:** Farmer **Age** 17
Enrolled at: Itawamba Co., MS **Enrolled By:** Capt. Booth **Promoted:** No **ROH:** No
Born: Mississippi **Marital Status:** S **Residence** Guntown, MS

Captured at Gettysburg on 7/1/1863. Sent to Fort Delaware. Released on oath on 6/11/1865.

Ellison, Robert
CO: D **Initial Rank:** Private
Joined: **Term (yrs):** 0 **Occupation:** **Age**
Enrolled at: **Enrolled By:** **Promoted:** No **ROH:** No
Born: **Marital Status:** **Residence**

See personal papers for additional information. No other records.

Ellzey, Berry M.
CO: G **Initial Rank:** Private
Joined: Wednesday, May 1, 1861 **Term (yrs):** 1 **Occupation:** Farmer **Age** 20
Enrolled at: Pontotoc Co., MS **Enrolled By:** Capt. Miller **Promoted:** No **ROH:** No
Born: Mississippi **Marital Status:** S **Residence** Pontotoc, MS

Severely wounded (hip) at 1st Manassas on 7/21/1861. Discharged for disability due to wound at Camp Fisher, VA on 10/27/1861 by order of General Johnston.

2nd Mississippi Alphabetical Roster (Annotated)

Ellzey, Elijah H.
CO: G   *Initial Rank:* Private
Joined: Tuesday, April 30, 1861   *Term (yrs):* 1   *Occupation:* Farmer   *Age* 19
Enrolled at: Pontotoc, MS   *Enrolled By:* Capt. Kilpatrick   *Promoted:* No   *ROH:* No
Born: Mississippi   *Marital Status:* S   *Residence* Pontotoc, MS

Killed in battle at 2nd Manassas on 8/29/1862.

English, John J.
CO: C   *Initial Rank:* Private
Joined: Wednesday, May 1, 1861   *Term (yrs):* 1   *Occupation:* Farmer   *Age* 22
Enrolled at: Itawamba Co., MS   *Enrolled By:* Capt. Bromley   *Promoted:* No   *ROH:* No
Born: *Marital Status:*   *Residence*

Wounded at Gaines Mill on 6/27/1862. Died of disease at Brandy Station, VA on 8/25/1862.

Ennis, James M.
CO: D, F   *Initial Rank:* Private
Joined: Wednesday, May 1, 1861   *Term (yrs):* 1   *Occupation:* Farmer   *Age* 24
Enrolled at: Tippah Co., MS   *Enrolled By:* Capt. Beck   *Promoted:* No   *ROH:* No
Born: Tennessee   *Marital Status:* S   *Residence* Jonesboro, TN

Also see 79th Tennessee Infantry. Transferred to Company F from Company D on 4/30/1862. Transferred to Co. E, 79th Tennessee Infantry Regiment on 12/2/1862 as a citizen of Tennessee.

Estell, Jackson V.
CO: G   *Initial Rank:* Private
Joined: Wednesday, May 1, 1861   *Term (yrs):* 1   *Occupation:* Farmer   *Age* 19
Enrolled at: Pontotoc Co., MS   *Enrolled By:* Capt. Miller   *Promoted:* No   *ROH:* No
Born: Alabama   *Marital Status:* S   *Residence* Pontotoc, MS

Discharged on 6/13/1863 due to heart disease.

Estell, Levi L.
CO: G   *Initial Rank:* Private
Joined: Thursday, March 20, 1862   *Term (yrs):* 3   *Occupation:* Farmer   *Age* 18
Enrolled at: Pontotoc, MS   *Enrolled By:* G. B. Mears   *Promoted:* No   *ROH:* No
Born: Alabama   *Marital Status:* S   *Residence* Pontotoc, MS

Died on 6/20/1862 (or 7/6/1862) of disease at Richmond, VA.

2nd Mississippi Alphabetical Roster (Annotated)

Estep, Rufus D.
CO: E *Initial Rank:* Private
Joined: Wednesday, May 1, 1861 *Term (yrs):* 1 *Occupation:* Farmer *Age* 50
Enrolled at: Itawamba Co., MS *Enrolled By:* Capt. Booth *Promoted:* No *ROH:* No
Born: *Marital Status:* M *Residence* Guntown, MS

Discharged on 7/23/1862 under act of Congress (over age?).

Estes, Samuel G.
CO: A *Initial Rank:* Private
Joined: Wednesday, May 1, 1861 *Term (yrs):* 1 *Occupation:* Printer *Age* 23
Enrolled at: Tishomingo Co., MS *Enrolled By:* Capt. Leeth *Promoted:* No *ROH:* No
Born: Alabama *Marital Status:* S *Residence* Jacinto, MS

Admitted to hospital in Richmond on 10/22/1863 wounded (company records provide no details as to date of wound or engagement). Returned to duty. Killed in battle on 10/27/1864 near Petersburg.

Eubanks, John B.
CO: C, B *Initial Rank:* Private
Joined: Saturday, March 1, 1862 *Term (yrs):* 3 *Occupation:* *Age*
Enrolled at: Verona, MS *Enrolled By:* Lt. Pounds *Promoted:* No *ROH:* No
Born: *Marital Status:* *Residence*

Captured at Gettysburg on 7/3/1863. Taken to DeCamp General Hospital, Davids Island, NY Harbor and paroled to City Point, VA on 9/8/1863 to await exchange. Returned to duty. Paroled at Appomattox Court House on 4/9/1865.

Evans, James R.
CO: C *Initial Rank:* Private
Joined: Wednesday, May 1, 1861 *Term (yrs):* 1 *Occupation:* Farmer *Age* 21
Enrolled at: Itawamba Co., MS *Enrolled By:* Capt. Bromley *Promoted:* No *ROH:* No
Born: *Marital Status:* *Residence*

Captured at Gettysburg on 7/3/1863. Taken to Point Lookout, MD. According to Federal records, became "Galvanized Yankee" and joined U.S. Army on 2/26/1864. Listed on May/Jun 1864 company muster rolls as "deserted."

2nd Mississippi Alphabetical Roster (Annotated)

Evans, Oliver P.

CO: E *Initial Rank:* Private

Joined: Wednesday, May 1, 1861 *Term (yrs):* 1 *Occupation:* Farmer *Age* 17

Enrolled at: Itawamba Co., MS *Enrolled By:* Capt. Booth *Promoted:* No *ROH:* No

Born: Alabama *Marital Status:* S *Residence* Guntown, MS

Admitted to hospital due to wound (date of wound or engagement not noted in company records) on 7/12/1863. Returned to duty on 8/8/1863. Listed in Mar/Apr 1864 muster as deserted near Orange Court House, VA on 2/10/1864. Taken custody of by Federal forces as a rebel deserter on 2/12/1864.

Ewing, James J.

CO: H *Initial Rank:*

Joined: Friday, March 1, 1861 *Term (yrs):* 1 *Occupation:* *Age*

Enrolled at: Chesterville, MS *Enrolled By:* Capt. Kilpatrick *Promoted:* No *ROH:* No

Born: *Marital Status:* *Residence*

Appears on a company muster roll. No other record.

Falkner, James W.

CO: L *Initial Rank:* 1st Lieutenant

Joined: Monday, March 3, 1862 *Term (yrs):* 3 *Occupation:* Lawyer *Age* 27

Enrolled at: Ripley, MS *Enrolled By:* Col. Falkner *Promoted:* No *ROH:* No

Born: Tennessee *Marital Status:* *Residence* Ripley, MS

Elected on 3/22/1862. Dropped from the rolls as a deserter on 10/1/1862. Company records note "desertion in cavalry in Mississippi." [Presumably, the new unit Col. Falkner raised after being replaced by Capt. John M. Stone during the regimental reorganization elections on 4/23/1862 — the 7th Mississippi Cavalry Regiment].

Falkner, Jeremiah

CO: H *Initial Rank:* Private

Joined: Saturday, August 10, 1861 *Term (yrs):* 1 *Occupation:* Merchant *Age* 21

Enrolled at: Camp Jones, VA *Enrolled By:* Lt. Stone *Promoted:* No *ROH:* No

Born: Alabama *Marital Status:* S *Residence* Tupelo, MS

Killed while on picket duty on 9/18/1864 (other notes say, "Killed sharp shooting near Petersburg Sept/64.")

Falkner, Mardis

CO: H *Initial Rank:* Private

Joined: Monday, April 29, 1861 *Term (yrs):* 1 *Occupation:* Carpenter *Age* 23

Enrolled at: Pontotoc Co., MS *Enrolled By:* Capt. Taylor *Promoted:* No *ROH:* No

Born: *Marital Status:* *Residence*

Died of disease at Blackwater, VA on 4/11/1863.

2nd Mississippi Alphabetical Roster (Annotated)

Falkner, William C.
CO: F, S **Initial Rank:** Captain
Joined: Monday, March 4, 1861 **Term (yrs):** 1 **Occupation:** **Age** 35
Enrolled at: Ripley, MS **Enrolled By:** J. R. Chalmers **Promoted:** Yes **ROH:** No
Born: Virginia **Marital Status:** M **Residence**

Also see 7th Mississippi Cavalry Regiment. Appointed Colonel of the regiment on 5/10/1861. Slightly wounded at 1st Manassas on 7/21/1861. Lost in close election to Captain John M. Stone of Company K during regimental reorganization on 4/23/1862. Resigned as Colonel and went back to Mississippi to raise the 7th Mississippi Cavalry Regiment (Partisan Rangers) which see.

Fallon, Daniel
CO: G **Initial Rank:** Private
Joined: Wednesday, May 1, 1861 **Term (yrs):** 1 **Occupation:** Watchmaker **Age** 25
Enrolled at: Pontotoc Co., MS **Enrolled By:** Capt. Miller **Promoted:** No **ROH:** No
Born: **Marital Status:** S **Residence** Pontotoc, MS

Captured at South Mountain, MD on 8/15/1862 and refused to be exchanged (Federal document dated near Sharpsburg on 8/24/1862). Listed as "deserted to the enemy" on company rolls.

Faris, J. M. A.
CO: A **Initial Rank:** Private
Joined: Monday, September 30, 1861 **Term (yrs):** 1 **Occupation:** Farmer **Age** 35
Enrolled at: Iuka, MS **Enrolled By:** Lt. Davenport **Promoted:** No **ROH:** No
Born: Tennessee **Marital Status:** **Residence**

Discharged on 5/27/1862 for over age.

Faris, John P.
CO: A **Initial Rank:** Private
Joined: Monday, September 30, 1861 **Term (yrs):** 1 **Occupation:** Farmer **Age** 29
Enrolled at: Iuka, MS **Enrolled By:** Lt. Davenport **Promoted:** No **ROH:** No
Born: Kentucky **Marital Status:** M **Residence** Rienzi, MS

Detailed for light duty in Meridian, Mississippi by medical examining board on 12/15/1864.

2nd Mississippi Alphabetical Roster (Annotated)

Faris, Micajah

	CO: A	**Initial Rank:** Private
Joined: Saturday, March 1, 1862	**Term (yrs):** 3 **Occupation:** Farmer	**Age** 16
Enrolled at: Jacinto, MS	**Enrolled By:** Lt. Clayton	**Promoted:** No **ROH:** Yes
Born: Mississippi	**Marital Status:** S	**Residence** Burnsville, MS

Listed as AWOL since 12/31/1864. Appears on a Federal roll of prisoners of war at Nashville, TN dated 5/27/1865. Captured near Burnsville, MS on 4/13/1865. Taken to prison in Louisville, KY. Released on oath at Nashville on 6/16/1865. ROH for Gettysburg, 7/1/1863.

Farmer, James F.

	CO: K	**Initial Rank:** Private
Joined: Saturday, March 1, 1862	**Term (yrs):** 3 **Occupation:**	**Age** 22
Enrolled at: Iuka, MS	**Enrolled By:** Lt. Latham	**Promoted:** Yes **ROH:** No
Born:	**Marital Status:**	**Residence**

Appointed 2nd Corporal on 8/1/1862. Listed on a Federal register of refugees and rebel deserters on 3/29/1865. Other records show he was received into Federal custody on 3/22/1865. Deserted to the enemy.

Fears, Andrew J.

	CO: H	**Initial Rank:** Private
Joined: Monday, April 29, 1861	**Term (yrs):** 1 **Occupation:** Farmer	**Age** 24
Enrolled at: Pontotoc Co., MS	**Enrolled By:** Capt. Taylor	**Promoted:** No **ROH:** No
Born: Alabama	**Marital Status:** S	**Residence** Tupelo, MS

Wounded (gunshot wound, right leg) and captured at Gettysburg on 7/1/1863. Died at Point Lookout, MD on 1/8/1864 of complications from wound.

Fears, John C.

	CO: H	**Initial Rank:** Private
Joined: Monday, April 29, 1861	**Term (yrs):** 1 **Occupation:** Farmer	**Age** 23
Enrolled at: Pontotoc Co., MS	**Enrolled By:** Capt. Taylor	**Promoted:** Yes **ROH:** No
Born: Alabama	**Marital Status:** S	**Residence** Chesterville, MS

Also see Co. F of the 11th Mississippi Cavalry Regiment Consolidated. Elected Jr. 2nd Lieutenant. on 4/23/1862. Wounded at Sharpsburg on 9/17/1862. Promoted to 1st Lieutenant. on 12/28/1863. Commission expired on 7/1/1864 — "resigned for promotion in the West." Company records list him as AWOL since 1/25/1864 and dropped him from the rolls by order of the Secretary of War dated 5/2/1864.

2nd Mississippi Alphabetical Roster (Annotated)

Ferguson, Calvin   CO: A   Initial Rank: Private
Joined: Wednesday, May 1, 1861   **Term (yrs):** 1   **Occupation:** Farmer   **Age** 25
Enrolled at: Corinth, MS   **Enrolled By:** Capt. Boone   **Promoted:** No   **ROH:** No
Born: Tennessee   **Marital Status:** S   **Residence** Burnsville, MS

Killed at Gaines Mill on 6/27/1862.

Ferguson, Willoby   CO: K   Initial Rank: Private
Joined: Wednesday, May 1, 1861   **Term (yrs):** 1   **Occupation:** Farmer   **Age** 20
Enrolled at: Tishomingo Co., MS   **Enrolled By:** Capt. Leeth   **Promoted:** No   **ROH:** No
Born: Mississippi   **Marital Status:**   **Residence**

Discharged at Camp Fisher, VA on 10/10/1861 for disability.

Ferrell, Alphonso T.   CO: D   Initial Rank: 4th Sergeant
Joined: Wednesday, May 1, 1861   **Term (yrs):** 1   **Occupation:** Farmer   **Age** 22
Enrolled at: Tippah Co., MS   **Enrolled By:** Capt. Beck   **Promoted:** No   **ROH:** No
Born: Mississippi   **Marital Status:** S   **Residence** Snow Creek, MS

Reduced to ranks on reorganization of the company on 4/22/1862. Killed in battle at Gaines Mill on 6/27/1862.

Fetting, Albert S.   CO: K   Initial Rank: Private
Joined: Wednesday, May 1, 1861   **Term (yrs):** 1   **Occupation:** Tinner   **Age** 18
Enrolled at: Tishomingo Co., MS   **Enrolled By:** Capt. Stone   **Promoted:** Yes   **ROH:** No
Born: **Marital Status:**   **Residence**

Appointed 4th Corporal on 4/30/1862. Wounded and captured by Federal cavalry at Falling Waters, MD on 7/14/1863. Sent to Point Lookout, MD. Released on oath of allegiance on 1/12/1864.

Fewel, Granderson T.   CO: B   Initial Rank: Private
Joined: Wednesday, May 1, 1861   **Term (yrs):** 1   **Occupation:** Engineer   **Age** 21
Enrolled at: Tippah Co., MS   **Enrolled By:** Capt. Buchanan   **Promoted:** No   **ROH:** No
Born: **Marital Status:**   **Residence**

Wounded on 6/27/1862 at Gaines Mill. Captured at Gettysburg on 7/1/1863. Sent to Fort Delaware. Released on oath on 6/11/1865.

2nd Mississippi Alphabetical Roster (Annotated)

Fife, Samuel T.
CO: E *Initial Rank:* Private
Joined: Tuesday, September 16, 1862 *Term (yrs):* 3 *Occupation:* *Age* 18
Enrolled at: Saltillo, MS *Enrolled By:* Lt. Burns *Promoted:* No *ROH:* Yes
Born: *Marital Status:* S *Residence* Saltillo, MS

Captured at Hatcher's Run on 4/2/1865. Taken to Point Lookout, MD. Released on oath on 6/26/1865. ROH for Weldon Railroad, 8/19/1864.

Finnerson, John
CO: D *Initial Rank:* Private
Joined: Wednesday, May 1, 1861 *Term (yrs):* 1 *Occupation:* Farmer *Age* 39
Enrolled at: Tippah Co., MS *Enrolled By:* Capt. Beck *Promoted:* No *ROH:* No
Born: North Carolina *Marital Status:* M *Residence* Pine Grove, MS

Died of disease on 6/27/1861 at Winchester, VA.

Fisher, James S.
CO: E *Initial Rank:* Private
Joined: Saturday, March 1, 1862 *Term (yrs):* 3 *Occupation:* Farmer *Age* 16
Enrolled at: Guntown, MS *Enrolled By:* Capt. Bates *Promoted:* No *ROH:* No
Born: Mississippi *Marital Status:* *Residence*

Discharged on 10/23/1862 for disability — underage

Fisher, Newton Jasper
CO: E *Initial Rank:* Private
Joined: Saturday, March 1, 1862 *Term (yrs):* 3 *Occupation:* Farmer *Age* 19
Enrolled at: Guntown, MS *Enrolled By:* Capt. Bates *Promoted:* No *ROH:* No
Born: Mississippi *Marital Status:* S *Residence* Saltillo, MS

Killed in battle on 7/1/1863 at Gettysburg.

Fisher, William B.
CO: E *Initial Rank:* Private
Joined: Saturday, March 1, 1862 *Term (yrs):* 3 *Occupation:* Laborer *Age* 20
Enrolled at: Guntown, MS *Enrolled By:* Capt. Bates *Promoted:* No *ROH:* No
Born: Alabama *Marital Status:* S *Residence* Saltillo, MS

Died of disease at Richmond, VA on 8/17/1862.

2nd Mississippi Alphabetical Roster (Annotated)

Flake, Martin V. B.
CO: A *Initial Rank:* Private
Joined: Wednesday, May 1, 1861 *Term (yrs):* 1 *Occupation:* Farmer *Age* 22
Enrolled at: Tishomingo Co., MS *Enrolled By:* Capt. Leeth *Promoted:* No *ROH:* No
Born: Mississippi *Marital Status:* S *Residence*
Discharged on 12/25/1861 due to disability.

Flanagan, Edward H.
CO: E *Initial Rank:* Private
Joined: Saturday, March 1, 1862 *Term (yrs):* 3 *Occupation:* Farmer *Age* 40
Enrolled at: Guntown, MS *Enrolled By:* Capt. Bates *Promoted:* No *ROH:* No
Born: Tennessee *Marital Status:* M *Residence*
Hospital records show admission for a wound at Richmond on 7/9/1863 (company records do not provide details on date of wound or engagement). Died of disease at Richmond on 9/22/1863 (also listed as 9/20/1863). [*Buried at Hollywood Cemetery, Richmond, VA. Soldiers Section T Lot:438. Note says he died on 9/19/1863.]

Flanagan, John J.
CO: E *Initial Rank:* Private
Joined: Saturday, March 1, 1862 *Term (yrs):* 3 *Occupation:* Farmer *Age* 17
Enrolled at: Guntown, MS *Enrolled By:* Capt. Bates *Promoted:* No *ROH:* No
Born: Tennessee *Marital Status:* S *Residence* Saltillo, MS
Captured at Gettysburg on 7/1/1863. Taken to Fort Delaware. Released on oath on 6/11/1865.

Flanagan, Michael C.
CO: E *Initial Rank:* Private
Joined: Wednesday, May 1, 1861 *Term (yrs):* 1 *Occupation:* Laborer *Age* 32
Enrolled at: Itawamba Co., MS *Enrolled By:* Capt. Booth *Promoted:* No *ROH:* No
Born: Ireland *Marital Status:* S *Residence* Guntown, MS
Deserted on 12/20/1862.

Fleming, Andrew F.
CO: B *Initial Rank:* Private
Joined: Wednesday, May 1, 1861 *Term (yrs):* 1 *Occupation:* Clerk *Age* 20
Enrolled at: Tippah Co., MS *Enrolled By:* Capt. Buchanan *Promoted:* No *ROH:* No
Born: Virginia *Marital Status:* *Residence*
Discharged for disability on 6/25/1861 at Winchester, VA.

2nd Mississippi Alphabetical Roster (Annotated)

Flinn, Jesse H.
Joined: Saturday, March 15, 1862 **Term (yrs):** 3 **Occupation:**   **CO:** C **Initial Rank:** Private **Age**
Enrolled at: Richmond, MS **Enrolled By:** Lt. Pounds **Promoted:** No **ROH:** No
Born: **Marital Status:** **Residence**

Wounded at Gaines Mill on 6/27/1862. Furloughed. Returned to duty. Admitted to hospital at Charlottesville, VA for wound on 7/12/1863 (company records do not provide date of wound or engagement). Listed as AWOL from 2/1/1864. "Deserted and at home" remarks on Nov/Dec 1864 muster roll.

Flinn, John C.
Joined: Wednesday, May 1, 1861 **Term (yrs):** 1 **Occupation:** Farmer **CO:** C **Initial Rank:** Private **Age** 20
Enrolled at: Itawamba Co., MS **Enrolled By:** Capt. Bromley **Promoted:** No **ROH:** Yes
Born: **Marital Status:** **Residence**

Wounded at Sharpsburg on 9/17/1862. Furloughed. Returned to duty. Wounded on 6/2/1864. Sent to hospital. Furloughed 40-days from 7/19/1864. Listed as AWOL since 8/26/1864, however, other records indicate he was assigned to the Medical College Hospital as a Lieutenant. in the Reserve Force of Mississippi. ROH for The Wilderness, 5/5/1864.

Flowers, Benjamin
Joined: Wednesday, May 1, 1861 **Term (yrs):** 1 **Occupation:** Farmer **CO:** D **Initial Rank:** Private **Age** 39
Enrolled at: Tippah Co., MS **Enrolled By:** Capt. Beck **Promoted:** No **ROH:** No
Born: North Carolina **Marital Status:** M **Residence**

Discharged on 7/27/1862 due to over age.

Floyd, Philip G.
Joined: Tuesday, March 11, 1862 **Term (yrs):** 3 **Occupation:**   **CO:** E **Initial Rank:** Private **Age** 17
Enrolled at: Guntown, MS **Enrolled By:** Capt. Bates **Promoted:** No **ROH:** No
Born: **Marital Status:** S **Residence** Guntown, MS

Died of disease at Guntown, MS on 9/25/1862.

Fontaine, Charles D.
Joined: Wednesday, May 1, 1861 **Term (yrs):** 1 **Occupation:** Lawyer **CO:** G **Initial Rank:** 2nd Lieutenant **Age** 46
Enrolled at: Pontotoc Co., MS **Enrolled By:** Capt. Kilpatrick **Promoted:** No **ROH:** No
Born: Virginia **Marital Status:** M **Residence** Pontotoc, MS

Resigned on 10/22/1861.

2nd Mississippi Alphabetical Roster (Annotated)

Fontaine, Charles D., Jr.
CO: G *Initial Rank:* Private
Joined: Wednesday, May 1, 1861 *Term (yrs):* 1 *Occupation:* Student *Age* 16
Enrolled at: Pontotoc Co., MS *Enrolled By:* Capt. Miller *Promoted:* No *ROH:* No
Born: Mississippi *Marital Status:* S *Residence* Pontotoc, MS

Discharged for disability (underage?) on 6/20/1861.

Foote, William H., Jr.
CO: F *Initial Rank:* 3rd Corporal
Joined: Wednesday, May 1, 1861 *Term (yrs):* 1 *Occupation:* Planter *Age* 20
Enrolled at: Tippah Co., MS *Enrolled By:* Capt. Davis *Promoted:* No *ROH:* No
Born: Mississippi *Marital Status:* *Residence*

Wounded at Gaines Mill on 6/27/1862 (arm amputated). On "unlimited" furlough. Discharged on 12/15/1863 due to disability due to wounds.

Ford, Charles A. H.
CO: F *Initial Rank:* Private
Joined: Wednesday, May 1, 1861 *Term (yrs):* 1 *Occupation:* Planter *Age* 24
Enrolled at: Tippah Co., MS *Enrolled By:* Capt. Davis *Promoted:* No *ROH:* No
Born: *Marital Status:* *Residence*

Died of disease at Camp Fisher, VA on 12/21/1861.

Ford, Francis M.
CO: E *Initial Rank:* Private
Joined: Tuesday, March 18, 1862 *Term (yrs):* 3 *Occupation:* Blacksmith *Age* 31
Enrolled at: Guntown, MS *Enrolled By:* Capt. Bates *Promoted:* No *ROH:* No
Born: *Marital Status:* M *Residence* Tupelo, MS

Served on detached service as brigade blacksmith from November 1862. Paroled at Appomattox Court House on 4/9/1865.

Ford, John P.
CO: G *Initial Rank:* Private
Joined: *Term (yrs):* 0 *Occupation:* *Age*
Enrolled at: *Enrolled By:* *Promoted:* No *ROH:* No
Born: *Marital Status:* *Residence*

Appears on Federal prisoner of war records as captured near Morris Hill, GA on 6/7/1864. Discharged: Terms: Rock Island, IL; When: 6/22/1864. Remarks, charges, &c: "Nashville, Tenn." No other records.

2nd Mississippi Alphabetical Roster (Annotated)

Ford, Newton
CO: E **Initial Rank:** Private
Joined: Wednesday, May 1, 1861 **Term (yrs):** 1 **Occupation:** Farmer **Age** 16
Enrolled at: Itawamba Co., MS **Enrolled By:** Capt. Booth **Promoted:** No **ROH:** No
Born: Mississippi **Marital Status:** S **Residence** Saltillo, MS

Discharged on 7/23/1862 under act of Congress (underage?).

Ford, Thomas
CO: F **Initial Rank:** 3rd Sergeant
Joined: Wednesday, May 1, 1861 **Term (yrs):** 1 **Occupation:** Planter **Age** 27
Enrolled at: Tippah Co., MS **Enrolled By:** Capt. Davis **Promoted:** Yes **ROH:** No
Born: **Marital Status:** **Residence**

Elected 1st Lieutenant. on 7/26/1861. Discharged on 4/25/1862 due to expiration of term of service.

Fore, Thomas
CO: H **Initial Rank:** Private
Joined: Saturday, March 1, 1862 **Term (yrs):** 3 **Occupation:** Laborer **Age** 23
Enrolled at: Chesterville, MS **Enrolled By:** Lt. Porter **Promoted:** No **ROH:** No
Born: Alabama **Marital Status:** S **Residence** Tupelo, MS

Received furlough in October 1862 and never returned — AWOL. Listed as deserted during May/Jun 1863 muster.

Forister, Alferd
CO: A **Initial Rank:** Private
Joined: **Term (yrs):** 0 **Occupation:** **Age**
Enrolled at: **Enrolled By:** **Promoted:** No **ROH:** No
Born: **Marital Status:** **Residence**

Appears on a Federal roll of prisoners of war paroled at Alton, IL to City Point, VA on 6/21/1863. Captured at Hernando, MS on 5/25/186?. Appears on a CSA hospital register, admitted on 6/29/1863 and furloughed for 40-days on 8/15/1863 from Richmond, VA. Also appears on a register of payments on descriptive lists (5/11/1863 - 6/30/1863). No other records.

Forsythe, James A. B.
CO: F **Initial Rank:** Private
Joined: Wednesday, May 1, 1861 **Term (yrs):** 1 **Occupation:** Farmer **Age** 22
Enrolled at: Tippah Co., MS **Enrolled By:** Capt. Davis **Promoted:** No **ROH:** No
Born: South Carolina **Marital Status:** **Residence**

Wounded (in arm) at Sharpsburg on 9/17/1862. Furloughed 30-days from 10/10/1862. Returned to duty. Killed at Gettysburg on 7/1/1863.

2nd Mississippi Alphabetical Roster (Annotated)

Fortenbury, Greenlief L.
CO: L, F **Initial Rank:** Private
Joined: Monday, March 3, 1862 **Term (yrs):** 3 **Occupation:** Farmer **Age** 18
Enrolled at: Ripley, MS **Enrolled By:** Col. Falkner **Promoted:** No **ROH:** No
Born: Tennessee **Marital Status:** **Residence**

Transferred to Company F from Company L on 4/30/1862. Captured at Petersburg (Hatcher's Run?) on 4/2/1865. Sent to Fort Delaware. Released on oath on 6/11/1865.

Fowler, Robert T.
CO: A **Initial Rank:** Private
Joined: Saturday, March 1, 1862 **Term (yrs):** 3 **Occupation:** Student **Age** 18
Enrolled at: Jacinto, MS **Enrolled By:** Lt. Clayton **Promoted:** No **ROH:** No
Born: Mississippi **Marital Status:** S **Residence** Kossuth, MS

Also see 26th Mississippi Infantry Regiment. Wounded at Gettysburg on 7/3/1863. Transferred to Co. B of the 26th Mississippi Infantry Regiment by order of General Davis to take effect on 5/1/1864.

Fowler, S. K.
CO: F **Initial Rank:** Sergeant
Joined: **Term (yrs):** 0 **Occupation:** **Age**
Enrolled at: **Enrolled By:** **Promoted:** No **ROH:** No
Born: **Marital Status:** **Residence** Charlottesville, VA

Appears on a roll of prisoners of war paroled, dated Meridian, MS on 5/13/1865. No other record.

Fox, Alexander
CO: K **Initial Rank:** Private
Joined: Wednesday, May 1, 1861 **Term (yrs):** 1 **Occupation:** Laborer **Age** 20
Enrolled at: Tishomingo Co., MS **Enrolled By:** Capt. Stone **Promoted:** No **ROH:** No
Born: **Marital Status:** **Residence**

Wounded (hand and shoulder) at battle of Gaines Mill on 6/27/1862. Listed as deserted from picket post at Harrison Ford in March. Date not known.

Foy, William T.
CO: K **Initial Rank:** Private
Joined: Wednesday, May 1, 1861 **Term (yrs):** 1 **Occupation:** Clerk **Age** 19
Enrolled at: Tishomingo Co., MS **Enrolled By:** Capt. Stone **Promoted:** No **ROH:** No
Born: **Marital Status:** S **Residence**

Killed at 1st Manassas on 7/21/1861.

2nd Mississippi Alphabetical Roster (Annotated)

Fraley, Benjamin F.   CO: K   Initial Rank: Private
Joined: Wednesday, May 1, 1861   **Term (yrs):** 1   **Occupation:** Plasterer   **Age** 20
Enrolled at: Tishomingo Co., MS   **Enrolled By:** Capt. Stone   **Promoted:** No   **ROH:** No
Born: **Marital Status:**   **Residence**

Wounded at Sharpsburg on 9/17/1862. Furloughed. Returned to duty and deserted to the enemy from the picket line on 5/5/186?. Name appears on a Federal oath of amnesty dated City Point, VA on 1/8/1865. Transportation furnished to Indianapolis, IN.

Francis, James O.   CO: C   Initial Rank: Private
Joined: Tuesday, October 1, 1861   **Term (yrs):** 1   **Occupation:**   **Age**
Enrolled at: Richmond, MS   **Enrolled By:** Lt. Davenport   **Promoted:** No   **ROH:** No
Born: Mississippi   **Marital Status:**   **Residence**

Died of disease in Ashland, VA on 4/17/1862.

Franklin, Thomas M.   CO: C   Initial Rank: Private
Joined: Wednesday, May 1, 1861   **Term (yrs):** 1   **Occupation:** Carpenter   **Age** 26
Enrolled at: Itawamba Co., MS   **Enrolled By:** Capt. Bromley   **Promoted:** No   **ROH:** No
Born: **Marital Status:** M   **Residence**

According to company records, deserted. Date not given, but circa Mar/Apr 1863. However, affidavit filed by wife claims he died on 10/6/1862 while on furlough.

Frazier, Alexander   CO: E   Initial Rank: Private
Joined: Tuesday, April 30, 1861   **Term (yrs):** 1   **Occupation:** Carpenter   **Age** 28
Enrolled at: Guntown, MS   **Enrolled By:** Capt. Booth   **Promoted:** No   **ROH:** No
Born: Scotland   **Marital Status:** S   **Residence** Guntown, MS

Wounded at Gaines Mill on 6/27/1862. Discharged by Special Order; reason — "Never acquired a domicile." Discharged on 7/29/1862.

Frazier, J. W. B.   CO: Initial Rank:
Joined: **Term (yrs):** 0   **Occupation:**   **Age**
Enrolled at: **Enrolled By:**   **Promoted:** No   **ROH:** No
Born: **Marital Status:**   **Residence**

Also see Wise's Virginia Artillery. No other record.

2nd Mississippi Alphabetical Roster (Annotated)

Frazier, James S.   *CO:* C, F   *Initial Rank:* Private
Joined: *Term (yrs):* 0   *Occupation:*   *Age*
Enrolled at: *Enrolled By:*   *Promoted:* No   *ROH:* No
Born: *Marital Status:*   *Residence*

Appears on several Federal prisoner of war documents, listing his company variously as C or F. Captured near Clifton, TN on 7/7/1864. Sent to prison at Louisville, KY. Sent to Camp Chase, OH on 8/5/1864. Died of disease at Camp Chase on 1/9/1865 (also listed as 12/9/1864). Grave #724, 1/3-mile south of Camp Chase. No other records.

Frazier, Samuel W.   *CO:* F   *Initial Rank:* Private
Joined: Wednesday, May 1, 1861   *Term (yrs):* 1   *Occupation:* Planter   *Age* 26
Enrolled at: Tippah Co., MS   *Enrolled By:* Capt. Davis   *Promoted:* No   *ROH:* No
Born: Tennessee   *Marital Status:*   *Residence*

Wounded at Gettysburg on 7/3/1863. Furloughed 60-days from 9/12/1863. Discharged on 1/9/1864 due to disability from wounds.

Freeman, John L.   *CO:* I   *Initial Rank:* Private
Joined: Wednesday, May 1, 1861   *Term (yrs):* 1   *Occupation:* Farmer   *Age* 18
Enrolled at: Pontotoc Co., MS   *Enrolled By:* Capt. Herring   *Promoted:* No   *ROH:* Yes
Born: *Marital Status:*   *Residence*

On detached duty with the Pioneer Corps on 6/8/1863. Wounded at the battle of The Wilderness on 5/5/1864. Sent to hospital at Lynchburg, VA. Admitted to hospital again on 2/12/1865 with gunshot wound to left forearm (date of wound or engagement not given in company records). Furloughed from the hospital at Danville, VA on 4/9/1865 for 60-days. ROH for The Wilderness, 5/5/1864.

Freeman, William   *CO:* I   *Initial Rank:* Private
Joined: Friday, May 31, 1861   *Term (yrs):* 1   *Occupation:* Farmer   *Age* 26
Enrolled at: Harpers Ferry, VA   *Enrolled By:* Capt. Herring   *Promoted:* Yes   *ROH:* No
Born: *Marital Status:*   *Residence*

Detailed with Infirmary Corps for May/June and July/Aug 1862 musters. Wounded and captured at Gettysburg on 7/3/1863. Died at Federal hospital near Gettysburg on 7/20/1863 as a result of wounds (Other records cite 8/1/1863 as the date of death). [*Buried at Hollywood Cemetery, Richmond, VA. Gettysburg Section Lot: 1. Note says he died on 7/20/1863.]

2nd Mississippi Alphabetical Roster (Annotated)

Freeman, William D.

CO: H **Initial Rank:** Private

Joined: Monday, April 29, 1861   **Term (yrs):** 1 **Occupation:** Tailor   **Age** 23

Enrolled at: Pontotoc Co., MS   **Enrolled By:** Capt. Taylor   **Promoted:** No **ROH:** No

Born: Alabama   **Marital Status:** S   **Residence** Tupelo, MS

Discharged due to disability at Camp Fisher, VA on 9/16/1861.

Freeman, Wyatt B.

CO: K **Initial Rank:** Private

Joined: Tuesday, November 19, 1861   **Term (yrs):** 1 **Occupation:**   **Age**

Enrolled at: Camp Fisher, VA   **Enrolled By:** Capt. Stone   **Promoted:** No **ROH:** No

Born: **Marital Status:**   **Residence**

No record after 11/1862.

Fretwell, Joseph Y.

CO: H **Initial Rank:** Private

Joined: Monday, April 29, 1861   **Term (yrs):** 1 **Occupation:** Farmer   **Age** 22

Enrolled at: Pontotoc Co., MS   **Enrolled By:** Capt. Taylor   **Promoted:** No **ROH:** No

Born: **Marital Status:** S   **Residence** Tupelo, MS

Furloughed about 8/10/1862. Listed as AWOL since about 10/1/1862. However Federal records indicate he was captured while on furlough near Verona, MS on 5/2/1863 and sent to Alton, IL. No further record.

Frierson, Boston L.

CO: H **Initial Rank:** 4th Sergeant

Joined: Monday, April 29, 1861   **Term (yrs):** 1 **Occupation:** Farmer   **Age** 37

Enrolled at: Pontotoc Co., MS   **Enrolled By:** Capt. Taylor   **Promoted:** Yes **ROH:** No

Born: Tennessee   **Marital Status:** M   **Residence** Chesterville, MS

Appointed 1st Sergeant on 5/24/1861. Promoted to Jr. 2nd Lieutenant. in Feb 1862. Relieved of duty on 4/23/1862 due to reorganization of company. Discharged.

2nd Mississippi Alphabetical Roster (Annotated)

Frierson, M. W.
Joined: *Term (yrs):* 0   *Occupation:*   *Age*
CO: S   *Initial Rank:* Chaplain
Enrolled at: *Enrolled By:*   *Promoted:* No   *ROH:* No
Born: *Marital Status:*   *Residence*

Also see 32nd Mississippi Infantry Regiment. Made Chaplain of the 2nd Mississippi when transferred from the 32nd Mississippi on 6/4/1863. According to Federal prisoner of war records, he was captured near Greencastle, PA on 7/5/1863 following the battle of Gettysburg. He was taken to Fort Delaware and sent to Baltimore, MD on 10/10/1863. He must have been released at some point because the last Confederate record shows him deceased at Meridian, MS in hospital on 1/26/1864 (or 1/27/1864). Cause not given. No other records.

Frierson, Thomas S. W.
CO: A   *Initial Rank:* Private
Joined: Wednesday, May 1, 1861   *Term (yrs):* 1   *Occupation:* Teacher   *Age* 22
Enrolled at: Tishomingo Co., MS   *Enrolled By:* Capt. Leeth   *Promoted:* No   *ROH:* No
Born: Alabama   *Marital Status:* S   *Residence* Jacinto, MS

Wounded at 2nd Manassas on 8/29/1862. In hospital at Warrenton and furloughed in 12/1862. Died on 12/8/1864 as a result of wounds at 2nd Manassas.

Frierson, William V., Jr.
CO: A   *Initial Rank:* Private
Joined: Wednesday, May 1, 1861   *Term (yrs):* 1   *Occupation:* Student   *Age* 20
Enrolled at: Tishomingo Co., MS   *Enrolled By:* Capt. Leeth   *Promoted:* Yes   *ROH:* No
Born: Alabama   *Marital Status:* S   *Residence* Jacinto, MS

Appointed 5th Sergeant on 10/13/1861. During Nov/Dec 1861 muster, listed as 4th Sergeant. Reduced to ranks on 4/22/1862 (reorganization?). Appointed 1st Sergeant on 3/21/1863. Wounded (left leg) and captured at Gettysburg on 7/1/1863. Paroled to City Point, VA on 11/17/1863 for exchange. Furloughed. Retired by medical examining board on 8/22/1864 due to wound received at Gettysburg.

Frost, Hezikiah J.
CO: H   *Initial Rank:* Private
Joined: Monday, April 29, 1861   *Term (yrs):* 1   *Occupation:* Farmer   *Age* 19
Enrolled at: Pontotoc Co., MS   *Enrolled By:* Capt. Taylor   *Promoted:* No   *ROH:* No
Born: Alabama   *Marital Status:* S   *Residence* Tupelo, MS

Wounded at 2nd Manassas on 8/29/1862. Returned to duty. Killed in battle at Gettysburg on 7/1/1863.

2nd Mississippi Alphabetical Roster (Annotated)

Fryar, Isaac

CO: B, L **Initial Rank:** Private
Joined: Wednesday, May 1, 1861 **Term (yrs):** 1 **Occupation:** Farmer **Age** 20
Enrolled at: Tippah Co., MS **Enrolled By:** Capt. Buchanan **Promoted:** No **ROH:** No
Born: Mississippi **Marital Status:** S **Residence** Ripley, MS

Transferred to Company L from Company B on 4/30/1862. Captured near Williamsport on 9/14/1862. Paroled and exchanged on 10/6/1862 and 11/10/1862, respectively, at Aiken's Landing, VA. Furloughed home in Aug, 1863. AWOL. Never reported back to his command. Deserted per Jul/Aug 1864 muster.

Fryar, John W.

CO: B, L **Initial Rank:** Private
Joined: Wednesday, May 1, 1861 **Term (yrs):** 1 **Occupation:** Farmer (Student) **Age** 18
Enrolled at: Tippah Co., MS **Enrolled By:** Capt. Buchanan **Promoted:** Yes **ROH:** No
Born: Mississippi **Marital Status:** S **Residence** Ripley, MS

Transferred to Company L from Company B on 4/30/1862. Promoted to 5th Sergeant on 3/1/1863. Captured at Gettysburg on 7/1/1863. Taken to Fort Delaware. Died of disease at Fort Delaware on 10/30/1863 (other records give 10/31/1863 as the date of death).

Fryar, Thomas J.

CO: F, L **Initial Rank:** Private
Joined: Saturday, March 1, 1862 **Term (yrs):** 3 **Occupation:** Farmer **Age** 19
Enrolled at: Ripley, MS **Enrolled By:** Capt. Powers **Promoted:** Yes **ROH:** No
Born: Mississippi **Marital Status:** S **Residence** Ripley, MS

Also see 23rd Mississippi Infantry Regiment. Transferred to Company L from Company F on 4/30/1862. Promoted to 4th Sergeant on 3/23/1862. Reduced to ranks on 10/1/1862. List of engagements shows him wounded on 5/10/1864 at Tally's Mill (no indication in company records). Captured at Hatcher's Run on 4/2/1865. Taken to Point Lookout, MD. Released on oath on 6/26/1865.

Fuller, J. V.

CO: C **Initial Rank:** Private
Joined: Saturday, March 1, 1862 **Term (yrs):** 3 **Occupation:** Farmer **Age** 26
Enrolled at: Verona, MS **Enrolled By:** Lt. Pounds **Promoted:** No **ROH:** No
Born: South Carolina **Marital Status:** M **Residence**

Furloughed for 30-days on 10/31/1862. Died in Mississippi of smallpox on 12/10/1862.

2nd Mississippi Alphabetical Roster (Annotated)

Fulton, Jeremiah
CO: D **Initial Rank:** Private
Joined: Wednesday, May 1, 1861 **Term (yrs):** 1 **Occupation:** Farmer **Age** 27
Enrolled at: Tippah Co., MS **Enrolled By:** Capt. Beck **Promoted:** No **ROH:** Yes
Born: Tennessee **Marital Status:** **Residence**

Wounded at 1st Manassas on 7/21/1861. Wounded at Gaines Mill on 6/27/1862. In hospital at Richmond. Returned to duty. Wounded at Gettysburg on 7/1/1863. Died at Martinsburg, VA on 7/25/1863 of wounds. ROH for Gettysburg, 7/1/1863.

Gailliard, William
CO: H **Initial Rank:** Private
Joined: Monday, April 29, 1861 **Term (yrs):** 1 **Occupation:** Gin Agent (Farmer) **Age** 35
Enrolled at: Pontotoc Co., MS **Enrolled By:** Capt. Taylor **Promoted:** No **ROH:** No
Born: South Carolina **Marital Status:** M **Residence** Chesterville, MS

Wounded (through the neck) at 1st Manassas on 7/21/1861. In hospital at University of Virginia. Died of wounds on 9/10/1861 at hospital in Charlottesville, VA.

Gaines, Robert A.
CO: H **Initial Rank:** Private
Joined: Monday, April 29, 1861 **Term (yrs):** 1 **Occupation:** Farmer **Age** 37
Enrolled at: Pontotoc Co., MS **Enrolled By:** Capt. Taylor **Promoted:** Yes **ROH:** No
Born: South Carolina **Marital Status:** S **Residence** Chesterville, MS

Appointed 4th Sergeant on 5/24/1861. Discharged on 7/29/1862 — over age. (List of engagements record card reports him wounded at 1st Manassas on 7/21/1861. Company muster rolls do not so indicate).

Gallagher, David L.
CO: A **Initial Rank:**
Joined: Wednesday, February 20, 1861 **Term (yrs):** 1 **Occupation:** **Age**
Enrolled at: Corinth, MS **Enrolled By:** R. Griffith **Promoted:** No **ROH:** No
Born: **Marital Status:** **Residence**

Appears on a company muster roll for state service. No other record.

Gallagher, William
CO: A **Initial Rank:** Private
Joined: Saturday, March 1, 1862 **Term (yrs):** 3 **Occupation:** Farmer **Age** 28
Enrolled at: Jacinto, MS **Enrolled By:** Lt. Clayton **Promoted:** No **ROH:** No
Born: Mississippi **Marital Status:** **Residence** Jacinto, MS

Discharged on 10/4/1862 due to disability.

2nd Mississippi Alphabetical Roster (Annotated)

Gallimore, William S.
CO: K **Initial Rank:** Private
Joined: Wednesday, May 1, 1861 **Term (yrs):** 1 **Occupation:** Farmer **Age** 21
Enrolled at: Tishomingo Co., MS **Enrolled By:** Capt. Stone **Promoted:** No **ROH:** No
Born: North Carolina **Marital Status:** **Residence**

Died of disease on 6/15/1864 at Whites Tavern, VA.

Gallion, John M.
CO: A **Initial Rank:** Private
Joined: Wednesday, May 1, 1861 **Term (yrs):** 1 **Occupation:** Farmer **Age** 26
Enrolled at: Tishomingo Co., MS **Enrolled By:** Capt. Leeth **Promoted:** No **ROH:** No
Born: **Marital Status:** S **Residence** Burnsville, MS

Wounded at 2nd Manassas on 8/29/1862. Sent to hospital at Staunton, VA. Furloughed. Listed as deserted on Mar/Apr 1863 muster "Obtained furlough about 20 Nov 1862 — has not since returned to the Regiment." However, another record shows he took the oath of allegiance at Fort Delaware on 6/11/1865, [implying he was probably captured while on furlough in Mississippi.]

Gambrell, Ira D.
CO: I **Initial Rank:** 2nd Sergeant
Joined: Wednesday, May 1, 1861 **Term (yrs):** 1 **Occupation:** Farmer **Age** 21
Enrolled at: Pontotoc Co., MS **Enrolled By:** Capt. Herring **Promoted:** Yes **ROH:** No
Born: **Marital Status:** **Residence**

Promoted to 1st Sergeant on 4/23/1862. Wounded at Sharpsburg on 9/17/1862. Furloughed. Appointed Jr. 2nd Lieutenant. on 12/18/1862. Killed at Suffolk while on scout detail on 5/9/1863.

Gambrell, James B.
CO: I **Initial Rank:** Private
Joined: Wednesday, May 1, 1861 **Term (yrs):** 1 **Occupation:** Farmer **Age** 19
Enrolled at: Pontotoc Co., MS **Enrolled By:** Capt. Herring **Promoted:** Yes **ROH:** No
Born: **Marital Status:** **Residence**

Appointed 4th Corporal on 6/1/1861. Promoted 3rd Corporal on 7/4/1861. Promoted to 2nd Corporal circa Nov/Dec 1861. Promoted to 4th Sergeant on 4/23/1862. Admitted to hospital in Richmond for treatment of a wound on 9/27/1862 (company records provide no details on date of wound or engagement). Promoted to 3rd Sergeant on 5/16/1863. Promoted to 1st Lieutenant. "to raise a Co. of Scouts (cavalry) in Miss by order of Secretary of War 8/18/1863."

2nd Mississippi Alphabetical Roster (Annotated)

Ganong, Charles H.
CO: K **Initial Rank:** Private
Joined: Wednesday, May 1, 1861 **Term (yrs):** 1 **Occupation:** Painter **Age** 18
Enrolled at: Tishomingo Co., MS **Enrolled By:** Capt. Stone **Promoted:** No **ROH:** No
Born: **Marital Status:** **Residence**

Furloughed in March 1863. AWOL. Listed as deserted on 4/18/1863.

Garner, James P.
CO: I **Initial Rank:** Private
Joined: Wednesday, May 1, 1861 **Term (yrs):** 1 **Occupation:** Shoemaker **Age** 28
Enrolled at: Pontotoc Co., MS **Enrolled By:** Capt. Herring **Promoted:** No **ROH:** No
Born: South Carolina **Marital Status:** **Residence**

Discharged for disability at Camp Fisher, VA on 11/30/1861.

Garner, John
CO: D **Initial Rank:** Private
Joined: Saturday, March 9, 1861 **Term (yrs):** 1 **Occupation:** **Age**
Enrolled at: Toombs Store, MS **Enrolled By:** John M. McGuirk **Promoted:** No **ROH:** No
Born: **Marital Status:** **Residence**

Appears on a company muster roll for state service. No other record.

Garret, William A.
CO: L **Initial Rank:** 5th Sergeant
Joined: Monday, March 3, 1862 **Term (yrs):** 3 **Occupation:** Farmer **Age** 19
Enrolled at: Ripley, MS **Enrolled By:** Col. Falkner **Promoted:** Yes **ROH:** No
Born: Mississippi **Marital Status:** S **Residence**

Promoted to 5th Sergeant on 3/23/1862. Discharged on 6/27/1862 due to disability.

Gary, James T.
CO: K **Initial Rank:** Private
Joined: Saturday, March 1, 1862 **Term (yrs):** 3 **Occupation:** Farmer **Age** 20
Enrolled at: Iuka, MS **Enrolled By:** Lt. Latham **Promoted:** No **ROH:** No
Born: Alabama **Marital Status:** **Residence**

Killed in battle at Seven Pines on 5/31/1862 (other records list his death at 5/29/1862).

2nd Mississippi Alphabetical Roster (Annotated)

Gelison, A. H.
CO: A **Initial Rank:** Sergeant
Joined: **Term (yrs):** 0 **Occupation:** **Age**
Enrolled at: **Enrolled By:** **Promoted:** No **ROH:** No
Born: **Marital Status:** **Residence**

Appears on a Federal record of prisoners of war at Fort McHenry, MD. Captured at Gettysburg on 7/4/1863. Sent to Fort Delaware. No other record.

Gentry, L. A.
CO: C **Initial Rank:** Private
Joined: Saturday, March 1, 1862 **Term (yrs):** 3 **Occupation:** **Age**
Enrolled at: Verona, MS **Enrolled By:** Lt. Pounds **Promoted:** No **ROH:** No
Born: **Marital Status:** **Residence**

Appears on a muster-in roll. No other record.

George, Charles
CO: K **Initial Rank:** Private
Joined: Saturday, March 1, 1862 **Term (yrs):** 3 **Occupation:** Farmer **Age** 35
Enrolled at: Iuka, MS **Enrolled By:** Lt. Latham **Promoted:** No **ROH:** No
Born: Tennessee **Marital Status:** **Residence**

Listed as "absent wounded" during May/June 1862 muster (company records provide no information as to date of wound or battle). Returned to duty. Wounded and left on the field at Sharpsburg on 9/17/1862. Died on 10/1/1862 from wounds at Frederick, MD.

George, Isaac N.
CO: K **Initial Rank:** 2nd Sergeant
Joined: Wednesday, May 1, 1861 **Term (yrs):** 1 **Occupation:** Merchant **Age** 24
Enrolled at: Tishomingo Co., MS **Enrolled By:** Capt. Stone **Promoted:** No **ROH:** No
Born: Tennessee **Marital Status:** **Residence**

Discharged on 2/1/1862 due to disability by order of Brig. Gen. Whiting.

Gholston, Agrippa C.
CO: H **Initial Rank:** Private
Joined: Monday, April 29, 1861 **Term (yrs):** 1 **Occupation:** Farmer **Age** 42
Enrolled at: Pontotoc Co., MS **Enrolled By:** Capt. Taylor **Promoted:** No **ROH:** No
Born: Georgia **Marital Status:** M **Residence** Chesterville, MS

Discharged on 8/19/1861 due to disability.

2nd Mississippi Alphabetical Roster (Annotated)

Gibbs, John
CO: E, A **Initial Rank:** Private
Joined: *Term (yrs):* 0 *Occupation:* *Age*
Enrolled at: *Enrolled By:* *Promoted:* No *ROH:* No
Born: *Marital Status:* *Residence*

Appears on several Federal prisoner of war records. Captured 5/25/1863. Location not given. Taken to Alton, IL. Exchanged on 6/12/1863. Listed as belonging to both Co. A and Co. E., 2nd Miss. No other records.

Gibson, Albert H.
CO: K **Initial Rank:** Private
Joined: Wednesday, May 1, 1861 *Term (yrs):* 1 *Occupation:* Farmer *Age* 18
Enrolled at: Tishomingo Co., MS *Enrolled By:* Capt. Stone *Promoted:* No *ROH:* No
Born: *Marital Status:* *Residence*

Wounded at Gaines Mill on 6/27/1862. Wounded and captured at Gettysburg on 7/1/1863. Sent to Fort Delaware. Released on oath on 6/11/1865.

Gibson, Calvin
CO: K **Initial Rank:** Private
Joined: Saturday, March 1, 1862 *Term (yrs):* 3 *Occupation:* Farmer *Age* 42
Enrolled at: Iuka, MS *Enrolled By:* Lt. Latham *Promoted:* No *ROH:* No
Born: Alabama *Marital Status:* *Residence*

Discharged on 7/15/1862 for disability.

Gibson, Jarrett W.
CO: K **Initial Rank:** Private
Joined: Wednesday, May 1, 1861 *Term (yrs):* 1 *Occupation:* Farmer *Age* 21
Enrolled at: Tishomingo Co., MS *Enrolled By:* Capt. Stone *Promoted:* No *ROH:* Yes
Born: Alabama *Marital Status:* *Residence*

Killed in action at Sharpsburg on 9/17/1862. ROH for Sharpsburg, 9/17/1862.

Gibson, William J.
CO: A **Initial Rank:** Private
Joined: Saturday, March 1, 1862 *Term (yrs):* 3 *Occupation:* Student *Age* 16
Enrolled at: Jacinto, MS *Enrolled By:* Lt. Clayton *Promoted:* Yes *ROH:* No
Born: Mississippi *Marital Status:* S *Residence* Rienzi, MS

Wounded (in left hip) at Gaines Mill on 6/27/1862. Furloughed in Sept. 1862 to Mississippi. Returned to duty by Nov/Dec 1863 muster. Promoted to 1st Corporal about Sep/Oct 1864. Captured at Petersburg (Hatcher's Run?) on 4/2/1865. Taken to Point Lookout, MD. Released on oath on 6/13/1865.

2nd Mississippi Alphabetical Roster (Annotated)

Gibson, William T.

CO: F **Initial Rank:** Private
Joined: Wednesday, May 1, 1861 **Term (yrs):** 1 **Occupation:** Planter **Age** 21
Enrolled at: Tippah Co., MS **Enrolled By:** Capt. Davis **Promoted:** No **ROH:** No
Born: **Marital Status:** **Residence**

Admitted to hospital at Richmond with wound on 7/9/1863 (company records do not indicate date of wound or engagement). Returned to duty on 8/11/1863. Furloughed sick to Mississippi for 60-days on 6/3/1864. Died of disease near Ripley, MS on 7/25/1864.

Gill, Samuel C.

CO: H, I **Initial Rank:** 2nd Corporal
Joined: Monday, April 29, 1861 **Term (yrs):** 1 **Occupation:** Merchant (Clerk) **Age** 29
Enrolled at: Pontotoc Co., MS **Enrolled By:** Capt. Taylor **Promoted:** Yes **ROH:** No
Born: Alabama **Marital Status:** S **Residence** Chesterville, MS

Listed as 2nd Sergeant during Mar/Apr 1862 muster roll. Transferred to Company I on 8/1/1862. No further record.

Gill, William M.

CO: H **Initial Rank:** Private
Joined: Saturday, March 15, 1862 **Term (yrs):** 3 **Occupation:** Farmer **Age** 23
Enrolled at: Chesterville, MS **Enrolled By:** Lt. Porter **Promoted:** No **ROH:** No
Born: Alabama **Marital Status:** S **Residence** Chesterville, MS

Also see 2nd (Harris') Battalion Mississippi Cavalry. Wounded at Gettysburg on 7/1/1863. In hospital at Lynchburg, VA. Furloughed to MS from 7/23/1863. AWOL since 2/25/1864. Listed as deserted in Mar/Apr, 1864 muster roll. [He apparently joined the above referenced cavalry unit while on furlough without a regular transfer from his unit.]

Gilley, James W.

CO: K **Initial Rank:** Private
Joined: Wednesday, May 1, 1861 **Term (yrs):** 1 **Occupation:** Farmer **Age** 19
Enrolled at: Tishomingo Co., MS **Enrolled By:** Capt. Stone **Promoted:** No **ROH:** No
Born: **Marital Status:** **Residence**

Died of disease at Winchester, VA on 8/8/1861.

2nd Mississippi Alphabetical Roster (Annotated)

Gillmore, William H.
CO: I **Initial Rank:** Private
Joined: Wednesday, May 1, 1861 **Term (yrs):** 1 **Occupation:** Farmer **Age** 25
Enrolled at: Pontotoc Co., MS **Enrolled By:** Capt. Herring **Promoted:** No **ROH:** No
Born: Alabama **Marital Status:** **Residence**

Admitted to hospital in Richmond on 11/30/1863 with wound to left hand (company records do not give details as to date of wound or engagement). Transferred to smallpox hospital on 1/21/1864. Died in hospital at Richmond, VA of smallpox on 2/10/1864.

Gilmer, James
CO: A **Initial Rank:** Private
Joined: Wednesday, May 1, 1861 **Term (yrs):** 1 **Occupation:** Farmer **Age** 20
Enrolled at: Tishomingo Co., MS **Enrolled By:** Capt. Leeth **Promoted:** No **ROH:** No
Born: Mississippi **Marital Status:** S **Residence** Jacinto, MS

Appears on Federal records as a prisoner of war captured at Glendale, MS on 4/18/1863. Sent to Alton, IL on 5/22/1863. Company records list him as deserted on 3/16/1863. No further record.

Gilmer, William
CO: A **Initial Rank:**
Joined: Wednesday, February 20, 1861 **Term (yrs):** 1 **Occupation:** **Age**
Enrolled at: Corinth, MS **Enrolled By:** R. Griffith **Promoted:** No **ROH:** No
Born: **Marital Status:** **Residence**

Appears on a company muster roll for state service. No other record.

Gilmore, Humphrey M.
CO: **Initial Rank:** Private
Joined: **Term (yrs):** 0 **Occupation:** **Age**
Enrolled at: **Enrolled By:** **Promoted:** No **ROH:** No
Born: **Marital Status:** **Residence**

Appears on a Federal roll of prisoners of war, dated St. Louis 6/27/1862. Captured at Corinth, MS on 6/1/1862. Prisoner of war. Sent to Alton, IL. Sent to Vicksburg, MS on 9/23/1862 for exchange at Aiken's Landing, VA on 11/11/1862. No other records.

2nd Mississippi Alphabetical Roster (Annotated)

Glenn, Joseph K.　　　　　　　　　　　CO: B　　Initial Rank: Private
Joined: Wednesday, May 1, 1861　　*Term (yrs):* 1　*Occupation:* Farmer　　　　　*Age* 18
Enrolled at: Tippah Co., MS　　*Enrolled By:* Capt. Buchanan　　*Promoted:* No　*ROH:* No
Born:　　　　　　*Marital Status:*　　　　　　*Residence*

Captured at the battle of Falling Waters on 7/14/1863. Sent to Point Lookout, MD. Transferred to Elmira, NY on 8/16/1864. Paroled and sent to James River for exchange on 3/10/1865.

Glidewell, John H.　　　　　　　　　　CO: B　　Initial Rank: Private
Joined: Monday, March 3, 1862　　*Term (yrs):* 3　*Occupation:* Farmer　　　　　*Age* 36
Enrolled at: Ripley, MS　　*Enrolled By:* Capt. Buchanan　　*Promoted:* No　*ROH:* No
Born: North Carolina　　*Marital Status:* M　　　　*Residence*

Discharged on 7/24/1862 for disability.

Glover, Francis M.　　　　　　　　　　CO: K　　Initial Rank: Private
Joined: Saturday, March 1, 1862　　*Term (yrs):* 3　*Occupation:* Farmer　　　　　*Age* 24
Enrolled at: Iuka, MS　　*Enrolled By:* Lt. Latham　　*Promoted:* No　*ROH:* No
Born: Tennessee　　*Marital Status:*　　　　*Residence*

Died on 12/5/1862 at Richmond, VA of disease (pneumonia). Date of death also given as 12/1/1862 in other records. [*Buried at Hollywood Cemetery, Richmond, VA. Soldiers Section Lot: Unknown.]

Golding, John H.　　　　　　　　　　CO: F　　Initial Rank: Private
Joined: Wednesday, May 1, 1861　　*Term (yrs):* 1　*Occupation:* Teacher　　　　　*Age* 39
Enrolled at: Tippah Co., MS　　*Enrolled By:* Capt. Davis　　*Promoted:* No　*ROH:* No
Born: Ireland　　*Marital Status:*　　　　*Residence*

Discharged on 7/31/1862 — over age.

Golding, Marcus L.　　　　　　　　　　CO: I　　Initial Rank: Private
Joined: Wednesday, May 1, 1861　　*Term (yrs):* 1　*Occupation:* Farmer　　　　　*Age* 19
Enrolled at: Pontotoc Co., MS　　*Enrolled By:* Capt. Herring　　*Promoted:* Yes　*ROH:* Yes
Born: South Carolina　　*Marital Status:*　　　　*Residence*

Listed as 4th Corporal during Mar/Apr 1862 muster roll. Promoted to 2nd Corporal on 4/23/1862. Killed in battle at Sharpsburg on 9/17/1862. ROH for Sharpsburg, 9/17/1862.

2nd Mississippi Alphabetical Roster (Annotated)

Golding, William S.
CO: I **Initial Rank:** Private
Joined: Tuesday, September 17, 1861 **Term (yrs):** 1 **Occupation:** Farmer **Age** 25
Enrolled at: Cherry Creek, MS **Enrolled By:** Lt. Davenport **Promoted:** No **ROH:** No
Born: South Carolina **Marital Status:** **Residence**

Wounded at 2nd Manassas on 8/29/1862. Died at Warrenton, VA on 9/21/1862 as a result of wounds.

Goldsmith, Samuel
CO: B **Initial Rank:** Private
Joined: Sunday, April 6, 1862 **Term (yrs):** 3 **Occupation:** Farmer **Age** 15
Enrolled at: Fredericksburg, VA **Enrolled By:** Capt. Buchanan **Promoted:** No **ROH:** No
Born: Washington D.C. **Marital Status:** S **Residence**

Deserted at Hagerstown, MD on 6/26/1863. Appears on a Federal record of prisoners of war who surrendered themselves and were taken to Old Capitol Prison in Washington, D.C. Took oath of allegiance on 7/17/1863.

Gooch, Pinkney D.
CO: A **Initial Rank:** Private
Joined: Wednesday, May 1, 1861 **Term (yrs):** 1 **Occupation:** Farmer (Mechanic) **Age** 27
Enrolled at: Tishomingo Co., MS **Enrolled By:** Capt. Leeth **Promoted:** No **ROH:** No
Born: Alabama **Marital Status:** S **Residence** Corinth, MS

Deserted to the enemy at Blackwater Bridge, VA on 5/11/1863.

Goode, William T.
CO: K **Initial Rank:** Private
Joined: Saturday, March 1, 1862 **Term (yrs):** 3 **Occupation:** Farmer **Age** 17
Enrolled at: Iuka, MS **Enrolled By:** Lt. Latham **Promoted:** No **ROH:** No
Born: Alabama **Marital Status:** S **Residence**

Reported "absent wounded" during May/Jun 1862 muster roll (company records do not provide details as to date of wound or engagement). Returned to duty. Wounded at Sharpsburg and captured on 9/17/1862. Died on 1/15/1863 at Federal hospital at Frederick, MD due to complications from amputation of left leg. Grave #189 at Mt. Olivet Hospital Cemetery, Frederick, MD.

2nd Mississippi Alphabetical Roster (Annotated)

Goodman, S. A.
CO: I **Initial Rank:** Private
Joined: **Term (yrs):** 0 **Occupation:** **Age**
Enrolled at: **Enrolled By:** **Promoted:** No **ROH:** No
Born: **Marital Status:** **Residence**

Appears on a list of Confederate soldiers who have died in the Danville, KY general hospitals since 10/14/1862. List dated Lexington, KY, 5/2/1863. Captured at Chaplain Hills (Perryville) on 10/8/1862. Died 10/22/1862. [Misidentified. Very unlikely this person is a member of the 2nd Mississippi since it was not with the Army of Tennessee at the battle of Perryville].

Gore, F. M.
CO: C **Initial Rank:** Private
Joined: Sunday, September 1, 1861 **Term (yrs):** 1 **Occupation:** Farmer **Age** 17
Enrolled at: Camp Fisher, VA **Enrolled By:** Capt. Bromley **Promoted:** No **ROH:** No
Born: Arkansas **Marital Status:** **Residence**

Discharged on 5/25/1862 due to underage (conscript act military exemption).

Gory, Albert G.
CO: I **Initial Rank:** Private
Joined: Monday, September 30, 1861 **Term (yrs):** 1 **Occupation:** Farmer **Age** 28
Enrolled at: Iuka, MS **Enrolled By:** Lt. Davenport **Promoted:** No **ROH:** No
Born: South Carolina **Marital Status:** **Residence**

Discharged on 2/26/1862 at Camp Fisher, VA due to disability.

Gossett, John W.
CO: B **Initial Rank:** Private
Joined: Wednesday, May 1, 1861 **Term (yrs):** 1 **Occupation:** Farmer **Age** 23
Enrolled at: Tippah Co., MS **Enrolled By:** Capt. Buchanan **Promoted:** No **ROH:** No
Born: **Marital Status:** **Residence**

Listed as AWOL from 6/26/1862 and deserted 8/8/1862 near Richmond.

Gossett, Littlejohn G.
CO: B **Initial Rank:** Private
Joined: Wednesday, September 18, 1861 **Term (yrs):** 1 **Occupation:** **Age**
Enrolled at: Ripley, MS **Enrolled By:** Lt. Davenport **Promoted:** No **ROH:** No
Born: South Carolina **Marital Status:** **Residence**

Died of disease on 12/15/1861 at Warrenton, VA.

2nd Mississippi Alphabetical Roster (Annotated)

Gossett, William R.
CO: B **Initial Rank:** Private
Joined: Wednesday, September 18, 1861 **Term (yrs):** 1 **Occupation:** **Age**
Enrolled at: Ripley, MS **Enrolled By:** Lt. Davenport **Promoted:** No **ROH:** No
Born: **Marital Status:** **Residence**

Deserted from the hospital at Richmond on 9/10/1864.

Goudy, Robert M.
CO: L **Initial Rank:** Private
Joined: Monday, March 3, 1862 **Term (yrs):** 3 **Occupation:** Farmer **Age** 35
Enrolled at: Ripley, MS **Enrolled By:** Col. Falkner **Promoted:** No **ROH:** No
Born: South Carolina **Marital Status:** M **Residence** Clayville, MS

Severely wounded at The Wilderness on 5/5/1864. At hospital. Furloughed on 12/29/1864 to Mississippi. Listed as AWOL from that point.

Goza, Hampton D.
CO: H **Initial Rank:** Private
Joined: Monday, February 24, 1862 **Term (yrs):** 3 **Occupation:** Farmer **Age** 30
Enrolled at: Chesterville, MS **Enrolled By:** Lt. Porter **Promoted:** No **ROH:** No
Born: Georgia **Marital Status:** M **Residence** Chesterville, MS

Wounded at The Wilderness on 5/5/1864. Returned to duty. Killed in battle at Weldon Railroad on 8/18/1864.

Grace, John L.
CO: B **Initial Rank:** Private
Joined: Wednesday, May 1, 1861 **Term (yrs):** 1 **Occupation:** Mason **Age** 26
Enrolled at: Tippah Co., MS **Enrolled By:** Capt. Buchanan **Promoted:** No **ROH:** No
Born: Mississippi **Marital Status:** **Residence**

Wounded at 1st Manassas on 7/21/1861. Discharged on 8/23/1861 for disability due to wound by order of General Johnston.

2nd Mississippi Alphabetical Roster (Annotated)

Grace, Virgil A.　　　　　　　　　　　　　　CO: B　　Initial Rank: Private
Joined: Wednesday, May 1, 1861　　*Term (yrs):* 1　*Occupation:* Student　　　　*Age* 20
Enrolled at: Tippah Co., MS　　*Enrolled By:* Capt. Buchanan　　*Promoted:* No　*ROH:* No
Born:　　　　*Marital Status:*　　　　*Residence*

Also see 7th Mississippi Cavalry Regiment. Captured at South Mountain, MD on 9/14/1862. Sent to Fort Delaware. Exchanged on 11/10/1862 at Aikens Landing, VA. Returned to duty. Wounded (left leg) and captured at Gettysburg on 7/3/1863. Sent to DeCamp General Hospital, Davids Island, NY Harbor. Paroled at City Point, VA on 9/27/1863. Exchanged on 1/1/1864. Furloughed. Furlough expired on 2/4/1864. AWOL from that point. Note in May/Jun 1864 muster remarks: "he joined another command [7th Mississippi Cavalry], and refused to return. Deserted."

Graham, James W. W.　　　　　　　　　　　　CO: K　　Initial Rank: Private
Joined: Tuesday, September 24, 1861　　*Term (yrs):* 1　*Occupation:*　　　　*Age*
Enrolled at: Iuka, MS　　*Enrolled By:* Lt. Davenport　　*Promoted:* Yes　*ROH:* No
Born:　　　　*Marital Status:*　　　　*Residence*

Listed as 2nd Sergeant in May/Jun 1862 muster roll. Listed as "absent on furlough" for same time period and "absent wounded" for Jul/Aug and Sep/Oct 1862 musters. (company records do not give date or wound or engagement). Hospital records show he was admitted on 10/1/1862 and had the index and middle fingers of his right hand amputated. He was furloughed for 30-days from 10/8/62. Captured at Gettysburg on 7/1/1863. Sent to Fort Delaware. Died in captivity on 4/17/1865 of disease (pneumonia). Location of grave: "Jersey Shore."

Graham, Walter C.　　　　　　　　　　　　　CO: B　　Initial Rank: Private
Joined: Tuesday, June 25, 1861　　*Term (yrs):* 1　*Occupation:* Student　　　*Age* 18
Enrolled at: Winchester, VA　　*Enrolled By:* Capt. Buchanan　　*Promoted:* No　*ROH:* No
Born: Mississippi　　*Marital Status:*　　　　*Residence*

Wounded on 5/31/1862 at battle of Seven Pines. Furloughed to 1/1/1863. Returned to duty as "present" during Jul/Aug 1863 muster roll. Discharged on 9/1/1863 due disability caused by wounds.

Grant, John　　　　　　　　　　　　　　　　CO: A　　Initial Rank: Private
Joined:　　　　　　　　　　　*Term (yrs):* 0　*Occupation:* Machinist　　　*Age* 21
Enrolled at:　　　　*Enrolled By:*　　　　*Promoted:* No　*ROH:* No
Born:　　　　*Marital Status:*　　　　*Residence*

Appears on Federal records of prisoners of war. Arrested on 7/19/1862 at Charleston, VA. Sent to Camp Chase, OH. Released on 8/25/1862 by order of the Secretary of War. No other records.

2nd Mississippi Alphabetical Roster (Annotated)

Grant, Willis B.
CO: I *Initial Rank:* Private
Joined: Wednesday, May 1, 1861 *Term (yrs):* 1 *Occupation:* Farmer *Age* 20
Enrolled at: Pontotoc Co., MS *Enrolled By:* Capt. Herring *Promoted:* No *ROH:* No
Born: Alabama *Marital Status:* *Residence*

Wounded (thigh) and captured at Gettysburg on 7/3/1863. Died at Federal hospital in Gettysburg on 7/11/1863 of wounds. [*Buried at Hollywood Cemetery, Richmond, VA. Gettysburg Section Lot: 1.]

Gray, Isaac N.
CO: B *Initial Rank:* Private
Joined: Wednesday, May 1, 1861 *Term (yrs):* 1 *Occupation:* Farmer *Age* 23
Enrolled at: Tippah Co., MS *Enrolled By:* Capt. Buchanan *Promoted:* No *ROH:* No
Born: *Marital Status:* *Residence*

Wounded on 8/28/1864. In hospital at Richmond. Furloughed 40-days from 9/23/1864.

Gray, Lawrence
CO: F, H *Initial Rank:* Private
Joined: Saturday, March 22, 1862 *Term (yrs):* 3 *Occupation:* Farmer *Age* 22
Enrolled at: Corinth, MS *Enrolled By:* Capt. Powers *Promoted:* No *ROH:* No
Born: South Carolina *Marital Status:* S *Residence* Chesterville, MS

Transferred to Company H from Company F on 4/1/1862. Captured at battle of The Wilderness on 5/5/1864. Taken to Point Lookout, MD. Exchanged on 3/17/1865. Furloughed to Mississippi.

Gray, Leonidas M.
CO: B, F *Initial Rank:* Private
Joined: Monday, March 3, 1862 *Term (yrs):* 3 *Occupation:* Farmer *Age* 32
Enrolled at: Ripley, MS *Enrolled By:* Capt. Buchanan *Promoted:* No *ROH:* No
Born: Tennessee *Marital Status:* M *Residence*

Transferred to Company F from Company B on 4/30/1862. Died of disease at Chimborazo Hospital #5 at Richmond, VA on 6/24/1862.

Gray, Robert T.
CO: H *Initial Rank:* 2nd Lieutenant
Joined: Tuesday, April 30, 1861 *Term (yrs):* 1 *Occupation:* Farmer *Age* 35
Enrolled at: Corinth, MS *Enrolled By:* Capt. Taylor *Promoted:* No *ROH:* No
Born: Alabama *Marital Status:* M *Residence* Chesterville, MS

Resigned on 5/24/1861 due to disability from sickness. Discharged.

2nd Mississippi Alphabetical Roster (Annotated)

Gray, Thomas J.
CO: C **Initial Rank:** Private
Joined: Saturday, March 1, 1862 **Term (yrs):** 3 **Occupation:** **Age**
Enrolled at: Verona, MS **Enrolled By:** Lt. Pounds **Promoted:** No **ROH:** No
Born: **Marital Status:** **Residence**

Variously listed as captured at Gettysburg on 7/6/1863 or in PA or in MD on 7/6/1863. (Federal records say he was captured on 7/5/1863 at Gettysburg). Sent to Fort Delaware. Released on oath on 6/11/1865.

Gray, William A.
CO: B **Initial Rank:** Private
Joined: Monday, March 3, 1862 **Term (yrs):** 3 **Occupation:** Farmer **Age** 20
Enrolled at: Ripley, MS **Enrolled By:** Capt. Buchanan **Promoted:** No **ROH:** No
Born: **Marital Status:** M **Residence**

Mortally wounded and captured at Gettysburg on 7/1/1863. Died in Federal hospital (same day?).

Green, Gaston
CO: C **Initial Rank:** Private
Joined: Tuesday, October 1, 1861 **Term (yrs):** 1 **Occupation:** **Age**
Enrolled at: Richmond, MS **Enrolled By:** Lt. Davenport **Promoted:** Yes **ROH:** No
Born: **Marital Status:** **Residence**

Appointed 2nd Sergeant on 4/23/1862. Wounded at 2nd Manassas on 8/29/1862. Furloughed 30-days as of 3/11/1863. Discharged due to disability caused by wounds on 5/15/1863.

Green, George W.
CO: F **Initial Rank:** Private
Joined: Monday, September 30, 1861 **Term (yrs):** 1 **Occupation:** Farmer **Age** 16
Enrolled at: Iuka, MS **Enrolled By:** Lt. Davenport **Promoted:** No **ROH:** No
Born: Mississippi **Marital Status:** **Residence**

Discharged for disability on 1/27/1862 at Camp Fisher, VA. Appears on an oath of allegiance dated 5/16/1865 at Memphis, TN.

Green, J. G.
CO: C **Initial Rank:** Private
Joined: Saturday, March 1, 1862 **Term (yrs):** 3 **Occupation:** **Age**
Enrolled at: Verona, MS **Enrolled By:** Lt. Pounds **Promoted:** No **ROH:** No
Born: **Marital Status:** **Residence**

Transferred by Special Order to Co. B of the 12th Battalion Mississippi Partisan Rangers (cavalry) dated 5/30/1863.

2nd Mississippi Alphabetical Roster (Annotated)

Green, J. J.
CO: H **Initial Rank:** Private
Joined: *Term (yrs):* 0 *Occupation:* *Age*
Enrolled at: *Enrolled By:* *Promoted:* No *ROH:* No
Born: *Marital Status:* *Residence*

Appears on a Federal roll of prisoners of war paroled at Point Lookout, MD on 2/18/1865. Captured at Gettysburg on 7/1/1863. No other record.

Green, James J.
CO: H **Initial Rank:** Private
Joined: Saturday, March 1, 1862 *Term (yrs):* 3 *Occupation:* Farmer *Age* 22
Enrolled at: Chesterville, MS *Enrolled By:* Lt. Porter *Promoted:* No *ROH:* No
Born: Alabama *Marital Status:* S *Residence*

Captured at Gettysburg on 7/1/1863. Sent to Fort Delaware. Exchanged on 2/18/1865.

Green, John A.
CO: F **Initial Rank:** Private
Joined: Wednesday, May 1, 1861 *Term (yrs):* 1 *Occupation:* *Age* 19
Enrolled at: Tippah Co., MS *Enrolled By:* Capt. Davis *Promoted:* No *ROH:* No
Born: *Marital Status:* *Residence*

Killed in battle at 1st Manassas on 7/21/1861.

Green, John W.
CO: C **Initial Rank:** Private
Joined: Saturday, March 1, 1862 *Term (yrs):* 3 *Occupation:* *Age*
Enrolled at: Verona, MS *Enrolled By:* Lt. Pounds *Promoted:* No *ROH:* No
Born: *Marital Status:* *Residence*

Killed in battle at Gettysburg on 7/1/1863.

Green, Joseph R.
CO: A **Initial Rank:** Private
Joined: Wednesday, May 1, 1861 *Term (yrs):* 1 *Occupation:* Farmer *Age* 21
Enrolled at: Tishomingo Co., MS *Enrolled By:* Capt. Leeth *Promoted:* No *ROH:* No
Born: Alabama *Marital Status:* S *Residence* Hickory Plains, MS

Admitted to Chimborazo Hospital #2 in Richmond on 6/8/1862 with gunshot wound of foot (battle?). Furloughed to Mississippi on 7/7/1862. Company records list as deserted in June 1862. However, his name also appears on a list of prisoners received at Camp Douglas, IL from Corinth, MS on 9/28/1862 (while he was still on furlough). [It appears he was captured while on furlough and was sent to a Northern prison. He probably did not actually desert. He may have been exchanged and transferred to the cavalry].

2nd Mississippi Alphabetical Roster (Annotated)

Green, Samuel
CO: L **Initial Rank:** Private
Joined: Monday, March 3, 1862 **Term (yrs):** 3 **Occupation:** Farmer **Age** 34
Enrolled at: Ripley, MS **Enrolled By:** Col. Falkner **Promoted:** No **ROH:** No
Born: South Carolina **Marital Status:** M **Residence** Dumas, MS

Hospital records show admission for treatment of wound on 7/9/1863 (battle?). Captured at The Wilderness on 5/5/1864. Taken to Point Lookout, MD. Exchanged on 2/10/1865. Died at Howard's Grove, VA in hospital on 2/23/1865.

Green, William J.
CO: H **Initial Rank:** Private
Joined: Saturday, March 1, 1862 **Term (yrs):** 3 **Occupation:** Farmer **Age** 29
Enrolled at: Chesterville, MS **Enrolled By:** Lt. Porter **Promoted:** No **ROH:** No
Born: Alabama **Marital Status:** S **Residence** Chesterville, MS

Received furlough on 7/13/1863 and never returned to his company (AWOL since 8/12/1863). Listed as deserted for Jan/Feb 1864 muster.

Greer, R. A.
CO: I **Initial Rank:** Private
Joined: **Term (yrs):** 0 **Occupation:** **Age**
Enrolled at: **Enrolled By:** **Promoted:** No **ROH:** No
Born: **Marital Status:** **Residence**

Appears on a Federal list of Confederates admitted into a Federal hospital at Frederick, MD during the months of Sept., Oct., Nov., and Dec. 1862. List not dated. Date of transfer, 9/19/1862 [probably wounded at Sharpsburg on 9/17/1862]. No other records.

Gregg, Robert E.
CO: G **Initial Rank:** Private
Joined: Wednesday, May 1, 1861 **Term (yrs):** 1 **Occupation:** Medical Student **Age** 26
Enrolled at: Pontotoc Co., MS **Enrolled By:** Capt. Miller **Promoted:** No **ROH:** No
Born: Alabama **Marital Status:** S **Residence** Pontotoc, MS

Discharged for disability at Camp Fisher, VA on 10/8/1861 by order of General Johnston.

2nd Mississippi Alphabetical Roster (Annotated)

Gregory, W. **CO:** K **Initial Rank:** Private
Joined: *Term (yrs):* 0 *Occupation:*   *Age*
Enrolled at: *Enrolled By:*   *Promoted:* No *ROH:* No
Born: *Marital Status:*   *Residence*

Appears on a Federal register of prisoners of war in custody of the Provost Marshal, Memphis, TN. Dated 11/10/1863. Released on oath of allegiance and sent North on 11/10/1863. No other records.

Griffin, David H. **CO:** F **Initial Rank:** Private
Joined: Saturday, March 1, 1862 *Term (yrs):* 3 *Occupation:* Farmer *Age* 24
Enrolled at: Ripley, MS *Enrolled By:* Capt. Powers *Promoted:* No *ROH:* No
Born: South Carolina *Marital Status:* S *Residence*

Captured at Gettysburg on 7/1/1863. Taken to Fort Delaware. Desired to take oath of allegiance. Released on 5/11/1865. Listed as deserted on company records.

Griffin, Eli **CO:** G **Initial Rank:** Private
Joined: Wednesday, May 1, 1861 *Term (yrs):* 1 *Occupation:* Farmer *Age* 19
Enrolled at: Pontotoc Co., MS *Enrolled By:* Capt. Miller *Promoted:* No *ROH:* No
Born: *Marital Status:* M *Residence* Pontotoc, MS

Wounded at 1st Manassas on 7/21/1861. Captured at Falling Waters, MD on 7/14/1863. Taken to Point Lookout, MD. Exchanged on 3/14/1865.

Griffin, James T. **CO:** E **Initial Rank:** Private
Joined: Friday, February 8, 1861 *Term (yrs):* 1 *Occupation:*   *Age*
Enrolled at: Saltillo, MS *Enrolled By:* R. Griffith *Promoted:* No *ROH:* Yes
Born: *Marital Status:*   *Residence*

Appears on a company muster roll and is listed on the Confederate Roll of Honor (G.O. #87, dated 12/10/1864), and a pay voucher. No other records. ROH but battle unknown.

Griffin, Leander **CO:** L **Initial Rank:** Private
Joined: Monday, March 3, 1862 *Term (yrs):* 3 *Occupation:* Farmer *Age* 21
Enrolled at: Ripley, MS *Enrolled By:* Col. Falkner *Promoted:* No *ROH:* Yes
Born: North Carolina *Marital Status:* M *Residence* Silver Springs, MS

Killed in battle at Sharpsburg on 9/17/1862. ROH for Sharpsburg, 9/17/1862.

2nd Mississippi Alphabetical Roster (Annotated)

Griffin, Presley G.
CO: **Initial Rank:** Private
Joined: **Term (yrs):** 0 **Occupation:** **Age**
Enrolled at: **Enrolled By:** **Promoted:** No **ROH:** No
Born: **Marital Status:** **Residence**

Appears on Federal prisoner of war records to be sent to Alton, IL and dated 6/27/1862. Captured 6/1/1862 at Corinth, MS. Sent to Vicksburg, MS for exchange on 9/23/1862. No other records.

Grimes, Jasper U.
CO: A **Initial Rank:** Private
Joined: Saturday, March 1, 1862 **Term (yrs):** 3 **Occupation:** Farmer **Age** 18
Enrolled at: Jacinto, MS **Enrolled By:** Lt. Clayton **Promoted:** No **ROH:** No
Born: Mississippi **Marital Status:** S **Residence** Burnsville, MS

Also see Jasper Grimes, 26th Mississippi Infantry Regiment. Captured at Hatcher's Run on 4/2/1862. Taken to Point Lookout, MD. Released on oath on 6/27/1865.

Grisham, Jasper
CO: F, D **Initial Rank:** Private
Joined: Monday, February 24, 1862 **Term (yrs):** 3 **Occupation:** Farmer **Age** 18
Enrolled at: Ripley, MS **Enrolled By:** Capt. Powers **Promoted:** No **ROH:** Yes
Born: Mississippi **Marital Status:** S **Residence** Salem, MS

Transferred to Co. D on 5/1/1862. Wounded in battle at Talley's Mill on 5/10/1864. Retired to Invalid Corps, P.A.C.S on 11/10/1864 due to disability caused by wounds. ROH for Talley's Mill, 5/10/1864.

Grisham, Robert E.
CO: D **Initial Rank:** Private
Joined: Wednesday, May 1, 1861 **Term (yrs):** 1 **Occupation:** Farmer **Age** 18
Enrolled at: Tippah Co., MS **Enrolled By:** Capt. Beck **Promoted:** No **ROH:** No
Born: Mississippi **Marital Status:** S **Residence** Salem, MS

Wounded at 1st Manassas on 7/21/1861. Wounded (left thigh) at Gettysburg on 7/1/1863. Listed as AWOL from 2/15/1864. Dropped from Roll on 12/31/1864 by order of Col. Stone. Deserted. Surrendered at La Grange, TN to Federal authorities on 5/22/1865. Paroled.

2nd Mississippi Alphabetical Roster (Annotated)

Guess, William E.
CO: E **Initial Rank:** Private
Joined: Wednesday, May 1, 1861 **Term (yrs):** 1 **Occupation:** Laborer **Age** 25
Enrolled at: Itawamba Co., MS **Enrolled By:** Capt. Booth **Promoted:** No **ROH:** No
Born: Georgia **Marital Status:** S **Residence** Guntown, MS

Captured at Petersburg (Hatcher's Run?) on 4/2/1865. Taken to Point Lookout, MD. Released on oath on 6/13/1865.

Guin, Thomas P.
CO: H **Initial Rank:** Private
Joined: Saturday, March 1, 1862 **Term (yrs):** 3 **Occupation:** Overseer **Age** 18
Enrolled at: Chesterville, MS **Enrolled By:** Lt. Porter **Promoted:** No **ROH:** No
Born: Kentucky **Marital Status:** S **Residence** Chesterville, MS

Discharged for disability on 11/1/1862 (other records indicate 10/30/1862 and 11/6//1862).

Guy, William H.
CO: F, L **Initial Rank:** Private
Joined: Wednesday, May 1, 1861 **Term (yrs):** 1 **Occupation:** Planter **Age** 22
Enrolled at: Tippah Co., MS **Enrolled By:** Capt. Davis **Promoted:** No **ROH:** No
Born: Alabama **Marital Status:** S **Residence** Dumas, MS

Discharged from Co. F on 10/20/1861 for disability. Reenlisted in Co. L on 3/3/1862 (or 2/10/1862). Wounded at Gettysburg on 7/3/1863. Wounded at The Wilderness on 5/5/1864. Mortally wounded at Fort Cherry (near Petersburg) and died on 10/12/1864 at Richmond in the Stuart Hospital.

Guyton, James F.
CO: B **Initial Rank:** Private
Joined: Wednesday, May 1, 1861 **Term (yrs):** 1 **Occupation:** Farmer **Age** 19
Enrolled at: Tippah Co., MS **Enrolled By:** Capt. Buchanan **Promoted:** No **ROH:** No
Born: **Marital Status:** **Residence**

Wounded at Sharpsburg on 9/17/1862. Sent to hospital. Captured on 7/3/1863 at Gettysburg. Taken to Point Lookout, MD. Exchanged on 5/3/1864. Furloughed for 30-days. Returned to duty on 7/20/1864. Wounded in battle on 10/1/1864. Sent to Brigade hospital. Returned to duty. Captured at Petersburg (Hatcher's Run?) on 4/2/1865. Taken to Point Lookout, MD. Released on oath on 6/12/1865.

2nd Mississippi Alphabetical Roster (Annotated)

Guyton, Joseph J.
CO: B, S **Initial Rank:** Private
Joined: Wednesday, May 1, 1861 **Term (yrs):** 1 **Occupation:** Druggist **Age** 21
Enrolled at: Tippah Co., MS **Enrolled By:** Capt. Buchanan **Promoted:** Yes **ROH:** No
Born: **Marital Status:** **Residence**

Appointed Quarter Master Sergeant on 5/1/1861. Transferred to regimental staff on 11/13/1861 by order of Col. Falkner. Appointed regimental Adjutant on 2/17/1862.

Guyton, Luther C.
CO: B **Initial Rank:** Private
Joined: Monday, March 3, 1862 **Term (yrs):** 3 **Occupation:** Farmer **Age** 20
Enrolled at: Ripley, MS **Enrolled By:** Capt. Buchanan **Promoted:** No **ROH:** Yes
Born: North Carolina **Marital Status:** S **Residence**

Wounded at 2nd Manassas on 8/29/1862. Sent to hospital at Lynchburg. Returned to duty. Wounded at The Wilderness on 5/5/1864 (gunshot wound of left forearm). Sent to hospital and furloughed from 5/24/1864 for 60-days. Returned to duty on 7/24/1864. Killed in battle near Petersburg on 10/2/1864. ROH for The Wilderness, 5/5/1864.

Haggarty, W.
CO: S **Initial Rank:** Sergeant Major
Joined: **Term (yrs):** 0 **Occupation:** **Age**
Enrolled at: **Enrolled By:** **Promoted:** No **ROH:** No
Born: **Marital Status:** **Residence**

See also Wm Hegarty. Appears on a Federal record of prisoners of war paroled at Montgomery, AL on 5/26/1865. Also appears on a signed parole, same location. No other records.

Hale, Joseph
CO: D **Initial Rank:** Private
Joined: Wednesday, May 1, 1861 **Term (yrs):** 1 **Occupation:** Farmer **Age** 36
Enrolled at: Tippah Co., MS **Enrolled By:** Capt. Beck **Promoted:** No **ROH:** No
Born: Virginia **Marital Status:** S **Residence** Jonesboro, TN

Discharged on 3/6/1862 for disability.

2nd Mississippi Alphabetical Roster (Annotated)

Hall, Claiborne A.
CO: C **Initial Rank:** Private
Joined: Wednesday, May 1, 1861 **Term (yrs):** 1 **Occupation:** Farmer **Age** 21
Enrolled at: Itawamba Co., MS **Enrolled By:** Capt. Bromley **Promoted:** No **ROH:** No
Born: **Marital Status:** **Residence**

See also Forrest's Provost Guard, C. A. Hall. Wounded at 2nd Manassas (which day?). Wounded at The Wilderness on 5/5/1864. Sent to hospital. Furloughed. Listed as AWOL since 12/29/1864, and deserted in the Jan/Feb 1865 muster roll.

Hall, J. W.
CO: G **Initial Rank:** Private
Joined: **Term (yrs):** 0 **Occupation:** **Age**
Enrolled at: **Enrolled By:** **Promoted:** No **ROH:** No
Born: **Marital Status:** **Residence**

Appears on a Federal roll of prisoners of war surrendered and paroled, dated 5/20/1865 at Jackson, MS. No other records.

Hall, John J.
CO: F **Initial Rank:**
Joined: Monday, March 4, 1861 **Term (yrs):** 1 **Occupation:** **Age**
Enrolled at: Ripley, MS **Enrolled By:** J. R. Chalmers **Promoted:** No **ROH:** No
Born: **Marital Status:** **Residence**

Appears on a company muster roll. No other records.

Hamilton, George C.
CO: K **Initial Rank:** Private
Joined: Saturday, March 1, 1862 **Term (yrs):** 3 **Occupation:** **Age** 20
Enrolled at: Iuka, MS **Enrolled By:** Lt. Latham **Promoted:** No **ROH:** No
Born: **Marital Status:** **Residence**

Wounded at Seven Pines on 5/31/1862. Furloughed. Admitted to hospital in Richmond on 5/7/1864 for wound (action not stated). Captured near the Weldon Railroad on 8/20/1864. Taken to Point Lookout, MD. Paroled and exchanged on 2/13/1865.

Hamilton, James W.
CO: B, L **Initial Rank:** Private
Joined: Monday, March 3, 1862 **Term (yrs):** 3 **Occupation:** Farmer **Age** 37
Enrolled at: Ripley, MS **Enrolled By:** Capt. Buchanan **Promoted:** No **ROH:** No
Born: Alabama **Marital Status:** M **Residence** Dumas, MS

Transferred to Co. L on 3/3/1862. Died at the Seminary Hospital in Richmond, VA on 4/30/1862 of rubella.

2nd Mississippi Alphabetical Roster (Annotated)

Hamilton, Pinckney

CO: F **Initial Rank:** Private
Joined: Wednesday, May 1, 1861 **Term (yrs):** 1 **Occupation:** Planter **Age** 37
Enrolled at: Tippah Co., MS **Enrolled By:** Capt. Davis **Promoted:** No **ROH:** No
Born: Mississippi **Marital Status:** **Residence**

Discharged on 7/31/1862 due to expiration of non-conscript term of service (over age?).

Hamker, William

CO: H **Initial Rank:**
Joined: Friday, March 1, 1861 **Term (yrs):** 1 **Occupation:** **Age**
Enrolled at: Chesterville, MS **Enrolled By:** Capt. Kilpatrick **Promoted:** No **ROH:** No
Born: **Marital Status:** **Residence**

Appears on a company muster roll. No other record.

Hammerschmidt, Peter

CO: B **Initial Rank:** Private
Joined: Wednesday, May 1, 1861 **Term (yrs):** 1 **Occupation:** Shoemaker **Age** 17
Enrolled at: Tippah Co., MS **Enrolled By:** Capt. Buchanan **Promoted:** No **ROH:** No
Born: **Marital Status:** **Residence**

Wounded at 1st Manassas on 7/21/1861. Wounded at Gaines Mill on 6/27/1862. Captured at Gettysburg on 7/1/1863. Sent to Fort Delaware. Released on oath on 6/11/1865.

Hammons, Toleman H.

CO: D **Initial Rank:** Private
Joined: Tuesday, October 1, 1861 **Term (yrs):** 1 **Occupation:** Farmer **Age** 22
Enrolled at: Iuka, MS **Enrolled By:** Lt. Davenport **Promoted:** No **ROH:** No
Born: Mississippi **Marital Status:** S **Residence** Pine Grove, MS

Wounded at 2nd Manassas on 8/29/1862 (according to engagements list. Not so noted in company muster roll remarks column for same period). Wounded at Sharpsburg on 9/17/1862. Captured at Gettysburg on 7/1/1863. Sent to Fort Delaware. Released on oath on 6/11/1865.

Hampton, Jacob T.

CO: D **Initial Rank:** Private
Joined: Wednesday, May 1, 1861 **Term (yrs):** 1 **Occupation:** Farmer **Age** 18
Enrolled at: Tippah Co., MS **Enrolled By:** Capt. Beck **Promoted:** No **ROH:** No
Born: Tennessee **Marital Status:** S **Residence** Jonesboro, TN

Deserted on 5/28/1862, "Carried away musket and accoutrements complete, $21.45."

2nd Mississippi Alphabetical Roster (Annotated)

Hampton, Thomas D.
CO: K *Initial Rank:* Private
Joined: Wednesday, May 1, 1861 *Term (yrs):* 1 *Occupation:* Farmer *Age* 24
Enrolled at: Tishomingo Co., MS *Enrolled By:* Capt. Stone *Promoted:* No *ROH:* Yes
Born: Mississippi *Marital Status:* *Residence*

Killed in battle at Gaines Mill on 6/27/1862. ROH for Seven Pines, 5/31/1862 and Gaines Mill, 6/27/1862.

Hancock, James M.
CO: A *Initial Rank:* Private
Joined: Wednesday, July 10, 1861 *Term (yrs):* 1 *Occupation:* Farmer *Age* 21
Enrolled at: Winchester, VA *Enrolled By:* Capt. Leeth *Promoted:* Yes *ROH:* No
Born: Mississippi *Marital Status:* S *Residence* Rienzi, MS

Wounded (in the hand) at Gaines Mill on 6/27/1862. According to engagements list, wounded at Sharpsburg on 9/17/1862 (not indicated in company muster records, although hospital records show him admitted on 10/3/1862 with a wound to the hip). Returned to duty on 10/6/1862. Appointed 5th Sergeant on 5/1/1864. Wounded on 5/5/1864 at battle of The Wilderness.

Handly, William C
CO: G *Initial Rank:* Private
Joined: Wednesday, May 1, 1861 *Term (yrs):* 1 *Occupation:* Farmer *Age* 22
Enrolled at: Pontotoc Co., MS *Enrolled By:* Capt. Miller *Promoted:* Yes *ROH:* Yes
Born: Mississippi *Marital Status:* S *Residence* Pontotoc, MS

Wounded at Gettysburg on 7/3/1863. Returned to duty on 8/10/1863. Furloughed 40-days from 11/27/1863. Promoted to Corporal in July 1864. ROH for The Wilderness, 5/6/1864 and Weldon Railroad, 8/18/1864.

Hanes, Alonzo J.
CO: L *Initial Rank:* Private
Joined: Wednesday, February 10, 1864 *Term (yrs):* 3 *Occupation:* Blacksmith *Age* 26
Enrolled at: Orange Court House, VA *Enrolled By:* *Promoted:* No *ROH:* No
Born: Virginia *Marital Status:* S *Residence* Campbell Court House, VA

Also see 28th Virginia Infantry Regiment. Transferred to Co. K 28th Virginia Infantry on 12/3/1864.

Hankine, Charles
CO: *Initial Rank:* Private
Joined: *Term (yrs):* 0 *Occupation:* *Age*
Enrolled at: *Enrolled By:* *Promoted:* No *ROH:* No
Born: *Marital Status:* *Residence*

Appears on a Federal roll of prisoners of war sent from Alton Military Prison, Alton, IL to Vicksburg, MS on 9/23/1862 for exchange. Captured at Corinth, MS on 6/1/1862. No other records.

2nd Mississippi Alphabetical Roster (Annotated)

Hankins, Samuel W.
CO: E **Initial Rank:** Private
Joined: Monday, February 24, 1862 **Term (yrs):** 3 *Occupation:* **Age** 16
Enrolled at: Guntown, MS *Enrolled By:* Capt. Bates *Promoted:* Yes *ROH:* No
Born: *Marital Status:* *Residence*

Listed as 4th Corporal during Mar/Apr 1863 muster roll. Wounded and captured at Gettysburg on 7/1/1863. Exchanged in Sept (?), 1863. Listed as 3rd Corporal during Sep/Oct 1863 muster. Furloughed in Sept 1863. AWOL from 1/1/1864. Listed as deserted, dropped from rolls Mar/Apr 1864 muster.

Hanks, James Henry
CO: H **Initial Rank:** Private
Joined: **Term (yrs):** 0 *Occupation:* **Age**
Enrolled at: *Enrolled By:* *Promoted:* No *ROH:* No
Born: *Marital Status:* *Residence*

Appears on a Federal roll of prisoners of war at Point Lookout, MD. Captured at Hatcher's Run on 4/2/1865. Released on 6/27/1865. No other record.

Hanners, Edwin C.
CO: K **Initial Rank:** Private
Joined: Wednesday, May 1, 1861 **Term (yrs):** 1 *Occupation:* Farmer **Age** 21
Enrolled at: Tishomingo Co., MS *Enrolled By:* Capt. Stone *Promoted:* No *ROH:* No
Born: *Marital Status:* *Residence*

Wounded at Gettysburg on 7/1/1863. Sent to hospital at Lynchburg, VA. Returned to duty. Listed as AWOL from 2/8/1864. Dropped from rolls as deserter during Mar/Apr 1864 muster.

Harbin, John L.
CO: F **Initial Rank:** Private
Joined: Wednesday, May 1, 1861 **Term (yrs):** 1 *Occupation:* Planter **Age** 19
Enrolled at: Tippah Co., MS *Enrolled By:* Capt. Davis *Promoted:* No *ROH:* Yes
Born: *Marital Status:* *Residence*

Records say killed in battle at 2nd Manassas on 8/29/1862 (other records show death on 8/30/1862). ROH for Second Manassas, 8/28/1862 (records conflicting, but ROH would indicate he was probably killed on 8/28/1862).

Hardcastle, Granison L.
CO: E **Initial Rank:** Private
Joined: Tuesday, February 25, 1862 **Term (yrs):** 3 *Occupation:* **Age** 19
Enrolled at: Guntown, MS *Enrolled By:* Capt. Bates *Promoted:* No *ROH:* No
Born: *Marital Status:* *Residence*

Killed at Sharpsburg on 9/17/1862.

2nd Mississippi Alphabetical Roster (Annotated)

Hardin, Pinckney G.
CO: F **Initial Rank:** Private
Joined: Wednesday, May 1, 1861 **Term (yrs):** 1 **Occupation:** Planter **Age** 22
Enrolled at: Tippah Co., MS **Enrolled By:** Capt. Davis **Promoted:** No **ROH:** No
Born: **Marital Status:** **Residence**

Captured at Martinsburg, VA on 7/17/1863. Sent to Point Lookout, MD. Appears on a list of paroled and exchanged prisoners at Camp Lee, near Richmond, VA in Feb 1865.

Hardwick, McDonald
CO: A **Initial Rank:** Private
Joined: Wednesday, May 1, 1861 **Term (yrs):** 1 **Occupation:** Clerk **Age** 24
Enrolled at: Tishomingo Co., MS **Enrolled By:** Capt. Leeth **Promoted:** No **ROH:** No
Born: Tennessee **Marital Status:** **Residence**

Killed in battle at 2nd Manassas on 8/29/1862.

Harland, Ambrose C.
CO: K **Initial Rank:** Private
Joined: Saturday, March 1, 1862 **Term (yrs):** 3 **Occupation:** **Age** 29
Enrolled at: Iuka, MS **Enrolled By:** Lt. Latham **Promoted:** No **ROH:** No
Born: **Marital Status:** **Residence**

Captured on 4/2/1865 near Petersburg (Hatcher's Run?). Taken to Point Lookout, MD. Released on oath on 6/13/1865.

Harland, George T.
CO: K **Initial Rank:** Private
Joined: Saturday, March 1, 1862 **Term (yrs):** 3 **Occupation:** **Age**
Enrolled at: Iuka, MS **Enrolled By:** Lt. Latham **Promoted:** No **ROH:** No
Born: **Marital Status:** **Residence**

Died of typhoid fever at Chimborazo Hospital #5 in Richmond, VA on 8/29/1862.

Harland, James T.
CO: K **Initial Rank:** Private
Joined: Wednesday, May 1, 1861 **Term (yrs):** 1 **Occupation:** Farmer **Age** 20
Enrolled at: Tishomingo Co., MS **Enrolled By:** Capt. Stone **Promoted:** No **ROH:** No
Born: **Marital Status:** **Residence**

Listed as "absent wounded" during Jul/Aug 1862 muster (what battle?). Furloughed. Returned to duty. Again, absent on wounded furlough in remarks column of May/Jun 1864 muster (what battle?). Returned to duty. Captured at Petersburg (Hatcher's Run?) on 4/2/1865. Taken to Fort Delaware. Released on oath on 6/11/1865.

2nd Mississippi Alphabetical Roster (Annotated)

Harland, John A.
CO: K **Initial Rank:** Private
Joined: Wednesday, May 1, 1861 **Term (yrs):** 1 **Occupation:** Clerk **Age** 23
Enrolled at: Tishomingo Co., MS **Enrolled By:** Capt. Stone **Promoted:** Yes **ROH:** No
Born: **Marital Status:** **Residence**

Appointed 1st Corporal on 3/1/1862. Listed as AWOL during Mar/Apr 1864 muster. Dropped from rolls as deserter during Jul/Aug 1864 muster.

Harland, Robert E.
CO: K **Initial Rank:** Private
Joined: Wednesday, May 1, 1861 **Term (yrs):** 1 **Occupation:** Farmer **Age** 19
Enrolled at: Tishomingo Co., MS **Enrolled By:** Capt. Stone **Promoted:** No **ROH:** No
Born: **Marital Status:** **Residence**

Hospital records show admission on 5/16/1864 for slight wound to right hip (what engagement?). Paroled at Appomattox Court House on 4/9/1865.

Harlow, James W.
CO: A **Initial Rank:** Private
Joined: Wednesday, July 10, 1861 **Term (yrs):** 1 **Occupation:** Farmer **Age** 22
Enrolled at: Winchester, VA **Enrolled By:** Capt. Leeth **Promoted:** No **ROH:** No
Born: Tennessee **Marital Status:** S **Residence** Rienzi, MS

Wounded at Gaines Mill on 6/27/1862. Returned to duty. Wounded at battle of The Wilderness on 5/5/1864. Sent to hospital, then furloughed. Retired to Invalid Corps, P.A.C.S. on 10/22/1864.

Harper, William
CO: K **Initial Rank:** Private
Joined: Saturday, March 1, 1862 **Term (yrs):** 3 **Occupation:** Farmer **Age** 21
Enrolled at: Iuka, MS **Enrolled By:** Lt. Latham **Promoted:** No **ROH:** No
Born: Georgia **Marital Status:** **Residence**

Died on 7/25/1862 at Richmond, VA of disease.

Harris, Albert
CO: F **Initial Rank:** Private
Joined: Wednesday, May 1, 1861 **Term (yrs):** 1 **Occupation:** Blacksmith **Age** 20
Enrolled at: Tippah Co., MS **Enrolled By:** Capt. Davis **Promoted:** No **ROH:** No
Born: **Marital Status:** **Residence**

Wounded and captured at Sharpsburg on 9/17/1862. Paroled from Fort McHenry, MD on 12/14/1862. Wounded and captured at Gettysburg on 7/3/1863. Paroled from DeCamp General Hospital, Davids Island, NY on 9/23/1863. Furloughed 60-days from 10/20/1863. Discharged on 9/30/1864 from disability due to wounds.

2nd Mississippi Alphabetical Roster (Annotated)

Harris, Cornelius L.
CO: D **Initial Rank:** Private
Joined: Wednesday, May 1, 1861 **Term (yrs):** 1 **Occupation:** Teacher **Age**
Enrolled at: Tippah Co., MS **Enrolled By:** Capt. Beck **Promoted:** Yes **ROH:** No
Born: **Marital Status:** M **Residence** Pine Grove, MS

Promoted to Ordnance Sergeant from 5/10/1861. Elected 2nd Lieutenant. on 7/26/1861. Promoted to 1st Lieutenant. on 11/14/1861. Discharged on 4/23/1862 due to reorganization of company and regiment.

Harris, James, Jr.
CO: A **Initial Rank:** Private
Joined: Wednesday, May 1, 1861 **Term (yrs):** 1 **Occupation:** Carpenter **Age** 28
Enrolled at: Tishomingo Co., MS **Enrolled By:** Capt. Leeth **Promoted:** Yes **ROH:** No
Born: Tennessee **Marital Status:** M **Residence** Jacinto, MS

Appointed 4th Sergeant on 7/23/1861. Reduced to ranks by sentence of Court Martial on 3/22/1864. Killed in battle at Talley's Mill on 5/10/1864.

Harris, John W.
CO: G **Initial Rank:** Private
Joined: Saturday, April 4, 1863 **Term (yrs):** 3 **Occupation:** Farmer **Age** 40
Enrolled at: Blackwater, VA **Enrolled By:** Lt. Dillard **Promoted:** No **ROH:** No
Born: Tennessee **Marital Status:** M **Residence** Pontotoc, MS

Also see Andrew J. Miears. Harris substituted for him on 4/4/1863. Deserted in Sept. 1863. Rejoined the company on 11/24/1863. Court Martialed and sentenced to one-year labor working on the fortifications around Richmond, to date from 1/26/1864. Sentence remitted during May/June 1864 time period. Sick at Richmond in hospital. Died on 7/17/1864 at Richmond.

Harris, Martin C.
CO: B **Initial Rank:** Private
Joined: Wednesday, May 1, 1861 **Term (yrs):** 1 **Occupation:** Laborer **Age** 23
Enrolled at: Tippah Co., MS **Enrolled By:** Capt. Buchanan **Promoted:** No **ROH:** No
Born: **Marital Status:** **Residence**

Listed as deserted for the period of Jul/Aug 1862 muster. Obtained sick furlough in Aug 1861 to North Carolina. No disability certificates received since Jan 1862.

2nd Mississippi Alphabetical Roster (Annotated)

Harris, Peter F.
CO: H **Initial Rank:** Private
Joined: Monday, April 29, 1861   **Term (yrs):** 1   **Occupation:** Teacher   **Age** 20
Enrolled at: Pontotoc Co., MS   **Enrolled By:** Capt. Taylor   **Promoted:** Yes   **ROH:** Yes
Born: **Marital Status:**   **Residence**

Appointed 3rd Corporal on 8/1/1861. Appointed to 3rd Sergeant circa Nov/Dec 1861. Appointed to 1st Sergeant on 4/22/1862. Made an orderly in May 1862. Wounded at Gaines Mill on 6/27/1862. Sent to hospital at Richmond. Returned to duty. Killed at Sharpsburg on 9/17/1862. ROH for Sharpsburg, 9/17/1862.

Harris, Robert
CO: C **Initial Rank:** 4th Corporal
Joined: Wednesday, May 1, 1861   **Term (yrs):** 1   **Occupation:** Farmer   **Age** 23
Enrolled at: Itawamba Co., MS   **Enrolled By:** Capt. Bromley   **Promoted:** Yes   **ROH:** Yes
Born: **Marital Status:**   **Residence**

Appointed 4th Sergeant on 8/1/1861. Reaffirmed appointment on 4/23/1862. Listed as 2nd Sergeant during Jul/Aug 1862 muster. Wounded and captured in battle at Sharpsburg on 9/17/1862. Paroled on 9/27/1862. Died of wounds (gunshot wound, left leg — amputated) at Frederick, MD on 10/9/1862 (other records indicate 10/8/1862). ROH for South Mountain (Boonsboro), 9/14/1862.

Harris, Sylvester
CO: C **Initial Rank:** Private
Joined: Saturday, March 1, 1862   **Term (yrs):** 3   **Occupation:** Farmer   **Age** 21
Enrolled at: Verona, MS   **Enrolled By:** Lt. Pounds   **Promoted:** No   **ROH:** No
Born: Tennessee   **Marital Status:** S   **Residence**

Captured at Gettysburg on 7/3/1863. No further record.

Harris, Terrel S.
CO: B **Initial Rank:** Private
Joined: Wednesday, May 1, 1861   **Term (yrs):** 1   **Occupation:** Farmer   **Age** 25
Enrolled at: Tippah Co., MS   **Enrolled By:** Capt. Buchanan   **Promoted:** No   **ROH:** No
Born: **Marital Status:**   **Residence**

Wounded and captured at Gettysburg on 7/1/1863. Taken to Fort Delaware. Died on 6/30/1864 of disease at Fort Delaware. "Buried upon the Island with a view to their future removal to the Prisoners of War burial ground, on the Jersey Shore, opposite Post."

2nd Mississippi Alphabetical Roster (Annotated)

Harris, Thomas C.
CO: C **Initial Rank:** Private
Joined: Saturday, March 1, 1862 **Term (yrs):** 3 **Occupation:** **Age**
Enrolled at: Verona, MS **Enrolled By:** Lt. Pounds **Promoted:** No **ROH:** No
Born: **Marital Status:** **Residence**

Captured at Falling Waters, MD on 7/14/1863. Sent to Point Lookout, MD. Transferred to Elmira, NY on 8/16/1864. Paroled at Elmira on 3/10/1865 and sent to James River for exchange. Also appears on a Federal register of paroles dated 5/24/1865 at Columbus, MS.

Harrison, James A.
CO: A **Initial Rank:** Private
Joined: Wednesday, May 1, 1861 **Term (yrs):** 1 **Occupation:** Farmer (student) **Age** 19
Enrolled at: Tishomingo Co., MS **Enrolled By:** Capt. Leeth **Promoted:** No **ROH:** No
Born: Alabama **Marital Status:** S **Residence** Highland, MS

Furloughed about 10/1/1862. Did not return. Deserted as of Mar/Apr 1862 muster.

Harrison, James M.
CO: C **Initial Rank:** Private
Joined: Wednesday, May 1, 1861 **Term (yrs):** 1 **Occupation:** Farmer **Age** 21
Enrolled at: Itawamba Co., MS **Enrolled By:** Capt. Bromley **Promoted:** No **ROH:** No
Born: South Carolina **Marital Status:** **Residence**

(??) Discharged for disability on 9/6/1861.

Harrison, Moses
CO: K **Initial Rank:** Private
Joined: Saturday, March 1, 1862 **Term (yrs):** 3 **Occupation:** **Age** 30
Enrolled at: Iuka, MS **Enrolled By:** Lt. Latham **Promoted:** No **ROH:** No
Born: **Marital Status:** **Residence**

Company records indicate that he obtained furlough and deserted to the enemy circa Jul/Aug 1862. However, Federal prisoner of war records indicate a Moses Harrison was captured and paroled at the battles of Iuka, Corinth, and Hatchie during the period 9/19/1862 - 10/6/1862. Dated 10/13/1862 at Corinth, MS. No other record.

Harrison, Thomas H.
CO: G **Initial Rank:** Private
Joined: Wednesday, May 1, 1861 **Term (yrs):** 1 **Occupation:** Carpenter **Age** 21
Enrolled at: Pontotoc Co., MS **Enrolled By:** Capt. Miller **Promoted:** No **ROH:** No
Born: South Carolina **Marital Status:** M **Residence** Pontotoc, MS

Discharged on 12/31/1861 due to disability.

2nd Mississippi Alphabetical Roster (Annotated)

Harrison, William F.
CO: G **Initial Rank:** Private
Joined: Wednesday, May 1, 1861 **Term (yrs):** 1 **Occupation:** Stage Driver **Age** 26
Enrolled at: Pontotoc Co., MS **Enrolled By:** Capt. Miller **Promoted:** No **ROH:** No
Born: Tennessee **Marital Status:** S **Residence** Pontotoc, MS

Although company records do not so indicate, accompanying list of engagements show William F. Harrison wounded at Gettysburg on 7/1/1863. Hospital records indicate admission for gunshot wound on 7/14/1863. Listed as absent on furlough from 2/7/1864. Expiration of furlough on 3/8/1864. "Deserted to the enemy."

Hartsfield, Alexander S.
CO: E **Initial Rank:** Private
Joined: Wednesday, May 1, 1861 **Term (yrs):** 1 **Occupation:** Farmer **Age** 17
Enrolled at: Itawamba Co., MS **Enrolled By:** Capt. Booth **Promoted:** No **ROH:** No
Born: Tennessee **Marital Status:** S **Residence** Baldwyn, MS

Wounded at Gettysburg on 7/1/1863. Furloughed. Returned to duty in June 1864. Captured at Hatcher's Run on 4/2/1865. Taken to Point Lookout, MD. Released on oath on 6/13/1865.

Hartsfield, Leroy
CO: E **Initial Rank:** Private
Joined: Saturday, March 1, 1862 **Term (yrs):** 3 **Occupation:** **Age** 47
Enrolled at: Guntown, MS **Enrolled By:** Capt. Bates **Promoted:** No **ROH:** No
Born: **Marital Status:** S **Residence** Guntown, MS

Died in camp at Ashland, VA of disease on 7/1/1862.

Hartsfield, William
CO: E **Initial Rank:** Private
Joined: Saturday, March 1, 1862 **Term (yrs):** 3 **Occupation:** **Age** 17
Enrolled at: Guntown, MS **Enrolled By:** Capt. Bates **Promoted:** No **ROH:** No
Born: **Marital Status:** **Residence** Guntown, MS

Died of disease at Richmond, VA on 8/1/1862.

Harvey, Andrew B.
CO: K **Initial Rank:** Private
Joined: Wednesday, May 1, 1861 **Term (yrs):** 1 **Occupation:** Farmer **Age** 18
Enrolled at: Tishomingo Co., MS **Enrolled By:** Capt. Stone **Promoted:** No **ROH:** No
Born: Mississippi **Marital Status:** **Residence**

Also see A. B. Harvey, 26th Mississippi Infantry Regiment. Wounded at 1st Manassas "wound in thigh & very severe". Placed in hospital at Charlottesville, VA. Furloughed 11/2/1861. Discharged for disability on 12/17/1861.

2nd Mississippi Alphabetical Roster (Annotated)

Harvey, Madison
CO: K **Initial Rank:** Private
Joined: Wednesday, May 1, 1861 **Term (yrs):** 1 **Occupation:** Farmer **Age** 17
Enrolled at: Tishomingo Co., MS **Enrolled By:** Capt. Stone **Promoted:** No **ROH:** No
Born: Tennessee **Marital Status:** **Residence**

Discharged on 5/27/1862 — underage.

Harvey, William F.
CO: K **Initial Rank:** 2nd Corporal
Joined: Wednesday, May 1, 1861 **Term (yrs):** 1 **Occupation:** Farmer **Age** 22
Enrolled at: Tishomingo Co., MS **Enrolled By:** Capt. Stone **Promoted:** Yes **ROH:** No
Born: **Marital Status:** **Residence**

Elected 2nd Lieutenant. and assigned to duty on 7/15/1862. Listed as Sr. 2nd Lieutenant. during Nov/Dec 1862 muster roll. Listed 1st Lieutenant. for Mar/Apr 1863 muster. Listed as Captain for Sep/Oct 1864 muster roll. Captured at Hatcher's Run on 4/2/1865. Taken to Johnson's Island, OH. Released on oath on 6/18/1865.

Harwell, C. F.
CO: C **Initial Rank:** Private
Joined: Tuesday, October 1, 1861 **Term (yrs):** 1 **Occupation:** Farmer **Age** 25
Enrolled at: Verona, MS **Enrolled By:** Lt. Davenport **Promoted:** No **ROH:** No
Born: Mississippi **Marital Status:** **Residence**

Killed in battle at Sharpsburg on 9/17/1862.

Harwell, John T.
CO: H **Initial Rank:** Private
Joined: Monday, April 29, 1861 **Term (yrs):** 1 **Occupation:** Clerk **Age** 18
Enrolled at: Pontotoc Co., MS **Enrolled By:** Capt. Taylor **Promoted:** No **ROH:** Yes
Born: Tennessee **Marital Status:** S **Residence** Tupelo, MS

List of engagements indicates he was wounded at The Wilderness on 5/5/1864, (however company records do not mention this). Killed at battle of Spotsylvania Court House on 5/12/1864. ROH for Talley's Mill, 5/10/1864.

Hasle, John T.
CO: D **Initial Rank:** Private
Joined: Wednesday, May 1, 1861 **Term (yrs):** 1 **Occupation:** Farmer **Age** 23
Enrolled at: Tippah Co., MS **Enrolled By:** Capt. Beck **Promoted:** No **ROH:** No
Born: Alabama **Marital Status:** S **Residence** Snow Creek, MS

Wounded at Sharpsburg on 9/17/1862. Furloughed for 60-days from 10/5/1862. Listed as deserted for Mar/Apr, 1863 muster roll. Dropped from rolls for prolonged AWOL.

2nd Mississippi Alphabetical Roster (Annotated)

Hassitt, John
CO: **Initial Rank:** Private
Joined: **Term (yrs):** 0 **Occupation:** **Age**
Enrolled at: **Enrolled By:** **Promoted:** No **ROH:** No
Born: **Marital Status:** **Residence**

Appears on a Federal roll of prisoners of war who died at Alton, IL Military Prison. Captured at Mt. Pleasant, MS on 8/17/1863. Died on 10/28/1863 of typhus fever. No other record.

Hathaway, Edward C.
CO: K **Initial Rank:** Private
Joined: Saturday, March 1, 1862 **Term (yrs):** 3 **Occupation:** **Age** 21
Enrolled at: Iuka, MS **Enrolled By:** Lt. Latham **Promoted:** No **ROH:** No
Born: **Marital Status:** **Residence**

Federal records indicate he deserted on 3/22/1865 and was taken into custody.

Hay, Nathaniel M.
CO: A, S **Initial Rank:** 2nd Corporal
Joined: Wednesday, May 1, 1861 **Term (yrs):** 1 **Occupation:** Clerk **Age** 21
Enrolled at: Tishomingo Co., MS **Enrolled By:** Capt. Leeth **Promoted:** Yes **ROH:** No
Born: North Carolina **Marital Status:** S **Residence** Corinth, MS

Listed as Commissary Sergeant for Nov/Dec 1863 muster roll (had been previously detailed as Assistant Commissary). Detailed as Regimental Commissary circa Jan/Feb 1864. Captured at Petersburg (Hatcher's Run?) on 4/2/1865. Taken to Fort Delaware. Released on oath on 6/11/1865.

Hayes, John W.
CO: K **Initial Rank:** Private
Joined: Monday, September 30, 1861 **Term (yrs):** 1 **Occupation:** Shoemaker **Age** 22
Enrolled at: Iuka, MS **Enrolled By:** Lt. Davenport **Promoted:** No **ROH:** No
Born: Alabama **Marital Status:** **Residence**

Discharged on 1/31/1862 due to disability by order of Brigadier General Whiting.

Haynes, James
CO: A **Initial Rank:** Private
Joined: Wednesday, February 20, 1861 **Term (yrs):** 1 **Occupation:** **Age**
Enrolled at: Corinth, MS **Enrolled By:** R. Griffith **Promoted:** No **ROH:** No
Born: **Marital Status:** **Residence**

Appears on a company muster roll. No other record.

2nd Mississippi Alphabetical Roster (Annotated)

Heard, Isaac N. *CO:* G *Initial Rank:* Private
Joined: Wednesday, May 1, 1861 *Term (yrs):* 1 *Occupation:* Printer *Age* 22
Enrolled at: Pontotoc Co., MS *Enrolled By:* Capt. Miller *Promoted:* No *ROH:* No
Born: Alabama *Marital Status:* S *Residence* Pontotoc, MS

Deserted in March (May?) 1862.

Heath, Henry G. *CO:* L *Initial Rank:* Private
Joined: Monday, March 3, 1862 *Term (yrs):* 3 *Occupation:* Farmer *Age* 39
Enrolled at: Ripley, MS *Enrolled By:* Col. Falkner *Promoted:* No *ROH:* No
Born: Georgia *Marital Status:* M *Residence* Ripley, MS

Wounded (in thigh) and captured and paroled at battle of 2nd Manassas on 8/29/1862. Sent to Warrenton, VA. Furloughed 60-days from 7/10/1863. AWOL. Dropped from rolls on 8/31/1864. Deserted. Federal prisoner of war records show he surrendered and was paroled at La Grange, TN on 5/24/1865. Remarks: "Left his command at Farmville, VA Aug 16, 1863."

Heckman, H. *CO:* *Initial Rank:* Private
Joined: *Term (yrs):* 0 *Occupation:* *Age*
Enrolled at: *Enrolled By:* *Promoted:* No *ROH:* No
Born: *Marital Status:* *Residence*

Federal records show he was captured at Sharpsburg (not dated). Appears on a parole list dated 9/27/1862. Also appears on a list of Confederates wounded at the Battle of Antietam and who died at various hospitals near Antietam, MD. Not dated. Cause unknown. Place of death: Linis Farm Hospital. No other record.

Hedden, Charles H. *CO:* B, F *Initial Rank:* Private
Joined: Monday, March 3, 1862 *Term (yrs):* 3 *Occupation:* Farmer *Age* 17
Enrolled at: Ripley, MS *Enrolled By:* Capt. Buchanan *Promoted:* No *ROH:* No
Born: Mississippi *Marital Status:* S *Residence*

Transferred to Co. F on 4/30/1862. Sent to hospital at Winchester on 10/20/1862 (what cause?). Mar/Apr 1863 muster roll remarks: "Died — sent to hospital at Winchester, VA Oct 15, 1862 (not heard from since, supposed died.)" Additional reference card notes "Coffin & hearse" dated Dec. 6, 1862.

2nd Mississippi Alphabetical Roster (Annotated)

Hedden, John S.
CO: F, L **Initial Rank:** Private
Joined: Wednesday, May 1, 1861 **Term (yrs):** 1 **Occupation:** Planter **Age** 24
Enrolled at: Tippah Co., MS **Enrolled By:** Capt. Davis **Promoted:** No **ROH:** No
Born: Mississippi **Marital Status:** **Residence**

Captured on 7/14/1863 at Falling Waters, MD. Taken to Point Lookout, MD. Died in prison on 1/7/1864 (another record says 1/6/1864).

Hegerty, William
CO: E **Initial Rank:** Private
Joined: Wednesday, May 1, 1861 **Term (yrs):** 1 **Occupation:** Laborer **Age** 24
Enrolled at: Itawamba Co., MS **Enrolled By:** Capt. Booth **Promoted:** No **ROH:** No
Born: Ireland **Marital Status:** S **Residence** Guntown, MS

Reference jacket says to also see W. Haggarty. Discharged 2/7/1863 by act of Congress for "not having acquired a domicile in the Confederate States."

Heist, Lewis J.
CO: G **Initial Rank:** Private
Joined: Wednesday, May 1, 1861 **Term (yrs):** 1 **Occupation:** Mechanic **Age** 39
Enrolled at: Pontotoc Co., MS **Enrolled By:** Capt. Miller **Promoted:** No **ROH:** No
Born: **Marital Status:** M **Residence** Pontotoc, MS

Discharged on 8/2/1862 — over age.

Helms, E. W.
CO: A **Initial Rank:** Private
Joined: Saturday, March 1, 1862 **Term (yrs):** 3 **Occupation:** Sawyer (?) **Age** 31
Enrolled at: Jacinto, MS **Enrolled By:** Lt. Clayton **Promoted:** No **ROH:** No
Born: North Carolina **Marital Status:** **Residence**

Discharged due to disability on 7/17/1862.

Helms, John W.
CO: H **Initial Rank:** Private
Joined: Monday, April 29, 1861 **Term (yrs):** 1 **Occupation:** Farmer **Age** 24
Enrolled at: Pontotoc Co., MS **Enrolled By:** Capt. Taylor **Promoted:** No **ROH:** No
Born: Georgia **Marital Status:** S **Residence** Chesterville, MS

Admitted to hospital in Richmond with gunshot wound on 7/9/1863 (company records provide no details as to date of wound or action). Returned to duty on 8/7/1863. Company muster roll remarks that he was wounded in The Wilderness (date not given but admitted to hospital at Richmond on 5/16/1864). Furloughed for 60-days from 5/27/1864. Paroled at Appomattox Court House on 4/9/1865.

2nd Mississippi Alphabetical Roster (Annotated)

Helms, Robert A.
CO: B **Initial Rank:** Private
Joined: Monday, March 3, 1862 **Term (yrs):** 3 **Occupation:** Teacher **Age** 22
Enrolled at: Ripley, MS **Enrolled By:** Capt. Buchanan **Promoted:** No **ROH:** Yes
Born: South Carolina **Marital Status:** S **Residence**

Captured at Hatcher's Run on 4/2/1865. Taken to Point Lookout, MD. Released on oath on 6/27/1865. ROH for Spotsylvania Court House, 5/12/1864.

Helms, William B.
CO: I **Initial Rank:** Private
Joined: Wednesday, May 1, 1861 **Term (yrs):** 1 **Occupation:** Farmer **Age** 22
Enrolled at: Pontotoc Co., MS **Enrolled By:** Capt. Herring **Promoted:** No **ROH:** No
Born: **Marital Status:** **Residence**

Captured at Gettysburg on 7/1/1863. Taken to Fort Delaware. Released on oath on 6/11/1865.

Helton, James
CO: A **Initial Rank:** Private
Joined: Saturday, March 1, 1862 **Term (yrs):** 3 **Occupation:** Farmer **Age** 18
Enrolled at: Jacinto, MS **Enrolled By:** Lt. Clayton **Promoted:** No **ROH:** No
Born: Mississippi **Marital Status:** S **Residence** Jacinto, MS

Captured on 9/15/1862 at South Mountain, MD. Taken to Fort Delaware. Declared exchanged on 11/10/1862. Captured at Gettysburg on 7/1/1863. Sent to Fort Delaware. Died on 5/2/1865 at Fort Delaware.

Helvenstein, Eugene
CO: E **Initial Rank:** Private
Joined: Saturday, June 1, 1861 **Term (yrs):** 1 **Occupation:** Farmer **Age** 23
Enrolled at: Harpers Ferry, VA **Enrolled By:** Capt. Booth **Promoted:** No **ROH:** No
Born: Georgia **Marital Status:** **Residence** Guntown, MS

Discharged due to disability on 12/25/1861 at Camp Fisher, VA.

Helvenstine, Thaddeus H.
CO: E **Initial Rank:** Private
Joined: Wednesday, May 1, 1861 **Term (yrs):** 1 **Occupation:** Farmer **Age** 19
Enrolled at: Itawamba Co., MS **Enrolled By:** Capt. Booth **Promoted:** No **ROH:** No
Born: Georgia **Marital Status:** **Residence** Guntown, MS

Discharged for disability on 7/30/1861 by order of General Johnston.

2nd Mississippi Alphabetical Roster (Annotated)

Henderson, James
CO: C **Initial Rank:** Private
Joined: Tuesday, October 1, 1861 **Term (yrs):** 1 **Occupation:** Farmer **Age** 37
Enrolled at: Verona, MS **Enrolled By:** Lt. Davenport **Promoted:** No **ROH:** No
Born: Tennessee **Marital Status:** **Residence**

Discharged on plea of military exemption on 5/25/1862 — over age.

Henderson, Robert B.
CO: B **Initial Rank:** Musician
Joined: Wednesday, May 1, 1861 **Term (yrs):** 1 **Occupation:** **Age** 24
Enrolled at: Tippah Co., MS **Enrolled By:** Capt. Buchanan **Promoted:** No **ROH:** No
Born: **Marital Status:** **Residence**

Listed as "Bugler" during May/Jun 1861 - Mar/Apr 1862 muster rolls; Private from that point forward. Hospital records show admission at Howard's Grove, VA on 8/3/1863 for gunshot wound (battle not stated). Furloughed 40-days from 10/5/1863. Wounded at the battle of The Wilderness on 5/6/1864. Listed as AWOL from 8/1/1864. Deserted from hospital in Columbia, SC on 9/1/1864.

Henderson, Robert H.
CO: A, S **Initial Rank:** 3rd Corporal
Joined: Wednesday, May 1, 1861 **Term (yrs):** 1 **Occupation:** Clerk **Age** 25
Enrolled at: Tishomingo Co., MS **Enrolled By:** Capt. Leeth **Promoted:** Yes **ROH:** No
Born: **Marital Status:** M **Residence** Danville, MS

Promoted to Captain and Assistant Commissary in staff position on 10/7/1861. Dropped from rolls on 8/2/1862.

Henderson, William C.
CO: C **Initial Rank:** Private
Joined: Wednesday, May 1, 1861 **Term (yrs):** 1 **Occupation:** Farmer **Age** 19
Enrolled at: Itawamba Co., MS **Enrolled By:** Capt. Bromley **Promoted:** No **ROH:** No
Born: **Marital Status:** **Residence**

Died of disease on 7/18/1861.

Henderson, William M.
CO: E **Initial Rank:** Private
Joined: Wednesday, May 1, 1861 **Term (yrs):** 1 **Occupation:** Farmer **Age** 37
Enrolled at: Itawamba Co., MS **Enrolled By:** Capt. Booth **Promoted:** No **ROH:** No
Born: Georgia **Marital Status:** M **Residence** Saltillo, MS

Discharged in July 1862 — over age.

2nd Mississippi Alphabetical Roster (Annotated)

Henley, Thomas J. *CO:* F *Initial Rank:* Private
Joined: Saturday, March 1, 1862 *Term (yrs):* 3 *Occupation:* Farmer *Age* 22
Enrolled at: Ripley, MS *Enrolled By:* Capt. Powers *Promoted:* No *ROH:* No
Born: Tennessee *Marital Status:* S *Residence*

Died of disease in hospital at Ashland, VA on 5/1/1862.

Henry, D. J. *CO:* *Initial Rank:* Private
Joined: *Term (yrs):* 0 *Occupation:* *Age*
Enrolled at: *Enrolled By:* *Promoted:* No *ROH:* No
Born: *Marital Status:* *Residence*

Name appears on a Federal list of prisoners of war surrendered at Tallahassee, FL on 5/10/1865. Paroled at Albany, GA on 5/17/1865. No other record.

Henry, James F. *CO:* G *Initial Rank:* Private
Joined: Wednesday, May 1, 1861 *Term (yrs):* 1 *Occupation:* Farmer *Age* 26
Enrolled at: Pontotoc Co., MS *Enrolled By:* Capt. Miller *Promoted:* No *ROH:* No
Born: Alabama *Marital Status:* M *Residence* Pontotoc, MS

Wounded at South Mountain, MD on 9/14/1862. Furloughed. Returned to duty on 11/10/1862. Wounded at Gettysburg on 7/1/1863. Sent to hospital in Richmond. Returned to duty on 11/15/1863. Accompanying list of engagements show him wounded on 5/10/1864 at Talley's Mill (company muster records do not so indicate). Wounded in battle (Bethesda Church) on 6/2/1864. Sent to hospital in Richmond. Returned to duty. Captured at Hatcher's Run on 4/2/1865. Taken to Point Lookout, MD. Released on oath on 6/27/1865.

Henson, J. H. *CO:* A *Initial Rank:* Private
Joined: Saturday, March 1, 1862 *Term (yrs):* 3 *Occupation:* *Age* 25
Enrolled at: Jacinto, MS *Enrolled By:* Lt. Clayton *Promoted:* No *ROH:* No
Born: *Marital Status:* *Residence*

Listed as AWOL since 1862. "Was never in a fight." Deserted. Furloughed from hospital and never heard from since.

2nd Mississippi Alphabetical Roster (Annotated)

Henson, John A.
CO: A **Initial Rank:** Private
Joined: Saturday, March 1, 1862 **Term (yrs):** 3 **Occupation:** Farmer **Age** 26
Enrolled at: Jacinto, MS **Enrolled By:** Lt. Clayton **Promoted:** No **ROH:** No
Born: Tennessee **Marital Status:** **Residence** Burnsville, MS

Died of disease at Lynchburg, VA on 8/19/1862 (although another record lists his death as 7/17/1862).

Henson, Joshua L.
CO: L **Initial Rank:** Private
Joined: Monday, March 3, 1862 **Term (yrs):** 3 **Occupation:** Farmer **Age** 29
Enrolled at: Ripley, MS **Enrolled By:** Col. Falkner **Promoted:** Yes **ROH:** No
Born: Tennessee **Marital Status:** M **Residence** Ripley, MS

Listed as 2nd Lieutenant. during May/Jun 1862 muster, elected on 3/22/1862. Promoted to 1st Lieutenant. on 11/30/1862. Promoted to Captain on 12/28/1863 to rank from 7/3/1863. AWOL from 11/28/1864.

Herd, H. B.
CO: B **Initial Rank:** Private
Joined: **Term (yrs):** 0 **Occupation:** **Age**
Enrolled at: **Enrolled By:** **Promoted:** No **ROH:** No
Born: **Marital Status:** **Residence**

Appears on a Federal roll of prisoners of war captured in GA from 3/22/1865 - 4/20/1865. Roll not dated. Captured at Selma, AL on 4/2/1865. No other record.

Heron, Thomas D.
CO: G **Initial Rank:**
Joined: Saturday, March 2, 1861 **Term (yrs):** 1 **Occupation:** **Age**
Enrolled at: Pontotoc Co., MS **Enrolled By:** Capt. Kilpatrick **Promoted:** No **ROH:** No
Born: **Marital Status:** **Residence**

Appears on a company muster roll. No other record.

Herridge, James M.
CO: K **Initial Rank:** Private
Joined: Saturday, March 1, 1862 **Term (yrs):** 3 **Occupation:** **Age** 17
Enrolled at: Iuka, MS **Enrolled By:** Lt. Latham **Promoted:** No **ROH:** No
Born: Kentucky **Marital Status:** **Residence**

Also see J. M. Harridge of the 26th Mississippi Infantry Regiment. Records indicate both "killed in action at 2nd Manassas on 8/29/1862" and "died of wounds on 8/30/1862."

2nd Mississippi Alphabetical Roster (Annotated)

Herridge, John W.
CO: K, L *Initial Rank:* Private
Joined: Wednesday, May 1, 1861 *Term (yrs):* 1 *Occupation:* Farmer *Age* 18
Enrolled at: Tishomingo Co., MS *Enrolled By:* Capt. Stone *Promoted:* No *ROH:* No
Born: Georgia *Marital Status:* S *Residence* Iuka, MS

Listed in Company L during Mar/Apr 1863 muster. Wounded in shoulder on picket near Suffolk, VA circa Mar/Apr 1863 (what date?). Furloughed. Deserted to the enemy on 2/6/1864 at Orange Court House, VA.

Herring, John B.
CO: I *Initial Rank:* Captain
Joined: Wednesday, May 1, 1861 *Term (yrs):* 1 *Occupation:* Farmer *Age* 32
Enrolled at: Pontotoc Co., MS *Enrolled By:* Col. Falkner *Promoted:* No *ROH:* No
Born: *Marital Status:* *Residence*

Also see 5th Mississippi Infantry Regiment. Retired from service on expiration of term of enlistment.

Herring, Robert A.
CO: F *Initial Rank:* Private
Joined: Wednesday, May 1, 1861 *Term (yrs):* 1 *Occupation:* Blacksmith *Age* 21
Enrolled at: Tippah Co., MS *Enrolled By:* Capt. Davis *Promoted:* No *ROH:* No
Born: *Marital Status:* *Residence*

Wounded at Bristoe Station on 10/14/1863. In hospital at Richmond. Furloughed for 30-days from 2/25/1864. Never returned. Deserted.

Herring, Thomas J.
CO: F *Initial Rank:* Private
Joined: Wednesday, May 1, 1861 *Term (yrs):* 1 *Occupation:* Planter *Age* 27
Enrolled at: Tippah Co., MS *Enrolled By:* Capt. Davis *Promoted:* No *ROH:* No
Born: *Marital Status:* *Residence*

Discharged for disability on 7/1/1861 at Winchester, VA.

Herron, Thomas F.
CO: G *Initial Rank:* 2nd Corporal
Joined: Wednesday, May 1, 1861 *Term (yrs):* 1 *Occupation:* Merchant *Age* 22
Enrolled at: Pontotoc Co., MS *Enrolled By:* Capt. Kilpatrick *Promoted:* Yes *ROH:* No
Born: *Marital Status:* S *Residence* Pontotoc, MS

Also see Green L. Kidd (substitute). Appointed 4th Sergeant on 7/26/1861. Appointed Ordnance Sergeant on 5/10/1862. Replaced by substitute G. L. Kidd on 5/11/1862. Discharged.

2nd Mississippi Alphabetical Roster (Annotated)

Hester, James M. B.   CO: A   Initial Rank: Private

Joined: Wednesday, May 1, 1861   *Term (yrs):* 1   *Occupation:* Farmer   **Age** 22

Enrolled at: Tishomingo Co., MS   *Enrolled By:* Capt. Leeth   *Promoted:* No   *ROH:* No

Born: Georgia   *Marital Status:* S   *Residence* Booneville, MS

Wounded at Gaines Mill on 6/27/1862. Furloughed. Discharged on 4/3/1863 on surgeons' certificate of disability due to wounds.

Hester, Robert F.   CO: A   Initial Rank: Private

Joined: Wednesday, May 1, 1861   *Term (yrs):* 1   *Occupation:* Farmer   **Age** 33

Enrolled at: Tishomingo Co., MS   *Enrolled By:* Capt. Leeth   *Promoted:* No   *ROH:* No

Born: Georgia   *Marital Status:* M   *Residence* Booneville, MS

Discharged on 12/25/1861 due to disability at Camp Fisher, VA.

Hicks, John J.   CO: D   Initial Rank: 3rd Sergeant

Joined: Wednesday, May 15, 1861   *Term (yrs):* 1   *Occupation:* Farmer   **Age** 30

Enrolled at: Harpers Ferry, VA   *Enrolled By:* Capt. Beck   *Promoted:* Yes   *ROH:* No

Born: Tennessee   *Marital Status:* S   *Residence* Snow Creek, MS

Elected 2nd Lieutenant. on 4/23/1862. Accompanying list of engagements show him wounded on 9/17/1862 at Sharpsburg (muster records do not so indicate). Promoted to Captain on 7/3/1863. Again, engagements list indicates he was wounded on 10/14/1863 at Bristoe Station (Company muster rolls do not so indicate). Severely wounded at The Wilderness on 5/5/1864. Sent to hospital in Richmond. Furloughed 60-days. Retired for disability due to wounds on 1/10/1865.

Hill, Andrew M.   CO: H   Initial Rank: Private

Joined: Monday, April 29, 1861   *Term (yrs):* 1   *Occupation:* Farmer   **Age** 28

Enrolled at: Pontotoc Co., MS   *Enrolled By:* Capt. Taylor   *Promoted:* No   *ROH:* No

Born: Alabama   *Marital Status:* S   *Residence* Chesterville, MS

Wounded at 1st Manassas on 7/21/1861. Discharged for disability due to wounds on 10/23/1861 by order of General Smith.

2nd Mississippi Alphabetical Roster (Annotated)

Hill, David J.
CO: B **Initial Rank:** Private
Joined: Wednesday, May 1, 1861 **Term (yrs):** 1 **Occupation:** Surveyor **Age** 33
Enrolled at: Tippah Co., MS **Enrolled By:** Capt. Buchanan **Promoted:** No **ROH:** No
Born: **Marital Status:** **Residence**

Wounded and captured at Gettysburg on 7/3/1863. Paroled at City Point, VA on 9/25/1863. Sent home on wounded furlough. Listed present for Jan/Feb 1864 muster. Captured at Hatcher's Run on 4/2/1865. Taken to Point Lookout, MD. Released on oath on 6/27/1865.

Hill, Henry J.
CO: A **Initial Rank:** Private
Joined: Wednesday, May 1, 1861 **Term (yrs):** 1 **Occupation:** Farmer **Age** 23
Enrolled at: Tishomingo Co., MS **Enrolled By:** Capt. Leeth **Promoted:** No **ROH:** No
Born: **Marital Status:** S **Residence**

Killed in battle at 1st Manassas on 7/21/1861.

Hill, John R.
CO: I **Initial Rank:** Private
Joined: Wednesday, May 1, 1861 **Term (yrs):** 1 **Occupation:** Farmer **Age** 19
Enrolled at: Pontotoc Co., MS **Enrolled By:** Capt. Herring **Promoted:** No **ROH:** No
Born: **Marital Status:** **Residence**

Wounded at Gettysburg on 7/1/1863. Sent to Staunton, VA. Furloughed to Columbia, SC for 60-days on 10/9/1863. Returned to duty.

Hinds, James K.
CO: E **Initial Rank:** Private
Joined: Wednesday, February 26, 1862 **Term (yrs):** 3 **Occupation:** **Age** 18
Enrolled at: Guntown, MS **Enrolled By:** Capt. Bates **Promoted:** No **ROH:** No
Born: **Marital Status:** **Residence**

See also James K. Hines of the 10th Mississippi Cavalry Regiment. Furloughed home sick on 8/31/1862. Deserted and joined cavalry.

2nd Mississippi Alphabetical Roster (Annotated)

Hobbs, Berry
CO: A, L **Initial Rank:** Private
Joined: Saturday, March 1, 1862 **Term (yrs):** 3 **Occupation:** Farmer **Age** 37
Enrolled at: Jacinto, MS **Enrolled By:** Lt. Clayton **Promoted:** No **ROH:** No
Born: Georgia **Marital Status:** M **Residence** Rienzi, MS

Transferred to Company L on 4/30/1862. Sick and sent to Liberty, VA on 5/1/1862. Dropped from rolls on 4/30/1863 as a deserter (however, his name appears on a register of those who were killed in battle or died of wounds or disease, dated 12/26/1862 at Mobile, AL general hospital branch #2. Death due to disease).

Hobbs, E. W.
CO: C **Initial Rank:** Private
Joined: Saturday, March 1, 1862 **Term (yrs):** 3 **Occupation:** **Age**
Enrolled at: Verona, MS **Enrolled By:** Lt. Pounds **Promoted:** No **ROH:** No
Born: **Marital Status:** **Residence**

Died at Blackwater, VA on 3/14/1863 of disease.

Hobbs, L. H.
CO: C **Initial Rank:** Private
Joined: Saturday, March 1, 1862 **Term (yrs):** 3 **Occupation:** **Age**
Enrolled at: Verona, MS **Enrolled By:** Lt. Pounds **Promoted:** No **ROH:** No
Born: **Marital Status:** **Residence**

Died of disease at Richmond on 9/26/1862 (other records say 9/25/1862 and 9/30/1862).

Hobson, James
CO: L, F **Initial Rank:** Private
Joined: Monday, March 3, 1862 **Term (yrs):** 3 **Occupation:** Farmer **Age** 22
Enrolled at: Ripley, MS **Enrolled By:** Col. Falkner **Promoted:** No **ROH:** No
Born: Mississippi **Marital Status:** **Residence**

Transferred to Company F during Mar/Apr 1862 muster roll (date not given). Discharged due to disability on 7/20/1862.

Hodges, Thomas C.
CO: K **Initial Rank:** Private
Joined: Wednesday, May 1, 1861 **Term (yrs):** 1 **Occupation:** Merchant **Age** 25
Enrolled at: Tishomingo Co., MS **Enrolled By:** Capt. Stone **Promoted:** Yes **ROH:** No
Born: **Marital Status:** **Residence**

Appointed 5th Sergeant on 9/1/1861. "Deserted before Richmond about end of July 1862." Federal records show him on a receipt for exchange of prisoners of war near Vicksburg, MS, dated 11/1/1862. Remarks in Federal records indicate he was paroled and "deserter from C.S.A."

2nd Mississippi Alphabetical Roster (Annotated)

Hodges, William
CO: E **Initial Rank:** Private
Joined: Monday, February 18, 1861 **Term (yrs):** 0 **Occupation:** **Age**
Enrolled at: Saltillo, MS **Enrolled By:** R. Griffith **Promoted:** No **ROH:** No
Born: **Marital Status:** **Residence**

Appears on a company muster roll. No other record.

Hogan, Michael
CO: A **Initial Rank:** Private
Joined: Wednesday, May 1, 1861 **Term (yrs):** 1 **Occupation:** Farmer **Age** 30
Enrolled at: Tishomingo Co., MS **Enrolled By:** Capt. Leeth **Promoted:** No **ROH:** No
Born: Ireland **Marital Status:** S **Residence** Rienzi, MS

Deserted on 6/14/1862 at Lynchburg, VA.

Holbrook, William S.
CO: D **Initial Rank:** 3rd Sergeant
Joined: Wednesday, May 1, 1861 **Term (yrs):** 1 **Occupation:** Physician **Age** 35
Enrolled at: Tippah Co., MS **Enrolled By:** Capt. Beck **Promoted:** No **ROH:** No
Born: Virginia **Marital Status:** M **Residence** Snow Creek, MS

Acting 3rd Sergeant to 6/15/1861. "Went to ranks by his own request to attend on sick of the regiment." Discharged on 7/27/1862 — over age.

Holcomb, R. S.
CO: D **Initial Rank:** Private
Joined: **Term (yrs):** 0 **Occupation:** **Age**
Enrolled at: **Enrolled By:** **Promoted:** No **ROH:** No
Born: **Marital Status:** **Residence**

Appears on a Federal list of prisoners of war forwarded to Memphis, TN for exchange. Captured on 9/14/1863 within the District of Corinth. Residence: Tippah Co., MS. Forwarded to Memphis for exchange. No other records.

Holcombe, George P.
CO: B **Initial Rank:** Private
Joined: Monday, March 3, 1862 **Term (yrs):** 3 **Occupation:** Student **Age** 16
Enrolled at: Ripley, MS **Enrolled By:** Capt. Buchanan **Promoted:** No **ROH:** No
Born: Mississippi **Marital Status:** S **Residence**

Wounded at 2nd Manassas on 8/29/1862. Sent to hospital. Returned to duty. Wounded at Gettysburg (date not given) and furloughed for 40-days from 7/22/1863. Captured in Tippah Co., MS by the 7th Kansas Cavalry while on wounded furlough on 9/9/1863. Sent to Alton, IL on 10/3/1863. Transferred to Fort Delaware on 2/29/1864. Exchanged on 12/5/1864. Still on disabled list as of 3/14/1865 at Lauderdale, MS.

2nd Mississippi Alphabetical Roster (Annotated)

Holcombe, Levi D.
CO: B **Initial Rank:** 3rd Corporal
Joined: Wednesday, May 1, 1861 **Term (yrs):** 1 **Occupation:** Student **Age** 18
Enrolled at: Tippah Co., MS **Enrolled By:** Capt. Buchanan **Promoted:** Yes **ROH:** No
Born: **Marital Status:** **Residence**

Appointed 2nd Sergeant on 4/30/1862. Wounded at 2nd Manassas on 8/29/1862. Sent to hospital. Returned to duty. Captured by Federal cavalry while on sick furlough in Mississippi on 7/21/1863 at Ripley, MS. Sent to Alton, IL on 8/11/1863. Sent to Camp Morton, IN on 8/21/1863. Transferred for exchange on 3/4/1865 to City Point, VA. Furloughed from hospital on 3/18/1865 for 30-days.

Holditch, Sydney F.
CO: I **Initial Rank:** 2nd Corporal
Joined: Wednesday, May 1, 1861 **Term (yrs):** 1 **Occupation:** Farmer **Age** 35
Enrolled at: Pontotoc Co., MS **Enrolled By:** Capt. Herring **Promoted:** Yes **ROH:** No
Born: South Carolina **Marital Status:** **Residence**

Promoted to 3rd Sergeant on 7/4/1861. Discharged due to disability on 2/26/1862 at Camp Fisher, VA.

Holland, Hugh L.
CO: D **Initial Rank:** 1st Corporal
Joined: Wednesday, May 1, 1861 **Term (yrs):** 1 **Occupation:** Farmer **Age**
Enrolled at: Tippah Co., MS **Enrolled By:** Capt. Beck **Promoted:** Yes **ROH:** No
Born: **Marital Status:** M **Residence** Hickory Flat, MS

1st Corporal to 5/10/1861. Promoted to 1st Lieutenant. Resigned on 6/28/1861 and discharged on 11/4/1861 due to disability.

Holly, John
CO: A, E **Initial Rank:** Private
Joined: Saturday, March 1, 1862 **Term (yrs):** 3 **Occupation:** Farmer **Age** 45
Enrolled at: Jacinto, MS **Enrolled By:** Lt. Clayton **Promoted:** No **ROH:** No
Born: Tennessee **Marital Status:** M **Residence** Baldwyn, MS

Transferred to Company E on 4/30/1862. Discharged due to disability in early 1863. [There is apparently some confusion in the records of John Holly and those of the younger John C. Holly, so it is possible that the comments apply to the other individual].

2nd Mississippi Alphabetical Roster (Annotated)

Holly, John C.
CO: A, E **Initial Rank:** Private
Joined: Saturday, March 1, 1862 **Term (yrs):** 3 **Occupation:** Farmer **Age** 19
Enrolled at: Jacinto, MS **Enrolled By:** Lt. Clayton **Promoted:** No **ROH:** No
Born: Alabama **Marital Status:** S **Residence** Baldwyn, MS

Transferred to Company E on 4/30/1862. Captured at Warrenton on 9/29/1862 and paroled. Died of disease on 4/1/1863. [There is apparently some confusion in the records of John Holly and those of the younger John C. Holly, so it is possible that the comments apply to the other individual].

Holman, Samuel W.
CO: C **Initial Rank:** Private
Joined: Friday, June 28, 1861 **Term (yrs):** 1 **Occupation:** Farmer **Age** 19
Enrolled at: Winchester, VA **Enrolled By:** Capt. Bromley **Promoted:** No **ROH:** No
Born: North Carolina **Marital Status:** **Residence**

Killed in battle at 2nd Manassas on 8/29/1862 (other records list his death on 8/31/1862).

Holmes, Wiley T.
CO: H **Initial Rank:** Private
Joined: Monday, April 29, 1861 **Term (yrs):** 1 **Occupation:** Farmer **Age** 44
Enrolled at: Pontotoc Co., MS **Enrolled By:** Capt. Taylor **Promoted:** No **ROH:** No
Born: North Carolina **Marital Status:** M **Residence** Chesterville, MS

Discharged on 7/29/1862 — over age.

Holt, Isaac J.
CO: K **Initial Rank:** Private
Joined: Saturday, March 1, 1862 **Term (yrs):** 3 **Occupation:** **Age** 36
Enrolled at: Iuka, MS **Enrolled By:** Lt. Latham **Promoted:** No **ROH:** No
Born: **Marital Status:** **Residence**

Wounded at battle of Bristoe Station on 10/14/1863. Furloughed home for 60-days from 1/5/1864. Listed as AWOL from end of furlough. Dropped from rolls during Nov/Dec 1864 muster for prolonged AWOL.

Holt, Joseph J.
CO: S **Initial Rank:** Asst. Surgeon
Joined: Saturday, April 27, 1861 **Term (yrs):** 1 **Occupation:** Surgeon **Age**
Enrolled at: **Enrolled By:** Jefferson Davis **Promoted:** Yes **ROH:** No
Born: **Marital Status:** **Residence**

Appointed Assistant Surgeon (with rank of Captain) by President Davis on 4/27/1861. Appointed Surgeon, P.A.C.S. on 6/1/1864 to rank from 11/1/1863. Paroled at Appomattox Court House on 4/9/1865.

2nd Mississippi Alphabetical Roster (Annotated)

Honey, Thomas J.　　　　　CO: A　　Initial Rank: Private

Joined: Saturday, March 1, 1862　　**Term (yrs):** 3　**Occupation:** Farmer　　**Age** 26

Enrolled at: Jacinto, MS　　**Enrolled By:** Lt. Clayton　　**Promoted:** No　**ROH:** No

Born: Tennessee　　**Marital Status:**　　**Residence** Iuka, MS

Died of disease at Lynchburg, VA on 9/10/1862.

Hooker, Emery E.　　　　　CO: H　　Initial Rank: Private

Joined: Thursday, August 15, 1861　　**Term (yrs):** 1　**Occupation:** Farmer　　**Age** 25

Enrolled at: Camp Jones, VA　　**Enrolled By:** Capt. Taylor　　**Promoted:** No　**ROH:** No

Born: Alabama　　**Marital Status:** S　　**Residence** Chesterville, MS

For much of the time from June 1863, served in detached service as a scout for General Heth. Killed in battle near Petersburg on 10/27/1864.

Hopkins, James H.　　　　　CO: E　　Initial Rank: Private

Joined: Wednesday, May 1, 1861　　**Term (yrs):** 1　**Occupation:** Farmer　　**Age** 19

Enrolled at: Itawamba Co., MS　　**Enrolled By:** Capt. Booth　　**Promoted:** No　**ROH:** No

Born: Mississippi　　**Marital Status:** S　　**Residence** Guntown, MS

Discharged for disability on 8/11/1861 by order of General Johnston.

Hopkins, James M.　　　　　CO: E　　Initial Rank: Private

Joined: Wednesday, May 1, 1861　　**Term (yrs):** 1　**Occupation:** Farmer　　**Age** 19

Enrolled at: Itawamba Co., MS　　**Enrolled By:** Capt. Booth　　**Promoted:** No　**ROH:** No

Born: Mississippi　　**Marital Status:** S　　**Residence** Guntown, MS

Captured at Gettysburg on 7/1/1863. Taken to Fort Delaware. Paroled on 9/14/1864. Exchanged on 9/18/1864. Furloughed 40-days from 9/27/1864. Appears on a Federal roll of prisoners of war paroled at Columbus, MS on 5/17/1865.

Horton, John H.　　　　　CO: K　　Initial Rank: Private

Joined: Wednesday, May 1, 1861　　**Term (yrs):** 1　**Occupation:** Farmer　　**Age** 20

Enrolled at: Iuka, MS　　**Enrolled By:** Capt. Stone　　**Promoted:** No　**ROH:** No

Born:　　**Marital Status:**　　**Residence**

May/Jun 1864 muster roll remarks: "Absent wounded furlough." Date and battle of wound not given, however, a hospital record shows his admission on 6/4/1864. Returned to duty. Captured near Petersburg (Hatcher's Run?) on 4/2/1865. Sent to Point Lookout, MD. Released on oath on 6/27/1865.

2nd Mississippi Alphabetical Roster (Annotated)

Hoskins, Jasper N.
CO: E **Initial Rank:** Private
Joined: Wednesday, May 1, 1861 **Term (yrs):** 1 **Occupation:** Farmer **Age** 21
Enrolled at: Itawamba Co., MS **Enrolled By:** Capt. Booth **Promoted:** Yes **ROH:** No
Born: Alabama **Marital Status:** S **Residence** Baldwyn, MS

Accompanying list of engagements show him wounded at Gettysburg on 7/1/1863 (company muster records do not so indicate, however hospital records show admission for gunshot wound on 7/13/1863). Captured on 8/19/1864 at the battle of Weldon Railroad. Sent to Point Lookout, MD. Became a "Galvanized Yankee" and joined the Federal army on 10/15/1864. Deserted.

Houston, Joseph A.
CO: D **Initial Rank:** Private
Joined: Tuesday, October 1, 1861 **Term (yrs):** 1 **Occupation:** **Age**
Enrolled at: Iuka, MS **Enrolled By:** Lt. Davenport **Promoted:** No **ROH:** No
Born: **Marital Status:** **Residence**

Captured at Gettysburg on 7/1/1863. Sent to Fort Delaware. Released on oath on 6/11/1865.

Houston, William B.
CO: D **Initial Rank:** Private
Joined: Tuesday, October 1, 1861 **Term (yrs):** 1 **Occupation:** Farmer **Age** 18
Enrolled at: Iuka, MS **Enrolled By:** Lt. Davenport **Promoted:** No **ROH:** Yes
Born: Mississippi **Marital Status:** S **Residence** Pine Grove, MS

Killed in battle at Gettysburg on 7/3/1863 (other records indicate he was killed on 7/1/1863). ROH for South Mountain (Boonsboro), 9/14/1862.

Houston, William W.
CO: K **Initial Rank:** Private
Joined: Saturday, March 1, 1862 **Term (yrs):** 3 **Occupation:** **Age** 20
Enrolled at: Iuka, MS **Enrolled By:** Lt. Latham **Promoted:** Yes **ROH:** No
Born: **Marital Status:** **Residence**

Wounded at Gaines Mill on 6/27/1862. Appointed 3rd Sergeant on 8/1/1862. Listed as absent on wounded furlough during May/Jun 1864 muster roll (date and battle not given although hospital records indicate he was admitted with gunshot wound on 5/8/1864). Furloughed home for 60-days from 5/29/1864. On detached duty in North Carolina from 2/15/1865.

2nd Mississippi Alphabetical Roster (Annotated)

Hovis, James W.
CO: B *Initial Rank:* 2nd Sergeant
Joined: Wednesday, May 1, 1861 *Term (yrs):* 1 *Occupation:* Cabinet Maker *Age* 27
Enrolled at: Tippah Co., MS *Enrolled By:* Capt. Buchanan *Promoted:* Yes *ROH:* No
Born: North Carolina *Marital Status:* *Residence*

Appointed 1st Sergeant on 4/30/1862. Wounded at Sharpsburg on 9/17/1862. Sent to hospital. Furloughed. Discharged by order of medical examining board to the Invalid Corps, P.A.C.S. on 8/26/1864 due to disability caused by wounds at Sharpsburg.

Hovis, Joseph E.
CO: B *Initial Rank:* Private
Joined: Wednesday, May 1, 1861 *Term (yrs):* 1 *Occupation:* Carriage Maker *Age* 19
Enrolled at: Tippah Co., MS *Enrolled By:* Capt. Buchanan *Promoted:* No *ROH:* No
Born: *Marital Status:* *Residence*

Discharged on 7/30/1862 due to military exemption.

Hovis, Lawson B.
CO: B, S *Initial Rank:* Adjutant (1Lt)
Joined: Wednesday, May 1, 1861 *Term (yrs):* 1 *Occupation:* *Age* 34
Enrolled at: Tippah Co., MS *Enrolled By:* Col. Falkner *Promoted:* No *ROH:* No
Born: *Marital Status:* *Residence*

Appointed Adjutant on 4/30/1861. Relieved from duty and discharged on 4/23/1862 due to reorganization of regiment.

Howard, A. C.
CO: C *Initial Rank:* Private
Joined: Saturday, March 1, 1862 *Term (yrs):* 3 *Occupation:* *Age*
Enrolled at: Verona, MS *Enrolled By:* Lt. Pounds *Promoted:* No *ROH:* Yes
Born: *Marital Status:* M *Residence*

Killed at Sharpsburg on 9/17/1862. ROH for Sharpsburg, 9/17/1862.

Howarton, Richard
CO: E *Initial Rank:* Private
Joined: Wednesday, May 1, 1861 *Term (yrs):* 1 *Occupation:* Farmer *Age* 32
Enrolled at: Itawamba Co., MS *Enrolled By:* Capt. Booth *Promoted:* No *ROH:* No
Born: Alabama *Marital Status:* S *Residence* Saltillo, MS

Discharge for disability on 2/7/1862 at Camp Fisher, VA.

2nd Mississippi Alphabetical Roster (Annotated)

Hoyle, Daniel H.
CO: H *Initial Rank:* 1st Corporal
Joined: Monday, April 29, 1861   *Term (yrs):* 1   *Occupation:* Tailor   *Age* 42
Enrolled at: Pontotoc Co., MS   *Enrolled By:* Capt. Taylor   *Promoted:* No   *ROH:* No
Born: Georgia   *Marital Status:* S   *Residence* Chesterville, MS

Reduced to ranks and detailed in Quartermaster Dept. of the regiment on 9/10/1861. Discharged on 7/29/1862 — over age.

Hoyle, James M.
CO: H *Initial Rank:* Private
Joined: Monday, April 29, 1861   *Term (yrs):* 1   *Occupation:* Physician   *Age* 24
Enrolled at: Pontotoc Co., MS   *Enrolled By:* Capt. Taylor   *Promoted:* Yes   *ROH:* No
Born: Georgia   *Marital Status:* M   *Residence* Chesterville, MS

Promoted to Assistant Surgeon, P.A.C.S on 10/28/1861.

Hubbard, George D.
CO: K *Initial Rank:* Private
Joined: Wednesday, May 1, 1861   *Term (yrs):* 1   *Occupation:* Mechanic   *Age* 28
Enrolled at: Tishomingo Co., MS   *Enrolled By:* Capt. Stone   *Promoted:* No   *ROH:* No
Born: Georgia   *Marital Status:*   *Residence*

Detailed as regimental and brigade ambulance blacksmith. Deserted to the enemy on 7/25/1863. Federal records indicate he was captured at Orleans, VA on 7/26/1863 and desired to take the oath of allegiance. Willing to work for U.S. government, but unwilling to enlist. Taken to Point Lookout, MD and transferred to Fortress Monroe, VA on 3/2/1864 "awaiting orders." No other record.

Hubbard, H. H.
CO: S *Initial Rank:* Surgeon
Joined: Saturday, April 27, 1861   *Term (yrs):* 1   *Occupation:* Surgeon   *Age*
Enrolled at: Vicksburg, MS   *Enrolled By:* Pres. Davis   *Promoted:* No   *ROH:* No
Born: *Marital Status:*   *Residence*

Appointed regimental surgeon by President Davis on 4/27/1861.

2nd Mississippi Alphabetical Roster (Annotated)

Hubbard, James M.   CO: H   Initial Rank: Private

Joined: Monday, April 29, 1861   **Term (yrs):** 1   **Occupation:** Farmer   **Age** 23
Enrolled at: Pontotoc Co., MS   **Enrolled By:** Capt. Taylor   **Promoted:** Yes   **ROH:** No
Born: Alabama   **Marital Status:** S   **Residence** Chesterville, MS

Appointed 3rd Sergeant on 4/22/1862. Listed as 2nd Sergeant during Jul/Aug 1862 muster roll. Wounded at Sharpsburg on 9/17/1862 (left leg amputated). Furloughed. Authority to appear before a medical examining board. Discharged for disability on 3/8/1865.

Hubbard, James S.   CO: K   Initial Rank: Private

Joined: Saturday, March 1, 1862   **Term (yrs):** 3   **Occupation:**   **Age** 19
Enrolled at: Iuka, MS   **Enrolled By:** Lt. Latham   **Promoted:** No   **ROH:** No
Born: **Marital Status:**   **Residence**

Listed in company records as having deserted to the enemy while in Pennsylvania. Federal records show him captured on 7/5/1863. Paroled at DeCamp General Hospital, Davids Island, New York Harbor (not dated). Also appears on a Federal list of sick and wounded Confederates in the hospitals in and about Gettysburg, PA after the battle (heading lists him as "nurse Co. K, 2 Regt Miss").

Hubbard, William T.   CO: K   Initial Rank: Private

Joined: Saturday, April 6, 1861   **Term (yrs):** 0   **Occupation:**   **Age**
Enrolled at: Iuka, MS   **Enrolled By:** W. M. Inge   **Promoted:** No   **ROH:** No
Born: **Marital Status:**   **Residence**

Appears on a company muster roll. No other record.

Hubbs, Madison   CO: C, E   Initial Rank: Private

Joined: Wednesday, February 27, 1861   **Term (yrs):** 1   **Occupation:**   **Age**
Enrolled at: Verona, MS   **Enrolled By:** Capt. Kilpatrick   **Promoted:** No   **ROH:** No
Born: **Marital Status:**   **Residence**

Appears on only one company muster roll. Appears on a Federal register of prisoners of war captured at Tupelo, MS on 7/14/1864 and sent to Alton, IL. Took oath of allegiance on 5/23/1865. Requested transportation to family in Pulaski Co., IL. No other record.

2nd Mississippi Alphabetical Roster (Annotated)

Hudson, Lewis J.   *CO:* F   *Initial Rank:* Private
Joined: Friday, June 7, 1861   *Term (yrs):* 1   *Occupation:* Planter   *Age* 24
Enrolled at: Harpers Ferry, VA   *Enrolled By:* Capt. Davis   *Promoted:* No   *ROH:* No
Born: *Marital Status:*   *Residence*

Killed in battle at 1st Manassas on 7/21/1861.

Hughes, Alexander H.   *CO:* K   *Initial Rank:* Private
Joined: Saturday, March 1, 1862   *Term (yrs):* 3   *Occupation:*   *Age* 29
Enrolled at: Iuka, MS   *Enrolled By:* Lt. Latham   *Promoted:* No   *ROH:* No
Born: *Marital Status:*   *Residence*

Wounded at Sharpsburg on 9/17/1862 (little finger, left hand). Furloughed. Returned to duty. Captured at Petersburg (Hatcher's Run?) on 4/2/1865. Taken to Fort Delaware. Released on oath on 6/11/1865.

Hughes, Dolphus E.   *CO:* C   *Initial Rank:* Private
Joined: Saturday, March 1, 1862   *Term (yrs):* 3   *Occupation:*   *Age*
Enrolled at: Verona, MS   *Enrolled By:* Lt. Pounds   *Promoted:* No   *ROH:* Yes
Born: *Marital Status:*   *Residence*

Hospital records show admission with a wound on 7/12/1863 (action or date of wound not stated). Hospital records also indicate admission for a wound on 3/28/1864 and returned to duty on 4/1/1864. Killed in action at Cold Harbor on 6/2/1864. ROH for Bethesda Church, 5/31/1864.

Hughes, J. B.   *CO:* E   *Initial Rank:*
Joined: *Term (yrs):* 0   *Occupation:*   *Age*
Enrolled at: *Enrolled By:*   *Promoted:* No   *ROH:* No
Born: *Marital Status:*   *Residence*

Appears on a list of the Calhoun Rifles dated 2/11/1861. No other record.

2nd Mississippi Alphabetical Roster (Annotated)

Hughes, James C.
CO: K **Initial Rank:** Private
Joined: Saturday, March 1, 1862   **Term (yrs):** 3 **Occupation:**   **Age** 26
Enrolled at: Iuka, MS   **Enrolled By:** Lt. Latham   **Promoted:** No **ROH:** No
Born: **Marital Status:**   **Residence**

Hospital records show admission for gunshot wound on 7/10/1863 at Richmond (date and battle received not indicated in records). Returned to duty on 7/30/1863. Wounded at battle of The Wilderness on 5/5/1864. Captured near Petersburg (Hatcher's Run?) on 4/2/1865. Taken to Point Lookout, MD. Released on oath on 6/27/1865.

Hughes, James W.
CO: C **Initial Rank:** Private
Joined: Wednesday, May 1, 1861   **Term (yrs):** 1 **Occupation:** Farmer   **Age** 19
Enrolled at: Itawamba Co., MS   **Enrolled By:** Capt. Bromley   **Promoted:** No **ROH:** No
Born: **Marital Status:**   **Residence**

Wounded at battle of 2nd Manassas (date not given). Returned to duty. Captured at Gettysburg on 7/1/1863. Sent to Fort Delaware. Released on oath on 6/11/1865.

Hughes, Robert S. C.
CO: E **Initial Rank:** Private
Joined: Wednesday, May 1, 1861   **Term (yrs):** 1 **Occupation:** Clerk   **Age** 19
Enrolled at: Itawamba Co., MS   **Enrolled By:** Capt. Booth   **Promoted:** No **ROH:** No
Born: Mississippi   **Marital Status:** S   **Residence** Guntown, MS

Discharged on 7/9/1861 by order of General Johnston. Appears to have re-enlisted on 3/22/1862 at Guntown, MS for 3-years or the war by Capt. Bates. Wounded and captured at Gettysburg on 7/3/1863. Died in captivity at Fort Delaware on 3/1/1864. Grave located "Jersey Shore opposite Post."

Hughes, Singleton
CO: E **Initial Rank:** Private
Joined: Wednesday, May 1, 1861   **Term (yrs):** 1 **Occupation:**   **Age**
Enrolled at: Itawamba Co., MS   **Enrolled By:** Capt. Booth   **Promoted:** No **ROH:** No
Born: **Marital Status:**   **Residence**

Appears on company muster-in roll. No other record.

2nd Mississippi Alphabetical Roster (Annotated)

Hughs, William M.
CO: C **Initial Rank:** Private
Joined: Wednesday, May 1, 1861 *Term (yrs):* 1 *Occupation:* Farmer **Age** 45
Enrolled at: Itawamba Co., MS *Enrolled By:* Capt. Bromley *Promoted:* No *ROH:* No
Born: South Carolina *Marital Status:* *Residence*

Discharged due to disability on 9/12/1861.

Hull, R.
CO: **Initial Rank:** Sergeant
Joined: *Term (yrs):* 0 *Occupation:* **Age**
Enrolled at: *Enrolled By:* *Promoted:* No *ROH:* No
Born: *Marital Status:* *Residence*

Appears on a Federal report of paroles given prisoners of war dated Richmond, VA on 5/12/1865. No other record.

Humphreys, Charles L.
CO: E **Initial Rank:** Private
Joined: Monday, September 30, 1861 *Term (yrs):* 1 *Occupation:* Farmer **Age** 21
Enrolled at: Corinth, MS *Enrolled By:* Lt. Davenport *Promoted:* Yes *ROH:* Yes
Born: Mississippi *Marital Status:* *Residence*

Promoted to 3rd Corporal circa Sep/Oct 1862. Wounded and captured at Gettysburg (date not given). Died at Federal hospital, Gettysburg, PA on 8/9/1863 (according to Federal records. Confederate records record his death as 7/15/1863). ROH for Gettysburg, 7/1/1863.

Humphreys, Charles W.
CO: B **Initial Rank:** Private
Joined: Monday, October 28, 1861 *Term (yrs):* 1 *Occupation:* Farmer **Age** 20
Enrolled at: Camp Fisher, VA *Enrolled By:* Capt. Buchanan *Promoted:* No *ROH:* No
Born: Mississippi *Marital Status:* S *Residence* Guntown, MS

Captured at Gettysburg on 7/1/1863. Sent to Fort Delaware. Released on oath on 6/11/1865.

Humphreys, David W.
CO: B, S **Initial Rank:** 2nd Lieutenant
Joined: Tuesday, April 30, 1861 *Term (yrs):* 1 *Occupation:* **Age**
Enrolled at: Ripley, MS *Enrolled By:* Col. Falkner *Promoted:* Yes *ROH:* No
Born: *Marital Status:* *Residence*

Appointed Major on 5/10/1861. Appointed Lieutenant. Colonel to rank from 4/16/1862. Wounded at Sharpsburg on 9/17/1862. Killed in battle at Gettysburg (while leading the remnant of the regiment in Pickett's Charge) on 7/3/1863.

2nd Mississippi Alphabetical Roster (Annotated)

Humphries, Francis M.
CO: A **Initial Rank:** Private
Joined: Saturday, March 1, 1862 **Term (yrs):** 3 **Occupation:** Farmer **Age** 27
Enrolled at: Jacinto, MS **Enrolled By:** Lt. Clayton **Promoted:** No **ROH:** No
Born: Mississippi **Marital Status:** S **Residence** Burnsville, MS

Captured at Petersburg (Hatcher's Run?) on 4/2/1865. Sent to Point Lookout, MD. Released on oath on 6/21/1865.

Humphries, H. L. D.
CO: A **Initial Rank:** Private
Joined: Saturday, March 1, 1862 **Term (yrs):** 3 **Occupation:** Farmer **Age** 22
Enrolled at: Jacinto, MS **Enrolled By:** Lt. Clayton **Promoted:** No **ROH:** No
Born: Mississippi **Marital Status:** **Residence**

Mortally wounded at Gaines Mill on 6/27/1862. Died of wounds on 7/17/1862.

Hunt, E. Newton
CO: B **Initial Rank:** Private
Joined: Wednesday, May 1, 1861 **Term (yrs):** 1 **Occupation:** Physician **Age** 26
Enrolled at: Tippah Co., MS **Enrolled By:** Capt. Buchanan **Promoted:** No **ROH:** No
Born: **Marital Status:** **Residence**

Assigned to duty in the hospital and as surgeon's assistant. Appointed hospital steward on 1/14/1863.

Hunt, J. D.
CO: A **Initial Rank:** Private
Joined: **Term (yrs):** 0 **Occupation:** **Age**
Enrolled at: **Enrolled By:** **Promoted:** No **ROH:** No
Born: **Marital Status:** **Residence**

Appears on a Federal roll of prisoners of war received at Camp Douglas, IL on 3/9/1864. Captured at Okolona, MS on 2/19/1864. No other record.

Hunt, John C.
CO: G **Initial Rank:** Private
Joined: Wednesday, May 1, 1861 **Term (yrs):** 1 **Occupation:** Student **Age** 18
Enrolled at: Pontotoc Co., MS **Enrolled By:** Capt. Miller **Promoted:** No **ROH:** No
Born: Mississippi **Marital Status:** S **Residence** Pontotoc, MS

Deserted from hospital in July 1863. Appears on a Federal register of prisoners of war at Memphis, TN — Deserters from rebel army. Dated 4/3/1864. Oath of allegiance taken.

2nd Mississippi Alphabetical Roster (Annotated)

Hussey, Josiah
CO: C *Initial Rank:* Private
Joined: Wednesday, May 1, 1861 *Term (yrs):* 1 *Occupation:* Farmer *Age* 30
Enrolled at: Itawamba Co., MS *Enrolled By:* Capt. Bromley *Promoted:* No *ROH:* No
Born: *Marital Status:* *Residence*

Listed as deserted from 3/28/1864. Appears on a list of prisoners of war belonging the Armstrong's brigade, Chalmer's division, Forrest's corps, captured 4/5/1865 at Plantersville, AL by the 18th Indiana Battalion. [May have joined the cavalry unit after deserting, or may have been simply picked up and misidentified when captured].

Hutchinson, George W.
CO: H *Initial Rank:* Private
Joined: Monday, February 24, 1862 *Term (yrs):* 3 *Occupation:* Carpenter *Age* 20
Enrolled at: Chesterville, MS *Enrolled By:* Lt. Porter *Promoted:* No *ROH:* No
Born: Georgia *Marital Status:* S *Residence* Chesterville, MS

Killed in battle at Sharpsburg on 9/17/1862.

Hyatt, Calvin J.
CO: K *Initial Rank:* 3rd Lieutenant
Joined: Wednesday, May 1, 1861 *Term (yrs):* 1 *Occupation:* Merchant *Age* 28
Enrolled at: Tishomingo Co., MS *Enrolled By:* *Promoted:* No *ROH:* No
Born: *Marital Status:* *Residence*

Listed as Jr. 2nd Lieutenant. on company muster-in roll. Relieved of duty on 4/23/1862 due to reorganization of company. Discharged.

Inman, Henry A. J.
CO: K *Initial Rank:* Private
Joined: Wednesday, May 1, 1861 *Term (yrs):* 1 *Occupation:* Merchant *Age* 28
Enrolled at: Tishomingo Co., MS *Enrolled By:* Capt. Stone *Promoted:* No *ROH:* No
Born: *Marital Status:* *Residence*

Wounded at 1st Manassas on 7/21/1861. In hospital at Charlottesville, VA. Furloughed to Alabama. Returned to duty. Captured at Gettysburg on 7/1/1863. Sent to Fort Delaware and then to Point Lookout, MD. Paroled on 3/17/1864. Exchanged. Furloughed 30-days. Never returned. Listed as deserted, dropped from rolls for prolonged AWOL during Nov/Dec 1864 muster roll.

2nd Mississippi Alphabetical Roster (Annotated)

Irvin, Green B.   CO: K   Initial Rank: Private
Joined: Wednesday, May 1, 1861   **Term (yrs):** 1   **Occupation:** Clerk   **Age** 23
Enrolled at: Tishomingo Co., MS   **Enrolled By:** Capt. Stone   **Promoted:** Yes   **ROH:** No
Born: **Marital Status:**   **Residence**

Listed as 4th Sergeant during May/Jun 1862 muster. Wounded at 2nd Manassas (date not given). Furloughed. AWOL. Listed as deserted during Jan/Feb 1864 muster roll.

Irvin, John   CO: K   Initial Rank: 2nd Lieutenant
Joined: Wednesday, May 1, 1861   **Term (yrs):** 1   **Occupation:** Carpenter   **Age** 26
Enrolled at: Tishomingo Co., MS   **Enrolled By:**   **Promoted:** No   **ROH:** No
Born: **Marital Status:**   **Residence**

Relieved from duty on 4/23/1862 due to reorganization of company. Discharged.

Irvin, Ptolmy V.   CO: L   Initial Rank: 3rd Sergeant
Joined: Monday, March 3, 1862   **Term (yrs):** 3   **Occupation:** Farmer   **Age** 34
Enrolled at: Ripley, MS   **Enrolled By:** Col. Falkner   **Promoted:** Yes   **ROH:** No
Born: Alabama   **Marital Status:**   **Residence** Ripley, MS

Promoted 3rd Sergeant on 3/23/1862. Died of disease at Liberty Hospital (various dates given: 12/1/1862, 2/6/1863 (hospital record), and 1/1/1863).

Ivey, Francis M.   CO: E   Initial Rank: Private
Joined: Wednesday, May 1, 1861   **Term (yrs):** 1   **Occupation:** Farmer   **Age** 30
Enrolled at: Itawamba Co., MS   **Enrolled By:** Capt. Booth   **Promoted:** No   **ROH:** No
Born: **Marital Status:** S   **Residence** Guntown, MS

Also see Ham's Regiment of Mississippi Cavalry. Detached service at hospital by order of Secretary of War. Listed as deserted for Jul/Aug 1863 company muster roll, but still shown as "present" on hospital muster roll.

Jackson, Andrew   CO: K   Initial Rank: Private
Joined: Wednesday, May 1, 1861   **Term (yrs):** 1   **Occupation:** Student   **Age** 18
Enrolled at: Tishomingo Co., MS   **Enrolled By:** Capt. Stone   **Promoted:** No   **ROH:** No
Born: **Marital Status:**   **Residence**

Wounded at Gaines Mill on 6/27/1862. Most of service time spent as detailed and detached from company. Captured at hospital in Richmond, VA on 4/3/1865.

2nd Mississippi Alphabetical Roster (Annotated)

Jackson, Ephram D.
CO: E   **Initial Rank:** Private
Joined: Saturday, March 1, 1862   **Term (yrs):** 3   **Occupation:**   **Age** 31
Enrolled at: Guntown, MS   **Enrolled By:** Capt. Bates   **Promoted:** No   **ROH:** No
Born: **Marital Status:** M   **Residence** Guntown, MS

Died of disease at Richmond, VA in Chimborazo Hospital on 9/11/1862 (typhoid fever).

Jackson, Henry N.
CO: E   **Initial Rank:** Private
Joined: Tuesday, March 4, 1862   **Term (yrs):** 3   **Occupation:** Farmer   **Age** 28
Enrolled at: Guntown, MS   **Enrolled By:** Capt. Bates   **Promoted:** No   **ROH:** No
Born: **Marital Status:** M   **Residence** Guntown, MS

Died in hospital at Richmond, VA on 11/24/1862 of disease (typhoid fever).

Jackson, John F.
CO: K   **Initial Rank:** Private
Joined: Wednesday, May 1, 1861   **Term (yrs):** 1   **Occupation:** Farmer   **Age** 20
Enrolled at: Tishomingo Co., MS   **Enrolled By:** Capt. Stone   **Promoted:** No   **ROH:** No
Born: **Marital Status:**   **Residence**

Wounded at Gettysburg on 7/1/1863. Sent to hospital in Richmond. Returned to duty. Captured near Petersburg (Hatcher's Run?) on 4/2/1865. Sent to Point Lookout, MD. Released on oath on 6/28/1865.

Jackson, John W.
CO: F   **Initial Rank:** Private
Joined: Tuesday, April 30, 1861   **Term (yrs):** 1   **Occupation:** Farmer   **Age** 39
Enrolled at: Ripley, MS   **Enrolled By:** Lt. Davenport   **Promoted:** No   **ROH:** No
Born: Alabama   **Marital Status:** M   **Residence**

Discharged for disability on 11/2/1861. Appears to have re-entered service on 3/1/1862 at Ripley, MS; enrolled by Capt. Powers for 3-years. Died of disease at Richmond on 7/15/1862.

Jackson, S. B.
CO: E   **Initial Rank:**
Joined: **Term (yrs):** 0   **Occupation:**   **Age**
Enrolled at: **Enrolled By:**   **Promoted:** No   **ROH:** No
Born: **Marital Status:**   **Residence**

Appears on a list of the Calhoun Rifles dated 2/11/1861. No other record.

2nd Mississippi Alphabetical Roster (Annotated)

Jackson, Steth S.
CO: L **Initial Rank:** Private
Joined: Monday, March 3, 1862 **Term (yrs):** 3 **Occupation:** Farmer **Age** 45
Enrolled at: Ripley, MS **Enrolled By:** Col. Falkner **Promoted:** No **ROH:** No
Born: Virginia **Marital Status:** M **Residence** Ripley, MS
Discharged for disability on 11/14/1862.

Jackson, William L.
CO: B **Initial Rank:** Private
Joined: Wednesday, May 1, 1861 **Term (yrs):** 1 **Occupation:** Farmer **Age** 23
Enrolled at: Tippah Co., MS **Enrolled By:** Capt. Buchanan **Promoted:** No **ROH:** No
Born: **Marital Status:** **Residence**
Spent much of service time detailed as regimental teamster. Captured at hospital in Richmond, VA on 4/3/1865. Paroled 5/8/1865.

James, Daniel A.
CO: K **Initial Rank:** Private
Joined: **Term (yrs):** 0 **Occupation:** Farmer **Age** 22
Enrolled at: **Enrolled By:** **Promoted:** No **ROH:** No
Born: **Marital Status:** **Residence**
Appears on a Confederate hospital record for wound, admitted (? Date not given). Sent to General Hospital on 9/25/1862. Appears on Federal rolls of prisoners of war, captured at Tuscumbia, AL on 3/3/1863. Sent to Alton, IL. Exchanged on 4/1/1863 at City Point, VA. No other records. [Evidence indicates he was probably wounded at Sharpsburg and on wounded furlough when captured].

Jenkins, James S.
CO: L **Initial Rank:** Private
Joined: Monday, April 18, 1864 **Term (yrs):** 3 **Occupation:** Farmer **Age** 17
Enrolled at: Meridian, MS **Enrolled By:** Lt. Henderson **Promoted:** No **ROH:** No
Born: Tennessee **Marital Status:** S **Residence** Ripley, MS
Accompanying list of engagements shows him wounded at The Wilderness on 5/5/1864 (company muster rolls do not so indicate). Captured at Hatcher's Run on 4/2/1865. Sent to Point Lookout, MD. Released on oath on 6/28/1865.

2nd Mississippi Alphabetical Roster (Annotated)

Jenkins, Ransom
CO: F, L **Initial Rank:** Private
Joined: Wednesday, May 1, 1861 **Term (yrs):** 1 **Occupation:** U.S. Army **Age** 24
Enrolled at: Tippah Co., MS **Enrolled By:** Capt. Davis **Promoted:** Yes **ROH:** No
Born: South Carolina **Marital Status:** S **Residence** Ripley, MS

Transferred to Company L on 4/30/1862. Listed as 3rd Lieutenant. for Mar/Apr 1863 muster. Wounded at Gettysburg on 7/1/1863. Promoted to 2nd Lieutenant. on 12/28/1863 to rank from 7/3/1863. Wounded at The Wilderness on 5/5/1864. Sent to hospital. Returned to duty. Killed in battle on 10/1/1864.

Jenkins, William J.
CO: F, L **Initial Rank:** Private
Joined: Wednesday, May 1, 1861 **Term (yrs):** 1 **Occupation:** Planter **Age** 21
Enrolled at: Tippah Co., MS **Enrolled By:** Capt. Davis **Promoted:** Yes **ROH:** No
Born: South Carolina **Marital Status:** M **Residence** Ripley, MS

Transferred to Company L on 4/30/1862. Promoted to 4th Corporal on 9/1/1862. Captured at Gettysburg on 7/1/1863. Sent to Fort Delaware. Released on oath on 6/11/1865.

Jennings, B. F.
CO: D **Initial Rank:**
Joined: **Term (yrs):** 0 **Occupation:** **Age**
Enrolled at: **Enrolled By:** **Promoted:** No **ROH:** No
Born: **Marital Status:** **Residence**

Appears on a Federal list of prisoners of war captured by the Army of the Potomac at the battle of Williamsburg, VA in May 1862 and sent to Fort Monroe, VA. List not dated. No other record.

Jeter, David F.
CO: L **Initial Rank:** Private
Joined: Monday, March 3, 1862 **Term (yrs):** 3 **Occupation:** Farmer **Age** 16
Enrolled at: Ripley, MS **Enrolled By:** Col. Falkner **Promoted:** No **ROH:** No
Born: South Carolina **Marital Status:** S **Residence** Union Mills, MS

Sick, sent to Liberty, VA on 5/1/1862. No further record.

Jeter, Richard C.
CO: L **Initial Rank:** Private
Joined: Monday, March 3, 1862 **Term (yrs):** 3 **Occupation:** Farmer **Age** 18
Enrolled at: Ripley, MS **Enrolled By:** Capt. Powers **Promoted:** No **ROH:** Yes
Born: South Carolina **Marital Status:** M **Residence** Union Mills, MS

Wounded (in thigh) at Gaines Mill on 6/27/1862. Killed in battle at The Wilderness on 5/5/1864. ROH for The Wilderness, 5/5/1864.

2nd Mississippi Alphabetical Roster (Annotated)

Jeter, William D. F.   CO: L   Initial Rank: Private
Joined: Monday, March 3, 1862   **Term (yrs):** 3   **Occupation:** Farmer   **Age** 16
Enrolled at: Ripley, MS   **Enrolled By:** Col. Falkner   **Promoted:** No   **ROH:** No
Born: South Carolina   **Marital Status:**   **Residence**

Sick. Sent to Williamsburg about 5/1/1862. No further record.

Jobe, J. Fletcher   CO: A   Initial Rank: Private
Joined: Saturday, March 1, 1862   **Term (yrs):** 3   **Occupation:** Farmer   **Age** 25
Enrolled at: Jacinto, MS   **Enrolled By:** Lt. Clayton   **Promoted:** No   **ROH:** No
Born: **Marital Status:** M   **Residence** Rienzi, MS

Died on 3/25/1862 at Rienzi, MS.

Johns, Henry H.   CO: B   Initial Rank: Private
Joined: Monday, March 3, 1862   **Term (yrs):** 3   **Occupation:** Farmer   **Age** 17
Enrolled at: Ripley, MS   **Enrolled By:** Capt. Buchanan   **Promoted:** No   **ROH:** Yes
Born: South Carolina   **Marital Status:** S   **Residence**

Killed in battle at Sharpsburg on 9/17/1862. ROH for Sharpsburg, 9/17/1862.

Johnson, Daniel A.   CO: F   Initial Rank: 2nd Corporal
Joined: Wednesday, May 1, 1861   **Term (yrs):** 1   **Occupation:** Planter   **Age** 24
Enrolled at: Tippah Co., MS   **Enrolled By:** Capt. Davis   **Promoted:** Yes   **ROH:** No
Born: **Marital Status:**   **Residence**

Appointed 5th Sergeant on 12/5/1861. Elected Jr. 2nd Lieutenant on 4/11/1862. Took command on 4/22/1862. Wounded at Sharpsburg on 9/17/1862. Furloughed 30-days. Returned to regiment on 11/23/1862. In hospital. Captured at Hatcher's Run on 4/2/1865. Sent to Johnson's Island. Released on oath on 6/18/1865.

Johnson, David A.   CO: H   Initial Rank: Private
Joined: Monday, April 29, 1861   **Term (yrs):** 1   **Occupation:** Carpenter   **Age** 21
Enrolled at: Pontotoc Co., MS   **Enrolled By:** Capt. Taylor   **Promoted:** No   **ROH:** No
Born: North Carolina   **Marital Status:** S   **Residence** Tupelo, MS

Captured at Gettysburg on 7/1/1863. Sent to Fort Delaware. Released on oath 6/11/1865.

2nd Mississippi Alphabetical Roster (Annotated)

Johnson, John A.
CO: D **Initial Rank:** Private
Joined: Wednesday, May 1, 1861 *Term (yrs):* 1 *Occupation:* Farmer *Age* 25
Enrolled at: Tippah Co., MS *Enrolled By:* Capt. Beck *Promoted:* No *ROH:* No
Born: Georgia *Marital Status:* S *Residence* Shelby Creek, MS

Accompany list of engagements show him wounded at Sharpsburg on 9/17/1862 and wounded at Gettysburg on 7/1/1863 (all company records say is that he took 40-days wounded furlough from 7/22/1863). AWOL since 10/2/1863. Dropped from rolls as deserter on orders of Col. Stone circa Mar/Apr 1864 muster.

Johnson, John W.
CO: D **Initial Rank:** Private
Joined: Thursday, September 19, 1861 *Term (yrs):* 1 *Occupation:* Farmer *Age* 21
Enrolled at: Salem, MS *Enrolled By:* Lt. Davenport *Promoted:* No *ROH:* No
Born: *Marital Status:* S *Residence* Pine Grove, MS

Discharged for disability on 1/18/1862. Unable to return home due to severity of illness. Died at Chimborazo Hospital #4 at Richmond, VA on 3/20/1862.

Johnson, Joseph
CO: A **Initial Rank:** Private
Joined: Saturday, March 1, 1862 *Term (yrs):* 3 *Occupation:* Farmer *Age* 26
Enrolled at: Jacinto, MS *Enrolled By:* Lt. Clayton *Promoted:* No *ROH:* No
Born: Tennessee *Marital Status:* M *Residence* Jacinto, MS

Wounded on 5/5/1864 at The Wilderness. AWOL from 7/1/1864. Dropped from rolls — deserted.

Johnson, Samuel
CO: G **Initial Rank:** Private
Joined: *Term (yrs):* 0 *Occupation:* *Age*
Enrolled at: *Enrolled By:* *Promoted:* No *ROH:* No
Born: *Marital Status:* *Residence*

Appears on a Federal register of prisoners of war dated 6/3/1863 at Memphis, TN. No other record.

Johnson, Thomas
CO: K **Initial Rank:** Private
Joined: Wednesday, May 1, 1861 *Term (yrs):* 1 *Occupation:* Carpenter *Age* 33
Enrolled at: Tishomingo Co., MS *Enrolled By:* Capt. Stone *Promoted:* No *ROH:* No
Born: Tennessee *Marital Status:* *Residence*

Discharged at Winchester, VA for disability on order of General Bee on 7/13/1861.

2nd Mississippi Alphabetical Roster (Annotated)

Johnson, Thomas
CO: D **Initial Rank:** Private
Joined: Wednesday, May 1, 1861 **Term (yrs):** 1 **Occupation:** Farmer **Age** 23
Enrolled at: Tippah Co., MS **Enrolled By:** Capt. Beck **Promoted:** Yes **ROH:** No
Born: Georgia **Marital Status:** S **Residence** Shelby Creek, MS

Wounded in battle at Gaines Mill on 6/27/1862. In hospital at Danville, VA. Returned to duty. Killed in railroad accident on 2/2/1863 in South Carolina (Wilmington & Manchester Railroad).

Johnson, William C.
CO: E **Initial Rank:** Private
Joined: Saturday, March 1, 1862 **Term (yrs):** 3 **Occupation:** Farmer **Age** 20
Enrolled at: Guntown, MS **Enrolled By:** Capt. Bates **Promoted:** No **ROH:** No
Born: Alabama **Marital Status:** S **Residence** Marietta, MS

Wounded at Sharpsburg on 9/17/1862. Furloughed home. Returned to duty. Captured at Gettysburg on 7/1/1863. Sent to Fort Delaware. Released on oath on 6/11/1865.

Johnson, William R.
CO: H **Initial Rank:** Private
Joined: Monday, April 29, 1861 **Term (yrs):** 1 **Occupation:** Farmer **Age** 31
Enrolled at: Pontotoc Co., MS **Enrolled By:** Capt. Taylor **Promoted:** No **ROH:** No
Born: Alabama **Marital Status:** M **Residence** Poplar Springs, MS

Wounded (in foot) at 1st Manassas on 7/21/1861. Discharged for disability due to wounds on 10/13/1861 at Camp Fisher, VA.

Johnson, William R.
CO: L **Initial Rank:** Private
Joined: Monday, March 3, 1862 **Term (yrs):** 3 **Occupation:** Farmer **Age** 26
Enrolled at: Ripley, MS **Enrolled By:** Col. Falkner **Promoted:** No **ROH:** No
Born: South Carolina **Marital Status:** S **Residence** Ripley, MS

Died of disease at Chimborazo Hospital #4 at Richmond, VA on 10/13/1862.

Johnston, John C.
CO: G **Initial Rank:** Private
Joined: Wednesday, September 18, 1861 **Term (yrs):** 1 **Occupation:** Farmer **Age** 19
Enrolled at: Pontotoc, MS **Enrolled By:** Lt. Davenport **Promoted:** No **ROH:** No
Born: Mississippi **Marital Status:** S **Residence** Pontotoc, MS

Captured at Gettysburg on 7/1/1863. Taken to Fort Delaware. Released on oath on 6/11/1865.

2nd Mississippi Alphabetical Roster (Annotated)

Johnston, John F.

	CO: F	**Initial Rank:** 4th Corporal
Joined: Wednesday, May 1, 1861	**Term (yrs):** 1 **Occupation:** Planter	**Age** 23
Enrolled at: Tippah Co., MS	**Enrolled By:** Capt. Davis	**Promoted:** No **ROH:** No
Born:	**Marital Status:**	**Residence**

Died of disease in hospital at Camp Fisher, VA on 10/11/1861 (other records say 10/12/1861).

Joiner, Charles J.

	CO: H	**Initial Rank:** Private
Joined: Monday, April 29, 1861	**Term (yrs):** 1 **Occupation:** Physician	**Age** 30
Enrolled at: Pontotoc Co., MS	**Enrolled By:** Capt. Taylor	**Promoted:** No **ROH:** No
Born: Alabama	**Marital Status:** M	**Residence** Chesterville, MS

Detailed Assistant Surgeon from 6/10/1861. Discharged on 7/12/1861 due to disability.

Jones, Bluford

	CO: K	**Initial Rank:** Private
Joined: Saturday, March 1, 1862	**Term (yrs):** 3 **Occupation:**	**Age** 40
Enrolled at: Iuka, MS	**Enrolled By:** Lt. Latham	**Promoted:** No **ROH:** No
Born:	**Marital Status:**	**Residence**

Captured at Martinsburg, VA on 11/25/1863 (another record says Front Royal, VA on 6/4/1863). Taken to Fort Delaware. Exchanged on 10/31/1864.

Jones, George H.

	CO: H, I	**Initial Rank:** Private
Joined: Saturday, March 15, 1862	**Term (yrs):** 3 **Occupation:** Farmer	**Age** 17
Enrolled at: Chesterville, MS	**Enrolled By:** Lt. Porter	**Promoted:** No **ROH:** No
Born: Tennessee	**Marital Status:** S	**Residence** Chesterville, MS

Transferred to Company I on 5/1/1863 by order of Col. Stone. Wounded and captured at Gettysburg on 7/1/1863. Taken to DeCamp General Hospital, Davids Island, NY and paroled at City Point, VA on 9/27/1863. Furloughed on parole for 60-days on 10/5/1863. Hospital records indicate left leg amputated due to wound on 7/1/1863 by the regimental surgeon, Dr. Hubbard.

Jones, John

	CO: A	**Initial Rank:** Private
Joined:	**Term (yrs):** 0 **Occupation:**	**Age**
Enrolled at:	**Enrolled By:**	**Promoted:** No **ROH:** No
Born:	**Marital Status:**	**Residence**

Appears on a Federal roll of prisoners of war dated Vicksburg, MS on 7/28/1863. Captured at Young's Point, MS on 6/12/1863. No other record.

2nd Mississippi Alphabetical Roster (Annotated)

Jones, John
CO: E *Initial Rank:* Private
Joined: Wednesday, May 1, 1861 *Term (yrs):* 1 *Occupation:* *Age*
Enrolled at: Iuka, MS *Enrolled By:* Capt. Stone *Promoted:* No *ROH:* No
Born: *Marital Status:* *Residence*

No record following Nov/Dec 1862 muster roll — "On extra daily duty."

Jones, John H.
CO: I *Initial Rank:* Private
Joined: *Term (yrs):* 0 *Occupation:* *Age*
Enrolled at: *Enrolled By:* *Promoted:* No *ROH:* No
Born: *Marital Status:* *Residence*

Appears on a Federal register of prisoners received and disposed of by the Provost Marshal General, Army of the Potomac. Dated 2/15/1864, "Rebel deserter." Also appears on a register of the Way Hospital in Meridian, MS, complaint: wounded; admitted: 3/26/1865; remarks: retired. No other records.

Jones, Marion F.
CO: E *Initial Rank:* Private
Joined: Saturday, March 1, 1862 *Term (yrs):* 3 *Occupation:* Farmer *Age* 18
Enrolled at: Guntown, MS *Enrolled By:* Capt. Bates *Promoted:* No *ROH:* No
Born: *Marital Status:* *Residence*

Died of disease at Ashland, VA on 4/30/1862.

Jones, Martin D.
CO: K *Initial Rank:* Private
Joined: Saturday, March 1, 1862 *Term (yrs):* 3 *Occupation:* Farmer *Age* 25
Enrolled at: Iuka, MS *Enrolled By:* Lt. Latham *Promoted:* No *ROH:* No
Born: Alabama *Marital Status:* *Residence*

Died of disease at Ashland, VA on 6/22/1862.

Jones, Rufus C.
CO: E *Initial Rank:* Private
Joined: Wednesday, May 1, 1861 *Term (yrs):* 1 *Occupation:* Farmer *Age* 21
Enrolled at: Itawamba Co., MS *Enrolled By:* Capt. Booth *Promoted:* Yes *ROH:* No
Born: Mississippi *Marital Status:* S *Residence* Ripley, MS

Listed as 5th Sergeant during Mar/Apr 1862 muster. Appears as 4th Sergeant during Jul/Aug 1862 muster. Rank given as 3rd Sergeant for Jan/Feb 1864 muster. Detached in Jan 1865 on recruiting service [probably with the detail accompanying Col. Stone].

2nd Mississippi Alphabetical Roster (Annotated)

Jones, Sargent M.
CO: A, I **Initial Rank:** Private
Joined: Saturday, March 1, 1862 **Term (yrs):** 3 **Occupation:** Farmer **Age** 26
Enrolled at: Jacinto, MS **Enrolled By:** Lt. Clayton **Promoted:** No **ROH:** No
Born: Mississippi **Marital Status:** **Residence**

Transferred from Company A to Company I circa Jul/Aug 1862. Wounded and captured at Gettysburg on 7/3/1863. Sent to Fort Delaware. Released on oath on 6/11/1865.

Jones, William D. J.
CO: B **Initial Rank:** Private
Joined: Wednesday, May 1, 1861 **Term (yrs):** 1 **Occupation:** Farmer **Age** 18
Enrolled at: Tippah Co., MS **Enrolled By:** Capt. Buchanan **Promoted:** No **ROH:** No
Born: **Marital Status:** **Residence**

Wounded on 8/29/1862 (?) 2nd Manassas. In hospital. During Mar/Apr 1863 muster listed as AWOL — deserted.

Jones, William H.
CO: D **Initial Rank:** Private
Joined: Wednesday, May 1, 1861 **Term (yrs):** 1 **Occupation:** Farmer **Age** 22
Enrolled at: Tippah Co., MS **Enrolled By:** Capt. Beck **Promoted:** No **ROH:** No
Born: Tennessee **Marital Status:** S **Residence** Shelby Creek, MS

Killed in battle at Gaines Mill on 6/27/1862.

Jones, William H.
CO: K, E **Initial Rank:** Private
Joined: Wednesday, May 1, 1861 **Term (yrs):** 1 **Occupation:** Boatman **Age** 22
Enrolled at: Tishomingo Co., MS **Enrolled By:** Capt. Stone **Promoted:** No **ROH:** No
Born: **Marital Status:** S **Residence** Iuka, MS

Detailed as regimental teamster. Transferred to Company E on 5/6/1862. Deserted from camp near Orange Court House, VA on 2/10/1864.

Jones, William P.
CO: F **Initial Rank:** Private
Joined: Wednesday, May 1, 1861 **Term (yrs):** 1 **Occupation:** Planter **Age** 21
Enrolled at: Tippah Co., MS **Enrolled By:** Capt. Davis **Promoted:** No **ROH:** No
Born: Mississippi **Marital Status:** **Residence**

Killed while on the skirmish line (sharpshooting) near Petersburg, VA on 9/21/1864.

2nd Mississippi Alphabetical Roster (Annotated)

Jordan, Charles W.
CO: L **Initial Rank:** Private
Joined: Monday, March 3, 1862 **Term (yrs):** 3 **Occupation:** Farmer **Age** 32
Enrolled at: Ripley, MS **Enrolled By:** Col. Falkner **Promoted:** No **ROH:** No
Born: Georgia **Marital Status:** M **Residence** Ripley, MS

Wounded at Malvern Hill on 7/1/1862 Captured at Gettysburg on 7/1/1863. Sent to Fort Delaware where he died of disease on 3/31/1865 (or 3/30/1865). Grave location: "Jersey Shore."

Jordan, Edwin
CO: L **Initial Rank:** 2nd Sergeant
Joined: Monday, March 3, 1862 **Term (yrs):** 3 **Occupation:** Farmer **Age** 35
Enrolled at: Ripley, MS **Enrolled By:** Col. Falkner **Promoted:** No **ROH:** No
Born: Georgia **Marital Status:** M **Residence** New Albany, MS

Accompanying list of engagements show him wounded at Seven Pines on 5/31/1862 (company records do not mention this). Captured at Gettysburg on 7/1/1863. Taken to Fort Delaware. Paroled and exchanged (date?). Admitted to Richmond hospital for wound on 9/22/1864. Furloughed 40-days from 9/27/1864.

Joslin, John F.
CO: K **Initial Rank:** Private
Joined: Saturday, March 1, 1862 **Term (yrs):** 3 **Occupation:** **Age** 21
Enrolled at: Iuka, MS **Enrolled By:** Lt. Latham **Promoted:** No **ROH:** No
Born: **Marital Status:** **Residence**

Received sick furlough during Jul/Aug 1862 time period. Never returned. Deserted.

Joslin, Samuel M.
CO: K **Initial Rank:** Private
Joined: Saturday, March 1, 1862 **Term (yrs):** 3 **Occupation:** Farmer **Age** 20
Enrolled at: Iuka, MS **Enrolled By:** Lt. Latham **Promoted:** No **ROH:** No
Born: Mississippi **Marital Status:** **Residence**

Died of disease in hospital at Ashland, VA on 6/8/1862.

2ⁿᵈ Mississippi Alphabetical Roster (Annotated)

Joslin, William

CO: K *Initial Rank:* Private

Joined: Wednesday, May 1, 1861 *Term (yrs):* 1 *Occupation:* Farmer *Age* 36

Enrolled at: Tishomingo Co., MS *Enrolled By:* Capt. Stone *Promoted:* No *ROH:* No

Born: *Marital Status:* *Residence*

Reported as deserted from furlough during Mar/Apr 1863 muster. However, he also appears on Federal prisoner of war records, captured within the District of Corinth. Dated 11/1/1863 at Chewalla, MS. Sent to Alton, IL. Died in military prison on 12/25/1863 of smallpox. Notes on records say, "Conscripted. Willing to enter federal army. Objects to exchange. Desires to take the oath of allegiance. Died Dec 20, 1863."

Julian, Ansel

CO: K *Initial Rank:* Private

Joined: Wednesday, May 1, 1861 *Term (yrs):* 1 *Occupation:* Farmer *Age* 22

Enrolled at: Tishomingo Co., MS *Enrolled By:* Capt. Stone *Promoted:* No *ROH:* No

Born: Georgia *Marital Status:* *Residence*

Killed in battle at Gaines Mill on 6/27/1862.

Kantenbuger, P.

CO: *Initial Rank:*

Joined: *Term (yrs):* 0 *Occupation:* *Age*

Enrolled at: *Enrolled By:* *Promoted:* No *ROH:* No

Born: *Marital Status:* *Residence*

Appears on a Federal record of prisoners of war dated 2/2/1863 at Old Capitol Prison, Washington, D.C. Charges: "Confederate soldier & deserter." Signed parole as P. Kautenberger, dated 1/17/1863. No other records.

Keelen, James

CO: K *Initial Rank:* Private

Joined: Saturday, April 6, 1861 *Term (yrs):* 1 *Occupation:* *Age*

Enrolled at: Iuka, MS *Enrolled By:* W. M. Inge *Promoted:* No *ROH:* No

Born: *Marital Status:* *Residence*

Appears on a company muster roll. No other record.

Keenum, Leander D.

CO: K *Initial Rank:* Private

Joined: Saturday, March 1, 1862 *Term (yrs):* 3 *Occupation:* *Age* 27

Enrolled at: Iuka, MS *Enrolled By:* Lt. Latham *Promoted:* No *ROH:* No

Born: *Marital Status:* *Residence*

Also see L. D. Keenum, 26th Mississippi Infantry Regiment. Wounded and captured at 2nd Manassas on 8/29/1862. Paroled. Furloughed. Captured while on furlough in Mississippi on 9/12/1863. Sent to Alton, IL.

2nd Mississippi Alphabetical Roster (Annotated)

Keith, J. B.
CO: A   *Initial Rank:* Private
Joined: *Term (yrs):* 0   *Occupation:*   *Age*
Enrolled at: *Enrolled By:*   *Promoted:* No   *ROH:* No
Born: *Marital Status:*   *Residence*

Appears on a Federal report of prisoners of war captured within the District of Corinth. Dated 10/27/1863. Residence: Tippah Co., MS. Took oath of allegiance and was released. No other record.

Kelly, Elisha
CO: G   *Initial Rank:* Private
Joined: Wednesday, May 1, 1861   *Term (yrs):* 1   *Occupation:* Grocer   *Age* 37
Enrolled at: Pontotoc Co., MS   *Enrolled By:* Capt. Miller   *Promoted:* No   *ROH:* No
Born: South Carolina   *Marital Status:* S   *Residence* Pontotoc, MS

Discharged for disability on 9/9/1861 at Camp Jones, VA by order of General Johnston.

Kelly, James
CO: E   *Initial Rank:* Private
Joined: Wednesday, May 1, 1861   *Term (yrs):* 1   *Occupation:* Farmer   *Age* 23
Enrolled at: Itawamba Co., MS   *Enrolled By:* Capt. Booth   *Promoted:* No   *ROH:* No
Born: Ireland   *Marital Status:* S   *Residence* Guntown, MS

Also see O'Kelly. Deserted on 9/16/1861 from Camp Jones, VA.

Kelly, John O.
CO: B   *Initial Rank:* Private
Joined: Wednesday, May 1, 1861   *Term (yrs):* 1   *Occupation:* Farmer   *Age* 27
Enrolled at: Tippah Co., MS   *Enrolled By:* Capt. Buchanan   *Promoted:* No   *ROH:* No
Born: *Marital Status:*   *Residence*

Wounded at 2nd Manassas on 8/29/1862. Sent to hospital. Returned to duty. Captured at Gettysburg on 7/1/1863. Sent to Fort Delaware. Released on oath on 6/7/1865.

Kelly, Thomas D.
CO: F, H   *Initial Rank:* Private
Joined: Sunday, March 23, 1862   *Term (yrs):* 3   *Occupation:* Farmer   *Age* 21
Enrolled at: Corinth, MS   *Enrolled By:* Capt. Powers   *Promoted:* No   *ROH:* No
Born: South Carolina   *Marital Status:* M   *Residence*

Also see Company C, 1st Mississippi Infantry Regiment. Transferred to Company H about 4/1/1862. Listed as AWOL since about 10/1/1862. However, he was transferred to Company C of the 1st Mississippi by order of General Smith in Oct 1862.

2nd Mississippi Alphabetical Roster (Annotated)

Kenan, James A.

	CO: K	**Initial Rank:** Private
Joined: Wednesday, May 1, 1861	**Term (yrs):** 1 **Occupation:** Laborer	**Age** 21
Enrolled at: Tishomingo Co., MS	**Enrolled By:** Capt. Stone	**Promoted:** No **ROH:** No
Born:	**Marital Status:**	**Residence**

Also see Confederate States Navy. Wounded at 1st Manassas on 7/21/1861. Sent to hospital at Charlottesville, VA. Returned to duty. Transferred to Confederate States Navy on 4/1/1864 by order of General Lee.

Kent, James W.

	CO: F	**Initial Rank:** Private
Joined: Wednesday, May 1, 1861	**Term (yrs):** 1 **Occupation:** Planter	**Age** 19
Enrolled at: Tippah Co., MS	**Enrolled By:** Capt. Davis	**Promoted:** No **ROH:** No
Born:	**Marital Status:**	**Residence**

Discharged for disability on 6/28/1861 at Winchester, VA.

Kent, Stephen W.

	CO: E	**Initial Rank:** Private
Joined: Saturday, March 1, 1862	**Term (yrs):** 3 **Occupation:** Farmer	**Age** 21
Enrolled at: Guntown, MS	**Enrolled By:** Capt. Bates	**Promoted:** No **ROH:** No
Born: Alabama	**Marital Status:** S	**Residence** Guntown, MS

List of engagements shows him wounded on 6/2/1864 at Bethesda Church; wounded again at the Weldon Railroad on 8/18/1864; and again, at Fort Bratton on 10/1/1864 (company records provide no confirmation of his being wounded on these dates or battles), however hospital records do show an admission on 6/5/1864.

Keown, Isaac

	CO: K	**Initial Rank:** Private
Joined: Saturday, April 6, 1861	**Term (yrs):** 1 **Occupation:**	**Age**
Enrolled at: Iuka, MS	**Enrolled By:** W. M. Inge	**Promoted:** No **ROH:** No
Born:	**Marital Status:**	**Residence**

Appears on a company muster roll. No other record.

Key, Christopher C.

	CO: A	**Initial Rank:** Private
Joined: Wednesday, May 1, 1861	**Term (yrs):** 1 **Occupation:** Mechanic	**Age** 23
Enrolled at: Tishomingo Co., MS	**Enrolled By:** Capt. Leeth	**Promoted:** No **ROH:** No
Born: Mississippi	**Marital Status:** S	**Residence** Jacinto, MS

Detailed as ambulance driver and regimental teamster for much of his career. Captured at Seven Pines on 5/31/1862. Exchanged on 8/5/1862. Paroled at Appomattox Court House on 4/9/1865.

2nd Mississippi Alphabetical Roster (Annotated)

Key, David L.   *CO:* A   *Initial Rank:* Private
Joined: Monday, November 25, 1861   *Term (yrs):* 1   *Occupation:* Farmer   *Age* 32
Enrolled at: Camp Fisher, VA   *Enrolled By:* Capt. Leeth   *Promoted:* No   *ROH:* No
Born: Tennessee   *Marital Status:* S   *Residence* Rienzi, MS

Discharged due to disability in March 1862 (company muster records indicate he deserted from sick furlough in Mississippi).

Key, William J.   *CO:* A   *Initial Rank:* Private
Joined: Wednesday, May 1, 1861   *Term (yrs):* 1   *Occupation:* Law Student   *Age* 23
Enrolled at: Tishomingo Co., MS   *Enrolled By:* Capt. Leeth   *Promoted:* No   *ROH:* Yes
Born: Tennessee   *Marital Status:* S   *Residence* Rienzi, MS

Wounded at Gaines Mill on 6/27/1862. Died of wounds at Lynchburg General Hospital #1 on 7/27/1862. ROH for Gaines Mill, 6/27/1862 and Malvern Hill, 7/1/1862. (Records do not match ROH citation. May have been wounded at Malvern Hill and not Gaines Mill).

Keys, George E.   *CO:* E   *Initial Rank:* Private
Joined: Saturday, March 8, 1862   *Term (yrs):* 3   *Occupation:* Farmer   *Age* 18
Enrolled at: Guntown, MS   *Enrolled By:* Capt. Bates   *Promoted:* No   *ROH:* No
Born: Alabama   *Marital Status:* S   *Residence* Danville, AL

Captured at Hatcher's Run on 4/2/1865. Taken to Point Lookout, MD. Released on oath on 6/28/1865.

Keys, William H.   *CO:* E   *Initial Rank:* Private
Joined: Wednesday, May 1, 1861   *Term (yrs):* 1   *Occupation:* Farmer   *Age* 21
Enrolled at: Itawamba Co., MS   *Enrolled By:* Capt. Booth   *Promoted:* Yes   *ROH:* No
Born: *Marital Status:*   *Residence*

Listed as 3rd Sergeant on Sep/Oct 1861 muster roll. Rank shown as 2nd Sergeant during Jul/Aug 1862 muster. Accompanying list of engagements indicate he was wounded on 7/3/1863 at Gettysburg and again wounded on 5/6/1864 at The Wilderness (these are not mentioned in the company records). He was wounded "by his own gun" on 8/18/1864 at the battle of Weldon Railroad and furloughed 40-days from 8/30/1864.

Kidd, Green L.   *CO:* G   *Initial Rank:* Private
Joined: Tuesday, June 10, 1862   *Term (yrs):* 2   *Occupation:* Farmer   *Age* 45
Enrolled at: Richmond, VA   *Enrolled By:* Capt. Crawford   *Promoted:* No   *ROH:* No
Born: Virginia   *Marital Status:* M   *Residence* Pontotoc, MS

Also see Thomas F. Herron (substituted for him). Killed at Gettysburg on 7/1/1863.

2nd Mississippi Alphabetical Roster (Annotated)

Kidd, William D.   CO: G   Initial Rank: Private

Joined: Wednesday, May 1, 1861   **Term (yrs):** 1   **Occupation:** Farmer   **Age** 21

Enrolled at: Pontotoc Co., MS   **Enrolled By:** Capt. Miller   **Promoted:** No   **ROH:** No

Born: Alabama   **Marital Status:** S   **Residence** Pontotoc, MS

Accompanying list of engagements show him wounded at The Wilderness on 5/6/1864 (company records do not so indicate). Deserted to the enemy on 3/2/1865.

Kile, C   CO: E   Initial Rank: Private

Joined: **Term (yrs):** 0   **Occupation:**   **Age**

Enrolled at: **Enrolled By:**   **Promoted:** No   **ROH:** No

Born: **Marital Status:**   **Residence**

Appears on a roll of prisoners of war dated Camp Douglas, IL on 8/1/1862. Captured at Springfield, MO. [Misidentified. This man probably does not belong to the 2nd Mississippi, but to the 2nd Missouri which is sometimes abbreviated identically in the Federal records as the 2nd Mississippi].

Killian, Reuben   CO: H   Initial Rank: Private

Joined: Monday, April 29, 1861   **Term (yrs):** 1   **Occupation:** Farmer   **Age** 23

Enrolled at: Pontotoc Co., MS   **Enrolled By:** Capt. Taylor   **Promoted:** No   **ROH:** No

Born: Alabama   **Marital Status:** M   **Residence** Alabama

Detailed as regimental teamster for much of his service. Listed as AWOL from furlough as of 2/26/1864. Listed as deserted during Jul/Aug 1864 muster roll.

Kimball, James W.   CO: K   Initial Rank: Private

Joined: Saturday, March 1, 1862   **Term (yrs):** 3   **Occupation:**   **Age**

Enrolled at: Iuka, MS   **Enrolled By:** Lt. Latham   **Promoted:** No   **ROH:** No

Born: **Marital Status:**   **Residence**

Captured at Hatcher's Run on 4/2/1865. Taken to Point Lookout, MD. Released on oath on 6/28/1865.

Kimbell, Gilbert B.   CO: B   Initial Rank: Private

Joined: Wednesday, May 1, 1861   **Term (yrs):** 1   **Occupation:** Student   **Age** 18

Enrolled at: Tippah Co., MS   **Enrolled By:** Capt. Buchanan   **Promoted:** No   **ROH:** No

Born: Mississippi   **Marital Status:**   **Residence**

Discharged on 12/31/1861 by order of General Whiting, however apparently re-enlisted on 3/3/1862 for 3-years. Detached on divisional ordnance guard duties. Discharged for disability on 4/8/1863.

2nd Mississippi Alphabetical Roster (Annotated)

Kimbell, James F.　　　　　　　　　　　　　　　*CO:* K　　*Initial Rank:* Private

Joined: Saturday, March 1, 1862　　*Term (yrs):* 3　*Occupation:*　　　　　　　　　　*Age* 36

Enrolled at: Iuka, MS　　*Enrolled By:* Lt. Latham　　*Promoted:* No　*ROH:* No

Born:　　　　*Marital Status:*　　　　*Residence*

Listed as sick at hospital through Jul/Aug 1862 muster. Present through Nov/Dec 1862 muster. No other record.

King, J. J.　　　　　　　　　　　　　　　*CO:* A　　*Initial Rank:* Private

Joined:　　*Term (yrs):* 0　*Occupation:*　　　　　　　　　　*Age*

Enrolled at:　　*Enrolled By:*　　*Promoted:* No　*ROH:* No

Born:　　　　*Marital Status:*　　　　*Residence*

Appears on a list of rebel sick and wounded prisoners of war received at DeCamp General Hospital, Davids Island, NY Harbor, July 17, 19, 22, 23, 24, 1863. Not dated. Where captured: Gettysburg. Date: 1-4 July 1863. No other record.

King, John S.　　　　　　　　　　　　　　　*CO:* F　　*Initial Rank:* Private

Joined: Saturday, March 1, 1862　　*Term (yrs):* 3　*Occupation:* Farmer　　　　*Age* 21

Enrolled at: Ripley, MS　　*Enrolled By:* Col. Falkner　　*Promoted:* No　*ROH:* No

Born: Mississippi　　*Marital Status:* S　　*Residence*

Captured at Gettysburg on 7/5/1863 (or 7/6/1863). Taken to Fort Delaware. Released on oath on 6/11/1865.

King, Thomas J.　　　　　　　　　　　　　　　*CO:* I　　*Initial Rank:* Private

Joined: Wednesday, May 1, 1861　　*Term (yrs):* 1　*Occupation:* Farmer　　　　*Age* 25

Enrolled at: Pontotoc Co., MS　　*Enrolled By:* Capt. Herring　　*Promoted:* No　*ROH:* No

Born: Georgia　　*Marital Status:*　　　　*Residence*

Died of disease in hospital on 6/25/1861 at Winchester, VA.

King, William H.　　　　　　　　　　　　　　　*CO:* F　　*Initial Rank:* Private

Joined: Wednesday, May 1, 1861　　*Term (yrs):* 1　*Occupation:* Planter　　　　*Age* 21

Enrolled at: Tippah Co., MS　　*Enrolled By:* Capt. Davis　　*Promoted:* No　*ROH:* No

Born:　　　　*Marital Status:*　　　　*Residence*

Wounded and captured at Sharpsburg on 9/17/1862. Exchanged. Sent to hospital, leg amputated (at right thigh by Dr. Eads) and then furloughed home as of 11/24/1863. AWOL thru last muster (Jan/Feb 1865).

2nd Mississippi Alphabetical Roster (Annotated)

Kinman, John
CO: D *Initial Rank:* Private
Joined: *Term (yrs):* 0 *Occupation:* Painter *Age*
Enrolled at: *Enrolled By:* *Promoted:* No *ROH:* No
Born: *Marital Status:* *Residence*

Appears on Federal prisoner of war records. Sent to Camp Douglas, IL, dated 9/29/1862. Brigade: Chalmers; Division: Bragg [records list variously as 2 Miss Batt and 2 Miss Battery and 2 Regt Miss. Misidentified. Probably did not belong to the 2nd Mississippi Infantry Regiment but to one of the other commands].

Kirk, John
CO: K *Initial Rank:* Private
Joined: Saturday, March 1, 1862 *Term (yrs):* 3 *Occupation:* Farmer *Age* 19
Enrolled at: Iuka, MS *Enrolled By:* Lt. Latham *Promoted:* No *ROH:* No
Born: Tennessee *Marital Status:* *Residence*

Killed in battle at Sharpsburg on 9/17/1862.

Kirksey, Christopher C.
CO: C *Initial Rank:* Private
Joined: Saturday, March 1, 1862 *Term (yrs):* 3 *Occupation:* *Age*
Enrolled at: Verona, MS *Enrolled By:* Lt. Pounds *Promoted:* No *ROH:* No
Born: *Marital Status:* *Residence*

Captured battle of 2nd Manassas at Warrenton (nurse) on 8/29/1862. Paroled and exchanged. Admitted to hospital in Richmond on 7/9/1863 with wound (action or date not stated in company records). Listed as AWOL from 7/3/1864. Listed as deserted during Jan/Feb 1865 muster roll.

Kizer, Benjamin F.
CO: A *Initial Rank:* Private
Joined: Wednesday, May 1, 1861 *Term (yrs):* 1 *Occupation:* Farmer *Age* 25
Enrolled at: Tishomingo Co., MS *Enrolled By:* Capt. Leeth *Promoted:* No *ROH:* No
Born: *Marital Status:* *Residence*

Deserted to the enemy at Blackwater Bridge, VA (near Suffolk) on 5/10/1863.

Kizer, Michael
CO: A *Initial Rank:* Private
Joined: Saturday, March 1, 1862 *Term (yrs):* 3 *Occupation:* Farmer *Age* 29
Enrolled at: Jacinto, MS *Enrolled By:* Lt. Clayton *Promoted:* No *ROH:* No
Born: Tennessee *Marital Status:* M *Residence* Booneville, MS

Also see 26th Mississippi Infantry Regiment. Initially detailed as teamster. Died of disease in camp near Blackwater Bridge, VA on 3/18/1863.

2nd Mississippi Alphabetical Roster (Annotated)

Knight, James C.
CO: I **Initial Rank:** Private
Joined: Wednesday, May 1, 1861 **Term (yrs):** 1 **Occupation:** Farmer **Age** 20
Enrolled at: Pontotoc Co., MS **Enrolled By:** Capt. Herring **Promoted:** No **ROH:** No
Born: **Marital Status:** **Residence**

Wounded at Sharpsburg on 9/17/1862. Furloughed. Returned to duty. Captured at Gettysburg on 7/3/1863. Died at Fort Delaware on 4/17/1865 of pneumonia. Locality of grave: "Jersey Shore."

Knight, William J.
CO: I **Initial Rank:** Private
Joined: Wednesday, May 1, 1861 **Term (yrs):** 1 **Occupation:** Carpenter **Age** 40
Enrolled at: Pontotoc Co., MS **Enrolled By:** Capt. Herring **Promoted:** No **ROH:** No
Born: South Carolina **Marital Status:** **Residence**

Discharged on 7/31/1862 — over age.

Knott, James S.
CO: E **Initial Rank:** Private
Joined: Wednesday, May 1, 1861 **Term (yrs):** 1 **Occupation:** Student **Age** 17
Enrolled at: Itawamba Co., MS **Enrolled By:** Capt. Booth **Promoted:** Yes **ROH:** No
Born: Alabama **Marital Status:** S **Residence** Guntown, MS

Promoted to 1st Corporal on 4/17/1862. Appears on a hospital admission record for gunshot wound on 7/9/1863 (date or battle not given in company records). Wanted to transfer to the cavalry. Furloughed 60-days from 4/23/1864. Dropped from rolls as deserter on 12/31/1864 for continued AWOL.

Knott, Rufus D.
CO: E **Initial Rank:** Private
Joined: Wednesday, May 1, 1861 **Term (yrs):** 1 **Occupation:** Clerk (farmer) **Age** 21
Enrolled at: Itawamba Co., MS **Enrolled By:** Capt. Booth **Promoted:** No **ROH:** No
Born: Alabama **Marital Status:** S **Residence** Guntown, MS

Discharged on 7/10/1861 for disability by order of General Johnston. Re-enlisted for 3-years on 3/1/1862. Died of disease at Ashland, VA on 4/24/1862.

2nd Mississippi Alphabetical Roster (Annotated)

Knox, John
CO: E *Initial Rank:* Private
Joined: *Term (yrs):* 0 *Occupation:* *Age*
Enrolled at: *Enrolled By:* *Promoted:* No *ROH:* No
Born: *Marital Status:* *Residence*

Appears on a Federal register of prisoners of war at Fort Delaware received from Alton, IL and dated April, 1864. He also appears on a register of payments on descriptive lists, period of service from 2/22/1862 to 6/30/1862. Paid on 7/15/1862 by S.R. Chisman. Amount $44.00. No other records.

Knox, Mathew
CO: B, L *Initial Rank:* Private
Joined: Wednesday, May 1, 1861 *Term (yrs):* 1 *Occupation:* Teacher *Age* 19
Enrolled at: Tippah Co., MS *Enrolled By:* Capt. Buchanan *Promoted:* Yes *ROH:* Yes
Born: Georgia *Marital Status:* S *Residence* Malin, MS

Wounded at 1st Manassas on 7/21/1861. Transferred to Company L on 4/30/1862. Transferred back to Company B on 11/1/1862. Wounded at Gettysburg (date not given) and sent to hospital at Richmond. Listed as 4th Corporal during May/Jun 1864 muster roll. Wounded at The Wilderness on 5/5/1864. Sent to hospital and furloughed for 60-days from 5/20/1864. Returned to duty. Captured at Petersburg (Hatcher's Run?) on 4/2/1865. Sent to Point Lookout, MD. Released on oath on 6/28/1865. ROH for Weldon Railroad, 8/19/1864.

Krause, Henry
CO: K *Initial Rank:* Private
Joined: Monday, September 30, 1861 *Term (yrs):* 1 *Occupation:* *Age*
Enrolled at: Iuka, MS *Enrolled By:* Lt. Davenport *Promoted:* No *ROH:* No
Born: *Marital Status:* *Residence*

Also see Confederate States Navy. Transferred to Navy on 4/1/1864 by order of General Lee.

Kyle, James R.
CO: E, H *Initial Rank:* Private
Joined: Saturday, June 1, 1861 *Term (yrs):* 1 *Occupation:* *Age* 22
Enrolled at: Saltillo, MS *Enrolled By:* Capt. Halder *Promoted:* No *ROH:* No
Born: *Marital Status:* S *Residence* Saltillo, MS

Also see 17th Mississippi Infantry Regiment. Transferred from the 17th Mississippi on 8/1/1861. According to accompanying list of engagements, was also wounded, captured and paroled at 2nd Manassas on 8/29/1862. Captured at Gettysburg on 7/1/1863. Taken to Fort Delaware. Released on oath on 6/11/1865.

2nd Mississippi Alphabetical Roster (Annotated)

Kyle, Samuel D.
CO: E, H **Initial Rank:** Private
Joined: Wednesday, May 1, 1861 **Term (yrs):** 1 **Occupation:** Farmer **Age** 18
Enrolled at: Itawamba Co., MS **Enrolled By:** Capt. Booth **Promoted:** No **ROH:** Yes
Born: South Carolina **Marital Status:** S **Residence** Saltillo, MS

Wounded (left side) and captured at 2nd Manassas on 8/30/1862. Paroled and exchanged. Furloughed home. Returned to duty. Wounded (arm) at The Wilderness on 5/6/1864. Captured at Hatcher's Run on 4/2/1865. Sent to Point Lookout, MD. Released on oath on 6/14/1865. ROH for The Wilderness, 5/6/1864.

Lafarge, Henry
CO: G **Initial Rank:** Private
Joined: Wednesday, May 1, 1861 **Term (yrs):** 1 **Occupation:** Steward **Age** 53
Enrolled at: Pontotoc Co., MS **Enrolled By:** Capt. Miller **Promoted:** No **ROH:** No
Born: England **Marital Status:** S **Residence** Pontotoc, MS

Discharged by order of General Lee on 8/2/1862 — over age.

Laird, James
CO: A **Initial Rank:** Private
Joined: Saturday, September 21, 1861 **Term (yrs):** 1 **Occupation:** Farmer **Age** 49
Enrolled at: Rienzi, MS **Enrolled By:** Lt. Davenport **Promoted:** No **ROH:** No
Born: Tennessee **Marital Status:** **Residence** Rienzi, MS

Discharged for disability on 11/29/1861 at Camp Fisher, VA.

Laird, John A.
CO: A **Initial Rank:** Private
Joined: Saturday, September 21, 1861 **Term (yrs):** 1 **Occupation:** Farmer **Age** 26
Enrolled at: Rienzi, MS **Enrolled By:** Lt. Davenport **Promoted:** No **ROH:** No
Born: Alabama **Marital Status:** S **Residence** Rienzi, MS

Killed in action (skirmish) near Windsor, VA on 5/22/1863.

Lakey, Pleasant H.
CO: F **Initial Rank:** Private
Joined: Saturday, March 1, 1862 **Term (yrs):** 3 **Occupation:** Farmer **Age** 27
Enrolled at: Ripley, MS **Enrolled By:** Col. Falkner **Promoted:** No **ROH:** No
Born: Indiana **Marital Status:** M **Residence**

Sent home on sick furlough for 30-days as of 10/10/1862. Never reported back. Deserted.

2nd Mississippi Alphabetical Roster (Annotated)

Lakey, William
Joined: Saturday, March 1, 1862 **Term (yrs):** 3 **CO:** F **Initial Rank:** Private **Occupation:** Farmer **Age** 43
Enrolled at: Ripley, MS **Enrolled By:** Col. Falkner **Promoted:** No **ROH:** No
Born: Indiana **Marital Status:** M **Residence**

Went home on sick furlough for 40-days from 6/24/1863. Never reported back. "Went to the enemy."

Lamb, James
Joined: Saturday, March 1, 1862 **Term (yrs):** 3 **CO:** C **Initial Rank:** Private **Occupation:** **Age**
Enrolled at: Verona, MS **Enrolled By:** Lt. Pounds **Promoted:** No **ROH:** No
Born: **Marital Status:** **Residence**

Wounded (in arm) at Gaines Mill on 6/27/1862. Furloughed. Returned to duty. Killed at Gettysburg on 7/3/1863 (actually, mortally wounded — died in Federal hospital).

Lancaster, Joseph C.
Joined: Monday, March 3, 1862 **Term (yrs):** 3 **CO:** B **Initial Rank:** Private **Occupation:** Farmer **Age** 22
Enrolled at: Ripley, MS **Enrolled By:** Capt. Buchanan **Promoted:** No **ROH:** No
Born: Alabama **Marital Status:** S **Residence**

Wounded at Gettysburg on 7/1/1863. Sent to hospital at Richmond. Furloughed. Captured "near" Ripley, MS on 6/10/1864. Sent to Alton, IL. Last record, Alton, IL prison hospital, 2/10/1865.

Lancaster, Samuel
Joined: Monday, March 3, 1862 **Term (yrs):** 3 **CO:** B **Initial Rank:** Private **Occupation:** Farmer **Age** 18
Enrolled at: Ripley, MS **Enrolled By:** Capt. Buchanan **Promoted:** No **ROH:** No
Born: Alabama **Marital Status:** S **Residence**

Wounded at battle of The Wilderness, May 1864 (specific date not given). Returned to duty. Detailed to Engineer Regiment since 2/12/1865. Captured near Petersburg (Hatcher's Run?) on 4/2/1865. Taken to Point Lookout, MD. Released on oath on 6/28/1865.

Landcaster, William R.
Joined: Wednesday, May 1, 1861 **Term (yrs):** 1 **CO:** C **Initial Rank:** Private **Occupation:** Farmer **Age** 26
Enrolled at: Itawamba Co., MS **Enrolled By:** Capt. Bromley **Promoted:** No **ROH:** No
Born: **Marital Status:** **Residence**

Discharged at Camp Fisher, VA for disability on 10/22/1861.

2nd Mississippi Alphabetical Roster (Annotated)

Lang, C.   *CO:*   *Initial Rank:* Private

Joined: *Term (yrs):* 0   *Occupation:*   *Age*

Enrolled at: *Enrolled By:*   *Promoted:* No   *ROH:* No

Born: *Marital Status:*   *Residence*

Appears on Federal prisoner of war records. Date and location of capture not given, but prior to 7/31/1862. Sent to Fort Monroe, VA from Fort McHenry, MD on 11/13/1861. Appears on Special Orders No. 138 for exchange (not dated). No other records.

Laning, James B.   *CO:* K   *Initial Rank:* Private

Joined: Saturday, April 6, 1861   *Term (yrs):* 1   *Occupation:*   *Age*

Enrolled at: Iuka, MS   *Enrolled By:* W. M. Inge   *Promoted:* No   *ROH:* No

Born: *Marital Status:*   *Residence*

Appears on a company muster roll. No other record.

Laslie, D. H.   *CO:* C   *Initial Rank:* Private

Joined: Saturday, March 1, 1862   *Term (yrs):* 3   *Occupation:* Blacksmith   *Age* 54

Enrolled at: Verona, MS   *Enrolled By:* Lt. Pounds   *Promoted:* No   *ROH:* No

Born: South Carolina   *Marital Status:*   *Residence*

Discharged on 9/1/1862 — over age.

Laslie, W. M.   *CO:* C   *Initial Rank:* Private

Joined: Saturday, March 1, 1862   *Term (yrs):* 3   *Occupation:*   *Age*

Enrolled at: Verona, MS   *Enrolled By:* Lt. Pounds   *Promoted:* No   *ROH:* No

Born: South Carolina   *Marital Status:*   *Residence*

Died of disease in Chimborazo Hospital #2, Richmond, VA on 5/18/1862 (dates of death on records range from 5/15/1862-5/31/1862).

Laslie, William   *CO:* C   *Initial Rank:* Private

Joined: Saturday, March 1, 1862   *Term (yrs):* 3   *Occupation:*   *Age*

Enrolled at: Verona, MS   *Enrolled By:* Lt. Pounds   *Promoted:* No   *ROH:* No

Born: *Marital Status:*   *Residence*

Died of disease on 5/17/1862 at Richmond, VA (another record says 5/15/1862). [*Buried at Hollywood Cemetery, Richmond, VA. Note says he died on 6/1/1862. Soldiers Section L Lot: 68.]

2nd Mississippi Alphabetical Roster (Annotated)

Lassiter, William L. **CO:** E **Initial Rank:** Private

Joined: Saturday, March 1, 1862 **Term (yrs):** 3 **Occupation:** Farmer **Age** 19

Enrolled at: Guntown, MS **Enrolled By:** Capt. Bates **Promoted:** No **ROH:** No

Born: Mississippi **Marital Status:** S **Residence** Guntown, MS

Accompanying list of engagements shows him captured at Gettysburg on 7/1/1863. Sent to Fort Delaware. Paroled on 7/30/1863, exchanged and back on duty by 12/1/1863. Captured at The Wilderness on 5/6/1864. Taken to Point Lookout, MD. Exchanged on 10/30/1864. Paroled, dated Columbus, MS on 5/17/1865.

Latham, Davenport M. **CO:** K **Initial Rank:** 3rd Sergeant

Joined: Wednesday, May 1, 1861 **Term (yrs):** 1 **Occupation:** Student **Age** 17

Enrolled at: Tishomingo Co., MS **Enrolled By:** Capt. Stone **Promoted:** Yes **ROH:** No

Born: Alabama **Marital Status:** **Residence**

Elected Jr. 2nd Lieutenant on 4/8/1862. Assigned to duty on 4/23/1862. Killed in action at Gaines Mill on 6/27/1862.

Latham, George W. **CO:** K **Initial Rank:** 1st Lieutenant

Joined: Wednesday, May 1, 1861 **Term (yrs):** 1 **Occupation:** Merchant **Age** 25

Enrolled at: Tishomingo Co., MS **Enrolled By:** Capt. Stone **Promoted:** Yes **ROH:** No

Born: Alabama **Marital Status:** **Residence**

Elected Captain from 1st Lieutenant on 3/10/1862. Assigned to duty on 4/23/1862. Killed in battle at 2nd Manassas on 8/29/1862.

Lauderdale, John C. **CO:** B **Initial Rank:** 4th Sergeant

Joined: Wednesday, May 1, 1861 **Term (yrs):** 1 **Occupation:** Saddler **Age** 28

Enrolled at: Tippah Co., MS **Enrolled By:** Capt. Buchanan **Promoted:** Yes **ROH:** No

Born: **Marital Status:** **Residence**

Slightly wounded by shell fragment at 1st Manassas on 7/21/1861. Listed as 3rd Sergeant for Jul/Aug 1861 muster. Elected 1st Lieutenant on 4/21/1862 and assigned to duty on 4/23/1862. Wounded at 2nd Manassas on 8/29/1862. Sent to hospital. Furloughed from 9/16/1862. Returned to duty. Killed at Gettysburg on 7/1/1863.

2nd Mississippi Alphabetical Roster (Annotated)

Lauler, Thomas *CO:* D *Initial Rank:* Private
Joined: Monday, July 21, 1862 *Term (yrs):* 3 *Occupation:*   *Age*
Enrolled at: Richmond, VA *Enrolled By:*   *Promoted:* No *ROH:* No
Born: *Marital Status:*   *Residence*

"Deserted July 21, 62 — Substitute." No other record.

Lavall, John *CO:* E *Initial Rank:* Private
Joined: Wednesday, May 1, 1861 *Term (yrs):* 1 *Occupation:* Laborer *Age* 28
Enrolled at: Itawamba Co., MS *Enrolled By:* Capt. Booth *Promoted:* No *ROH:* No
Born: Ireland *Marital Status:* S *Residence* Guntown, MS

Deserted about 9/17/1862.

Lawson, Davenport P. *CO:* A *Initial Rank:* Private
Joined: Wednesday, May 1, 1861 *Term (yrs):* 1 *Occupation:* Fireman *Age* 20
Enrolled at: Tishomingo Co., MS *Enrolled By:* Capt. Leeth *Promoted:* No *ROH:* No
Born: Tennessee *Marital Status:* S *Residence* Burnsville, MS

Deserted to enemy 4/14/1863, near Suffolk, VA.

Leach, William T. *CO:* D *Initial Rank:* Private
Joined: Wednesday, May 1, 1861 *Term (yrs):* 1 *Occupation:* Farmer *Age* 19
Enrolled at: Tippah Co., MS *Enrolled By:* Capt. Beck *Promoted:* No *ROH:* No
Born: Tennessee *Marital Status:* S *Residence* Jonesboro, TN

Detailed from 6/30/1861 as teamster. Deserted on 5/28/1862. "Carried away musket and accoutrements complete. $21.45."

Leathers, Doctor Franklin *CO:* E *Initial Rank:* Private
Joined: Saturday, March 1, 1862 *Term (yrs):* 3 *Occupation:* Farmer *Age* 29
Enrolled at: Guntown, MS *Enrolled By:* Capt. Bates *Promoted:* No *ROH:* No
Born: Georgia *Marital Status:* M *Residence* Saltillo, MS

Captured at Gettysburg on 7/1/1863. Taken to Fort Delaware. Died of disease while a prisoner of war on 6/1/1864 (other records indicate he died on 2/24/1864). Grave location: "On Jersey Shore opposite Post."

2nd Mississippi Alphabetical Roster (Annotated)

Leatherwood, John N. CO: B Initial Rank: Private
Joined: Wednesday, May 1, 1861 **Term (yrs):** 1 **Occupation:** Farmer **Age** 21
Enrolled at: Tippah Co., MS **Enrolled By:** Capt. Buchanan **Promoted:** No **ROH:** No
Born: Mississippi **Marital Status:** **Residence**

Discharged for disability on 2/26/1862 at Camp Fisher, VA by order of General Whiting.

Leavell, John K. G. CO: I Initial Rank: Private
Joined: Wednesday, May 1, 1861 **Term (yrs):** 1 **Occupation:** Farmer **Age** 22
Enrolled at: Pontotoc Co., MS **Enrolled By:** Capt. Herring **Promoted:** Yes **ROH:** No
Born: Mississippi **Marital Status:** **Residence**

Wounded in battle at 1st Manassas on 7/21/1861. Taken to hospital at Charlottesville, VA. Returned to duty. Promoted to 4th Corporal on 11/5/1861. Promoted to 5th Sergeant on 4/23/1862. Promoted to 4th Sergeant on 5/16/1863. Killed at Gettysburg on 7/2/1863.

Leavell, Richard M. CO: I Initial Rank: 2nd Lieutenant
Joined: Wednesday, May 1, 1861 **Term (yrs):** 1 **Occupation:** Teacher **Age** 22
Enrolled at: Pontotoc Co., MS **Enrolled By:** Capt. Herring **Promoted:** Yes **ROH:** No
Born: **Marital Status:** **Residence**

Elected Captain and assigned to duty on 4/23/1862. Captured at Gettysburg on 7/1/1863. Taken to Fort Delaware, then to Johnson's Island, OH. Forwarded to Point Lookout, MD for exchange on 3/21/1865. Released on oath on 5/31/1865.

Lee, Andrew J. CO: L Initial Rank: Private
Joined: Monday, March 3, 1862 **Term (yrs):** 3 **Occupation:** Farmer **Age** 19
Enrolled at: Ripley, MS **Enrolled By:** Col. Falkner **Promoted:** No **ROH:** No
Born: Alabama **Marital Status:** S **Residence** Ripley, MS

Wounded in battle on 8/19/1864 at the Weldon Railroad. Furloughed to Mississippi due to wound. Company records list him as AWOL since 12/29/1864, however Federal records indicate he was captured on 3/6/1865 at Ripley, MS and on 4/18/1865 was sent to Vicksburg, MS for exchange. Paroled from Federal hospital in Vicksburg on 6/15/1865.

2nd Mississippi Alphabetical Roster (Annotated)

Lee, Francis M.
CO: A **Initial Rank:** Private
Joined: Saturday, March 1, 1862   *Term (yrs):* 3 *Occupation:* Farmer   *Age* 25
Enrolled at: Jacinto, MS   *Enrolled By:* Lt. Clayton   *Promoted:* No   *ROH:* No
Born: South Carolina   *Marital Status:* M   *Residence* Jacinto, MS

Hospital records show admission for wound on 7/9/1863 (date of wound or engagement not given in company records). Wounded (both hands) in battle of The Wilderness on 5/5/1864. Sent to hospital. Returned to duty.

Lee, George W.
CO: B **Initial Rank:** Private
Joined: Wednesday, May 1, 1861   *Term (yrs):* 1 *Occupation:* Farmer   *Age* 21
Enrolled at: Tippah Co., MS   *Enrolled By:* Capt. Buchanan   *Promoted:* No   *ROH:* No
Born: Georgia   *Marital Status:*   *Residence*

Died of disease at Camp Fisher, VA on 1/29/1862.

Lee, William C.
CO: B, L **Initial Rank:** Private
Joined: Wednesday, September 18, 1861   *Term (yrs):* 1 *Occupation:* Farmer   *Age* 18
Enrolled at: Ripley, MS   *Enrolled By:* Lt. Davenport   *Promoted:* No   *ROH:* No
Born: Alabama   *Marital Status:* S   *Residence* Ripley, MS

Transferred to Company L on 3/1/1863. Deserted to the enemy at Blackwater Bridge, VA on 5/15/1863.

Leeth, James M.
CO: A **Initial Rank:** Captain
Joined: Wednesday, May 1, 1861   *Term (yrs):* 1 *Occupation:* Farmer   *Age* 32
Enrolled at: Tishomingo Co., MS   *Enrolled By:* Col. Falkner   *Promoted:* No   *ROH:* No
Born: *Marital Status:*   *Residence*

Relieved of command by reorganization of the Company, 4/22/1862. Discharged.

Leland, William W.
CO: G **Initial Rank:** 2nd Lieutenant
Joined: Wednesday, May 1, 1861   *Term (yrs):* 1 *Occupation:* Merchant   *Age* 45
Enrolled at: Pontotoc Co., MS   *Enrolled By:* Capt. Kilpatrick   *Promoted:* No   *ROH:* No
Born: *Marital Status:* M   *Residence* Pontotoc, MS

Resigned by reason of disability on 8/1/1861.

2nd Mississippi Alphabetical Roster (Annotated)

Leonard, A.
CO: *Initial Rank:*
Joined: *Term (yrs):* 0 *Occupation:* *Age*
Enrolled at: *Enrolled By:* *Promoted:* No *ROH:* No
Born: *Marital Status:* *Residence*

Appears on a register of prisoners received and disposed of by the Provost Marshal General, Army of the Potomac. Dated 1/8/1865. Charge: "Rebel Deserter." Remarks: "Took the oath at City Point." No other record.

Lesley, Edward
CO: E *Initial Rank:* 4th Corporal
Joined: Wednesday, May 1, 1861 *Term (yrs):* 1 *Occupation:* Farmer *Age* 23
Enrolled at: Itawamba Co., MS *Enrolled By:* Capt. Booth *Promoted:* No *ROH:* No
Born: Mississippi *Marital Status:* S *Residence* Saltillo, MS

Listed as 3rd Sergeant during Jul/Aug 1862 muster roll. Captured at Gettysburg on 7/1/1863. Sent to Fort Delaware. Released on oath on 6/11/865.

Lesley, G. G.
CO: C *Initial Rank:* Private
Joined: Saturday, March 1, 1862 *Term (yrs):* 3 *Occupation:* *Age*
Enrolled at: Verona, MS *Enrolled By:* Lt. Pounds *Promoted:* No *ROH:* No
Born: *Marital Status:* *Residence*

Wounded (right hand with loss of fingers) at Gaines Mill on 6/27/1862. Furloughed. Company records list as AWOL. Obtained medical certificate of disability on 5/23/1864.

Lesley, J. N.
CO: C *Initial Rank:* Private
Joined: Saturday, March 1, 1862 *Term (yrs):* 3 *Occupation:* Farmer *Age* 24
Enrolled at: Verona, MS *Enrolled By:* Lt. Pounds *Promoted:* No *ROH:* No
Born: Mississippi *Marital Status:* *Residence*

Wounded and captured at Gettysburg on 7/3/1863. Died as a result of wounds in Federal hospital at Gettysburg on 10/4/1863 (another Federal hospital record lists the date of death as 8/5/1863 — cause: fractured left thigh. Grave #2; Location: 9 Sec. Genl. Hospital). [*Reinterred to Hollywood Cemetery, Richmond, VA. Note says he died 10/5/1863. Gettysburg Section Lot: 1.]

2nd Mississippi Alphabetical Roster (Annotated)

Lesley, Samuel O.
CO: E *Initial Rank:* Private
Joined: Saturday, March 1, 1862 *Term (yrs):* 3 *Occupation:* Farmer *Age* 18
Enrolled at: Guntown, MS *Enrolled By:* Capt. Bates *Promoted:* No *ROH:* No
Born: Mississippi *Marital Status:* S *Residence* Saltillo, MS
Died of disease at Richmond, VA on 5/8/1862.

Lesley, Wilson
CO: C, D *Initial Rank:* Private
Joined: Saturday, March 1, 1862 *Term (yrs):* 3 *Occupation:* Farmer *Age* 24
Enrolled at: Verona, MS *Enrolled By:* Lt. Pounds *Promoted:* No *ROH:* No
Born: Alabama *Marital Status:* M *Residence* Richmond, MS
Transferred to Company D on 10/19/1862. In hospital records, admitted for gunshot wound on 7/12/1863 at Richmond (however, company records provide no details on date of wound or action). Given sick furlough for 40-days from 8/11/1863. Listed as AWOL from 10/20/1863. Company records list as dropped from rolls for prolonged AWOL circa Mar/Apr 1864 by order of Col. Stone. Deserted. [However, Federal records show he was taken prisoner on 11/19/1863 — location not given, but in custody of Provost Marshal in Memphis, TN. He was released on oath of allegiance on 11/21/1863].

Leslie, Andrew V. B.
CO: D *Initial Rank:* Private
Joined: Wednesday, May 1, 1861 *Term (yrs):* 1 *Occupation:* Farmer *Age* 23
Enrolled at: Tippah Co., MS *Enrolled By:* Capt. Beck *Promoted:* No *ROH:* No
Born: Alabama *Marital Status:* M *Residence* Pine Grove, MS
Record reads the same as previous Wilson Leslie. May be the same person.

Leslie, Jacob
CO: C *Initial Rank:* Private
Joined: Saturday, March 1, 1862 *Term (yrs):* 3 *Occupation:* Farmer *Age* 62
Enrolled at: Verona, MS *Enrolled By:* Lt. Pounds *Promoted:* No *ROH:* No
Born: South Carolina *Marital Status:* *Residence*
Discharged on 9/9/1862 — over age.

2nd Mississippi Alphabetical Roster (Annotated)

Lett, James
CO: BFL **Initial Rank:** Private
Joined: Saturday, March 1, 1862 **Term (yrs):** 3 **Occupation:** Farmer **Age** 26
Enrolled at: Ripley, MS **Enrolled By:** Capt. Buchanan **Promoted:** No **ROH:** No
Born: Alabama **Marital Status:** M **Residence** Ripley, MS

Transferred to Company L on 4/30/1862. Transferred to Company F on 11/1/1862. Wounded at Weldon Railroad on 8/19/1864. In hospital. Furloughed for 30-days. AWOL from 9/26/1864. Surrendered to Federal forces at LaGrange, TN on 5/24/1865. Paroled.

Levett, William F. M.
CO: E **Initial Rank:** Private
Joined: Saturday, March 1, 1862 **Term (yrs):** 3 **Occupation:** **Age** 19
Enrolled at: Guntown, MS **Enrolled By:** Capt. Bates **Promoted:** No **ROH:** Yes
Born: **Marital Status:** **Residence**

Wounded at Sharpsburg on 9/17/1862. Furloughed. Returned to duty. Wounded on 5/12/1864. In hospital. Returned to duty. Appears on a list of paroled Confederate prisoners of war. No date. No location. ROH for Talley's Mill, 5/10/1864.

Lewallen, Andrew
CO: K **Initial Rank:** Private
Joined: Tuesday, April 1, 1862 **Term (yrs):** 3 **Occupation:** **Age** 24
Enrolled at: Iuka, MS **Enrolled By:** Lt. Latham **Promoted:** No **ROH:** No
Born: **Marital Status:** **Residence**

Also see Andrew Lewellen of the 26th Mississippi Infantry Regiment. Wounded (left thigh) at Gettysburg on 7/1/1863 and captured on 7/5/1863 in the field hospital. Taken to DeCamp General Hospital at Davids Island, NY Harbor and paroled. Furloughed. AWOL from expiration of furlough. Dropped as deserter during Jul/Aug, 1864 muster.

Lewallen, George W.
CO: L **Initial Rank:** Private
Joined: Monday, March 3, 1862 **Term (yrs):** 3 **Occupation:** Farmer **Age** 28
Enrolled at: Ripley, MS **Enrolled By:** Col. Falkner **Promoted:** No **ROH:** No
Born: Tennessee **Marital Status:** M **Residence** Ripley, MS

Discharged for disability on 7/23/1862.

2nd Mississippi Alphabetical Roster (Annotated)

Lewellen, Joseph H.

CO: B, L **Initial Rank:** Private
Joined: Wednesday, May 1, 1861 **Term (yrs):** 1 **Occupation:** Farmer **Age** 25
Enrolled at: Tippah Co., MS **Enrolled By:** Capt. Buchanan **Promoted:** No **ROH:** No
Born: Mississippi **Marital Status:** S **Residence** Ripley, MS

Transferred to Company L on 4/30/1862. Severely wounded (arm) at 2nd Manassas on 8/28/1862. Sent to Warrenton hospital. Furloughed 90-days. Returned to duty. Discharge for disability due to wound in August, 1864.

Lewelling, John

CO: K **Initial Rank:** Private
Joined: Monday, September 30, 1861 **Term (yrs):** 1 **Occupation:** Farmer **Age**
Enrolled at: Iuka, MS **Enrolled By:** Lt. Davenport **Promoted:** No **ROH:** Yes
Born: Alabama **Marital Status:** **Residence**

Wounded at Gaines Mill on 6/27/1862. Admitted to hospital in Richmond on 7/10/1863 with gunshot wound (action or date of wound not stated in records). Returned to duty on 7/29/1863. Killed in action at battle of Spotsylvania on 5/12/1864. ROH for The Wilderness, 5/6/1864; Talley's Mill, 5/10/1864; and Spotsylvania Court House, 5/12/1864.

Lewis, Bynum

CO: F, L **Initial Rank:** Private
Joined: Saturday, March 1, 1862 **Term (yrs):** 3 **Occupation:** Farmer **Age** 18
Enrolled at: Ripley, MS **Enrolled By:** Capt. Powers **Promoted:** No **ROH:** No
Born: South Carolina **Marital Status:** S **Residence**

Transferred to Company L on 4/30/1862. Listed as "wounded at hospital" during Jul/Aug 1864 muster (date or action not given).

Lewis, James P.

CO: D **Initial Rank:** Private
Joined: Thursday, September 19, 1861 **Term (yrs):** 1 **Occupation:** Student **Age** 19
Enrolled at: Salem, MS **Enrolled By:** Lt. Davenport **Promoted:** No **ROH:** Yes
Born: Virginia **Marital Status:** S **Residence** Salem, MS

Wounded and captured at Gettysburg on 7/1/1863. Died at Davids Island, NY in Federal custody on 7/20/1863 as a result of wounds. ROH for Gaines Mill, 6/27/1862.

2nd Mississippi Alphabetical Roster (Annotated)

Lewis, Moses

CO: L **Initial Rank:** Private
Joined: Monday, March 3, 1862 **Term (yrs):** 3 **Occupation:** Farmer **Age** 20
Enrolled at: Ripley, MS **Enrolled By:** Col. Falkner **Promoted:** No **ROH:** No
Born: South Carolina **Marital Status:** S **Residence** Dumas, MS

Killed in battle at Falling Waters, MD on 7/14/1863 in a charge of Federal cavalry.

Lichman, G.

CO: E **Initial Rank:**
Joined: **Term (yrs):** 0 **Occupation:** **Age**
Enrolled at: **Enrolled By:** **Promoted:** No **ROH:** No
Born: **Marital Status:** **Residence**

Appears on a Federal list of prisoners of war captured by the Army of the Potomac at the battle of Williamsburg, VA in May 1862 and sent to Fort Monroe, VA. Not dated. No other record.

Liddell, Samuel B.

CO: F **Initial Rank:** Private
Joined: Wednesday, May 1, 1861 **Term (yrs):** 1 **Occupation:** Planter **Age** 20
Enrolled at: Tippah Co., MS **Enrolled By:** Capt. Davis **Promoted:** Yes **ROH:** No
Born: South Carolina **Marital Status:** **Residence**

Appointed 2nd Sergeant on 4/24/1862. Wounded at Malvern Hill on 7/1/1862. Furloughed 30-days from 7/29/1862. Returned to duty. Mortally wounded and captured at Gettysburg on 7/1/1863. Some records say he died in Federal hospital the same day, others on 7/4/1863. Confederate records list him as killed in battle on 7/1/1863.

Liles, William W.

CO: F **Initial Rank:** Private
Joined: Wednesday, May 1, 1861 **Term (yrs):** 1 **Occupation:** Planter **Age** 18
Enrolled at: Tippah Co., MS **Enrolled By:** Capt. Davis **Promoted:** No **ROH:** No
Born: **Marital Status:** **Residence**

Wounded (left thigh) and captured at Sharpsburg on 9/17/1862. Paroled on 9/27/1862 and exchanged at Fortress Monroe, VA on 10/27/1862. Furloughed 60-days from 12/5/1862. Returned to duty. Furloughed from hospital on 9/10/1864. AWOL since.

2nd Mississippi Alphabetical Roster (Annotated)

Lilly, William L.   CO: H   Initial Rank: Private

Joined: Monday, April 29, 1861   **Term (yrs):** 1   **Occupation:** Farmer   **Age** 21
Enrolled at: Pontotoc Co., MS   **Enrolled By:** Capt. Taylor   **Promoted:** No   **ROH:** No
Born: South Carolina   **Marital Status:** S   **Residence** Chesterville, MS

Wounded and captured at 2nd Manassas on 8/29/1862. Paroled on 9/29/1862. Furloughed. Returned to duty. Retired from service by medical examining board in April 1864.

Lindsey, John S.   CO: A   Initial Rank: Private

Joined: Wednesday, May 1, 1861   **Term (yrs):** 1   **Occupation:** Farmer   **Age** 24
Enrolled at: Tishomingo Co., MS   **Enrolled By:** Capt. Leeth   **Promoted:** No   **ROH:** No
Born: Mississippi   **Marital Status:** S   **Residence** Booneville, MS

May have been detailed as a nurse at battle of 2nd Manassas and captured and paroled the following month (name unclear on records). Wounded (right knee) in battle of Bethesda Church on 6/2/1864. Died of wounds at Lynchburg Virginia hospital on 6/26/1864.

Lindsey, Samuel H.   CO: G, A   Initial Rank: Private

Joined: Wednesday, May 1, 1861   **Term (yrs):** 1   **Occupation:** Planter   **Age** 20
Enrolled at: Pontotoc Co., MS   **Enrolled By:** Capt. Miller   **Promoted:** No   **ROH:** No
Born: Alabama   **Marital Status:** S   **Residence** Pontotoc, MS

Wounded (slight wound in hand) in battle at Gaines Mill on 6/27/1862. Returned to duty. Wounded on 7/1/1863 at Gettysburg and captured on 7/5/1863 near Cashtown. Taken to Fort Delaware. Released on oath on 6/11/1865.

Lindsey, William   CO: D   Initial Rank: Private

Joined: **Term (yrs):** 0   **Occupation:**   **Age** 16
Enrolled at: **Enrolled By:**   **Promoted:** No   **ROH:** No
Born: **Marital Status:**   **Residence** Fayette Co., TN

Appears on a Federal register of prisoners of war dated 10/4/1864 at Memphis, TN — "Deserters form rebel army." Also appears on an oath of allegiance to the United States at Memphis, TN dated 10/4/1864. Remarks: "Deserter oath." No other records.

2nd Mississippi Alphabetical Roster (Annotated)

Linly, William H.
CO: E *Initial Rank:* Private
Joined: Wednesday, May 1, 1861 *Term (yrs):* 1 *Occupation:* Farmer *Age* 21
Enrolled at: Itawamba Co., MS *Enrolled By:* Capt. Booth *Promoted:* No *ROH:* No
Born: Georgia *Marital Status:* S *Residence* Guntown, MS
Discharged for disability at Camp Jones, VA on 8/22/1861.

Livingston, Allen W.
CO: F,B *Initial Rank:* Private
Joined: Wednesday, May 1, 1861 *Term (yrs):* 1 *Occupation:* Farmer *Age* 19
Enrolled at: Tippah Co., MS *Enrolled By:* Capt. Davis *Promoted:* No *ROH:* No
Born: Tennessee *Marital Status:* *Residence*
Transferred to Company B on 6/1/1861. Slightly wounded at 1st Manassas on 7/21/1861. Discharged for disability on 10/18/1861 at Camp Fisher, VA by order of General Smith.

Livingston, Henry H.
CO: B *Initial Rank:* Private
Joined: Wednesday, May 1, 1861 *Term (yrs):* 1 *Occupation:* Brick mason *Age* 37
Enrolled at: Tippah Co., MS *Enrolled By:* Capt. Buchanan *Promoted:* No *ROH:* No
Born: Alabama *Marital Status:* *Residence*
Discharged for disability at Camp Fisher, VA on 11/21/1861 by order of General Smith.

Lockhart, Amos T.
CO: I *Initial Rank:* Private
Joined: Wednesday, May 1, 1861 *Term (yrs):* 1 *Occupation:* Farmer *Age* 20
Enrolled at: Pontotoc Co., MS *Enrolled By:* Capt. Herring *Promoted:* No *ROH:* No
Born: *Marital Status:* *Residence*
Died of disease (pneumonia) at Camp Fisher, VA on 12/23/1861.

Lockhart, Nathaniel
CO: I *Initial Rank:* Private
Joined: Wednesday, May 1, 1861 *Term (yrs):* 1 *Occupation:* Farmer *Age* 22
Enrolled at: Pontotoc Co., MS *Enrolled By:* Capt. Herring *Promoted:* No *ROH:* No
Born: Mississippi *Marital Status:* *Residence*
Killed at Sharpsburg on 9/17/1862.

2nd Mississippi Alphabetical Roster (Annotated)

Logan, Thomas S.
CO: H **Initial Rank:** Private
Joined: Monday, April 29, 1861 **Term (yrs):** 1 **Occupation:** Carpenter **Age** 24
Enrolled at: Pontotoc Co., MS **Enrolled By:** Capt. Taylor **Promoted:** No **ROH:** No
Born: North Carolina **Marital Status:** S **Residence** Tupelo, MS

Wounded (in arm) at Sharpsburg on 9/17/1862. Furloughed. Returned to duty. Captured at Gettysburg on 7/1/1863. Taken to Fort Delaware. Released on oath on 6/11/1865.

Lokey, John D.
CO: F **Initial Rank:** Private
Joined: Wednesday, May 1, 1861 **Term (yrs):** 1 **Occupation:** Planter **Age** 22
Enrolled at: Tippah Co., MS **Enrolled By:** Capt. Davis **Promoted:** Yes **ROH:** No
Born: **Marital Status:** **Residence**

Listed as 2nd Corporal during May/Jun 1862 muster. Slightly wounded at Gaines Mill on 6/27/1862. Promoted to 3rd Sergeant on 7/31/1862. Wounded at The Wilderness on 5/5/1864. Sent to hospital at Augusta, GA. Returned to duty. Listed as "deserted from camp near Petersburg, VA, Feby 15, 1865."

Long, James M.
CO: E **Initial Rank:** Private
Joined: Saturday, March 1, 1862 **Term (yrs):** 3 **Occupation:** Farmer **Age** 18
Enrolled at: Guntown, MS **Enrolled By:** Capt. Bates **Promoted:** No **ROH:** No
Born: **Marital Status:** S **Residence** Guntown, MS

Much of his career was listed as "absent, sick in hospital." Hospital records show he was sick with typhoid fever and died from pneumonia at Richmond, VA on 11/30/1863.

Long, Philip S.
CO: H **Initial Rank:** Private
Joined: Monday, April 29, 1861 **Term (yrs):** 1 **Occupation:** Farmer **Age** 24
Enrolled at: Pontotoc Co., MS **Enrolled By:** Capt. Taylor **Promoted:** No **ROH:** No
Born: Tennessee **Marital Status:** S **Residence** Palmetto, MS

Wounded in battle at 1st Manassas on 7/21/1861. Sent to hospital at Culpepper. Discharged for disability due to wounds on 10/22/1861 by order of General Smith.

Long, Richard B.
CO: A **Initial Rank:** Private
Joined: Wednesday, May 1, 1861 **Term (yrs):** 1 **Occupation:** Clerk **Age** 28
Enrolled at: Tishomingo Co., MS **Enrolled By:** Capt. Leeth **Promoted:** No **ROH:** No
Born: Alabama **Marital Status:** S **Residence** Jacinto, MS

Discharged due to disability on 4/27/1862.

2ⁿᵈ Mississippi Alphabetical Roster (Annotated)

Long, Richard C.
CO: E *Initial Rank:* Private
Joined: Friday, February 28, 1862 *Term (yrs):* 3 *Occupation:* Farmer *Age* 41
Enrolled at: Guntown, MS *Enrolled By:* Capt. Bates *Promoted:* No *ROH:* No
Born: *Marital Status:* M *Residence* Guntown, MS

Hospital records show he was admitted at Richmond with a wound on 7/9/1863 (date of wound and action not given in company records). During Jan/Feb 1865 muster roll, listed as AWOL since 9/1/1864.

Long, Thomas E.
CO: G *Initial Rank:* Private
Joined: Wednesday, May 1, 1861 *Term (yrs):* 1 *Occupation:* Farmer *Age* 18
Enrolled at: Pontotoc Co., MS *Enrolled By:* Capt. Miller *Promoted:* No *ROH:* No
Born: Mississippi *Marital Status:* S *Residence* Pontotoc, MS

Killed in battle at 2nd Manassas on 8/29/1862.

Long, Timothy
CO: H *Initial Rank:* Musician
Joined: Monday, April 29, 1861 *Term (yrs):* 1 *Occupation:* Laborer *Age* 25
Enrolled at: Pontotoc Co., MS *Enrolled By:* Capt. Taylor *Promoted:* No *ROH:* No
Born: Ireland *Marital Status:* S *Residence* Chesterville, MS

Discharged due to disability on 7/21/1862.

Long, William E.
CO: E *Initial Rank:* Private
Joined: Wednesday, May 1, 1861 *Term (yrs):* 1 *Occupation:* *Age*
Enrolled at: Itawamba Co., MS *Enrolled By:* Capt. Booth *Promoted:* No *ROH:* No
Born: *Marital Status:* *Residence*

Appears on a company muster-in roll and a state service muster roll (prior to regimental organization). No other records.

Looney, John S.
CO: C *Initial Rank:* Private
Joined: Saturday, March 1, 1862 *Term (yrs):* 3 *Occupation:* *Age*
Enrolled at: Richmond, MS *Enrolled By:* Lt. Pounds *Promoted:* No *ROH:* No
Born: *Marital Status:* *Residence*

Wounded at 2nd Manassas on 8/29/1862. Sent to hospital. Furloughed. Returned to duty. Captured at Gettysburg on 7/1/1863. Sent to Fort Delaware. Released on oath on 6/11/1865.

2nd Mississippi Alphabetical Roster (Annotated)

Looney, William H.
CO: A *Initial Rank:* Private
Joined: Saturday, March 1, 1862 *Term (yrs):* 3 *Occupation:* Farmer *Age* 22
Enrolled at: Jacinto, MS *Enrolled By:* Lt. Clayton *Promoted:* No *ROH:* Yes
Born: Mississippi *Marital Status:* M *Residence* Corinth, MS

Mortally wounded at Sharpsburg on 9/17/1862. Died of wounds on 9/18/1862. ROH for Sharpsburg, 9/17/1862.

Loveless, George M.
CO: K *Initial Rank:* Private
Joined: Saturday, March 1, 1862 *Term (yrs):* 3 *Occupation:* Farmer *Age* 17
Enrolled at: Iuka, MS *Enrolled By:* Lt. Latham *Promoted:* No *ROH:* No
Born: Georgia *Marital Status:* *Residence*

Died at Huguenot Springs Hospital, VA of disease on 9/20/1862 (other records list his death as 9/1/1862).

Lowrey, Jacob A.
CO: H *Initial Rank:* Private
Joined: Monday, April 29, 1861 *Term (yrs):* 1 *Occupation:* Farmer *Age* 21
Enrolled at: Pontotoc Co., MS *Enrolled By:* Capt. Taylor *Promoted:* No *ROH:* No
Born: Alabama *Marital Status:* S *Residence* Chesterville, MS

Wounded in battle at Gaines Mill on 6/27/1862. In hospital at Richmond. Furloughed. Returned to duty. Wounded and captured at Gettysburg (captured 7/5/1863, date of wound not given). Paroled at U.S. Army General Hospital in Chester, PA. Appears on muster roll of a detachment of paroled and exchanged prisoners at Camp Lee, VA dated 9/25/1863. No further record.

Lowrey, William B.
CO: D *Initial Rank:* Private
Joined: Saturday, March 9, 1861 *Term (yrs):* 0 *Occupation:* *Age*
Enrolled at: Toombs Store, MS *Enrolled By:* John M. McGuirk *Promoted:* No *ROH:* No
Born: *Marital Status:* *Residence*

Appears on a company muster roll. No other record.

Lowrey, William J.
CO: L *Initial Rank:* Private
Joined: Monday, March 3, 1862 *Term (yrs):* 3 *Occupation:* Farmer *Age* 32
Enrolled at: Ripley, MS *Enrolled By:* Col. Falkner *Promoted:* No *ROH:* No
Born: Georgia *Marital Status:* M *Residence* Claysville, MS

Captured at Sharpsburg on 9/17/1862. Paroled and taken to hospital at Winchester. Last heard from on 10/1/1862. "Supposed to be dead and dropped from the rolls on 4/30/1863."

2nd Mississippi Alphabetical Roster (Annotated)

Lowry, David
CO: C, G **Initial Rank:** Private
Joined: Tuesday, October 1, 1861 **Term (yrs):** 1 **Occupation:** Farmer **Age** 20
Enrolled at: Verona, MS **Enrolled By:** Lt. Davenport **Promoted:** No **ROH:** No
Born: Mississippi **Marital Status:** S **Residence** Pontotoc, MS

Transferred to Company G on 4/30/1862. Died of disease at hospital in Richmond on 7/15/1862. [*Buried at Hollywood Cemetery, Richmond, VA. Soldiers Section M Lot:17. Lists Name as Daniel David Lowry.]

Lowry, R. G.
CO: B **Initial Rank:** Private
Joined: **Term (yrs):** 0 **Occupation:** **Age**
Enrolled at: **Enrolled By:** **Promoted:** No **ROH:** No
Born: **Marital Status:** **Residence**

Reference envelope says to see 2nd Mississippi Cavalry. No other record.

Lucas, James T.
CO: K **Initial Rank:** Private
Joined: Saturday, March 1, 1862 **Term (yrs):** 3 **Occupation:** Farmer **Age** 42
Enrolled at: Iuka, MS **Enrolled By:** Lt. Latham **Promoted:** No **ROH:** No
Born: Georgia **Marital Status:** **Residence**

Died at Charlottesville, VA on 7/7/1862 of disease (typhoid fever).

Lucas, Richard A.
CO: K **Initial Rank:** Private
Joined: Saturday, March 1, 1862 **Term (yrs):** 3 **Occupation:** **Age** 18
Enrolled at: Iuka, MS **Enrolled By:** Lt. Latham **Promoted:** No **ROH:** No
Born: **Marital Status:** **Residence**

Captured at Gettysburg on 7/3/1863. Sent to Fort Delaware. Became "Galvanized Yankee" and joined the U.S. Service (artillery) on 7/27/1863. Deserted.

Lummus, William G.
CO: K, H **Initial Rank:** Private
Joined: Saturday, March 1, 1862 **Term (yrs):** 3 **Occupation:** **Age** 18
Enrolled at: Iuka, MS **Enrolled By:** Lt. Latham **Promoted:** No **ROH:** No
Born: **Marital Status:** **Residence**

Captured at Gettysburg on 7/1/1863. Sent to Fort Delaware. Released on oath on 6/11/1865. (Some confusion in Federal records as the name also appears under the title of 20th Miss).

2nd Mississippi Alphabetical Roster (Annotated)

Lummus, William T. CO: K   Initial Rank: Private
Joined: Saturday, March 1, 1862   **Term (yrs):** 3   **Occupation:**   **Age** 42
Enrolled at: Iuka, MS   **Enrolled By:** Lt. Latham   **Promoted:** No   **ROH:** No
Born: **Marital Status:**   **Residence**

Captured circa May/Jun 1862 (date or action not given). Paroled to Camp Lee, VA. Returned to duty (date not given). Captured at South Mountain on 9/15/1862 and sent to Fort Delaware. Exchanged on 11/10/1862. Mortally wounded at The Wilderness (date not given). Died at Charlottesville, VA on 5/15/1864.

Luna, D   CO: A   Initial Rank: Private
Joined: **Term (yrs):** 0   **Occupation:**   **Age**
Enrolled at: **Enrolled By:**   **Promoted:** No   **ROH:** No
Born: **Marital Status:**   **Residence**

Appears on a Confederate regimental return dated Nov 1862. Date: 11/15/1862. Place: Lynchburg. Remarks: Died. No other record.

Luna, Isaac D.   CO: F   Initial Rank: Private
Joined: Wednesday, May 1, 1861   **Term (yrs):** 1   **Occupation:** Planter   **Age** 21
Enrolled at: Tippah Co., MS   **Enrolled By:** Capt. Davis   **Promoted:** No   **ROH:** No
Born: Tennessee   **Marital Status:**   **Residence**

Wounded and captured at Gettysburg (wounded in left arm and thorax on 7/1/1863 and captured 7/5/1863). Paroled at DeCamp General Hospital, Davids Island, NY (not dated). Furloughed on 9/13/1863. Died in Ripley, MS on 10/10/1863.

Luna, James W.   CO: F   Initial Rank: 1st Corporal
Joined: Wednesday, May 1, 1861   **Term (yrs):** 1   **Occupation:** Planter   **Age** 30
Enrolled at: Tippah Co., MS   **Enrolled By:** Capt. Davis   **Promoted:** No   **ROH:** No
Born: Tennessee   **Marital Status:**   **Residence**

Wounded at Malvern Hill on 7/1/1862. Killed in battle at Gettysburg on 7/1/1863 (according to Federal records, was wounded and captured and died in Federal hospital (date not given)).

2nd Mississippi Alphabetical Roster (Annotated)

Luna, John C.
CO: F **Initial Rank:** Private
Joined: Wednesday, May 1, 1861 **Term (yrs):** 1 **Occupation:** Planter **Age** 21
Enrolled at: Tippah Co., MS **Enrolled By:** Capt. Davis **Promoted:** No **ROH:** No
Born: **Marital Status:** **Residence**

Killed in battle at Sharpsburg on 9/17/1862.

Luna, William L.
CO: F **Initial Rank:** Private
Joined: Wednesday, May 1, 1861 **Term (yrs):** 1 **Occupation:** Planter **Age** 32
Enrolled at: Tippah Co., MS **Enrolled By:** Capt. Davis **Promoted:** No **ROH:** Yes
Born: **Marital Status:** **Residence**

Wounded at 1st Manassas on 7/21/1861. Wounded at Sharpsburg on 9/17/1862. Furloughed. Returned to duty. Wounded (right forearm, requiring amputation) and captured at Gettysburg (captured on 7/5/1863, date of wound not given). Paroled at DeCamp General Hospital, Davids Island, NY Harbor (not dated). Furloughed from Williamsburg, VA Confederate Hospital on 9/13/1863. Listed on final company muster rolls as AWOL from 10/31/1863. ROH for Gettysburg, 7/1/1863.

Lyle, Thomas M.
CO: K **Initial Rank:** Private
Joined: Wednesday, May 1, 1861 **Term (yrs):** 1 **Occupation:** Physician **Age** 35
Enrolled at: Tishomingo Co., MS **Enrolled By:** Capt. Stone **Promoted:** No **ROH:** No
Born: **Marital Status:** **Residence**

Apparently never mustered into service. Remarks on May/Jun 1861 muster roll say, "Was sick in Lynchburg. Was never mustered into service. Gone home." No other record.

Lyles, J. T.
CO: C **Initial Rank:** Private
Joined: Saturday, March 1, 1862 **Term (yrs):** 3 **Occupation:** Farmer **Age** 16
Enrolled at: Verona, MS **Enrolled By:** Lt. Pounds **Promoted:** No **ROH:** No
Born: **Marital Status:** **Residence**

Wounded in left arm on 7/1/1863 and captured at Gettysburg (captured on 7/5/1863). Paroled at DeCamp General Hospital, Davids Island, NY Harbor (not dated). Furloughed from Williamsburg hospital on 9/13/1863. Listed as AWOL from 1/1/1864 and deserter as of May/Jun 1864 muster roll.

2nd Mississippi Alphabetical Roster (Annotated)

Lyons, G. K. *CO:* B *Initial Rank:*
Joined: *Term (yrs):* 0 *Occupation:*   *Age*
Enrolled at: *Enrolled By:*   *Promoted:* No *ROH:* No
Born: *Marital Status:*   *Residence*

Appears to have been wounded and captured at Gettysburg. On Federal records of prisoners of war at the hospitals in and about Gettysburg. No other records.

Lyons, Joseph N *CO:* I *Initial Rank:* Private
Joined: Monday, April 29, 1861 *Term (yrs):* 1 *Occupation:* Farmer *Age* 22
Enrolled at: Cherry Creek, MS *Enrolled By:* Capt. Herring *Promoted:* No *ROH:* No
Born: Alabama *Marital Status:*   *Residence*

Severely wounded (in hip) at 1st Manassas on 7/21/1861. Discharged on 9/21/1861 due to disability from wound.

Lyons, Thomas J. *CO:* G *Initial Rank:* Private
Joined: Wednesday, May 1, 1861 *Term (yrs):* 1 *Occupation:* Farmer *Age* 22
Enrolled at: Pontotoc Co., MS *Enrolled By:* Capt. Miller *Promoted:* No *ROH:* No
Born: Mississippi *Marital Status:* S *Residence* Pontotoc, MS

Detailed as regimental teamster. Placed under arrest at Petersburg, VA on 2/19/1865 for desertion.

Mabry, Thomas T. *CO:* C *Initial Rank:* Private
Joined: Wednesday, May 1, 1861 *Term (yrs):* 1 *Occupation:* Farmer *Age* 24
Enrolled at: Itawamba Co., MS *Enrolled By:* Capt. Bromley *Promoted:* Yes *ROH:* No
Born: *Marital Status:*   *Residence*

Wounded (right thigh) in battle at Gaines Mill on 6/27/1862. Furloughed. Returned to duty. Listed as 2nd Sergeant during Mar/Apr 1862 muster. Wounded (left shoulder) and captured at Falling Waters, MD on 7/14/1863. Paroled at Baltimore, MD on 8/23/1863 and delivered to City Point, VA. Furloughed for 40-days on 9/11/1863 and returned to parole camp at Camp Lee, VA. Returned to duty. Captured at Petersburg (Hatcher's Run?) on 4/2/1865. Taken to Fort Delaware. Released on oath on 6/11/1865.

2nd Mississippi Alphabetical Roster (Annotated)

Mabry, William R. *CO:* H *Initial Rank:* Private
Joined: Saturday, August 10, 1861 *Term (yrs):* 1 *Occupation:* Farmer *Age* 29
Enrolled at: Camp Jones, VA *Enrolled By:* Lt. Stone *Promoted:* No *ROH:* No
Born: Georgia *Marital Status:* S *Residence*

Wounded at Gettysburg on 7/1/1863. Returned to duty. Wounded at The Wilderness on 5/5/1864. Returned to duty. Wounded at the Weldon Railroad on 8/18/1864. Sent to hospital. Returned to duty. Captured at Hatcher's Run on 4/2/1865. Taken to Point Lookout, MD. Released on oath on 6/29/1865.

Madrus, Charles W. *CO:* E *Initial Rank:* Private
Joined: Friday, February 8, 1861 *Term (yrs):* 0 *Occupation:* *Age*
Enrolled at: Saltillo, MS *Enrolled By:* R. Griffith *Promoted:* No *ROH:* No
Born: *Marital Status:* *Residence*

Appears on a company muster roll. No other record.

Mahon, John G. *CO:* I *Initial Rank:* Private
Joined: Wednesday, May 1, 1861 *Term (yrs):* 1 *Occupation:* Farmer *Age* 22
Enrolled at: Pontotoc Co., MS *Enrolled By:* Capt. Herring *Promoted:* Yes *ROH:* No
Born: *Marital Status:* *Residence*

Promoted to 4th Corporal on 4/23/1862. Wounded at Gaines Mill on 6/27/1862. Sent to hospital in Richmond. Returned to duty. Listed as 1st Corporal during May/Jun 1863 muster. Wounded (right lung) and captured at Gettysburg on 7/3/1863. Paroled at DeCamp General Hospital, Davids Island, NY Harbor (not dated). Admitted to Confederate hospital in Williamsburg, VA on 9/8/1863. Furloughed on 9/13/1863 for 30-days. Returned to duty. Listed as sick in brigade hospital during last muster (Jan/Feb, 1865).

Mahorba, Samuel M. *CO:* F *Initial Rank:*
Joined: Monday, March 4, 1861 *Term (yrs):* 0 *Occupation:* *Age*
Enrolled at: Ripley, MS *Enrolled By:* J. R. Chalmers *Promoted:* No *ROH:* No
Born: *Marital Status:* *Residence*

Appears on a company muster roll. No other record.

2nd Mississippi Alphabetical Roster (Annotated)

Mallory, William T.
CO: B **Initial Rank:** Private
Joined: Wednesday, May 1, 1861 **Term (yrs):** 1 **Occupation:** Farmer **Age** 24
Enrolled at: Tippah Co., MS **Enrolled By:** Capt. Buchanan **Promoted:** No **ROH:** No
Born: Alabama **Marital Status:** **Residence**

Discharged for disability on 2/26/1862 at Camp Fisher, VA by order of General Whiting.

Manahan, William E.
CO: G **Initial Rank:** Private
Joined: Friday, May 10, 1861 **Term (yrs):** 1 **Occupation:** Clerk **Age** 30
Enrolled at: Lynchburg, VA **Enrolled By:** Capt. Miller **Promoted:** No **ROH:** Yes
Born: South Carolina **Marital Status:** S **Residence** Pontotoc, MS

Wounded (leg amputated by Dr. Hubbard) in battle at Seven Pines on 5/31/1862. Furloughed. Authority to appear before medical examining board. Retired to Invalid Corps, P.A.C.S. by order of medical examining board on 12/1/1864. Discharged. ROH for Seven Pines, 5/31/1862.

Maness, Benjamin H.
CO: A **Initial Rank:** Private
Joined: Wednesday, May 1, 1861 **Term (yrs):** 1 **Occupation:** Clerk **Age** 19
Enrolled at: Tishomingo Co., MS **Enrolled By:** Capt. Leeth **Promoted:** No **ROH:** No
Born: Mississippi **Marital Status:** S **Residence** Burns Store, MS

Wounded at 2nd Manassas on 8/29/1862. Furloughed. Killed "in personal difficulty" (in a fight) near Barnes Store while on furlough in MS on 1/2/1863.

Maness, William J.
CO: A **Initial Rank:** Private
Joined: Wednesday, May 1, 1861 **Term (yrs):** 1 **Occupation:** Physician **Age** 25
Enrolled at: Tishomingo Co., MS **Enrolled By:** Capt. Leeth **Promoted:** No **ROH:** No
Born: Tennessee **Marital Status:** M **Residence** Burns Store, MS

"Deserted April 12, 1863."

Marcy, Osburn
CO: C **Initial Rank:** Private
Joined: Saturday, March 1, 1862 **Term (yrs):** 3 **Occupation:** **Age**
Enrolled at: Verona, MS **Enrolled By:** Lt. Pounds **Promoted:** No **ROH:** No
Born: **Marital Status:** **Residence**

Listed as AWOL from 9/11/1863. Deserted as of May/Jun 1864 muster roll.

2nd Mississippi Alphabetical Roster (Annotated)

Marion, Robert H.
CO: C **Initial Rank:** Private
Joined: Wednesday, May 1, 1861 **Term (yrs):** 1 **Occupation:** Farmer **Age** 20
Enrolled at: Itawamba Co., MS **Enrolled By:** Capt. Bromley **Promoted:** Yes **ROH:** No
Born: **Marital Status:** **Residence**

Appointed 4th Corporal on 8/1/1861. Appears on list as Private again beginning May/Jun 1863 muster. Listed as AWOL from 2/25/1864. Deserted from 3/14/1864 reported during Jul/Aug 1864 muster roll.

Marlin, David
CO: H **Initial Rank:** Private
Joined: Monday, April 29, 1861 **Term (yrs):** 1 **Occupation:** Teacher **Age** 26
Enrolled at: Pontotoc Co., MS **Enrolled By:** Capt. Taylor **Promoted:** Yes **ROH:** No
Born: Ireland **Marital Status:** S **Residence** Chesterville, MS

Listed as 5th Sergeant during Nov/Dec 1861 muster. Was elected 1st Lieutenant on 4/14/1862 and assigned to duty on 4/22/1862. Mortally wounded and died at Gettysburg on 7/3/1863.

Maroney, John B.
CO: G **Initial Rank:** Private
Joined: Thursday, March 20, 1862 **Term (yrs):** 3 **Occupation:** Farmer **Age** 14
Enrolled at: Pontotoc, MS **Enrolled By:** G. B. Mears **Promoted:** No **ROH:** No
Born: Arkansas **Marital Status:** S **Residence** Pontotoc, MS

Wounded at Sharpsburg on 9/17/1862. Sent to hospital in Richmond. Discharged (underage) by order of General G. W. Smith on 11/10/1862.

Marrow, Abraham
CO: K **Initial Rank:** Private
Joined: Wednesday, May 1, 1861 **Term (yrs):** 1 **Occupation:** Laborer **Age** 22
Enrolled at: Tishomingo Co., MS **Enrolled By:** Capt. Stone **Promoted:** No **ROH:** No
Born: Tennessee **Marital Status:** **Residence**

Killed in battle at Sharpsburg on 9/17/1862.

Marrs, Albert C.
CO: H **Initial Rank:** Private
Joined: Monday, April 29, 1861 **Term (yrs):** 1 **Occupation:** Farmer **Age** 21
Enrolled at: Pontotoc Co., MS **Enrolled By:** Capt. Taylor **Promoted:** No **ROH:** Yes
Born: Alabama **Marital Status:** S **Residence** Tupelo, MS

Wounded in battle at Gaines Mill on 6/27/1862. In hospital at Richmond. Returned to duty. Killed in battle at Sharpsburg on 9/17/1862. ROH for Gaines Mill, 6/27/1862.

2nd Mississippi Alphabetical Roster (Annotated)

Marrs, William H. H.   CO: H   Initial Rank: Private
Joined: Saturday, August 10, 1861   **Term (yrs):** 1   **Occupation:** Farmer   **Age**
Enrolled at: Camp Jones, VA   **Enrolled By:** Lt. Stone   **Promoted:** No   **ROH:** No
Born: Alabama   **Marital Status:**   **Residence**
Discharged for disability on 12/24/1861 at Camp Fisher, VA.

Marsh, Zachariah S.   CO: K   Initial Rank: Private
Joined: Saturday, March 1, 1862   **Term (yrs):** 3   **Occupation:** Mechanic   **Age** 31
Enrolled at: Iuka, MS   **Enrolled By:** Lt. Latham   **Promoted:** No   **ROH:** No
Born: Tennessee   **Marital Status:**   **Residence**
Killed in battle at Sharpsburg on 9/17/1862.

Marshall, Calvin T.   CO: G   Initial Rank: Private
Joined: Wednesday, May 1, 1861   **Term (yrs):** 1   **Occupation:** Blacksmith   **Age** 35
Enrolled at: Pontotoc Co., MS   **Enrolled By:** Capt. Miller   **Promoted:** No   **ROH:** No
Born: Tennessee   **Marital Status:** M   **Residence** Pontotoc, MS
Discharged — over age — on 8/2/1862

Marshall, James A.   CO: C   Initial Rank: Private
Joined: Friday, June 28, 1861   **Term (yrs):** 1   **Occupation:** Farmer   **Age** 18
Enrolled at: Winchester, VA   **Enrolled By:** Capt. Bromley   **Promoted:** No   **ROH:** No
Born: **Marital Status:**   **Residence**
Killed in battle at Gettysburg on 7/1/1863.

Martin, Anderson D.   CO: C   Initial Rank: Private
Joined: Wednesday, May 1, 1861   **Term (yrs):** 1   **Occupation:** Farmer   **Age** 22
Enrolled at: Itawamba Co., MS   **Enrolled By:** Capt. Bromley   **Promoted:** No   **ROH:** No
Born: South Carolina   **Marital Status:**   **Residence**
Discharged for disability at Camp Jones, VA on 9/12/1861.

2nd Mississippi Alphabetical Roster (Annotated)

Martin, Fredrick
CO: *Initial Rank:* Private
Joined: *Term (yrs):* 0 *Occupation:* *Age*
Enrolled at: *Enrolled By:* *Promoted:* No *ROH:* No
Born: *Marital Status:* *Residence*

Appears on a Federal register of oaths taken by rebel deserters, HQ Provost Marshal, Bermuda Hundred, VA. Dated 3/27/1865. Remarks: "Oath not administered." No other record.

Martin, George
CO: C *Initial Rank:* Private
Joined: Saturday, March 1, 1862 *Term (yrs):* 3 *Occupation:* *Age*
Enrolled at: Verona, MS *Enrolled By:* Lt. Pounds *Promoted:* No *ROH:* No
Born: *Marital Status:* *Residence*

Admitted to hospital in Richmond on 7/15/1863 with wound (date of wound and name of engagement not given in company records). Returned to duty on 8/7/1863. Captured at Petersburg (Hatcher's Run?) on 4/2/1865. Taken to Fort Delaware. Released on oath on 6/10/1865.

Martin, John M
CO: F *Initial Rank:* Private
Joined: Wednesday, May 1, 1861 *Term (yrs):* 1 *Occupation:* Planter *Age* 22
Enrolled at: Tippah Co., MS *Enrolled By:* Capt. Davis *Promoted:* No *ROH:* No
Born: *Marital Status:* *Residence*

Last company muster (Jan/Feb 1865) lists him in hospital at Richmond, VA. He was transferred to Farmville on 4/1/1865. He appears on a Federal list of prisoners of war paroled at Lynchburg, VA on 4/15/1865 (or 4/13/1865).

Martin, Joseph T.
CO: B *Initial Rank:* Private
Joined: Tuesday, June 18, 1861 *Term (yrs):* 1 *Occupation:* Grocer *Age* 26
Enrolled at: Winchester, VA *Enrolled By:* Capt. Buchanan *Promoted:* No *ROH:* No
Born: Kentucky *Marital Status:* *Residence*

Wounded at Gaines Mill on 6/27/1862. Returned to duty. Wounded on 8/29/1862 at 2nd Manassas. Sent to hospital. Returned to duty. Hospital records show admission on 7/9/1863 with wound (date of wound and battle not noted in company records). Returned to duty 8/7/1863. Sep/Oct 1863 muster lists him on detached duty in Ordnance Dept. in Augusta, GA thru Mar/Apr 1864 muster. Returned to duty. Captured at Hatcher's Run on 4/2/1865. Taken to Point Lookout, MD. Released on oath on 6/29/1865.

2nd Mississippi Alphabetical Roster (Annotated)

Martin, Thomas B.   CO: K   Initial Rank: Private

Joined: Wednesday, May 1, 1861   **Term (yrs):** 1   **Occupation:** Laborer   **Age** 18

Enrolled at: Tishomingo Co., MS   **Enrolled By:** Capt. Stone   **Promoted:** No   **ROH:** No

Born: Mississippi   **Marital Status:**   **Residence**

Killed at The Wilderness on 5/5/1864.

Martindale, Claiborne   CO: F   Initial Rank: Private

Joined: Saturday, March 1, 1862   **Term (yrs):** 3   **Occupation:** Farmer   **Age** 37

Enrolled at: Ripley, MS   **Enrolled By:** Capt. Powers   **Promoted:** No   **ROH:** No

Born: Alabama   **Marital Status:** M   **Residence**

Died of disease (smallpox) on 1/22/1863 at Danville, VA.

Martindale, Jesse   CO: K   Initial Rank: Private

Joined: Wednesday, May 1, 1861   **Term (yrs):** 1   **Occupation:** Laborer   **Age** 21

Enrolled at: Tishomingo Co., MS   **Enrolled By:** Capt. Stone   **Promoted:** No   **ROH:** No

Born: **Marital Status:**   **Residence**

Captured at South Mountain, MD on 9/15/1862. Taken to Fort Delaware. Paroled to Aikens Landing, VA on 10/2/1862 and declared exchanged on 11/10/1862. Wounded at The Wilderness (not dated). Furloughed. Returned to duty. Captured at Richmond, VA in brigade hospital on 4/3/1865. Sent to Point Lookout, MD. Died in custody on 5/8/1865 at Point Lookout. Buried in prison cemetery — plot #6924.

Martindale, Miles   CO: K   Initial Rank: Private

Joined: Saturday, March 1, 1862   **Term (yrs):** 3   **Occupation:**   **Age** 25

Enrolled at: Iuka, MS   **Enrolled By:** Lt. Latham   **Promoted:** No   **ROH:** No

Born: **Marital Status:**   **Residence**

Wounded in battle of The Wilderness (date not given). Returned to duty. "Deserted to the enemy from picket line on 2/13/1865." Appears on Federal prisoner of war lists as rebel deserter.

Marton, W. M.   CO: B   Initial Rank:

Joined: **Term (yrs):** 0   **Occupation:**   **Age**

Enrolled at: **Enrolled By:**   **Promoted:** No   **ROH:** No

Born: **Marital Status:**   **Residence**

Appears on Federal prisoner records as captured at Gettysburg (not dated) and in a register of sick and wounded Confederates in the hospital in and about Gettysburg, PA following the battle. No other records.

2nd Mississippi Alphabetical Roster (Annotated)

Mask, John S.
CO: F, L **Initial Rank:** Private
Joined: Saturday, March 1, 1862 **Term (yrs):** 3 **Occupation:** Farmer **Age** 22
Enrolled at: Ripley, MS **Enrolled By:** Capt. Powers **Promoted:** No **ROH:** No
Born: North Carolina **Marital Status:** S **Residence** Union Mills, MS

Transferred to Company L on 4/30/1862. Wounded (in foot) at Sharpsburg on 9/17/1862. Furloughed. Returned to duty. Wounded at The Wilderness on 5/5/1864. Returned to duty. Wounded at Fort Cherry on 10/1/1864. Furloughed 40-days from 10/26/1864.

Massey, William J.
CO: L **Initial Rank:** Private
Joined: Monday, March 3, 1862 **Term (yrs):** 3 **Occupation:** Farmer **Age** 32
Enrolled at: Ripley, MS **Enrolled By:** Col. Falkner **Promoted:** No **ROH:** No
Born: Alabama **Marital Status:** **Residence**

Died of disease at Richmond, VA on 8/14/1862.

Matthews, Benjamin F.
CO: G **Initial Rank:** Private
Joined: Wednesday, May 1, 1861 **Term (yrs):** 1 **Occupation:** Farmer **Age** 34
Enrolled at: Pontotoc Co., MS **Enrolled By:** Capt. Miller **Promoted:** No **ROH:** No
Born: Georgia **Marital Status:** S **Residence** Pontotoc, MS

Listed as AWOL since 3/28/1862. Deserted as of Jul/Aug 1862 muster.

Maw, Charles W.
CO: E **Initial Rank:** Private
Joined: Wednesday, May 1, 1861 **Term (yrs):** 1 **Occupation:** Mechanic **Age** 25
Enrolled at: Itawamba Co., MS **Enrolled By:** Capt. Booth **Promoted:** No **ROH:** No
Born: South Carolina **Marital Status:** S **Residence** Guntown, MS

Wounded at Gaines Mill on 6/27/1862. Returned to duty on 11/25/1862. Wounded at The Wilderness on 5/6/1864. Furloughed. Returned to duty. Captured at Petersburg (Hatcher's Run?) on 4/2/1865. Taken to Fort Delaware. Released on oath on 6/11/1865.

Maxcy, Edward V.
CO: H **Initial Rank:** Private
Joined: Monday, April 29, 1861 **Term (yrs):** 1 **Occupation:** Farmer **Age** 19
Enrolled at: Pontotoc Co., MS **Enrolled By:** Capt. Taylor **Promoted:** Yes **ROH:** No
Born: Alabama **Marital Status:** S **Residence** Chesterville, MS

Appointed 1st Corporal on 6/1/1863. Captured at Gettysburg on 7/1/1863. Taken to Fort Delaware. Released on oath on 6/11/1865.

2nd Mississippi Alphabetical Roster (Annotated)

Maxey, Thomas
CO: D **Initial Rank:** Private
Joined: Saturday, March 9, 1861 **Term (yrs):** 0 **Occupation:** **Age**
Enrolled at: Toombs Store, MS **Enrolled By:** John M. McGuirk **Promoted:** No **ROH:** No
Born: **Marital Status:** **Residence**

Appears on a company muster roll. No other record.

May, Benjamin
CO: F **Initial Rank:** Private
Joined: Saturday, March 1, 1862 **Term (yrs):** 3 **Occupation:** Farmer **Age** 46
Enrolled at: Ripley, MS **Enrolled By:** Capt. Powers **Promoted:** No **ROH:** No
Born: Alabama **Marital Status:** M **Residence**

Discharged at Richmond, VA on 7/16/1862 due to disability.

May, Francis M.
CO: G **Initial Rank:** Private
Joined: Monday, September 16, 1861 **Term (yrs):** 1 **Occupation:** Farmer **Age** 20
Enrolled at: Pontotoc, MS **Enrolled By:** Lt. Davenport **Promoted:** No **ROH:** No
Born: Mississippi **Marital Status:** S **Residence** Pontotoc, MS

Wounded at Sharpsburg (engagements list says South Mountain, MD on 9/14/1862) on 9/17/1862. Furloughed. Returned to duty on 11/20/1862. Wounded (date and action not given) and admitted to hospital in Richmond on 2/24/1865. Furloughed 4/1/1865 for 60-days.

Mayfield, John A.
CO: C **Initial Rank:** Private
Joined: Wednesday, May 1, 1861 **Term (yrs):** 1 **Occupation:** Farmer **Age** 25
Enrolled at: Itawamba Co., MS **Enrolled By:** Capt. Bromley **Promoted:** Yes **ROH:** No
Born: **Marital Status:** **Residence**

Appointed 4th Sergeant on 7/22/1863. Captured near Petersburg (Hatcher's Run?) on 4/2/1865. Taken to Point Lookout, MD. Released on oath on 6/29/1865.

Mayo, James L.
CO: A **Initial Rank:** Private
Joined: Wednesday, May 1, 1861 **Term (yrs):** 1 **Occupation:** Laborer **Age** 18
Enrolled at: Tishomingo Co., MS **Enrolled By:** Capt. Leeth **Promoted:** No **ROH:** No
Born: Alabama **Marital Status:** S **Residence** Burnsville, MS

Wounded at Gaines Mill on 6/27/1862. Sent to hospital at Richmond. Returned to duty. Mortally wounded and captured at Gettysburg on 7/1/1863. Died of wounds on 7/20/1863.

2nd Mississippi Alphabetical Roster (Annotated)

Mays, Stephen T.
CO: E *Initial Rank:* Private
Joined: Wednesday, May 1, 1861 *Term (yrs):* 1 *Occupation:* Farmer *Age* 42
Enrolled at: Itawamba Co., MS *Enrolled By:* Capt. Booth *Promoted:* Yes *ROH:* No
Born: *Marital Status:* M *Residence* Guntown, MS

Elected 1st Lieutenant on 8/20/1861. Discharged on 4/17/1862 upon expiration of term of service.

McAllister, John A.
CO: L *Initial Rank:* Private
Joined: Monday, March 3, 1862 *Term (yrs):* 3 *Occupation:* Farmer *Age* 22
Enrolled at: Ripley, MS *Enrolled By:* Col. Falkner *Promoted:* No *ROH:* Yes
Born: South Carolina *Marital Status:* S *Residence* Molina, MS

Wounded (in shoulder) at Seven Pines on 5/31/1862. Sent to Richmond hospital. Furloughed. Returned to duty. Wounded at Weldon Railroad on 8/19/1864 and sent to hospital. Furloughed on 9/1/1864 for 30-days. Listed as AWOL from 11/9/1864 on wounded furlough on last muster (Jan/Feb 1865). Surrendered and paroled at LaGrange, TN on 5/25/1865. ROH for Seven Pines, 5/31/1862.

McAnally, Thomas J.
CO: A *Initial Rank:* Private
Joined: Saturday, March 1, 1862 *Term (yrs):* 3 *Occupation:* Farmer *Age* 18
Enrolled at: Jacinto, MS *Enrolled By:* Lt. Clayton *Promoted:* No *ROH:* Yes
Born: Mississippi *Marital Status:* S *Residence* Jacinto, MS

Killed in battle at The Wilderness on 5/6/1864. ROH for Gettysburg, 7/1/1863.

McBride, J. C.
CO: B *Initial Rank:* Private
Joined: *Term (yrs):* 0 *Occupation:* *Age*
Enrolled at: *Enrolled By:* *Promoted:* No *ROH:* No
Born: *Marital Status:* *Residence*

Appears on a Federal report of prisoners of war paroled at Memphis, TN for six days ending 5/31/1865. Not dated. No other record.

McBride, John A.
CO: F *Initial Rank:* Private
Joined: Wednesday, May 1, 1861 *Term (yrs):* 1 *Occupation:* Blacksmith *Age* 19
Enrolled at: Tippah Co., MS *Enrolled By:* Capt. Davis *Promoted:* Yes *ROH:* No
Born: *Marital Status:* *Residence*

Appointed 2nd Sergeant on 7/26/1861. Appointed 1st Sergeant on 4/24/1862. Captured at Gettysburg on 7/1/1863. Sent to Fort Delaware. Released on oath on 6/11/1865.

2nd Mississippi Alphabetical Roster (Annotated)

McBride, Samuel A.
CO: F *Initial Rank:* Private
Joined: Wednesday, May 1, 1861   *Term (yrs):* 1 *Occupation:* Planter   *Age* 21
Enrolled at: Tippah Co., MS   *Enrolled By:* Capt. Davis   *Promoted:* No   *ROH:* No
Born: *Marital Status:*   *Residence*
Killed in battle at 1st Manassas on 7/21/1861.

McBride, William Riley
CO: F *Initial Rank:* Private
Joined: Wednesday, May 1, 1861   *Term (yrs):* 1 *Occupation:* Planter   *Age* 21
Enrolled at: Tippah Co., MS   *Enrolled By:* Capt. Davis   *Promoted:* No   *ROH:* No
Born: Mississippi   *Marital Status:*   *Residence*
Discharged for disability on 11/18/1861 at Camp Fisher, VA.

McCabe, James
CO: K *Initial Rank:* Private
Joined: Saturday, March 1, 1862   *Term (yrs):* 3 *Occupation:*   *Age* 18
Enrolled at: Iuka, MS   *Enrolled By:* Lt. Latham   *Promoted:* No   *ROH:* No
Born: *Marital Status:*   *Residence*
Deserted on 5/25/1863.

McCarley, Green
CO: B *Initial Rank:* Private
Joined: Wednesday, May 1, 1861   *Term (yrs):* 1 *Occupation:* Farmer   *Age* 22
Enrolled at: Tippah Co., MS   *Enrolled By:* Capt. Buchanan   *Promoted:* No   *ROH:* No
Born: *Marital Status:*   *Residence*
Wounded and captured at Gettysburg on 7/1/1863. Taken to DeCamp General Hospital, Davids Island, NY Harbor where he died as a result of his wounds on 10/13/1863. Grave #899.

McCarty, D. Virginius
CO: H *Initial Rank:* Private
Joined: Monday, April 29, 1861   *Term (yrs):* 1 *Occupation:* Clerk   *Age* 17
Enrolled at: Pontotoc Co., MS   *Enrolled By:* Capt. Taylor   *Promoted:* No   *ROH:* No
Born: *Marital Status:* S   *Residence* Tupelo, MS
Mortally wounded at 1st Manassas on 7/21/1861. Died the following day (7/22/1861) in camp.

2nd Mississippi Alphabetical Roster (Annotated)

McCarty, Jacob
CO: L **Initial Rank:** Private
Joined: Monday, March 3, 1862   **Term (yrs):** 3   **Occupation:** Farmer   **Age** 24
Enrolled at: Ripley, MS   **Enrolled By:** Col. Falkner   **Promoted:** No   **ROH:** Yes
Born: Mississippi   **Marital Status:** M   **Residence** Dumas, MS

Killed in battle at Sharpsburg on 9/17/1862. ROH for South Mountain (Boonsboro), 9/14/1862.

McCarty, James
CO: C **Initial Rank:** Private
Joined: Saturday, March 1, 1862   **Term (yrs):** 3   **Occupation:**   **Age**
Enrolled at: Verona, MS   **Enrolled By:** Lt. Pounds   **Promoted:** No   **ROH:** No
Born: **Marital Status:**   **Residence**

Captured near Petersburg (Hatcher's Run?) on 4/2/1865. Taken to Point Lookout, MD. Released on oath on 6/29/1865.

McCarty, William D.
CO: C **Initial Rank:** Private
Joined: Saturday, March 1, 1862   **Term (yrs):** 3   **Occupation:** Farmer   **Age** 33
Enrolled at: Verona, MS   **Enrolled By:** Lt. Pounds   **Promoted:** No   **ROH:** No
Born: South Carolina   **Marital Status:**   **Residence**

Discharged due to disability on 8/6/1862.

McCarver, James M.
CO: F **Initial Rank:** Private
Joined: Wednesday, May 1, 1861   **Term (yrs):** 1   **Occupation:** Planter   **Age** 23
Enrolled at: Tippah Co., MS   **Enrolled By:** Capt. Davis   **Promoted:** No   **ROH:** No
Born: **Marital Status:**   **Residence**

Died of disease (pneumonia) at Camp Fisher, VA on 12/12/1861 (another record says 12/13/1861).

McCarver, James R.
CO: I **Initial Rank:** Private
Joined: Wednesday, May 1, 1861   **Term (yrs):** 1   **Occupation:** Farmer   **Age** 22
Enrolled at: Pontotoc Co., MS   **Enrolled By:** Capt. Herring   **Promoted:** No   **ROH:** No
Born: **Marital Status:**   **Residence**

Wounded at Sharpsburg on 9/17/1862. Furloughed. Returned to duty. Hospital records show admission for wound on 11/10/1863 (date of wound or engagement not listed). Returned to duty on 11/25/1863. Listed as AWOL from 3/24/1864 and deserted 3/25/1864 on Jul/Aug 1864 company muster roll.

2nd Mississippi Alphabetical Roster (Annotated)

McCarver, John W.
CO: B **Initial Rank:** Private
Joined: Monday, March 3, 1862 **Term (yrs):** 3 **Occupation:** Farmer **Age** 21
Enrolled at: Ripley, MS **Enrolled By:** Capt. Buchanan **Promoted:** No **ROH:** No
Born: Tennessee **Marital Status:** M **Residence**

Company records mark him as "deserted at Fredericksburg, VA June 13, 1863." However, Federal records also show him on rolls of Gettysburg captured lists, dated 7/5/1863. Taken to Fort Delaware and released on oath of allegiance on 6/7/1864.

McCay, Isaac W.
CO: A **Initial Rank:** Private
Joined: Wednesday, May 1, 1861 **Term (yrs):** 1 **Occupation:** Laborer **Age** 21
Enrolled at: Tishomingo Co., MS **Enrolled By:** Capt. Leeth **Promoted:** No **ROH:** No
Born: North Carolina **Marital Status:** S **Residence** Booneville, MS

Discharged for disability at Camp Fisher, VA on 1/8/1862.

McClain, Major T.
CO: E **Initial Rank:** Private
Joined: Saturday, March 8, 1862 **Term (yrs):** 3 **Occupation:** Farmer **Age** 22
Enrolled at: Guntown, MS **Enrolled By:** Capt. Bates **Promoted:** No **ROH:** No
Born: **Marital Status:** S **Residence** Guntown, MS

Captured at Gettysburg on 7/1/1863. Sent to Fort Delaware. Released on oath on 6/11/1865.

McCollam, Levi
CO: I **Initial Rank:** Private
Joined: **Term (yrs):** 0 **Occupation:** **Age**
Enrolled at: **Enrolled By:** **Promoted:** No **ROH:** No
Born: **Marital Status:** **Residence**

Appears on several Federal prisoner of war records. Captured 7/18/1863 in Tishomingo Co., MS by the 18th Missouri Infantry and forwarded to Memphis, TN for exchange. Sent to Camp Morton, IN on 8/22/1863. Died on 8/26/1864 of disease. Buried in grave #1090 in Green Lawn Cemetery. No other records.

McCombs, William H.
CO: E **Initial Rank:** Private
Joined: Wednesday, May 1, 1861 **Term (yrs):** 1 **Occupation:** Farmer **Age** 21
Enrolled at: Itawamba Co., MS **Enrolled By:** Capt. Booth **Promoted:** No **ROH:** No
Born: South Carolina **Marital Status:** S **Residence** Guntown, MS

Captured at Gettysburg on 7/1/1863. Sent to Fort Delaware. Released on oath on 6/11/1865.

2nd Mississippi Alphabetical Roster (Annotated)

McCowan, William C. CO: B Initial Rank: Private
Joined: Saturday, March 8, 1862 *Term (yrs):* 3 *Occupation:* Farmer *Age* 18
Enrolled at: Ripley, MS *Enrolled By:* Capt. Buchanan *Promoted:* No *ROH:* No
Born: Mississippi *Marital Status:* S *Residence*

Killed at Gettysburg on 7/3/1863. [*Buried at Hollywood Cemetery, Richmond, VA. Gettysburg Section Lot: 1.]

McCoy, James CO: K Initial Rank: Private
Joined: Saturday, March 1, 1862 *Term (yrs):* 3 *Occupation:* *Age* 22
Enrolled at: Iuka, MS *Enrolled By:* Lt. Latham *Promoted:* No *ROH:* No
Born: *Marital Status:* *Residence*

Wounded 7/1/1863 at Gettysburg and captured on 7/5/1863. Paroled at DeCamp General Hospital, Davids Island, NY Harbor (not dated). Appears on a muster roll of paroled and exchanged prisoners at Camp Lee, VA, dated 9/17/1863. Listed as AWOL on company rolls during Jan/Feb 1864 muster roll. Dropped from rolls as deserter during Mar/Apr 1864 muster for prolonged AWOL.

McCoy, Louis CO: K Initial Rank: Private
Joined: Saturday, March 1, 1862 *Term (yrs):* 3 *Occupation:* *Age* 29
Enrolled at: Iuka, MS *Enrolled By:* Lt. Latham *Promoted:* No *ROH:* No
Born: *Marital Status:* *Residence*

Died of disease at Richmond, VA, Chimborazo Hospital #5, on 8/16/1862.

McCrory, Elvis CO: A Initial Rank: Private
Joined: Wednesday, May 1, 1861 *Term (yrs):* 1 *Occupation:* Physician *Age* 24
Enrolled at: Tishomingo Co., MS *Enrolled By:* Capt. Leeth *Promoted:* No *ROH:* No
Born: Tennessee *Marital Status:* S *Residence*

Detailed to hospital duties and to Assistant Surgeon. Appointed Assistant Surgeon on 10/29/1861 to hospital in Staunton, VA.

McCully, Daniel CO: E Initial Rank: Private
Joined: Wednesday, May 1, 1861 *Term (yrs):* 1 *Occupation:* Farmer *Age* 18
Enrolled at: Itawamba Co., MS *Enrolled By:* Capt. Booth *Promoted:* No *ROH:* No
Born: *Marital Status:* S *Residence* Saltillo, MS

Captured at Gettysburg on 7/1/1863. Sent to Fort Delaware. Died of disease in prison on 12/27/1864 (or 12/26/1864). Locality of grave: "Jersey Shore."

2nd Mississippi Alphabetical Roster (Annotated)

McCully, Ephram H. *CO:* E *Initial Rank:* Private
Joined: Wednesday, May 1, 1861 *Term (yrs):* 1 *Occupation:* Farmer *Age* 21
Enrolled at: Itawamba Co., MS *Enrolled By:* Capt. Booth *Promoted:* No *ROH:* No
Born: *Marital Status:* S *Residence* Saltillo, MS

Detailed on detached service with the Pioneer Corps from 6/12/1863. Paroled at Appomattox Court House on 4/9/1865.

McCully, James *CO:* E *Initial Rank:* Private
Joined: Wednesday, May 1, 1861 *Term (yrs):* 1 *Occupation:* Farmer *Age* 27
Enrolled at: Itawamba Co., MS *Enrolled By:* Capt. Booth *Promoted:* Yes *ROH:* Yes
Born: *Marital Status:* S *Residence* Saltillo, MS

Listed as 3rd Corporal during Jul/Aug 1862 muster roll. Killed in battle at Sharpsburg on 9/17/1862. ROH for Seven Pines, 5/31/1862.

McCully, John T. *CO:* E *Initial Rank:* Private
Joined: Wednesday, May 1, 1861 *Term (yrs):* 1 *Occupation:* Farmer *Age* 25
Enrolled at: Itawamba Co., MS *Enrolled By:* Capt. Booth *Promoted:* No *ROH:* No
Born: South Carolina *Marital Status:* S *Residence* Saltillo, MS

Died of disease at Camp Fisher, VA on 2/26/1862. Other records show him applying for a discharge for disability in Dec 1861.

McCurley, John *CO:* G *Initial Rank:* Private
Joined: Wednesday, May 1, 1861 *Term (yrs):* 1 *Occupation:* Mechanic *Age* 24
Enrolled at: Pontotoc Co., MS *Enrolled By:* Capt. Miller *Promoted:* Yes *ROH:* No
Born: *Marital Status:* *Residence*

Listed as Corporal during May/Jun 1861 muster. Appointed 2nd Sergeant on 7/26/1861. Appointed 3rd Lieutenant on 4/23/1862. Appointed Brevet 2nd Lieutenant on 12/3/1862. Captured at Gettysburg (Cashtown) on 7/5/1863. Sent to Johnson's Island, OH. Paroled and transferred to Point Lookout, MD on 3/14/1865 for exchange.

2nd Mississippi Alphabetical Roster (Annotated)

McDaniel, James   CO: K   Initial Rank: Private

Joined: Tuesday, December 15, 1863   *Term (yrs):* 3   *Occupation:*   *Age*

Enrolled at: Iuka, MS   *Enrolled By:* Lt. Castlebery   *Promoted:* No   *ROH:* No

Born: *Marital Status:*   *Residence*

Recruit from conscript camp. Deserted at battle of The Wilderness. Federal records show him captured at Louisa Court House, VA on 6/11/1864. Sent to Elmira, NY on 7/25/1864. Desirous to take oath of allegiance and go to Nashville, TN. Released on 5/17/1865 on oath.

McDaniel, John W.   CO: B   Initial Rank: Private

Joined: Wednesday, May 1, 1861   *Term (yrs):* 1   *Occupation:*   *Age* 18

Enrolled at: Tippah Co., MS   *Enrolled By:* Capt. Buchanan   *Promoted:* No   *ROH:* No

Born: *Marital Status:*   *Residence*

Wounded at 1st Manassas on 7/21/1861. Sent to Charlottesville hospital. Amputated leg at thigh. Died at Charlottesville, VA on 9/9/1861 of wounds received at battle of 1st Manassas.

McDole, Robert J.   CO: G   Initial Rank: Private

Joined: Wednesday, May 1, 1861   *Term (yrs):* 1   *Occupation:* Farmer   *Age* 19

Enrolled at: Pontotoc Co., MS   *Enrolled By:* Capt. Miller   *Promoted:* Yes   *ROH:* Yes

Born: Mississippi   *Marital Status:* S   *Residence* Pontotoc, MS

Appointed Corporal on 5/10/1862. Wounded battle of 2nd Manassas on 8/29/1862. Returned to duty on 10/11/1862. Wounded (gunshot wound, left thigh) at Gettysburg on 7/1/1863. Sent to hospital in Richmond. Furloughed for 35-days from 8/13/1863. Returned to duty. Died on 8/10/1864 at hospital in Richmond, VA (cause not given). ROH for Bethesda Church, 6/2/1864.

McDonald, J. A.   CO: C   Initial Rank: Private

Joined: Saturday, March 1, 1862   *Term (yrs):* 3   *Occupation:*   *Age*

Enrolled at: Verona, MS   *Enrolled By:* Lt. Pounds   *Promoted:* No   *ROH:* No

Born: *Marital Status:*   *Residence*

Wounded at Gaines Mill on 6/27/1862. Returned to duty. Furloughed on sick leave from 7/25/1863 for 40-days. Did not return. During May/Jun 1864 muster, listed as "Deserted at Home."

2nd Mississippi Alphabetical Roster (Annotated)

McDonald, James
CO: E **Initial Rank:** Private
Joined: Thursday, May 1, 1862 *Term (yrs):* 1 *Occupation:* Carpenter **Age** 24
Enrolled at: Itawamba Co., MS *Enrolled By:* Capt. Booth *Promoted:* No *ROH:* No
Born: Alabama *Marital Status:* *Residence*

Died of disease at Camp Fisher, VA on 12/14/1861.

McDonald, James A.
CO: F **Initial Rank:** Private
Joined: Saturday, March 22, 1862 *Term (yrs):* 3 *Occupation:* Farmer **Age** 23
Enrolled at: Corinth, MS *Enrolled By:* Capt. Powers *Promoted:* No *ROH:* No
Born: Alabama *Marital Status:* S *Residence*

Appears on a company muster-in roll dated 3/1/1862. No other records.

McDonald, James H.
CO: E **Initial Rank:** Private
Joined: Saturday, February 22, 1862 *Term (yrs):* 3 *Occupation:* **Age** 18
Enrolled at: Guntown, MS *Enrolled By:* Capt. Bates *Promoted:* No *ROH:* No
Born: *Marital Status:* *Residence*

Wounded at Gaines Mill on 6/27/1862. Furloughed. Returned to duty. Captured at Gettysburg on 7/1/1863. Sent to Fort Delaware. Released on oath on 6/11/1865.

McDonald, John J.
CO: C **Initial Rank:** Private
Joined: Saturday, March 1, 1862 *Term (yrs):* 3 *Occupation:* **Age**
Enrolled at: Verona, MS *Enrolled By:* Lt. Pounds *Promoted:* No *ROH:* No
Born: *Marital Status:* *Residence*

Wounded (in hand) at Gaines Mill on 6/27/1862. Furloughed on 7/14/1862 for 30-days. Returned to duty. Wounded at The Wilderness on 5/5/1864. Sent to hospital in Lynchburg, VA.

McDonald, Lewis J.
CO: B **Initial Rank:** Private
Joined: Wednesday, May 1, 1861 *Term (yrs):* 1 *Occupation:* Farmer **Age** 26
Enrolled at: Tippah Co., MS *Enrolled By:* Capt. Buchanan *Promoted:* No *ROH:* No
Born: *Marital Status:* *Residence*

Wounded (right shoulder) at battle of Seven Pines on 5/31/1862. Furloughed. Returned to duty. Wounded at Gettysburg 7/1/1863 and sent to hospital at Lynchburg, VA. Furloughed. Returned to duty 8/14/1864. Captured at Hatcher's Run on 4/2/1865. Taken to Point Lookout, MD. Released on oath on 6/29/1865.

2nd Mississippi Alphabetical Roster (Annotated)

McDowell, James

CO: I   *Initial Rank:* Private
Joined: Wednesday, May 1, 1861   *Term (yrs):* 1   *Occupation:* Laborer   *Age* 35
Enrolled at: Pontotoc Co., MS   *Enrolled By:* Capt. Herring   *Promoted:* No   *ROH:* No
Born: *Marital Status:*   *Residence*

Died of disease (typhoid fever) at Camp Bee, VA on 7/18/1861.

McDuffie, George

CO: F   *Initial Rank:* Private
Joined: Tuesday, February 25, 1862   *Term (yrs):* 3   *Occupation:* Farmer   *Age* 21
Enrolled at: Ripley, MS   *Enrolled By:* Capt. Powers   *Promoted:* No   *ROH:* No
Born: Georgia   *Marital Status:* S   *Residence*

Appears on company muster-in roll. No other records.

McElhannon, James

CO: A   *Initial Rank:* Private
Joined: Saturday, September 21, 1861   *Term (yrs):* 1   *Occupation:* Farmer   *Age* 29
Enrolled at: Rienzi, MS   *Enrolled By:* Lt. Davenport   *Promoted:* No   *ROH:* No
Born: Georgia   *Marital Status:* M   *Residence* Rienzi, MS

Died of disease at Staunton, VA on 11/4/1862.

McElhannon, Marcus

CO: A   *Initial Rank:* Private
Joined: Wednesday, May 1, 1861   *Term (yrs):* 1   *Occupation:* Farmer   *Age* 25
Enrolled at: Tishomingo Co., MS   *Enrolled By:* Capt. Leeth   *Promoted:* No   *ROH:* No
Born: Georgia   *Marital Status:* S   *Residence* Rienzi, MS

Detailed as regimental wagon master for much of career. Captured at Hatcher's Run on 4/2/1865. Taken to Point Lookout, MD. Released on oath on 6/29/1865.

McElvin, J. E.

CO: H   *Initial Rank:* Sergeant
Joined: *Term (yrs):* 0   *Occupation:*   *Age*
Enrolled at: *Enrolled By:*   *Promoted:* No   *ROH:* No
Born: *Marital Status:*   *Residence*

Appears on Federal prisoner of war records. Captured at Murfreesboro, TN on 1/2/1863. Sent to Baltimore on 5/29/1863. Another record says captured at Stone River, 1/2/1863. A third record indicates individual was paroled at Fort McHenry, MD on 6/3/1863 and sent to Fort Monroe, VA for exchange. No other records. [Misidentified. Unlikely that a member of the 2nd Miss would be fighting with the Army of Tennessee at Stones River.]

2nd Mississippi Alphabetical Roster (Annotated)

McElwayne, David Andr
CO: A, I *Initial Rank:* Private
Joined: *Term (yrs):* 0 *Occupation:* *Age*
Enrolled at: *Enrolled By:* *Promoted:* No *ROH:* No
Born: *Marital Status:* *Residence*

Records jacket says to see David A. McElwain, 2nd Miss. State Cavalry. No other records.

McFaddin, Van B.
CO: E *Initial Rank:* Private
Joined: Monday, February 24, 1862 *Term (yrs):* 3 *Occupation:* Merchant *Age* 30
Enrolled at: Guntown, MS *Enrolled By:* Capt. Bates *Promoted:* No *ROH:* No
Born: *Marital Status:* M *Residence* Guntown, MS

Assigned to extra duty as Quartermaster Clerk for much of career. Furloughed on 2/2/1865.

McFearson, Wallace
CO: E *Initial Rank:* Private
Joined: Wednesday, May 1, 1861 *Term (yrs):* 1 *Occupation:* Farmer *Age* 19
Enrolled at: Itawamba Co., MS *Enrolled By:* Capt. Booth *Promoted:* No *ROH:* No
Born: Alabama *Marital Status:* S *Residence* Saltillo, MS

Wounded at Sharpsburg on 9/17/1862. Furloughed. Returned to duty. Deserted on 7/25/1863 from hospital at Richmond, VA.

McGee, William R.
CO: E *Initial Rank:* 1st Sergeant
Joined: Wednesday, May 1, 1861 *Term (yrs):* 1 *Occupation:* Carpenter *Age* 40
Enrolled at: Itawamba Co., MS *Enrolled By:* Capt. Booth *Promoted:* No *ROH:* No
Born: *Marital Status:* M *Residence* Guntown, MS

Listed as Private during May/Jun 1861 muster roll. Deserted on 7/25/1863 from hospital in Richmond.

McGill, John W.
CO: H *Initial Rank:* Private
Joined: Friday, March 21, 1862 *Term (yrs):* 3 *Occupation:* Laborer *Age* 16
Enrolled at: Shannon, MS *Enrolled By:* Lt. Porter *Promoted:* No *ROH:* No
Born: Mississippi *Marital Status:* S *Residence* Verona, MS

Discharged on 8/7/1863 — underage.

2nd Mississippi Alphabetical Roster (Annotated)

McGregor, Amos F.   CO: I   Initial Rank: Private
Joined: Wednesday, May 1, 1861   **Term (yrs):** 1   **Occupation:** Farmer   **Age** 22
Enrolled at: Pontotoc Co., MS   **Enrolled By:** Capt. Herring   **Promoted:** No   **ROH:** No
Born: **Marital Status:**   **Residence**

Wounded at Gettysburg on 7/1/1863. Sent to hospital at Charlottesville, VA. Furloughed from Lynchburg for 30-days from 10/9/1863. Listed as AWOL and deserted 2/10/1864 during Nov/Dec 1864 company muster roll.

McGregor, James E.   CO: G   Initial Rank: Private
Joined: Wednesday, May 1, 1861   **Term (yrs):** 1   **Occupation:** Shoemaker   **Age** 26
Enrolled at: Pontotoc Co., MS   **Enrolled By:** Capt. Miller   **Promoted:** No   **ROH:** No
Born: Tennessee   **Marital Status:** M   **Residence** Pontotoc, MS

Under arrest and awaiting sentence of Court Martial, "deserted to the enemy from camp on Blackwater, VA, March 17, 1863." Taken by Federal forces and sent to Fort McHenry, MD. Prepared spy charges and charged on 1/5/1864. Sent to Penitentiary at Albany, NY on 7/29/1864, Special Order 251.

McGregor, Robert L.   CO: I   Initial Rank: Private
Joined: Wednesday, May 1, 1861   **Term (yrs):** 1   **Occupation:** Farmer   **Age** 20
Enrolled at: Pontotoc Co., MS   **Enrolled By:** Capt. Herring   **Promoted:** No   **ROH:** No
Born: Mississippi   **Marital Status:**   **Residence**

Wounded at 2nd Manassas on 8/30/1862. Furloughed. Returned to duty and detailed to hospital in Richmond. Died of disease (smallpox) at Richmond, VA on 3/29/1864 (other records say 3/27/1864).

McHansard, James   CO: F   Initial Rank: Private
Joined: Saturday, March 1, 1862   **Term (yrs):** 3   **Occupation:** Farmer   **Age** 36
Enrolled at: Ripley, MS   **Enrolled By:** Capt. Powers   **Promoted:** No   **ROH:** No
Born: Tennessee   **Marital Status:** M   **Residence**

Died of disease at Fredericksburg, VA on 4/6/1862.

McHenry, John A.   CO: C   Initial Rank: 1st Corporal
Joined: Wednesday, May 1, 1861   **Term (yrs):** 1   **Occupation:** Farmer   **Age** 33
Enrolled at: Itawamba Co., MS   **Enrolled By:** Capt. Bromley   **Promoted:** No   **ROH:** No
Born: **Marital Status:**   **Residence**

Reduced to ranks on 8/1/1861. Mortally wounded at the battle of Weldon Railroad on 8/19/1864. Died as a result of wounds on 8/28/1864 at Richmond, VA.

2nd Mississippi Alphabetical Roster (Annotated)

McIntosh, Albert W.

CO: K **Initial Rank:** Private

Joined: Saturday, March 1, 1862 **Term (yrs):** 3 **Occupation:** Student **Age** 15

Enrolled at: Iuka, MS **Enrolled By:** Lt. Latham **Promoted:** No **ROH:** No

Born: Alabama **Marital Status:** S **Residence**

Discharged due to disability (underage?) on 9/22/1862.

McIntosh, James M.

CO: K **Initial Rank:** Private

Joined: Wednesday, May 1, 1861 **Term (yrs):** 1 **Occupation:** Engineer **Age** 22

Enrolled at: Tishomingo Co., MS **Enrolled By:** Capt. Stone **Promoted:** Yes **ROH:** No

Born: Alabama **Marital Status:** **Residence**

Appointed 1st Corporal on 5/30/1861. Discharged on 2/18/1862 at Camp Fisher, VA for disability.

McIntosh, John A.

CO: K **Initial Rank:** Private

Joined: Wednesday, May 1, 1861 **Term (yrs):** 1 **Occupation:** Engineer **Age** 19

Enrolled at: Tishomingo Co., MS **Enrolled By:** Capt. Stone **Promoted:** Yes **ROH:** No

Born: **Marital Status:** **Residence**

Appointed 3rd Sergeant on 4/30/1862. Wounded 7/1/1863 (left thigh) and captured at Gettysburg on (captured at Confederate field hospital on 7/5/1863). Taken to DeCamp General Hospital, Davids Island, NY Harbor and paroled (not dated but probably Sep/Oct 1863 time period). Furloughed. Returned to duty. Appointed 4th Sergeant during Jan/Feb 1864 muster roll. Hospital records show admission for gunshot wound to left hand on 5/11/1864 (company records do not indicate date or engagement). Furloughed for 60-days from 5/28/1864. Returned to duty on 11/26/1864. Captured at Petersburg (Hatcher's Run?) on 4/2/1865. Taken to Point Lookout, MD. Released on oath on 6/15/1865.

McKay, J. C.

CO: E **Initial Rank:** Private

Joined: **Term (yrs):** 0 **Occupation:** **Age**

Enrolled at: **Enrolled By:** **Promoted:** No **ROH:** No

Born: **Marital Status:** **Residence**

Appears on a Federal roll of prisoners of war received at Camp Douglas, IL on 3/9/1864. Captured at Aberdeen (MS?) on 2/17/1864. No other record.

2nd Mississippi Alphabetical Roster (Annotated)

McKay, James — *CO:* A, K, D, F   *Initial Rank:* Private
Joined: Saturday, March 1, 1862   *Term (yrs):* 3   *Occupation:* Engineer   *Age* 33
Enrolled at: Jacinto, MS   *Enrolled By:* Lt. Clayton   *Promoted:* Yes   *ROH:* No
Born: Nova Scotia   *Marital Status:* S   *Residence* Baldwyn, MS

Listed as "absent wounded" during Jul/Aug 1863 muster (date of wound and engagement not noted). Promoted Brevet 2nd Lieutenant on 7/3/1863. Elected 2nd Lieutenant on 11/26/1863. Temporarily transferred to Company K on 2/11/1864. Commanding Companies D and F since 5/6/1864. Mortally wounded at Weldon Railroad on 8/18/1864. Died of wound on 8/19/1864.

McKay, Trussie B. — *CO:* B   *Initial Rank:* Private
Joined: Wednesday, May 1, 1861   *Term (yrs):* 1   *Occupation:* Clerk   *Age* 21
Enrolled at: Tippah Co., MS   *Enrolled By:* Capt. Buchanan   *Promoted:* Yes   *ROH:* Yes
Born: *Marital Status:*   *Residence*

Appointed 4th Sergeant on 4/30/1862. Wounded in battle of 2nd Manassas on 8/29/1862. Sent to hospital. Returned to duty. Killed in battle at Gettysburg on 7/1/1863 (may have died in Federal hospital after the battle). ROH for South Mountain (Boonsboro), 9/14/1862.

McKee, Robert — *CO:* K   *Initial Rank:* Private
Joined: Saturday, March 1, 1862   *Term (yrs):* 3   *Occupation:*   *Age* 28
Enrolled at: Iuka, MS   *Enrolled By:* Lt. Latham   *Promoted:* No   *ROH:* No
Born: *Marital Status:*   *Residence*

Deserted on 5/25/1863. Taken by Federal forces at Corinth, MS on 9/9/1863. Took oath of allegiance. Remarks: "Passed North."

McKeown, Isaac — *CO:* K   *Initial Rank:* Private
Joined: Wednesday, May 1, 1861   *Term (yrs):* 1   *Occupation:* Carpenter   *Age* 29
Enrolled at: Tishomingo Co., MS   *Enrolled By:* Capt. Stone   *Promoted:* No   *ROH:* Yes
Born: Alabama   *Marital Status:*   *Residence*

Wounded and captured at Gettysburg on 7/1/1863 (wounded date, captured in Confederate hospital on 7/5/1863). Taken to Point Lookout, MD, paroled on 8/16/1863 and exchanged on 3/3/1864. Returned to duty. Mortally wounded at The Wilderness (not dated). Died on way to hospital on 5/8/1864. ROH for The Wilderness, 5/5/1864.

2nd Mississippi Alphabetical Roster (Annotated)

McKeown, James *CO:* K *Initial Rank:* Private
Joined: Saturday, March 1, 1862 *Term (yrs):* 3 *Occupation:* Farmer *Age* 20
Enrolled at: Iuka, MS *Enrolled By:* Lt. Latham *Promoted:* No *ROH:* No
Born: Mississippi *Marital Status:* *Residence*

Mortally wounded at Gaines Mill on 6/27/1862. Died of wounds at Richmond, VA on 7/5/1862.

McKinney, Franklin S. *CO:* H *Initial Rank:* Private
Joined: Saturday, March 1, 1862 *Term (yrs):* 3 *Occupation:* Student *Age* 18
Enrolled at: Chesterville, MS *Enrolled By:* Lt. Porter *Promoted:* No *ROH:* Yes
Born: Alabama *Marital Status:* S *Residence* Chesterville, MS

Killed in battle at Seven Pines on 5/31/1862. ROH for Seven Pines, 5/31/1862.

McKinney, William C. H. *CO:* H *Initial Rank:* Private
Joined: Saturday, March 1, 1862 *Term (yrs):* 3 *Occupation:* Student *Age* 20
Enrolled at: Chesterville, MS *Enrolled By:* Lt. Porter *Promoted:* No *ROH:* No
Born: Alabama *Marital Status:* S *Residence* Chesterville, MS

Captured at Gettysburg on 7/1/1863. Sent to Fort Delaware. Released on oath on 6/11/1865.

McMickin, Andrew J. *CO:* G *Initial Rank:* Private
Joined: Wednesday, May 1, 1861 *Term (yrs):* 1 *Occupation:* Farmer *Age* 23
Enrolled at: Pontotoc Co., MS *Enrolled By:* Capt. Miller *Promoted:* No *ROH:* No
Born: Mississippi *Marital Status:* S *Residence* Pontotoc, MS

Severely wounded (in arm) at 1st Manassas on 7/21/1861. Sent to hospital at Charlottesville, VA. Discharged for disability due to wound on 10/31/1861 by order of General Johnston.

2nd Mississippi Alphabetical Roster (Annotated)

McNally, Patrick   *CO:* G   *Initial Rank:* Private

Joined: Wednesday, May 1, 1861   *Term (yrs):* 1   *Occupation:* Laborer   *Age* 45

Enrolled at: Pontotoc Co., MS   *Enrolled By:* Capt. Miller   *Promoted:* No   *ROH:* Yes

Born: Ireland   *Marital Status:* S   *Residence* Pontotoc, MS

Also see Thomas J. Rye. Wounded at Seven Pines on 5/31/1862. In hospital at Lynchburg, VA. Returned to duty. Muster roll dated Nov/Dec 1862 remarks: "Discharged by order of Genl G.W. Smith by virtue of conscription act, being overage." However, subsequent company records still carry him on the rolls as "present." [Subsequent records may actually refer to the man he substituted for, Thomas J. Rye]. Wounded at Gettysburg on 7/1/1863. Sent to hospital in Lynchburg, VA. Returned to duty on 11/10/1863. Wounded at The Wilderness on 5/5/1864. Returned to duty on 5/16/1864. Paroled at Appomattox Court House, VA on 4/9/1865 (under name of P. McConnally?). ROH for Weldon Railroad, 8/19/1864.

McNutt, J. R.   *CO:* E   *Initial Rank:*

Joined: *Term (yrs):* 0   *Occupation:*   *Age*

Enrolled at: *Enrolled By:*   *Promoted:* No   *ROH:* No

Born: *Marital Status:*   *Residence*

Appears on a list of the Calhoun Rifles, dated 2/11/1861. No other record.

McPeak, Daniel E.   *CO:* C   *Initial Rank:* Private

Joined: Wednesday, May 1, 1861   *Term (yrs):* 1   *Occupation:* Farmer   *Age* 26

Enrolled at: Itawamba Co., MS   *Enrolled By:* Capt. Bromley   *Promoted:* No   *ROH:* No

Born: Tennessee   *Marital Status:*   *Residence*

Discharged for disability at Winchester, VA on 9/12/1861.

McPherson, Henry   *CO:* H   *Initial Rank:* Private

Joined: Monday, April 29, 1861   *Term (yrs):* 1   *Occupation:* Farmer   *Age* 19

Enrolled at: Pontotoc Co., MS   *Enrolled By:* Capt. Taylor   *Promoted:* Yes   *ROH:* Yes

Born: Alabama   *Marital Status:* S   *Residence* Chesterville, MS

Wounded in battle at 2nd Manassas on 8/29/1862. In hospital at Lynchburg, VA. Returned to duty. "Captured a stand of colors [shot Color Corporal Henry Spayd in the leg and seized the colors of the 149th Pennsylvania] on 7/1/1863 at Gettysburg in front of lines. Declined promotion therefor." Killed at The Wilderness on 5/6/1864. He appears on a register of appointments, CSA to Ensign & 1st Lieutenant. Date of appointment: 6/6/1864. To take rank: 5/4/1864 [However, Pvt. McPherson was killed before it could take effect.] ROH for Gettysburg, 7/3/1863.

2nd Mississippi Alphabetical Roster (Annotated)

McPherson, Lewis A.
CO: H   **Initial Rank:** Private
Joined: Monday, April 29, 1861   **Term (yrs):** 1   **Occupation:** Farmer   **Age** 21
Enrolled at: Pontotoc Co., MS   **Enrolled By:** Capt. Taylor   **Promoted:** No   **ROH:** No
Born: **Marital Status:**   **Residence**

Discharged for disability on 11/26/1861 by order of Gen. Smith.

McRae, Alexander
CO: A   **Initial Rank:** Private
Joined: Wednesday, May 1, 1861   **Term (yrs):** 1   **Occupation:** Carpenter   **Age** 23
Enrolled at: Tishomingo Co., MS   **Enrolled By:** Capt. Leeth   **Promoted:** No   **ROH:** No
Born: **Marital Status:** S   **Residence** Rienzi, MS

Died of disease at Camp Fisher, VA on 2/3/1862.

McReynolds, Peyton R.
CO: I   **Initial Rank:** Private
Joined: Wednesday, May 1, 1861   **Term (yrs):** 1   **Occupation:** Farmer   **Age** 21
Enrolled at: Pontotoc Co., MS   **Enrolled By:** Capt. Herring   **Promoted:** No   **ROH:** No
Born: **Marital Status:**   **Residence**

Wounded (right thigh) in battle at Sharpsburg on 9/17/1862 (hospital records indicate date of wound as 9/13/1862). Furloughed. Returned to duty. Hospital records show admission on 7/27/1863 for wound (records give no details as to date or engagement). Also show admission on 11/10/1863 for wound to foot (no details — same wound?) "Deserted to the enemy on 3/24/1864."

McRory, W. D. T.
CO: A   **Initial Rank:** Private
Joined: Monday, November 25, 1861   **Term (yrs):** 1   **Occupation:** Farmer   **Age** 36
Enrolled at: Camp Fisher, VA   **Enrolled By:** Capt. Leeth   **Promoted:** No   **ROH:** No
Born: Tennessee   **Marital Status:** S   **Residence** Rienzi, MS

Discharged on 5/27/1862 — over age.

McSwine, William
CO: **Initial Rank:** Private
Joined: **Term (yrs):** 0   **Occupation:**   **Age**
Enrolled at: **Enrolled By:**   **Promoted:** No   **ROH:** No
Born: **Marital Status:**   **Residence**

Appears on a Federal roll of prisoners of war, of detailed men, Post of Grenada, MS. Surrendered at Citronelle, AL and paroled at Grenada, MS. Dated 5/18/1865. [Residence listed as Yalobusha Co., MS — most of the 2nd Miss hailed from another part of the State. May be misidentified]. No other record.

2nd Mississippi Alphabetical Roster (Annotated)

McWhorter, J. F.   CO: A   Initial Rank: Private

Joined: Saturday, March 1, 1862   *Term (yrs):* 3   *Occupation:* Farmer   *Age* 23

Enrolled at: Jacinto, MS   *Enrolled By:* Lt. Clayton   *Promoted:* No   *ROH:* No

Born: Tennessee   *Marital Status:* S   *Residence* Kossuth, MS

Mortally wounded at Gaines Mill on 6/27/1862. Died of wounds on 6/29/1862.

Meador, Benjamin S.   CO: B   Initial Rank: Private

Joined: Wednesday, May 1, 1861   *Term (yrs):* 1   *Occupation:* Carpenter   *Age* 32

Enrolled at: Tippah Co., MS   *Enrolled By:* Capt. Buchanan   *Promoted:* No   *ROH:* No

Born: *Marital Status:*   *Residence*

Discharged on 7/31/1862 due to "military exemption."

Meadows, James W.   CO: G   Initial Rank: Private

Joined: Thursday, March 20, 1862   *Term (yrs):* 3   *Occupation:* Farmer   *Age* 16

Enrolled at: Pontotoc, MS   *Enrolled By:* G. B. Mears   *Promoted:* No   *ROH:* No

Born: Mississippi   *Marital Status:* S   *Residence* Pontotoc, MS

Died of disease at Richmond, VA on 8/5/1862.

Means, Edwin P.   CO: E   Initial Rank: Private

Joined: Wednesday, May 1, 1861   *Term (yrs):* 1   *Occupation:* Farmer   *Age* 22

Enrolled at: Itawamba Co., MS   *Enrolled By:* Capt. Booth   *Promoted:* No   *ROH:* No

Born: Alabama   *Marital Status:* S   *Residence* Saltillo, MS

Died of disease on furlough at Saltillo, MS on 2/12/1864.

Mears, Goldsboro B.   CO: G   Initial Rank: Private

Joined: Wednesday, May 1, 1861   *Term (yrs):* 1   *Occupation:* Law Student   *Age* 26

Enrolled at: Pontotoc Co., MS   *Enrolled By:* Capt. Miller   *Promoted:* Yes   *ROH:* No

Born: Tennessee   *Marital Status:* S   *Residence* Pontotoc, MS

Also see 42nd Mississippi Infantry Regiment. Appointed Corporal on 8/1/1861. Detailed on recruiting service circa 4/1/1862 and promoted to Captain of Company K of the 42nd Mississippi. Transferred.

2nd Mississippi Alphabetical Roster (Annotated)

Mears, Thomas L.   CO: G   Initial Rank: Private
Joined: Thursday, March 20, 1862   **Term (yrs):** 3   **Occupation:** Farmer   **Age** 18
Enrolled at: Pontotoc, MS   **Enrolled By:** G. B. Mears   **Promoted:** No   **ROH:** No
Born: Tennessee   **Marital Status:** S   **Residence** Pontotoc, MS

Wounded (left thigh) and captured at 2nd Manassas on 8/29/1862. Paroled on 9/29/1862. Died of wounds at Warrenton, VA on 10/1/1862 (other records say 10/15/1862).

Megar, William R.   CO: K   Initial Rank: Private
Joined: Wednesday, May 1, 1861   **Term (yrs):** 1   **Occupation:** Grocer   **Age** 25
Enrolled at: Tishomingo Co., MS   **Enrolled By:** Capt. Stone   **Promoted:** No   **ROH:** No
Born: **Marital Status:**   **Residence**

Discharged for disability on 8/12/1861 by order of General Johnston.

Melton, John F.   CO: E   Initial Rank: Private
Joined: Thursday, March 13, 1862   **Term (yrs):** 3   **Occupation:** Farmer   **Age** 18
Enrolled at: Guntown, MS   **Enrolled By:** Capt. Bates   **Promoted:** No   **ROH:** No
Born: Mississippi   **Marital Status:**   **Residence** Guntown, MS

Died of disease at Richmond, VA on 5/1/1862.

Melton, Levi B.   CO: F   Initial Rank: Private
Joined: Wednesday, May 1, 1861   **Term (yrs):** 1   **Occupation:** Planter   **Age** 20
Enrolled at: Tippah Co., MS   **Enrolled By:** Capt. Davis   **Promoted:** No   **ROH:** No
Born: Alabama   **Marital Status:**   **Residence**

Discharged for disability at Camp Fisher, VA on 11/24/1861.

Melton, Marion   CO: E   Initial Rank: Private
Joined: Wednesday, May 1, 1861   **Term (yrs):** 1   **Occupation:** Farmer   **Age** 18
Enrolled at: Itawamba Co., MS   **Enrolled By:** Capt. Booth   **Promoted:** No   **ROH:** No
Born: **Marital Status:** S   **Residence** Guntown, MS

Died of disease 7/17/1861.

2nd Mississippi Alphabetical Roster (Annotated)

Merchant, Richard F.
CO: C **Initial Rank:** Private
Joined: Wednesday, May 1, 1861 **Term (yrs):** 1 **Occupation:** Farmer **Age** 21
Enrolled at: Itawamba Co., MS **Enrolled By:** Capt. Bromley **Promoted:** No **ROH:** No
Born: **Marital Status:** **Residence**

Killed in battle at 1st Manassas on 7/21/1861.

Messer, Elijah
CO: F **Initial Rank:** Private
Joined: Wednesday, May 1, 1861 **Term (yrs):** 1 **Occupation:** Planter **Age** 20
Enrolled at: Tippah Co., MS **Enrolled By:** Capt. Davis **Promoted:** No **ROH:** No
Born: **Marital Status:** **Residence**

Wounded (left arm and chest) at Gettysburg on 7/3/1863. Sent to hospital in Richmond. Furloughed. Furlough extended by medical examining board to 2/2/1864. Did not report back to duty upon expiration of furlough. Listed as deserted during Jul/Aug 1864 muster roll.

Messer, Marion
CO: F **Initial Rank:** Private
Joined: Wednesday, May 1, 1861 **Term (yrs):** 1 **Occupation:** Planter **Age** 22
Enrolled at: Tippah Co., MS **Enrolled By:** Capt. Davis **Promoted:** Yes **ROH:** No
Born: **Marital Status:** **Residence**

Listed as 4th Corporal during May/Jun 1862 muster. Listed as 3rd Corporal during Jul/Aug 1863 muster roll. Received furlough of indulgence for 50-days on 1/25/1864 to MS. Did not return. Listed as deserted during Jul/Aug 1864 muster.

Mickls, John
CO: E **Initial Rank:**
Joined: **Term (yrs):** 0 **Occupation:** **Age**
Enrolled at: **Enrolled By:** **Promoted:** No **ROH:** No
Born: **Marital Status:** **Residence**

Appears on a list of the Calhoun Rifles dated 2/11/1861. No other record.

Middleton, James
CO: L **Initial Rank:** 4th Corporal
Joined: Monday, March 3, 1862 **Term (yrs):** 3 **Occupation:** Farmer **Age** 43
Enrolled at: Ripley, MS **Enrolled By:** Capt. Powers **Promoted:** Yes **ROH:** Yes
Born: Tennessee **Marital Status:** M **Residence** Moline, MS

Promoted to 4th Corporal on 3/23/1862. Killed in battle at Sharpsburg on 9/17/1862. ROH for Second Manassas, 8/28/1862 (either ROH citation or company records in error. ROH citation says KIA at Second Manassas; company records say KIA at Sharpsburg).

2nd Mississippi Alphabetical Roster (Annotated)

Miears, Andrew J.　　　　　　　　　　CO: G　　Initial Rank: Private

Joined: Wednesday, May 1, 1861　　**Term (yrs):** 1　**Occupation:** Merchant　　　**Age** 23
Enrolled at: Pontotoc Co., MS　　**Enrolled By:** Capt. Miller　　**Promoted:** Yes　**ROH:** No
Born: Alabama　　**Marital Status:** S　　**Residence** Pontotoc, MS

See also John W. Harris (substitute). Discharged by providing a substitute in March 1862. Appears on a Federal register of prisoners of war dated Memphis, TN on 10/21/1864. Took oath of allegiance.

Milam, Wiley F.　　　　　　　　　　CO: I　　Initial Rank: Private

Joined: Wednesday, May 1, 1861　　**Term (yrs):** 1　**Occupation:** Farmer　　　**Age** 24
Enrolled at: Pontotoc Co., MS　　**Enrolled By:** Capt. Herring　　**Promoted:** No　**ROH:** Yes
Born:　　**Marital Status:**　　**Residence**

Wounded in battle on 6/2/1864. Sent to hospital at Richmond, VA. Returned to duty. Captured near Petersburg (Hatcher's Run?) on 4/2/2865. Taken to Point Lookout, MD. Released on oath on 6/29/1865. ROH for Bethesda Church, 5/31/1864.

Miles, William E.　　　　　　　　　　CO: C　　Initial Rank: Private

Joined: Saturday, March 1, 1862　　**Term (yrs):** 3　**Occupation:**　　　**Age**
Enrolled at: Verona, MS　　**Enrolled By:** Lt. Pounds　　**Promoted:** No　**ROH:** No
Born:　　**Marital Status:**　　**Residence**

Last company muster (Jan/Feb 1865) lists him as absent, in corps guard house for desertion.

Miller, Archibald　　　　　　　　　　CO: C　　Initial Rank: Private

Joined: Saturday, March 1, 1862　　**Term (yrs):** 3　**Occupation:**　　　**Age**
Enrolled at: Verona, MS　　**Enrolled By:** Lt. Pounds　　**Promoted:** No　**ROH:** No
Born:　　**Marital Status:**　　**Residence**

Died of disease at Richmond, VA on 5/15/1862. [*Buried at Hollywood Cemetery, Richmond, VA. Soldiers Section F Lot: 125.]

Miller, Ebenezer E.　　　　　　　　　　CO: G　　Initial Rank:

Joined: Saturday, March 2, 1861　　**Term (yrs):** 0　**Occupation:**　　　**Age**
Enrolled at: Pontotoc, MS　　**Enrolled By:** Capt. Kilpatrick　　**Promoted:** No　**ROH:** No
Born:　　**Marital Status:**　　**Residence**

Appears on a company muster roll. No other record.

2nd Mississippi Alphabetical Roster (Annotated)

Miller, Edwin
CO: G *Initial Rank:* Private
Joined: Wednesday, May 1, 1861 *Term (yrs):* 1 *Occupation:* Student *Age* 18
Enrolled at: Pontotoc Co., MS *Enrolled By:* Capt. Miller *Promoted:* No *ROH:* No
Born: Mississippi *Marital Status:* S *Residence* Pontotoc, MS

See also 42nd Mississippi Infantry Regiment as Edwin H. Miller. Transferred to Company A of the 42nd Mississippi on 7/12/1862 by order of the Secretary of War.

Miller, Elijah T.
CO: E *Initial Rank:* Private
Joined: Wednesday, May 1, 1861 *Term (yrs):* 1 *Occupation:* Farmer *Age* 18
Enrolled at: Itawamba Co., MS *Enrolled By:* Capt. Booth *Promoted:* No *ROH:* No
Born: Tennessee *Marital Status:* S *Residence* Guntown, MS

Captured at South Mountain, MD on 9/15/1862. Taken to Fort Delaware. Paroled at Aikens Landing, VA on 10/2/1862. Declared exchanged on 11/10/1862. Deserted from hospital at Richmond on 7/25/1863. Captured by Federal forces on 11/14/1863 in the District of Corinth. Took oath of allegiance.

Miller, George
CO: G *Initial Rank:* Private
Joined: Wednesday, May 1, 1861 *Term (yrs):* 1 *Occupation:* Student *Age* 20
Enrolled at: Pontotoc Co., MS *Enrolled By:* Capt. Miller *Promoted:* No *ROH:* No
Born: Mississippi *Marital Status:* S *Residence* Pontotoc, MS

Also see 42nd Mississippi Infantry Regiment. Transferred to Company A of the 42nd Mississippi on 7/12/1862 by order of the Secretary of War.

Miller, Henry
CO: L *Initial Rank:* Private
Joined: Thursday, July 24, 1862 *Term (yrs):* 2 *Occupation:* Saddler *Age* 20
Enrolled at: Richmond, VA *Enrolled By:* Capt. Storey *Promoted:* No *ROH:* No
Born: Maryland *Marital Status:* S *Residence*

See also Samuel N. Talbert. Deserted same day as sworn in (7/14/1862). Substitute for Samuel N. Talbert.

Miller, Houson A.
CO: G *Initial Rank:* Private
Joined: Wednesday, May 1, 1861 *Term (yrs):* 1 *Occupation:* Tinner *Age* 19
Enrolled at: Pontotoc Co., MS *Enrolled By:* Capt. Miller *Promoted:* Yes *ROH:* No
Born: South Carolina *Marital Status:* S *Residence* Pontotoc, MS

Detailed as regimental musician to the band from 6/1/1861 through Mar/Apr 1862 muster. Killed in battle at Gettysburg on 7/1/1863.

2nd Mississippi Alphabetical Roster (Annotated)

Miller, Hugh R.
CO: G **Initial Rank:** Captain
Joined: Wednesday, May 1, 1861 *Term (yrs):* 1 *Occupation:* Lawyer **Age** 49
Enrolled at: Pontotoc Co., MS *Enrolled By:* Capt. Kilpatrick *Promoted:* No *ROH:* No
Born: South Carolina *Marital Status:* M *Residence* Pontotoc, MS

"Superceded by election, April 21, 1862." Discharged due to reorganization of Company on 4/23/1862. [Later, became Colonel of the 42nd Mississippi Infantry].

Miller, James D.
CO: G **Initial Rank:** Private
Joined: Wednesday, May 1, 1861 *Term (yrs):* 1 *Occupation:* Planter **Age** 26
Enrolled at: Pontotoc Co., MS *Enrolled By:* Capt. Miller *Promoted:* No *ROH:* No
Born: Mississippi *Marital Status:* S *Residence* Pontotoc, MS

Admitted to hospital in Richmond with a gunshot wound on 9/26/1862 (date of wound and engagement not given in company records). Returned to duty on 10/23/1862. Wounded at Gettysburg on 7/1/1863 and captured on 7/5/1863. Taken to DeCamp General Hospital, Davids Island, NY Harbor and paroled on 8/24/1863. Exchanged. Wounded at The Wilderness on 5/5/1864. In hospital at Lynchburg, VA. Listed as AWOL and dropped from the rolls as a deserter for prolonged AWOL during Nov/Dec 1864 muster by order of Col. Stone. Surrendered and paroled, dated Columbus, MS on 5/17/1865.

Miller, Joel H.
CO: K **Initial Rank:** Musician
Joined: Wednesday, May 1, 1861 *Term (yrs):* 1 *Occupation:* Painter **Age** 18
Enrolled at: Tishomingo Co., MS *Enrolled By:* Capt. Stone *Promoted:* No *ROH:* No
Born: South Carolina *Marital Status:* *Residence*

Listed as drummer from May/Jun 1861 muster. Wounded in battle at 1st Manassas on 7/21/1861. Furloughed home. Returned to duty. Discharged for disability due to wound on 1/1/1862 by order of General Whiting.

Miller, John F.
CO: I **Initial Rank:** Private
Joined: *Term (yrs):* 0 *Occupation:* **Age**
Enrolled at: *Enrolled By:* *Promoted:* No *ROH:* No
Born: *Marital Status:* *Residence*

Appears on several Federal prisoner of war records. Captured on 7/18/1863 at Ripley, MS by the 18th Missouri Infantry. Sent to Alton, IL on 9/2/1863. Released on oath of allegiance on 5/30/1865. No other records.

2nd Mississippi Alphabetical Roster (Annotated)

Miller, Newton
CO: E **Initial Rank:** Private
Joined: Monday, February 18, 1861 **Term (yrs):** 0 **Occupation:** **Age**
Enrolled at: Saltillo, MS **Enrolled By:** R. Griffith **Promoted:** No **ROH:** No
Born: **Marital Status:** **Residence**

Appears on a company muster roll and a list of the Calhoun Rifles dated 2/11/1861. No other records.

Miller, Richmond L.
CO: B **Initial Rank:** Private
Joined: Monday, March 3, 1862 **Term (yrs):** 3 **Occupation:** Farmer **Age** 28
Enrolled at: Ripley, MS **Enrolled By:** Capt. Buchanan **Promoted:** No **ROH:** No
Born: Tennessee **Marital Status:** M **Residence**

Wounded at Gettysburg on 7/1/1863. Furloughed from hospital in Richmond on 7/30/1863 for 40-days. Discharged from service by medical examining board because of disability due to wounds received at Gettysburg (remarks in Mar/Apr 1864 muster roll).

Miller, Thomas J.
CO: G **Initial Rank:** Private
Joined: Thursday, August 15, 1861 **Term (yrs):** 1 **Occupation:** Farmer **Age** 20
Enrolled at: Camp Jones, VA **Enrolled By:** Capt. Miller **Promoted:** No **ROH:** No
Born: Mississippi **Marital Status:** S **Residence** Pontotoc, MS

Wounded in battle at Gettysburg on 7/3/1863. Furloughed to 9/2/1863. Furlough extended to 3/17/1864. Furlough expired on 4/25/1864. Returned to duty on 11/15/1864. Discharged due to disability by order of the medical examining board on 12/15/1864. Surrendered and paroled, dated Columbus, MS on 5/17/1865.

Miller, William D. K.
CO: A, B **Initial Rank:** Private
Joined: Saturday, March 1, 1862 **Term (yrs):** 3 **Occupation:** Farmer **Age** 32
Enrolled at: Jacinto, MS **Enrolled By:** Lt. Clayton **Promoted:** No **ROH:** No
Born: Tennessee **Marital Status:** **Residence** Blackland, MS

Transferred to Company B on 4/30/1862. Captured at Gettysburg on 7/1/1863. Taken to Fort Delaware. Died of disease (typhoid fever) in prison on 9/23/1863.

Miller, William H.
CO: F **Initial Rank:** Private
Joined: Wednesday, May 1, 1861 **Term (yrs):** 1 **Occupation:** Planter **Age** 22
Enrolled at: Tippah Co., MS **Enrolled By:** Capt. Davis **Promoted:** No **ROH:** Yes
Born: **Marital Status:** **Residence**

Listed as "present" though most of company musters. ROH for Falling Waters, 7/14/1863.

2nd Mississippi Alphabetical Roster (Annotated)

Mills, William B.
Joined: Saturday, April 6, 1861 *Term (yrs):* 0 *Occupation:* *CO:* C *Initial Rank:* *Age*
Enrolled at: Richmond, MS *Enrolled By:* Capt. Bromley *Promoted:* No *ROH:* No
Born: *Marital Status:* *Residence*

Appears on a company muster roll. No other record.

Millsaps, Jacob T.
Joined: Wednesday, May 1, 1861 *Term (yrs):* 1 *Occupation:* Farmer *CO:* I *Initial Rank:* Private *Age* 21
Enrolled at: Pontotoc Co., MS *Enrolled By:* Capt. Herring *Promoted:* No *ROH:* No
Born: *Marital Status:* *Residence*

Wounded during Suffolk Campaign, circa Mar/Apr 1863. Furloughed from hospital on 5/23/1863 for 30-days. Company rolls remark: "Deserted June 23, 1863." However Federal prisoner of war records show he was captured at Ripley, MS on 7/8/1863. He was first sent to Camp Morton, IN and then to Fort Delaware on 3/19/1864. Released on oath on 6/11/1865. [This would seem to indicate that, although he was AWOL during the time he was captured, it may have been premature to declare him a deserter].

Minnix, William H.
Joined: Wednesday, May 1, 1861 *Term (yrs):* 1 *Occupation:* Laborer *CO:* K *Initial Rank:* Private *Age* 20
Enrolled at: Tishomingo Co., MS *Enrolled By:* Capt. Stone *Promoted:* No *ROH:* No
Born: *Marital Status:* *Residence*

Listed as AWOL from 4/18/1863 during Mar/Apr 1863 company muster. Declared deserter during Jul/Aug, 1863 muster.

Mitchel, Rufus H.
Joined: Monday, September 30, 1861 *Term (yrs):* 1 *Occupation:* Physician *CO:* A *Initial Rank:* Private *Age* 25
Enrolled at: Iuka, MS *Enrolled By:* Lt. Davenport *Promoted:* No *ROH:* No
Born: Tennessee *Marital Status:* M *Residence* Corinth, MS

Discharged due to disability on 3/28/1862.

2nd Mississippi Alphabetical Roster (Annotated)

Mitchel, Zariah D.
CO: L, B **Initial Rank:** Private
Joined: Monday, March 3, 1862 **Term (yrs):** 3 **Occupation:** Farmer **Age** 21
Enrolled at: Ripley, MS **Enrolled By:** Capt. Powers **Promoted:** No **ROH:** No
Born: Alabama **Marital Status:** M **Residence** Ripley, MS

Transferred to Company B on 11/1/1862. Transferred back to Company L on 3/1/1863. Listed as AWOL from 4/15/1864. Deserted, dropped from rolls during Jul/Aug 1864 muster roll — "reported to be in Tenn."

Mitchell, John L.
CO: H **Initial Rank:** Private
Joined: Monday, April 29, 1861 **Term (yrs):** 1 **Occupation:** Farmer **Age** 26
Enrolled at: Pontotoc Co., MS **Enrolled By:** Capt. Taylor **Promoted:** No **ROH:** No
Born: Alabama **Marital Status:** **Residence**

Severely wounded (in foot) in battle at 1st Manassas on 7/21/1861. In Univ. of Virginia hospital. Discharged for disability due to wounds on 11/13/1862.

Mitchell, William A.
CO: C **Initial Rank:** Private
Joined: Wednesday, May 1, 1861 **Term (yrs):** 1 **Occupation:** Blacksmith **Age** 39
Enrolled at: Itawamba Co., MS **Enrolled By:** Capt. Bromley **Promoted:** No **ROH:** No
Born: Georgia **Marital Status:** **Residence**

Discharged on plea of military exemption (over age) on 5/16/1862.

Moffett, Silas L.
CO: G **Initial Rank:** Private
Joined: Wednesday, May 1, 1861 **Term (yrs):** 1 **Occupation:** Farmer **Age** 30
Enrolled at: Pontotoc Co., MS **Enrolled By:** Capt. Miller **Promoted:** No **ROH:** No
Born: South Carolina **Marital Status:** S **Residence** Pontotoc, MS

Wounded at 1st Manassas on 7/21/1861. Wounded at The Wilderness on 5/5/1864 (shell wound in left thigh). Furloughed for 60-days from 5/20/1864. Listed as AWOL from 12/1/1864. Surrendered and paroled at Columbus, MS on 5/17/1865.

Molet, John D.
CO: B **Initial Rank:** Private
Joined: Wednesday, May 1, 1861 **Term (yrs):** 1 **Occupation:** Student **Age** 16
Enrolled at: Chattanooga, TN **Enrolled By:** Capt. Buchanan **Promoted:** No **ROH:** No
Born: **Marital Status:** **Residence**

Discharged due to disability on 9/2/1861 at Camp Fisher, VA.

2nd Mississippi Alphabetical Roster (Annotated)

Molloy, John Thomas
CO: I **Initial Rank:** Private
Joined: Wednesday, May 1, 1861 **Term (yrs):** 1 **Occupation:** Farmer **Age** 22
Enrolled at: Pontotoc Co., MS **Enrolled By:** Capt. Herring **Promoted:** No **ROH:** No
Born: South Carolina **Marital Status:** **Residence**

Discharged for disability on 1/24/1862. Took oath of allegiance on 4/21/1864 at Memphis, TN.

Monday, Westley O.
CO: B **Initial Rank:** Private
Joined: Monday, March 3, 1862 **Term (yrs):** 3 **Occupation:** Farmer **Age** 35
Enrolled at: Ripley, MS **Enrolled By:** Capt. Buchanan **Promoted:** No **ROH:** No
Born: Alabama **Marital Status:** M **Residence**

Wounded ("accidental") at Sharpsburg on 9/17/1862. Sent to hospital. Returned to duty. Captured at Falling Waters, MD on 7/14/1863. Sent to Point Lookout, MD. Paroled at Point Lookout 11/15/1864 to Venus Point, Savannah River for exchange.

Monk, George W.
CO: E **Initial Rank:** Private
Joined: Wednesday, May 1, 1861 **Term (yrs):** 1 **Occupation:** Farmer **Age** 28
Enrolled at: Itawamba Co., MS **Enrolled By:** Capt. Booth **Promoted:** Yes **ROH:** Yes
Born: Alabama **Marital Status:** S **Residence** Tupelo, MS

Listed as 4th Sergeant during May 1861. Discharged on 8/21/1861 for disability by order of General Johnston. Re-enlisted on 2/22/1862 for 3-years or the war as a Private at Guntown, MS by Capt. Bates. Killed in action at Bristoe Station on 10/14/1863. ROH for South Mountain (Boonsboro), 9/14/1862.

Monk, Richard J.
CO: E **Initial Rank:** Private
Joined: Tuesday, March 18, 1862 **Term (yrs):** 3 **Occupation:** Farmer **Age** 27
Enrolled at: Guntown, MS **Enrolled By:** Capt. Bates **Promoted:** No **ROH:** No
Born: **Marital Status:** M **Residence** Tupelo, MS

Died of disease at Ashland, VA on 4/30/1862.

2nd Mississippi Alphabetical Roster (Annotated)

Monroe, James M.
CO: A, C **Initial Rank:** Private
Joined: Wednesday, May 1, 1861 **Term (yrs):** 1 **Occupation:** Painter **Age** 19
Enrolled at: Tishomingo Co., MS **Enrolled By:** Capt. Leeth **Promoted:** No **ROH:** No
Born: Mississippi **Marital Status:** **Residence**

Discharged on 1/8/1862 due to disability at Camp Fisher, VA. Taken into Federal custody in Mississippi on 8/7/1862 and sent to Camp Chase, OH on 9/2/1862. Transferred to Johnson's Island on 9/6/1862. Exchanged at Vicksburg, MS in Dec 1862.

Monroe, Lewis A.
CO: A **Initial Rank:** Private
Joined: Wednesday, May 1, 1861 **Term (yrs):** 1 **Occupation:** Farmer **Age** 21
Enrolled at: Tishomingo Co., MS **Enrolled By:** Capt. Leeth **Promoted:** No **ROH:** No
Born: North Carolina **Marital Status:** S **Residence** Rienzi, MS

Also see 26th Mississippi Infantry Regiment. Transferred to Company B of the 26th Mississippi on 5/1/1864 by order of General Heth.

Monroe, Reuben H.
CO: K **Initial Rank:** Private
Joined: Wednesday, May 1, 1861 **Term (yrs):** 1 **Occupation:** Farmer **Age** 21
Enrolled at: Tishomingo Co., MS **Enrolled By:** Capt. Stone **Promoted:** No **ROH:** No
Born: **Marital Status:** **Residence**

Wounded at Gaines Mill on 6/27/1862. Listed as AWOL from 2/25/1864 and dropped from rolls as a deserter during Mar/Apr 1864 muster for prolonged AWOL.

Montgomery, William M.
CO: G **Initial Rank:** Private
Joined: Wednesday, May 1, 1861 **Term (yrs):** 1 **Occupation:** Planter **Age** 36
Enrolled at: Pontotoc Co., MS **Enrolled By:** Capt. Miller **Promoted:** No **ROH:** No
Born: **Marital Status:** M **Residence** Pontotoc, MS

Wounded at 1st Manassas on 7/21/1861. Sent to hospital at Lynchburg, VA. Listed as AWOL from 7/22/1861 and deserted as of 8/1/1861.

Montgomery, William P.
CO: C **Initial Rank:**
Joined: Saturday, April 6, 1861 **Term (yrs):** 0 **Occupation:** **Age**
Enrolled at: Richmond, MS **Enrolled By:** Capt. Bromley **Promoted:** No **ROH:** No
Born: **Marital Status:** **Residence**

Appears on a company muster roll. No other record.

2nd Mississippi Alphabetical Roster (Annotated)

Moody, William C.
CO: B **Initial Rank:** Private
Joined: Wednesday, May 1, 1861 *Term (yrs):* 1 *Occupation:* Druggist **Age** 24
Enrolled at: Tippah Co., MS *Enrolled By:* Capt. Buchanan *Promoted:* Yes *ROH:* No
Born: *Marital Status:* *Residence*

On daily duty in hospital from 5/24/1861. Elected 2nd Lieutenant on 4/21/1862 and assigned to duty on 4/23/1862. Promoted to 1st Lieutenant during Jul/Aug 1863 time period. Wounded (right leg) and captured at Gettysburg on 7/3/1863. Taken to Johnson's Island, OH. Exchanged on 3/14/1865.

Moody, William H.
CO: A **Initial Rank:** Private
Joined: Wednesday, May 1, 1861 *Term (yrs):* 1 *Occupation:* Merchant **Age** 21
Enrolled at: Tishomingo Co., MS *Enrolled By:* Capt. Leeth *Promoted:* Yes *ROH:* No
Born: Mississippi *Marital Status:* S *Residence* Burnsville, MS

Elected Brevet 2nd Lieutenant on 3/21/1863. Wounded and captured at Gettysburg on 7/3/1863. Died on or about 7/3/1863 of wounds.

Mooney, Alfred P.
CO: D **Initial Rank:** 4th Corporal
Joined: Wednesday, May 1, 1861 *Term (yrs):* 1 *Occupation:* Farmer **Age** 24
Enrolled at: Tippah Co., MS *Enrolled By:* Capt. Beck *Promoted:* Yes *ROH:* No
Born: North Carolina *Marital Status:* S *Residence* Snow Creek, MS

Appointed 2nd Sergeant on 7/31/1862. Accompanying list of engagements shows him wounded at Gettysburg on 7/3/1863 (company records do not mention this, although hospital records show admission for a wound in the left hand on 7/14/1863). Wounded at The Wilderness on 5/5/1864. Returned to duty. Captured at Petersburg (Hatcher's Run?) on 4/2/1865. Taken to Fort Delaware. Released on oath on 6/11/1865.

Mooney, Peter
CO: D **Initial Rank:** Private
Joined: Wednesday, May 1, 1861 *Term (yrs):* 1 *Occupation:* Farmer **Age** 18
Enrolled at: Tippah Co., MS *Enrolled By:* Capt. Beck *Promoted:* No *ROH:* No
Born: North Carolina *Marital Status:* S *Residence* Snow Creek, MS

Wounded at 1st Manassas on 7/21/1861. Returned to duty. Deserted to the enemy during a skirmish near Windsor, VA on 5/23/1863.

2nd Mississippi Alphabetical Roster (Annotated)

Moore, Allen
CO: G *Initial Rank:* Private
Joined: Wednesday, May 1, 1861 *Term (yrs):* 1 *Occupation:* Farmer *Age* 42
Enrolled at: Pontotoc Co., MS *Enrolled By:* Capt. Miller *Promoted:* No *ROH:* No
Born: Georgia *Marital Status:* M *Residence* Pontotoc, MS

Detailed as musician by Major Humphreys (temporarily commanding regiment) during Mar/Apr 1862 muster. Discharged by virtue of the Conscription Act (too old) on 8/2/1862 by order of General Lee.

Moore, George W.
CO: K *Initial Rank:* Private
Joined: Tuesday, April 1, 1862 *Term (yrs):* 3 *Occupation:* *Age* 21
Enrolled at: Iuka, MS *Enrolled By:* Lt. Latham *Promoted:* No *ROH:* No
Born: *Marital Status:* *Residence*

Also see G. W. Moore, 26th Mississippi Infantry Regiment. Wounded in battle at Sharpsburg on 9/17/1862. Furloughed. Did not return. Listed as deserted during Mar/Apr 1863 muster.

Moore, John A.
CO: B, F *Initial Rank:* Private
Joined: Wednesday, May 1, 1861 *Term (yrs):* 1 *Occupation:* Farmer *Age* 21
Enrolled at: Tippah Co., MS *Enrolled By:* Capt. Buchanan *Promoted:* No *ROH:* No
Born: *Marital Status:* *Residence*

Transferred to Company F on 6/1/1861. Captured at Warrenton, VA on 9/29/1862. Paroled. Listed as deserted during Jul/Aug 1863 muster.

Moore, John G.
CO: F *Initial Rank:* Private
Joined: Saturday, March 1, 1862 *Term (yrs):* 3 *Occupation:* Farmer *Age* 26
Enrolled at: Ripley, MS *Enrolled By:* Capt. Powers *Promoted:* No *ROH:* No
Born: North Carolina *Marital Status:* M *Residence*

Reported death by drowning at Richmond, VA on 5/31/1862. However, hospital records show he died of disease at Chimborazo Hospital #3 at Richmond on 6/23/1862.

Moore, John L.
CO: D *Initial Rank:* 3rd Lieutenant
Joined: Saturday, March 9, 1861 *Term (yrs):* 0 *Occupation:* *Age*
Enrolled at: Toombs Store, MS *Enrolled By:* John McGuirk *Promoted:* No *ROH:* No
Born: *Marital Status:* *Residence*

Appears on a company muster roll. No other record.

2nd Mississippi Alphabetical Roster (Annotated)

Moore, John M.
CO: K **Initial Rank:** Private
Joined: Tuesday, April 1, 1862 **Term (yrs):** 3 **Occupation:** Farmer **Age** 18
Enrolled at: Iuka, MS **Enrolled By:** Lt. Latham **Promoted:** Yes **ROH:** Yes
Born: Mississippi **Marital Status:** **Residence**

Wounded (date or action not noted in records) circa Mar/Apr 1862. Listed as 3rd Corporal during Mar/Apr, 1863 muster roll. Killed in action at Spotsylvania on 5/12/1864. ROH for Malvern Hill, 7/1/1862.

Moore, Joseph J.
CO: K **Initial Rank:** Private
Joined: Wednesday, May 1, 1861 **Term (yrs):** 1 **Occupation:** **Age** 20
Enrolled at: Tishomingo Co., MS **Enrolled By:** Capt. Stone **Promoted:** Yes **ROH:** No
Born: **Marital Status:** **Residence**

Appointed 5th Sergeant on 8/1/1862. Wounded and captured by Federal cavalry near Williamsport (Falling Waters?), MD and paroled (date not given, but admitted to hospital in Richmond on 7/17/1863). Detailed with Col. Stone to arrest deserters and absentees in Mississippi on 1/8/1865.

Moore, Martin V.
CO: A **Initial Rank:**
Joined: Wednesday, February 20, 1861 **Term (yrs):** 0 **Occupation:** **Age**
Enrolled at: Corinth, MS **Enrolled By:** R. Griffith **Promoted:** No **ROH:** No
Born: **Marital Status:** **Residence**

Appears on a company muster roll. No other record.

Moore, Samuel
CO: F **Initial Rank:** Private
Joined: Wednesday, May 1, 1861 **Term (yrs):** 1 **Occupation:** Planter **Age** 22
Enrolled at: Tippah Co., MS **Enrolled By:** Capt. Davis **Promoted:** No **ROH:** No
Born: **Marital Status:** **Residence**

Wounded at Gettysburg on 7/1/1863. Sent to hospital in Richmond, VA. Deserted from hospital on 7/21/1863.

Moore, Stephen H.
CO: A **Initial Rank:** Private
Joined: Saturday, March 1, 1862 **Term (yrs):** 3 **Occupation:** Farmer **Age** 25
Enrolled at: Jacinto, MS **Enrolled By:** Lt. Clayton **Promoted:** No **ROH:** No
Born: Alabama **Marital Status:** **Residence**

Discharged for disability on 6/15/1862.

2nd Mississippi Alphabetical Roster (Annotated)

Moore, William A.

Joined: Monday, February 24, 1862   **CO:** H   **Initial Rank:** Private
Joined: Monday, February 24, 1862   **Term (yrs):** 3   **Occupation:** Mechanic   **Age** 27
Enrolled at: Chesterville, MS   **Enrolled By:** Lt. Porter   **Promoted:** Yes   **ROH:** No
Born: Alabama   **Marital Status:** M   **Residence** Chesterville, MS

Appointed 3rd Corporal on 6/1/1863. Killed in battle at Gettysburg on 7/3/1863.

Moore, William J.

CO: K   **Initial Rank:** Private
Joined: Wednesday, May 1, 1861   **Term (yrs):** 1   **Occupation:** Farmer   **Age** 26
Enrolled at: Tishomingo Co., MS   **Enrolled By:** Capt. Stone   **Promoted:** Yes   **ROH:** No
Born: **Marital Status:**   **Residence**

Listed as 5th Sergeant during Mar/Apr 1863 muster roll. Admitted to hospital on 7/13/1863. Furloughed on 7/25/1863 for 40-days. Company records say "wounded furlough" but date of wound and engagement not given. Did not return. During Mar/Apr 1864 muster, remarks say, "Dropped from the rolls as a deserter for prolonged absence without leave."

Moore, William L.

CO: K   **Initial Rank:** Private
Joined: Wednesday, May 1, 1861   **Term (yrs):** 1   **Occupation:**   **Age** 23
Enrolled at: Tishomingo Co., MS   **Enrolled By:** Capt. Stone   **Promoted:** No   **ROH:** No
Born: Mississippi   **Marital Status:**   **Residence**

Discharged for disability at Camp Fisher, VA on 9/10/1861 by order of General Johnston.

Moore, William T.

CO: D   **Initial Rank:** 3rd Corporal
Joined: Wednesday, May 1, 1861   **Term (yrs):** 1   **Occupation:** Farmer   **Age** 22
Enrolled at: Tippah Co., MS   **Enrolled By:** Capt. Beck   **Promoted:** No   **ROH:** Yes
Born: Tennessee   **Marital Status:** S   **Residence** Pine Grove, MS

Reduced to ranks by his own request on 8/12/1861. According to accompanying engagements list, he was wounded at Gettysburg on 7/3/1863 (company records do not so note, however hospital records show admission for wound on 7/12/1863). Captured at Petersburg (Hatcher's Run?) on 4/2/1865. Sent to Fort Delaware. Released on oath on 6/11/1865. ROH for Gettysburg, 7/3/1863.

2nd Mississippi Alphabetical Roster (Annotated)

Mooser, Isaac A.
CO: G **Initial Rank:** Private
Joined: Wednesday, May 1, 1861 **Term (yrs):** 1 **Occupation:** Merchant **Age** 25
Enrolled at: Pontotoc Co., MS **Enrolled By:** Capt. Miller **Promoted:** No **ROH:** No
Born: Germany **Marital Status:** S **Residence** Pontotoc, MS

Also see Miles Cary, his substitute. Discharged on 7/13/1862 by reason of providing a substitute.

Morgan, John B.
CO: F **Initial Rank:**
Joined: Monday, March 4, 1861 **Term (yrs):** 0 **Occupation:** **Age**
Enrolled at: Ripley, MS **Enrolled By:** J. R. Chalmers **Promoted:** No **ROH:** No
Born: **Marital Status:** **Residence**

Appears on a company muster roll. No other record.

Morgan, William
CO: F **Initial Rank:** Private
Joined: Wednesday, May 1, 1861 **Term (yrs):** 1 **Occupation:** Planter **Age** 36
Enrolled at: Tippah Co., MS **Enrolled By:** Capt. Davis **Promoted:** No **ROH:** No
Born: Alabama **Marital Status:** **Residence**

Discharged on 7/31/1862 — over age.

Morgan, William A.
CO: F **Initial Rank:** Private
Joined: Wednesday, May 1, 1861 **Term (yrs):** 1 **Occupation:** Planter **Age** 21
Enrolled at: Tippah Co., MS **Enrolled By:** Capt. Davis **Promoted:** No **ROH:** No
Born: Mississippi **Marital Status:** **Residence**

Severely wounded (through right thigh) at 1st Manassas on 7/21/1861. Discharged for disability due to wounds on 11/12/1861 at Camp Fisher, VA.

2nd Mississippi Alphabetical Roster (Annotated)

Morrill, F. A.
CO: L *Initial Rank:* Private
Joined: *Term (yrs):* 0 *Occupation:* *Age*
Enrolled at: *Enrolled By:* *Promoted:* No *ROH:* No
Born: *Marital Status:* *Residence*

Appears on a Federal list of Confederates admitted into U.S.A. General Hospital No. 1, Frederick, MD, during the months of September, October, November and December 1862 (not dated). Date of transfer: 9/18/1862. Also appears on a Confederate list of monies of deceased soldiers, dated 7/13/1863 and a register of Officers and Soldiers killed in battle or died of wounds or disease (not dated). [It appears from circumstantial evidence, that he was probably wounded and captured at Sharpsburg on 9/17/1862. Paroled and later died, either on furlough or in hospital, the other records being lost or destroyed].

Morris, Benjamin R.
CO: L *Initial Rank:* Private
Joined: Monday, March 3, 1862 *Term (yrs):* 3 *Occupation:* Farmer *Age* 30
Enrolled at: Ripley, MS *Enrolled By:* Col. Falkner *Promoted:* No *ROH:* No
Born: Alabama *Marital Status:* M *Residence* Union Mills, MS

Wounded in battle at 2nd Manassas on 8/29/1862. Sent to hospital at Warrenton, VA. Captured and paroled at Warrenton on 9/29/1862. Furloughed. Did not return. Dropped from rolls as deserter during Mar/Apr 1864 muster roll.

Morris, George W.
CO: B *Initial Rank:* Private
Joined: Saturday, March 1, 1862 *Term (yrs):* 3 *Occupation:* Farmer *Age* 21
Enrolled at: Verona, MS *Enrolled By:* Lt. Pounds *Promoted:* No *ROH:* No
Born: Mississippi *Marital Status:* *Residence*

Killed in battle at 2nd Manassas on 8/29/1862.

Morris, O. F.
CO: C *Initial Rank:* Private
Joined: Saturday, March 1, 1862 *Term (yrs):* 3 *Occupation:* Farmer *Age* 26
Enrolled at: Verona, MS *Enrolled By:* Lt. Pounds *Promoted:* No *ROH:* No
Born: *Marital Status:* *Residence*

Died at Lynchburg, VA of disease on 5/10/1862.

2nd Mississippi Alphabetical Roster (Annotated)

Moser, Barney

CO: I **Initial Rank:** Private

Joined: Monday, September 30, 1861 **Term (yrs):** 1 **Occupation:** Farmer **Age** 22

Enrolled at: Iuka, MS **Enrolled By:** Lt. Davenport **Promoted:** No **ROH:** No

Born: Mississippi **Marital Status:** **Residence**

Captured at Gettysburg on 7/1/1863. Sent to Fort Delaware. Died of disease (smallpox) on 12/15/1863 in captivity at Fort Delaware. Locality of grave: "Jersey Shore, Opposite Post."

Mullins, Marion M.

CO: C **Initial Rank:** Private

Joined: Wednesday, May 1, 1861 **Term (yrs):** 1 **Occupation:** Farmer **Age** 24

Enrolled at: Itawamba Co., MS **Enrolled By:** Capt. Bromley **Promoted:** No **ROH:** No

Born: **Marital Status:** **Residence**

Also see 1st (Johnston's) Mississippi Infantry. Discharged due to disability on 11/15/1861 at Camp Fisher, VA.

Murphy, James

CO: L **Initial Rank:** Private

Joined: Sunday, July 13, 1862 **Term (yrs):** 2 **Occupation:** Seaman **Age** 36

Enrolled at: Richmond, VA **Enrolled By:** Capt. Clayton **Promoted:** Yes **ROH:** No

Born: England **Marital Status:** M **Residence** Baltimore, MD

Substitute for [Marcus] Bynum, Co. A. Promoted to 3rd Corporal on 9/1/1862. Accompanying list of engagements shows him wounded at Sharpsburg on 9/17/1862 (company records do not so indicate). Captured at Gettysburg on 7/1/1863. Taken to Fort Delaware. Paroled on 10/30/1864 and exchanged on 11/12/1864 at Savannah, GA. Furloughed for 30-days. Reported for duty on 12/23/1864. Captured at Hatcher's Run on 4/2/1865. Taken to Point Lookout, MD. Released on oath on 6/15/1865.

Murphy, John

CO: B, L **Initial Rank:** Private

Joined: Monday, March 3, 1862 **Term (yrs):** 3 **Occupation:** Laborer **Age** 30

Enrolled at: Ripley, MS **Enrolled By:** Capt. Buchanan **Promoted:** No **ROH:** No

Born: Ireland **Marital Status:** M **Residence** Arizabo, MS

Transferred to Company L on 4/30/1862. Wounded (in arm) at Sharpsburg on 9/17/1862. Furloughed from hospital. Returned to duty. Severely wounded (right shoulder) at Gettysburg (date not given). Furloughed. Captured by Federal forces in Mississippi in Tupelo on 7/14/1864. Sent to Alton, IL. Paroled for exchange on 2/17/1865.

2nd Mississippi Alphabetical Roster (Annotated)

Murphy, Lewis *CO:* A *Initial Rank:* Private
Joined: *Term (yrs):* 0 *Occupation:* *Age*
Enrolled at: *Enrolled By:* *Promoted:* No *ROH:* No
Born: *Marital Status:* *Residence*

Appears on Federal prisoner of war records. Captured in Claiborne Co., MS on 5/5/1863. Sent to Alton, IL. Exchanged on 6/12/1863. No other records.

Murphy, William B. *CO:* A *Initial Rank:* Private
Joined: Wednesday, May 1, 1861 *Term (yrs):* 1 *Occupation:* Farmer *Age* 20
Enrolled at: Tishomingo Co., MS *Enrolled By:* Capt. Leeth *Promoted:* No *ROH:* No
Born: Tennessee *Marital Status:* S *Residence* Rienzi, MS

Wounded at 2nd Manassas on 8/29/1862. Returned to duty. Captured at Gettysburg on 7/1/1863. Sent to Fort Delaware. [Either escaped or was paroled and exchanged because company records show him "absent on furlough" for Jul/Aug 1863 muster roll]. Captured while on furlough at Edwards Depot, MS on 9/5/1863. Sent to Alton, IL and transferred to Fort Delaware on 2/29/1864. Released on oath on 6/11/1865. [Color-bearer at Gettysburg on 7/1/1863. Was captured, along with the regiment's colors at the Railroad Cut by Corporal Frank Wallar of the 6th Wisconsin Infantry Regiment (for which Wallar was awarded a Congressional Medal of Honor)].

Murthra, John *CO:* F *Initial Rank:* Private
Joined: *Term (yrs):* 0 *Occupation:* *Age*
Enrolled at: *Enrolled By:* *Promoted:* No *ROH:* No
Born: *Marital Status:* *Residence*

See John Murtha, Wood's Regiment Confederate Cavalry. No other record.

Music, Daniel E. *CO:* K *Initial Rank:* Private
Joined: Saturday, March 1, 1862 *Term (yrs):* 3 *Occupation:* *Age* 29
Enrolled at: Iuka, MS *Enrolled By:* Lt. Latham *Promoted:* No *ROH:* No
Born: *Marital Status:* *Residence*

Furloughed during Sep/Oct 1862 muster. Did not return. Listed as deserter as of Mar/Apr 1863 muster roll.

2nd Mississippi Alphabetical Roster (Annotated)

Nance, John O.　　　　　　　　　　CO: B　　Initial Rank: Private

Joined: Monday, March 3, 1862　　**Term (yrs):** 3　**Occupation:** Farmer　　**Age** 19

Enrolled at: Ripley, MS　　**Enrolled By:** Capt. Buchanan　　**Promoted:** No　**ROH:** No

Born: Tennessee　　**Marital Status:** S　　**Residence**

Captured at Gettysburg on 7/3/1863. Escaped. Furloughed 30-days from 12/18/1863. Returned to duty. Wounded in battle on 10/28/1864. Sent to hospital in Richmond, VA. Furloughed 60-days from 11/16/1864. Paroled (location not given) on 5/12/1865.

Nance, Thomas H.　　　　　　　　　CO: B　　Initial Rank: Private

Joined: Wednesday, May 1, 1861　　**Term (yrs):** 1　**Occupation:** Farmer　　**Age** 24

Enrolled at: Tippah Co., MS　　**Enrolled By:** Capt. Buchanan　　**Promoted:** Yes　**ROH:** No

Born:　　**Marital Status:**　　**Residence**

Listed as 2nd Corporal during Nov/Dec 1861 muster and 1st Corporal for Mar/Apr 1862 muster. Wounded on 6/27/1862 at Gaines Mill. Furloughed. Returned to duty. Wounded at Gettysburg 7/1/1863 and furloughed for 40-days from 7/28/1863. Died of wounds at Ripley, MS on 9/9/1863.

Nash, Richard　　　　　　　　　　　CO: A　　Initial Rank: Private

Joined: Wednesday, May 1, 1861　　**Term (yrs):** 1　**Occupation:** Laborer　　**Age** 19

Enrolled at: Tishomingo Co., MS　　**Enrolled By:** Capt. Leeth　　**Promoted:** No　**ROH:** No

Born: Mississippi　　**Marital Status:** S　　**Residence** Jacinto, MS

Wounded in battle at Malvern Hill on 7/1/1862 according to company records (however, he appears on a list of casualties dated 6/27/1862 which would place his wounding at Gaines Mill). Furloughed. Did not return. Listed as deserter during Mar/Apr 1863 muster roll.

Neal, Benjamin A.　　　　　　　　　CO: D　　Initial Rank: Private

Joined: Tuesday, October 1, 1861　　**Term (yrs):** 1　**Occupation:** Farmer　　**Age** 34

Enrolled at: Iuka, MS　　**Enrolled By:** Lt. Davenport　　**Promoted:** No　**ROH:** No

Born: Alabama　　**Marital Status:** M　　**Residence** Pine Grove, MS

Furloughed (reason not given) 30-days from 10/5/1862. Did not return. Listed as deserter during Mar/Apr 1863 muster. Dropped from rolls for prolonged AWOL.

2nd Mississippi Alphabetical Roster (Annotated)

Neeley, Alexander S.

CO: B, L **Initial Rank:** Private

Joined: Wednesday, May 1, 1861 **Term (yrs):** 1 **Occupation:** Wagon maker **Age** 23

Enrolled at: Tippah Co., MS **Enrolled By:** Capt. Buchanan **Promoted:** No **ROH:** No

Born: Tennessee **Marital Status:** S **Residence** Arizabo, MS

Transferred to Company L on 4/30/1862. Detailed as ambulance driver from Sep/Oct 1862 time period. Transferred back to Company B on 3/1/1863. Listed as present with company for Jan/Feb 1865 muster. Captured at Petersburg (Hatcher's Run?) on 4/2/1865. Taken to Point Lookout, MD. Released on oath on 6/29/1865.

Neeley, William N.

CO: L **Initial Rank:** Private

Joined: Monday, March 3, 1862 **Term (yrs):** 3 **Occupation:** Farmer **Age** 19

Enrolled at: Ripley, MS **Enrolled By:** Col. Falkner **Promoted:** No **ROH:** No

Born: Tennessee **Marital Status:** S **Residence**

Wounded in battle at Weldon Railroad on 8/19/1864. Sent to hospital. Leg amputated. Furloughed 60-days from 10/13/1864. Jan/Feb 1865 muster remarks: "absent — sick since Aug 18, 1864, supposed to be retired."

Neely, Isaac R.

CO: A **Initial Rank:** Private

Joined: Wednesday, July 10, 1861 **Term (yrs):** 1 **Occupation:** Farmer **Age** 22

Enrolled at: Winchester, VA **Enrolled By:** Capt. Leeth **Promoted:** No **ROH:** No

Born: Tennessee **Marital Status:** S **Residence** Rienzi, MS

Furloughed with leave Jan/Feb 1865 "indulgence."

Neely, Robert A.

CO: A **Initial Rank:** Private

Joined: Wednesday, July 10, 1861 **Term (yrs):** 1 **Occupation:** Carpenter **Age** 30

Enrolled at: Winchester, VA **Enrolled By:** Capt. Leeth **Promoted:** Yes **ROH:** No

Born: Tennessee **Marital Status:** M **Residence** Rienzi, MS

Appointed 1st Corporal on 4/22/1862. Promoted 5th Sergeant on 10/16/1862. Wounded at Gettysburg on 7/1/1863. Furloughed. Returned to duty. Promoted to 4th Sergeant circa May/Jun 1864. Listed as 3rd Sergeant during Jul/Aug 1864 muster. Promoted to Jr. 2nd Lieutenant on 9/30/1864 by election. Captured at Hatcher's Run on 4/2/1865. Sent to Johnson's Island, OH. Released on oath on 6/19/1865.

2nd Mississippi Alphabetical Roster (Annotated)

Neely, Samuel G.   CO: A   Initial Rank: Private
Joined: Wednesday, July 10, 1861   *Term (yrs):* 1   *Occupation:* Farmer   *Age* 19
Enrolled at: Winchester, VA   *Enrolled By:* Capt. Leeth   *Promoted:* Yes   *ROH:* Yes
Born: Tennessee   *Marital Status:* S   *Residence* Rienzi, MS

Wounded (slight, in leg) at 1st Manassas on 7/21/1861. Wounded at 2nd Manassas on 8/29/1862. Sent to hospital at Richmond, VA. Returned to duty. Wounded at Sharpsburg on 9/17/1862 (according to engagements list; not indicated in company records). Returned to duty. Wounded at Gettysburg (again, according to engagements list), on 7/1/1863. Hospital records do show him admitted on 7/16/1863 with a wound to the right thigh. Returned to duty. Appointed 4th Corporal on 5/1/1864. Mortally wounded (in abdomen) in battle at the Weldon Railroad on 8/19/1864. Died on 8/21/1864 of wounds [only Confederate soldier named to the ROH 5 times;]. ROH for The Wilderness, 5/6/1864; Talley's Mill, 5/10/1864; Spotsylvania Court House, 5/12/1864; Bethesda Church, 5/31/1864; and Weldon Railroad, 8/18/1864 (mortally wounded).

Neely, William H.   CO: A   Initial Rank: Private
Joined: Wednesday, May 1, 1861   *Term (yrs):* 1   *Occupation:* Laborer   *Age* 21
Enrolled at: Tishomingo Co., MS   *Enrolled By:* Capt. Leeth   *Promoted:* No   *ROH:* No
Born: Tennessee   *Marital Status:* S   *Residence* Rienzi, MS

Discharged due to disability on 9/10/1861 at Camp Fisher, VA.

Neely, William S.   CO: I   Initial Rank: 3rd Sergeant
Joined: Wednesday, May 1, 1861   *Term (yrs):* 1   *Occupation:* Teacher   *Age* 26
Enrolled at: Pontotoc Co., MS   *Enrolled By:* Capt. Herring   *Promoted:* No   *ROH:* No
Born: *Marital Status:*   *Residence*

Died of disease at Winchester, VA on 7/3/1861.

Nelson, Charles R.   CO: E   Initial Rank: Private
Joined: Wednesday, May 1, 1861   *Term (yrs):* 1   *Occupation:* Farmer   *Age* 21
Enrolled at: Itawamba Co., MS   *Enrolled By:* Capt. Booth   *Promoted:* No   *ROH:* No
Born: Alabama   *Marital Status:* S   *Residence* Guntown, MS

Wounded at 1st Manassas on 7/21/1861. Discharged for disability on 1/6/1862. However, apparently re-enlisted on 3/1/1862 at Guntown, MS by Capt. Bates for 3-years or the war. Served on detached service in hospitals as nurse and Ward Master in Richmond from 7/27/1863. Hospital records show he was admitted for a wound on 7/5/1863 (date of wound or cause not given). Paroled at hospital in Richmond on 4/3/1865.

2nd Mississippi Alphabetical Roster (Annotated)

Nelson, Lucius W. D.　　　　　　　　　　　CO: C　　Initial Rank: Private
Joined: Wednesday, May 1, 1861　　*Term (yrs):* 1　*Occupation:* Clerk　　　　*Age* 19
Enrolled at: Itawamba Co., MS　　*Enrolled By:* Capt. Bromley　　*Promoted:* No　*ROH:* No
Born:　　　　　　　　　　*Marital Status:*　　　　　　　*Residence*

Killed in battle at 1st Manassas on 7/21/1861.

Nelson, W. B.　　　　　　　　　　　　　　CO: H　　Initial Rank: Private
Joined:　　　　　　　　　　　　　*Term (yrs):* 0　*Occupation:*　　　　　　　*Age*
Enrolled at:　　　　　　　　　　　*Enrolled By:*　　　　　　　*Promoted:* No　*ROH:* No
Born:　　　　　　　　　　*Marital Status:*　　　　　　　*Residence*

Appears on a Federal roll of prisoners of war. Captured at Selma, AL on 4/2/1862 (roll not dated). [May be mistaken regimental identity for the 2nd Missouri]. No other record.

Nerwood, N. L.　　　　　　　　　　　　　CO: E　　Initial Rank: Private
Joined:　　　　　　　　　　　　　*Term (yrs):* 0　*Occupation:*　　　　　　　*Age*
Enrolled at:　　　　　　　　　　　*Enrolled By:*　　　　　　　*Promoted:* No　*ROH:* No
Born:　　　　　　　　　　*Marital Status:*　　　　　　　*Residence*

Appears on a Federal roll of prisoners of war dated Talladega, AL. Paroled on 5/12/1865. No other records.

Newberry, John B.　　　　　　　　　　　　CO: E　　Initial Rank: Private
Joined: Wednesday, May 1, 1861　　*Term (yrs):* 1　*Occupation:* Farmer　　　*Age* 20
Enrolled at: Itawamba Co., MS　　*Enrolled By:* Capt. Booth　　*Promoted:* No　*ROH:* No
Born: Alabama　　　　　　*Marital Status:* S　　　　　　*Residence* Saltillo, MS

Wounded (left hand) at The Wilderness on 5/5/1864. Furloughed 60-days from 6/2/1864. Listed as AWOL as of last (Jan/Feb 1865) muster roll.

Newman, Benjamin Franklin　　　　　　　　CO: A,I　Initial Rank: Private
Joined:　　　　　　　　　　　　　*Term (yrs):* 0　*Occupation:*　　　　　　　*Age*
Enrolled at:　　　　　　　　　　　*Enrolled By:*　　　　　　　*Promoted:* No　*ROH:* No
Born:　　　　　　　　　　*Marital Status:*　　　　　　　*Residence*

Reference envelope says to also see B. F. Newman, 1st Mississippi Cavalry. Appears on a register of the Medical Director's Office, Richmond, VA for period "to Sept 27, 1864." Remarks: "Ripley, Miss." No other record.

2nd Mississippi Alphabetical Roster (Annotated)

Newman, Martin D.　　　　　　　　　　　　　CO: D　　Initial Rank: Private
Joined: Wednesday, May 1, 1861　　*Term (yrs):* 1　*Occupation:* Farmer　　　　*Age* 40
Enrolled at: Tippah Co., MS　　*Enrolled By:* Capt. Beck　　*Promoted:* No　*ROH:* No
Born: South Carolina　　*Marital Status:* M　　*Residence* Hickory Flat, MS

Discharged on 7/31/1862 — over age.

Newsom, William H.　　　　　　　　　　　　CO: G　　Initial Rank: Private
Joined: Wednesday, May 1, 1861　　*Term (yrs):* 1　*Occupation:* Clerk　　　　*Age* 22
Enrolled at: Pontotoc Co., MS　　*Enrolled By:* Capt. Miller　　*Promoted:* No　*ROH:* No
Born: Tennessee　　*Marital Status:* S　　*Residence* Pontotoc, MS

Wounded (finger) at battle of 1st Manassas on 7/21/1861. Discharged for disability due to wounds on 9/5/1861 at Camp Jones, VA by order of General Johnston.

Newton, Thomas J.　　　　　　　　　　　　CO: F　　Initial Rank: Private
Joined: Wednesday, May 1, 1861　　*Term (yrs):* 1　*Occupation:* Collector　　　　*Age* 34
Enrolled at: Tippah Co., MS　　*Enrolled By:* Capt. Davis　　*Promoted:* Yes　*ROH:* No
Born:　　*Marital Status:*　　*Residence*

Appointed 4th Sergeant on 7/26/1861. Slightly wounded at Gaines Mill on 6/27/1862. Returned to duty. Wounded (left leg) at The Wilderness on 5/5/1864 (according to company muster remarks. However, hospital records show admission for gunshot wound on 7/8/1864). Sent to hospital at Lynchburg, VA. Furloughed 60-days from 8/11/1864. Listed as AWOL from 10/31/1864 during last (Jan/Feb 1865) muster roll.

Nicholson, David L.　　　　　　　　　　　　CO: A　　Initial Rank: Private
Joined: Wednesday, May 1, 1861　　*Term (yrs):* 1　*Occupation:* Clerk (farmer)　　*Age* 20
Enrolled at: Tishomingo Co., MS　　*Enrolled By:* Capt. Leeth　　*Promoted:* No　*ROH:* No
Born: Alabama　　*Marital Status:* S　　*Residence* Hickory Plains, MS

Killed in battle at 2nd Manassas on 8/29/1862.

Nicholson, Leonidas　　　　　　　　　　　　CO: A, L　　Initial Rank: Private
Joined: Saturday, August 10, 1861　　*Term (yrs):* 1　*Occupation:* Farmer　　　*Age* 23
Enrolled at: Camp Jones, VA　　*Enrolled By:* Capt. Leeth　　*Promoted:* No　*ROH:* No
Born: Alabama　　*Marital Status:* S　　*Residence* Iuka, MS

Transferred to Company L on 4/30/1862. Listed as AWOL on sick furlough in MS from 9/11/1864 during last (Jan/Feb 1865) muster.

2nd Mississippi Alphabetical Roster (Annotated)

Nicholson, Thomas J.
CO: A **Initial Rank:** Private
Joined: Monday, September 30, 1861 **Term (yrs):** 1 **Occupation:** Student **Age** 19
Enrolled at: Iuka, MS **Enrolled By:** Lt. Davenport **Promoted:** No **ROH:** No
Born: Alabama **Marital Status:** S **Residence** Hickory Plains, MS

Given a furlough "of indulgence" on 2/10/1864 for 30-days. Did not return. Remarks on Jan/Feb 1865 muster list him as deserter. "Joined another command since last muster."

Nixon, Abner
CO: I **Initial Rank:** Private
Joined: Wednesday, May 1, 1861 **Term (yrs):** 1 **Occupation:** Farmer **Age** 35
Enrolled at: Pontotoc Co., MS **Enrolled By:** Capt. Herring **Promoted:** Yes **ROH:** No
Born: **Marital Status:** **Residence**

Promoted to 2nd Lieutenant on 4/23/1862 and assigned to duty. Killed in battle at Sharpsburg on 9/17/1862.

Nolan, John M.
CO: D **Initial Rank:** Private
Joined: Wednesday, May 1, 1861 **Term (yrs):** 1 **Occupation:** Farmer **Age** 21
Enrolled at: Tippah Co., MS **Enrolled By:** Capt. Beck **Promoted:** No **ROH:** No
Born: Tennessee **Marital Status:** S **Residence** Snow Creek, MS

Accompanying list of engagements shows him wounded at Sharpsburg on 9/17/1862 (company records do not so indicate). Captured on 10/1/1864 in battle at Fort Bratton, VA. Taken to Point Lookout, MD. Became "Galvanized Yankee" and joined U.S. service on 10/8/1864. Deserted.

Noon, Daniel
CO: B **Initial Rank:** Private
Joined: Wednesday, May 1, 1861 **Term (yrs):** 1 **Occupation:** Laborer **Age** 37
Enrolled at: Tippah Co., MS **Enrolled By:** Capt. Buchanan **Promoted:** No **ROH:** No
Born: **Marital Status:** **Residence**

Spent much of time on detached service in hospital at Richmond and Greensboro, NC. Paroled at Greensboro, NC on 5/1/1865.

2nd Mississippi Alphabetical Roster (Annotated)

Nooner, William L. CO: B Initial Rank: Private
Joined: Wednesday, May 1, 1861 **Term (yrs):** 1 **Occupation:** Farmer **Age** 21
Enrolled at: Tippah Co., MS **Enrolled By:** Capt. Buchanan **Promoted:** No **ROH:** No
Born: **Marital Status:** **Residence**

Wounded in battle at Sharpsburg on 9/17/1862. Sent to hospital. Returned to duty. Detailed as scout for Major General Heth from 7/1/1863 to last company muster. Admitted to hospital for treatment of wound at Richmond, VA on 7/14/1863 (action or date of wound not given in records). Returned to duty on 8/8/1863.

Norland, James T. CO: K Initial Rank: Private
Joined: Wednesday, May 1, 1861 **Term (yrs):** 1 **Occupation:** **Age**
Enrolled at: Tishomingo Co., MS **Enrolled By:** Capt. Stone **Promoted:** No **ROH:** No
Born: **Marital Status:** **Residence**

Appears on a company muster-in roll. No other record.

Norris, Thomas J. CO: L Initial Rank: Private
Joined: Monday, March 3, 1862 **Term (yrs):** 3 **Occupation:** Farmer **Age** 30
Enrolled at: Ripley, MS **Enrolled By:** Capt. Powers **Promoted:** No **ROH:** No
Born: Alabama **Marital Status:** M **Residence** Union Mills, MS

Died of disease (typhoid fever) at Richmond, VA on 6/17/1862.

Northcross, Richard CO: F Initial Rank: Private
Joined: Monday, September 30, 1861 **Term (yrs):** 1 **Occupation:** **Age**
Enrolled at: Iuka, MS **Enrolled By:** Lt. Davenport **Promoted:** No **ROH:** Yes
Born: **Marital Status:** **Residence**

Killed in battle at Gaines Mill on 6/27/1862. ROH for Gaines Mill, 6/27/1862.

Norton, Jacob A. CO: B Initial Rank: Private
Joined: Wednesday, May 1, 1861 **Term (yrs):** 1 **Occupation:** Farmer **Age** 21
Enrolled at: Tippah Co., MS **Enrolled By:** Capt. Buchanan **Promoted:** No **ROH:** No
Born: **Marital Status:** **Residence**

Wounded at Gaines Mill on 6/27/1862. Returned to duty. Wounded in battle at Bristoe Station on 10/14/1863. Sent to hospital. Returned to duty. Wounded at The Wilderness on 5/6/1864. Sent to hospital. Returned to duty on 8/1/1864. Wounded at the Weldon Railroad on 8/18/1864 (or 8/19/1864 — two conflicting records). Furloughed 40-days from 8/30/1864. Paroled at Appomattox Court House, VA on 4/9/1865.

2nd Mississippi Alphabetical Roster (Annotated)

Norton, John A.
CO: F **Initial Rank:** Private
Joined: Wednesday, May 1, 1861 **Term (yrs):** 1 **Occupation:** Planter **Age** 19
Enrolled at: Tippah Co., MS **Enrolled By:** Capt. Davis **Promoted:** No **ROH:** No
Born: **Marital Status:** **Residence**

Killed in battle at 1st Manassas on 7/21/1861.

Norton, Josiah H.
CO: B **Initial Rank:** Private
Joined: Wednesday, September 18, 1861 **Term (yrs):** 1 **Occupation:** Clerk **Age** 24
Enrolled at: Ripley, MS **Enrolled By:** Lt. Davenport **Promoted:** No **ROH:** No
Born: Mississippi **Marital Status:** **Residence**

Discharged due to disability on 11/11/1861 by order of General Smith. [same as Miles H. Norton?]

Norton, Miles H.
CO: B **Initial Rank:** Private
Joined: Wednesday, May 1, 1861 **Term (yrs):** 1 **Occupation:** Clerk **Age** 24
Enrolled at: Tippah Co., MS **Enrolled By:** Capt. Buchanan **Promoted:** No **ROH:** No
Born: Mississippi **Marital Status:** **Residence**

Discharged on 11/2/1862 for disability by order of General Smith [same as Josiah H. Norton?]

Norton, W. H.
CO: B **Initial Rank:** Private
Joined: **Term (yrs):** 0 **Occupation:** **Age**
Enrolled at: **Enrolled By:** **Promoted:** No **ROH:** No
Born: **Marital Status:** **Residence**

Appears on a register of General Hospital, Howard's Grove, VA in Richmond, VA. Dated, 7/25/1863. No other record.

Norton, William C.
CO: B **Initial Rank:** Private
Joined: Monday, March 3, 1862 **Term (yrs):** 3 **Occupation:** Farmer **Age** 18
Enrolled at: Ripley, MS **Enrolled By:** Capt. Buchanan **Promoted:** No **ROH:** No
Born: Mississippi **Marital Status:** S **Residence**

Wounded at Gettysburg on 7/1/1863. Left leg amputated below left knee by Surgeon Hubbard on the field. Captured on 7/5/1863. Paroled at DeCamp General Hospital, Davids Island, NY Harbor on 9/8/1863. Taken to City Point, VA for exchange. Furloughed. Retired by medical examining board to the Invalid Corps, P.A.C.S. on 9/22/1864. Discharged.

2nd Mississippi Alphabetical Roster (Annotated)

Norton, William M.
CO: B **Initial Rank:** Private
Joined: Monday, March 3, 1862 **Term (yrs):** 3 **Occupation:** Farmer **Age** 17
Enrolled at: Ripley, MS **Enrolled By:** Capt. Buchanan **Promoted:** No **ROH:** No
Born: Mississippi **Marital Status:** S **Residence**
Killed in action at The Wilderness on 5/5/1864.

Norvell, James M.
CO: F **Initial Rank:** Private
Joined: Wednesday, May 1, 1861 **Term (yrs):** 1 **Occupation:** Planter **Age** 26
Enrolled at: Tippah Co., MS **Enrolled By:** Capt. Davis **Promoted:** Yes **ROH:** No
Born: **Marital Status:** **Residence**
Appointed 4th Corporal on 4/24/1862. Captured at Gettysburg on 7/1/1863. Taken to Fort Delaware. Released on oath on 6/11/1865.

Norwood, George W.
CO: H **Initial Rank:** Private
Joined: Monday, April 29, 1861 **Term (yrs):** 1 **Occupation:** Carpenter **Age** 29
Enrolled at: Pontotoc Co., MS **Enrolled By:** Capt. Taylor **Promoted:** No **ROH:** No
Born: Alabama **Marital Status:** M **Residence** Chesterville, MS
Wounded and captured at Gettysburg on 7/1/1863 (captured on 7/5/1863). Returned to duty (probably paroled and exchanged circa Sep 1863). Wounded on 6/2/1864. In hospital at Richmond. Furloughed. Returned to duty 12/10/1864. Captured near Petersburg, VA on 3/25/1865. Sent to Point Lookout, MD. Released on oath on 5/14/1865.

Nowlin, Mark H.
CO: G **Initial Rank:** Private
Joined: Thursday, March 20, 1862 **Term (yrs):** 3 **Occupation:** Student **Age** 16
Enrolled at: Pontotoc, MS **Enrolled By:** G. B. Mears **Promoted:** No **ROH:** No
Born: Nebraska **Marital Status:** S **Residence** Pontotoc, MS
Killed in battle at Sharpsburg on 9/17/1862.

2nd Mississippi Alphabetical Roster (Annotated)

Nowlin, William C.
CO: G **Initial Rank:** Private
Joined: Wednesday, May 1, 1861 **Term (yrs):** 1 **Occupation:** Mechanic **Age** 21
Enrolled at: Pontotoc Co., MS **Enrolled By:** Capt. Milller **Promoted:** Yes **ROH:** No
Born: Mississippi **Marital Status:** S **Residence** Pontotoc, MS

Wounded in battle at 2nd Manassas on 8/29/1862. Returned to duty on 9/28/1862. Listed as 5th Sergeant during Mar/Apr 1863 muster. Wounded in battle at Gettysburg on 7/1/1863. Sent to hospital. Furloughed for 30-days from 7/30/1863. Did not return upon expiration of furlough. Listed as deserter during Jan/Feb 1864 muster.

Null, Jacob
CO: K **Initial Rank:** Private
Joined: Saturday, March 1, 1862 **Term (yrs):** 3 **Occupation:** Farmer **Age** 21
Enrolled at: Iuka, MS **Enrolled By:** Lt. Latham **Promoted:** No **ROH:** No
Born: Mississippi **Marital Status:** **Residence**

Died of disease at Ashland, VA on 5/14/1862.

Null, Shelby J.
CO: K **Initial Rank:** Private
Joined: Saturday, March 1, 1862 **Term (yrs):** 3 **Occupation:** Farmer **Age** 19
Enrolled at: Iuka, MS **Enrolled By:** Lt. Latham **Promoted:** No **ROH:** No
Born: Mississippi **Marital Status:** **Residence**

Died of disease at Danville, VA on 7/6/1862 (another record says 7/7/1862).

Null, Thomas
CO: K **Initial Rank:** Private
Joined: Saturday, March 1, 1862 **Term (yrs):** 3 **Occupation:** Farmer **Age** 26
Enrolled at: Iuka, MS **Enrolled By:** Lt. Latham **Promoted:** No **ROH:** No
Born: Mississippi **Marital Status:** **Residence**

Died of disease at Ashland, VA on 6/14/1862.

Nunnalee, James M.
CO: H **Initial Rank:** Private
Joined: Monday, March 17, 1862 **Term (yrs):** 3 **Occupation:** Student **Age** 17
Enrolled at: Chesterville, MS **Enrolled By:** Lt. Porter **Promoted:** No **ROH:** Yes
Born: Mississippi **Marital Status:** S **Residence** Tupelo, MS

Furloughed for 30-days as of 2/19/1865 for "having furnished recruit" (furlough of indulgence). ROH for Falling Waters, 7/14/1863.

2nd Mississippi Alphabetical Roster (Annotated)

Nutt, Robert P.   CO: D   Initial Rank: Private
Joined: Thursday, September 19, 1861   *Term (yrs):* 1   *Occupation:* Farmer   *Age* 16
Enrolled at: Salem, MS   *Enrolled By:* Lt. Davenport   *Promoted:* No   *ROH:* No
Born: Mississippi   *Marital Status:* S   *Residence* Pine Grove, MS

Discharged on 7/27/1862 — underage.

Nutt, Thompson   CO: D   Initial Rank: Private
Joined: Wednesday, May 1, 1861   *Term (yrs):* 1   *Occupation:* Farmer   *Age* 33
Enrolled at: Tippah Co., MS   *Enrolled By:* Capt. Beck   *Promoted:* Yes   *ROH:* No
Born: Mississippi   *Marital Status:* M   *Residence* Pine Grove, MS

Promoted to 5th Sergeant on 8/20/1861. Promoted to 1st Sergeant on 11/20/1861. Elected 1st Lieutenant on 4/23/1862. Wounded at Gaines Mill on 6/27/1862. Sent to hospital in Richmond. Returned to duty. Wounded (in foot) at Sharpsburg on 9/17/1862. Furloughed 60-days from 10/8/1862. Captured while on furlough in MS and paroled at Holly Spring, MS (about Dec 1862). Resigned due to disability on 8/8/1863.

O'Connell, James   CO: E   Initial Rank: Private
Joined: Wednesday, May 1, 1861   *Term (yrs):* 1   *Occupation:* Farmer   *Age* 22
Enrolled at: Itawamba Co., MS   *Enrolled By:* Capt. Booth   *Promoted:* No   *ROH:* No
Born: Ireland   *Marital Status:* S   *Residence* Guntown, MS

Deserted on 7/30/1862. Picked up at Bull Run, VA by Federal forces on 3/27/1863. Took oath of allegiance on 4/29/1863.

Ogan, Thomas   CO: D   Initial Rank: Private
Joined: *Term (yrs):* 0   *Occupation:*   *Age*
Enrolled at: *Enrolled By:*   *Promoted:* No   *ROH:* No
Born: *Marital Status:*   *Residence*

Appears on a Federal roll of Confederate prisoners. Captured near Pulaski, TN on 12/24/1864. Remarks: "Deserter." Dated Nashville, TN, 12/27/1864. No other record.

O'Kelly, James   CO: E   Initial Rank: Private
Joined: Monday, February 18, 1861   *Term (yrs):* 0   *Occupation:*   *Age*
Enrolled at: Saltillo, MS   *Enrolled By:* R. Griffith   *Promoted:* No   *ROH:* No
Born: *Marital Status:*   *Residence*

Also see Kelly. Appears on a company muster roll. No other record.

2nd Mississippi Alphabetical Roster (Annotated)

O'Kely, F. *CO:* E *Initial Rank:*
Joined: *Term (yrs):* 0 *Occupation:* *Age*
Enrolled at: *Enrolled By:* *Promoted:* No *ROH:* No
Born: *Marital Status:* *Residence*

Appears on a list of the Calhoun Rifles. Dated 2/11/1861. No other record.

Oliver, Isaac S. *CO:* D *Initial Rank:* Private
Joined: Wednesday, May 1, 1861 *Term (yrs):* 1 *Occupation:* Mechanic *Age* 25
Enrolled at: Tippah Co., MS *Enrolled By:* Capt. Beck *Promoted:* No *ROH:* No
Born: Wisconsin *Marital Status:* S *Residence* Salem, MS

Deserted on 5/28/1862.

Orndorff, J. K. *CO:* *Initial Rank:* Private
Joined: *Term (yrs):* 0 *Occupation:* *Age*
Enrolled at: *Enrolled By:* *Promoted:* No *ROH:* No
Born: *Marital Status:* *Residence* Jefferson, VA

Appears on an Oath of Allegiance to the United States, subscribed to at Fort Delaware, Del., June 11, 1865. Released on 6/11/1865. No other record.

Osborne, George W. *CO:* H *Initial Rank:* Private
Joined: Monday, April 29, 1861 *Term (yrs):* 1 *Occupation:* Farmer *Age* 19
Enrolled at: Pontotoc Co., MS *Enrolled By:* Capt. Taylor *Promoted:* No *ROH:* No
Born: Alabama *Marital Status:* S *Residence* Verona, MS

Listed as deserter in Sep/Oct 1862 muster. "Was given furlough of 30 days about the 10th of July 1862 & has not returned to the company."

Osborne, William W. *CO:* D *Initial Rank:* Private
Joined: Wednesday, May 1, 1861 *Term (yrs):* 1 *Occupation:* *Age* 24
Enrolled at: Tippah Co., MS *Enrolled By:* Capt. Beck *Promoted:* No *ROH:* No
Born: *Marital Status:* *Residence*

Transferred (what regiment?) on 6/7/1862 by order of Maj. Gen. T. H. Holmes. Company muster rolls carry him as a deserter from Mar/Apr 1863 muster.

2nd Mississippi Alphabetical Roster (Annotated)

Osburn, William M.
CO: B *Initial Rank:* Private
Joined: *Term (yrs):* 0 *Occupation:* *Age*
Enrolled at: *Enrolled By:* *Promoted:* No *ROH:* No
Born: *Marital Status:* *Residence*

Also see 48th North Carolina Infantry Regiment. Transferred to 48th North Carolina on 6/7/1862 by order of Maj. Gen. T. H. Holmes.

Overbey, Nimrod W.
CO: I *Initial Rank:* Private
Joined: Wednesday, May 1, 1861 *Term (yrs):* 1 *Occupation:* Farmer *Age* 35
Enrolled at: Pontotoc Co., MS *Enrolled By:* Capt. Herring *Promoted:* No *ROH:* No
Born: South Carolina *Marital Status:* *Residence*

Discharged on 7/31/1862 — over age.

Overcash, John A.
CO: K *Initial Rank:* Private
Joined: Saturday, March 1, 1862 *Term (yrs):* 3 *Occupation:* *Age* 22
Enrolled at: Iuka, MS *Enrolled By:* Lt. Latham *Promoted:* No *ROH:* No
Born: *Marital Status:* *Residence*

Also see John Overcash, 26th Mississippi Infantry Regiment. Admitted to hospital with gunshot wound to left foot (date of wound or engagement not given in company records) on 6/4/1864. Furloughed 40-days from 6/6/1864. Listed as AWOL from 7/15/1864. Deserted, dropped from rolls for prolonged AWOL during Nov/Dec 1864 muster (but see 26th Mississippi Infantry records).

Owen, Samuel S.
CO: C, S *Initial Rank:* 1st Sergeant
Joined: Wednesday, May 1, 1861 *Term (yrs):* 1 *Occupation:* Farmer *Age* 26
Enrolled at: Itawamba Co., MS *Enrolled By:* Capt. Bromley *Promoted:* Yes *ROH:* No
Born: *Marital Status:* *Residence*

Also see staff. Appointed Adjutant and assigned to duty on 4/23/1862.

Owens, Alexander D.
CO: I *Initial Rank:* Private
Joined: Wednesday, May 1, 1861 *Term (yrs):* 1 *Occupation:* Farmer *Age* 23
Enrolled at: Pontotoc Co., MS *Enrolled By:* Capt. Herring *Promoted:* No *ROH:* No
Born: *Marital Status:* *Residence*

Captured at Gettysburg on 7/1/1863. Taken to Fort Delaware. Released on oath on 6/11/1865.

2nd Mississippi Alphabetical Roster (Annotated)

Owens, Andrew B.

CO: K *Initial Rank:* Private

Joined: Tuesday, April 30, 1861 *Term (yrs):* 0 *Occupation:* Laborer *Age* 18

Enrolled at: Iuka, MS *Enrolled By:* Capt. Stone *Promoted:* No *ROH:* No

Born: *Marital Status:* *Residence*

Appears on a company muster roll for May/Jun 1861. Notes say: "not mustered into service. Left sick in hospital at Corinth, Miss. Has not since joined company." No other record.

Owens, Andrew F.

CO: K *Initial Rank:* Private

Joined: Wednesday, May 1, 1861 *Term (yrs):* 1 *Occupation:* *Age* 18

Enrolled at: Tishomingo Co., MS *Enrolled By:* Capt. Stone *Promoted:* No *ROH:* No

Born: *Marital Status:* *Residence*

Also see 26th Mississippi Infantry Regiment. Appears to have re-enlisted on 3/1/1862 at Iuka, MS by Lt. Latham for 3-years (not apparent if he was discharged from prior 12-month enlistment). Captured by Federal cavalry at Falling Waters, MD on 7/14/1863. Taken to Point Lookout, MD. Exchanged on 3/14/1865 at Aiken's Landing, VA. Took oath of allegiance at Nashville, TN on 5/7/1865.

Owens, Joseph S.

CO: I *Initial Rank:* Private

Joined: Wednesday, May 1, 1861 *Term (yrs):* 1 *Occupation:* Farmer *Age* 26

Enrolled at: Pontotoc Co., MS *Enrolled By:* Capt. Herring *Promoted:* Yes *ROH:* No

Born: South Carolina *Marital Status:* *Residence*

Promoted to 3rd Corporal on 4/23/1862. Listed as 1st Sergeant during Mar/Apr 1863 muster. Promoted to Jr 2nd Lieutenant on 5/16/1863. Killed in battle on 5/10/1864 (Talley's Mill?) (another record shows his death from wounds on 5/12/1864).

Owens, Richard

CO: I *Initial Rank:* Private

Joined: Friday, August 28, 1863 *Term (yrs):* 3 *Occupation:* *Age*

Enrolled at: Columbia, SC *Enrolled By:* Maj. Melton *Promoted:* No *ROH:* No

Born: *Marital Status:* *Residence*

Discharged on 5/31/1864 — underage.

2nd Mississippi Alphabetical Roster (Annotated)

Paden, William D.
CO: A *Initial Rank:* 3rd Sergeant
Joined: Wednesday, May 1, 1861 *Term (yrs):* 1 *Occupation:* Deputy Sheriff *Age* 28
Enrolled at: Tishomingo Co., MS *Enrolled By:* Capt. Leeth *Promoted:* No *ROH:* No
Born: South Carolina *Marital Status:* S *Residence* Jacinto, MS

Detailed as Assistant Commissary. Discharged due to military exemption on 7/31/1862.

Palmer, John
CO: C *Initial Rank:* Private
Joined: Wednesday, May 1, 1861 *Term (yrs):* 1 *Occupation:* Farmer *Age* 28
Enrolled at: Itawamba Co., MS *Enrolled By:* Capt. Bromley *Promoted:* Yes *ROH:* No
Born: *Marital Status:* *Residence*

Listed as 4th Corporal during May/Jun 1863 muster roll. Captured at Gettysburg on 7/1/1863. Taken to Fort Delaware. Released on oath on 6/7/1865.

Palmer, Richard A.
CO: G *Initial Rank:* 1st Lieutenant
Joined: Wednesday, May 1, 1861 *Term (yrs):* 1 *Occupation:* Teacher *Age* 29
Enrolled at: Pontotoc Co., MS *Enrolled By:* Capt. Kilpatrick *Promoted:* No *ROH:* No
Born: South Carolina *Marital Status:* S *Residence* Pontotoc, MS

Killed in battle at 1st Manassas on 7/21/1861.

Parish, John H.
CO: A *Initial Rank:* Private
Joined: Wednesday, May 1, 1861 *Term (yrs):* 1 *Occupation:* Farmer *Age* 23
Enrolled at: Tishomingo Co., MS *Enrolled By:* Capt. Leeth *Promoted:* No *ROH:* No
Born: *Marital Status:* *Residence*

Wounded at 2nd Manassas on 8/29/1862. Returned to duty. Wounded(?) and captured at Gettysburg on 7/3/1863. Sent to Fort Delaware. Released on oath 5/31/1865.

Parish, Thomas T.
CO: A *Initial Rank:* Private
Joined: Wednesday, May 1, 1861 *Term (yrs):* 1 *Occupation:* Farmer *Age* 24
Enrolled at: Tishomingo Co., MS *Enrolled By:* Capt. Leeth *Promoted:* No *ROH:* No
Born: Alabama *Marital Status:* S *Residence* Rienzi, MS

Wounded on 8/29/1862 at 2nd Manassas. Sent to hospital at Lynchburg, VA. Captured at Gettysburg on 7/1/1863. Sent to Fort Delaware. Paroled and exchanged (? admitted to Richmond hospital on 3/18/1865). No further record.

2nd Mississippi Alphabetical Roster (Annotated)

Parish, William A.
CO: A **Initial Rank:** Private
Joined: Saturday, September 21, 1861 **Term (yrs):** 1 **Occupation:** Farmer **Age** 30
Enrolled at: Rienzi, MS **Enrolled By:** Lt. Davenport **Promoted:** No **ROH:** No
Born: Alabama **Marital Status:** M **Residence** Rienzi, MS

Listed as deserter. "Left on furlough Feb 1st and has not returned" (May/Jun 1863 muster). Record remarks: "Elected Lieutenant of cavalry in Miss in 1863."

Parker, Joseph H.
CO: B **Initial Rank:** Private
Joined: Wednesday, May 1, 1861 **Term (yrs):** 1 **Occupation:** Farmer **Age** 21
Enrolled at: Tippah Co., MS **Enrolled By:** Capt. Buchanan **Promoted:** No **ROH:** Yes
Born: **Marital Status:** **Residence**

Wounded at Gaines Mill on 6/27/1862. Returned to duty. Killed in battle at 2nd Manassas on 8/29/1862. ROH for Malvern Hill, 7/1/1862.

Parks, James D.
CO: A **Initial Rank:** Private
Joined: Wednesday, May 1, 1861 **Term (yrs):** 1 **Occupation:** Buggy trimmer **Age** 23
Enrolled at: Tishomingo Co., MS **Enrolled By:** Capt. Leeth **Promoted:** No **ROH:** No
Born: Tennessee **Marital Status:** S **Residence** Jacinto, MS

Wounded at 1st Manassas on 7/21/1861. Sent to hospital at Charlottesville, VA (left leg amputated at thigh). Discharged due to disability caused by wounds on 10/4/1861.

Parr, John W.
CO: B **Initial Rank:** 2nd Corporal
Joined: Wednesday, May 1, 1861 **Term (yrs):** 1 **Occupation:** Farmer **Age** 37
Enrolled at: Tippah Co., MS **Enrolled By:** Capt. Buchanan **Promoted:** No **ROH:** No
Born: **Marital Status:** **Residence**

Wounded at 1st Manassas on 7/21/1861. Sent to hospital at Charlottesville, VA. Appointed regimental wagon master by order of Col. Falkner on 10/28/1861. Discharged on 5/25/1862 — over age.

Pass, A. Sidney
CO: H **Initial Rank:** Ordnance Sergeant
Joined: **Term (yrs):** 0 **Occupation:** **Age**
Enrolled at: **Enrolled By:** **Promoted:** No **ROH:** No
Born: **Marital Status:** **Residence**

Appears on several Federal prisoner of war records. Wounded and captured at Pittsburg Landing (Shiloh) on 4/7/1862. Sent to Camp Chase, OH. Transferred to Vicksburg, MS on 8/25/1862 for exchange. [Misidentified. This man is almost certainly not a member of the 2nd Mississippi Infantry Regiment].

2nd Mississippi Alphabetical Roster (Annotated)

Patrick, Andrew J.
CO: A **Initial Rank:** Private
Joined: Wednesday, May 1, 1861 **Term (yrs):** 1 **Occupation:** Mechanic **Age** 19
Enrolled at: Tishomingo Co., MS **Enrolled By:** Capt. Leeth **Promoted:** No **ROH:** No
Born: Mississippi **Marital Status:** M **Residence** Burnsville, MS

Killed in battle at Gaines Mill on 6/27/1862.

Patrick, George W.
CO: A **Initial Rank:** 2nd Lieutenant
Joined: Wednesday, May 1, 1861 **Term (yrs):** 1 **Occupation:** Carpenter **Age** 32
Enrolled at: Tishomingo Co., MS **Enrolled By:** Capt. Leeth **Promoted:** Yes **ROH:** No
Born: **Marital Status:** M **Residence** Jacinto, MS

Listed as 1st Lieutenant during Jul/Aug 1861 muster. Resigned on 7/12/1861.

Patrick, James M.
CO: A **Initial Rank:** 4th Corporal
Joined: Wednesday, May 1, 1861 **Term (yrs):** 1 **Occupation:** Clerk **Age** 22
Enrolled at: Tishomingo Co., MS **Enrolled By:** Capt. Leeth **Promoted:** Yes **ROH:** No
Born: Alabama **Marital Status:** S **Residence** Burnsville, MS

Reduced to ranks on 4/23/1862. Appointed 3rd Corporal on 5/20/1862. Promoted to 2nd Corporal on 10/16/1862. Killed in battle at Gettysburg on 7/3/1863. *Buried at Hollywood Cemetery, Richmond, VA. Section: Gettysburg Section Lot: 1.

Patterson, J. R.
CO: B **Initial Rank:** 2nd Lieutenant
Joined: **Term (yrs):** 0 **Occupation:** **Age**
Enrolled at: **Enrolled By:** **Promoted:** No **ROH:** No
Born: **Marital Status:** **Residence**

Appears on a Federal register of prisoners of war. Captured at Hatcher's Run on 4/2/1865. Taken to Johnson's Island, OH. No other record.

Patton, Duncan M.
CO: F **Initial Rank:** Private
Joined: Wednesday, May 1, 1861 **Term (yrs):** 1 **Occupation:** Planter **Age** 22
Enrolled at: Tippah Co., MS **Enrolled By:** Capt. Davis **Promoted:** Yes **ROH:** No
Born: **Marital Status:** **Residence**

Elected 2nd Lieutenant on 12/3/1861. Discharged on 4/25/1862 — expiration of term of service.

2nd Mississippi Alphabetical Roster (Annotated)

Patton, Jerome B.   *CO:* F   *Initial Rank:* Private
Joined: Wednesday, May 1, 1861   *Term (yrs):* 1 *Occupation:* Planter   *Age* 24
Enrolled at: Tippah Co., MS   *Enrolled By:* Capt. Davis   *Promoted:* No   *ROH:* No
Born: *Marital Status:*   *Residence*

Also see 7th Mississippi Cavalry Regiment. Detailed as regimental teamster. Given a furlough of indulgence for 30-days on 2/5/1864. Did not return. Listed as deserted during Jul/Aug 1864 muster roll.

Patton, Mathew L.   *CO:* F   *Initial Rank:* Private
Joined: Monday, September 30, 1861 *Term (yrs):* 1 *Occupation:*   *Age*
Enrolled at: Ripley, MS   *Enrolled By:* Lt. Davenport   *Promoted:* No   *ROH:* No
Born: *Marital Status:*   *Residence*

Wounded at Gettysburg on 7/3/1863. Furloughed 40-days from 7/22/1863. Did not return. Listed as deserted during Jul/Aug 1863 muster roll. Surrendered and was paroled at LaGrange, TN on 5/25/1865.

Payne, J. C.   *CO:* G   *Initial Rank:* Private
Joined: *Term (yrs):* 0 *Occupation:*   *Age*
Enrolled at: *Enrolled By:*   *Promoted:* No   *ROH:* No
Born: *Marital Status:*   *Residence*

Appears on a Federal roll of prisoners of war paroled at Columbus, MS on 5/17/1865. No other record.

Payne, John A.   *CO:* E, A *Initial Rank:* Private
Joined: *Term (yrs):* 0 *Occupation:*   *Age*
Enrolled at: *Enrolled By:*   *Promoted:* No   *ROH:* No
Born: *Marital Status:*   *Residence*

Appears on Federal prisoner of war records, Department of the Cumberland. Captured at Franklin, TN on 12/17/1864. [Misidentified. This man probably belonged to the 2nd/6th Missouri Infantry Regiment, not the 2nd Mississippi]. No other records.

Payne, Thomas F. M.   *CO:* A   *Initial Rank:* Private
Joined: Wednesday, May 1, 1861   *Term (yrs):* 1 *Occupation:* Farmer   *Age* 21
Enrolled at: Tishomingo Co., MS   *Enrolled By:* Capt. Leeth   *Promoted:* No   *ROH:* No
Born: Mississippi   *Marital Status:* S   *Residence* Hazel Green, MS

Also see Ham's Regiment Mississippi Cavalry. AWOL since 8/1/1862. Listed as deserted during Mar/Apr, 1863 muster. Elected Captain in Ham's Regiment Mississippi Cavalry without regular transfer.

2nd Mississippi Alphabetical Roster (Annotated)

Pearce, Lazarus D. *CO:* B *Initial Rank:* Private

Joined: Saturday, March 1, 1862 *Term (yrs):* 3 *Occupation:* Farmer *Age* 34

Enrolled at: 3 Creek, AR *Enrolled By:* Capt. Reedy *Promoted:* No *ROH:* No

Born: North Carolina *Marital Status:* M *Residence*

Wounded at Gaines Mill on 6/27/1862. Returned to duty. Captured at Gettysburg on 7/3/1863. Taken to Fort Delaware. On Confederate records, listed as having died of disease at Fort Delaware on 6/30/1864. However, shown as released on oath on 6/11/1865, according to Federal records.

Peden, Warren W. *CO:* D *Initial Rank:* Private

Joined: *Term (yrs):* 0 *Occupation:* *Age*

Enrolled at: *Enrolled By:* *Promoted:* No *ROH:* No

Born: *Marital Status:* *Residence*

Appears on Federal prisoner of war records, however, heading variously lists organization as 2 Miss Battery and 2 Miss. Batt. Sent to Camp Douglas, Il in Sept 1862. Brigade: Chalmers, Division: Bragg [Misidentified. Not a member of the 2nd Mississippi Infantry Regiment]. No other records.

Peek, Lewis B. *CO:* K *Initial Rank:* Private

Joined: Wednesday, May 1, 1861 *Term (yrs):* 1 *Occupation:* Carpenter *Age* 27

Enrolled at: Tishomingo Co., MS *Enrolled By:* Capt. Stone *Promoted:* No *ROH:* No

Born: Alabama *Marital Status:* S *Residence*

Died of pneumonia at Camp Fisher, VA on 12/17/1861 (other records say 12/21/1861).

Pegram, Amos J. *CO:* B *Initial Rank:* Private

Joined: Wednesday, May 1, 1861 *Term (yrs):* 1 *Occupation:* Farmer *Age* 19

Enrolled at: Tippah Co., MS *Enrolled By:* Capt. Buchanan *Promoted:* No *ROH:* Yes

Born: *Marital Status:* *Residence*

Wounded at Gaines Mill on 6/27/1862. Missing since then. No further record. ROH for Gaines Mill, 6/27/1862.

2nd Mississippi Alphabetical Roster (Annotated)

Pegues, Miles T.
CO: G *Initial Rank:* Private
Joined: Wednesday, May 1, 1861 *Term (yrs):* 1 *Occupation:* Teacher *Age* 22
Enrolled at: Pontotoc Co., MS *Enrolled By:* Capt. Miller *Promoted:* No *ROH:* No
Born: Mississippi *Marital Status:* S *Residence* Pontotoc, MS

Wounded in battle at 1st Manassas on 7/21/1861. Returned to duty. Detailed as brigade courier from Jul/Aug, 1863 muster. Returned to company on 10/27/1864. Deserted from hospital in Richmond on 2/23/1865. Paroled at Columbus, MS on 5/17/1865.

Pennybaker, Samuel L.
CO: F *Initial Rank:* Private
Joined: Wednesday, May 1, 1861 *Term (yrs):* 1 *Occupation:* Farmer *Age* 19
Enrolled at: Tippah Co., MS *Enrolled By:* Capt. Davis *Promoted:* No *ROH:* No
Born: *Marital Status:*   *Residence*

Wounded (left thigh) at Bristoe Station on 10/14/1863. Sent to hospital at Richmond. Returned to duty. Wounded in battle at Deep Bottom on 6/25/1864. Sent to hospital. Furloughed 60-days from 7/21/1864. Listed as AWOL from 11/20/1864. Surrendered to Federal forces in Mississippi on 4/9/1865. Paroled at Holly Springs on 6/9/1865.

Perry, Frederick G.
CO: G *Initial Rank:* Private
Joined: Wednesday, May 1, 1861 *Term (yrs):* 1 *Occupation:* Farmer *Age* 27
Enrolled at: Pontotoc Co., MS *Enrolled By:* Capt. Miller *Promoted:* No *ROH:* No
Born: South Carolina *Marital Status:* M *Residence* Pontotoc, MS

Wounded in battle at 2nd Manassas on 8/30/1862. Sent to hospital. Returned to duty on 11/18/1862. Deserted to the enemy in camp on the Blackwater, VA on 3/30/1863.

Perry, S.
CO: E *Initial Rank:* Private
Joined: *Term (yrs):* 0 *Occupation:*   *Age*
Enrolled at: *Enrolled By:*   *Promoted:* No *ROH:* No
Born: *Marital Status:*   *Residence*

Appears on Federal prisoner of war records. Captured at Williamsburg, VA on 5/4/1862. Sent to Fort Delaware. Exchanged at Aiken's Landing, VA on 8/5/1862. No other records.

2nd Mississippi Alphabetical Roster (Annotated)

Pester, James *CO:* H *Initial Rank:*
Joined: Friday, March 1, 1861 *Term (yrs):* 0 *Occupation:* *Age*
Enrolled at: Chesterville, MS *Enrolled By:* Capt. Kilpatrick *Promoted:* No *ROH:* No
Born: *Marital Status:* *Residence*

Appears on a company muster roll. No other record.

Pettigrew, James L. *CO:* C *Initial Rank:* Private
Joined: Saturday, March 1, 1862 *Term (yrs):* 3 *Occupation:* *Age*
Enrolled at: Verona, MS *Enrolled By:* Lt. Pounds *Promoted:* No *ROH:* No
Born: *Marital Status:* *Residence*

Hospital records show admission for gunshot wound on 7/17/1863 (company records do not indicate date of wound or engagement). Returned to duty on 8/17/1863. Wounded in battle on 10/1/1864. In hospital at Richmond. Furloughed 60-days from 11/10/1864. Listed as AWOL during last (Jan/Feb 1865) company muster.

Pettigrew, John W. F. *CO:* C *Initial Rank:* Private
Joined: Saturday, March 1, 1862 *Term (yrs):* 3 *Occupation:* *Age*
Enrolled at: Verona, MS *Enrolled By:* Lt. Pounds *Promoted:* No *ROH:* No
Born: *Marital Status:* *Residence*

Appears on a company muster-in roll. No other record.

Pettigrew, Thomas F. *CO:* C *Initial Rank:* Private
Joined: Monday, March 3, 1862 *Term (yrs):* 3 *Occupation:* Farmer *Age* 19
Enrolled at: Ripley, MS *Enrolled By:* Capt. Powers *Promoted:* No *ROH:* No
Born: Mississippi *Marital Status:* *Residence*

Hospital records show admission for wound on 7/17/1863 (company records do not indicate date of wound or action). Returned to duty on 8/17/1863. Killed in action on 10/1/1864.

2nd Mississippi Alphabetical Roster (Annotated)

Pettigrew, William L.

CO: C *Initial Rank:* Private
Joined: Saturday, March 1, 1862 *Term (yrs):* 3 *Occupation:* *Age*
Enrolled at: Verona, MS *Enrolled By:* Lt. Pounds *Promoted:* No *ROH:* No
Born: *Marital Status:* *Residence*

Wounded at Sharpsburg on 9/17/1862. In hospital at Lynchburg, VA. Returned to duty. Wounded at The Wilderness on 5/5/1864. Returned to duty. Admitted to hospital with wound on 9/27/1864 (company records do not give date of wound or engagement). Furloughed 60-days from 10/7/1864. Listed as AWOL during last (Jan/Feb 1865) company muster.

Phelps, John F.

CO: C *Initial Rank:* Private
Joined: Saturday, March 1, 1862 *Term (yrs):* 3 *Occupation:* *Age*
Enrolled at: Verona, MS *Enrolled By:* Lt. Pounds *Promoted:* No *ROH:* No
Born: *Marital Status:* *Residence*

Also see 1st Mississippi Infantry Regiment. Transferred to 1st Mississippi in Sep 1861.

Phillips, Joseph M.

CO: K *Initial Rank:* Private
Joined: Wednesday, May 1, 1861 *Term (yrs):* 1 *Occupation:* Clerk *Age* 21
Enrolled at: Tishomingo Co., MS *Enrolled By:* Capt. Stone *Promoted:* Yes *ROH:* No
Born: *Marital Status:* *Residence*

Listed as Brevet 2nd Lieutenant during Mar/Apr 1863 muster. Wounded and captured at Gettysburg on 7/3/1863. Sent to Johnson's Island, OH. Transferred to Point Lookout, MD on 3/14/1865 for exchange.

Phillips, Josiah W.

CO: D *Initial Rank:* Private
Joined: Saturday, March 9, 1861 *Term (yrs):* 0 *Occupation:* *Age*
Enrolled at: Toombs Store, MS *Enrolled By:* John McGuirk *Promoted:* No *ROH:* No
Born: *Marital Status:* *Residence*

Appears on a company muster roll. No other record.

Philpot, J. W.

CO: G *Initial Rank:* Private
Joined: *Term (yrs):* 0 *Occupation:* *Age*
Enrolled at: *Enrolled By:* *Promoted:* No *ROH:* No
Born: *Marital Status:* *Residence*

Reference envelope says to also see J. M. Philpot, 2nd Mississippi State Cavalry. No other record.

2nd Mississippi Alphabetical Roster (Annotated)

Philpot, R. J., Jr. CO: G Initial Rank: Private
Joined: Term (yrs): 0 Occupation: Age
Enrolled at: Enrolled By: Promoted: No ROH: No
Born: Marital Status: Residence

Reference envelope says to also see J. M. Philpot, 2nd Mississippi State Cavalry. No other record.

Philpot, R. J., Sr. CO: G Initial Rank:
Joined: Term (yrs): 0 Occupation: Age
Enrolled at: Enrolled By: Promoted: No ROH: No
Born: Marital Status: Residence

Reference envelope says to also see J. M. Philpot, 2nd Mississippi State Cavalry. No other record.

Pickens, Josephus J. CO: G Initial Rank: Private
Joined: Wednesday, May 1, 1861 Term (yrs): 1 Occupation: Farmer Age 21
Enrolled at: Pontotoc Co., MS Enrolled By: Capt. Miller Promoted: No ROH: No
Born: South Carolina Marital Status: S Residence Pontotoc, MS

Severely wounded (leg) in battle at 1st Manassas. Sent to hospital at Charlottesville, VA. Discharged due to disability caused by wounds on 12/4/1861 by order of General Whiting.

Pickens, Peter K. CO: G Initial Rank: Private
Joined: Wednesday, May 1, 1861 Term (yrs): 1 Occupation: Mechanic Age 27
Enrolled at: Pontotoc Co., MS Enrolled By: Capt. Miller Promoted: No ROH: No
Born: South Carolina Marital Status: S Residence Pontotoc, MS

Severely wounded in battle at Seven Pines on 5/31/1862. Sent to hospital at Danville, VA. Discharged for disability due to wounds on 9/29/1862 by order of General Smith.

Pickens, Samuel J. CO: F Initial Rank: Private
Joined: Saturday, March 1, 1862 Term (yrs): 3 Occupation: Farmer Age 22
Enrolled at: Ripley, MS Enrolled By: Capt. Powers Promoted: No ROH: No
Born: Alabama Marital Status: M Residence

Wounded and captured at Gettysburg on 7/3/1863 (Federal records say captured on 7/5/1863). Arm amputated. Paroled at DeCamp General Hospital, Davids Island, NY Harbor to City Point, VA on 9/8/1863 for exchange. Furloughed 60-days from 9/10/1864. AWOL upon expiration of furlough.

2nd Mississippi Alphabetical Roster (Annotated)

Pickins, Richmond C.
CO: F   **Initial Rank:** Private
Joined: Saturday, March 1, 1862   **Term (yrs):** 3   **Occupation:** Farmer   **Age** 24
Enrolled at: Ripley, MS   **Enrolled By:** Capt. Powers   **Promoted:** No   **ROH:** No
Born: Alabama   **Marital Status:** S   **Residence**

Supposed killed in battle at Seven Pines on 5/31/1862. "In the battle — never found — supposed dead." Dropped from rolls on 12/31/1862.

Pierce, Benjamin F.
CO: H   **Initial Rank:** Private
Joined: Monday, April 29, 1861   **Term (yrs):** 1   **Occupation:** Clerk   **Age** 21
Enrolled at: Pontotoc Co., MS   **Enrolled By:** Capt. Taylor   **Promoted:** No   **ROH:** No
Born: Tennessee   **Marital Status:** S   **Residence** Tupelo, MS

Also see 11th Mississippi Infantry Regiment. Appointed Bugler on 5/27/1861. Transferred to the band of the 11th Mississippi on 11/14/1862 by order #136.

Pierce, Thomas L.
CO: G   **Initial Rank:** Musician
Joined: Wednesday, May 1, 1861   **Term (yrs):** 1   **Occupation:** Clerk   **Age** 22
Enrolled at: Pontotoc Co., MS   **Enrolled By:** Capt. Kilpatrick   **Promoted:** No   **ROH:** No
Born: Tennessee   **Marital Status:** S   **Residence** Pontotoc, MS

Also see 11th Mississippi Infantry Regiment. Transferred to the band of the 11th Mississippi on 7/15/1862 by order of General Lee.

Pinson, William H.
CO: D   **Initial Rank:** Private
Joined: Wednesday, May 1, 1861   **Term (yrs):** 1   **Occupation:**   **Age** 19
Enrolled at: Tippah Co., MS   **Enrolled By:** Capt. Beck   **Promoted:** No   **ROH:** No
Born: **Marital Status:**   **Residence**

Severely wounded (leg) at Sharpsburg on 9/17/1862. In hospital at Charlottesville and furloughed. Did not return upon expiration of furlough. Listed as deserted and dropped from roll on 12/31/1864 by order of Col. Stone.

2nd Mississippi Alphabetical Roster (Annotated)

Pittman, John L. *CO:* F *Initial Rank:* Private
Joined: Wednesday, May 1, 1861 *Term (yrs):* 1 *Occupation:* Planter *Age* 21
Enrolled at: Tippah Co., MS *Enrolled By:* Capt. Davis *Promoted:* Yes *ROH:* No
Born: *Marital Status:* *Residence*

Apparently wounded (left elbow) at Seven Pines on 5/31/1862 (hospital records show admission for gunshot wound on 6/1/1862). Returned to duty on 6/7/1862. Appointed 2nd Corporal on 10/1/1862. Company records of Sep/Oct 1862 muster indicate he is on wounded furlough (date of wound and engagement not given). Wounded at Gettysburg (not dated — left arm) and sent to hospital in Richmond. Furloughed 60-days from 9/24/1863. Did not return to company. Listed as deserted, "supposed to have gone to the enemy in Miss." Surrendered and paroled at La Grange, TN on 5/22/1865.

Pitts, A. M. *CO:* A *Initial Rank:* Private
Joined: *Term (yrs):* 0 *Occupation:* *Age*
Enrolled at: *Enrolled By:* *Promoted:* No *ROH:* No
Born: *Marital Status:* *Residence*

Appears on a Federal register of prisoners of war at Fort Delaware. Captured at Gettysburg on 7/5/1863. Died on 10/22/1863 (cause not given). No other record.

Pitts, Benjamin *CO:* A *Initial Rank:*
Joined: Wednesday, February 20, 1861 *Term (yrs):* 0 *Occupation:* *Age*
Enrolled at: Corinth, MS *Enrolled By:* R. Griffith *Promoted:* No *ROH:* No
Born: *Marital Status:* *Residence*

Appears on a company muster roll. No other record.

Pitts, Isaac T. *CO:* I *Initial Rank:* Private
Joined: Wednesday, May 1, 1861 *Term (yrs):* 1 *Occupation:* Farmer *Age* 28
Enrolled at: Pontotoc Co., MS *Enrolled By:* Capt. Herring *Promoted:* Yes *ROH:* No
Born: South Carolina *Marital Status:* *Residence*

Appointed 4th Corporal on 7/4/1861. Died of disease (typhoid fever) at Warrenton, VA on 10/2/1861.

2nd Mississippi Alphabetical Roster (Annotated)

Pitts, John *CO:* A *Initial Rank:* Private
Joined: Saturday, March 1, 1862 *Term (yrs):* 3 *Occupation:* Farmer *Age* 21
Enrolled at: Jacinto, MS *Enrolled By:* Lt. Clayton *Promoted:* No *ROH:* No
Born: Alabama *Marital Status:* S *Residence* Jacinto, MS

Furloughed on 9/10/1863 from hospital. Captured by Federal forces in Tishomingo Co., MS. Sent to Fort Delaware.

Pitts, John Minett *CO:* I *Initial Rank:* Private
Joined: Wednesday, May 1, 1861 *Term (yrs):* 1 *Occupation:* Farmer *Age* 20
Enrolled at: Pontotoc Co., MS *Enrolled By:* Capt. Herring *Promoted:* No *ROH:* No
Born: Alabama *Marital Status:* S *Residence*

Captured at Gettysburg on 7/5/1863. Taken to Fort Delaware. Died in captivity on 10/22/1863 of disease.

Pitts, John P. *CO:* F *Initial Rank:* Private
Joined: Monday, March 24, 1862 *Term (yrs):* 3 *Occupation:* Farmer *Age* 22
Enrolled at: Bienville, MS *Enrolled By:* Capt. Powers *Promoted:* No *ROH:* No
Born: Alabama *Marital Status:* S *Residence*

Also see 26th Mississippi Infantry Regiment. Furloughed 40-days with typhoid fever to Okolona, MS from 9/3/1863. No other records.

Pitts, Robert B. *CO:* I *Initial Rank:* 2nd Lieutenant
Joined: Wednesday, May 1, 1861 *Term (yrs):* 1 *Occupation:* Farmer *Age* 23
Enrolled at: Pontotoc Co., MS *Enrolled By:* Capt. Herring *Promoted:* No *ROH:* No
Born: *Marital Status:* *Residence*

Retired from service on expiration of term of enlistment (about March 1862).

Pitts, S. N. *CO:* A *Initial Rank:* Private
Joined: *Term (yrs):* 0 *Occupation:* *Age*
Enrolled at: *Enrolled By:* *Promoted:* No *ROH:* No
Born: *Marital Status:* *Residence*

Appears on a Federal register of prisoners of war at Fort Delaware. Captured at Gettysburg on 7/5/1863. Remarks: "Dead." No other record.

2nd Mississippi Alphabetical Roster (Annotated)

Pitts, William
CO: G **Initial Rank:** Private
Joined: Wednesday, May 1, 1861 **Term (yrs):** 1 **Occupation:** Farmer **Age** 27
Enrolled at: Pontotoc Co., MS **Enrolled By:** Capt. Miller **Promoted:** No **ROH:** No
Born: South Carolina **Marital Status:** **Residence**

Discharged for disability at Camp Fisher, VA on 1/28/1862.

Pitts, William C.
CO: I **Initial Rank:** Private
Joined: Wednesday, May 1, 1861 **Term (yrs):** 1 **Occupation:** Farmer **Age** 32
Enrolled at: Pontotoc Co., MS **Enrolled By:** Capt. Herring **Promoted:** No **ROH:** No
Born: South Carolina **Marital Status:** **Residence**

Discharged for disability at Camp Fisher, VA on 10/15/1861.

Pitts, Younger
CO: A **Initial Rank:** Private
Joined: Saturday, March 1, 1862 **Term (yrs):** 3 **Occupation:** Grocer **Age** 48
Enrolled at: Jacinto, MS **Enrolled By:** Lt. Clayton **Promoted:** Yes **ROH:** No
Born: Virginia **Marital Status:** S **Residence** Baldwyn, MS

Appointed 2nd Sergeant on 4/22/1862. Wounded at Sharpsburg on 9/17/1862. Sent to hospital at Richmond. Furloughed. Company records list him as AWOL and deserted for Mar/Apr 1864 muster for prolonged AWOL. [However, medical records indicate he might have been discharged to the Invalid Corps, P.A.C.S. by a medical examining board. If so, word apparently never got back to his company].

Plunkett, James R.
CO: D **Initial Rank:** Private
Joined: Saturday, March 9, 1861 **Term (yrs):** 0 **Occupation:** **Age**
Enrolled at: Toombs Store, MS **Enrolled By:** John McGuirk **Promoted:** No **ROH:** No
Born: **Marital Status:** **Residence**

Appears on a company muster roll. No other record.

Plunkett, Joseph P.
CO: D **Initial Rank:** Private
Joined: Wednesday, May 1, 1861 **Term (yrs):** 1 **Occupation:** Farmer **Age** 22
Enrolled at: Tippah Co., MS **Enrolled By:** Capt. Beck **Promoted:** No **ROH:** No
Born: Georgia **Marital Status:** S **Residence** Shelby Creek, MS

Severely wounded at 1st Manassas on 7/21/1861. Sent to hospital at Culpeper, VA. Discharged for disability due to wounds on 6/13/1862.

2nd Mississippi Alphabetical Roster (Annotated)

Plunkett, Thomas P.
CO: D **Initial Rank:** Private
Joined: Wednesday, May 1, 1861 **Term (yrs):** 1 **Occupation:** Farmer **Age** 24
Enrolled at: Tippah Co., MS **Enrolled By:** Capt. Beck **Promoted:** No **ROH:** No
Born: Georgia **Marital Status:** S **Residence** Shelby Creek, MS

Died of disease at Lynchburg, VA on 5/19/1861.

Pogue, Daniel
CO: D **Initial Rank:** Private
Joined: Wednesday, May 1, 1861 **Term (yrs):** 1 **Occupation:** Farmer **Age** 42
Enrolled at: Tippah Co., MS **Enrolled By:** Capt. Beck **Promoted:** No **ROH:** No
Born: New York **Marital Status:** S **Residence** Salem, MS

According to accompanying list of engagements, was wounded at Sharpsburg on 9/17/1862 (company records do not so indicate). Wounded in battle at The Wilderness on 5/6/1864. Sent to hospital in Lynchburg, VA. Returned to duty. Captured at Petersburg (Hatcher's Run?) on 4/2/1865. Sent to Fort Delaware. Released on oath on 6/11/1865.

Poland, L. G.
CO: **Initial Rank:** Private
Joined: **Term (yrs):** 0 **Occupation:** **Age**
Enrolled at: **Enrolled By:** **Promoted:** No **ROH:** No
Born: **Marital Status:** **Residence**

Appears on a Federal register of refugees and rebel deserters, Provost Marshal General, Washington, D.C., dated 7/10/1865. Transportation furnished to Columbus, MS. No other record.

Pollock, Isaac J.
CO: B **Initial Rank:** Private
Joined: Wednesday, September 18, 1861 **Term (yrs):** 1 **Occupation:** Mechanic **Age** 28
Enrolled at: Ripley, MS **Enrolled By:** Lt. Davenport **Promoted:** No **ROH:** No
Born: Alabama **Marital Status:** **Residence**

Discharged for disability on 12/8/1861 by order of General Whiting.

2nd Mississippi Alphabetical Roster (Annotated)

Porter, F.
CO: E   *Initial Rank:* Private
Joined: *Term (yrs):* 0   *Occupation:*   *Age*
Enrolled at: *Enrolled By:*   *Promoted:* No   *ROH:* No
Born: *Marital Status:*   *Residence*

Appears on a Federal list of prisoners of war captured and paroled by the U.S. forces in the battles of Iuka, Sept. 19; of Corinth on the 3d and 4th, and of Hatchie on the 5th and 6th of October 1862. Paroled at Corinth, MS on 10/13/1862. No other record. [Misidentified. Unlikely this person belonged to the 2nd Mississippi Infantry Regiment].

Porter, James
CO: H   *Initial Rank:* Private
Joined: Monday, July 21, 1862   *Term (yrs):* 3   *Occupation:*   *Age*
Enrolled at: Richmond, VA   *Enrolled By:* Capt. Cunningham   *Promoted:* No   *ROH:* No
Born: Maryland   *Marital Status:*   *Residence*

Also see Samuel Richman. Deserted. Was mustered as substitute for S. Richman and deserted about 7/29/1862.

Porter, James W.
CO: H   *Initial Rank:* 3rd Sergeant
Joined: Monday, April 29, 1861   *Term (yrs):* 1   *Occupation:* Student   *Age* 24
Enrolled at: Pontotoc Co., MS   *Enrolled By:* Capt. Taylor   *Promoted:* Yes   *ROH:* No
Born: Alabama   *Marital Status:* S   *Residence* Verona, MS

Was elected 2nd Lieutenant on 8/1/1861. Discharged due to reorganization of company and expiration of term of enlistment on 4/23/1862.

Potts, Jesse
CO: C   *Initial Rank:* Private
Joined: Saturday, March 1, 1862   *Term (yrs):* 3   *Occupation:* Farmer   *Age* 35
Enrolled at: Verona, MS   *Enrolled By:* Lt. Pounds   *Promoted:* No   *ROH:* No
Born: South Carolina   *Marital Status:* M   *Residence*

Died of disease at Richmond, VA on 8/10/1862.

Pounds, William M.
CO: C   *Initial Rank:* 1st Lieutenant
Joined: Wednesday, May 1, 1861   *Term (yrs):* 1   *Occupation:* Farmer   *Age* 33
Enrolled at: Itawamba Co., MS   *Enrolled By:* Capt. Kilpatrick   *Promoted:* No   *ROH:* No
Born: *Marital Status:*   *Residence*

No record after Jan/Feb 1862 muster.

2nd Mississippi Alphabetical Roster (Annotated)

Powell, David
CO: A   *Initial Rank:* Private

Joined: *Term (yrs):* 0   *Occupation:*   *Age*

Enrolled at: *Enrolled By:*   *Promoted:* No   *ROH:* No

Born: *Marital Status:*   *Residence*

Appears on a Federal descriptive list of rebel prisoners arrested. Dated 11/28/1864; location: Newark, OH on 11/27/1864. Transportation requisition to Columbus (KY?); "a rebel prisoner." No other records.

Powell, Henry W.
CO: H   *Initial Rank:* Private

Joined: Monday, April 29, 1861   *Term (yrs):* 1   *Occupation:* Farmer   *Age* 20

Enrolled at: Pontotoc Co., MS   *Enrolled By:* Capt. Taylor   *Promoted:* Yes   *ROH:* No

Born: Alabama   *Marital Status:* S   *Residence* Chesterville, MS

Listed as 1st Corporal during May/Jun 1862 muster. Wounded at 2nd Manassas on 8/29/1862. Returned to duty. Promoted to 3rd Sergeant on 6/1/1863. Captured at Gettysburg on 7/1/1863. Taken to Fort Delaware. Released on oath on 6/11/1865.

Powell, William A.
CO: H   *Initial Rank:* Private

Joined: Saturday, March 1, 1862   *Term (yrs):* 3   *Occupation:* Farmer   *Age* 18

Enrolled at: Chesterville, MS   *Enrolled By:* Lt. Porter   *Promoted:* No   *ROH:* No

Born: Alabama   *Marital Status:* S   *Residence* Chesterville, MS

Died of disease at Ashland, VA on 5/8/1862.

Powell, William C.
CO: E   *Initial Rank:* Private

Joined: Wednesday, May 1, 1861   *Term (yrs):* 1   *Occupation:* Teamster   *Age* 36

Enrolled at: Itawamba Co., MS   *Enrolled By:* Capt. Booth   *Promoted:* Yes   *ROH:* No

Born: Georgia   *Marital Status:* M   *Residence* Guntown, MS

Discharged on 7/23/1862 — over age.

2nd Mississippi Alphabetical Roster (Annotated)

Powers, Henry H.
CO: B, F **Initial Rank:** Private
Joined: Wednesday, May 1, 1861 **Term (yrs):** 1 **Occupation:** Lawyer **Age** 29
Enrolled at: Tippah Co., MS **Enrolled By:** Capt. Buchanan **Promoted:** Yes **ROH:** No
Born: **Marital Status:** **Residence**

Transferred to Company F on 11/18/1861 by order of Col. Falkner. Elected 2nd Lieutenant on 11/18/1861. Elected Captain on 12/3/1861. Re-elected Captain on 4/11/1862. Slightly wounded at Malvern Hill on 7/1/1862. Returned to duty. Wounded at Gettysburg on 7/3/1863. Captured at Gettysburg on 7/5/1863. Sent to Johnson's Island, OH. Paroled and forwarded to Point Lookout, MD for exchange on 3/14/1865. Surrendered and paroled dated Columbus, MS on 5/9/1865 (signed as Capt. Co. L 2nd Miss Regt).

Powers, John W.
CO: D **Initial Rank:** Private
Joined: **Term (yrs):** 0 **Occupation:** **Age**
Enrolled at: **Enrolled By:** **Promoted:** No **ROH:** No
Born: **Marital Status:** **Residence**

Appears on Federal prisoner of war records received at Camp Douglas, IL on 9/23/1862 from Corinth, MS. Headings list unit variously as 2nd Miss Battery and 2nd Miss Battln. [Misidentified. This man does not belong to the 2nd Mississippi Infantry Regiment]. No other records.

Prescott, James A.
CO: D **Initial Rank:** Private
Joined: Tuesday, October 1, 1861 **Term (yrs):** 1 **Occupation:** Farmer **Age** 16
Enrolled at: Iuka, MS **Enrolled By:** Lt. Davenport **Promoted:** No **ROH:** No
Born: Mississippi **Marital Status:** S **Residence** Salem, MS

Discharged on 7/31/1862 — underage.

Prescott, Zachariah D.
CO: D **Initial Rank:** Private
Joined: Saturday, April 27, 1861 **Term (yrs):** 1 **Occupation:** Farmer **Age** 25
Enrolled at: Pine Grove, MS **Enrolled By:** Capt. Beck **Promoted:** Yes **ROH:** Yes
Born: Tennessee **Marital Status:** S **Residence** Pine Grove, MS

Listed as 1st Sergeant circa Mar/Apr 1862. Wounded at Gaines Mill on 6/27/1862. Sent to hospital at Richmond, VA. Returned to duty. Wounded on 9/17/1862 at Sharpsburg. Returned to duty. According to list of engagements, was wounded at Gettysburg on 7/3/1863 (company records do not so indicate). Severely wounded at The Wilderness on 5/5/1864. Sent to hospital. Furloughed 60-days from 7/15/1864. Returned to duty. Captured at Petersburg (Hatcher's Run) on 4/2/1865. Sent to Fort Delaware. Released on oath on 6/11/1865. ROH for The Wilderness, 5/5/1864.

2nd Mississippi Alphabetical Roster (Annotated)

Preston, W. R. *CO:* K *Initial Rank:* Private
Joined: *Term (yrs):* 0 *Occupation:* *Age*
Enrolled at: *Enrolled By:* *Promoted:* No *ROH:* No
Born: *Marital Status:* *Residence*

Appears on a roll of prisoners of war picked up at points between Chickasaw Landing and Macon, GA, from March 22 to April 20, 1865. Captured at Selma, AL on 4/2/1865. [Misidentified. This man is probably a member of the 2nd/6th Missouri Infantry which was stationed in the area at the time].

Prewett, James R. *CO:* K *Initial Rank:* Private
Joined: Wednesday, May 1, 1861 *Term (yrs):* 1 *Occupation:* Laborer *Age* 25
Enrolled at: Tishomingo Co., MS *Enrolled By:* Capt. Stone *Promoted:* No *ROH:* No
Born: *Marital Status:* *Residence*

Deserted on 6/5/1863. Taken into Federal custody on 6/8/1863 near Suffolk, VA. Was administered the oath of allegiance on 6/24/1864. Listed on company rolls as present during Sep/Oct 1864 muster roll. Nov/Dec muster remarks: "According to sentence of Court Martial he forfeits all pay from 5 June 1863 to 25 July 1864." Jan/Feb, 1865 muster remarks: "Deserted 1 Feb 1865."

Prewett, Micajah C. *CO:* K *Initial Rank:* 3rd Corporal
Joined: Wednesday, May 1, 1861 *Term (yrs):* 1 *Occupation:* Farmer *Age* 27
Enrolled at: Tishomingo Co., MS *Enrolled By:* Capt. Stone *Promoted:* No *ROH:* No
Born: *Marital Status:* *Residence*

Company muster roll lists him as deserted from sick furlough during Mar/Apr 1863. Federal records show he was captured while on furlough at Glendale, MS on 2/12/1863. Sent to Alton, IL and paroled to City Point, VA for exchange on 4/1/1863. No other records.

Prewitt, Francis M. *CO:* K *Initial Rank:* Private
Joined: Saturday, April 6, 1861 *Term (yrs):* 0 *Occupation:* *Age*
Enrolled at: Iuka, MS *Enrolled By:* W. M. Inge *Promoted:* No *ROH:* No
Born: *Marital Status:* *Residence*

Appears on a company muster roll. No other record.

2nd Mississippi Alphabetical Roster (Annotated)

Price, John B.
CO: E **Initial Rank:** Private
Joined: Monday, February 18, 1861 **Term (yrs):** 0 **Occupation:** **Age**
Enrolled at: Saltillo, MS **Enrolled By:** R. Griffith **Promoted:** No **ROH:** No
Born: **Marital Status:** **Residence**

Appears on a list of the Calhoun Rifles dated 2/11/1861 and on a company muster roll. No other records.

Price, Stephen
CO: C **Initial Rank:** Private
Joined: Wednesday, May 1, 1861 **Term (yrs):** 1 **Occupation:** Farmer **Age** 39
Enrolled at: Itawamba Co., MS **Enrolled By:** Capt. Bromley **Promoted:** No **ROH:** No
Born: **Marital Status:** **Residence**

Discharged due to disability on 11/15, 1861 at Camp Fisher, VA.

Prince, Joel
CO: F **Initial Rank:** Private
Joined: Wednesday, May 1, 1861 **Term (yrs):** 1 **Occupation:** Miller **Age** 22
Enrolled at: Tippah Co., MS **Enrolled By:** Capt. Davis **Promoted:** No **ROH:** No
Born: **Marital Status:** **Residence**

Mortally wounded at battle of Seven Pines on 5/31/1862. Died in hospital at Richmond on 6/16/1862 from wounds.

Prince, Thomas A.
CO: B **Initial Rank:** Private
Joined: Wednesday, May 1, 1861 **Term (yrs):** 1 **Occupation:** Tailor **Age** 25
Enrolled at: Tippah Co., MS **Enrolled By:** Capt. Buchanan **Promoted:** No **ROH:** No
Born: South Carolina **Marital Status:** **Residence**

Mortally wounded at Seven Pines on 5/31/1862. Died at Richmond on 6/6/1862 from wounds.

Pryor, John H.
CO: E **Initial Rank:** Private
Joined: Saturday, March 1, 1862 **Term (yrs):** 3 **Occupation:** Farmer **Age** 26
Enrolled at: Guntown, MS **Enrolled By:** Capt. Bates **Promoted:** No **ROH:** No
Born: Tennessee **Marital Status:** M **Residence** Guntown, MS

Accompanying list of engagements shows him wounded at Gettysburg on 7/1/1863 (company records do not confirm this). Deserted on 7/25/1863 from hospital at Richmond, VA.

2nd Mississippi Alphabetical Roster (Annotated)

Quillin, Henderson — CO: E — Initial Rank: Private
- **Joined:** Friday, February 28, 1862
- **Term (yrs):** 3
- **Occupation:** Laborer
- **Age** 31
- **Enrolled at:** Guntown, MS
- **Enrolled By:** Capt. Bates
- **Promoted:** No
- **ROH:** No
- **Born:** Tennessee
- **Marital Status:** M
- **Residence** Guntown, MS

Present through most of the regiment's battles. Captured at Petersburg (Hatcher's Run) on 4/2/1865. Taken to Fort Delaware. Released on oath on 6/11/1865.

Quinn, David N. — CO: K — Initial Rank: Private
- **Joined:** Wednesday, May 1, 1861
- **Term (yrs):** 1
- **Occupation:** Teacher
- **Age** 19
- **Enrolled at:** Tishomingo Co., MS
- **Enrolled By:** Capt. Stone
- **Promoted:** No
- **ROH:** No
- **Born:** Georgia
- **Marital Status:**
- **Residence**

Discharged for disability at Camp Fisher, VA on 10/19/1861 by order of General Smith.

Quinn, George W. — CO: H — Initial Rank: Private
- **Joined:**
- **Term (yrs):** 0
- **Occupation:**
- **Age**
- **Enrolled at:**
- **Enrolled By:**
- **Promoted:** No
- **ROH:** No
- **Born:**
- **Marital Status:**
- **Residence**

Reference envelope says to see G. W. Quinn, Wood's Regiment Confederate Cavalry. No other record.

Raby, James H. — CO: F — Initial Rank: Private
- **Joined:** Saturday, March 1, 1862
- **Term (yrs):** 3
- **Occupation:** Farmer
- **Age** 20
- **Enrolled at:** Ripley, MS
- **Enrolled By:** Capt. Powers
- **Promoted:** No
- **ROH:** No
- **Born:** Tennessee
- **Marital Status:** S
- **Residence**

Wounded at The Wilderness on 5/5/1864. Sent to hospital in Richmond. Furloughed 30-days from 6/15/1864. Did not return. Listed as deserted during Nov/Dec 1864 muster.

Raines, James A. — CO: H — Initial Rank: Private
- **Joined:** Monday, April 29, 1861
- **Term (yrs):** 1
- **Occupation:** Farmer
- **Age** 19
- **Enrolled at:** Pontotoc Co., MS
- **Enrolled By:** Capt. Taylor
- **Promoted:** Yes
- **ROH:** Yes
- **Born:** Alabama
- **Marital Status:** S
- **Residence** Tupelo, MS

Appointed 4th Corporal in Aug 1862. Severely wounded and captured at Gettysburg on 7/1/1863 (right foot amputated). Paroled at Hammond U.S. General Hospital, Point Lookout, MD on 4/27/1864 and transferred to City Point, VA for exchange. Furloughed. Has authority to appear before medical examining board for retirement. ROH for Gettysburg, 7/1/1863.

2nd Mississippi Alphabetical Roster (Annotated)

Raines, Oliver T. **CO:** E **Initial Rank:** Private
Joined: Wednesday, February 26, 1862 **Term (yrs):** 3 **Occupation:** Farmer **Age** 18
Enrolled at: Guntown, MS **Enrolled By:** Capt. Bates **Promoted:** No **ROH:** No
Born: Mississippi **Marital Status:** S **Residence** Guntown, MS

Captured at Gettysburg on 7/1/1863. Taken to Fort Delaware. Released on oath on 6/11/1865.

Ralph, John L. **CO:** F **Initial Rank:** Private
Joined: Monday, September 30, 1861 **Term (yrs):** 1 **Occupation:** **Age**
Enrolled at: Iuka, MS **Enrolled By:** Lt. Davenport **Promoted:** No **ROH:** Yes
Born: **Marital Status:** S **Residence**

Killed in battle at Sharpsburg on 9/17/1862. ROH for Malvern Hill, 7/1/1862.

Ralph, William H. H. **CO:** F **Initial Rank:** Private
Joined: Saturday, March 1, 1862 **Term (yrs):** 3 **Occupation:** Farmer **Age** 22
Enrolled at: Ripley, MS **Enrolled By:** Capt. Powers **Promoted:** No **ROH:** Yes
Born: Mississippi **Marital Status:** S **Residence**

Wounded on 9/15/1864. Furloughed 60-days from 10/8/1864. Listed as AWOL during Jan/Feb 1865 muster roll. ROH for Spotsylvania Court House, 5/12/1864.

Ralston, George G. **CO:** A **Initial Rank:** Private
Joined: Wednesday, May 1, 1861 **Term (yrs):** 1 **Occupation:** Mechanic **Age** 27
Enrolled at: Tishomingo Co., MS **Enrolled By:** Capt. Leeth **Promoted:** Yes **ROH:** No
Born: **Marital Status:** **Residence**

Appointed 5th Sergeant on 4/22/1862. Elected Jr. 2nd Lieutenant on 10/16/1862. Promoted to 1st Lieutenant on 3/1/1863. Wounded at Gettysburg on 7/1/1863. Captured 7/4/1863 at Gettysburg. Leg amputated. Died of wounds at the U.S. General Hospital in Chester, PA on 7/30/1863. Grave #188 in Chester Cemetery, PA.

Ralston, William M. **CO:** A **Initial Rank:** Private
Joined: Friday, June 7, 1861 **Term (yrs):** 1 **Occupation:** Mechanic **Age** 36
Enrolled at: Winchester, VA **Enrolled By:** Col. Falkner **Promoted:** Yes **ROH:** No
Born: Tennessee **Marital Status:** S **Residence** Burnsville, MS

Also see 17th Mississippi Infantry Regiment. Transferred from the 17th Mississippi on 6/8/1861. Appointed Orderly Sergeant on 7/15/1861. Elected 1st Lieutenant on 4/22/1862. Killed in battle at 2nd Manassas on 8/29/1862.

2nd Mississippi Alphabetical Roster (Annotated)

Ramsey, A. O.   *CO:* G   *Initial Rank:* Private
Joined: *Term (yrs):* 0   *Occupation:*   *Age*
Enrolled at: *Enrolled By:*   *Promoted:* No   *ROH:* No
Born: *Marital Status:*   *Residence*

Appears on a Federal register of prisoners of war, dated Memphis, TN. Date of capture not given. Location not given. Receive on 9/15/1863. Released on 9/16/1863. No other record.

Raper, Robert   *CO:* E   *Initial Rank:* Private
Joined: Monday, March 17, 1862   *Term (yrs):* 3   *Occupation:* Farmer   *Age* 20
Enrolled at: Guntown, MS   *Enrolled By:* Capt. Bates   *Promoted:* No   *ROH:* No
Born: *Marital Status:*   *Residence* Guntown, MS

Died of disease in Richmond, VA on 5/4/1862.

Ratliff, James R.   *CO:* E   *Initial Rank:* Private
Joined: Wednesday, May 1, 1861   *Term (yrs):* 1   *Occupation:* Farmer   *Age* 20
Enrolled at: Itawamba Co., MS   *Enrolled By:* Capt. Booth   *Promoted:* No   *ROH:* No
Born: *Marital Status:* S   *Residence* Guntown, MS

Listed as present during last (Jan/Feb 1865) company muster.

Ray, J. F.   *CO:* C   *Initial Rank:* Sergeant
Joined: *Term (yrs):* 0   *Occupation:*   *Age*
Enrolled at: *Enrolled By:*   *Promoted:* No   *ROH:* No
Born: *Marital Status:*   *Residence*

Appears on a Federal register of prisoners of war at Fort Delaware. Captured at Cashtown on 7/5/1863. Became "Galvanized Yankee" and joined U. S. 3rd Maryland Cavalry in July 1863. Deserted. No other record.

Ray, James   *CO:* I   *Initial Rank:* Private
Joined: *Term (yrs):* 0   *Occupation:*   *Age*
Enrolled at: *Enrolled By:*   *Promoted:* No   *ROH:* No
Born: *Marital Status:*   *Residence*

Appears on a Federal register of prisoners of war at Fort Delaware. Received from Gettysburg, July 1863. No other record.

2nd Mississippi Alphabetical Roster (Annotated)

Ray, James W.   *CO:* D   *Initial Rank:* Private
Joined: Wednesday, May 1, 1861   *Term (yrs):* 1   *Occupation:* Farmer   *Age* 20
Enrolled at: Tippah Co., MS   *Enrolled By:* Capt. Beck   *Promoted:* Yes   *ROH:* No
Born: Tennessee   *Marital Status:* S   *Residence* Pine Grove, MS

Listed as 4th Corporal for Jul/Aug 1862 muster roll. Accompanying list of engagements shows him wounded at Sharpsburg on 9/17/1862 (company records do not confirm this). Died of disease at Richmond, VA on 11/24/1862.

Ray, John H. Z.   *CO:* B   *Initial Rank:* Private
Joined: Wednesday, May 1, 1861   *Term (yrs):* 1   *Occupation:* Farmer   *Age* 19
Enrolled at: Tippah Co., MS   *Enrolled By:* Capt. Buchanan   *Promoted:* Yes   *ROH:* No
Born: *Marital Status:*   *Residence*

Wounded at 2nd Manassas on 8/29/1862. Sent to hospital. Returned to duty. Wounded (in foot) and captured at Gettysburg on 7/1/1863. Paroled to City Point, VA on 11/17/1863 and exchanged on 1/1/1864. Furloughed. Returned to duty. Retired to Invalid Corps, P.A.C.S. Surrendered at La Grange, TN on 5/30/1865 and paroled.

Ray, Joseph   *CO:* D   *Initial Rank:* Private
Joined: Tuesday, October 1, 1861   *Term (yrs):* 1   *Occupation:* Farmer   *Age* 18
Enrolled at: Iuka, MS   *Enrolled By:* Lt. Davenport   *Promoted:* No   *ROH:* No
Born: Mississippi   *Marital Status:* S   *Residence* Pine Grove, MS

Discharged for disability on 12/7/1861 by order of General Whiting.

Ray, Turner   *CO:* I   *Initial Rank:* Private
Joined: Wednesday, May 1, 1861   *Term (yrs):* 1   *Occupation:* Farmer   *Age* 31
Enrolled at: Pontotoc Co., MS   *Enrolled By:* Capt. Herring   *Promoted:* No   *ROH:* No
Born: *Marital Status:*   *Residence*

Wounded at Sharpsburg on 9/17/1862. Furloughed. Returned to duty. Captured at Gettysburg on 7/1/1863. Sent to Fort Delaware. Released on oath on 6/11/1865.

2nd Mississippi Alphabetical Roster (Annotated)

Rea, Andrew M.

CO: C, H *Initial Rank:* Private

Joined: Tuesday, October 1, 1861 *Term (yrs):* 1 *Occupation:* Mechanic *Age* 25

Enrolled at: Richmond, MS *Enrolled By:* Lt. Davenport *Promoted:* No *ROH:* Yes

Born: *Marital Status:* M *Residence* Verona, MS

Transferred to Company H in June 1862. Severely wounded at Gettysburg on 7/1/1863. Sent to hospital in Richmond. Furloughed on 7/25/1863 for 40-days. Admitted to hospital 10/10/1863 (ankylosis of left elbow). Assigned to duty as nurse at Howards Grove Hospital on 11/10/1863. Returned to duty on 3/11/1864. Severely wounded and captured at the Weldon Railroad on 8/18/1864 (left leg amputated at thigh). Taken to Fort McHenry, MD. Exchanged on 2/20.1865. Wounded (?) and admitted to hospital on 3/4/1865. Furloughed 3/11/1865 for 30-days. Surrendered and paroled in North Carolina under terms arranged between Johnston and Sherman on 5/12/1865. ROH for Spotsylvania Court House, 5/12/1864.

Rea, Thomas S.

CO: C, H *Initial Rank:* Private

Joined: Tuesday, October 1, 1861 *Term (yrs):* 1 *Occupation:* Mechanic *Age* 28

Enrolled at: Richmond, MS *Enrolled By:* Lt. Davenport *Promoted:* No *ROH:* No

Born: *Marital Status:* M *Residence* Verona, MS

Transferred to Company H in June 1862. Captured at Gettysburg on 7/1/1863. Sent to Fort Delaware. Released on oath on 6/11/1865.

Reagh, Anderson M.

CO: C, F *Initial Rank:* Private

Joined: Monday, September 30, 1861 *Term (yrs):* 1 *Occupation:* *Age*

Enrolled at: Ripley, MS *Enrolled By:* Lt. Davenport *Promoted:* No *ROH:* No

Born: Mississippi *Marital Status:* *Residence*

Transferred to Company F on 4/30/1862. Deserted. Gave himself over to Federal authorities at Carlisle, PA on 7/1/1863. Sent to Fort Delaware. Became "Galvanized Yankee" and joined the 3rd Maryland Cavalry (U.S.) on 9/22/1863.

Reagh, J. C.

CO: F *Initial Rank:* Private

Joined: Monday, September 30, 1861 *Term (yrs):* 1 *Occupation:* brick maker *Age* 20

Enrolled at: Ripley, MS *Enrolled By:* Lt. Davenport *Promoted:* No *ROH:* No

Born: Alabama *Marital Status:* *Residence*

Discharged for disability on 1/10/1862.

2nd Mississippi Alphabetical Roster (Annotated)

Reece, Charles A.
CO: A **Initial Rank:** Private
Joined: Saturday, March 1, 1862 **Term (yrs):** 3 **Occupation:** Farmer **Age** 18
Enrolled at: Jacinto, MS **Enrolled By:** Lt. Clayton **Promoted:** No **ROH:** No
Born: Alabama **Marital Status:** S **Residence** Rienzi, MS

Also see 26th Mississippi Infantry Regiment. Wounded at Malvern Hill on 7/1/1862 according to company muster records (however, other records show him on a list of those wounded on 6/27/1862 at Gaines Mill). Furloughed. "Returned to the 26th Mississippi to which he originally belonged."

Reece, James O.
CO: A **Initial Rank:** Private
Joined: Wednesday, May 1, 1861 **Term (yrs):** 1 **Occupation:** Farmer **Age** 26
Enrolled at: Tishomingo Co., MS **Enrolled By:** Capt. Leeth **Promoted:** No **ROH:** No
Born: Alabama **Marital Status:** S **Residence** Rienzi, MS

Discharged due to disability on 5/12/1861.

Reed, James A.
CO: G **Initial Rank:** Private
Joined: Wednesday, May 1, 1861 **Term (yrs):** 1 **Occupation:** Smith **Age** 19
Enrolled at: Pontotoc Co., MS **Enrolled By:** Capt. Miller **Promoted:** No **ROH:** No
Born: South Carolina **Marital Status:** S **Residence** Pontotoc, MS

Killed in battle at Seven Pines on 5/31/1862.

Reed, James R.
CO: A **Initial Rank:** Private
Joined: Saturday, March 1, 1862 **Term (yrs):** 3 **Occupation:** Farmer **Age** 30
Enrolled at: Jacinto, MS **Enrolled By:** Lt. Clayton **Promoted:** No **ROH:** No
Born: Alabama **Marital Status:** M **Residence** Jacinto, MS

Killed in battle at Gettysburg on 7/1/1863.

Reeder, William L.
CO: I **Initial Rank:** Private
Joined: Wednesday, May 1, 1861 **Term (yrs):** 1 **Occupation:** Farmer **Age** 27
Enrolled at: Pontotoc Co., MS **Enrolled By:** Capt. Herring **Promoted:** No **ROH:** No
Born: **Marital Status:** **Residence**

Killed in battle at Sharpsburg on 9/17/1862.

2nd Mississippi Alphabetical Roster (Annotated)

Renean, William L.   CO: K   Initial Rank: 4th Sergeant

Joined: Wednesday, May 1, 1861   **Term (yrs):** 1   **Occupation:** Clerk   **Age** 22

Enrolled at: Tishomingo Co., MS   **Enrolled By:** Capt. Stone   **Promoted:** No   **ROH:** No

Born: Alabama   **Marital Status:**   **Residence**

Mortally wounded in battle at Seven Pines on 5/31/1862. Died of wounds at Richmond, VA on 6/21/1862.

Renfro, James A.   CO: F   Initial Rank: Private

Joined: Wednesday, May 1, 1861   **Term (yrs):** 1   **Occupation:** Planter   **Age** 26

Enrolled at: Tippah Co., MS   **Enrolled By:** Capt. Davis   **Promoted:** No   **ROH:** No

Born: Mississippi   **Marital Status:**   **Residence**

Discharged due to disability on 11/13/1861 at Camp Fisher, VA.

Reynolds, Arthur M.   CO: A   Initial Rank: Private

Joined: Wednesday, May 1, 1861   **Term (yrs):** 1   **Occupation:** Student   **Age** 18

Enrolled at: Tishomingo Co., MS   **Enrolled By:** Capt. Leeth   **Promoted:** No   **ROH:** No

Born: Tennessee   **Marital Status:** S   **Residence** Jacinto, MS

Also see Company D, 26th Mississippi Infantry Regiment. Wounded (not dated) and captured at Gettysburg on 7/5/1863. Paroled at DeCamp General Hospital, Davids Island, NY Harbor to City Point, VA on 9/8/1863. Furloughed. Returned to duty. Wounded "in trenches" on 5/31/1864. Sent to hospital in Richmond. Transferred to Company D of the 26th Mississippi in July 1864.

Reynolds, George W.   CO: A   Initial Rank: Private

Joined: Wednesday, May 1, 1861   **Term (yrs):** 1   **Occupation:** Student   **Age** 17

Enrolled at: Tishomingo Co., MS   **Enrolled By:** Capt. Leeth   **Promoted:** Yes   **ROH:** No

Born: Mississippi   **Marital Status:** S   **Residence** Burnsville, MS

Also see 26th Mississippi Infantry Regiment. Promoted to 3rd Corporal on 7/3/1863. Transferred to 26th Mississippi in July 1864.

2nd Mississippi Alphabetical Roster (Annotated)

Reynolds, Gilford G.

CO: A **Initial Rank:** Private
Joined: Saturday, March 1, 1862 **Term (yrs):** 3 **Occupation:** Farmer **Age** 26
Enrolled at: Jacinto, MS **Enrolled By:** Lt. Clayton **Promoted:** No **ROH:** No
Born: Tennessee **Marital Status:** M **Residence** Jacinto, MS

Captured at South Mountain, MD on 9/16/1862. Paroled to Aikens Landing, VA on 10/2/1862. Declared exchanged on 11/10/1862. Returned to duty. Wounded at Gettysburg on 7/1/1863 and captured on 7/5/1863. Sent to DeCamp General Hospital, Davids Island, NY Harbor and paroled to City Point, VA on 9/16/1863. Furloughed. Did not return. Dropped from rolls as deserter on 12/31/1864.

Reynolds, Lafayette P.

CO: A **Initial Rank:** 1st Lieutenant
Joined: Wednesday, May 1, 1861 **Term (yrs):** 1 **Occupation:** Lawyer **Age** 27
Enrolled at: Tishomingo Co., MS **Enrolled By:** Capt. Leeth **Promoted:** No **ROH:** No
Born: **Marital Status:** S **Residence** Jacinto, MS

Relieved of command due to reorganization of company on 4/22/1862. Resigned.

Reynolds, Monroe M.

CO: K **Initial Rank:** Private
Joined: Saturday, March 1, 1862 **Term (yrs):** 3 **Occupation:** Mechanic **Age** 42
Enrolled at: Iuka, MS **Enrolled By:** Lt. Latham **Promoted:** No **ROH:** No
Born: Tennessee **Marital Status:** **Residence**

Died of disease at Ashland, VA on 6/17/1862.

Reynolds, P. R.

CO: **Initial Rank:** Private
Joined: **Term (yrs):** 0 **Occupation:** **Age**
Enrolled at: **Enrolled By:** **Promoted:** No **ROH:** No
Born: **Marital Status:** **Residence**

Appears on a Federal register of prisoners received and disposed of by the Provost Marshal General, Army of the Potomac. Dated 3/27/1864. Charge: "Rebel deserter." Appears on a register of oathers and deserters, Provost Marshal General, Washington, D.C. Dated 3/29/1864. Action Taken: "Taken the oath of allegiance. Trans[portation] fur[nished] to Phil[adelphia] Pa." No other records.

2nd Mississippi Alphabetical Roster (Annotated)

Reynolds, Robert H.
CO: D   **Initial Rank:** Private
Joined: Wednesday, May 1, 1861   **Term (yrs):** 1   **Occupation:** Farmer   **Age** 20
Enrolled at: Tippah Co., MS   **Enrolled By:** Capt. Beck   **Promoted:** No   **ROH:** No
Born: Mississippi   **Marital Status:** S   **Residence** Snow Creek, MS
Deserted on 5/28/1862.

Reynolds, Thomas G.
CO: A   **Initial Rank:** Private
Joined: Friday, June 21, 1861   **Term (yrs):** 1   **Occupation:** Farmer   **Age** 21
Enrolled at: Winchester, VA   **Enrolled By:** Capt. Leeth   **Promoted:** No   **ROH:** No
Born: **Marital Status:**   **Residence**
Also see 17th Mississippi Infantry Regiment. Transferred from the 17th Mississippi on 6/8/1861. Died of disease at Warrenton, VA on 10/11/1861.

Rice, David E.
CO: K   **Initial Rank:** Private
Joined: Saturday, March 1, 1862   **Term (yrs):** 3   **Occupation:**   **Age** 32
Enrolled at: Iuka, MS   **Enrolled By:** Lt. Latham   **Promoted:** No   **ROH:** No
Born: **Marital Status:**   **Residence**
Deserted before arriving at Richmond about 5/1/1861.

Rice, James M.
CO: E   **Initial Rank:** Private
Joined: Wednesday, August 7, 1861   **Term (yrs):** 1   **Occupation:**   **Age**
Enrolled at: Camp Jones, VA   **Enrolled By:** Col. Falkner   **Promoted:** No   **ROH:** No
Born: **Marital Status:**   **Residence**
Severely wounded and captured at Sharpsburg on 9/17/1862. Paroled on 9/27/1862. Exchanged on 12/15/1862 at Fortress Monroe, VA. Discharged due to disability caused by wounds on 4/15/1863. Picked up by Federal forces at Corinth, MS on 10/14/1863 (or 10/6/1863). Sent to Alton, IL prison. Remarks: "Conscripted. Object to being exchanged. Desires to take the oath of allegiance without reservation or evasion." Transferred to Fort Delaware on 4/4/1864. Released on oath on 6/7/1865.

Richardson, Benjamin F.
CO: E   **Initial Rank:** Private
Joined: Friday, February 28, 1862   **Term (yrs):** 3   **Occupation:** Mechanic   **Age** 26
Enrolled at: Guntown, MS   **Enrolled By:** Capt. Bates   **Promoted:** Yes   **ROH:** No
Born: Alabama   **Marital Status:** M   **Residence** Marietta, MS
Promoted to 3rd Lieutenant on 1/15/1863. Killed in battle at Gettysburg on 7/3/1863.

2nd Mississippi Alphabetical Roster (Annotated)

Richie, Albert
CO: B **Initial Rank:** Private
Joined: Wednesday, May 1, 1861 **Term (yrs):** 1 **Occupation:** Painter **Age** 24
Enrolled at: Tippah Co., MS **Enrolled By:** Capt. Buchanan **Promoted:** No **ROH:** No
Born: **Marital Status:** **Residence** Ripley, MS

Detailed as scout for Major General Heth on 7/1/1863 through last company muster. Appears on a Federal record of paroled prisoners of war remaining in Richmond, VA. Dated 5/10/1865.

Richie, Luther A.
CO: B **Initial Rank:** Private
Joined: Wednesday, May 1, 1861 **Term (yrs):** 1 **Occupation:** Clerk **Age** 21
Enrolled at: Tippah Co., MS **Enrolled By:** Capt. Buchanan **Promoted:** Yes **ROH:** No
Born: **Marital Status:** **Residence** Guntown, MS

Listed as 5th Sergeant during Nov/Dec 1862 muster. Promoted to Jr 2nd Lieutenant on 8/14/1863. Wounded near Cold Harbor on 6/10/1864. Sent to hospital in Richmond, VA. Furloughed 60-days from 7/9/1864. Returned to duty. Captured at Hatcher's Run on 4/2/1865. Sent to Johnson's Island, OH. Released on oath on 6/19/1865.

Richie, Wilson M.
CO: B **Initial Rank:** Private
Joined: Wednesday, September 18, 1861 **Term (yrs):** 1 **Occupation:** Farmer **Age**
Enrolled at: Ripley, MS **Enrolled By:** Lt. Davenport **Promoted:** No **ROH:** No
Born: South Carolina **Marital Status:** **Residence**

Discharged for disability on 3/27/1862 by order of General Whiting.

Richman, Samuel
CO: H **Initial Rank:** Private
Joined: Monday, April 29, 1861 **Term (yrs):** 1 **Occupation:** Merchant **Age** 28
Enrolled at: Pontotoc Co., MS **Enrolled By:** Capt. Taylor **Promoted:** No **ROH:** No
Born: **Marital Status:** S **Residence** Chesterville, MS

Also see James Porter (substitute). Discharged on 7/21/1861 by reason of having furnished a substitute.

Riddle, Ariel
CO: C **Initial Rank:** Private
Joined: Wednesday, May 1, 1861 **Term (yrs):** 1 **Occupation:** Carpenter **Age** 25
Enrolled at: Itawamba Co., MS **Enrolled By:** Capt. Bromley **Promoted:** No **ROH:** No
Born: **Marital Status:** **Residence**

Died (cause not given) at Lynchburg, VA on 5/24/1861 (another record says 5/26/1861).

2nd Mississippi Alphabetical Roster (Annotated)

Riggan, Benjamin J.
CO: H *Initial Rank:* Private
Joined: Saturday, August 10, 1861 *Term (yrs):* 1 *Occupation:* Farmer *Age* 21
Enrolled at: Camp Jones, VA *Enrolled By:* Lt. Stone *Promoted:* No *ROH:* No
Born: Alabama *Marital Status:* S *Residence* Chesterville, MS

Listed as present for last muster (Jan/Feb 1865).

Riggs, Augustus L.
CO: K *Initial Rank:* Private
Joined: Wednesday, May 1, 1861 *Term (yrs):* 1 *Occupation:* Carpenter *Age* 32
Enrolled at: Tishomingo Co., MS *Enrolled By:* Capt. Stone *Promoted:* No *ROH:* No
Born: Alabama *Marital Status:* *Residence*

Wounded at Gettysburg on 7/1/1863. Captured at Confederate field hospital at Gettysburg on 7/5/1863. Taken to DeCamp General Hospital, Davids Island, NY Harbor and then, in Oct 1863 to Fort Wood, Bedloe's Island, NY Harbor where he died on 12/5/1863. #of grave: 952. Location: Cypress Hill.

Riley, James A.
CO: B, L *Initial Rank:* Private
Joined: Monday, March 3, 1862 *Term (yrs):* 3 *Occupation:* Farmer *Age* 36
Enrolled at: Ripley, MS *Enrolled By:* Capt. Buchanan *Promoted:* No *ROH:* No
Born: Alabama *Marital Status:* M *Residence*

Transferred to Company L on 4/30/1862. Mortally wounded and captured at Gettysburg on 7/1/1863. Died of wounds (not dated), but shortly after capture.

Ritchie, James
CO: *Initial Rank:* Private
Joined: *Term (yrs):* 0 *Occupation:* *Age*
Enrolled at: *Enrolled By:* *Promoted:* No *ROH:* No
Born: *Marital Status:* *Residence*

Appears on a Federal register of prisoners of war. Captured at Camp Wildcat, KY (not dated). Remarks: "Released on taking oath." [Misidentified. Doubtful that this man belongs to the 2nd Mississippi].

2nd Mississippi Alphabetical Roster (Annotated)

Roberson, James B.
CO: F **Initial Rank:** Private
Joined: Wednesday, May 1, 1861 **Term (yrs):** 1 **Occupation:** Planter **Age** 21
Enrolled at: Tippah Co., MS **Enrolled By:** Capt. Davis **Promoted:** No **ROH:** No
Born: **Marital Status:** **Residence**

Admitted to hospital at Charlottesville, VA on 7/23/1861 for wound of arm (company records do not give date of wound or action but must have been 1st Manassas on 7/21/1861). Returned to duty on 8/31/1861. Died of disease (pneumonia) at Camp Jones, VA on 9/22/1861.

Roberson, Thomas J.
CO: F **Initial Rank:** 4th Sergeant
Joined: Wednesday, May 1, 1861 **Term (yrs):** 1 **Occupation:** Planter **Age** 22
Enrolled at: Tippah Co., MS **Enrolled By:** Capt. Davis **Promoted:** Yes **ROH:** No
Born: **Marital Status:** **Residence**

Listed as 2nd Sergeant for May/Jun 1861 muster roll. Discharged due to disability on 7/18/1861 at Camp Bee, VA.

Roberts, Alfred R.
CO: C **Initial Rank:** Private
Joined: Saturday, March 15, 1862 **Term (yrs):** 3 **Occupation:** Blacksmith **Age** 43
Enrolled at: Richmond, MS **Enrolled By:** Lt. Pounds **Promoted:** No **ROH:** No
Born: **Marital Status:** **Residence**

Confusing hospital records indicate he may have been wounded (left leg) in July 1863 (cannot be verified by records). Furloughed for 35-days from 8/28/1863. Listed as deserted, AWOL since 12/5/1864 for Jan/Feb 1865 muster.

Roberts, Atlas K.
CO: H **Initial Rank:** Private
Joined: Monday, April 29, 1861 **Term (yrs):** 1 **Occupation:** Farmer **Age** 19
Enrolled at: Pontotoc Co., MS **Enrolled By:** Capt. Taylor **Promoted:** Yes **ROH:** Yes
Born: Alabama **Marital Status:** S **Residence** Chesterville, MS

Appointed 2nd Corporal on 4/22/1862. Appointed 3rd Sergeant on 8/8/1862. Wounded at 2nd Manassas on 8/29/1862. Returned to duty. Promoted to 1st Sergeant on 10/1/1862. Elected Jr. 2nd Lieutenant on 5/17/1863. Killed at Gettysburg on 7/1/1863 [in leading a raiding party to capture the colors of the 149th Pennsylvania]. ROH for Malvern Hill, 7/1/1862.

2nd Mississippi Alphabetical Roster (Annotated)

Roberts, E. S.
CO: H *Initial Rank:* Lieutenant
Joined: *Term (yrs):* 0 *Occupation:* *Age*
Enrolled at: *Enrolled By:* *Promoted:* No *ROH:* No
Born: *Marital Status:* *Residence*

Appears on a Federal record of prisoners of war at Old Capitol Prison, Washington, D.C. Remarks: "Came into our lines of his own accord." Dated 10/6/1862. No other records.

Roberts, Elvis C.
CO: H *Initial Rank:* Private
Joined: Monday, April 29, 1861 *Term (yrs):* 1 *Occupation:* Farmer *Age* 19
Enrolled at: Pontotoc Co., MS *Enrolled By:* Capt. Taylor *Promoted:* No *ROH:* No
Born: Mississippi *Marital Status:* S *Residence* Chesterville, MS

Discharged (accidentally shot himself in left hip) on 7/12/1861 due to disability. Re-joined in May 1863. Accompanying list of engagements shows him wounded at Gettysburg on 7/1/1863 (company records do not so indicate). Company muster rolls list him as deserted about mid-July 1863.

Roberts, G. R.
CO: B *Initial Rank:* Private
Joined: Monday, March 3, 1862 *Term (yrs):* 3 *Occupation:* Farmer *Age* 23
Enrolled at: Ripley, MS *Enrolled By:* Capt. Buchanan *Promoted:* No *ROH:* No
Born: Alabama *Marital Status:* S *Residence*

Wounded (?) and captured at Sharpsburg on 9/17/1862. Paroled on 9/27/1862.

Roberts, Joseph A.
CO: C *Initial Rank:* Private
Joined: Tuesday, October 1, 1861 *Term (yrs):* 1 *Occupation:* Merchant *Age*
Enrolled at: Richmond, MS *Enrolled By:* Lt. Davenport *Promoted:* No *ROH:* No
Born: Mississippi *Marital Status:* *Residence*

Killed in battle at Sharpsburg on 9/17/1862.

Roberts, Killis M.
CO: H *Initial Rank:* Private
Joined: Monday, April 29, 1861 *Term (yrs):* 1 *Occupation:* Farmer *Age* 23
Enrolled at: Pontotoc Co., MS *Enrolled By:* Capt. Taylor *Promoted:* No *ROH:* No
Born: Mississippi *Marital Status:* S *Residence* Chesterville, MS

Discharged on 12/18/1861 due to disability by order of General Whiting.

2nd Mississippi Alphabetical Roster (Annotated)

Roberts, Lewis

CO:	**Initial Rank:** Private	
Joined:	**Term (yrs):** 0 **Occupation:**	**Age**
Enrolled at:	**Enrolled By:**	**Promoted:** No **ROH:** No
Born:	**Marital Status:**	**Residence**

Appears on a Federal register of prisoners of war, dated 2/20/1865 at Memphis, TN — Deserters from rebel army. No other record.

Roberts, Reuben M.

CO: C	**Initial Rank:** Private	
Joined: Wednesday, May 1, 1861	**Term (yrs):** 1 **Occupation:** Farmer	**Age** 16
Enrolled at: Itawamba Co., MS	**Enrolled By:** Capt. Bromley	**Promoted:** Yes **ROH:** No
Born:	**Marital Status:**	**Residence**

Appointed 3rd Corporal on 4/23/1862. Wounded in battle at Gaines Mill on 6/27/1862. Sent to hospital at Lynchburg, VA. Returned to duty. Wounded (in arm) on 6/2/1864. Furloughed. Did not return. Nov/Dec 1864 muster remarks: "Joined the cavalry in Miss. Deserted." However, he was paroled at Appomattox Court House on 4/9/1865 and still claiming to be a member of the 2nd Mississippi.

Roberts, Robert M.

CO: C	**Initial Rank:** Private	
Joined: Tuesday, October 1, 1861	**Term (yrs):** 1 **Occupation:**	**Age**
Enrolled at: Camp Fisher, VA	**Enrolled By:** Capt. Bromley	**Promoted:** No **ROH:** No
Born:	**Marital Status:**	**Residence**

Detached on hospital detail for much of service, thru last company muster (Jan/Feb 1865).

Roberts, Ruffin A.

CO: C	**Initial Rank:** Private	
Joined: Wednesday, May 1, 1861	**Term (yrs):** 1 **Occupation:** Farmer	**Age** 22
Enrolled at: Itawamba Co., MS	**Enrolled By:** Capt. Bromley	**Promoted:** Yes **ROH:** Yes
Born:	**Marital Status:**	**Residence**

Wounded at Malvern Hill on 7/1/1862 (severe contusion, left thigh). Returned to duty on 8/29/1862. Listed as 1st Corporal during Nov/Dec 1862 muster roll. Listed as 4th Sergeant during May/Jun 1863 muster. Killed in battle at Gettysburg on 7/1/1863. ROH for Seven Pines, 5/31/1862.

2nd Mississippi Alphabetical Roster (Annotated)

Robertson, James M.
CO: B **Initial Rank:** Private
Joined: Monday, March 3, 1862 **Term (yrs):** 3 **Occupation:** Farmer **Age** 18
Enrolled at: Ripley, MS **Enrolled By:** Capt. Buchanan **Promoted:** No **ROH:** No
Born: North Carolina **Marital Status:** S **Residence**

Killed in battle at Gettysburg on 7/1/1863.

Robinson, ?
CO: C **Initial Rank:**
Joined: **Term (yrs):** 0 **Occupation:** **Age**
Enrolled at: **Enrolled By:** **Promoted:** No **ROH:** No
Born: **Marital Status:** **Residence**

Appears on a Federal roll of prisoners of war at the hospitals in and about Gettysburg (not dated). Captured at Gettysburg. Remarks: "Died." No other record.

Robinson, Abner C.
CO: E **Initial Rank:** Private
Joined: Wednesday, May 1, 1861 **Term (yrs):** 1 **Occupation:** Farmer **Age** 23
Enrolled at: Itawamba Co., MS **Enrolled By:** Capt. Booth **Promoted:** No **ROH:** No
Born: Tennessee **Marital Status:** S **Residence** Danville, MS

Killed in battle at Sharpsburg on 9/17/1862 (actually listed on Federal records as having been mortally wounded and captured. Place of death at J. H. Grove's farm (not dated).

Robinson, Alfred
CO: K **Initial Rank:** Private
Joined: Saturday, March 1, 1862 **Term (yrs):** 3 **Occupation:** **Age** 22
Enrolled at: Iuka, MS **Enrolled By:** Lt. Latham **Promoted:** No **ROH:** No
Born: **Marital Status:** **Residence**

Deserted on 6/5/1863. Taken into Federal custody near Suffolk, VA on 6/8/1863. Was administered oath of allegiance on 6/24/1863.

Robinson, Ambrose
CO: K **Initial Rank:** Private
Joined: Saturday, March 1, 1862 **Term (yrs):** 3 **Occupation:** **Age** 32
Enrolled at: Iuka, MS **Enrolled By:** Lt. Latham **Promoted:** No **ROH:** No
Born: **Marital Status:** **Residence**

Wounded (gunshot in hand) at Gaines Mill on 6/27/1862. Furloughed for 60-days from 7/4/1862. Never returned. Listed as deserted in Mar/Apr 1863 muster roll.

2nd Mississippi Alphabetical Roster (Annotated)

Robinson, Arthur R.
CO: A **Initial Rank:** Private
Joined: Wednesday, May 1, 1861 **Term (yrs):** 1 **Occupation:** Mechanic **Age** 19
Enrolled at: Tishomingo Co., MS **Enrolled By:** Capt. Leeth **Promoted:** No **ROH:** No
Born: Tennessee **Marital Status:** **Residence**

Admitted to hospital in Charlottesville, VA on 10/13/1862 for wound in foot (date of wound or engagement not given in company records). Captured on 7/5/1863 at Gettysburg. Sent to Fort Delaware. Died in captivity of disease on 12/23/1863. Locality of grave: "Jersey Shore opposite Post."

Robinson, Cornelius
CO: D,F **Initial Rank:** Private
Joined: Wednesday, May 1, 1861 **Term (yrs):** 1 **Occupation:** Farmer **Age** 21
Enrolled at: Tippah Co., MS **Enrolled By:** Capt. Beck **Promoted:** No **ROH:** No
Born: **Marital Status:** S **Residence** Shelby Creek, MS

Transferred to Company F on 4/30/1862. Federal prisoner of war records show he was wounded and captured at Gettysburg on 7/1/1863. Sent to Fort Delaware where he died of disease on 10/16/1863.

Robinson, George W.
CO: K **Initial Rank:** Private
Joined: Thursday, May 16, 1861 **Term (yrs):** 1 **Occupation:** Wagoner **Age** 34
Enrolled at: Lynchburg, VA **Enrolled By:** Capt. Stone **Promoted:** No **ROH:** No
Born: Tennessee **Marital Status:** **Residence**

Discharged due to disability at Camp Fisher, VA on 10/19/1861 by order of General Smith.

Robinson, Marcus L.
CO: E **Initial Rank:** Jr. 2nd Lieutenant
Joined: Wednesday, May 1, 1861 **Term (yrs):** 1 **Occupation:** Mechanic **Age** 26
Enrolled at: Itawamba Co., MS **Enrolled By:** Capt. Booth **Promoted:** Yes **ROH:** No
Born: **Marital Status:** S **Residence** Guntown, MS

Elected Captain (April?) 1862. Resigned on 11/15/1862 due to disability.

Robinson, Michael
CO: F **Initial Rank:** Private
Joined: Wednesday, May 1, 1861 **Term (yrs):** 1 **Occupation:** Planter **Age** 23
Enrolled at: Tippah Co., MS **Enrolled By:** Capt. Davis **Promoted:** No **ROH:** No
Born: **Marital Status:** **Residence**

Captured at Gettysburg on 7/1/1863. Taken to Fort Delaware. Released on oath on 6/11/1865.

2nd Mississippi Alphabetical Roster (Annotated)

Robinson, Thomas H. B.
CO: D *Initial Rank:* Private
Joined: Saturday, April 27, 1861 *Term (yrs):* 1 *Occupation:* Farmer *Age* 24
Enrolled at: Pine Grove, MS *Enrolled By:* Capt. Beck *Promoted:* No *ROH:* No
Born: Tennessee *Marital Status:* S *Residence:* Salem, MS

Discharged due to disability on 3/6/1862.

Robinson, Thomas J. S.
CO: L *Initial Rank:* Private
Joined: Monday, March 3, 1862 *Term (yrs):* 3 *Occupation:* Farmer *Age* 18
Enrolled at: Ripley, MS *Enrolled By:* Capt. Powers *Promoted:* No *ROH:* Yes
Born: Mississippi *Marital Status:* S *Residence:* Dumas, MS

Accompanying list of engagements shows him wounded at Gettysburg on 7/1/1863 (not noted in company records). Killed in battle at Weldon Railroad on 8/19/1864. ROH for Weldon Railroad, 8/18/1864.

Robinson, William
CO: L *Initial Rank:* Private
Joined: Monday, March 3, 1862 *Term (yrs):* 3 *Occupation:* Farmer *Age* 31
Enrolled at: Ripley, MS *Enrolled By:* Col. Falkner *Promoted:* No *ROH:* No
Born: Mississippi *Marital Status:* M *Residence*

Discharged for disability at Richmond on 9/26/1863.

Rodgers, Benjamin
CO: G *Initial Rank:* Private
Joined: Thursday, March 20, 1862 *Term (yrs):* 3 *Occupation:* Farmer *Age* 35
Enrolled at: Pontotoc, MS *Enrolled By:* G. B. Mears *Promoted:* No *ROH:* No
Born: Alabama *Marital Status:* M *Residence:* Pontotoc, MS

Severely wounded (right leg) at Gettysburg on 7/1/1863 and captured on 7/5/1863 at Gettysburg. Paroled and exchanged (date unknown but admitted to hospital in Richmond on 9/29/1863). Furloughed for 20-days as of 10/15/1863. Listed as AWOL during Mar/Apr 1864 muster. During Jul/Aug 1864 muster, "Deserted by failing to return upon expiration of furlough."

2nd Mississippi Alphabetical Roster (Annotated)

Rodgers, James *CO:* B *Initial Rank:* Private
Joined: *Term (yrs):* 0 *Occupation:* *Age*
Enrolled at: *Enrolled By:* *Promoted:* No *ROH:* No
Born: *Marital Status:* *Residence*

Appears on a Federal roll of prisoners of war paroled at Vicksburg, MS, dated 7/10/1863. Captured at Vicksburg, MS on 7/4/1863. No other records. [This person is almost certainly misidentified — the regiment was never at Vicksburg. He may belong to the 2nd/6th Missouri Consolidated — the abbreviation would be the same "2 Miss Inf"].

Rodgers, James B. *CO:* C *Initial Rank:* Private
Joined: Wednesday, May 1, 1861 *Term (yrs):* 1 *Occupation:* Justice of the Peace *Age* 39
Enrolled at: Itawamba Co., MS *Enrolled By:* Capt. Bromley *Promoted:* No *ROH:* No
Born: *Marital Status:* *Residence*

Discharged (reason not given) on 10/29/1861.

Rodgers, Ransom *CO:* G *Initial Rank:* Private
Joined: *Term (yrs):* 0 *Occupation:* *Age*
Enrolled at: *Enrolled By:* *Promoted:* No *ROH:* No
Born: *Marital Status:* *Residence*

Appears on several Federal prisoner of war records. Rebel sick and wounded prisoners of war captured at Gettysburg on 7/5/1863 and sent to DeCamp General Hospital, Davids Island, NY Harbor. Paroled at DeCamp General Hospital and delivered to City Point, VA on 9/27/1863. No other records.

Rodgers, William E. *CO:* F *Initial Rank:* 1st Lieutenant
Joined: Wednesday, May 1, 1861 *Term (yrs):* 1 *Occupation:* Clerk *Age* 42
Enrolled at: Tippah Co., MS *Enrolled By:* Capt. Davis *Promoted:* No *ROH:* No
Born: *Marital Status:* *Residence*

Resigned due to disability on 7/16/1861 at Camp Bee, VA.

2nd Mississippi Alphabetical Roster (Annotated)

Rollin, Samuel
CO: C *Initial Rank:* Private
Joined: Tuesday, October 1, 1861 *Term (yrs):* 1 *Occupation:* *Age*
Enrolled at: Richmond, MS *Enrolled By:* Lt. Davenport *Promoted:* No *ROH:* No
Born: *Marital Status:* *Residence*

Admitted for gunshot wound to left arm to the hospital in Richmond on 5/10/1864 (date of wound or engagement not given in company records). Hospital records also show admission for wound to right arm above elbow joint on 6/5/1864 (again, company records provide no details). Returned to duty on 7/1/1864. Listed as present through Jan/Feb 1865 company muster.

Rollins, William R.
CO: A *Initial Rank:* Private
Joined: Saturday, March 1, 1862 *Term (yrs):* 3 *Occupation:* Farmer *Age* 33
Enrolled at: Jacinto, MS *Enrolled By:* Lt. Clayton *Promoted:* No *ROH:* No
Born: Tennessee *Marital Status:* M *Residence* Jacinto, MS

Wounded (left thigh) at Gettysburg on 7/1/1863 and captured on 7/5/1863. Paroled at DeCamp General Hospital, Davids Island, NY Harbor on 9/16/1863 to City Point, VA. Furloughed to MS. Did not return. Dropped from rolls as deserter on 12/31/1864.

Rook, Benjamin F.
CO: H *Initial Rank:* Private
Joined: Monday, April 29, 1861 *Term (yrs):* 1 *Occupation:* Farmer *Age* 26
Enrolled at: Pontotoc Co., MS *Enrolled By:* Capt. Taylor *Promoted:* Yes *ROH:* No
Born: South Carolina *Marital Status:* M *Residence* Tupelo, MS

Appointed 5th Sergeant on 4/22/1862. Wounded at Sharpsburg on 9/17/1862. In hospital at Winchester, VA. Captured and paroled while in hospital at Winchester (paroled on 12/4/1862). Furloughed. Returned to duty. Accidentally wounded on 6/23/1864. Sent to hospital in Richmond. Furloughed 40-days from 7/30/1864. Discharged by ruling of medical examining board for disability due to wounds. Dated Okolona, MS on 4/12/1865. Surrendered and paroled at Citronelle, AL. Dated 5/20/1865 at Mobile, AL ("Stragglers of Berry's Regiment, Confederate States Army").

Rook, John H.
CO: H *Initial Rank:* Private
Joined: Monday, April 29, 1861 *Term (yrs):* 1 *Occupation:* Farmer *Age* 22
Enrolled at: Pontotoc Co., MS *Enrolled By:* Capt. Taylor *Promoted:* No *ROH:* No
Born: South Carolina *Marital Status:* S *Residence* Tupelo, MS

Discharged due to disability on 1/28/1862 at Camp Fisher, VA by order of General Whiting.

2nd Mississippi Alphabetical Roster (Annotated)

Rooker, John C.   CO: D   Initial Rank: Private
Joined: Saturday, March 9, 1861   **Term (yrs):** 0   **Occupation:**   **Age**
Enrolled at: Toombs Store, MS   **Enrolled By:** John McGuirk   **Promoted:** No   **ROH:** No
Born: **Marital Status:**   **Residence**

Appears on a company muster roll. No other record.

Roper, H.   CO: E   Initial Rank: Private
Joined: **Term (yrs):** 0   **Occupation:**   **Age**
Enrolled at: **Enrolled By:**   **Promoted:** No   **ROH:** No
Born: **Marital Status:**   **Residence**

Appears on a Federal roll of prisoners of war. Surrendered and paroled. Dated 5/17/1865 at Columbus, MS. Residence listed as Itawamba, Co., MS. No other record. [Same person as S. Roper?]

Roper, S.   CO: E   Initial Rank: Private
Joined: **Term (yrs):** 0   **Occupation:**   **Age**
Enrolled at: **Enrolled By:**   **Promoted:** No   **ROH:** No
Born: **Marital Status:**   **Residence**

Appears on a Federal roll of prisoners of war. Surrendered and paroled. Dated 5/17/1865 at Columbus, MS. Residence listed as Itawamba, Co., MS. No other record. [same person as H. Roper?]

Rose, Francis M.   CO: I   Initial Rank: Private
Joined: Tuesday, September 10, 1861   **Term (yrs):** 1   **Occupation:** Farmer   **Age** 22
Enrolled at: Guntown, MS   **Enrolled By:** Lt. Davenport   **Promoted:** No   **ROH:** No
Born: Georgia   **Marital Status:**   **Residence**

Wounded (left thigh) at Gettysburg on 7/1/1863. Sent to hospital at Richmond, VA. Furloughed. Discharged due to disability caused by wounds on 7/23/1864.

Rose, John P.   CO: A   Initial Rank: Private
Joined: Wednesday, May 1, 1861   **Term (yrs):** 1   **Occupation:** Laborer   **Age** 25
Enrolled at: Tishomingo Co., MS   **Enrolled By:** Capt. Leeth   **Promoted:** No   **ROH:** No
Born: **Marital Status:** M   **Residence** Burnsville, MS

Mortally wounded at 1st Manassas on 7/21/1861. Died of wounds on 8/1/1861 (or 8/2/1861) at Manassas, VA.

2nd Mississippi Alphabetical Roster (Annotated)

Ross, Robert N.
CO: D,F **Initial Rank:** Private
Joined: Wednesday, May 1, 1861 **Term (yrs):** 1 **Occupation:** Farmer **Age** 20
Enrolled at: Tippah Co., MS **Enrolled By:** Capt. Beck **Promoted:** No **ROH:** No
Born: Mississippi **Marital Status:** S **Residence** Pine Grove, MS

Also see Capt. Ahls Battery, United States Army. Wounded at 1st Manassas on 7/21/1861. Returned to duty. Transferred to Company F on 4/30/1862. Transferred back to Company D on 5/1/1862. Deserted on 6/30/1863 at Cashtown, PA from camp. Taken into custody by Federal forces and sent to Fort Delaware. Became a "Galvanized Yankee" and joined U.S. Service. Discharged from Fort Delaware on 8/1/1863.

Ross, William C
CO: D **Initial Rank:** Private
Joined: Tuesday, October 1, 1861 **Term (yrs):** 1 **Occupation:** Farmer **Age** 46
Enrolled at: Iuka, MS **Enrolled By:** Lt. Davenport **Promoted:** No **ROH:** No
Born: Tennessee **Marital Status:** M **Residence** Pine Grove, MS

Discharged on 2/7/1862 for disability at Camp Fisher, VA.

Rowell, James C.
CO: B **Initial Rank:** Private
Joined: Wednesday, May 1, 1861 **Term (yrs):** 1 **Occupation:** Farmer **Age** 24
Enrolled at: Tippah Co., MS **Enrolled By:** Capt. Buchanan **Promoted:** No **ROH:** No
Born: **Marital Status:** **Residence**

Listed as "present" during most of company musters. Captured near Petersburg (Hatcher's Run?) on 4/2/1865. Taken to Point Lookout, MD. Released on oath on 6/17/1865.

Rowland, Henry M.
CO: K **Initial Rank:** Private
Joined: Saturday, March 1, 1862 **Term (yrs):** 3 **Occupation:** **Age** 22
Enrolled at: Iuka, MS **Enrolled By:** Lt. Latham **Promoted:** No **ROH:** No
Born: **Marital Status:** **Residence**

Wounded (right hip) at Gettysburg on 7/1/1863. Captured on 7/5/1863. Paroled at DeCamp General Hospital, Davids Island, NY Harbor and taken to City Point, VA for exchange on 10/28/1863. Furloughed for 20-days from 11/11/1863. Did not return. Listed as deserted for prolonged AWOL during Mar/Apr 1864 muster roll.

2nd Mississippi Alphabetical Roster (Annotated)

Rucker, Abbott C.
CO: F **Initial Rank:** 2nd Lieutenant

Joined: Monday, March 4, 1861 **Term (yrs):** 0 **Occupation:** **Age**

Enrolled at: Ripley, MS **Enrolled By:** J. R. Chalmers **Promoted:** No **ROH:** No

Born: **Marital Status:** **Residence**

Appears on a company muster roll. No other record.

Rucker, John W.
CO: H **Initial Rank:** Private

Joined: Saturday, March 1, 1862 **Term (yrs):** 3 **Occupation:** Farmer **Age** 18

Enrolled at: Chesterville, MS **Enrolled By:** Lt. Porter **Promoted:** No **ROH:** No

Born: Alabama **Marital Status:** S **Residence** Chesterville, MS

Captured in battle at Falling Waters, MD on 7/14/1863. Taken to Point Lookout, MD. Became "Galvanized Yankee" and joined U. S. Service on 1/26/1864. Deserted.

Ruse, James O.
CO: A **Initial Rank:** Private

Joined: Wednesday, May 1, 1861 **Term (yrs):** 1 **Occupation:** Farmer **Age** 26

Enrolled at: Corinth, MS **Enrolled By:** Capt. Leeth **Promoted:** No **ROH:** No

Born: **Marital Status:** **Residence**

Discharged on 5/28/1861 due to disability by order of General Johnston.

Rutledge, Walter G.
CO: B, S **Initial Rank:** Private

Joined: Wednesday, May 1, 1861 **Term (yrs):** 1 **Occupation:** Mail carrier **Age** 20

Enrolled at: Tippah Co., MS **Enrolled By:** Capt. Buchanan **Promoted:** Yes **ROH:** No

Born: **Marital Status:** **Residence**

Appointed Sergeant Major of regiment from 10/28/1861. Admitted to hospital in Richmond with wound on 3/9/1865.

Ryan, Ed
CO: **Initial Rank:** Private

Joined: **Term (yrs):** 0 **Occupation:** **Age**

Enrolled at: **Enrolled By:** **Promoted:** No **ROH:** No

Born: **Marital Status:** **Residence**

Appears on a Federal register of prisoners of war captured at Wild Cat, KY. Remarks: "Released on taking oath." [Misidentified. Not likely a member of the 2nd Mississippi].

2nd Mississippi Alphabetical Roster (Annotated)

Rye, Thomas J. *CO:* G *Initial Rank:* 3rd Corporal
Joined: Wednesday, May 1, 1861 *Term (yrs):* 1 *Occupation:* Clerk *Age* 21
Enrolled at: Pontotoc Co., MS *Enrolled By:* Capt. Kilpatrick *Promoted:* Yes *ROH:* No
Born: Mississippi *Marital Status:* S *Residence* Pontotoc, MS

Also see Patrick McNally (his substitute). Appointed 3rd Sergeant on 5/10/1862. Discharged by reason of having furnished a substitute on 12/1/1862.

Salmon, Richard T. *CO:* I *Initial Rank:* Private
Joined: Wednesday, May 1, 1861 *Term (yrs):* 1 *Occupation:* Farmer *Age* 25
Enrolled at: Pontotoc Co., MS *Enrolled By:* Capt. Herring *Promoted:* No *ROH:* No
Born: *Marital Status:* *Residence*

Died of disease (typhoid fever pneumonia) on 11/61/1861 at Camp Fisher, VA.

Sampson, G. W. *CO:* I *Initial Rank:* Private
Joined: *Term (yrs):* 0 *Occupation:* *Age*
Enrolled at: *Enrolled By:* *Promoted:* No *ROH:* No
Born: *Marital Status:* *Residence*

Appears on a Federal roll of prisoners of war paroled at DeCamp General Hospital, Davids Island, NY Harbor. Captured at Gettysburg on 7/5/1863. Transported to City Point, VA to await exchange on 9/16/1863. No other records.

Sanders, John A. *CO:* C, H *Initial Rank:* Private
Joined: Wednesday, May 1, 1861 *Term (yrs):* 1 *Occupation:* Farmer *Age* 30
Enrolled at: Itawamba Co., MS *Enrolled By:* Capt. Bromley *Promoted:* No *ROH:* No
Born: *Marital Status:* M *Residence* Verona, MS

Transferred to Company H in June 1863. Wounded at Williamsport, MD (Falling Waters?) — not dated. Admitted to hospital in Richmond for gunshot wound of right forefinger (requiring amputation) on 7/17/1863. Furloughed for 30-days from 9/7/1863. Did not return. Listed as deserted during Mar/Apr 1864 muster.

2nd Mississippi Alphabetical Roster (Annotated)

Sanderson, H. S. *CO:* K *Initial Rank:* Private
Joined: *Term (yrs):* 0 *Occupation:* *Age*
Enrolled at: *Enrolled By:* *Promoted:* No *ROH:* No
Born: *Marital Status:* *Residence*

Appears on a Federal register of prisoners of war. Dated Memphis, TN on 6/3/1863. Captured at Florence, AL on 5/29/1863. Sent to Alton, IL on 6/5/1863. No other record.

Sanderson, J. H. *CO:* B *Initial Rank:* Private
Joined: *Term (yrs):* 0 *Occupation:* *Age*
Enrolled at: *Enrolled By:* *Promoted:* No *ROH:* No
Born: *Marital Status:* *Residence*

Appears on a Federal roll of prisoners of war surrendered and paroled at Columbus, MS on 5/19/1865. No other record.

Sargent, Aaron T. *CO:* C *Initial Rank:* Private
Joined: Tuesday, October 1, 1861 *Term (yrs):* 1 *Occupation:* *Age*
Enrolled at: Richmond, MS *Enrolled By:* Lt. Davenport *Promoted:* No *ROH:* Yes
Born: *Marital Status:* *Residence*

Also see Company C, Inge's Regiment Mississippi Cavalry. Furloughed from hospital for 60-days from 8/23/1863. Did not return (according to records). Company records list him as deserted for Jan/Feb 1865 muster. However, he appears to have obtained a transfer, dated 1/10/1865, to Inge's Cavalry Regiment. ROH for Talley's Mill, 5/10/1864 (inconsistent if he did not return from 8/23/1863; given ROH citation, assume he did return to regiment prior to transfer to cavalry).

Sargent, James L. *CO:* C *Initial Rank:* 2nd Lieutenant
Joined: Wednesday, May 1, 1861 *Term (yrs):* 1 *Occupation:* Farmer *Age* 28
Enrolled at: Itawamba Co., MS *Enrolled By:* Capt. Bromley *Promoted:* No *ROH:* No
Born: *Marital Status:* *Residence*

No record after Jan/Feb 1862 muster roll.

Sargent, John *CO:* C *Initial Rank:* Private
Joined: Wednesday, May 1, 1861 *Term (yrs):* 1 *Occupation:* Farmer *Age* 22
Enrolled at: Itawamba Co., MS *Enrolled By:* Capt. Bromley *Promoted:* No *ROH:* No
Born: *Marital Status:* *Residence*

Captured at Gettysburg on 7/1/1863. Taken to Point Lookout, MD. Died in captivity on 4/22/1864 of disease.

2nd Mississippi Alphabetical Roster (Annotated)

Sargent, Phillip O.   *CO:* C   *Initial Rank:* Private

Joined: Tuesday, October 1, 1861   *Term (yrs):* 1   *Occupation:* Farmer   *Age* 19

Enrolled at: Richmond, MS   *Enrolled By:* Lt. Davenport   *Promoted:* No   *ROH:* No

Born: Alabama   *Marital Status:*   *Residence*

Discharged due to disability at Camp Fisher, VA on 2/26/1862.

Sargent, Romulus D.   *CO:* C   *Initial Rank:* Private

Joined: Wednesday, May 1, 1861   *Term (yrs):* 1   *Occupation:* Farmer   *Age* 22

Enrolled at: Itawamba Co., MS   *Enrolled By:* Capt. Bromley   *Promoted:* Yes   *ROH:* No

Born: *Marital Status:*   *Residence*

Elected 2nd Lieutenant on 4/22/1862. Wounded at 2nd Manassas on 8/29/1862. Sent to hospital. Returned to duty. Listed as 1st Lieutenant during Sep/Oct 1862 muster roll. Captured at Gettysburg on 7/1/1863 (listed as Captain on Jul/Aug 1863 muster roll). Sent to Johnson's Island, OH. Paroled and forwarded to Point Lookout, MD for exchange on 3/14/1865.

Sargent, Wilburn   *CO:* B   *Initial Rank:* Private

Joined: Wednesday, May 1, 1861   *Term (yrs):* 1   *Occupation:* Student   *Age* 18

Enrolled at: Tippah Co., MS   *Enrolled By:* Capt. Buchanan   *Promoted:* No   *ROH:* No

Born: *Marital Status:*   *Residence*

Wounded in battle at 1st Manassas on 7/21/1861. Furloughed from 8/25/1861. Returned to duty. Placed in confinement and hard labor for 6-months, circa Jan/Feb 1864 muster. Deserted near Walthall Junction, VA on 6/19/1864.

Sargent, William J.   *CO:* C   *Initial Rank:* Private

Joined: Wednesday, February 27, 1861   *Term (yrs):* 0   *Occupation:*   *Age*

Enrolled at: Verona, MS   *Enrolled By:* Capt. Kilpatrick   *Promoted:* No   *ROH:* No

Born: *Marital Status:*   *Residence*

Appears on a company muster roll. No other record.

2nd Mississippi Alphabetical Roster (Annotated)

Saunders, J. S.　　　　　　　　　　　　　　　　　*CO:*　　　*Initial Rank:* Private
Joined:　　　　　　　　　　　*Term (yrs):* 0　*Occupation:*　　　　　　　　　　*Age*
Enrolled at:　　　　　　　*Enrolled By:*　　　　　　　*Promoted:* No　*ROH:* No
Born:　　　　　　　*Marital Status:*　　　　　　*Residence*

Appears on a Federal register of prisoners of war. Dated Memphis, TN on 5/7/1863. Captured at Tupelo, MS on (not dated). Sent to Alton, IL on 5/22/1863. No other records.

Saunders, James W.　　　　　　　　　　　　　　　*CO:* F　*Initial Rank:* 2nd Sergeant
Joined: Wednesday, May 1, 1861　　*Term (yrs):* 1　*Occupation:* Planter　　　*Age* 23
Enrolled at: Tippah Co., MS　*Enrolled By:* Capt. Davis　　　*Promoted:* Yes　*ROH:* No
Born: South Carolina　*Marital Status:* S　　　*Residence*

Appointed Orderly Sergeant on 6/1/1861. Elected 1st Lieutenant on 4/11/1862 and took command on 4/22/1862. Wounded at Sharpsburg on 9/17/1862. Furloughed 30-days. Returned to duty. Wounded in battle at Gettysburg on 7/3/1863. Captured on 7/5/1863. Sent to Johnson's Island, OH. Paroled and forwarded to Point Lookout, MD for exchange on 3/14/1865.

Saunders, John W.　　　　　　　　　　　　　　　　*CO:* D　*Initial Rank:* Private
Joined: Friday, March 8, 1861　　*Term (yrs):* 0　*Occupation:*　　　　　　　*Age*
Enrolled at: Toombs Store, MS　*Enrolled By:* John McGuirk　*Promoted:* No　*ROH:* No
Born:　　　　　　*Marital Status:*　　　　　　*Residence*

Appears on a company muster roll. No other record.

Saunders, Michael H.　　　　　　　　　　　　　　　*CO:* B, L　*Initial Rank:* Private
Joined: Wednesday, May 1, 1861　　*Term (yrs):* 1　*Occupation:* Student　　*Age* 25
Enrolled at: Tippah Co., MS　*Enrolled By:* Capt. Buchanan　*Promoted:* No　*ROH:* No
Born: Kentucky　*Marital Status:* S　　　*Residence*

Discharged for disability on 8/25/1861. Apparently re-enlisted in Company L on 3/3/1862 for 3-years at Ripley, MS by Col. Falkner. Transferred back to Company B same day. Captured at Gettysburg on 7/1/1863. Sent to Fort Delaware. Released on oath on 6/11/1865.

2nd Mississippi Alphabetical Roster (Annotated)

Saunders, Thomas
CO: D *Initial Rank:* Private
Joined: Wednesday, May 1, 1861 *Term (yrs):* 1 *Occupation:* Farmer *Age* 23
Enrolled at: Tippah Co., MS *Enrolled By:* Capt. Beck *Promoted:* No *ROH:* No
Born: Mississippi *Marital Status:* M *Residence* Pine Grove, MS

Discharged on 5/20/1861 for disability.

Saunders, Thomas J.
CO: B,F *Initial Rank:* Private
Joined: Monday, March 3, 1862 *Term (yrs):* 3 *Occupation:* Farmer *Age* 21
Enrolled at: Ripley, MS *Enrolled By:* Capt. Buchanan *Promoted:* No *ROH:* No
Born: South Carolina *Marital Status:* S *Residence*

Transferred to Company F on 4/30/1862. Wounded at Sharpsburg on 9/17/1862. Furloughed 30-days from 10/11/1862. Returned to duty. Killed at Gettysburg on 7/1/1863.

Scales, Alfred M.
CO: C *Initial Rank:* 3rd Corporal
Joined: Wednesday, May 1, 1861 *Term (yrs):* 1 *Occupation:* Clerk *Age* 20
Enrolled at: Itawamba Co., MS *Enrolled By:* Capt. Bromley *Promoted:* Yes *ROH:* No
Born: *Marital Status:* *Residence*

Appointed 3rd Sergeant on 8/1/1861. Confirmed on 4/23/1862. Listed as 1st Sergeant during Jul/Aug 1862 muster. Wounded at 2nd Manassas on 8/29/1862 according to company records. However, hospital records show admission for a wound on 7/6/1863 [company records may be incorrect — or, he may have been wounded in Gettysburg also]. Furloughed. Returned to duty per Jan/Feb 1864 muster roll. No records afterward.

Scales, P. A.
CO: C *Initial Rank:* Private
Joined: Tuesday, October 1, 1861 *Term (yrs):* 1 *Occupation:* *Age*
Enrolled at: Camp Fisher, VA *Enrolled By:* Capt. Bromley *Promoted:* Yes *ROH:* No
Born: *Marital Status:* *Residence*

Ordered to take command of Company C on 4/22/1862, appointed Captain from the ranks. Resigned on 10/2/1862 due to ill health.

2nd Mississippi Alphabetical Roster (Annotated)

Scales, R. E.
CO: C **Initial Rank:** Private
Joined: Sunday, September 1, 1861 **Term (yrs):** 1 **Occupation:** **Age**
Enrolled at: Camp Jones, VA **Enrolled By:** Capt. Bromley **Promoted:** No **ROH:** No
Born: **Marital Status:** **Residence**

Wounded (left foot) in battle at Gaines Mill on 6/27/1862. Died of wounds at Richmond, VA on 9/24/1862 (leg required amputation on 7/30/1862). [*Buried in Hollywood Cemetery, Richmond, VA. Soldiers Section S Lot: 152.]

Scalley, George W.
CO: B **Initial Rank:** Private
Joined: Wednesday, September 18, 1861 **Term (yrs):** 1 **Occupation:** Mechanic **Age** 24
Enrolled at: Ripley, MS **Enrolled By:** Lt. Davenport **Promoted:** No **ROH:** No
Born: Tennessee **Marital Status:** **Residence**

Discharged due to disability at Camp Fisher, VA on 1/1/1862.

Scally, John N.
CO: B **Initial Rank:** 2nd Lieutenant
Joined: Wednesday, May 1, 1861 **Term (yrs):** 1 **Occupation:** Lawyer **Age** 28
Enrolled at: Tippah Co., MS **Enrolled By:** Col. Falkner **Promoted:** No **ROH:** No
Born: **Marital Status:** **Residence**

Wounded by shell fragment in arm and side (three ribs broken) at battle of 1st Manassas on 7/21/1861. Returned to duty on 8/4/1861. Relieved of command due to reorganization of company and regiment on 4/23/1862. Discharged.

Scott, Bowland C.
CO: I **Initial Rank:** Private
Joined: Friday, May 31, 1861 **Term (yrs):** 1 **Occupation:** Teacher **Age** 25
Enrolled at: Harpers Ferry, VA **Enrolled By:** Capt. Herring **Promoted:** No **ROH:** No
Born: **Marital Status:** **Residence**

Died of pneumonia at Camp Fisher, VA on 9/29/1861. [Same person as Charles R. Scott?]

Scott, Charles R.
CO: I **Initial Rank:** Private
Joined: Wednesday, May 1, 1861 **Term (yrs):** 1 **Occupation:** Farmer **Age** 25
Enrolled at: Pontotoc Co., MS **Enrolled By:** Capt. Herring **Promoted:** No **ROH:** No
Born: South Carolina **Marital Status:** **Residence**

Died of disease (typhoid fever) at Camp Fisher, VA on 9/22/1861. [Same person as Bowland C. Scott?]

2nd Mississippi Alphabetical Roster (Annotated)

Scott, James M.   *CO:* I   *Initial Rank:* Private
Joined: Wednesday, May 1, 1861   *Term (yrs):* 1   *Occupation:* Farmer   *Age* 26
Enrolled at: Pontotoc Co., MS   *Enrolled By:* Capt. Herring   *Promoted:* No   *ROH:* Yes
Born: Georgia   *Marital Status:*   *Residence*

Killed in battle at Gaines Mill on 6/27/1862. ROH for Gaines Mill, 6/27/1862.

Scott, Samuel B.   *CO:* E   *Initial Rank:* Private
Joined: Wednesday, May 1, 1861   *Term (yrs):* 1   *Occupation:* Farmer   *Age* 19
Enrolled at: Itawamba Co., MS   *Enrolled By:* Capt. Booth   *Promoted:* No   *ROH:* No
Born: *Marital Status:* M   *Residence* Guntown, MS

Captured near Petersburg (Hatcher's Run?) on 4/2/1865. Taken to Point Lookout, MD. Released on oath on 6/19/1865.

Scott, William   *CO:* E   *Initial Rank:* Private
Joined: Wednesday, May 1, 1861   *Term (yrs):* 1   *Occupation:* Farmer   *Age* 21
Enrolled at: Itawamba Co., MS   *Enrolled By:* Capt. Booth   *Promoted:* No   *ROH:* No
Born: *Marital Status:* S   *Residence* Guntown, MS

Died of disease at Camp Jones, VA on 8/11/1861.

Seaker, J. M.   *CO:* B   *Initial Rank:* Private
Joined: *Term (yrs):* 0   *Occupation:*   *Age*
Enrolled at: *Enrolled By:*   *Promoted:* No   *ROH:* No
Born: *Marital Status:*   *Residence*

Appears on a Federal roll of prisoners of war in custody of the Provost Marshal, Memphis, TN. Captured at Tupelo, MS on 5/7/1863. Sent to Alton, IL on 5/22/1863. No other records.

Seargeant, James R.   *CO:* B   *Initial Rank:* Private
Joined: Monday, March 3, 1862   *Term (yrs):* 3   *Occupation:* Farmer   *Age* 33
Enrolled at: Ripley, MS   *Enrolled By:* Capt. Buchanan   *Promoted:* No   *ROH:* No
Born: Tennessee   *Marital Status:* M   *Residence*

Wounded in battle at South Mountain, MD (not dated). Sent to hospital. Returned to duty. Wounded (in hand) on 6/2/1862. Sent to hospital. Returned to duty. Hospital records indicated admission on 7/9/1863 with wound (company records do not indicate date of wound or action). Captured at Petersburg (Hatcher's Run?) on 4/2/2865. Sent to Fort Delaware. Released on oath on 6/11/1865.

2nd Mississippi Alphabetical Roster (Annotated)

Sellers, C.
CO: A *Initial Rank:* Private
Joined: Saturday, March 1, 1862 *Term (yrs):* 3 *Occupation:* *Age* 24
Enrolled at: Jacinto, MS *Enrolled By:* Lt. Clayton *Promoted:* No *ROH:* No
Born: *Marital Status:* *Residence*

Listed as deserted on 3/1/1862 (the day he enlisted).

Sellman, Benjamin T.
CO: E *Initial Rank:* Private
Joined: Wednesday, May 1, 1861 *Term (yrs):* 1 *Occupation:* Farmer *Age* 18
Enrolled at: Itawamba Co., MS *Enrolled By:* Capt. Booth *Promoted:* No *ROH:* No
Born: *Marital Status:* *Residence* Guntown, MS

Also see 17th Mississippi Infantry Regiment. Transferred to the 17th Mississippi July 1861.

Selph, Montgomery C.
CO: D, F *Initial Rank:* Private
Joined: Wednesday, May 1, 1861 *Term (yrs):* 1 *Occupation:* Farmer *Age* 22
Enrolled at: Tippah Co., MS *Enrolled By:* Capt. Beck *Promoted:* Yes *ROH:* No
Born: *Marital Status:* S *Residence* Hickory Flat, MS

Wounded at 1st Manassas on 7/21/1861. In hospital at Richmond, VA. Returned to duty. Transferred to Company F on 4/30/1862. Promoted to 2nd Corporal on 7/31/1862. Appointed 5th Sergeant on 10/1/1862. Listed as AWOL for last (Jan/Feb 1865) muster (was furloughed 3/19/1864 for 60-days due to illness).

Shackleford, W. A. H.
CO: H *Initial Rank:* Captain
Joined: *Term (yrs):* 0 *Occupation:* *Age*
Enrolled at: *Enrolled By:* *Promoted:* No *ROH:* No
Born: *Marital Status:* *Residence*

From Reference envelope, See also W. A. H. Shackleford, 26th Mississippi Infantry Regiment. No other record.

Shackleford, William H.
CO: E *Initial Rank:* Private
Joined: Wednesday, May 1, 1861 *Term (yrs):* 1 *Occupation:* Carpenter *Age* 26
Enrolled at: Itawamba Co., MS *Enrolled By:* Capt. Booth *Promoted:* No *ROH:* No
Born: Georgia *Marital Status:* S *Residence* Guntown, MS

Died of disease at Franklin, VA on 3/15/1863.

2nd Mississippi Alphabetical Roster (Annotated)

Shankle, Irvin
CO: D **Initial Rank:** Private
Joined: Saturday, March 9, 1861 **Term (yrs):** 0 **Occupation:** **Age**
Enrolled at: Toombs Store, MS **Enrolled By:** John McGuirk **Promoted:** No **ROH:** No
Born: **Marital Status:** **Residence**

Appears on a company muster roll. No other record.

Shannaha, J.
CO: **Initial Rank:** Private
Joined: **Term (yrs):** 0 **Occupation:** **Age**
Enrolled at: **Enrolled By:** **Promoted:** No **ROH:** No
Born: **Marital Status:** **Residence**

Appears on Federal prisoner of war records. Captured at Yorktown, VA on 5/13/1862. Paroled and exchanged at Aiken's Landing, VA on 8/5/1862. No other records.

Sheehorn, C. L.
CO: A **Initial Rank:** Private
Joined: Saturday, March 1, 1862 **Term (yrs):** 3 **Occupation:** **Age** 27
Enrolled at: Jacinto, MS **Enrolled By:** Lt. Clayton **Promoted:** No **ROH:** No
Born: **Marital Status:** **Residence**

Apparently died of disease about June 1862 (was listed as sick in hospital in prior musters — reference card dated 6/10/1862, labeled Shehorn - C.L., Co. A. 2nd Miss. "For burial." [*Buried in Hollywood Cemetery, Richmond, VA. Note says died 5/24/1862. Buried in Soldiers Section J Lot: 113.]

Sheehorn, Michael
CO: A **Initial Rank:** Private
Joined: Saturday, March 1, 1862 **Term (yrs):** 3 **Occupation:** **Age** 21
Enrolled at: Jacinto, MS **Enrolled By:** Lt. Clayton **Promoted:** No **ROH:** No
Born: **Marital Status:** S **Residence**

Also see 26th Mississippi Infantry Regiment. Wounded at Gaines Mill on 6/27/1862. Returned to his original regiment about October 1862.

2nd Mississippi Alphabetical Roster (Annotated)

Shelton, Elijah H.
CO: G **Initial Rank:** Private
Joined: Thursday, March 20, 1862 **Term (yrs):** 3 **Occupation:** Farmer **Age** 20
Enrolled at: Pontotoc, MS **Enrolled By:** G. B. Mears **Promoted:** No **ROH:** No
Born: Tennessee **Marital Status:** S **Residence** Pontotoc, MS

Wounded (in thigh) at The Wilderness on 5/5/1864. Furloughed from hospital for 30-days from 6/18/1864. Did not return. Marked as deserted, dropped from the rolls for prolonged AWOL by order of Col. Stone (Nov/Dec, 1864 muster).

Shelton, Patrick
CO: H **Initial Rank:** Private
Joined: Tuesday, March 18, 1862 **Term (yrs):** 3 **Occupation:** **Age** 31
Enrolled at: Chesterville, MS **Enrolled By:** Lt. Porter **Promoted:** No **ROH:** No
Born: **Marital Status:** **Residence**

Died of disease (pneumonia) in the hospital at Lynchburg, VA on 4/7/1862.

Sherrill, Samuel P.
CO: A **Initial Rank:** Private
Joined: Wednesday, February 20, 1861 **Term (yrs):** 0 **Occupation:** **Age**
Enrolled at: Corinth, MS **Enrolled By:** R. Griffith **Promoted:** No **ROH:** No
Born: **Marital Status:** **Residence**

Appears on a company muster roll. No other record.

Shields, Bassel S.
CO: K **Initial Rank:** Private
Joined: Wednesday, May 1, 1861 **Term (yrs):** 1 **Occupation:** Farmer **Age** 19
Enrolled at: Tishomingo Co., MS **Enrolled By:** Capt. Stone **Promoted:** No **ROH:** No
Born: Tennessee **Marital Status:** **Residence**

Listed as "absent wounded" for May/Jun 1862 muster roll (date of wound or engagement not given). Severely wounded at Sharpsburg on 9/17/1862 (requiring amputation of left arm at shoulder joint). Furloughed from hospital for 60-days from 12/9/1862. Discharged for disability due to wounds by order of General Lee on 8/6/1863.

Shirley, Newton N.
CO: I **Initial Rank:** Private
Joined: Tuesday, September 10, 1861 **Term (yrs):** 1 **Occupation:** **Age** 26
Enrolled at: Guntown, MS **Enrolled By:** Lt. Davenport **Promoted:** No **ROH:** No
Born: South Carolina **Marital Status:** **Residence**

Killed in battle at Gettysburg on 7/1/1863.

2nd Mississippi Alphabetical Roster (Annotated)

Shole, William
CO: E *Initial Rank:* Private
Joined: Wednesday, May 1, 1861 *Term (yrs):* 1 *Occupation:* *Age* 23
Enrolled at: Itawamba Co., MS *Enrolled By:* Capt. Booth *Promoted:* No *ROH:* No
Born: *Marital Status:* *Residence*

Appears on a company muster-in roll. No other record.

Shone, Joseph A.
CO: D *Initial Rank:* Private
Joined: Wednesday, May 1, 1861 *Term (yrs):* 1 *Occupation:* Mechanic *Age* 32
Enrolled at: Tippah Co., MS *Enrolled By:* Capt. Beck *Promoted:* No *ROH:* No
Born: *Marital Status:* S *Residence* Salem, MS

Discharged due to disability on 8/30/1861.

Shook, W. M.
CO: K *Initial Rank:* Corporal
Joined: *Term (yrs):* 0 *Occupation:* *Age*
Enrolled at: *Enrolled By:* *Promoted:* No *ROH:* No
Born: *Marital Status:* *Residence*

Reference envelope: See also Alfred M. Shook, 4th (McLemore's) Tennessee Cavalry. No other record.

Short, Calvin
CO: A *Initial Rank:* Private
Joined: Saturday, March 1, 1862 *Term (yrs):* 3 *Occupation:* Farmer *Age* 19
Enrolled at: Jacinto, MS *Enrolled By:* Lt. Clayton *Promoted:* No *ROH:* No
Born: *Marital Status:* S *Residence*

Wounded at 2nd Manassas on 8/29/1862. Furloughed. Did not return. Nov/Dec 1863 muster remarks: "Deserted since Nov 1st, 1863 — Supposed to be in Northern Alabama."

Short, Ruben L.
CO: B *Initial Rank:* Private
Joined: Monday, March 3, 1862 *Term (yrs):* 3 *Occupation:* Laborer *Age* 30
Enrolled at: Ripley, MS *Enrolled By:* Capt. Buchanan *Promoted:* No *ROH:* No
Born: Tennessee *Marital Status:* M *Residence*

Died of disease in hospital at Lynchburg, VA on 7/4/1862.

2nd Mississippi Alphabetical Roster (Annotated)

Shuttlesworth, Joseph W.

CO: I **Initial Rank:** Private

Joined: Friday, May 31, 1861 **Term (yrs):** 1 **Occupation:** Farmer **Age** 30

Enrolled at: Harpers Ferry, VA **Enrolled By:** Capt. Herring **Promoted:** No **ROH:** No

Born: South Carolina **Marital Status:** **Residence**

Killed in battle at Sharpsburg on 9/17/1862 according to company records. However, Federal records show his name on a parole of prisoners of war, dated 9/27/1862.

Shuttleworth, George W.

CO: I **Initial Rank:** Private

Joined: Wednesday, May 1, 1861 **Term (yrs):** 1 **Occupation:** Farmer **Age** 26

Enrolled at: Pontotoc Co., MS **Enrolled By:** Capt. Herring **Promoted:** No **ROH:** No

Born: **Marital Status:** **Residence**

Captured at Falling Waters, MD on 7/14/1863. Taken to Point Lookout, MD. Exchanged on 2/10/1865. Listed as on parole furlough for last company muster (Jan/Feb 1865).

Simmons, John J.

CO: H **Initial Rank:** Private

Joined: Saturday, August 10, 1861 **Term (yrs):** 1 **Occupation:** Dentist **Age** 37

Enrolled at: Camp Jones, VA **Enrolled By:** Lt. Stone **Promoted:** No **ROH:** No

Born: Alabama **Marital Status:** M **Residence** Tupelo, MS

Discharged due to disability — over age — on 4/23/1862.

Simmons, R. A.

CO: I **Initial Rank:** Private

Joined: **Term (yrs):** 0 **Occupation:** **Age**

Enrolled at: **Enrolled By:** **Promoted:** No **ROH:** No

Born: **Marital Status:** **Residence**

Appears on a Federal roll of prisoners of war received at Fort Delaware from City Point, VA. On 4/4/1865. Captured at Petersburg (Hatcher's Run?) on 4/2/1865. No other record.

2nd Mississippi Alphabetical Roster (Annotated)

Simpson, George W.

CO: H,I **Initial Rank:** Private

Joined: Saturday, March 1, 1862 **Term (yrs):** 3 **Occupation:** Farmer **Age** 18

Enrolled at: Chesterville, MS **Enrolled By:** Lt. Porter **Promoted:** No **ROH:** No

Born: Alabama **Marital Status:** S **Residence** Chesterville, MS

Transferred to Company I on 5/1/1862. Wounded (right leg) and captured at Gettysburg on 7/3/1863 (wounded); captured on 7/5/1863. Paroled at Fort McHenry, MD and transferred to Fort Delaware on 7/10/1863. Admitted to hospital at Williamsburg, VA on 9/15/1863. Furloughed, still on parole. Declared AWOL from 2/29/1864. Jul/Aug 1864 muster lists as deserted 3/1/1864.

Simpson, James H.

CO: B **Initial Rank:** Private

Joined: Wednesday, May 1, 1861 **Term (yrs):** 1 **Occupation:** Student **Age** 22

Enrolled at: Tippah Co., MS **Enrolled By:** Capt. Buchanan **Promoted:** No **ROH:** No

Born: **Marital Status:** **Residence**

Wounded in battle at 2nd Manassas on 8/29/1862. Sent to hospital. Returned to duty. Captured at Gettysburg on 7/1/1863. Taken to Fort Delaware. Released on oath on 6/11/1865.

Simpson, James W.

CO: I **Initial Rank:** Private

Joined: Wednesday, May 1, 1861 **Term (yrs):** 1 **Occupation:** Farmer **Age** 20

Enrolled at: Pontotoc Co., MS **Enrolled By:** Capt. Herring **Promoted:** Yes **ROH:** No

Born: **Marital Status:** **Residence**

Listed as 2nd Corporal from Mar/Apr 1863 muster. Listed as AWOL from 2/24/1864. Declared deserter during Jul/Aug 1864 muster roll.

Sims, Drury F.

CO: I **Initial Rank:** Private

Joined: Friday, August 28, 1863 **Term (yrs):** 3 **Occupation:** Farmer **Age** 18

Enrolled at: Columbia, SC **Enrolled By:** Maj. Milton **Promoted:** No **ROH:** Yes

Born: South Carolina **Marital Status:** **Residence**

"Killed instantly in battle" 5/10/1864 near Spotsylvania Court House, VA. ROH for Talley's Mill, 5/10/1864.

2nd Mississippi Alphabetical Roster (Annotated)

Sims, George R.
CO: B **Initial Rank:** Private
Joined: Wednesday, May 1, 1861 **Term (yrs):** 1 **Occupation:** Laborer **Age** 20
Enrolled at: Tippah Co., MS **Enrolled By:** Capt. Buchanan **Promoted:** No **ROH:** No
Born: **Marital Status:** **Residence**

Wounded accidentally sometime during Mar/Apr 1863 time period. Returned to duty. Wounded (in hip) and captured at Gettysburg on 7/1/1863. Paroled to City Point, VA from West's Buildings Hospital in Baltimore, MD on 11/12/1863. Retired to Invalid Corps, P.A.C.S. on 5/2/1864 due to disability caused by wound. Retirement temporary for only 6-months. Returned to company November 1864. Captured near Petersburg (Hatcher's Run?) on 4/2/1865. Taken to Point Lookout, MD. Released on oath on 6/30/1865.

Sims, Richard A.
CO: I **Initial Rank:** Private
Joined: Wednesday, May 1, 1861 **Term (yrs):** 1 **Occupation:** Farmer **Age** 24
Enrolled at: Pontotoc Co., MS **Enrolled By:** Capt. Herring **Promoted:** No **ROH:** Yes
Born: **Marital Status:** **Residence**

Wounded and captured at Gettysburg on 7/3/1863. Sent to hospital on Davids Island, NY Harbor. Listed as present for Sep/Oct 1863 muster (paroled?). According to hospital records, admitted on May 7, 1864 for wound at Charlottesville, VA (company records do not mention date of wound or engagement). Captured at Petersburg (Hatcher's Run?) not dated, but probably 4/2/1865. Sent to Fort Delaware and received on 4/4/1865. Released on oath on 6/11/1865. ROH for Weldon Railroad, 8/19/1864.

Sims, William J.
CO: I **Initial Rank:** Private
Joined: Wednesday, May 1, 1861 **Term (yrs):** 1 **Occupation:** Farmer **Age** 21
Enrolled at: Pontotoc Co., MS **Enrolled By:** Capt. Herring **Promoted:** No **ROH:** Yes
Born: South Carolina **Marital Status:** **Residence**

Mortally wounded at battle of Seven Pines on 5/31/1862. Died at Chimborazo Hospital #4 in Richmond, VA on 6/1/1862. ROH for Seven Pines, 5/31/1862.

Sisk, Jefferson W.
CO: C **Initial Rank:** Private
Joined: Wednesday, May 1, 1861 **Term (yrs):** 1 **Occupation:** Farmer **Age** 19
Enrolled at: Itawamba Co., MS **Enrolled By:** Capt. Bromley **Promoted:** No **ROH:** No
Born: Tennessee **Marital Status:** **Residence**

Received a dishonorable discharge for theft on 9/12/1861.

2nd Mississippi Alphabetical Roster (Annotated)

Sissom, Andrew
CO: F **Initial Rank:** Private
Joined: Wednesday, May 1, 1861 **Term (yrs):** 1 **Occupation:** Farmer **Age** 37
Enrolled at: Tippah Co., MS **Enrolled By:** Capt. Davis **Promoted:** No **ROH:** No
Born: Alabama **Marital Status:** **Residence**

Discharged for disability on 12/26/1861 at Camp Fisher, VA.

Skinner, Calvin
CO: D **Initial Rank:** Private
Joined: Wednesday, May 1, 1861 **Term (yrs):** 1 **Occupation:** Farmer **Age** 27
Enrolled at: Tippah Co., MS **Enrolled By:** Capt. Beck **Promoted:** No **ROH:** No
Born: Mississippi **Marital Status:** S **Residence** Snow Creek, MS

Discharged for disability on 11/26/1861 at Camp Fisher, VA by order of General Smith.

Slaughter, Peter W.
CO: D **Initial Rank:** Private
Joined: Wednesday, May 1, 1861 **Term (yrs):** 1 **Occupation:** Mechanic **Age** 25
Enrolled at: Tippah Co., MS **Enrolled By:** Capt. Beck **Promoted:** No **ROH:** No
Born: **Marital Status:** M **Residence** Salem, MS

Also see Peter Slaughter, 2nd Battalion Virginia Infantry, Local Defense Troops. Detailed to shoe manufacturing shop in Richmond, VA during Nov/Dec 1862 muster. Dropped from rolls — deserted — on 10/30/1863 for prolonged AWOL from furlough.

Sledge, James M.
CO: A **Initial Rank:** Private
Joined: Wednesday, May 1, 1861 **Term (yrs):** 1 **Occupation:** Farmer **Age** 25
Enrolled at: Tishomingo Co., MS **Enrolled By:** Capt. Leeth **Promoted:** No **ROH:** No
Born: Georgia **Marital Status:** S **Residence** Rienzi, MS

Captured at Gettysburg on 7/1/1863. Sent to Fort Delaware. Released on oath on 6/11/1865.

Smith, Allen G.
CO: B **Initial Rank:** Private
Joined: Wednesday, May 1, 1861 **Term (yrs):** 1 **Occupation:** Farmer **Age** 19
Enrolled at: Tippah Co., MS **Enrolled By:** Capt. Buchanan **Promoted:** No **ROH:** No
Born: South Carolina **Marital Status:** **Residence**

Killed in battle at 2nd Manassas on 8/30/1862.

2nd Mississippi Alphabetical Roster (Annotated)

Smith, Balam J. M. C.
CO: A **Initial Rank:** Private
Joined: Wednesday, May 1, 1861 **Term (yrs):** 1 **Occupation:** Farmer **Age** 27
Enrolled at: Tishomingo Co., MS **Enrolled By:** Capt. Leeth **Promoted:** No **ROH:** No
Born: Georgia **Marital Status:** S **Residence** Mud Creek, AL

Also see 26th Alabama Infantry Regiment. Captured at South Mountain, MD on 9/15/1862. Taken to Fort Delaware. Paroled to Aikens Landing, VA on 10/2/1862. Declared exchanged on 11/10/1862. Admitted to hospital in Williamsburg on 7/27/1863 with wound (company records do not provide date of wound or engagement information). Big toe amputated at 2nd phalange. Transferred to 26th Alabama on 9/11/1863.

Smith, Byrd B.
CO: B **Initial Rank:** Private
Joined: Wednesday, May 1, 1861 **Term (yrs):** 1 **Occupation:** Farmer **Age** 28
Enrolled at: Tippah Co., MS **Enrolled By:** Capt. Buchanan **Promoted:** Yes **ROH:** No
Born: Tennessee **Marital Status:** **Residence**

Also see John Coleman (substitute). Appointed 3rd Corporal on 4/30/1862. Discharged on 7/18/1862 due to having provided a substitute.

Smith, E. H.
CO: C **Initial Rank:** Private
Joined: Saturday, March 1, 1862 **Term (yrs):** 3 **Occupation:** **Age**
Enrolled at: Verona, MS **Enrolled By:** Lt. Pounds **Promoted:** No **ROH:** No
Born: **Marital Status:** **Residence**

Appears on a company muster-in roll. No other record.

Smith, Edward C
CO: K **Initial Rank:** Private
Joined: Wednesday, June 11, 1862 **Term (yrs):** 3 **Occupation:** **Age**
Enrolled at: Richmond, VA **Enrolled By:** Lt. Latham **Promoted:** No **ROH:** No
Born: **Marital Status:** **Residence**

Muster roll remarks: "Deserted 11 June 1862 as substitute." No other records.

Smith, Elijah
CO: B **Initial Rank:** Private
Joined: Monday, March 3, 1862 **Term (yrs):** 3 **Occupation:** Farmer **Age** 25
Enrolled at: Ripley, MS **Enrolled By:** Capt. Buchanan **Promoted:** No **ROH:** No
Born: North Carolina **Marital Status:** M **Residence**

Died of disease at Ashland, VA on 5/21/1862.

2nd Mississippi Alphabetical Roster (Annotated)

Smith, Francis M.
CO: G **Initial Rank:** Private
Joined: Wednesday, May 1, 1861 **Term (yrs):** 1 **Occupation:** Planter **Age** 20
Enrolled at: Pontotoc Co., MS **Enrolled By:** Capt. Miller **Promoted:** No **ROH:** Yes
Born: South Carolina **Marital Status:** S **Residence** Pontotoc, MS

For Jul/Aug 1863 muster roll, remarks say, "Returned to duty Aug 31st, 1863." [This may indicate he could have been absent wounded or sick, but the company records provide no details]. Detailed to go with Col. Stone to Mississippi to collect deserters and absentees on 1/9/1865. ROH for Bristoe Station, 10/14/1863.

Smith, George W.
CO: F **Initial Rank:** Private
Joined: Wednesday, May 1, 1861 **Term (yrs):** 1 **Occupation:** Planter **Age** 20
Enrolled at: Tippah Co., MS **Enrolled By:** Capt. Davis **Promoted:** No **ROH:** No
Born: **Marital Status:** **Residence**

Captured at Gettysburg on 7/3/1863. Sent to Fort Delaware. Released on oath on 6/11/1865.

Smith, H. R.
CO: F **Initial Rank:** Private
Joined: Thursday, August 25, 1864 **Term (yrs):** 3 **Occupation:** **Age**
Enrolled at: Petersburg, VA **Enrolled By:** Lt. Johnson **Promoted:** No **ROH:** No
Born: **Marital Status:** **Residence**

Absent, sick in hospital. AWOL during last two (Nov/Dec 1864 and Jan/Feb 1865) muster rolls.

Smith, Harvey W.
CO: B, L **Initial Rank:** Private
Joined: Wednesday, May 1, 1861 **Term (yrs):** 1 **Occupation:** Farmer **Age** 23
Enrolled at: Tippah Co., MS **Enrolled By:** Capt. Buchanan **Promoted:** Yes **ROH:** No
Born: Mississippi **Marital Status:** S **Residence** Ripley, MS

Transferred to Company L on 4/30/1862. Promoted to 3rd Sergeant in Sep 1862. Captured at Gettysburg on 7/1/1863. Taken to Fort Delaware. Released on oath on 6/11/1865.

Smith, James B.
CO: F **Initial Rank:** Private
Joined: Wednesday, May 1, 1861 **Term (yrs):** 1 **Occupation:** Planter **Age** 45
Enrolled at: Tippah Co., MS **Enrolled By:** Capt. Davis **Promoted:** No **ROH:** No
Born: **Marital Status:** **Residence**

Killed in battle at Seven Pines on 5/31/1862.

2nd Mississippi Alphabetical Roster (Annotated)

Smith, James L.
CO: A,I **Initial Rank:** Private
Joined: Saturday, March 1, 1862 **Term (yrs):** 3 **Occupation:** Mill wright **Age** 33
Enrolled at: Jacinto, MS **Enrolled By:** Lt. Clayton **Promoted:** No **ROH:** No
Born: South Carolina **Marital Status:** **Residence**

Transferred to Company I on 4/30/1862. Died of disease (pneumonia) at General Hospital #2, Lynchburg, VA on 9/1/1863 (other records put date at 9/3/1863).

Smith, James R.
CO: I **Initial Rank:** Private
Joined: Wednesday, May 1, 1861 **Term (yrs):** 1 **Occupation:** Carpenter **Age** 17
Enrolled at: Pontotoc Co., MS **Enrolled By:** Capt. Herring **Promoted:** No **ROH:** No
Born: **Marital Status:** **Residence**

Died (cause not given) at Winchester, VA on 7/1/1861.

Smith, James W.
CO: I **Initial Rank:** 1st Corporal
Joined: Wednesday, May 1, 1861 **Term (yrs):** 1 **Occupation:** Farmer **Age** 34
Enrolled at: Pontotoc Co., MS **Enrolled By:** Capt. Herring **Promoted:** No **ROH:** No
Born: **Marital Status:** **Residence**

"Left sick at Corinth. Returned home. Discharged." (May/Jun 1861 muster remarks)

Smith, Jerome B.
CO: F **Initial Rank:** Private
Joined: Saturday, March 1, 1862 **Term (yrs):** 3 **Occupation:** Farmer **Age** 28
Enrolled at: Ripley, MS **Enrolled By:** Capt. Powers **Promoted:** No **ROH:** Yes
Born: Virginia **Marital Status:** M **Residence**

Killed in battle at Sharpsburg on 9/17/1862. "Buried on the Battle field of Antietam." ROH for Seven Pines, 5/31/1862.

Smith, John
CO: L **Initial Rank:** Private
Joined: Monday, March 3, 1862 **Term (yrs):** 3 **Occupation:** Farmer **Age** 18
Enrolled at: Ripley, MS **Enrolled By:** Col. Falkner **Promoted:** No **ROH:** No
Born: Mississippi **Marital Status:** M **Residence** Ripley, MS

Deserted to Mississippi, 12/1/1864.

2nd Mississippi Alphabetical Roster (Annotated)

Smith, John H.
CO: F **Initial Rank:** Orderly Sergeant
Joined: Wednesday, May 1, 1861 **Term (yrs):** 1 **Occupation:** Carpenter **Age** 30
Enrolled at: Tippah Co., MS **Enrolled By:** Capt. Davis **Promoted:** Yes **ROH:** No
Born: **Marital Status:** **Residence**

Was Orderly Sergeant to 5/9/1861, then elected 2nd Lieutenant to replace [Abbott C.] Rucker. Killed in battle at 1st
Manassas on 7/21/1861.

Smith, John M.
CO: G **Initial Rank:** Private
Joined: Monday, September 16, 1861 **Term (yrs):** 1 **Occupation:** Farmer **Age** 37
Enrolled at: Pontotoc, MS **Enrolled By:** Lt. Davenport **Promoted:** No **ROH:** No
Born: South Carolina **Marital Status:** M **Residence** Pontotoc, MS

Discharged due to Conscription Act — over age — on 7/31/1862 by order of General Lee.

Smith, John P.
CO: F **Initial Rank:** Private
Joined: Wednesday, May 1, 1861 **Term (yrs):** 1 **Occupation:** Planter **Age** 19
Enrolled at: Tippah Co., MS **Enrolled By:** Capt. Davis **Promoted:** Yes **ROH:** No
Born: **Marital Status:** **Residence**

Captured at Gettysburg on 7/1/1863. Sent to Fort Delaware. Released on oath on 5/31/1865. Listed as 3rd
Corporal from Sep/Oct 1861 muster.

Smith, John W.
CO: G **Initial Rank:** Private
Joined: Monday, September 16, 1861 **Term (yrs):** 1 **Occupation:** Farmer **Age** 35
Enrolled at: Pontotoc, MS **Enrolled By:** Lt. Davenport **Promoted:** No **ROH:** No
Born: South Carolina **Marital Status:** S **Residence** Pontotoc, MS

Discharged in August 1862 — over age.

Smith, Joseph
CO: K **Initial Rank:** Private
Joined: Saturday, March 1, 1862 **Term (yrs):** 3 **Occupation:** **Age** 27
Enrolled at: Iuka, MS **Enrolled By:** Lt. Latham **Promoted:** No **ROH:** No
Born: **Marital Status:** **Residence**

Mar/Apr 1862 muster remarks: "Left at Iuka sick. Deserted and gone to the Yankees in the west."

2nd Mississippi Alphabetical Roster (Annotated)

Smith, Lemuel   *CO:* B, F   *Initial Rank:* Private

Joined: Monday, March 3, 1862   *Term (yrs):* 3   *Occupation:* Farmer   *Age* 45

Enrolled at: Ripley, MS   *Enrolled By:* Capt. Buchanan   *Promoted:* No   *ROH:* No

Born: North Carolina   *Marital Status:* M   *Residence*

Transferred to Company F on 4/30/1862. Admitted to hospital in Richmond with wound on 7/9/1863 (company records provide no details on date of wound or engagement). Discharged due to disability on 9/4/1863 at Orange Court House, VA.

Smith, Lemuel B.   *CO:* F   *Initial Rank:* 1st Lieutenant

Joined: *Term (yrs):* 0   *Occupation:*   *Age*

Enrolled at: *Enrolled By:*   *Promoted:* No   *ROH:* No

Born: *Marital Status:*   *Residence*

Appears on Federal prisoner of war records. Captured at De Soto, MS on 4/22/1863. Sent to Alton, IL. Forwarded to Johnson's Island, OH. Sent to City Point, VA for exchange on 2/24/1865. No other records.

Smith, Minett Martin   *CO:* I   *Initial Rank:* Private

Joined: Wednesday, May 1, 1861   *Term (yrs):* 1   *Occupation:* Farmer   *Age* 19

Enrolled at: Pontotoc Co., MS   *Enrolled By:* Capt. Herring   *Promoted:* Yes   *ROH:* No

Born: *Marital Status:*   *Residence*

Promoted to 1st Corporal on 4/23/1862. Wounded (right shoulder) and captured at Sharpsburg on 9/17/1862. Paroled from Fort McHenry, MD on 10/25/1862 and sent to Aikens Landing, VA. Furloughed to Mississippi on 11/5/1862. Promoted to 5th Sergeant on 5/16/1863. Returned to duty. Wounded and captured on 10/1/1864 near Petersburg. Sent to Elmira, NY. Released on oath on 6/14/1865.

Smith, R. W.   *CO:* G   *Initial Rank:* Private

Joined: Tuesday, April 30, 1861   *Term (yrs):* 1   *Occupation:* Farmer   *Age* 18

Enrolled at: Pontotoc Co., MS   *Enrolled By:*   *Promoted:* No   *ROH:* No

Born: *Marital Status:* S   *Residence* Pontotoc, MS

Appears on a record of the company, from 4/30/1861 to 3/15/1865. Dated near Petersburg, 3/15/1865. Died (cause not given) at Ashland, VA on 5/1/1862. No other records.

2nd Mississippi Alphabetical Roster (Annotated)

Smith, S. *CO:* F *Initial Rank:* Private
Joined: *Term (yrs):* 0 *Occupation:* *Age*
Enrolled at: *Enrolled By:* *Promoted:* No *ROH:* No
Born: *Marital Status:* *Residence*

Appears on a Federal register of prisoners of war at Fort Delaware. Captured at Gettysburg, July ?, 1863. Released 5/31/1865. No other record.

Smith, Stephen D. *CO:* E *Initial Rank:* 2nd Sergeant
Joined: Wednesday, May 1, 1861 *Term (yrs):* 1 *Occupation:* Farmer *Age* 26
Enrolled at: Itawamba Co., MS *Enrolled By:* Capt. Booth *Promoted:* Yes *ROH:* No
Born: Mississippi *Marital Status:* S *Residence* Guntown, MS

Listed as 1st Sergeant for Jul/Aug 1862 muster roll. Wounded (flesh wound, left thigh) at Sharpsburg on 9/17/1862. Furloughed. Returned to duty. Captured at Gettysburg on 7/1/1863. Sent to Fort Delaware. Released on oath on 6/11/1865.

Smith, William C. *CO:* K *Initial Rank:* Private
Joined: Saturday, March 1, 1862 *Term (yrs):* 3 *Occupation:* *Age* 18
Enrolled at: Iuka, MS *Enrolled By:* Lt. Latham *Promoted:* No *ROH:* No
Born: *Marital Status:* *Residence*

Admitted to hospital for illness on 3/9/1865. Transferred to Danville on 4/1/1865. Surrendered and paroled at Lynchburg, VA, April ?, 1865. Also appears on a Federal record of Confederate soldiers paroled at Montgomery, AL during the month of May 1865. Dated 5/31/1865.

Smith, William F. *CO:* H *Initial Rank:* Private
Joined: Monday, April 29, 1861 *Term (yrs):* 1 *Occupation:* Student *Age* 18
Enrolled at: Pontotoc Co., MS *Enrolled By:* Capt. Taylor *Promoted:* No *ROH:* No
Born: Alabama *Marital Status:* S *Residence* Tupelo, MS

Killed in battle at Gettysburg on 7/1/1863.

Smith, William R. *CO:* A *Initial Rank:* Private
Joined: Saturday, March 1, 1862 *Term (yrs):* 3 *Occupation:* Farmer *Age* 41
Enrolled at: Jacinto, MS *Enrolled By:* Lt. Clayton *Promoted:* No *ROH:* No
Born: Tennessee *Marital Status:* *Residence* Burnsville, MS

Discharged due to disability on 12/10/1862.

2nd Mississippi Alphabetical Roster (Annotated)

Smith, William R.   CO: G   Initial Rank: Private
Joined: Wednesday, May 1, 1861   *Term (yrs):* 1   *Occupation:* Student   *Age* 18
Enrolled at: Pontotoc Co., MS   *Enrolled By:* Capt. Miller   *Promoted:* No   *ROH:* No
Born: *Marital Status:* S   *Residence* Pontotoc, MS
Discharged due to disability on 8/29/1861.

Smither, John W.   CO: K   Initial Rank: Private
Joined: Saturday, March 1, 1862   *Term (yrs):* 3   *Occupation:*   *Age* 23
Enrolled at: Iuka, MS   *Enrolled By:* Lt. Latham   *Promoted:* No   *ROH:* No
Born: *Marital Status:*   *Residence*
Deserted to the enemy from the picket line on 2/13/1865.

Sory, Artaxerxes W.   CO: I   Initial Rank: 1st Sergeant
Joined: Wednesday, May 1, 1861   *Term (yrs):* 1   *Occupation:* Farmer   *Age* 27
Enrolled at: Pontotoc Co., MS   *Enrolled By:* Capt. Herring   *Promoted:* Yes   *ROH:* No
Born: *Marital Status:*   *Residence*
Promoted to 1st Lieutenant on 4/23/1862. Assigned to duty 4/23/1862. Wounded (in chest) in battle at The Wilderness on 5/5/1864. Sent to hospital in Charlottesville, VA. Returned to duty. Captured at Hatcher's Run on 4/2/1865. Sent to Johnson's Island, OH. Released on oath on 6/20/1865.

South, Abner O.   CO: F   Initial Rank: Private
Joined: Wednesday, May 1, 1861   *Term (yrs):* 1   *Occupation:* Planter   *Age* 34
Enrolled at: Tippah Co., MS   *Enrolled By:* Capt. Davis   *Promoted:* No   *ROH:* No
Born: Alabama   *Marital Status:*   *Residence*
Discharged due to disability on 10/13/1861 at Camp Fisher, VA.

Southall, John W.   CO: K   Initial Rank: Private
Joined: Thursday, June 20, 1861   *Term (yrs):* 1   *Occupation:* Planter   *Age* 24
Enrolled at: Winchester, VA   *Enrolled By:* Capt. Stone   *Promoted:* No   *ROH:* No
Born: *Marital Status:*   *Residence*
Paroled at Lynchburg, VA on April ?, 1865.

2nd Mississippi Alphabetical Roster (Annotated)

Southall, Richard J.   CO: K   Initial Rank: Private

Joined: Thursday, June 20, 1861   *Term (yrs):* 1 *Occupation:* Planter   *Age* 21
Enrolled at: Winchester, VA   *Enrolled By:* Capt. Stone   *Promoted:* No   *ROH:* No
Born: *Marital Status:*   *Residence*

Admitted to hospital in Charlottesville, VA with wound on 7/12/1863 (company records include no details on date of wound or engagement). Furloughed 30-days from 7/30/1863. Listed as present during last company muster (Jan/Feb 1865).

Sparks, William   CO: E   Initial Rank: Private

Joined: Wednesday, May 1, 1861   *Term (yrs):* 1 *Occupation:* Farmer   *Age* 28
Enrolled at: Itawamba Co., MS   *Enrolled By:* Capt. Booth   *Promoted:* No   *ROH:* No
Born: *Marital Status:*   *Residence* Guntown, MS

Discharged due to disability on 8/29/1861 at Camp Jones, VA.

Spears, William   CO: C   Initial Rank: Private

Joined: Wednesday, May 1, 1861   *Term (yrs):* 1 *Occupation:* Farmer   *Age* 40
Enrolled at: Itawamba Co., MS   *Enrolled By:* Capt. Bromley   *Promoted:* No   *ROH:* No
Born: South Carolina   *Marital Status:*   *Residence*

Discharged due to disability on 7/30/1861— over age.

Spencer, John   CO: A   Initial Rank: Private

Joined: Wednesday, May 1, 1861   *Term (yrs):* 1 *Occupation:* Laborer   *Age* 21
Enrolled at: Tishomingo Co., MS   *Enrolled By:* Capt. Leeth   *Promoted:* No   *ROH:* No
Born: Alabama   *Marital Status:* S   *Residence* Rienzi, MS

Discharged on 8/17/1861 due to disability.

Spencer, William P.   CO: G   Initial Rank: Private

Joined: Wednesday, May 1, 1861   *Term (yrs):* 1 *Occupation:* Lawyer   *Age* 26
Enrolled at: Pontotoc Co., MS   *Enrolled By:* Capt. Miller   *Promoted:* Yes   *ROH:* No
Born: *Marital Status:* S   *Residence* Pontotoc, MS

Listed as 2nd Corporal from Sep/Oct 1861 muster roll. Reduced to ranks on 3/31/1862. Elected 3rd Lieutenant on 4/21/1862. Cashiered for cowardice by sentence of General Court Martial on 8/18/1862. Dismissed from service.

2nd Mississippi Alphabetical Roster (Annotated)

Spight, William B.
CO: B,D **Initial Rank:** Private
Joined: Wednesday, May 1, 1861 **Term (yrs):** 1 **Occupation:** Clerk **Age** 19
Enrolled at: Tippah Co., MS **Enrolled By:** Capt. Buchanan **Promoted:** No **ROH:** No
Born: Mississippi **Marital Status:** **Residence**

Transferred to Company D on 7/21/1862. Discharged due to disability on 7/21/1862.

Spooner, William
CO: F **Initial Rank:** Private
Joined: Thursday, July 31, 1862 **Term (yrs):** 2 **Occupation:** Teacher **Age** 40
Enrolled at: Richmond, VA **Enrolled By:** Capt. Powers **Promoted:** No **ROH:** No
Born: **Marital Status:** **Residence**

Also see Solomon G. Street. Substituted for S. G. Street. Deserted on 8/25/1862. However, records show he was in hospitals for treatment. He was arrested and turned over to Capt. Alexander by order of the Medical Director on 8/15/1863.

Springer, Allen
CO: D, F **Initial Rank:** Private
Joined: Wednesday, May 1, 1861 **Term (yrs):** 1 **Occupation:** Farmer **Age** 20
Enrolled at: Tippah Co., MS **Enrolled By:** Capt. Beck **Promoted:** No **ROH:** No
Born: **Marital Status:** S **Residence** Hickory Flat, MS

Transferred to Company F on 4/30/1862. Wounded at Malvern Hill on 7/1/1862. Furloughed 30-days from 7/4/1862. Returned to duty. Deserted from Goldsborough, NC on 2/22/1863.

Springer, Jessee
CO: B **Initial Rank:** Private
Joined: Monday, March 3, 1862 **Term (yrs):** 3 **Occupation:** Farmer **Age** 25
Enrolled at: Ripley, MS **Enrolled By:** Capt. Buchanan **Promoted:** No **ROH:** No
Born: Alabama **Marital Status:** S **Residence**

Died of disease at Ashland, VA on 5/7/1862.

Sproles, J. R.
CO: A **Initial Rank:** Private
Joined: **Term (yrs):** 0 **Occupation:** **Age**
Enrolled at: **Enrolled By:** **Promoted:** No **ROH:** No
Born: **Marital Status:** **Residence**

Appears on a Federal list of prisoners of war captured and paroled by the U. S. forces in the battles of Iuka, Corinth, and Hatchie. Dated Corinth, MS on 10/13/1862. [Misidentified. Unlikely this person belonged to the 2nd Mississippi – possibly the 2nd Missouri instead]. No other record.

2nd Mississippi Alphabetical Roster (Annotated)

Spurgeon, John
CO: F **Initial Rank:** Private
Joined: Saturday, March 1, 1862 **Term (yrs):** 3 **Occupation:** Farmer **Age** 23
Enrolled at: Ripley, MS **Enrolled By:** Capt. Powers **Promoted:** No **ROH:** No
Born: Alabama **Marital Status:** M **Residence**

Hospital records indicate admission to hospital (not dated), with gunshot wound. Returned to duty on 7/23/1862 (company records do not provide any details of date of wound or engagement). Killed in battle at 2nd Manassas on 8/29/1862 (other records say he died on 8/30/1862).

St. Clair, Charles
CO: **Initial Rank:** Private
Joined: **Term (yrs):** 0 **Occupation:** **Age**
Enrolled at: **Enrolled By:** **Promoted:** No **ROH:** No
Born: **Marital Status:** **Residence**

Appears on a Federal register of refugees and rebel deserters at Washington, D.C. Received 7/10/1865. Transportation furnished to Lexington, MO [Probably misidentified – perhaps a member of the 2nd/6th Missouri Consolidated, not the 2nd Mississippi]. No other record.

Stalnaker, Adam W.
CO: L **Initial Rank:** Private
Joined: Monday, March 3, 1862 **Term (yrs):** 3 **Occupation:** Farmer **Age** 35
Enrolled at: Ripley, MS **Enrolled By:** Col. Falkner **Promoted:** No **ROH:** No
Born: Georgia **Marital Status:** M **Residence** Union Mills, MS

Also see 2nd Mississippi Cavalry Regiment. Furloughed on 9/16/1862 for 30-days. Did not return. Dropped from rolls as deserter on 4/30/1863. Appears on a Federal register of prisoners of war dated Memphis, TN on 6/3/1863. Captured at Florence, AL on 5/29/1863. Sent to Alton, IL. Exchanged on 6/12/1863. His name also appears on Confederate records showing his death from disease as a paroled prisoner, on 6/30/1863 (or 6/29/1863) in Petersburg, VA.

Stalnaker, Richard R.
CO: L **Initial Rank:** Private
Joined: Monday, March 3, 1862 **Term (yrs):** 3 **Occupation:** Farmer **Age** 39
Enrolled at: Ripley, MS **Enrolled By:** Col. Falkner **Promoted:** No **ROH:** No
Born: Georgia **Marital Status:** **Residence**

Died of disease at Richmond, VA on 9/10/1862.

2nd Mississippi Alphabetical Roster (Annotated)

Stanfield, William D.
CO: F **Initial Rank:** Private
Joined: Wednesday, May 1, 1861 **Term (yrs):** 1 **Occupation:** Planter **Age** 22
Enrolled at: Tippah Co., MS **Enrolled By:** Capt. Davis **Promoted:** No **ROH:** No
Born: **Marital Status:** **Residence**

Wounded at Gettysburg on 7/3/1863. Returned to duty. Hospital records show his admission at Williamsburg, VA for a wound on 6/3/1864 (company records do not provide details as to date of wound or engagement). Last company muster roll dated Jan/Feb 1865 listed as in hospital at Richmond. Hospital records indicate he died of disease at the General Hospital at Howard's Grove in Richmond, VA on 3/19/1865.

Stanley, J. M.
CO: H **Initial Rank:** Private
Joined: **Term (yrs):** 0 **Occupation:** **Age**
Enrolled at: **Enrolled By:** **Promoted:** No **ROH:** No
Born: **Marital Status:** **Residence**

Appears on a Federal roll of prisoners of war exchanged at Rough and Ready, GA on 9/19/1864 and 9/22/1864. Captured at Cedarstown, (GA?) on 8/21/1864. [Probably misidentified — more likely a member of the 2nd/6th Missouri Consolidated Regiment, which the Federals abbreviated identically to the 2nd Mississippi].

Stanley, James T.
CO: K, F **Initial Rank:** Private
Joined: Wednesday, May 1, 1861 **Term (yrs):** 1 **Occupation:** Laborer **Age** 20
Enrolled at: Tishomingo Co., MS **Enrolled By:** Capt. Stone **Promoted:** No **ROH:** Yes
Born: **Marital Status:** **Residence**

Wounded at Malvern Hill on 7/1/1862. Returned to duty. For Mar/Apr 1863 muster roll, remarks say, "wounded" — no details of date of wound or engagement. Hospital records show him admitted to the hospital in Richmond for a wound on 7/9/1863 (company records provide no details on date of wound or engagement). Hospital records show him admitted for a wound on 8/12/1863 at Richmond (again, company records provide no details — may simply be a transfer to another hospital from the July wound). Returned to duty on 10/9/1863. Last muster (Jan/Feb 1865) lists him as "absent without leave since 5 Feb 1865." Federal records show him on a register of prisoners of war. Captured near Iuka, MS on 4/22/1865. Forwarded to Louisville, KY on 5/9/1865. Released on oath on 6/20/1865. A Federal hospital record shows his death from disease (dysentery) on 6/22/1865 at Louisville "Paroled Confederate charity patient." ROH for Weldon Railroad, 8/18/1864.

Stanton, Patrick
CO: K **Initial Rank:** Private
Joined: Wednesday, May 1, 1861 **Term (yrs):** 1 **Occupation:** Hostler **Age** 34
Enrolled at: Tishomingo Co., MS **Enrolled By:** Capt. Stone **Promoted:** No **ROH:** No
Born: Ireland **Marital Status:** **Residence**

Discharged by order of Secretary of War on 7/14/1864, "Never acquired a domicile" in the Confederate States.

2nd Mississippi Alphabetical Roster (Annotated)

Stephens, J. H. P.
CO: *Initial Rank:* Lieutenant
Joined: *Term (yrs):* 0 *Occupation:* *Age*
Enrolled at: *Enrolled By:* *Promoted:* No *ROH:* No
Born: *Marital Status:* *Residence*

Appears on a Federal report of prisoners of war paroled on 5/17/1865 and 5/18/1865, dated Memphis, TN. No other record.

Stephens, John A.
CO: I *Initial Rank:* 4th Sergeant
Joined: Wednesday, May 1, 1861 *Term (yrs):* 1 *Occupation:* Farmer *Age* 28
Enrolled at: Pontotoc Co., MS *Enrolled By:* Capt. Herring *Promoted:* Yes *ROH:* No
Born: *Marital Status:* *Residence*

Promoted to 2nd Lieutenant on 4/23/1862. Assigned to duty 4/23/1862. Captured at Gettysburg on 7/1/1863. Sent to Johnson's Island, OH. Paroled and forwarded to Point Lookout, MD for exchange on 3/14/1865. Also appears on a Federal register of paroles given at Post of Columbus, MS, dated 5/23/1865.

Stephens, John J.
CO: D *Initial Rank:* Private
Joined: Wednesday, May 1, 1861 *Term (yrs):* 1 *Occupation:* Farmer *Age* 28
Enrolled at: Tippah Co., MS *Enrolled By:* Capt. Beck *Promoted:* No *ROH:* No
Born: *Marital Status:* S *Residence* Snow Creek, MS

Discharged for disability on 8/14/1861 at Camp Jones, Va.

Stephens, Robert M.
CO: I *Initial Rank:* Private
Joined: Wednesday, May 1, 1861 *Term (yrs):* 1 *Occupation:* Farmer *Age* 26
Enrolled at: Pontotoc Co., MS *Enrolled By:* Capt. Herring *Promoted:* Yes *ROH:* No
Born: South Carolina *Marital Status:* *Residence*

Promoted to 4th Corporal on 10/7/1861. Discharged due to disability on 2/26/1862 ("amputation of fingers") at Camp Fisher, VA [apparently, an accident with an axe].

Stephens, Robert R.
CO: C *Initial Rank:* Private
Joined: Wednesday, May 1, 1861 *Term (yrs):* 1 *Occupation:* Farmer *Age* 20
Enrolled at: Itawamba Co., MS *Enrolled By:* Capt. Bromley *Promoted:* No *ROH:* No
Born: *Marital Status:* *Residence*

Died (of disease?) on 10/2/1861 in the hospital at Winchester, VA.

2nd Mississippi Alphabetical Roster (Annotated)

Stephens, William O.   CO: C   Initial Rank: Private
Joined: Wednesday, May 1, 1861   **Term (yrs):** 1   **Occupation:** Farmer   **Age** 20
Enrolled at: Itawamba Co., MS   **Enrolled By:** Capt. Bromley   **Promoted:** No   **ROH:** No
Born: **Marital Status:**   **Residence**

Furloughed. Did not return to company. Listed as deserted in Mar/Apr 1863 muster roll.

Stephenson, Andrew R.   CO: E   Initial Rank: Private
Joined: Wednesday, May 1, 1861   **Term (yrs):** 1   **Occupation:** Carpenter   **Age** 26
Enrolled at: Itawamba Co., MS   **Enrolled By:** Capt. Booth   **Promoted:** Yes   **ROH:** No
Born: **Marital Status:**   **Residence**

Listed as 5th Sergeant on Sep/Oct 1861 muster. Promoted to 3rd Lieutenant during Mar/Apr 1862 muster. Promoted to 2nd Lieutenant on 4/17/1862. Wounded on 6/27/1862 at Gaines Mill. Placed in arrest on or about 6/27/1862. Court Martial sentence dismissed from service on 8/13/1862. Discharged.

Stevens, J.   CO: Initial Rank: Private
Joined: **Term (yrs):** 0   **Occupation:**   **Age**
Enrolled at: **Enrolled By:**   **Promoted:** No   **ROH:** No
Born: **Marital Status:**   **Residence**

Appears on a Federal register of prisoners of war at Memphis, TN. Captured at Tupelo, MS on 5/7/1863. Sent to Alton, IL on 5/22/1863. No other record.

Stevens, John   CO: C   Initial Rank: Private
Joined: Wednesday, May 1, 1861   **Term (yrs):** 1   **Occupation:** Farmer   **Age** 25
Enrolled at: Itawamba Co., MS   **Enrolled By:** Capt. Bromley   **Promoted:** Yes   **ROH:** No
Born: **Marital Status:**   **Residence**

Wounded in battle at 2nd Manassas on 8/29/1862. Furloughed from hospital. Returned to duty. Listed as 1st Corporal during Mar/Apr 1864 muster roll. Captured at Petersburg (Hatcher's Run?) on 4/2/1865. Sent to Fort Delaware. Released on oath on 6/11/1865.

Steward, James S.   CO: F   Initial Rank: Private
Joined: Wednesday, May 1, 1861   **Term (yrs):** 1   **Occupation:** Farmer   **Age** 17
Enrolled at: Tippah Co., MS   **Enrolled By:** Capt. Davis   **Promoted:** No   **ROH:** No
Born: Mississippi   **Marital Status:**   **Residence**

Discharged on 7/31/1862, expiration of term of service — non-conscript, underage.

2nd Mississippi Alphabetical Roster (Annotated)

Stewart, Benton W.   CO: G   Initial Rank: Private
Joined: Wednesday, May 1, 1861   **Term (yrs):** 1   **Occupation:** Farmer   **Age** 27
Enrolled at: Pontotoc Co., MS   **Enrolled By:** Capt. Miller   **Promoted:** No   **ROH:** No
Born: Alabama   **Marital Status:** S   **Residence** Pontotoc, MS

Wounded at Sharpsburg on 9/17/1862. Furloughed. Discharged due to disability from wound on 4/17/1863.

Stewart, John A.   CO: F   Initial Rank: Private
Joined: Tuesday, March 10, 1863   **Term (yrs):** 3   **Occupation:** Mason   **Age** 37
Enrolled at: Orizaba, MS   **Enrolled By:** Lt. Bearden   **Promoted:** No   **ROH:** No
Born: Georgia   **Marital Status:**   **Residence**

Discharged due to disability (epilepsy) on 4/30/1863.

Stewart, Mark T.   CO: G   Initial Rank: Private
Joined: Wednesday, May 1, 1861   **Term (yrs):** 1   **Occupation:** Farmer   **Age** 22
Enrolled at: Pontotoc Co., MS   **Enrolled By:** Capt. Miller   **Promoted:** No   **ROH:** No
Born: **Marital Status:** S   **Residence** Pontotoc, MS

Wounded at 1st Manassas on 7/21/1861. Returned to duty. Died of disease at Bowling Green, VA on 4/19/1862.

Stewart, William Andrew   CO: K   Initial Rank: Private
Joined: Saturday, March 1, 1862   **Term (yrs):** 3   **Occupation:**   **Age** 28
Enrolled at: Iuka, MS   **Enrolled By:** Lt. Latham   **Promoted:** No   **ROH:** No
Born: South Carolina   **Marital Status:**   **Residence**

Deserted on 6/27/1863. Taken into Federal custody at Emmitsburg, MD on 6/28/1863. Sent to Fort Delaware. Became "Galvanized Yankee" and joined 3rd Maryland Cavalry (U. S.) on 9/22/1863.

Stewart, William H.   CO: H   Initial Rank: Private
Joined: Monday, April 29, 1861   **Term (yrs):** 1   **Occupation:** Clerk   **Age** 21
Enrolled at: Pontotoc Co., MS   **Enrolled By:** Capt. Taylor   **Promoted:** No   **ROH:** No
Born: Mississippi   **Marital Status:** S   **Residence** Arizabo, MS

Died of disease at hospital in Goldsboro, NC on 4/7/1863.

2nd Mississippi Alphabetical Roster (Annotated)

Stitt, John N. *CO:* F *Initial Rank:* Private
Joined: Wednesday, May 1, 1861 *Term (yrs):* 1 *Occupation:* Planter *Age* 21
Enrolled at: Tippah Co., MS *Enrolled By:* Capt. Davis *Promoted:* No *ROH:* No
Born: *Marital Status:*   *Residence*

Discharged due to disability on 8/5/1861 at Camp Jones, VA.

Stocks, Henry C. *CO:* E *Initial Rank:* Private
Joined: Wednesday, May 1, 1861 *Term (yrs):* 1 *Occupation:* Farmer *Age* 18
Enrolled at: Itawamba Co., MS *Enrolled By:* Capt. Booth *Promoted:* No *ROH:* No
Born: Mississippi *Marital Status:* S *Residence* Baldwyn, MS

Wounded in battle at Sharpsburg on 9/17/1862. Furloughed 60-days from 10/10/1862 to Mississippi. Returned to duty. Hospital records show admission with wound on 7/12/1863 (company records do not list date of wound or engagement). Returned to duty on 8/7/1863. Deserted from camp near Orange Court House, VA on 2/10/1864. Taken into Federal custody on 2/12/1864.

Stockton, Joseph *CO:* C *Initial Rank:* Private
Joined: Saturday, March 1, 1862 *Term (yrs):* 3 *Occupation:*   *Age*
Enrolled at: Verona, MS *Enrolled By:* Lt. Pounds *Promoted:* No *ROH:* No
Born: *Marital Status:*   *Residence*

For Jul/Aug 1864 muster, remarks say, "Wounded & in hospital at Richmond, VA (no details of date of wound or engagement). Listed as AWOL from 11/7/1864. Deserted for prolonged AWOL during Jan/Feb 1865 muster roll.

Stone, John J. *CO:* H *Initial Rank:* 1st Lieutenant
Joined: Monday, April 29, 1861 *Term (yrs):* 1 *Occupation:* Minister *Age* 50
Enrolled at: Pontotoc, MS *Enrolled By:* Capt. Taylor *Promoted:* No *ROH:* No
Born: Alabama *Marital Status:* M *Residence* Chesterville, MS

Resigned his commission due to disability on 2/8/1862.

2nd Mississippi Alphabetical Roster (Annotated)

Stone, John M.
CO: K,S **Initial Rank:** Captain
Joined: Wednesday, May 1, 1861 **Term (yrs):** 1 **Occupation:** RR Agent **Age** 30
Enrolled at: Tishomingo Co., MS **Enrolled By:** **Promoted:** Yes **ROH:** No
Born: Tennessee **Marital Status:** S **Residence** Columbus, MS

Elected Colonel and assigned to duty on 4/23/1862. Wounded at Sharpsburg on 9/17/1862. Wounded at Gettysburg on 7/1/1863. Commanding Davis' Brigade during battle of The Wilderness on 5/5/1864. Dispatched to Mississippi to round up absentees and deserters in January 1865 [Lt. Col. Blair's Diary says he left on 13 Jan.]. Captured during fight at Salisbury, NC while trying to return to his command on 4/12/1865. Sent to Johnson's Island, OH. Released on oath on 7/25/1865.

Stone, William W.
CO: H **Initial Rank:** Private
Joined: Monday, April 29, 1861 **Term (yrs):** 1 **Occupation:** Teacher **Age** 23
Enrolled at: Pontotoc Co., MS **Enrolled By:** Capt. Taylor **Promoted:** No **ROH:** No
Born: South Carolina **Marital Status:** **Residence**

Discharged due to disability on 9/10/1861 at Camp Fisher, VA by order of General Johnston.

Storey, Henry H.
CO: C **Initial Rank:** Private
Joined: Wednesday, May 1, 1861 **Term (yrs):** 1 **Occupation:** Farmer **Age** 20
Enrolled at: Itawamba Co., MS **Enrolled By:** Capt. Bromley **Promoted:** No **ROH:** Yes
Born: **Marital Status:** **Residence**

Admitted to hospital in Richmond, VA with wound on 10/4/1862 (company records do not record date of wound or engagement). Killed in battle at Gettysburg on 7/3/1863. ROH for Gettysburg, 7/1/1863.

Storey, John F.
CO: C **Initial Rank:** Private
Joined: Wednesday, May 1, 1861 **Term (yrs):** 1 **Occupation:** Clerk **Age** 24
Enrolled at: Itawamba Co., MS **Enrolled By:** Capt. Bromley **Promoted:** Yes **ROH:** No
Born: **Marital Status:** **Residence**

Appointed 2nd Sergeant on 8/1/1861. Assigned to duty as 1st Lieutenant on 4/22/1862. Wounded at 2nd Manassas on 8/29/1862. Sent to hospital. Promoted Captain circa Sep/Oct 1862 time period. Furloughed from 11/10/1862 for 40-days. Returned to duty. Killed in battle at Gettysburg on 7/3/1862.

2nd Mississippi Alphabetical Roster (Annotated)

Storey, Robert
CO: L **Initial Rank:** Captain
Joined: Monday, March 3, 1862 **Term (yrs):** 3 **Occupation:** Farmer **Age** 38
Enrolled at: Ripley, MS **Enrolled By:** Col. Falkner **Promoted:** No **ROH:** No
Born: South Carolina **Marital Status:** M **Residence** Ripley, MS

Elected Captain on 3/22/1862. Died of disease at Richmond, VA on 7/2/1863.

Storey, Thomas
CO: L,F **Initial Rank:** 2nd Lieutenant
Joined: Monday, March 3, 1862 **Term (yrs):** 3 **Occupation:** Farmer **Age** 25
Enrolled at: Ripley, MS **Enrolled By:** Col. Falkner **Promoted:** Yes **ROH:** No
Born: Mississippi **Marital Status:** M **Residence** Ripley, MS

Elected 2nd Lieutenant on 3/22/1862. Wounded (flesh wound in calf) at Gettysburg on 7/3/1863. Furloughed Promoted to 1st Lieutenant on 12/28/1863 to date from 7/3/1863. Returned to duty. Wounded (right arm) at the Weldon Railroad on 8/19/1864. Furloughed to Mississippi. Listed as AWOL from 12/3/1864 on wounded furlough during last company muster roll (Jan/Feb 1865).

Stovall, George D.
CO: C **Initial Rank:** Private
Joined: Wednesday, May 1, 1861 **Term (yrs):** 1 **Occupation:** Farmer **Age** 17
Enrolled at: Itawamba Co., MS **Enrolled By:** Capt. Bromley **Promoted:** No **ROH:** No
Born: Tennessee **Marital Status:** **Residence**

Discharged on plea of military exemption on 5/25/1862 (underage).

Stovall, James K. P.
CO: C,E **Initial Rank:** Private
Joined: Wednesday, May 1, 1861 **Term (yrs):** 1 **Occupation:** Clerk **Age** 20
Enrolled at: Itawamba Co., MS **Enrolled By:** Capt. Bromley **Promoted:** Yes **ROH:** No
Born: Tennessee **Marital Status:** S **Residence** Richmond, MS

Transferred to Company E on 6/17/1862. Promoted to 5th Sergeant on 9/25/1862. Wounded during Jul/Aug, 1863 muster report (date of wound or engagement not noted but admitted to hospital on 7/12/1863). Sent to hospital at Charlottesville, VA. Furloughed. Returned to duty on 9/1/1863. Captured near Petersburg (Hatcher's Run?) on 4/2/1865. Taken to Point Lookout, MD. Released on oath on 6/19/1865.

2nd Mississippi Alphabetical Roster (Annotated)

Strain, Brice B.
CO: H **Initial Rank:** Musician
Joined: Monday, April 29, 1861 **Term (yrs):** 1 **Occupation:** Farmer **Age** 20
Enrolled at: Pontotoc Co., MS **Enrolled By:** Capt. Taylor **Promoted:** Yes **ROH:** No
Born: Alabama **Marital Status:** S **Residence** Chesterville, MS

Promoted to 3rd Sergeant on 10/1/1862. Promoted to 1st Sergeant on 6/1/1863. Wounded (right thigh) at Gettysburg on 7/1/1863. Sent to hospital at Richmond, VA. Returned to duty. Reduced to ranks, ordered by Lieutenant. Gen. Hill to forfeit 6-month's pay and do hard labor in camp three months (Gen. Order No. 33, 11/7/1864). Deserted on 2/7/1865.

Strain, James H.
CO: H **Initial Rank:** Private
Joined: Saturday, March 15, 1862 **Term (yrs):** 3 **Occupation:** Cadet **Age** 19
Enrolled at: Chesterville, MS **Enrolled By:** Lt. Porter **Promoted:** Yes **ROH:** No
Born: Alabama **Marital Status:** S **Residence** Chesterville, MS

Elected Jr. 2nd Lieutenant on 8/19/1863. Promoted to 2nd Lieutenant on 12/28/1863 to date from 7/3/1863. Wounded (in thigh) at The Wilderness on 5/5/1864. Sent to hospital at Richmond, VA. Furloughed. Listed as Captain and "present" during last company muster (Jan/Feb 1865).

Street, Elliott A.
CO: F **Initial Rank:** Private
Joined: Wednesday, May 1, 1861 **Term (yrs):** 1 **Occupation:** Planter **Age** 21
Enrolled at: Tippah Co., MS **Enrolled By:** Capt. Davis **Promoted:** No **ROH:** No
Born: **Marital Status:** **Residence**

Listed as deserted during May/Jun 1863 muster roll.

Street, Solomon G.
CO: F **Initial Rank:** Private
Joined: Wednesday, May 1, 1861 **Term (yrs):** 1 **Occupation:** Carpenter **Age** 30
Enrolled at: Tippah Co., MS **Enrolled By:** Capt. Davis **Promoted:** No **ROH:** No
Born: **Marital Status:** **Residence**

Also see William Spooner (substitute). Appointed 3rd Sergeant on 7/20/1861. Discharged on 7/31/1862 by reason of having furnished a substitute at Richmond, VA.

2nd Mississippi Alphabetical Roster (Annotated)

Strickland, Condary D.
CO: E **Initial Rank:** Private
Joined: Thursday, February 20, 1862 **Term (yrs):** 3 **Occupation:** Farmer **Age** 22
Enrolled at: Guntown, MS **Enrolled By:** Capt. Bates **Promoted:** No **ROH:** No
Born: Mississippi **Marital Status:** S **Residence** Guntown, MS

Captured at Gettysburg on 7/1/1863. Sent to Fort Delaware. Released on oath on 6/11/1865.

Strickland, H. F.
CO: K **Initial Rank:** Private
Joined: **Term (yrs):** 0 **Occupation:** **Age**
Enrolled at: **Enrolled By:** **Promoted:** No **ROH:** No
Born: **Marital Status:** **Residence**

Appears on a Federal roll of prisoners of war paroled at Talladega, AL. Dated 5/15/1865 at Talladega. No other record.

Strickland, S.
CO: E **Initial Rank:** Private
Joined: **Term (yrs):** 0 **Occupation:** **Age**
Enrolled at: **Enrolled By:** **Promoted:** No **ROH:** No
Born: **Marital Status:** **Residence**

Appears on a Federal roll of prisoners of war surrendered and paroled, dated Columbus, MS on 5/17/1865. No other record.

Strickland, Thomas K.
CO: E **Initial Rank:** 3rd Sergeant
Joined: Wednesday, May 1, 1861 **Term (yrs):** 1 **Occupation:** Blacksmith **Age** 34
Enrolled at: Itawamba Co., MS **Enrolled By:** Capt. Booth **Promoted:** No **ROH:** No
Born: **Marital Status:** S **Residence** Guntown, MS

Wounded at 1st Manassas on 7/21/1861 (both legs and chest). Discharged due to disability caused by wounds on 8/29/1861.

Strickland, W.
CO: E **Initial Rank:**
Joined: **Term (yrs):** 0 **Occupation:** **Age**
Enrolled at: **Enrolled By:** **Promoted:** No **ROH:** No
Born: **Marital Status:** **Residence**

Appears on a list of the Calhoun Rifles, dated 2/11/1861. No other record.

2nd Mississippi Alphabetical Roster (Annotated)

Stricklin, Edward W.
CO: F,L   **Initial Rank:** Private
Joined: Wednesday, May 1, 1861   **Term (yrs):** 1   **Occupation:** Planter   **Age** 29
Enrolled at: Tippah Co., MS   **Enrolled By:** Capt. Davis   **Promoted:** No   **ROH:** No
Born: **Marital Status:**   **Residence**

Transferred to Company L on 11/1/1862. Wounded at Gettysburg on 7/1/1863. Furloughed. Did not return. Listed as deserted during Mar/Apr 1864 muster.

Suber, David P.
CO: I   **Initial Rank:** Private
Joined: Wednesday, May 1, 1861   **Term (yrs):** 1   **Occupation:** Teacher   **Age** 24
Enrolled at: Pontotoc Co., MS   **Enrolled By:** Capt. Herring   **Promoted:** No   **ROH:** Yes
Born: **Marital Status:**   **Residence**

Killed in battle at 2nd Manassas on 8/29/1862. ROH for Second Manassas, 8/28/1862.

Sugar, John
CO: C   **Initial Rank:** Private
Joined: **Term (yrs):** 0   **Occupation:**   **Age**
Enrolled at: **Enrolled By:**   **Promoted:** No   **ROH:** No
Born: **Marital Status:**   **Residence**

Appears on a Federal register of prisoners of war at Fort Delaware. Captured at Gettysburg on 7/1/1863. Received at Fort Delaware on 7/6/1863. No other record.

Suggs, Joseph J.
CO: B   **Initial Rank:** Private
Joined: Wednesday, May 1, 1861   **Term (yrs):** 1   **Occupation:** Merchant   **Age** 20
Enrolled at: Tippah Co., MS   **Enrolled By:** Capt. Buchanan   **Promoted:** No   **ROH:** No
Born: **Marital Status:**   **Residence**

Died of disease at Ripley, MS on sick furlough on 4/19/1862.

Sullivan, Edward D.
CO: F   **Initial Rank:** Private
Joined: Wednesday, May 1, 1861   **Term (yrs):** 1   **Occupation:** Teacher   **Age** 34
Enrolled at: Tippah Co., MS   **Enrolled By:** Capt. Davis   **Promoted:** Yes   **ROH:** No
Born: **Marital Status:**   **Residence**

Appointed 4th Sergeant on 7/1/1861. Killed in battle at 1st Manassas on 7/21/1861.

2nd Mississippi Alphabetical Roster (Annotated)

Sullivan, Francis
CO: E **Initial Rank:** Private
Joined: *Term (yrs):* 0 *Occupation:* *Age*
Enrolled at: *Enrolled By:* *Promoted:* No *ROH:* No
Born: *Marital Status:* *Residence*

Appears on a Federal roll of prisoners of war at Camp Douglas, IL applying for oath of allegiance, Dec, —, 1864 (roll not dated). Captured at Woodville, MS on 10/5/1864. Remarks: "Claims to have been loyal. Enlisted to avoid conscription. Was captured, desires to take oath of allegiance to the United States & become a loyal citizen." No other record.

Sullivan, William H.
CO: H **Initial Rank:** Private
Joined: Monday, April 29, 1861 *Term (yrs):* 1 *Occupation:* Farmer *Age* 21
Enrolled at: Pontotoc Co., MS *Enrolled By:* Capt. Taylor *Promoted:* No *ROH:* No
Born: Alabama *Marital Status:* S *Residence* Tupelo, MS

Admitted to hospital in Richmond with wound on 10/18/1862 (date of wound or engagement not provided in company records). Returned to duty on 11/25/1862. Wounded and captured at Gettysburg on 7/3/1863. Taken to Fort Delaware. Released on oath on 6/11/1865.

Suratt, Malkijah
CO: A,S **Initial Rank:** Private
Joined: Wednesday, May 1, 1861 *Term (yrs):* 1 *Occupation:* Farmer *Age* 42
Enrolled at: Tishomingo Co., MS *Enrolled By:* Capt. Leeth *Promoted:* Yes *ROH:* No
Born: Tennessee *Marital Status:* M *Residence* Rienzi, MS

Appointed Assistant Quartermaster by order of the Secretary of War on 7/18/1861. Commissioned Quartermaster (rank of Captain) on 7/23/1861. Captured at Gettysburg (Greencastle, PA) on 7/5/1863. Sent to Johnson's Island, OH. Paroled and forwarded to Point Lookout, MD for exchange on 3/14/1865.

Suratt, Thomas E.
CO: A **Initial Rank:** Private
Joined: Saturday, March 1, 1862 *Term (yrs):* 3 *Occupation:* Student *Age* 20
Enrolled at: Jacinto, MS *Enrolled By:* Lt. Clayton *Promoted:* No *ROH:* No
Born: Mississippi *Marital Status:* S *Residence* Booneville, MS

Killed in battle at Sharpsburg on 9/17/1862.

2nd Mississippi Alphabetical Roster (Annotated)

Sutherland, James

CO: K,B *Initial Rank:* Private
Joined: Wednesday, May 1, 1861 *Term (yrs):* 1 *Occupation:* Farmer *Age* 21
Enrolled at: Tishomingo Co., MS *Enrolled By:* Capt. Stone *Promoted:* No *ROH:* No
Born: Tennessee *Marital Status:* *Residence*

Transferred to Company B on 4/29/1862. Wounded (in leg) on 5/31/1862 at battle of Seven Pines. Sent to hospital in Richmond. Furloughed 50-days from 11/22/1862. Did not return. Listed as deserted at Iuka, MS for Mar/Apr 1864 muster roll. However, other records show he applied for a disability discharge that appears to have been approved on 7/23/1862. Also, Federal records show him captured near Iuka, MS on 10/20/1863. Disposition not stated. [should not have been identified as a deserter].

Sutherland, James W.

CO: A *Initial Rank:* Private
Joined: Wednesday, May 1, 1861 *Term (yrs):* 1 *Occupation:* Carpenter *Age* 24
Enrolled at: Tishomingo Co., MS *Enrolled By:* Capt. Leeth *Promoted:* No *ROH:* No
Born: *Marital Status:* M *Residence* Rienzi, MS

Suffered an accidental wound to hand. Discharged for disability on 9/2/1861.

Suttlemeyer, James W.

CO: L *Initial Rank:* Private
Joined: Monday, March 3, 1862 *Term (yrs):* 3 *Occupation:* Farmer *Age* 43
Enrolled at: Ripley, MS *Enrolled By:* Col. Falkner *Promoted:* No *ROH:* No
Born: North Carolina *Marital Status:* M *Residence* Silver Springs, MS

Dropped from rolls as deserter at Blackwater, VA on 6/4/1863. Taken into custody by Federal authorities on 6/15/1863. Had oath of allegiance administered on 6/24/1863.

Sutton, Francis M.

CO: K *Initial Rank:* Private
Joined: Saturday, March 1, 1862 *Term (yrs):* 3 *Occupation:* *Age* 22
Enrolled at: Iuka, MS *Enrolled By:* Lt. Latham *Promoted:* No *ROH:* No
Born: *Marital Status:* *Residence*

Wounded and captured at Williamsport, MD on 7/8/1863. Died of wounds at the Seminary Hospital, Hagerstown, MD on 7/19/1863.

2nd Mississippi Alphabetical Roster (Annotated)

Sutton, George W.
CO: K **Initial Rank:** Private
Joined: Wednesday, May 1, 1861 **Term (yrs):** 1 **Occupation:** Farmer **Age** 19
Enrolled at: Tishomingo Co., MS **Enrolled By:** Capt. Stone **Promoted:** No **ROH:** No
Born: **Marital Status:** **Residence**

Admitted to hospital in Richmond with wound on 7/13/1863 (date of wound or engagement not given in company records). Returned to duty on 8/7/1863. Furloughed on 12/28/1864. Listed as AWOL since 2/5/1865 for last company muster (Jan/Feb 1865).

Sutton, John A.
CO: K **Initial Rank:** Private
Joined: Wednesday, May 1, 1861 **Term (yrs):** 1 **Occupation:** Farmer **Age** 34
Enrolled at: Tishomingo Co., MS **Enrolled By:** Capt. Stone **Promoted:** No **ROH:** No
Born: Alabama **Marital Status:** **Residence**

Discharged upon expiration of term of service — over age — on 5/27/1862.

Sutton, William H.
CO: K **Initial Rank:** Private
Joined: Saturday, March 1, 1862 **Term (yrs):** 3 **Occupation:** **Age** 28
Enrolled at: Iuka, MS **Enrolled By:** Lt. Latham **Promoted:** No **ROH:** No
Born: **Marital Status:** **Residence**

Wounded in battle at Seven Pines on 5/31/1862. Furloughed. Died of wounds (exact time of death, unknown. About 8/1/1862 on his way to Mississippi on furlough, according to records).

Swaine, Wilson B.
CO: L **Initial Rank:** Private
Joined: Monday, March 3, 1862 **Term (yrs):** 3 **Occupation:** Farmer **Age** 24
Enrolled at: Ripley, MS **Enrolled By:** Col. Falkner **Promoted:** No **ROH:** No
Born: Mississippi **Marital Status:** M **Residence** Silver Springs, MS

Furloughed for 40-days from 10/21/1863 (cause not stated). Failed to return. Dropped from rolls as deserter on 3/1/1864.

2nd Mississippi Alphabetical Roster (Annotated)

Swallow, Andrew CO: K *Initial Rank:* Private
Joined: *Term (yrs):* 0 *Occupation:* *Age*
Enrolled at: *Enrolled By:* *Promoted:* No *ROH:* No
Born: *Marital Status:* *Residence*

Appears on a Federal list of Rebel sick and wounded prisoners of war received at DeCamp General Hospital, Davids Island, NY Harbor from Gettysburg. List not dated. Captured at Gettysburg between 7/1/1863 and 7/4/1863. No other record.

Sweet, Marion N. CO: D *Initial Rank:* Private
Joined: Saturday, March 9, 1861 *Term (yrs):* 0 *Occupation:* *Age*
Enrolled at: Toombs Store, MS *Enrolled By:* John McGuirk *Promoted:* No *ROH:* No
Born: *Marital Status:* *Residence*

Appears on a company muster roll. No other record.

Sweney, Milton CO: B *Initial Rank:* Private
Joined: Wednesday, September 18, 1861 *Term (yrs):* 1 *Occupation:* *Age*
Enrolled at: Ripley, MS *Enrolled By:* Lt. Davenport *Promoted:* No *ROH:* No
Born: *Marital Status:* *Residence*

Wounded (leg) and captured at Gettysburg on 7/1/1863 (captured on 7/5/1863). Taken to DeCamp General Hospital, Davids Island, NY Harbor and paroled to City Point, VA on 9/16/1863. Furloughed from hospital in Richmond on 12/10/1863 "until exchanged." Exchanged on 1/1/1864. Returned to duty. Listed as present for last muster roll dated Jan/Feb 1865.

Swilker, John CO: *Initial Rank:* Private
Joined: *Term (yrs):* 0 *Occupation:* *Age*
Enrolled at: *Enrolled By:* *Promoted:* No *ROH:* No
Born: *Marital Status:* *Residence*

Appears on Federal prisoner of war records. Captured at Fair Oaks on 5/31/1862 and 6/1/1862 and sent to Fort Delaware. Exchanged at Aikens Landing, VA on 8/5/1862. [Misidentified. This man is probably a member of the 2nd Mississippi Infantry Battalion as noted in some of the record headers "2 Miss Batt'n" and "2 Bn. Miss."] No other records.

2nd Mississippi Alphabetical Roster (Annotated)

Swiney, Thomas   CO: A   Initial Rank:

Joined: Wednesday, February 20, 1861   *Term (yrs):* 0   *Occupation:*   *Age*

Enrolled at: Corinth, MS   *Enrolled By:* R. Griffith   *Promoted:* No   *ROH:* No

Born: *Marital Status:*   *Residence*

Appears on a company muster roll. No other record.

Swinn, George S.   CO: Initial Rank: Private

Joined: *Term (yrs):* 0   *Occupation:*   *Age* 33

Enrolled at: *Enrolled By:*   *Promoted:* No   *ROH:* No

Born: *Marital Status:*   *Residence*

Appears on a Federal register of prisoners of war. Dated Memphis, TN on 3/14/186?. "Deserters from rebel army." No other record.

Swinney, Wiley J.   CO: A   Initial Rank: Private

Joined: Wednesday, May 1, 1861   *Term (yrs):* 1   *Occupation:* Farmer   *Age* 18

Enrolled at: Tishomingo Co., MS   *Enrolled By:* Capt. Leeth   *Promoted:* No   *ROH:* No

Born: Mississippi   *Marital Status:* S   *Residence* Booneville, MS

Wounded (right thigh) in battle at Gaines Mill on 6/27/1862. Furloughed. Discharged on 4/7/1863 on surgeon's certificate of disability due to wound.

Swinny, William A.   CO: E, B   Initial Rank: Private

Joined: Wednesday, March 12, 1862   *Term (yrs):* 3   *Occupation:*   *Age* 17

Enrolled at: Guntown, MS   *Enrolled By:* Capt. Bates   *Promoted:* No   *ROH:* No

Born: *Marital Status:* S   *Residence* Baldwyn, MS

Transferred to Company B on 11/1/1862. Wounded (left hip) and captured at Gettysburg on 7/1/1863 (captured on 7/5/1863). Sent to DeCamp General Hospital, Davids Island, NY Harbor and paroled to City Point, VA on 9/16/1863. Furloughed from hospital at Richmond. Exchanged on 1/1/1864. Failed to return. Company records remarks: "Died." However, he appears on a Federal roll of prisoners of war surrendered and paroled at Meridian, MS on 5/12/1865.

2nd Mississippi Alphabetical Roster (Annotated)

Tabler, John W. H.
CO: C **Initial Rank:** Private
Joined: Saturday, March 1, 1862 **Term (yrs):** 3 **Occupation:** **Age**
Enrolled at: Verona, MS **Enrolled By:** Lt. Pounds **Promoted:** No **ROH:** No
Born: **Marital Status:** **Residence**

Admitted to hospital in Richmond on 6/5/1864 (no cause given). Returned to duty on 6/21/1864. Admitted to hospital in Richmond with wound on 8/20/1864 (date of wound or engagement not mentioned in company records). Furloughed for 30-days as of 8/25/1864. Did not return. Listed as deserted during last (Jan/Feb 1865) company muster roll.

Tabor, Thomas A.
CO: E **Initial Rank:** Private
Joined: Wednesday, May 1, 1861 **Term (yrs):** 1 **Occupation:** Farmer **Age** 23
Enrolled at: Itawamba Co., MS **Enrolled By:** Capt. Booth **Promoted:** No **ROH:** No
Born: Mississippi **Marital Status:** S **Residence** Guntown, MS

Discharged on 7/25/1862 for disability.

Talbert, Samuel N.
CO: B,L **Initial Rank:** Private
Joined: Tuesday, June 25, 1861 **Term (yrs):** 1 **Occupation:** Farmer **Age** 31
Enrolled at: Winchester, VA **Enrolled By:** Capt. Buchanan **Promoted:** No **ROH:** No
Born: South Carolina **Marital Status:** S **Residence**

Also see Henry Miller (substitute). Transferred to Company L on 7/17/1862. Discharged on 7/24/1862 by reason of furnishing a substitute.

Talbot, William H.
CO: B **Initial Rank:** Private
Joined: Monday, March 3, 1862 **Term (yrs):** 3 **Occupation:** Druggist **Age** 16
Enrolled at: Ripley, MS **Enrolled By:** Capt. Buchanan **Promoted:** No **ROH:** No
Born: Mississippi **Marital Status:** S **Residence**

Mortally wounded and captured at Sharpsburg on 9/17/1862. Died (date not given) at John Poffenberger's farm near Antietam.

2nd Mississippi Alphabetical Roster (Annotated)

Talbott, Allen
CO: B **Initial Rank:** Private
Joined: Wednesday, May 1, 1861   *Term (yrs):* 1 *Occupation:* Farmer   *Age* 20
Enrolled at: Tippah Co., MS   *Enrolled By:* Capt. Buchanan   *Promoted:* Yes   *ROH:* No
Born: *Marital Status:*   *Residence*

Wounded (thigh) at 1st Manassas on 7/21/1861. Sent to hospital at Charlottesville, VA. Returned to duty. Appointed 2nd Corporal on 4/30/1862. Detailed as brigade Quartermaster Sergeant from Sep/Oct 1863 muster to Jul/Aug 1864 muster. Paroled at Appomattox Court House, VA on 4/9/1865.

Tally, John F.
CO: C **Initial Rank:** Private
Joined: Wednesday, May 1, 1861   *Term (yrs):* 1 *Occupation:* Farmer   *Age* 21
Enrolled at: Itawamba Co., MS   *Enrolled By:* Capt. Bromley   *Promoted:* No   *ROH:* No
Born: Alabama   *Marital Status:*   *Residence*

Discharged due to disability at Camp Fisher, VA on 9/16/1861.

Tankersley, James H.
CO: A **Initial Rank:**
Joined: Wednesday, February 20, 1861   *Term (yrs):* 0 *Occupation:*   *Age*
Enrolled at: Corinth, MS   *Enrolled By:* R. Griffith   *Promoted:* No   *ROH:* No
Born: *Marital Status:*   *Residence*

Appears on a company muster roll. No other record.

Tapp, Curtis
CO: I **Initial Rank:** Private
Joined: Tuesday, September 17, 1861   *Term (yrs):* 1 *Occupation:* Farmer   *Age* 37
Enrolled at: Cherry Creek, MS   *Enrolled By:* Lt. Davenport   *Promoted:* No   *ROH:* No
Born: Georgia   *Marital Status:*   *Residence*

Discharged on 8/1/1862 — over age non-conscript.

2nd Mississippi Alphabetical Roster (Annotated)

Tapscott, Lycurgus L.   CO: A,I   Initial Rank: Private

Joined: Saturday, March 1, 1862   **Term (yrs):** 3   **Occupation:** Farmer   **Age** 23
Enrolled at: Jacinto, MS   **Enrolled By:** Lt. Clayton   **Promoted:** No   **ROH:** No
Born: North Carolina   **Marital Status:** S   **Residence** Kossuth, MS

Transferred to Company I on 4/30/1862. Transferred back to Company A on 1/16/1863. Wounded (left leg) 7/1/1863 and captured (7/5/1863) at Gettysburg. Sent to DeCamp General Hospital, Davids Island, NY Harbor. Paroled to City Point, VA on 9/16/1863. Furloughed from hospital in Williamsburg, VA on 9/13/1863. Returned to duty. Captured at Petersburg (Hatcher's Run?) on 4/2/1865. Taken to Point Lookout, MD. Released on oath on 6/21/1865.

Tarpley, William J.   CO: I   Initial Rank: Private

Joined: Saturday, March 1, 1862   **Term (yrs):** 3   **Occupation:** Farmer   **Age** 24
Enrolled at: Jacinto, MS   **Enrolled By:** Lt. Clayton   **Promoted:** No   **ROH:** No
Born: **Marital Status:** M   **Residence** Rienzi, MS

Transferred to Company I on 4/30/1862. Discharged for disability on 9/19/1862 at the General Hospital, Huguenot Springs, VA.

Tarver, Benjamin L.   CO: F   Initial Rank: Private

Joined: Saturday, March 1, 1862   **Term (yrs):** 3   **Occupation:** Farmer   **Age** 22
Enrolled at: Ripley, MS   **Enrolled By:** Capt. Powers   **Promoted:** No   **ROH:** No
Born: Georgia   **Marital Status:** S   **Residence**

Admitted to hospital in Richmond with gunshot wound to left hand on 7/20/1863 (date of wound or engagement not given in company records). Returned to duty on 8/17/1863. Wounded at The Wilderness on 5/5/1864. Furloughed 60-days from 6/25/1864. Listed as AWOL for last company muster (Jan/Feb 1865). Appears on a Federal report of prisoners of war paroled at Holly Springs, MS. Surrendered on 5/4/1865.

Tarver, R.   CO: Initial Rank: Private

Joined: **Term (yrs):** 0   **Occupation:**   **Age**
Enrolled at: **Enrolled By:**   **Promoted:** No   **ROH:** No
Born: **Marital Status:**   **Residence**

Also see 3rd Mississippi Infantry, State Troops. Appears on a Federal list of prisoners, taken and paroled during the March to the Mobile and Ohio Railroad. Dated Holly Springs, MS on 12/25/1862. No other record.

2nd Mississippi Alphabetical Roster (Annotated)

Tate, William M.   *CO:* B,L   *Initial Rank:* 4th Corporal

Joined: Wednesday, May 1, 1861   *Term (yrs):* 1   *Occupation:* Farmer   *Age* 20

Enrolled at: Tippah Co., MS   *Enrolled By:* Capt. Buchanan   *Promoted:* No   *ROH:* No

Born: South Carolina   *Marital Status:* S   *Residence* Molina, MS

Transferred to Company L on 4/30/1862. Wounded (in shoulder) at Sharpsburg on 9/17/1862. Sent to hospital at Winchester. Died of wounds at Staunton, VA on 11/10/1862.

Taylor, Charles   *CO:* B   *Initial Rank:* Private

Joined: *Term (yrs):* 0   *Occupation:*   *Age*

Enrolled at: *Enrolled By:*   *Promoted:* No   *ROH:* No

Born: *Marital Status:*   *Residence*

Appears on a Federal report of prisoners of war who have died at U. S. A. General Hospital, Chester, PA, from Oct. 1 to 31, 1863 (report not dated). Captured at Gettysburg on 7/3/1863. Died on 10/22/1863. Number of grave: 220. Locality of grave: Chester Cemetery.

Taylor, Eli   *CO:* F   *Initial Rank:* Private

Joined: Monday, September 30, 1861   *Term (yrs):* 1   *Occupation:* Blacksmith   *Age* 26

Enrolled at: Iuka, MS   *Enrolled By:* Lt. Davenport   *Promoted:* No   *ROH:* No

Born: Tennessee   *Marital Status:*   *Residence*

Discharged on 12/8/1861 due to disability at Camp Fisher, VA.

Taylor, John   *CO:* C   *Initial Rank:* Private

Joined: Saturday, March 1, 1862   *Term (yrs):* 3   *Occupation:*   *Age*

Enrolled at: Verona, MS   *Enrolled By:* Lt. Pounds   *Promoted:* No   *ROH:* No

Born: *Marital Status:*   *Residence*

Admitted to hospital in Richmond with wound on 10/18/1862 (date of wound or engagement not noted in company records). Returned to duty on 11/25/1862. Wounded in battle at The Wilderness on 5/5/1864. Sent to hospital. Returned to duty. Listed as present for last company muster dated Jan/Feb 1865.

2nd Mississippi Alphabetical Roster (Annotated)

Taylor, John W.
CO: **Initial Rank:** Private
Joined: **Term (yrs):** 0   **Occupation:**   **Age**
Enrolled at: **Enrolled By:**   **Promoted:** No   **ROH:** No
Born: **Marital Status:**   **Residence**

Appears on Federal prisoner of war records. Captured at Corinth, MS on 6/1/1862. Sent to Alton, IL. Paroled from Alton to Vicksburg, MS for exchange on 9/23/1862. No other records.

Taylor, Samuel H.
CO: H   **Initial Rank:** Captain
Joined: Monday, April 29, 1861   **Term (yrs):** 1   **Occupation:** Farmer   **Age** 46
Enrolled at: Pontotoc Co., MS   **Enrolled By:** Col. Falkner   **Promoted:** No   **ROH:** No
Born: Virginia   **Marital Status:** M   **Residence** Tupelo, MS

Also see general & staff officers, C.S.A. Relieved from duty on 4/23/1862 due to reorganization of company. Discharged.

Taylor, Thomas J.
CO: K   **Initial Rank:** Private
Joined: Saturday, March 1, 1862   **Term (yrs):** 3   **Occupation:**   **Age** 26
Enrolled at: Iuka, MS   **Enrolled By:** Lt. Latham   **Promoted:** No   **ROH:** No
Born: **Marital Status:**   **Residence**

Captured at Williamsburg, VA (not dated). Paroled and exchanged. Wounded in battle at Seven Pines on 5/31/1862. Furloughed. Returned to duty. Admitted to hospital at Richmond on 10/10/1863 with wound to right leg (company records do not detail date of wound or engagement). Returned to duty on 2/4/1864. Captured at Hatcher's Run on 4/2/1865. Sent to Point Lookout, MD. Camp hospital records say he died on 6/27/1865 at Point Lookout, MD).

Terrill, Samuel F.
CO: C   **Initial Rank:** Private
Joined: Saturday, March 1, 1862   **Term (yrs):** 3   **Occupation:** Farmer   **Age** 23
Enrolled at: Verona, MS   **Enrolled By:** Lt. Pounds   **Promoted:** No   **ROH:** No
Born: Georgia   **Marital Status:**   **Residence**

Apparently discharged on account of disability from hospital on 11/29/1862. However, records indicated he returned to duty with the company and died of disease at Richmond, VA on 2/2/1864.

2nd Mississippi Alphabetical Roster (Annotated)

Terry, Henry C.
CO: K **Initial Rank:** Private
Joined: Saturday, March 1, 1862 **Term (yrs):** 3 **Occupation:** **Age** 24
Enrolled at: Iuka, MS **Enrolled By:** Lt. Latham **Promoted:** Yes **ROH:** No
Born: **Marital Status:** **Residence**

Elected 2nd Lieutenant on 4/8/1862. Assigned to duty on 4/23/1862. Listed as 1st Lieutenant during Jul/Aug, 1862 muster. Wounded in battle at 2nd Manassas on 8/29/1862. Furloughed. Returned to duty. Listed as Captain during Mar/Apr 1863 muster. Killed in action at The Wilderness on 5/5/1864.

Terry, William C.
CO: L **Initial Rank:** Private
Joined: Monday, April 14, 1862 **Term (yrs):** 3 **Occupation:** Farmer **Age** 26
Enrolled at: Grenada, MS **Enrolled By:** Col. Miller **Promoted:** No **ROH:** No
Born: Alabama **Marital Status:** M **Residence**

Also see 42nd Mississippi Infantry Regiment. Transferred from Company B of the 42nd Mississippi in August 1864. Wounded at the Weldon Railroad on 8/19/1864. Sent to hospital. Last (Jan/Feb 1865) company muster lists as AWOL since 12/27/1864 on sick furlough to Mississippi. Surrendered at La Grange, TN on 5/17/1865. Paroled.

Thomas, Albert G.
CO: A **Initial Rank:** Private
Joined: Wednesday, May 1, 1861 **Term (yrs):** 1 **Occupation:** Farmer **Age** 22
Enrolled at: Tishomingo Co., MS **Enrolled By:** Capt. Leeth **Promoted:** No **ROH:** No
Born: **Marital Status:** **Residence**

Killed in battle at 1st Manassas on 7/21/1861.

Thomas, John D.
CO: E **Initial Rank:** Private
Joined: Wednesday, May 1, 1861 **Term (yrs):** 1 **Occupation:** Farmer **Age** 22
Enrolled at: Itawamba Co., MS **Enrolled By:** Capt. Booth **Promoted:** Yes **ROH:** No
Born: Mississippi **Marital Status:** S **Residence** Guntown, MS

Also see 11th Mississippi Infantry Regiment. Promoted to 3rd Corporal on 4/17/1862. Transferred to Company I, 11th Mississippi Infantry on 8/4/1862.

2nd Mississippi Alphabetical Roster (Annotated)

Thomas, John F. *CO:* L *Initial Rank:* Private
Joined: Thursday, August 13, 1863 *Term (yrs):* 3 *Occupation:* Plasterer *Age* 29
Enrolled at: Enterprise, MS *Enrolled By:* Maj. Berry *Promoted:* No *ROH:* No
Born: Tennessee *Marital Status:* M *Residence* Moscow, TN

Accompanying list of engagements shows him wounded at The Wilderness on 5/5/1864 (company records do not so indicate). Captured near Petersburg (Hatcher's Run?) on 4/2/1865. Taken to Point Lookout, MD. Released on oath on 6/21/1865.

Thomas, John G. *CO:* D *Initial Rank:* Private
Joined: Saturday, March 9, 1861 *Term (yrs):* 0 *Occupation:* *Age*
Enrolled at: Toombs Store, MS *Enrolled By:* John McGuirk *Promoted:* No *ROH:* No
Born: *Marital Status:* *Residence*

Appears on a company muster roll. No other record.

Thomas, John L. *CO:* E *Initial Rank:* Private
Joined: Wednesday, May 1, 1861 *Term (yrs):* 1 *Occupation:* Farmer *Age* 22
Enrolled at: Itawamba Co., MS *Enrolled By:* Capt. Booth *Promoted:* No *ROH:* No
Born: *Marital Status:* S *Residence* Guntown, MS

Discharged due to disability on 12/19/1861 at Camp Fisher, VA.

Thomas, Richard A. *CO:* *Initial Rank:* Private
Joined: *Term (yrs):* 0 *Occupation:* *Age*
Enrolled at: *Enrolled By:* *Promoted:* No *ROH:* No
Born: *Marital Status:* *Residence*

Also see R. A. Thomas, 12th Mississippi Infantry Regiment. No other record.

Thomas, William A. *CO:* B,D *Initial Rank:* Private
Joined: Monday, March 3, 1862 *Term (yrs):* 3 *Occupation:* Farmer *Age* 21
Enrolled at: Ripley, MS *Enrolled By:* Capt. Buchanan *Promoted:* No *ROH:* Yes
Born: South Carolina *Marital Status:* M *Residence* Pine Grove, MS

Transferred to Company D on 4/30/1862. Wounded near Petersburg on 9/17/1864. Sent to hospital in Richmond. Last company muster roll (Jan/Feb 1865) lists him as AWOL since 2/20/1865. Surrendered at La Grange, TN on 5/20/1865. ROH for The Wilderness, 5/6/1864.

2nd Mississippi Alphabetical Roster (Annotated)

Thomas, William A.
CO: D **Initial Rank:** Private
Joined: Wednesday, May 1, 1861 **Term (yrs):** 1 **Occupation:** Waggoner **Age** 20
Enrolled at: Tippah Co., MS **Enrolled By:** Capt. Beck **Promoted:** No **ROH:** No
Born: South Carolina **Marital Status:** **Residence**

Discharged for disability at Lynchburg, VA on 5/22/1861. However, must have later rejoined company, because subsequent hospital records show him admitted on 9/17/1864 and furloughed 60-days from 10/28/1864.

Thomas, William E.
CO: E **Initial Rank:** Private
Joined: Wednesday, May 1, 1861 **Term (yrs):** 1 **Occupation:** Farmer **Age** 18
Enrolled at: Itawamba Co., MS **Enrolled By:** Capt. Booth **Promoted:** No **ROH:** No
Born: Mississippi **Marital Status:** S **Residence** Guntown, MS

Mortally wounded in battle at 2nd Manassas on 8/30/1862. Died as a result of wound at Charlottesville, VA on 9/30/1862.

Thomason, James B.
CO: H **Initial Rank:** Private
Joined: Monday, April 29, 1861 **Term (yrs):** 1 **Occupation:** Clerk **Age** 21
Enrolled at: Pontotoc Co., MS **Enrolled By:** Capt. Taylor **Promoted:** No **ROH:** No
Born: Alabama **Marital Status:** S **Residence** Tupelo, MS

Given sick furlough in April 1863. Did not return. Listed as deserted during May/Jun 1863 muster roll.

Thompson, Benjamin F.
CO: B **Initial Rank:** Private
Joined: Wednesday, May 1, 1861 **Term (yrs):** 1 **Occupation:** Farmer **Age**
Enrolled at: Tippah Co., MS **Enrolled By:** Capt. Buchanan **Promoted:** No **ROH:** No
Born: **Marital Status:** **Residence**

Slightly wounded at 1st Manassas on 7/21/1861. Returned to duty. Wounded and captured at Seven Pines on 5/31/1862 (Leg amputated at thigh). Paroled and released for exchange on 8/31/1862. Furloughed from hospital. Listed as AWOL from 10/1/1863 during last (Jan/Feb 1865) company muster roll.

2nd Mississippi Alphabetical Roster (Annotated)

Thompson, Henry L.
CO: D   **Initial Rank:** 1st Corporal
Joined: Wednesday, May 1, 1861   **Term (yrs):** 1   **Occupation:** Farmer   **Age**
Enrolled at: Tippah Co., MS   **Enrolled By:** Capt. Beck   **Promoted:** Yes   **ROH:** No
Born: **Marital Status:** S   **Residence** Pine Grove, MS

Wounded at 1st Manassas on 7/21/1861. Furloughed 30-days from 8/16/1861. Returned to duty. Elected Jr. 2nd Lieutenant on 4/23/1862. Severely wounded (in back) in battle at Gaines Mill on 6/27/1862. Sent to hospital in Richmond, VA. Furloughed. Did not return to company. Dropped from rolls on 5/21/1863 for prolonged AWOL (being disabled of wound received in battle Gaines Farm and not reporting regularly).

Thompson, J. A.
CO: E   **Initial Rank:**
Joined: **Term (yrs):** 0   **Occupation:**   **Age**
Enrolled at: **Enrolled By:**   **Promoted:** No   **ROH:** No
Born: **Marital Status:**   **Residence**

Appears on a list of the Calhoun Rifles, dated 2/11/1861. No other record.

Thompson, Thomas G. N.
CO: F   **Initial Rank:** Private
Joined: Wednesday, May 1, 1861   **Term (yrs):** 1   **Occupation:** Planter   **Age** 21
Enrolled at: Tippah Co., MS   **Enrolled By:** Capt. Davis   **Promoted:** No   **ROH:** Yes
Born: **Marital Status:**   **Residence**

Killed in battle at Sharpsburg on 9/17/1862. ROH for South Mountain (Boonsboro), 9/14/1862.

Thompson, William M. T.
CO: H   **Initial Rank:** Private
Joined: Monday, April 29, 1861   **Term (yrs):** 1   **Occupation:** Teacher   **Age** 27
Enrolled at: Pontotoc Co., MS   **Enrolled By:** Capt. Taylor   **Promoted:** No   **ROH:** No
Born: Tennessee   **Marital Status:** S   **Residence** Tupelo, MS

Captured at 1st Manassas on 7/21/1861. Paroled. Returned to duty. Wounded in battle at Sharpsburg on 9/17/1862. Sent to hospital in Richmond. Returned to duty. Hospital records show admission for wound on 7/9/1863 (date of wound or engagement not mentioned in company records). Furloughed 60-days from 1/4/1864. Returned to duty. Last company muster (Jan/Feb 1865) remarks: "Sent to hospital sick Dec 20, 1864." Hospital records show he was furloughed 40-days from 2/18/1865. Retired for medical disability on 2/23/1865.

2nd Mississippi Alphabetical Roster (Annotated)

Thorn, John C.   *CO:* C   *Initial Rank:* Private
Joined: Wednesday, May 1, 1861   *Term (yrs):* 1   *Occupation:* Doctor   *Age* 31
Enrolled at: Itawamba Co., MS   *Enrolled By:* Capt. Bromley   *Promoted:* No   *ROH:* No
Born: *Marital Status:*   *Residence*

Died of disease at Goldsboro, NC on 2/10/1863.

Thorn, John T.   *CO:* B   *Initial Rank:* Private
Joined: Wednesday, May 1, 1861   *Term (yrs):* 1   *Occupation:* Farmer   *Age* 25
Enrolled at: Tippah Co., MS   *Enrolled By:* Capt. Buchanan   *Promoted:* No   *ROH:* No
Born: South Carolina   *Marital Status:*   *Residence*

Killed in battle at 1st Manassas on 7/21/1861.

Thornton, T. B.   *CO:* F   *Initial Rank:* Private
Joined: *Term (yrs):* 0   *Occupation:*   *Age*
Enrolled at: *Enrolled By:*   *Promoted:* No   *ROH:* No
Born: *Marital Status:*   *Residence*

Appears on a Federal report of prisoners of war paroled for 5/17/1865 and 5/18/1865 at Memphis, TN (not dated). No other record.

Threlkeld, Samuel C.   *CO:* I   *Initial Rank:* Private
Joined: Wednesday, May 1, 1861   *Term (yrs):* 1   *Occupation:* Farmer   *Age* 49
Enrolled at: Pontotoc Co., MS   *Enrolled By:* Capt. Herring   *Promoted:* No   *ROH:* No
Born: *Marital Status:*   *Residence*

Died at Strasburg, VA on 7/29/1861 (cause not stated).

Ticer, J. Pinkney   *CO:* B   *Initial Rank:* Private
Joined: Friday, August 23, 1861   *Term (yrs):* 1   *Occupation:*   *Age*
Enrolled at: Camp Jones, VA   *Enrolled By:* Capt. Buchanan   *Promoted:* Yes   *ROH:* Yes
Born: *Marital Status:*   *Residence*

Wounded at battle of Seven Pines on 5/31/1862. Returned to duty. Captured at Falling Waters, MD on 7/14/1863. Sent to Point Lookout, MD. Exchanged on 2/10/1865. Present at Camp Lee (near Richmond — parole camp) during camp muster dated Feb 1865. ROH for Gettysburg, 7/3/1863.

2nd Mississippi Alphabetical Roster (Annotated)

Tidwell, James M.
CO: D,F **Initial Rank:** Private
Joined: Tuesday, October 1, 1861 **Term (yrs):** 1 **Occupation:** Farmer **Age**
Enrolled at: Iuka, MS **Enrolled By:** Lt. Davenport **Promoted:** No **ROH:** No
Born: **Marital Status:** M **Residence** Pine Grove, MS

Also see Capt. Ahl's Battery, Pennsylvania Artillery. Transferred to Company F on 4/30/1862. Deserted on 6/28/1863 "went to the Yankees." Taken into Federal custody on 7/4/1863 in Pennsylvania. Sent to Fort Delaware. Became "Galvanized Yankee" and joined U. S. service — Capt. Ahl's Battery (not dated).

Tigert, David P.
CO: L **Initial Rank:** Orderly Sergeant
Joined: Monday, March 3, 1862 **Term (yrs):** 3 **Occupation:** Farmer **Age** 35
Enrolled at: Ripley, MS **Enrolled By:** Col. Falkner **Promoted:** Yes **ROH:** Yes
Born: Tennessee **Marital Status:** M **Residence** Ripley, MS

Promoted to 1st Sergeant on 3/23/1862. Captured at Petersburg (Hatcher's Run?) on 4/2/1865. Taken to Point Lookout, MD. Released on oath on 6/21/1865. ROH for Bethesda Church, 5/31/1864.

Tilman, D. S.
CO: K **Initial Rank:** Private
Joined: **Term (yrs):** 0 **Occupation:** **Age**
Enrolled at: **Enrolled By:** **Promoted:** No **ROH:** No
Born: **Marital Status:** **Residence**

Appears on a Federal roll of prisoners of war. Captured at Selma, AL on 4/2/1865. No other record. [Misidentified. Probably belongs to the 2nd/6th Missouri Infantry Regiment Consolidated which was in the area (and would be also be abbreviated "2 Regt Miss")]

Todd, Thomas K.
CO: D **Initial Rank:** Private
Joined: Wednesday, May 1, 1861 **Term (yrs):** 1 **Occupation:** Farmer **Age** 16
Enrolled at: Tippah Co., MS **Enrolled By:** Capt. Beck **Promoted:** No **ROH:** No
Born: Mississippi **Marital Status:** S **Residence** Salem, MS

Wounded (in foot) in battle at 1st Manassas on 7/21/1861. Returned to duty. Discharged by Conscript Act on 7/271/862 — under 18-years old.

2nd Mississippi Alphabetical Roster (Annotated)

Tolund, James M.
Joined: Saturday, March 1, 1862 *Term (yrs):* 3 *Occupation:* Farmer *CO:* K *Initial Rank:* Private *Age* 43
Enrolled at: Iuka, MS *Enrolled By:* Lt. Latham *Promoted:* No *ROH:* No
Born: Alabama *Marital Status:* *Residence*
Killed in battle at Gaines Mill on 6/27/1862.

Toombs, Albert G.
Joined: Wednesday, May 1, 1861 *Term (yrs):* 1 *Occupation:* Merchant *CO:* D *Initial Rank:* Private *Age* 27
Enrolled at: Tippah Co., MS *Enrolled By:* Capt. Beck *Promoted:* No *ROH:* No
Born: Tennessee *Marital Status:* S *Residence* Pine Grove, MS
Discharged for disability at Camp Fisher, VA on 2/27/1862.

Topp, Robert C.
Joined: Saturday, March 2, 1861 *Term (yrs):* 0 *Occupation:* *CO:* G *Initial Rank:* *Age*
Enrolled at: Pontotoc, MS *Enrolled By:* Capt. Kilpatrick *Promoted:* No *ROH:* No
Born: *Marital Status:* *Residence*
Appears on a company muster roll. No other record.

Topp, William H.
Joined: Wednesday, May 1, 1861 *Term (yrs):* 1 *Occupation:* Merchant *CO:* G *Initial Rank:* 2nd Sergeant *Age* 38
Enrolled at: Pontotoc Co., MS *Enrolled By:* Capt. Kilpatrick *Promoted:* Yes *ROH:* No
Born: Tennessee *Marital Status:* M *Residence* Pontotoc, MS
Appointed 1st Sergeant on 7/26/1861. Discharged on 8/2/1862 by order of General Lee — over age.

Trammell, Benjamin F.
Joined: Saturday, March 1, 1862 *Term (yrs):* 3 *Occupation:* *CO:* K *Initial Rank:* Private *Age* 25
Enrolled at: Iuka, MS *Enrolled By:* Lt. Latham *Promoted:* No *ROH:* Yes
Born: *Marital Status:* *Residence*
Wounded in battle at the Weldon Railroad on 8/19/1864. Furloughed 60-days from hospital on 10/25/1864. Listed as absent wounded during final (Jan/Feb 1865) company muster. ROH for Weldon Railroad, 8/19/1864.

2nd Mississippi Alphabetical Roster (Annotated)

Traylor, David H.
CO: C **Initial Rank:** 2nd Corporal
Joined: Wednesday, May 1, 1861 **Term (yrs):** 1 **Occupation:** Farmer **Age** 31
Enrolled at: Itawamba Co., MS **Enrolled By:** Capt. Bromley **Promoted:** No **ROH:** No
Born: **Marital Status:** **Residence**

Killed in battle at 1st Manassas on 7/21/1861.

Traylor, Thomas W.
CO: C **Initial Rank:** Private
Joined: Saturday, March 1, 1862 **Term (yrs):** 3 **Occupation:** **Age**
Enrolled at: Verona, MS **Enrolled By:** Lt. Pounds **Promoted:** Yes **ROH:** No
Born: **Marital Status:** **Residence**

Wounded at Gaines Mill on 6/27/1862. Sent to hospital in Richmond, VA. Furloughed on 9/29/1862 for 30-days. Returned to duty. Admitted to hospital in Charlottesville, VA with wound on 7/12/1863 (company records do not give date of wound or engagement). Returned to duty on 9/2/1863. Listed as 5th Sergeant for May/Jun 1864 muster. Wounded at The Wilderness (left thigh) on 5/5/1864. Furloughed 60-days from 5/24/1864. Returned to duty. Captured at Petersburg (Hatcher's Run?) on 4/2/1865. Sent to Fort Delaware. Released on oath on 6/11/1865.

Tremble, Marcus L.
CO: A **Initial Rank:** Private
Joined: Saturday, March 1, 1862 **Term (yrs):** 3 **Occupation:** Farmer **Age** 20
Enrolled at: Jacinto, MS **Enrolled By:** Lt. Clayton **Promoted:** No **ROH:** No
Born: Mississippi **Marital Status:** M **Residence** Jacinto, MS

Died of disease at Richmond, VA (Chimborazo Hospital #3) on 6/18/1862.

Tremble, Robert C.
CO: A **Initial Rank:** Private
Joined: Saturday, March 1, 1862 **Term (yrs):** 3 **Occupation:** Farmer **Age** 22
Enrolled at: Jacinto, MS **Enrolled By:** Lt. Clayton **Promoted:** No **ROH:** No
Born: Mississippi **Marital Status:** M **Residence** Jacinto, MS

Furloughed from hospital sick on 7/23/1864. Did not return. Last muster (Jan/Feb 1865) lists him as AWOL since 1/1/1865.

2nd Mississippi Alphabetical Roster (Annotated)

Trice, Morgan A.   *CO:* H   *Initial Rank:* Private

Joined: Monday, April 29, 1861   *Term (yrs):* 1 *Occupation:* Carpenter   *Age* 35

Enrolled at: Pontotoc Co., MS   *Enrolled By:* Capt. Taylor   *Promoted:* No   *ROH:* No

Born: Tennessee   *Marital Status:* M   *Residence* Blount Springs, AL

Also see Camp of Instruction, Talladega, AL. Discharged on 7/29/1862 — over age.

Trott, James F.   *CO:* A   *Initial Rank:* Private

Joined: Wednesday, May 1, 1861   *Term (yrs):* 1 *Occupation:* Clerk   *Age* 23

Enrolled at: Tishomingo Co., MS   *Enrolled By:* Capt. Leeth   *Promoted:* No   *ROH:* No

Born: *Marital Status:* S   *Residence* Rienzi, MS

Discharged for disability on 6/23/1861 by order of General Johnston.

Tubb, Abraham S.   *CO:* K   *Initial Rank:* Private

Joined: Wednesday, May 1, 1861   *Term (yrs):* 1 *Occupation:* Musician   *Age* 28

Enrolled at: Tishomingo Co., MS   *Enrolled By:* Capt. Stone   *Promoted:* No   *ROH:* No

Born: Tennessee   *Marital Status:*   *Residence*

Wounded (shoulder) in battle at 1st Manassas on 7/21/1861. Sent to hospital in Charlottesville, VA. Discharged due to disability caused by wound on 9/13/1861.

Tudor, John G.   *CO:* F   *Initial Rank:* Private

Joined: Wednesday, May 1, 1861   *Term (yrs):* 1 *Occupation:* Planter   *Age* 24

Enrolled at: Tippah Co., MS   *Enrolled By:* Capt. Davis   *Promoted:* No   *ROH:* No

Born: *Marital Status:*   *Residence*

According to company records, furloughed 34-days from 2/1/1863. Never returned to company. Deserted. However, Federal records show he was captured at Pocahontas, MS on 12/2/1863 and sent to Alton, IL on 12/29/1863. Sent to Fort Delaware on 4/4/1864. Released on oath on 6/11/1865. [he should not be listed as a deserter since he was unable to return to his command due to capture].

2nd Mississippi Alphabetical Roster (Annotated)

Turner, George H. *CO:* C *Initial Rank:* Private
Joined: Wednesday, May 1, 1861   *Term (yrs):* 1   *Occupation:* Farmer   *Age* 22
Enrolled at: Itawamba Co., MS   *Enrolled By:* Capt. Bromley   *Promoted:* No   *ROH:* Yes
Born: *Marital Status:*   *Residence*

Wounded at 1st Manassas on 7/21/1861. Sent to hospital at Charlottesville, VA. Returned to duty. Wounded at 2nd Manassas on 8/29/1862. Sent to hospital. Returned to duty. Killed in action at the Weldon Railroad on 8/18/1864. ROH for Weldon Railroad, 8/18/1864.

Turner, J. J. *CO:* C *Initial Rank:* Private
Joined: Tuesday, October 1, 1861   *Term (yrs):* 1   *Occupation:*   *Age*
Enrolled at: Richmond, MS   *Enrolled By:* Lt. Davenport   *Promoted:* No   *ROH:* No
Born: *Marital Status:*   *Residence*

Discharged on plea of military exemption on 5/25/1862.

Turner, J. R. *CO:* K *Initial Rank:* Private
Joined: *Term (yrs):* 0   *Occupation:*   *Age*
Enrolled at: *Enrolled By:*   *Promoted:* No   *ROH:* No
Born: *Marital Status:*   *Residence*

Appears on a Federal list of Confederate prisoners who have died in General Hospitals in the Department of the Ohio. Dated Cincinnati, OH, 4/20/1863. Captured at Shiloh, TN (not dated). Date of death, 5/12/1862 at the General Hospital, Camp Dennison, OH. No other record. [Misidentified. Unlikely a member of the 2nd Mississippi would have been captured at Shiloh].

Turner, Joseph P. *CO:* C *Initial Rank:* Private
Joined: Wednesday, May 1, 1861   *Term (yrs):* 1   *Occupation:* Farmer   *Age* 19
Enrolled at: Itawamba Co., MS   *Enrolled By:* Capt. Bromley   *Promoted:* No   *ROH:* No
Born: Alabama   *Marital Status:*   *Residence*

Wounded (left thigh) and captured at Gettysburg on 7/3/1863 (other records say 7/1/1863 or 7/5/1863). Taken to DeCamp General Hospital, Davids Island, NY Harbor. Paroled to City Point, VA on 1/5/1864 to await exchange. Furloughed 30-days from hospital in Richmond on 3/20/1863. Still listed as "absent" during the last (Jan/Feb 1865) company muster.

2nd Mississippi Alphabetical Roster (Annotated)

Turner, William E. *CO:* A *Initial Rank:* Private
Joined: Wednesday, May 1, 1861 *Term (yrs):* 1 *Occupation:* Clerk *Age* 23
Enrolled at: Tishomingo Co., MS *Enrolled By:* Capt. Leeth *Promoted:* Yes *ROH:* No
Born: Tennessee *Marital Status:* S *Residence* Jacinto, MS

Appointed 3rd Corporal on 7/23/1861. Wounded in battle at Sharpsburg on 9/17/1862. Promoted to 1st Corporal. Returned to duty. Severely wounded at Gettysburg on 7/1/1863. Furloughed. Returned to duty. Honorably retired to Invalid Corps, P.A.C.S. from service on 4/1/1864 due to disability caused by wound received at Gettysburg. Surrendered and paroled at Meridian, MS on 5/12/1865.

Usher, John D. *CO:* G *Initial Rank:* 1st Lieutenant
Joined: *Term (yrs):* 0 *Occupation:* *Age*
Enrolled at: *Enrolled By:* *Promoted:* No *ROH:* No
Born: *Marital Status:* *Residence*

Appears on Federal prisoner of war records. Captured at Franklin, TN on 11/30/1864. Sent to Johnson's Island, OH. [misidentified — the 2nd Mississippi was not at the battle of Franklin. Probably mislabeled for the 2nd/6th Missouri Infantry Consolidated].

Ussery, Leander F. *CO:* K *Initial Rank:* Private
Joined: Wednesday, May 1, 1861 *Term (yrs):* 1 *Occupation:* Planter *Age* 26
Enrolled at: Tishomingo Co., MS *Enrolled By:* Capt. Stone *Promoted:* No *ROH:* No
Born: Alabama *Marital Status:* *Residence*

Also see Gordon's Cavalry. Transferred to Gordon's Cavalry (Chickasaw Rangers) on 10/7/1961.

Vairin, Augustus L. P. *CO:* B, L *Initial Rank:* 1st Sergeant
Joined: Wednesday, May 1, 1861 *Term (yrs):* 1 *Occupation:* Watchmaker *Age* 41
Enrolled at: Tippah Co., MS *Enrolled By:* Capt. Buchanan *Promoted:* No *ROH:* No
Born: *Marital Status:* S *Residence* Ripley, MS

Transferred to Company L from Company B on 4/30/1862 (reduced to ranks). Transferred back to Company B on 1/20/1863. Wounded and captured at Gettysburg on 7/3/1863. Taken to DeCamp General Hospital, Davids Island, NY Harbor. Paroled and sent to City Point, VA for exchange on 10/28/1863. Sent to hospital in Richmond, VA. Furloughed. Returned to duty on 8/29/1864. Was detailed to guard forage at Bellfield, VA from 11/12/1864 thru last (Jan/Feb 1865) company muster. Hospital records show he was admitted during April, 1865 to the General Hospital at Greensboro, NC.

2nd Mississippi Alphabetical Roster (Annotated)

Vance, John B.
CO: H *Initial Rank:* 2nd Lieutenant
Joined: Monday, April 29, 1861 *Term (yrs):* 1 *Occupation:* Farmer *Age* 30
Enrolled at: Pontotoc Co., MS *Enrolled By:* Capt. Taylor *Promoted:* No *ROH:* No
Born: South Carolina *Marital Status:* S *Residence* Chesterville, MS

Resigned on 7/26/1861 due to disability due to disease.

Vanhook, John L.
CO: B *Initial Rank:* Private
Joined: Wednesday, May 1, 1861 *Term (yrs):* 1 *Occupation:* Farmer *Age* 17
Enrolled at: Tippah Co., MS *Enrolled By:* Capt. Buchanan *Promoted:* No *ROH:* No
Born: *Marital Status:* *Residence*

Captured on 2/14/1864 at Port Gibson, MS while on furlough. Sent to Camp Douglas, IL. Sent to New Orleans, LA for exchange on 5/4/1865. Exchanged on 5/23/1865.

Vanzant, John L.
CO: G *Initial Rank:* Private
Joined: Wednesday, May 1, 1861 *Term (yrs):* 1 *Occupation:* Farmer *Age* 25
Enrolled at: Pontotoc Co., MS *Enrolled By:* Capt. Miller *Promoted:* No *ROH:* Yes
Born: Tennessee *Marital Status:* S *Residence* Pontotoc, MS

Killed in battle at Sharpsburg on 9/17/1862. ROH for South Mountain (Boonsboro), 9/14/1862.

Varnum, James M.
CO: D *Initial Rank:* Private
Joined: Wednesday, May 1, 1861 *Term (yrs):* 1 *Occupation:* Farmer *Age* 22
Enrolled at: Tippah Co., MS *Enrolled By:* Capt. Beck *Promoted:* No *ROH:* No
Born: Mississippi *Marital Status:* S *Residence* Shelby Creek, MS

Discharged due to disability on 12/19/1861 by order of General Whiting.

Vaughan, Ebenezer H.
CO: G *Initial Rank:* Private
Joined: Monday, September 16, 1861 *Term (yrs):* 1 *Occupation:* Farmer *Age* 26
Enrolled at: Pontotoc, MS *Enrolled By:* Lt. Davenport *Promoted:* No *ROH:* No
Born: Mississippi *Marital Status:* S *Residence* Pontotoc, MS

Discharged for disability on 12/10/1861 by order of General Whiting.

2nd Mississippi Alphabetical Roster (Annotated)

Vaughn, Albert W.   *CO:* D   *Initial Rank:* Private
Joined: *Term (yrs):* 0   *Occupation:* Merchant   *Age*
Enrolled at: *Enrolled By:*   *Promoted:* No   *ROH:* No
Born: *Marital Status:*   *Residence*

Appears on Federal prisoner of war records. Sent to Camp Douglas, IL (circa 9/23/1862 — not dated). Brigade: Chalmers; Division: Bragg. One list heading also reads as 2 Miss. Battn. [Misidentified — this man belongs to another unit, not the 2nd Mississippi Infantry Regiment but a cavalry command].

Vaughn, William C.   *CO:* E   *Initial Rank:* Private
Joined: Saturday, February 22, 1862   *Term (yrs):* 3   *Occupation:* Carpenter   *Age* 31
Enrolled at: Guntown, MS   *Enrolled By:* Capt. Bates   *Promoted:* Yes   *ROH:* No
Born: South Carolina   *Marital Status:* M   *Residence* Guntown, MS

Appointed 3rd Corporal on 4/30/1862. Discharged by reason of disability on 7/25/1862.

Vernor, Zenas E.   *CO:* B   *Initial Rank:* Private
Joined: Monday, July 15, 1861   *Term (yrs):* 1   *Occupation:*   *Age*
Enrolled at: Winchester, VA   *Enrolled By:* Capt. Buchanan   *Promoted:* No   *ROH:* Yes
Born: *Marital Status:*   *Residence*

Wounded (left leg) at The Wilderness on 5/5/1864. Returned to duty. Wounded in battle on 10/1/1864. Furloughed 40-days from 10/7/1864. Did not return. Listed as AWOL since 12/1/1864 during last (Jan/Feb, 1865) company muster roll. Paroled at Holly Springs, MS on 5/27/1865. ROH for Weldon Railroad, 8/18/1864.

Vester, Robert   *CO:* F   *Initial Rank:* Private
Joined: Tuesday, April 30, 1861   *Term (yrs):* 1   *Occupation:* Planter   *Age* 19
Enrolled at: Ripley, MS   *Enrolled By:* Capt. Davis   *Promoted:* No   *ROH:* No
Born: *Marital Status:*   *Residence*

Deserted during battle at 1st Manassas on 7/21/1861.

Vincent, Charles S.   *CO:* C   *Initial Rank:* Private
Joined: Wednesday, May 1, 1861   *Term (yrs):* 1   *Occupation:* Farmer   *Age* 23
Enrolled at: Itawamba Co., MS   *Enrolled By:* Capt. Bromley   *Promoted:* No   *ROH:* Yes
Born: *Marital Status:* M   *Residence*

Killed in battle at 2nd Manassas on 8/29/1862. ROH for Second Manassas, 8/28/1862.

2nd Mississippi Alphabetical Roster (Annotated)

Vinson, William A.
CO: C **Initial Rank:** Private
Joined: Wednesday, May 1, 1861 **Term (yrs):** 1 **Occupation:** Farmer **Age** 22
Enrolled at: Itawamba Co., MS **Enrolled By:** Capt. Bromley **Promoted:** No **ROH:** No
Born: **Marital Status:**   **Residence**

Listed as present during most of the company musters, including the last muster during Jan/Feb 1865. Surrendered and paroled, dated Columbus, MS on 5/19/1865.

Wade, James L.
CO: H **Initial Rank:** Private
Joined: Monday, April 29, 1861 **Term (yrs):** 1 **Occupation:** Farmer **Age** 23
Enrolled at: Pontotoc Co., MS **Enrolled By:** Capt. Taylor **Promoted:** No **ROH:** No
Born: South Carolina **Marital Status:** S **Residence** Popular Springs, MS

Killed in battle on 10/1/1864 near Fort McRae (Fort Bratton).

Wade, Thomas J.
CO: A **Initial Rank:** Private
Joined: Wednesday, May 1, 1861 **Term (yrs):** 1 **Occupation:** Clerk **Age** 22
Enrolled at: Tishomingo Co., MS **Enrolled By:** Capt. Leeth **Promoted:** No **ROH:** No
Born: Tennessee **Marital Status:** S **Residence** Burnsville, MS

Deserted to the enemy on 4/12/1863.

Wafford, Marmaduke
CO: K **Initial Rank:** 1st Corporal
Joined: Wednesday, May 1, 1861 **Term (yrs):** 1 **Occupation:** Boatman **Age** 50
Enrolled at: Tishomingo Co., MS **Enrolled By:** Capt. Stone **Promoted:** No **ROH:** No
Born: **Marital Status:**   **Residence**

Died (cause not given) at Harpers Ferry, VA on 5/24/1861.

Waits, C.
CO: E **Initial Rank:**
Joined: **Term (yrs):** 0 **Occupation:**   **Age**
Enrolled at: **Enrolled By:**   **Promoted:** No **ROH:** No
Born: **Marital Status:**   **Residence**

Appears on a list of the Calhoun Rifles dated 2/11/1861. No other record.

2nd Mississippi Alphabetical Roster (Annotated)

Waits, John *CO:* E *Initial Rank:*
Joined: *Term (yrs):* 0 *Occupation:* **Age**
Enrolled at: *Enrolled By:* *Promoted:* No *ROH:* No
Born: *Marital Status:* *Residence*

Appears on a list of the Calhoun Rifles dated 2/11/1861. No other record.

Walding, James A. *CO:* D *Initial Rank:* Private
Joined: Wednesday, May 1, 1861 *Term (yrs):* 1 *Occupation:* Farmer **Age** 22
Enrolled at: Tippah Co., MS *Enrolled By:* Capt. Beck *Promoted:* Yes *ROH:* Yes
Born: Mississippi *Marital Status:* S *Residence* Snow Creek, MS

Promoted to 3rd Corporal on 4/23/1862. Admitted for wound to hospital at Williamsburg, VA on 7/27/1863 (company records do not give date of wound or engagement). Captured in battle of The Wilderness on 5/5/1864. Sent to Elmira, NY. Released on oath on 6/21/1865. ROH for Bristoe Station, 10/14/1863.

Waldo, John N. *CO:* H *Initial Rank:* Private
Joined: Monday, April 29, 1861 *Term (yrs):* 1 *Occupation:* Farmer **Age** 39
Enrolled at: Pontotoc Co., MS *Enrolled By:* Capt. Taylor *Promoted:* No *ROH:* No
Born: South Carolina *Marital Status:* M *Residence* Pontotoc, MS

Discharged due to disability on 8/13/1861

Walker, Alfred R. *CO:* C *Initial Rank:* 2nd Lieutenant
Joined: Wednesday, May 1, 1861 *Term (yrs):* 1 *Occupation:* Clerk **Age** 20
Enrolled at: Itawamba Co., MS *Enrolled By:* Capt. Bromley *Promoted:* No *ROH:* No
Born: *Marital Status:* *Residence*

No record after Feb 1862.

Walker, Andrew R. *CO:* A *Initial Rank:* Private
Joined: Wednesday, May 1, 1861 *Term (yrs):* 1 *Occupation:* Student **Age** 20
Enrolled at: Tishomingo Co., MS *Enrolled By:* Capt. Leeth *Promoted:* Yes *ROH:* No
Born: *Marital Status:* *Residence*

Elected Brevet 2nd Lieutenant from ranks on 4/22/1862. Promoted to Captain on 9/30/1862. Killed near Petersburg on 9/13/1864.

2nd Mississippi Alphabetical Roster (Annotated)

Walker, Benjamin F.
CO: F **Initial Rank:** Private
Joined: Saturday, March 1, 1862 **Term (yrs):** 3 **Occupation:** Farmer **Age** 19
Enrolled at: Ripley, MS **Enrolled By:** Capt. Davis **Promoted:** No **ROH:** No
Born: Tennessee **Marital Status:** S **Residence**

Wounded in battle at Sharpsburg on 9/17/1862. Furloughed 30-days from 10/11/1862. Did not return to company. Listed as deserted for Nov/Dec 1863 muster roll. Surrendered and paroled at La Grange, TN on 5/31/1865.

Walker, David T.
CO: C **Initial Rank:** Private
Joined: Wednesday, May 1, 1861 **Term (yrs):** 1 **Occupation:** Clerk **Age** 27
Enrolled at: Itawamba Co., MS **Enrolled By:** Capt. Bromley **Promoted:** Yes **ROH:** No
Born: **Marital Status:** **Residence**

Listed as 3rd Lieutenant during Sep/Oct 1862 muster; 2nd Lieutenant during Mar/Apr 1863 muster; and 1st Lieutenant during May/Jun 1863 muster. Captured at Gettysburg on 7/1/1863. Sent to Johnson's Island, OH. Forwarded to Fort Delaware for exchange. Released on oath on 6/12/1865.

Walker, George M.
CO: F, D **Initial Rank:** Private
Joined: Saturday, March 1, 1862 **Term (yrs):** 3 **Occupation:** Farmer **Age** 20
Enrolled at: Ripley, MS **Enrolled By:** Capt. Powers **Promoted:** No **ROH:** No
Born: Georgia **Marital Status:** S **Residence** Shelby Creek, MS

Transferred to Company D from Company F on 5/1/1862. Killed in battle at Gettysburg on 7/1/1863.

Walker, Hampton C.
CO: E **Initial Rank:** Private
Joined: Saturday, February 22, 1862 **Term (yrs):** 3 **Occupation:** Farmer **Age** 22
Enrolled at: Guntown, MS **Enrolled By:** Capt. Bates **Promoted:** No **ROH:** No
Born: Mississippi **Marital Status:** S **Residence** Marietta, MS

Hospital records show admission for a wound at Williamsburg, VA on 6/3/1864 (company records do not detail date of wound or engagement). Returned to duty. Captured in battle at Fort Bratton on 10/1/1864. Taken to Point Lookout, MD. Released on oath on 6/22/1865.

2nd Mississippi Alphabetical Roster (Annotated)

Walker, James A.
CO: E **Initial Rank:** Private
Joined: Saturday, March 1, 1862 **Term (yrs):** 3 **Occupation:** Farmer **Age** 19
Enrolled at: Guntown, MS **Enrolled By:** Capt. Bates **Promoted:** No **ROH:** No
Born: Mississippi **Marital Status:** S **Residence** Marietta, MS

Captured at Gettysburg on 7/1/1863. Sent to Fort Delaware. Released on oath on May 31, 1865.

Walker, James B.
CO: C **Initial Rank:** Private
Joined: Tuesday, October 1, 1861 **Term (yrs):** 1 **Occupation:** **Age**
Enrolled at: Richmond, MS **Enrolled By:** Lt. Davenport **Promoted:** No **ROH:** No
Born: **Marital Status:** **Residence**

Died of disease (typhoid fever) at Petersburg, VA on 6/5/1863.

Walker, James H.
CO: D **Initial Rank:** Private
Joined: Wednesday, May 1, 1861 **Term (yrs):** 1 **Occupation:** Farmer **Age** 22
Enrolled at: Tippah Co., MS **Enrolled By:** Capt. Beck **Promoted:** No **ROH:** Yes
Born: Georgia **Marital Status:** S **Residence** Shelby Creek, MS

Wounded in battle at 2nd Manassas on 8/29/1862. Furloughed. Returned to duty. Captured at Gettysburg on 7/1/1863. Sent to Fort Delaware. Released on oath on 6/11/1865. ROH for Seven Pines, 5/31/1862.

Walker, John
CO: A **Initial Rank:** Private
Joined: Saturday, March 1, 1862 **Term (yrs):** 3 **Occupation:** Laborer **Age** 18
Enrolled at: Jacinto, MS **Enrolled By:** Lt. Clayton **Promoted:** No **ROH:** No
Born: Mississippi **Marital Status:** S **Residence** Burnsville, MS

Died of disease (typhoid fever) at Charlottesville, VA on 6/25/1862.

Walker, John
CO: E **Initial Rank:** Private
Joined: Wednesday, May 1, 1861 **Term (yrs):** 1 **Occupation:** **Age**
Enrolled at: Itawamba Co., MS **Enrolled By:** Capt. Booth **Promoted:** No **ROH:** No
Born: **Marital Status:** **Residence**

Appears on a muster-in roll and a list of the Calhoun Rifles dated 2/11/1861. No other records.

2nd Mississippi Alphabetical Roster (Annotated)

Walker, John M.
CO: A **Initial Rank:** Private
Joined: Wednesday, May 1, 1861 **Term (yrs):** 1 **Occupation:** Teacher **Age** 24
Enrolled at: Tishomingo Co., MS **Enrolled By:** Capt. Leeth **Promoted:** No **ROH:** No
Born: Tennessee **Marital Status:** S **Residence** Jacinto, MS

Detailed as courier to Colonel Law and later to Maj. Gen. Davis from May/Jun 1862 muster through last company muster of Jan/Feb 1865. Last muster remarks reads: "Absent with leave on furlough of indulgence."

Walker, Robert M.
CO: D **Initial Rank:** Private
Joined: Wednesday, May 1, 1861 **Term (yrs):** 1 **Occupation:** Farmer **Age** 24
Enrolled at: Tippah Co., MS **Enrolled By:** Capt. Beck **Promoted:** No **ROH:** No
Born: Georgia **Marital Status:** S **Residence** Shelby Creek, MS

Captured at 1st Manassas on 7/21/1861. Paroled and on furlough in Mississippi. Returned to duty. Captured at Falling Waters, MD on 7/14/1863. Sent to Point Lookout, MD. Exchanged on 9/18/1864. Listed as AWOL for last (Jan/Feb 1865) company muster. Surrendered and paroled at La Grange, TN on 5/22/1865.

Walker, Thomas L.
CO: F **Initial Rank:** Private
Joined: Saturday, March 1, 1862 **Term (yrs):** 3 **Occupation:** Farmer **Age** 26
Enrolled at: Ripley, MS **Enrolled By:** Capt. Powers **Promoted:** No **ROH:** No
Born: South Carolina **Marital Status:** S **Residence**

Died of disease at Lynchburg, VA on 7/24/1862.

Wall, John I
CO: E **Initial Rank:** Private
Joined: Monday, March 17, 1862 **Term (yrs):** 3 **Occupation:** **Age** 21
Enrolled at: Guntown, MS **Enrolled By:** Capt. Bates **Promoted:** No **ROH:** No
Born: **Marital Status:** S **Residence** Guntown, MS

Deserted on 5/15/1862.

Wall, John J.
CO: F **Initial Rank:** Private
Joined: Wednesday, May 1, 1861 **Term (yrs):** 1 **Occupation:** Planter **Age** 38
Enrolled at: Tippah Co., MS **Enrolled By:** Capt. Davis **Promoted:** Yes **ROH:** No
Born: **Marital Status:** **Residence**

Elected 2nd Lieutenant on 7/20/1861. No record after Oct 1861.

2nd Mississippi Alphabetical Roster (Annotated)

Wallace, Thomas D. *CO:* F *Initial Rank:* Private

Joined: Saturday, March 1, 1862 *Term (yrs):* 3 *Occupation:* Farmer *Age* 34

Enrolled at: Ripley, MS *Enrolled By:* Lt. Ford *Promoted:* No *ROH:* No

Born: Tennessee *Marital Status:* M *Residence*

Discharged due to disability on 4/1/1863.

Wallis, James C. *CO:* K *Initial Rank:* Private

Joined: Saturday, March 1, 1862 *Term (yrs):* 3 *Occupation:* *Age* 25

Enrolled at: Iuka, MS *Enrolled By:* Lt. Latham *Promoted:* No *ROH:* No

Born: *Marital Status:* *Residence*

Company records indicate he was awarded a "wounded furlough" (date of wound or engagement not given). Hospital records show admission at Richmond on 7/13/1863, but not for treatment of a wound. Furloughed 40-days from 7/25/1863. Did not return. Company records list him as deserted from the Nov/Dec 1863 muster. However, Federal records show he was captured (in Mississippi) by Federal forces and sent to the Provost Marshal in Memphis, TN on 10/21/1863. Released on 10/24/1863.

Wallis, Newton C. *CO:* K *Initial Rank:* Private

Joined: Saturday, March 1, 1862 *Term (yrs):* 3 *Occupation:* *Age* 20

Enrolled at: Iuka, MS *Enrolled By:* Lt. Latham *Promoted:* No *ROH:* No

Born: *Marital Status:* *Residence*

Richmond hospital records show admission for wound on 7/9/1863 (company records do not indicate date of wound or engagement). Returned to duty on 7/30/1863. Also, hospital records at Richmond show he was admitted for treatment of a wound (right thigh) on 5/10/1864 (company records again provide no details on date of wound or engagement, but hospital records show he was wounded on 5/5/1864 at The Wilderness). Furloughed 60-days from 5/25/1864. Last company muster lists him as AWOL from 7/31/1864. However, he also appears on a muster roll of Company E of the 1st Regiment Troops and Defences, Macon, GA for Nov/Dec 1864. Captured at Macon, GA either 4/20/1865 or 4/21/1865. Released on oath at Nashville, TN on 7/30/1865.

Walters, Evander M. *CO:* A *Initial Rank:* Private

Joined: Wednesday, May 1, 1861 *Term (yrs):* 1 *Occupation:* Clerk *Age* 23

Enrolled at: Tishomingo Co., MS *Enrolled By:* Capt. Leeth *Promoted:* No *ROH:* No

Born: South Carolina *Marital Status:* S *Residence* Burnsville, MS

Also see 4th Georgia Infantry Regiment. Transferred to Company I of the 4th Georgia on 8/4/1862.

2nd Mississippi Alphabetical Roster (Annotated)

Ward, Evans J.
CO: H **Initial Rank:** Private
Joined: Monday, April 29, 1861 **Term (yrs):** 1 **Occupation:** Mechanic **Age** 23
Enrolled at: Pontotoc Co., MS **Enrolled By:** Capt. Taylor **Promoted:** No **ROH:** No
Born: Alabama **Marital Status:** S **Residence** Chesterville, MS

Wounded (flesh wound in thigh) in battle at Gaines Mill on 6/27/1862. Sent to hospital in Richmond, VA. Furloughed. Returned to duty. Furloughed for sickness on 2/1/1863. Did not return. Listed as deserted on 12/20/1863.

Ward, James C.
CO: K **Initial Rank:** Private
Joined: Wednesday, May 1, 1861 **Term (yrs):** 1 **Occupation:** Farmer **Age** 28
Enrolled at: Tishomingo Co., MS **Enrolled By:** Capt. Stone **Promoted:** No **ROH:** No
Born: **Marital Status:** **Residence**

Wounded at Gaines Mill on 6/27/1862. Furloughed. Captured at Tuscumbia, AL on 2/22/1863 by Federal forces. Sent to Alton, IL. Paroled to City Point, VA for exchange on 4/1/1863. Returned to duty. Wounded in battle at The Wilderness 5/5/1864. Returned to duty. "Deserted to the enemy from the picket line 17 Feby 1865."

Ward, James M.
CO: L **Initial Rank:** 1st Corporal
Joined: Monday, March 3, 1862 **Term (yrs):** 3 **Occupation:** Teacher **Age** 24
Enrolled at: Ripley, MS **Enrolled By:** Col. Falkner **Promoted:** No **ROH:** Yes
Born: Mississippi **Marital Status:** M **Residence** Ripley, MS

Killed in battle at Malvern Hill on 7/1/1862. ROH for Malvern Hill, 7/1/1862.

Ward, John M.
CO: G **Initial Rank:** Private
Joined: Wednesday, May 1, 1861 **Term (yrs):** 1 **Occupation:** Printer **Age** 30
Enrolled at: Pontotoc Co., MS **Enrolled By:** Capt. Miller **Promoted:** No **ROH:** No
Born: **Marital Status:** S **Residence** Pontotoc, MS

Killed in battle at 1st Manassas on 7/21/1861.

Wardlaw, John H.
CO: G **Initial Rank:** Private
Joined: Monday, September 16, 1861 **Term (yrs):** 1 **Occupation:** Farmer **Age** 54
Enrolled at: Pontotoc, MS **Enrolled By:** Lt. Davenport **Promoted:** No **ROH:** No
Born: South Carolina **Marital Status:** M **Residence** Pontotoc, MS

Discharged on 1/3/1862 at Camp Fisher, VA for disability (and over age).

2nd Mississippi Alphabetical Roster (Annotated)

Ware, John W.
CO: H   *Initial Rank:* Private
Joined: Monday, April 29, 1861   *Term (yrs):* 1   *Occupation:* Clerk   *Age* 22
Enrolled at: Pontotoc Co., MS   *Enrolled By:* Capt. Taylor   *Promoted:* No   *ROH:* No
Born: Mississippi   *Marital Status:* S   *Residence* Tupelo, MS

Severely wounded (leg amputated at thigh) and captured at Gettysburg on 7/1/1863. Sent to DeCamp General Hospital, Davids Island, NY Harbor. Paroled to City Point, VA for exchange on 9/27/1863. Furloughed from hospital in Richmond for 20-days from 10/8/1863. Last company muster (Jan/Feb 1865) remarks: "Has authority to appear before Medical Examining Board for retirement."

Wareham, Richard C.
CO: F   *Initial Rank:* Private
Joined: Wednesday, May 1, 1861   *Term (yrs):* 1   *Occupation:* Dentist   *Age* 30
Enrolled at: Tippah Co., MS   *Enrolled By:* Capt. Davis   *Promoted:* No   *ROH:* No
Born: *Marital Status:*   *Residence*

Discharged due to disability caused by gunshot wound (circumstances not given) on 10/28/1861. Appears as a signature on an Inspection Report of Davis' Brigade dated 1/30/1865 near Petersburg. Signs report as Ord. Officer. No other records.

Watkins, William
CO: A   *Initial Rank:* Private
Joined: *Term (yrs):* 0   *Occupation:*   *Age*
Enrolled at: *Enrolled By:*   *Promoted:* No   *ROH:* No
Born: *Marital Status:*   *Residence*

Appears on Federal prisoner of war records. Captured near White Station, MS (?). Not dated. Received at Memphis, TN on 2/3/1865. Sent to Vicksburg, MS for exchange on 3/12/1865. No other records.

Watson, Augustus
CO: C   *Initial Rank:* Private
Joined: Wednesday, May 1, 1861   *Term (yrs):* 1   *Occupation:* Farmer   *Age* 19
Enrolled at: Itawamba Co., MS   *Enrolled By:* Capt. Bromley   *Promoted:* No   *ROH:* No
Born: *Marital Status:*   *Residence*

Captured at Gettysburg on 7/1/1863. Sent to Fort Delaware. Released on oath on 6/11/1865.

2nd Mississippi Alphabetical Roster (Annotated)

Watson, Hezekiah C.

CO: E   **Initial Rank:** Private

Joined: Friday, February 28, 1862   **Term (yrs):** 3   **Occupation:**   **Age** 28

Enrolled at: Guntown, MS   **Enrolled By:** Capt. Bates   **Promoted:** No   **ROH:** No

Born: **Marital Status:**   **Residence**

Died of disease at Ashland, VA on 4/26/1862.

Watt, James T.

CO: E   **Initial Rank:** Private

Joined: Wednesday, May 1, 1861   **Term (yrs):** 1   **Occupation:** Mechanic   **Age** 27

Enrolled at: Itawamba Co., MS   **Enrolled By:** Capt. Booth   **Promoted:** No   **ROH:** No

Born: South Carolina   **Marital Status:** S   **Residence** Guntown, MS

Detailed on detached extra duty as teamster and regimental and brigade carpenter and wheelwright for much of his time of service. So listed during last company muster (Jan/Feb 1865). Captured near Petersburg (Hatcher's Run?) on 4/2/1865. Sent to Point Lookout, MD. Released on oath on 6/22/1865.

Watts, John W.

CO: K   **Initial Rank:** Private

Joined: Wednesday, May 1, 1861   **Term (yrs):** 1   **Occupation:** Laborer   **Age** 22

Enrolled at: Tishomingo Co., MS   **Enrolled By:** Capt. Stone   **Promoted:** No   **ROH:** No

Born: **Marital Status:**   **Residence**

Wounded at Gettysburg on 7/1/1863. Deserted from hospital circa Nov 1863.

Weatherington, Benton

CO: H   **Initial Rank:** Private

Joined: Saturday, March 15, 1862   **Term (yrs):** 3   **Occupation:** Student   **Age** 18

Enrolled at: Chesterville, MS   **Enrolled By:** Lt. Porter   **Promoted:** No   **ROH:** Yes

Born: Georgia   **Marital Status:** S   **Residence** Chesterville, MS

Wounded (both legs) in battle at Sharpsburg on 9/17/1862. Furloughed. Returned to duty. Severely wounded (left shoulder and face) at The Wilderness on 5/5/1864. Furloughed 60-days from 5/19/1864. Listed as AWOL from 7/31/1864 during last company muster roll (Jan/Feb 1865). [Great grandfather of author. Younger brother to George W. Weatherington]. ROH for South Mountain (Boonsboro), 9/14/1862.

Weatherington, George W.

CO: H   **Initial Rank:** Private

Joined: Saturday, August 10, 1861   **Term (yrs):** 1   **Occupation:** Teacher   **Age** 22

Enrolled at: Camp Jones, VA   **Enrolled By:** Lt. Stone   **Promoted:** No   **ROH:** No

Born: Georgia   **Marital Status:** S   **Residence** Chesterville, MS

Wounded in battle at 2nd Manassas on 8/29/1862. Returned to duty. Killed in battle at Gettysburg on 7/1/1863. [Older brother to Benton Weatherington].

2nd Mississippi Alphabetical Roster (Annotated)

Weathers, Gustavus A.
CO: A **Initial Rank:** Private
Joined: Wednesday, May 1, 1861 **Term (yrs):** 1 **Occupation:** Mechanic **Age** 27
Enrolled at: Tishomingo Co., MS **Enrolled By:** Capt. Leeth **Promoted:** Yes **ROH:** No
Born: **Marital Status:** **Residence**

Listed as 1st Corporal during Nov/Dec 1861 muster. Elected 2nd Lieutenant on 4/22/1862. Promoted to 1st Lieutenant on 8/30/1862. Dismissed from service by sentence of Court Martial on 2/10/1863.

Weaver, Robert
CO: K **Initial Rank:** Private
Joined: Wednesday, May 1, 1861 **Term (yrs):** 1 **Occupation:** Farmer **Age** 20
Enrolled at: Tishomingo Co., MS **Enrolled By:** Capt. Stone **Promoted:** No **ROH:** No
Born: **Marital Status:** **Residence**

Mortally wounded in battle at 1st Manassas on 7/21/1861. Died of wounds on 8/10/1861.

Webb, Andrew J.
CO: F **Initial Rank:** Private
Joined: Wednesday, May 1, 1861 **Term (yrs):** 1 **Occupation:** Planter **Age** 19
Enrolled at: Tippah Co., MS **Enrolled By:** Capt. Davis **Promoted:** No **ROH:** No
Born: **Marital Status:** **Residence**

Wounded in battle at 2nd Manassas on 8/30/1862. Captured and paroled from hospital at Warrenton, VA on 9/29/1862. Furloughed 60-days from 9/29/1862. Returned to duty. Wounded on 9/13/1864. Furloughed 30-days from 9/20/1864. Last company muster roll lists him as AWOL from 11/30/1864. Paroled at Memphis, TN on 5/20/1865.

Webb, Henry T.
CO: B **Initial Rank:** Private
Joined: Wednesday, May 1, 1861 **Term (yrs):** 1 **Occupation:** Farmer **Age** 21
Enrolled at: Tippah Co., MS **Enrolled By:** Capt. Buchanan **Promoted:** No **ROH:** No
Born: Mississippi **Marital Status:** **Residence**

Wounded (through calf) at 1st Manassas on 7/21/1861. Sent to hospital at Charlottesville, VA. Returned to duty. Discharged due to disability at Camp Fisher, VA on 12/31/1861.

Weedin, Eli M.
CO: D **Initial Rank:** Private
Joined: Wednesday, May 1, 1861 **Term (yrs):** 1 **Occupation:** Farmer **Age** 34
Enrolled at: Tippah Co., MS **Enrolled By:** Capt. Beck **Promoted:** No **ROH:** No
Born: Tennessee **Marital Status:** M **Residence** Hickory Flats, MS

Discharged on 7/27/1862 — over age.

2nd Mississippi Alphabetical Roster (Annotated)

Weems, James F.
CO: E **Initial Rank:** Private
Joined: Wednesday, February 26, 1862 **Term (yrs):** 3 **Occupation:** Farmer **Age** 17
Enrolled at: Guntown, MS **Enrolled By:** Capt. Bates **Promoted:** No **ROH:** No
Born: Mississippi **Marital Status:** S **Residence** Guntown, MS

Listed as present for last company muster (Jan/Feb 1865). Paroled at Appomattox Court House, VA on 4/9/1865.

Weems, William K.
CO: E **Initial Rank:** Private
Joined: Saturday, March 1, 1862 **Term (yrs):** 3 **Occupation:** Farmer **Age** 21
Enrolled at: Guntown, MS **Enrolled By:** Capt. Bates **Promoted:** No **ROH:** No
Born: Mississippi **Marital Status:** S **Residence** Guntown, MS

Wounded (left thigh) and captured at Gettysburg on 7/1/1863. Taken to DeCamp General Hospital, Davids Island, NY Harbor. Paroled to City Point, VA on 9/8/1863 for exchange. Admitted to hospital at Petersburg, VA on 9/8/1863. Furloughed 30-days from 9/16/1863. Did not return to company. Listed as deserted during Mar/Apr 1864 muster roll.

Wells, Charles C.
CO: H **Initial Rank:** Private
Joined: Monday, April 29, 1861 **Term (yrs):** 1 **Occupation:** Farmer **Age** 39
Enrolled at: Pontotoc Co., MS **Enrolled By:** Capt. Taylor **Promoted:** Yes **ROH:** No
Born: South Carolina **Marital Status:** M **Residence** Tupelo, MS

Appointed 1st Corporal on 3/12/1862. Discharged on 7/29/1862 — over age.

Wells, Henry Pickens
CO: I **Initial Rank:** Private
Joined: Wednesday, May 1, 1861 **Term (yrs):** 1 **Occupation:** Farmer **Age** 20
Enrolled at: Pontotoc Co., MS **Enrolled By:** Capt. Herring **Promoted:** No **ROH:** No
Born: **Marital Status:** **Residence**

Captured at Gettysburg on 7/1/1863. Taken to Fort Delaware. Released on oath on 6/7/1865.

Wells, Jesse Shaw
CO: I **Initial Rank:** Private
Joined: Wednesday, May 1, 1861 **Term (yrs):** 1 **Occupation:** Farmer **Age** 24
Enrolled at: Pontotoc Co., MS **Enrolled By:** Capt. Herring **Promoted:** No **ROH:** No
Born: **Marital Status:** **Residence**

Wounded (left arm and left leg) in battle at Gettysburg on 7/1/1863. Sent to hospital in Richmond, VA. Furloughed 40-days from 11/9/1863. Returned to duty. Sent to Brigade hospital sick on 10/20/1864 by order of Colonel Stone. Returned to duty. Listed as present for last company muster roll (Jan/Feb 1865).

2nd Mississippi Alphabetical Roster (Annotated)

Wells, Ludy Young
CO: I **Initial Rank:** Private
Joined: Wednesday, May 1, 1861 **Term (yrs):** 1 **Occupation:** Farmer **Age** 21
Enrolled at: Pontotoc Co., MS **Enrolled By:** Capt. Herring **Promoted:** No **ROH:** No
Born: South Carolina **Marital Status:** S **Residence**

Wounded in battle at Sharpsburg on 9/17/1862. Furloughed 60-days from 10/10/1862. Returned to duty. Wounded and captured at Gettysburg on 7/1/1863. Died in Federal hospital near Gettysburg on 7/5/1863 (another record says 7/13/1863).

Wells, Martin M.
CO: I **Initial Rank:** 4th Corporal
Joined: Wednesday, May 1, 1861 **Term (yrs):** 1 **Occupation:** **Age** 23
Enrolled at: Pontotoc Co., MS **Enrolled By:** Capt. Herring **Promoted:** Yes **ROH:** No
Born: **Marital Status:** **Residence**

Promoted to 3rd Corporal in place of George C. Young during May/Jun 1861 period. Promoted to 1st Corporal on 7/4/1861. Promoted to 3rd Sergeant on 4/23/1862. Promoted to 2nd Sergeant in place of G. C. Young on 5/16/1863. Captured at Hatcher's Run on 4/2/1865. Taken to Point Lookout, MD. Released on oath on 6/22/1865.

Wells, William H.
CO: I **Initial Rank:** Private
Joined: Saturday, December 13, 1862 **Term (yrs):** 2 **Occupation:** Farmer **Age** 19
Enrolled at: Enterprise, MS **Enrolled By:** Capt. Miller **Promoted:** No **ROH:** No
Born: South Carolina **Marital Status:** **Residence**

Died of disease (measles) at Richmond, VA on 7/20/1864.

Welty, Lafayette
CO: B,L **Initial Rank:** Private
Joined: Monday, March 3, 1862 **Term (yrs):** 3 **Occupation:** Farmer **Age** 19
Enrolled at: Ripley, MS **Enrolled By:** Capt. Buchanan **Promoted:** No **ROH:** No
Born: Tennessee **Marital Status:** M **Residence**

Transferred to Company L from Company B on 11/1/1862. Wounded at Gettysburg on 7/3/1863. Sent to hospital in Richmond, VA. Furloughed 40-days from 7/25/1863. Did not return to company. Listed as deserted for Mar/Apr 1864 muster roll.

2nd Mississippi Alphabetical Roster (Annotated)

West, Lewis *CO:* K *Initial Rank:* Private
Joined: Wednesday, May 1, 1861 *Term (yrs):* 1 *Occupation:* Laborer *Age* 18
Enrolled at: Tishomingo Co., MS *Enrolled By:* Capt. Stone *Promoted:* No *ROH:* No
Born: *Marital Status:* *Residence*

Left sick in hospital at Corinth, MS. Never joined company in Virginia. Never mustered into Confederate service.

West, R. A. *CO:* C *Initial Rank:* Private
Joined: Saturday, March 1, 1862 *Term (yrs):* 3 *Occupation:* Farmer *Age* 33
Enrolled at: Verona, MS *Enrolled By:* Lt. Pounds *Promoted:* No *ROH:* No
Born: South Carolina *Marital Status:* *Residence*

Admitted with wound to hospital in Richmond, VA on 7/9/1863 (date of wound or engagement not provided in company records). Discharged on 11/6/1863 due to disability caused by wound.

West, Simon M. *CO:* L *Initial Rank:* Private
Joined: Monday, March 3, 1862 *Term (yrs):* 3 *Occupation:* Farmer *Age* 32
Enrolled at: Ripley, MS *Enrolled By:* Col. Falkner *Promoted:* No *ROH:* No
Born: Tennessee *Marital Status:* M *Residence* Union Mills, MS

Wounded in battle at Gettysburg on 7/1/1863. Furloughed 7/25/1863 for 40-days. Did not return to company. Struck from rolls as deserter on 3/1/1864.

Westbrook, William W. *CO:* C *Initial Rank:* Private
Joined: Wednesday, May 1, 1861 *Term (yrs):* 1 *Occupation:* Farmer *Age* 22
Enrolled at: Itawamba Co., MS *Enrolled By:* Capt. Bromley *Promoted:* No *ROH:* No
Born: *Marital Status:* *Residence*

Mortally wounded in battle at 1st Manassas on 7/21/1861. Died of wounds on 7/24/1861 at Charlottesville, VA. Remarks: "Found dead in cars." [reference to transport by railroad cars to Charlottesville from Manassas battlefield.]

2nd Mississippi Alphabetical Roster (Annotated)

Westmoreland, Henderson H. M.
CO: C **Initial Rank:** Private
Joined: Wednesday, May 1, 1861 **Term (yrs):** 1 **Occupation:** Farmer **Age** 19
Enrolled at: Itawamba Co., MS **Enrolled By:** Capt. Bromley **Promoted:** No **ROH:** No
Born: **Marital Status:** **Residence**

Appears to have been discharged due to disability on 9/6/1861. Rejoined company on 3/1/1862 at Verona, MS, enrolled by Lt. Pounds for 3-years. Wounded (right foot requiring amputation of little toe at 1st joint) and captured at Gettysburg on 7/3/1863 (captured on 7/5/1863). Taken to DeCamp General Hospital, Davids Island, NY Harbor and paroled to City Point, VA on 9/8/1863 for exchange. Furloughed from hospital at Williamsburg, VA on 9/13/1863. Did not return. Company muster roll dated May/Jun 1864 lists him as deserted.

Westmoreland, Jerome W.
CO: H **Initial Rank:** Private
Joined: Monday, April 29, 1861 **Term (yrs):** 1 **Occupation:** Farmer **Age** 22
Enrolled at: Pontotoc Co., MS **Enrolled By:** Capt. Taylor **Promoted:** Yes **ROH:** Yes
Born: Tennessee **Marital Status:** S **Residence** Tupelo, MS

Appointed 3rd Sergeant on 8/1/1861. Reduced to ranks according to Nov/Dec 1861 muster roll. Severely wounded in battle at 2nd Manassas on 8/29/1862 (leg amputated). Furloughed. Discharged at Warrenton, VA on 10/17/1862 by Medical Examining Board. ROH for Second Manassas, 8/28/1862.

Westmoreland, Mortimore T.
CO: H **Initial Rank:** Private
Joined: Saturday, August 10, 1861 **Term (yrs):** 1 **Occupation:** Farmer **Age** 24
Enrolled at: Camp Jones, VA **Enrolled By:** Lt. Stone **Promoted:** No **ROH:** No
Born: Tennessee **Marital Status:** M **Residence** Tupelo, MS

Received furlough on 9/15/1861. Failed to return. Deserted.

Wheeler, Charles N.
CO: G **Initial Rank:** Private
Joined: Wednesday, May 1, 1861 **Term (yrs):** 1 **Occupation:** Clerk **Age** 26
Enrolled at: Pontotoc Co., MS **Enrolled By:** Capt. Miller **Promoted:** No **ROH:** No
Born: New York **Marital Status:** S **Residence** Pontotoc, MS

Captured at Seven Pines on 5/31/1862. Sent to Fort Delaware. Exchanged at Aiken's Landing, VA on 8/5/1862. Deserted in August.

2nd Mississippi Alphabetical Roster (Annotated)

Wheeler, J. T. *CO:* C *Initial Rank:* Private
Joined: Saturday, March 1, 1862 *Term (yrs):* 3 *Occupation:* *Age*
Enrolled at: Verona, MS *Enrolled By:* Lt. Pounds *Promoted:* No *ROH:* No
Born: *Marital Status:* *Residence*

"Represented himself to War Dept. as an officer. Obtained a furlough and deserted Aug 1862."

Whitaker, Lorenzo D. *CO:* K *Initial Rank:* Private
Joined: Saturday, March 1, 1862 *Term (yrs):* 3 *Occupation:* *Age* 19
Enrolled at: Iuka, MS *Enrolled By:* Lt. Latham *Promoted:* No *ROH:* No
Born: *Marital Status:* *Residence*

Wounded and captured at Gettysburg on 7/2/1863. Sent to Fort Delaware (must not have been wounded seriously). Released on oath on 6/11/1865.

Whitaker, William H. *CO:* K *Initial Rank:* Private
Joined: Wednesday, May 1, 1861 *Term (yrs):* 1 *Occupation:* Student *Age* 20
Enrolled at: Tishomingo Co., MS *Enrolled By:* Capt. Stone *Promoted:* No *ROH:* No
Born: *Marital Status:* *Residence*

Discharged by reason of disability on 4/28/1862.

Whitcher, Vincent A. *CO:* B *Initial Rank:* Private
Joined: Wednesday, May 8, 1861 *Term (yrs):* 1 *Occupation:* Lawyer *Age* 28
Enrolled at: Lynchburg, VA *Enrolled By:* Capt. Buchanan *Promoted:* No *ROH:* No
Born: *Marital Status:* *Residence*

No record after June 1861.

White, Arvin *CO:* C *Initial Rank:* Private
Joined: Saturday, June 29, 1861 *Term (yrs):* 1 *Occupation:* Farmer *Age* 19
Enrolled at: Winchester, VA *Enrolled By:* Capt. Bromley *Promoted:* No *ROH:* No
Born: *Marital Status:* *Residence*

Died of disease at Richmond, VA, Chimborazo Hospital #2, on 5/12/1862.

2nd Mississippi Alphabetical Roster (Annotated)

White, Byron B.　　　　　　　　　　　　　　　　*CO:* A　　*Initial Rank:* Private

Joined: Saturday, March 1, 1862　　　*Term (yrs):* 3　*Occupation:* Farmer　　　　　　*Age* 24

Enrolled at: Jacinto, MS　　　*Enrolled By:* Lt. Clayton　　　*Promoted:* No　*ROH:* No

Born: Alabama　　　*Marital Status:* M　　　*Residence* Burnsville, MS

Wounded (flesh wound, left thigh) and captured at Gettysburg on 7/5/1863 (captured). Sent to Hammond General Hospital, Point Lookout, MD from Chester, PA hospital on 10/4/1863. Paroled to City Point, VA on 3/17/1864 for exchange. Returned to duty. Severely wounded at The Wilderness on 5/5/1864. Furloughed from hospital in Richmond, VA. Last company muster (Jan/Feb 1865) remarks: "Absent with leave on wounded furlough."

White, Daniel M.　　　　　　　　　　　　　　　　*CO:* B,L　　*Initial Rank:* Private

Joined: Wednesday, September 18, 1861　　*Term (yrs):* 1　*Occupation:* Farmer　　　*Age* 21

Enrolled at: Ripley, MS　　　*Enrolled By:* Lt. Davenport　　　*Promoted:* Yes　*ROH:* Yes

Born: Mississippi　　　*Marital Status:* S　　　*Residence* Ripley, MS

Transferred to Company L from Company B on 4/30/1862. Promoted to 2nd Corporal on 9/1/1862. Killed in battle at Gettysburg on 7/1/1863. ROH for Gettysburg, 7/1/1863.

White, Isaac N.　　　　　　　　　　　　　　　　*CO:* H　　*Initial Rank:*

Joined: Friday, March 1, 1861　　　*Term (yrs):* 0　*Occupation:*　　　　　　　*Age*

Enrolled at: Chesterville, MS　　　*Enrolled By:* Capt. Kilpatrick　　　*Promoted:* No　*ROH:* No

Born:　　　*Marital Status:*　　　*Residence*

Appears on a company muster roll. No other record.

White, L.　　　　　　　　　　　　　　　　*CO:* E　　*Initial Rank:*

Joined:　　　*Term (yrs):* 0　*Occupation:*　　　　　　　*Age*

Enrolled at:　　　*Enrolled By:*　　　*Promoted:* No　*ROH:* No

Born:　　　*Marital Status:*　　　*Residence*

Appears on a list of the Calhoun Rifles dated 2/11/1861. No other record.

Whitehead, H. J.　　　　　　　　　　　　　　　　*CO:* B　　*Initial Rank:* Private

Joined:　　　*Term (yrs):* 0　*Occupation:*　　　　　　　*Age*

Enrolled at:　　　*Enrolled By:*　　　*Promoted:* No　*ROH:* No

Born:　　　*Marital Status:*　　　*Residence*

Appears on Federal prisoner of war records on a roll of prisoners at the hospitals in and about Gettysburg, captured July 1, 2 and 3, 1863. Complaint: "Arm." No other records.

2nd Mississippi Alphabetical Roster (Annotated)

Whitehead, Jasper N.   CO: B   Initial Rank: Private

Joined: Wednesday, September 18, 1861   **Term (yrs):** 1   **Occupation:**   **Age**
Enrolled at: Ripley, MS   **Enrolled By:** Lt. Davenport   **Promoted:** No   **ROH:** No
Born: **Marital Status:**   **Residence**

Wounded in battle at 2nd Manassas on 8/29/1862. Sent to hospital. Returned to duty. Wounded (leg and thigh) and captured at Gettysburg on 7/3/1863. Taken to the General Hospital in Chester, PA. Paroled to City Point, VA on 8/20/1863 for exchange. Furloughed on 9/3/1863. Returned to duty. Wounded on 6/2/1864. Sent to hospital in Richmond, VA. Furloughed on 6/8/1864 for 60-days. Last company muster roll (Jan/Feb 1865) remarks: "Absent without leave since 1 December 1864."

Whiteside, Robert G.   CO: A   Initial Rank: Private

Joined: Wednesday, July 10, 1861   **Term (yrs):** 1   **Occupation:** Farmer   **Age** 37
Enrolled at: Winchester, VA   **Enrolled By:** Capt. Leeth   **Promoted:** No   **ROH:** No
Born: Tennessee   **Marital Status:** S   **Residence** Rienzi, MS

Discharged 5/27/1862 — over age.

Whitesides, Moses H.   CO: H,I   Initial Rank: Private

Joined: Saturday, March 15, 1862   **Term (yrs):** 3   **Occupation:** Farmer   **Age** 18
Enrolled at: Chesterville, MS   **Enrolled By:** Lt. Porter   **Promoted:** No   **ROH:** No
Born: Tennessee   **Marital Status:** S   **Residence** Chesterville, MS

Transferred to Company I from Company H on 5/1/1863 by order of Colonel Stone. Hospital records show he was admitted for a wound (gunshot wound, left hip) at Richmond, VA on 7/21/1863 (date of wound or engagement not given in company records). Returned to duty on 8/24/1863. Mortally wounded (head) at Bristoe Station on 10/14/1863. Died of wounds on 11/6/1863 at Richmond, VA (other records show death on 11/5/1863).

Whitfield, John   CO: A   Initial Rank: Private

Joined: Wednesday, July 10, 1861   **Term (yrs):** 1   **Occupation:** Farmer   **Age** 24
Enrolled at: Winchester, VA   **Enrolled By:** Capt. Leeth   **Promoted:** No   **ROH:** No
Born: Tennessee   **Marital Status:** S   **Residence** Burnsville, MS

Severely wounded (leg) in battle at 1st Manassas on 7/21/1861. Sent to hospital at Charlottesville, VA. Discharged due to disability caused by wound on 10/22/1861.

2nd Mississippi Alphabetical Roster (Annotated)

Whitfield, Josiah
CO: A **Initial Rank:** Private
Joined: Saturday, March 1, 1862 **Term (yrs):** 3 **Occupation:** Farmer **Age** 28
Enrolled at: Jacinto, MS **Enrolled By:** Lt. Clayton **Promoted:** No **ROH:** No
Born: Tennessee **Marital Status:** **Residence** Burnsville, MS

Died of disease (smallpox) at Lynchburg, VA on 1/20/1863.

Whitley, J. J.
CO: E **Initial Rank:**
Joined: **Term (yrs):** 0 **Occupation:** **Age**
Enrolled at: **Enrolled By:** **Promoted:** No **ROH:** No
Born: **Marital Status:** **Residence**

Appears on Federal prisoner of war records of sick and wounded Confederates in the hospitals in and about Gettysburg. Captured at Gettysburg (not dated). Gunshot wound to hip and face. Died of wounds on 7/16/1863. No other records. [*Buried at Hollywood Cemetery, Richmond, VA. Gettysburg Section Lot: 1.]

Whitley, Robert
CO: E **Initial Rank:** Private
Joined: Wednesday, May 1, 1861 **Term (yrs):** 1 **Occupation:** Laborer **Age** 23
Enrolled at: Itawamba Co., MS **Enrolled By:** Capt. Booth **Promoted:** Yes **ROH:** No
Born: Alabama **Marital Status:** S **Residence** Guntown, MS

Wounded at 1st Manassas on 7/21/1861 (through calf). Returned to duty. Wounded (in hand) in battle at Gaines Mill on 6/27/1862. Furloughed to Mississippi. Returned to duty. Promoted to 4th Corporal on 9/24/1862. Promoted to 2nd Lieutenant on 1/15/1863. Captured at Gettysburg on 7/1/1863. Sent to Fort Delaware. Transferred to Johnson's Island, OH on 7/20/1863. Transferred to Point Lookout, MD on 3/21/1865. Released on oath on 6/12/1865.

Whitlow, Philip
CO: G **Initial Rank:** Private
Joined: Wednesday, May 1, 1861 **Term (yrs):** 1 **Occupation:** Farmer **Age** 25
Enrolled at: Pontotoc Co., MS **Enrolled By:** Capt. Miller **Promoted:** No **ROH:** No
Born: North Carolina **Marital Status:** M **Residence** Pontotoc, MS

Deserted 3/28/1862. "Reenlisted, went home on furlough and has not returned."

2nd Mississippi Alphabetical Roster (Annotated)

Whitten, James M.
CO: B   **Initial Rank:** Private
Joined: Monday, March 4, 1861   **Term (yrs):** 0   **Occupation:**   **Age**
Enrolled at: Ripley, MS   **Enrolled By:** J. R. Chalmers   **Promoted:** No   **ROH:** No
Born: **Marital Status:**   **Residence**

Appears on a company muster roll. No other record.

Whitten, John C.
CO: B   **Initial Rank:** Private
Joined: Wednesday, May 1, 1861   **Term (yrs):** 1   **Occupation:** Laborer   **Age** 19
Enrolled at: Tippah Co., MS   **Enrolled By:** Capt. Buchanan   **Promoted:** No   **ROH:** No
Born: **Marital Status:**   **Residence**

Mortally wounded (hip and foot) at 2nd Manassas on 8/29/1862. Sent to hospital at Warrenton, VA. Died of wounds on 9/12/1862 (another record gives date of death as 9/24/1862).

Whitten, John J.
CO: B   **Initial Rank:** Private
Joined: Friday, March 21, 1862   **Term (yrs):** 3   **Occupation:** Farmer   **Age** 33
Enrolled at: Shannon, MS   **Enrolled By:** Lt. Porter   **Promoted:** No   **ROH:** No
Born: Tennessee   **Marital Status:** M   **Residence**

Killed in battle at Gettysburg on 7/1/1863.

Whittington, George W.
CO: B   **Initial Rank:** Private
Joined: Wednesday, September 18, 1861   **Term (yrs):** 1   **Occupation:** Farmer   **Age** 24
Enrolled at: Ripley, MS   **Enrolled By:** Lt. Davenport   **Promoted:** No   **ROH:** No
Born: Alabama   **Marital Status:**   **Residence**

Discharged for disability on 1/1/1862. However, apparently re-enlisted on 2/17/1863 at Hickory Flat, MS by Lt. Bearden for 3-years. Last company muster roll (Jan/Feb 1865) indicates he was sick in the hospital at Richmond from 6/1/1864. Hospital records show he was transferred to Lynchburg, VA on 7/10/1864. Federal records show he was paroled at Holly Springs, MS on 5/31/1865.

Wiener, Samuel
CO: K   **Initial Rank:** Private
Joined: Wednesday, May 1, 1861   **Term (yrs):** 1   **Occupation:** Merchant   **Age** 26
Enrolled at: Tishomingo Co., MS   **Enrolled By:** Capt. Stone   **Promoted:** No   **ROH:** No
Born: **Marital Status:**   **Residence**

Also see Madison Light Artillery. Transferred to Madison Light Artillery on 5/1/1863.

2nd Mississippi Alphabetical Roster (Annotated)

Wiggle, Alfred R.
CO: C   **Initial Rank:** Private
Joined: Wednesday, May 1, 1861   **Term (yrs):** 1   **Occupation:** Farmer   **Age** 21
Enrolled at: Itawamba Co., MS   **Enrolled By:** Capt. Bromley   **Promoted:** No   **ROH:** No
Born: **Marital Status:**   **Residence**
Mortally wounded in battle at 2nd Manassas on 8/29/1862. Died of wounds at Warrenton, VA on 10/10/1862.

Wilds, Francis
CO: A   **Initial Rank:** Private
Joined: Saturday, March 1, 1862   **Term (yrs):** 3   **Occupation:** Farmer   **Age** 28
Enrolled at: Jacinto, MS   **Enrolled By:** Lt. Clayton   **Promoted:** No   **ROH:** No
Born: Tennessee   **Marital Status:** M   **Residence** Burnsville, MS
Deserted at Blackwater Bridge, VA on 5/10/1863.

Wiley, William E.
CO: G   **Initial Rank:** Private
Joined: Wednesday, May 1, 1861   **Term (yrs):** 1   **Occupation:** Farmer   **Age** 22
Enrolled at: Pontotoc Co., MS   **Enrolled By:** Capt. Miller   **Promoted:** No   **ROH:** No
Born: **Marital Status:** S   **Residence** Pontotoc, MS
Killed in battle at 1st Manassas on 7/21/1861.

Wilkerson, Jackson
CO: D   **Initial Rank:** Private
Joined: Saturday, March 9, 1861   **Term (yrs):** 0   **Occupation:**   **Age**
Enrolled at: Toombs Store, MS   **Enrolled By:** John McGuirk   **Promoted:** No   **ROH:** No
Born: **Marital Status:**   **Residence**
Appears on a company muster roll. No other record. [Same as Stephen Wilkerson?].

Wilkerson, Stephen
CO: D   **Initial Rank:** Private
Joined: Saturday, March 9, 1861   **Term (yrs):** 0   **Occupation:**   **Age**
Enrolled at: Toombs Store, MS   **Enrolled By:** John McGuirk   **Promoted:** No   **ROH:** No
Born: **Marital Status:**   **Residence**
Appears on a company muster roll. No other record. [Same as Jackson Wilkerson?].

2nd Mississippi Alphabetical Roster (Annotated)

Wilkerson, William C.
CO: A **Initial Rank:** Private
Joined: Saturday, March 1, 1862 **Term (yrs):** 3 **Occupation:** Farmer **Age** 38
Enrolled at: Jacinto, MS **Enrolled By:** Lt. Clayton **Promoted:** No **ROH:** No
Born: Tennessee **Marital Status:** M **Residence** Booneville, MS
Discharged due to disability on 11/26/1863.

Williams, Andrew J.
CO: A **Initial Rank:** Private
Joined: Wednesday, May 1, 1861 **Term (yrs):** 1 **Occupation:** Farmer **Age** 24
Enrolled at: Corinth, MS **Enrolled By:** Capt. Leeth **Promoted:** No **ROH:** No
Born: Mississippi **Marital Status:** **Residence**
Discharged due to disability on 1/8/1862 at Camp Fisher, VA.

Williams, Benjamin
CO: A **Initial Rank:** Private
Joined: Tuesday, April 30, 1861 **Term (yrs):** 1 **Occupation:** Farmer **Age**
Enrolled at: Corinth, MS **Enrolled By:** **Promoted:** No **ROH:** No
Born: **Marital Status:** M **Residence** Corinth, MS
Discharged due to disability in January 1862.

Williams, Charles W., Jr.
CO: A **Initial Rank:** Musician
Joined: Wednesday, May 1, 1861 **Term (yrs):** 1 **Occupation:** Farmer **Age** 18
Enrolled at: Tishomingo Co., MS **Enrolled By:** Capt. Leeth **Promoted:** Yes **ROH:** No
Born: **Marital Status:** **Residence**
Promoted to bugler on 6/10/1861. Wounded in battle at Squirrel Level Road on (?) according to accompanying list of engagements (not noted in company muster rolls). Captured near Petersburg (Hatcher's Run?) on 4/2/2865. Taken to Point Lookout, MD. Released on oath on 6/22/1865.

Williams, Erasmus M.
CO: E **Initial Rank:** Private
Joined: Tuesday, March 18, 1862 **Term (yrs):** 3 **Occupation:** Farmer **Age** 20
Enrolled at: Guntown, MS **Enrolled By:** Capt. Bates **Promoted:** No **ROH:** No
Born: Alabama **Marital Status:** M **Residence** Tupelo, MS
Also see 26th Mississippi Infantry Regiment. Transferred to Company H of the 26th Mississippi on 10/14/1862.

2nd Mississippi Alphabetical Roster (Annotated)

Williams, G. B. *CO:* A *Initial Rank:* Private
Joined: Saturday, March 1, 1862 *Term (yrs):* 3 *Occupation:* Farmer *Age* 27
Enrolled at: Jacinto, MS *Enrolled By:* Lt. Clayton *Promoted:* No *ROH:* No
Born: Tennessee *Marital Status:* *Residence* Jacinto, MS
Died of disease (pneumonia) at Lynchburg, VA on 7/3/1862.

Williams, James G. *CO:* C,H *Initial Rank:* Private
Joined: Saturday, March 1, 1862 *Term (yrs):* 3 *Occupation:* Farmer *Age* 30
Enrolled at: Verona, MS *Enrolled By:* Lt. Pounds *Promoted:* No *ROH:* No
Born: Alabama *Marital Status:* S *Residence* Chesterville, MS
Transferred to Company H from Company C in March or April 1862. Deserted from the hospital around 10/1/1862.

Williams, Jefferson *CO:* K *Initial Rank:* Private
Joined: Wednesday, May 1, 1861 *Term (yrs):* 1 *Occupation:* Student *Age* 18
Enrolled at: Tishomingo Co., MS *Enrolled By:* Capt. Stone *Promoted:* No *ROH:* No
Born: *Marital Status:* *Residence*
Killed in battle at 1st Manassas on 7/21/1861.

Williams, S. H. *CO:* H *Initial Rank:* Private
Joined: Saturday, March 1, 1862 *Term (yrs):* 3 *Occupation:* Farmer *Age* 33
Enrolled at: Chesterville, MS *Enrolled By:* Lt. Porter *Promoted:* No *ROH:* No
Born: Alabama *Marital Status:* M *Residence* Chesterville, MS
Deserted from hospital in Richmond on 9/20/1862. Appears on a Federal prisoner of war list during the march to the Mobile and Ohio Railroad. Dated Holly Springs, MS on 12/15/1862. Paroled: (not dated).

Williams, William T. *CO:* C *Initial Rank:* Private
Joined: Wednesday, May 1, 1861 *Term (yrs):* 1 *Occupation:* Farmer *Age* 17
Enrolled at: Itawamba Co., MS *Enrolled By:* Capt. Bromley *Promoted:* No *ROH:* No
Born: *Marital Status:* *Residence*
Also see 45th Mississippi Infantry Regiment. Transferred to Company B of the 45th Mississippi on 5/28/1863.

2nd Mississippi Alphabetical Roster (Annotated)

Williamson, James F.   CO: G   Initial Rank: Private

Joined: Wednesday, May 1, 1861   **Term (yrs):** 1   **Occupation:** Blacksmith   **Age** 27

Enrolled at: Pontotoc Co., MS   **Enrolled By:** Capt. Miller   **Promoted:** No   **ROH:** No

Born: Alabama   **Marital Status:** S   **Residence** Pontotoc, MS

Wounded in battle at 1st Manassas on 7/21/1861. Sent to hospital at Lynchburg, VA. Discharged due to disability from wounds on 10/6/1861 by order of General Johnston.

Willis, Dillon A.   CO: K   Initial Rank: Private

Joined: Wednesday, May 1, 1861   **Term (yrs):** 1   **Occupation:** Farmer   **Age** 19

Enrolled at: Tishomingo Co., MS   **Enrolled By:** Capt. Stone   **Promoted:** No   **ROH:** No

Born: **Marital Status:** S   **Residence**

Captured at South Mountain, MD on 9/15/1862. Sent to Fort Delaware. Paroled to await exchange to Aikens Landing, VA on 10/2/1862. Exchanged on 11/10/1862. Deserted from parole camp in November 1863. Took oath of allegiance at Nashville, TN on 4/6/1865.

Willis, Gideon W.   CO: D   Initial Rank: Private

Joined: Tuesday, October 1, 1861   **Term (yrs):** 1   **Occupation:**   **Age**

Enrolled at: Iuka, MS   **Enrolled By:** Lt. Davenport   **Promoted:** Yes   **ROH:** No

Born: **Marital Status:**   **Residence**

Appointed 5th Sergeant on 11/20/1861. Elected Jr. 2nd Lieutenant on 5/21/1863. Wounded and captured at Gettysburg on 7/3/1863. Sent to Johnson's Island, OH. Forwarded to Point Lookout, MD on 5/21/1865 for exchange. Released on oath on 6/12/1865.

Willis, Nathaniel D.   CO: A   Initial Rank: Private

Joined: Wednesday, May 1, 1861   **Term (yrs):** 1   **Occupation:** Dentist   **Age** 30

Enrolled at: Tishomingo Co., MS   **Enrolled By:** Capt. Leeth   **Promoted:** No   **ROH:** No

Born: North Carolina   **Marital Status:** S   **Residence** Rienzi, MS

Accompanying list of engagements has him wounded at Gettysburg on 7/1/1863 (company muster rolls do not confirm this, however, hospital records do show him admitted at Richmond, VA with a wound on 7/13/1863). Last company muster (Jan/Feb 1865) lists him as "Absent with leave on sick furlough." Another hospital record shows him admitted for sickness at the Way Hospital in Meridian, MS on 2/1/1865. Remarks: "Furlough."

2nd Mississippi Alphabetical Roster (Annotated)

Willis, Robert F. CO: D Initial Rank: Private
Joined: Tuesday, October 1, 1861 **Term (yrs):** 1 **Occupation:** Farmer **Age** 21
Enrolled at: Iuka, MS **Enrolled By:** Lt. Davenport **Promoted:** No **ROH:** No
Born: Mississippi **Marital Status:** S **Residence** Salem, MS

Severely wounded (left leg) in battle at Sharpsburg on 9/17/1862. Furloughed from hospital. Discharged due to disability caused by wounds on 8/5/1863.

Wilson, E. G. CO: C Initial Rank: 2nd Lieutenant
Joined: **Term (yrs):** 0 **Occupation:** **Age**
Enrolled at: **Enrolled By:** **Promoted:** No **ROH:** No
Born: **Marital Status:** **Residence**

See 10th Mississippi Cavalry. No other record.

Wilson, George A. CO: E Initial Rank: 1st Corporal
Joined: Wednesday, May 1, 1861 **Term (yrs):** 1 **Occupation:** Farmer **Age** 23
Enrolled at: Itawamba Co., MS **Enrolled By:** Capt. Booth **Promoted:** No **ROH:** No
Born: Alabama **Marital Status:** S **Residence** Guntown, MS

Muster roll shows him reduced to ranks during Nov/Dec 1861 muster. Detailed duty as teamster until Sep/Oct, 1862 muster. Killed in battle at Gettysburg on 7/1/1863.

Wilson, George W. CO: D Initial Rank: Private
Joined: Saturday, March 9, 1861 **Term (yrs):** 0 **Occupation:** **Age**
Enrolled at: Toombs Store, MS **Enrolled By:** John McGuirk **Promoted:** No **ROH:** No
Born: **Marital Status:** **Residence**

Appears on a company muster roll. No other record.

Wilson, John W. CO: D Initial Rank: Private
Joined: Wednesday, May 1, 1861 **Term (yrs):** 1 **Occupation:** Farmer **Age** 19
Enrolled at: Tippah Co., MS **Enrolled By:** Capt. Beck **Promoted:** No **ROH:** Yes
Born: Mississippi **Marital Status:** S **Residence** Snow Creek, MS

Wounded at Gaines Mill on 6/27/1862. Sent to hospital in Richmond, VA. Returned to duty. Wounded on 8/19/1864 at the Weldon Railroad. Sent to hospital in Richmond, VA. Furloughed 60-days from 9/9/1864. Last company muster (Jan/Feb 1865) remarks: "Absent without leave since 2/20/1865." ROH for Bethesda Church, 5/31/1864.

2nd Mississippi Alphabetical Roster (Annotated)

Wilson, Moses
CO: B **Initial Rank:** Private
Joined: Wednesday, September 18, 1861 **Term (yrs):** 1 **Occupation:** Farmer **Age** 23
Enrolled at: Ripley, MS **Enrolled By:** Lt. Davenport **Promoted:** No **ROH:** No
Born: Mississippi **Marital Status:** **Residence**

Died of disease (pneumonia from typhoid fever) at Richmond, VA, Chimborazo Hospital #4, on 11/25/1861.

Wilson, Robert H.
CO: D **Initial Rank:** Private
Joined: Wednesday, May 1, 1861 **Term (yrs):** 1 **Occupation:** Farmer **Age** 16
Enrolled at: Tippah Co., MS **Enrolled By:** Capt. Beck **Promoted:** No **ROH:** No
Born: Mississippi **Marital Status:** S **Residence** Snow Creek, MS

Accompanying lists of engagements shows him wounded at Seven Pines on 5/31/1862 (company records do not confirm this). Discharged on 7/27/1862 — underage. Captured near Holly Springs, MS by Federal forces (not dated). Received by Provost Marshal in Memphis, TN on 2/20/1864. Released on amnesty oath on 2/20/1864.

Winborne, Joseph W.
CO: D **Initial Rank:** Private
Joined: Saturday, March 9, 1861 **Term (yrs):** 0 **Occupation:** **Age**
Enrolled at: Toombs Store, MS **Enrolled By:** John McGuirk **Promoted:** No **ROH:** No
Born: **Marital Status:** **Residence**

Appears on a company muster roll. No other record.

Winburn, Jesse
CO: B **Initial Rank:** Private
Joined: Monday, March 3, 1862 **Term (yrs):** 3 **Occupation:** Farmer **Age** 30
Enrolled at: Ripley, MS **Enrolled By:** Capt. Buchanan **Promoted:** No **ROH:** No
Born: Missouri **Marital Status:** M **Residence**

Killed in battle at Gettysburg on 7/1/1863 (Federal records indicated he was wounded and captured and later died (date not given) in one of the Federal hospitals near the battlefield).

Winslow, John W.
CO: D **Initial Rank:** Private
Joined: **Term (yrs):** 0 **Occupation:** **Age**
Enrolled at: **Enrolled By:** **Promoted:** No **ROH:** No
Born: **Marital Status:** **Residence**

Appears on a Federal report of prisoners of war paroled at Holly Springs, MS. Dated 5/29/1865. No other record.

2nd Mississippi Alphabetical Roster (Annotated)

Winston, Eaton G.
CO: C **Initial Rank:** Private
Joined: Wednesday, May 1, 1861 **Term (yrs):** 1 **Occupation:** Farmer **Age** 37
Enrolled at: Itawamba Co., MS **Enrolled By:** Capt. Bromley **Promoted:** Yes **ROH:** No
Born: **Marital Status:** **Residence**

Discharged due to disability on 11/20/1861. However, he appears to have re-enlisted on 3/1/1862 at Verona, MS for 3-years by Lieutenant. Pounds. Listed as Brevet 2nd Lieutenant during Mar/Apr 1862 muster. Resigned in August 1862 due to disability.

Winston, George D.
CO: G **Initial Rank:** Musician
Joined: Wednesday, May 1, 1861 **Term (yrs):** 1 **Occupation:** Editor **Age** 27
Enrolled at: Pontotoc Co., MS **Enrolled By:** Capt. Kilpatrick **Promoted:** Yes **ROH:** No
Born: Virginia **Marital Status:** S **Residence** Pontotoc, MS

Also see 11th Mississippi Infantry Regiment. Detailed to the regimental band from 6/1/1861. Promoted to 3rd Sergeant in June 1862. Transferred to the band of the 11th Mississippi on 7/15/1862 by order of General Lee.

Winston, William
CO: G **Initial Rank:** Private
Joined: Wednesday, May 1, 1861 **Term (yrs):** 1 **Occupation:** Physician **Age** 35
Enrolled at: Pontotoc Co., MS **Enrolled By:** Capt. Miller **Promoted:** No **ROH:** No
Born: Virginia **Marital Status:** S **Residence** Pontotoc, MS

Also see 11th Mississippi Infantry Regiment. Detailed as a musician to the regiment since 6/1/1861. Detailed to attend sick at Ashland and as Hospital Steward; then in regimental hospital during Mar/Apr 1862 thru Sep/Oct 1862 musters. Transferred to the band of the 11th Mississippi on 11/25/1862 by order of General Smith.

Winters, James M.
CO: E **Initial Rank:** Private
Joined: Wednesday, May 1, 1861 **Term (yrs):** 1 **Occupation:** Farmer **Age** 27
Enrolled at: Itawamba Co., MS **Enrolled By:** Capt. Booth **Promoted:** No **ROH:** No
Born: Tennessee **Marital Status:** **Residence** Guntown, MS

Discharge due to disability at Camp Fisher, VA on 10/14/1861 by order of General Smith.

2nd Mississippi Alphabetical Roster (Annotated)

Wise, John B.
CO: C **Initial Rank:** Private
Joined: Saturday, March 1, 1862 **Term (yrs):** 3 **Occupation:** **Age**
Enrolled at: Verona, MS **Enrolled By:** Lt. Pounds **Promoted:** No **ROH:** No
Born: **Marital Status:** **Residence**

Also see 15th Arkansas Infantry Regiment. May/Jun 1864 company muster roll indicates "wounded and in hospital" but provides no details as to date of wound or engagement. He was admitted to the hospital in Richmond on 6/10/1864 and furloughed 40-days from 6/18/1864. Did not return to company. Nov/Dec 1864 muster remarks: "Joined 15th Arkansas Regiment."

Witherspoon, John G.
CO: H **Initial Rank:** Private
Joined: Monday, April 29, 1861 **Term (yrs):** 1 **Occupation:** Farmer **Age** 27
Enrolled at: Pontotoc Co., MS **Enrolled By:** Capt. Taylor **Promoted:** No **ROH:** No
Born: Alabama **Marital Status:** S **Residence** Tupelo, MS

Discharged due to disability on 12/24/1861 at Camp Fisher, VA by order of General Whiting.

Witherspoon, Paul F.
CO: H **Initial Rank:** 2nd Sergeant
Joined: Monday, April 29, 1861 **Term (yrs):** 1 **Occupation:** Farmer **Age** 29
Enrolled at: Pontotoc Co., MS **Enrolled By:** Capt. Taylor **Promoted:** Yes **ROH:** No
Born: Alabama **Marital Status:** M **Residence** Tupelo, MS

Promoted to 1st Sergeant in February 1862. Discharged due to disability about 4/14/1862.

Witherspoon, Thomas D.
CO: S **Initial Rank:** Chaplain
Joined: Sunday, August 18, 1861 **Term (yrs):** 1 **Occupation:** Chaplain **Age**
Enrolled at: Manassas, VA **Enrolled By:** President Davis **Promoted:** No **ROH:** No
Born: **Marital Status:** **Residence**

Also see 11th Mississippi Infantry Regiment. No record after February 1862.

Wiygul, A. B. Mayfield
CO: C **Initial Rank:** Private
Joined: Tuesday, October 1, 1861 **Term (yrs):** 1 **Occupation:** **Age**
Enrolled at: Richmond, MS **Enrolled By:** Lt. Davenport **Promoted:** No **ROH:** No
Born: **Marital Status:** **Residence**

Listed as "present" during most of the company musters. Detailed on 1/9/1865 to accompany Colonel Stone back to Mississippi to pick up deserters and absentees.

2nd Mississippi Alphabetical Roster (Annotated)

Wolf, Alexander D.
CO: B **Initial Rank:** Private
Joined: Wednesday, May 1, 1861   **Term (yrs):** 1 **Occupation:** Farmer   **Age** 33
Enrolled at: Tippah Co., MS   **Enrolled By:** Capt. Buchanan   **Promoted:** No   **ROH:** No
Born: **Marital Status:**   **Residence**

Wounded (in face) in battle at 1st Manassas on 7/21/1861. Returned to duty on 8/9/1861. Discharged due to disability on 12/4/1862.

Wommack, William C
CO: F **Initial Rank:** Private
Joined: Saturday, March 1, 1862   **Term (yrs):** 3 **Occupation:** Farmer   **Age** 23
Enrolled at: Ripley, MS   **Enrolled By:** Capt. Powers   **Promoted:** No   **ROH:** No
Born: Tennessee   **Marital Status:** M   **Residence**

Although listed as "present" for most of the company musters, AWOL since 2/26/1865 for last (Jan/Feb 1865) muster roll.

Wood, James M.
CO: I **Initial Rank:** Private
Joined: Wednesday, May 1, 1861   **Term (yrs):** 1 **Occupation:** Farmer   **Age** 23
Enrolled at: Pontotoc Co., MS   **Enrolled By:** Capt. Herring   **Promoted:** Yes   **ROH:** No
Born: **Marital Status:**   **Residence**

Promoted to 4th Corporal on 5/16/1863. Captured at Gettysburg on 7/1/1863. Sent to Fort Delaware. Released on oath on 6/11/1865.

Wood, James N.
CO: K **Initial Rank:** Private
Joined: Wednesday, May 1, 1861   **Term (yrs):** 1 **Occupation:** Farmer   **Age** 20
Enrolled at: Tishomingo Co., MS   **Enrolled By:** Capt. Stone   **Promoted:** No   **ROH:** No
Born: **Marital Status:**   **Residence**

Listed as "absent wounded" during May/Jun 1864 muster roll (date of wound or engagement not detailed in company records). Listed as "absent wounded since 1st October 1864" during Sep/Oct 1864 muster (assumption that wound occurred on 10/1/1864). He was admitted to the hospital on 10/2/1864 and furloughed 60-days from 11/9/1864. Last company muster roll lists him as "absent sick since 7 Jan. 1865."

2nd Mississippi Alphabetical Roster (Annotated)

Woodard, Thomas S.
CO: E **Initial Rank:** Private
Joined: Saturday, March 1, 1862 **Term (yrs):** 3 **Occupation:** Farmer **Age** 17
Enrolled at: Guntown, MS **Enrolled By:** Capt. Bates **Promoted:** No **ROH:** Yes
Born: Mississippi **Marital Status:** S **Residence** Guntown, MS

Hospital records show he was admitted for a wound on 9/6/1862 (date of wound or engagement not detailed in company records). Returned to duty on 10/3/1862. Killed in action "on the lines before Suffolk, VA, Apr 30, 1863." ROH for Second Manassas, 8/28/1862.

Woodfin, Robert
CO: H **Initial Rank:** Private
Joined: Monday, April 29, 1861 **Term (yrs):** 1 **Occupation:** **Age**
Enrolled at: Pontotoc Co., MS **Enrolled By:** Capt. Taylor **Promoted:** No **ROH:** No
Born: **Marital Status:** **Residence**

No record after muster-in on 5/10/1861. Remarks: "Absent on furlough."

Woodlaw, John H.
CO: C **Initial Rank:** Private
Joined: Wednesday, May 1, 1861 **Term (yrs):** 1 **Occupation:** Farmer **Age** 27
Enrolled at: Itawamba Co., MS **Enrolled By:** Capt. Bromley **Promoted:** No **ROH:** No
Born: South Carolina **Marital Status:** **Residence**

Discharged due to disability at Camp Fisher, VA on 9/10/1861.

Woods, Egbert S. G.
CO: F **Initial Rank:** Private
Joined: Saturday, March 1, 1862 **Term (yrs):** 3 **Occupation:** Farmer **Age** 26
Enrolled at: Ripley, MS **Enrolled By:** Capt. Powers **Promoted:** No **ROH:** No
Born: Mississippi **Marital Status:** M **Residence**

Also see 15th Consolidated Tennessee Cavalry Regiment (also called 2nd Organization and Stewart's-Logwood's Regiment) and the 23rd Mississippi Infantry Regiment (also called the 2nd or 3rd Regiment) Davidson's Regiment. Wounded (in neck) at Gaines Mill on 6/27/1862. Furloughed 30-days. Returned to duty. Deserted in June 1863 (see other units, above).

Woods, John L.
CO: B **Initial Rank:** Private
Joined: Wednesday, May 1, 1861 **Term (yrs):** 1 **Occupation:** Merchant **Age** 32
Enrolled at: Tippah Co., MS **Enrolled By:** Capt. Buchanan **Promoted:** No **ROH:** No
Born: Tennessee **Marital Status:** **Residence**

Discharged due to disability at Camp Jones, VA on 8/23/1861.

2nd Mississippi Alphabetical Roster (Annotated)

Woods, William H.
CO: D *Initial Rank:* Private
Joined: Wednesday, May 1, 1861 *Term (yrs):* 1 *Occupation:* Farmer *Age* 27
Enrolled at: Tippah Co., MS *Enrolled By:* Capt. Beck *Promoted:* No *ROH:* No
Born: Tennessee *Marital Status:* S *Residence* Grand Junction, TN

Died at Fredericksburg, VA of disease in April 1862 (exact date unknown).

Woodward, Ivy R.
CO: E *Initial Rank:* 3rd Corporal
Joined: Wednesday, May 1, 1861 *Term (yrs):* 1 *Occupation:* Farmer *Age* 21
Enrolled at: Itawamba Co., MS *Enrolled By:* Capt. Booth *Promoted:* Yes *ROH:* No
Born: Alabama *Marital Status:* S *Residence* Guntown, MS

Promoted to 2nd Corporal during Jul/Aug 1862 timeframe. Captured at Gettysburg on 7/1/1863. Sent to Fort Delaware. Released on oath on 6/11/1865.

Woodward, Wesley
CO: E *Initial Rank:* 2nd Lieutenant
Joined: Wednesday, May 1, 1861 *Term (yrs):* 1 *Occupation:* Farmer *Age* 27
Enrolled at: Itawamba Co., MS *Enrolled By:* Gen. Barksdale *Promoted:* No *ROH:* No
Born: Alabama *Marital Status:* S *Residence* Guntown, MS

Relieved of command due to expiration of term of service on 4/17/1862. Discharged.

Worthy, Fleming J.
CO: I *Initial Rank:* Private
Joined: Wednesday, May 1, 1861 *Term (yrs):* 1 *Occupation:* Farmer *Age* 20
Enrolled at: Pontotoc Co., MS *Enrolled By:* Capt. Herring *Promoted:* No *ROH:* No
Born: *Marital Status:* *Residence*

Wounded (right shoulder) and captured at Gettysburg on 7/3/1863 (captured 7/5/1863). Taken to DeCamp General Hospital, Davids Island, NY Harbor. Paroled to City Point, VA on 9/8/1863. Admitted to hospital in Williamsburg, VA on 9/8/1863. Furloughed on 9/13/1863. Captured at Pontotoc, MS while on furlough on 2/10/1864. Sent to Camp Douglas, IL on 3/3/1864. Released on oath on 6/13/1865.

2nd Mississippi Alphabetical Roster (Annotated)

Wray, John T.
CO: G **Initial Rank:** Private
Joined: Wednesday, May 1, 1861 **Term (yrs):** 1 **Occupation:** Planter **Age** 23
Enrolled at: Pontotoc Co., MS **Enrolled By:** Capt. Miller **Promoted:** Yes **ROH:** Yes
Born: Mississippi **Marital Status:** S **Residence** Pontotoc, MS

Records indicated he was appointed Lieutenant (grade unknown) on 6/14/1862. However, subsequent muster rolls show him as 4th Sergeant during Jul/Aug 1862. Listed as 2nd Sergeant for Nov/Dec 1862 muster, and 1st Sergeant for Mar/Apr 1863 muster roll. Captured at Gettysburg (near Cashtown) on 7/5/1863. Paroled at Fort McHenry, MD and transferred to Fort Delaware on 7/10/1863. No other records. ROH for Second Manassas, 8/28/1862.

Wren, William
CO: C **Initial Rank:** Private
Joined: Wednesday, May 1, 1861 **Term (yrs):** 1 **Occupation:** Farmer **Age** 19
Enrolled at: Itawamba Co., MS **Enrolled By:** Capt. Bromley **Promoted:** No **ROH:** No
Born: **Marital Status:** **Residence**

Discharged due to disability (loss of vision) at Camp Fisher, VA on 11/20/1861.

Wright, G. L.
CO: A **Initial Rank:** Private
Joined: Saturday, March 1, 1862 **Term (yrs):** 3 **Occupation:** **Age** 34
Enrolled at: Jacinto, MS **Enrolled By:** Lt. Clayton **Promoted:** No **ROH:** No
Born: **Marital Status:** **Residence**

Sick in hospital. No record after Nov/Dec 1862 muster roll. Final company "record" dated Petersburg, 3/21/1865 remarks: "Know nothing of his whereabouts. Was never in battle."

Wylie, Jackson A.
CO: C **Initial Rank:** Private
Joined: Saturday, March 1, 1862 **Term (yrs):** 3 **Occupation:** **Age**
Enrolled at: Verona, MS **Enrolled By:** Lt. Pounds **Promoted:** No **ROH:** No
Born: **Marital Status:** **Residence**

Wounded on 10/1/1864. Sent to hospital in Richmond, VA. Furloughed 60-days from 11/2/1864. Last (Jan/Feb, 1865) muster roll lists him as AWOL.

2nd Mississippi Alphabetical Roster (Annotated)

Wylie, Leroy W. **CO:** C **Initial Rank:** Private
Joined: Wednesday, May 1, 1861 *Term (yrs):* 1 *Occupation:* Farmer *Age* 19
Enrolled at: Itawamba Co., MS *Enrolled By:* Capt. Bromley *Promoted:* No *ROH:* No
Born: *Marital Status:* *Residence*

Present during most company muster rolls. Captured at Petersburg (Hatcher's Run?) on 4/2/1865. Sent to Fort Delaware. Released on oath on 6/11/1865.

Yancey, Robert L. **CO:** L **Initial Rank:** Private
Joined: Monday, March 3, 1862 *Term (yrs):* 3 *Occupation:* Farmer *Age* 18
Enrolled at: Ripley, MS *Enrolled By:* Col. Falkner *Promoted:* No *ROH:* No
Born: Virginia *Marital Status:* S *Residence* Ripley, MS

Wounded on 9/15/1864 (? Hospital records show him admitted on 9/27/1864). Furloughed 40-days from 10/8/1864. Last company muster roll (Jan/Feb 1865) lists him as AWOL on wounded furlough in Tippah Co., MS.

Yeager, Monroe **CO:** I **Initial Rank:** Private
Joined: Wednesday, May 1, 1861 *Term (yrs):* 1 *Occupation:* Clerk *Age* 18
Enrolled at: Pontotoc Co., MS *Enrolled By:* Capt. Herring *Promoted:* No *ROH:* Yes
Born: Mississippi *Marital Status:* *Residence*

Wounded in battle at 2nd Manassas on 8/30/1862. Returned to duty. Killed in battle at Gettysburg on 7/3/1863. ROH for Gettysburg, 7/3/1863.

Young, George C. **CO:** I **Initial Rank:** 3rd Corporal
Joined: Wednesday, May 1, 1861 *Term (yrs):* 1 *Occupation:* Farmer *Age* 20
Enrolled at: Pontotoc Co., MS *Enrolled By:* Capt. Herring *Promoted:* Yes *ROH:* No
Born: *Marital Status:* *Residence*

Promoted to 2nd Corporal in place of Sidney F. Holditch (not dated, about June 1861). Promoted to 5th Sergeant on 11/5/1861. Promoted to 2nd Sergeant on 4/23/1862. Promoted to 1st Sergeant in place of J. S. Owens on 5/16/1863. Wounded (chest) in battle at Gettysburg on 7/1/1863. Sent to hospital in Richmond, VA. Transferred to hospital at Lynchburg, VA on 10/6/1863. Returned to duty. Furloughed on 4/22/1864 for 60-days. Returned to duty. Listed as "present" for last company muster (Jan/Feb 1865).

2nd Mississippi Alphabetical Roster (Annotated)

Young, Isaac   *CO:* L   *Initial Rank:* Private

Joined: Monday, March 3, 1862   *Term (yrs):* 3   *Occupation:* Farmer   *Age* 35

Enrolled at: Ripley, MS   *Enrolled By:* Col. Falkner   *Promoted:* No   *ROH:* No

Born: Tennessee   *Marital Status:*   *Residence*

Died of disease at hospital in Huguenot Springs, VA on 9/28/1862.

Young, Robert   *CO:* C   *Initial Rank:* Private

Joined: Wednesday, May 1, 1861   *Term (yrs):* 1   *Occupation:* Farmer   *Age* 20

Enrolled at: Itawamba Co., MS   *Enrolled By:* Capt. Bromley   *Promoted:* No   *ROH:* No

Born: *Marital Status:*   *Residence*

Deserted from 2/18/1864.

Young, Robert M.   *CO:* B, L   *Initial Rank:* Private

Joined: Wednesday, May 1, 1861   *Term (yrs):* 1   *Occupation:* Clerk   *Age* 19

Enrolled at: Tippah Co., MS   *Enrolled By:* Capt. Buchanan   *Promoted:* Yes   *ROH:* No

Born: Mississippi   *Marital Status:* S   *Residence* Ripley, MS

Transferred to Company L from Company B on 4/30/1862. Promoted to 5th Sergeant on 8/1/1862. Transferred back to Company B from Company L on 4/1/1863. Wounded (gunshot wound; arm fractured) at Gettysburg (not dated). Furloughed 50-days from 8/15/1863. Returned to company, in hospital. Retired to Invalid Corps, P.A.C.S. on 9/8/1864 due to disability caused by wounds.

Young, Thomas P.   *CO:* S   *Initial Rank:* Captain

Joined: *Term (yrs):* 0   *Occupation:*   *Age*

Enrolled at: *Enrolled By:*   *Promoted:* No   *ROH:* No

Born: *Marital Status:*   *Residence*

Appears on a Field and Staff muster roll for July and August, 186?. Appointed Assistant Commissary by the President. Signs as Capt. Commanding Dept. Apparently resigned on 8/30/1861. No further record.

Younger, William   *CO:* H   *Initial Rank:* Private

Joined: Monday, April 29, 1861   *Term (yrs):* 1   *Occupation:* Farmer   *Age* 19

Enrolled at: Pontotoc Co., MS   *Enrolled By:* Capt. Taylor   *Promoted:* No   *ROH:* No

Born: Mississippi   *Marital Status:* S   *Residence* Tupelo, MS

Discharged due to disability on 12/24/1861 at Camp Fisher, VA.

2nd Mississippi Infantry Regiment Roll of Honor Introduction

The 2nd Mississippi Roll of Honor Introduction

The 2nd Mississippi Infantry Regiment had the distinction of having more individuals named to the Confederate *Roll of Honor* – 141 individuals with 153 listings – than any other regiment in Confederate service. Several individuals were named to the roll more than once, and remarkably, Corporal Sam Neeley was named to the Confederate *Roll of Honor* five times before succumbing to his wounds received at the fight at the Weldon Railroad in 1864.

The Confederate *Roll of Honor* resulted from General Orders No. 93 from the Adjutant and Inspector General's Office, dated November 22, 1862. It reads:

> No. 27. – AN ACT to authorize the grant of medals and badges of distinction as a reward for courage and good conduct on the field of battle.
>
> *The Congress of the Confederate States of America do enact,* That the President be and is hereby, authorized to bestow medals, with proper devices, upon such officers of the armies of the Confederate States as shall be conspicuous for courage and good conduct on the field of battle, and also to confer a badge of distinction upon one private or non-commissioned officer of each company after every signal victory it shall have assisted to achieve. The non-commissioned officers and privates of the company who may be present on the first dress-parade thereafter may choose, by a majority of their votes, the soldier best entitled to receive such distinction, whose name shall be communicated to the President by commanding officers of the company; and if the award fall upon a deceased soldier the badge thus awarded him shall be delivered to his widow, or if there be no widow, to any relation the President may adjudge entitled to receive it.[12]

Because of the wartime difficulties of procuring the appropriate medals and badges, the government posted General Orders No. 131, which instead established the *Roll of Honor* as the method of honoring those soldiers selected under the guidelines of General Orders No. 93. The names published on this roll were to be read at the head of every regiment at the first dress-parade after its receipt and was also to be published in at least one newspaper in each State.[13]

---

[12] *O.R.*, 11, pt. 2, p. 992.
[13] *Ibid.*

2nd Mississippi Infantry Regiment Roll of Honor Introduction

Therefore, the Confederate **Roll of Honor** was the rough equivalent to the Union's Medal of Honor as a method of recognizing bravery and courage on the field of battle. The primary difference between the two awards being that the Confederate soldiers so chosen were selected by their peers and not nominated by a superior officer. Additionally, regimental participation was voluntary, so unfortunately not all Confederate regiments acknowledged individuals in this manner.

It should be noted that the battle dates for multi-day battles where only a single selection took place was the first day of the engagement period. Thus, for Second Manassas, the date is listed as August 28, 1862 even though the fighting continued through August 30th. **KIA** means the individual was killed in action.

2nd Mississippi Roll of Honor Listing

Last Name	First Name	MI	Rank	CO	Battle Name	Date	KIA
Akers	James	L.	Private	K	South Mountain (Boonsboro)	9/14/62	no
					Gettysburg, July 3	7/3/63	yes
Aldridge	Isaac	N.	Private	K	Second Manassas	8/28/62	no
Anderson	James	L.	Private	C	Weldon Railroad, August 19	8/19/64	yes
Andrews	Henry		Private	I	Malvern Hill	7/1/62	no
Atkins	James	A.	Sergeant	C	Malvern Hill	7/1/62	no
Ayers	William	T.	Private	F	Talley's Mill	5/10/64	no
					Bethesda Church, June 3	6/3/64	no
Bazemore	William	D.	Private	C	Gettysburg, July 3	7/3/63	yes
Bell	William		Private	C	Gaines Mill	6/27/62	yes
Bennett	Miles	J.	Sergeant	B	Gettysburg, July 1	7/1/63	no
Bennett	Richard	G.	Private	B	The Wilderness, May 6	5/6/64	no
Billingsley	Thomas	W.	Private	I	The Wilderness, May 6	5/6/64	no
					Weldon Railroad, August 18	8/18/64	yes
Black	James	P.	Sergeant	F	Sharpsburg	9/17/62	yes
Blythe	Lewis	J.	Private	F	Gettysburg, July 3	7/3/63	no
Boone	Reuben	L.	Private	A	South Mountain (Boonsboro)	9/14/62	no
Braddock	Perry	G.	Corporal	B	Falling Waters	7/14/63	no
Brown	John	J.	Private	F	The Wilderness, May 6	5/6/64	no
Browning	Elijah		Private	I	South Mountain (Boonsboro)	9/14/62	no
Bryan	William	H.	Private	L	Gaines Mill	6/27/62	no
Bryant	Joseph	S.	Private	E	The Wilderness, May 5	5/5/64	no
Butler	Armistead	M.	Corporal	F	Bristoe Station	10/14/63	no
Byrn	William	H.	Private	B	Talley's Mill	5/10/64	no
Carpenter	Owen	F.	Private	L	Gettysburg, July 3	7/3/63	yes
Carr	John	W.	Private	H	Bethesda Church, 31 May	5/31/64	no
Carter	Thomas	S.	Corporal	A	The Wilderness, May 5	5/5/64	yes
Champion	George	W.	Private	C	The Wilderness, May 6	5/6/64	no
Chism	David	G.	Private	K	Bethesda Church, 31 May	5/31/64	no
Christman	John	C.	Private	A	Second Manassas	8/28/62	no
Clark	Micagah	L., Jr.	Private	L	Bethesda Church, June 2	6/2/64	no
Clark	Pleasant		Private	H	The Wilderness, May 5	5/5/64	yes
Cobb	Greenberry		Private	H	The Wilderness, May 6	5/6/64	no
Cobb	William	D.	Private	I	Gettysburg, July 1	7/1/63	yes
Cochran	William	M.	Private	B	Bethesda Church, 31 May	5/31/64	no
Compton	Joseph	E.	Private	E	Gaines Mill	6/27/62	yes
Condrey	William	J.	Private	K	Gettysburg, July 1	7/1/63	yes
Cooper	Thomas	J. S.	Corporal	G	Malvern Hill	7/1/62	no
Cotton	John	H.	Private	B	Seven Pines	5/31/62	yes
Cutbirth	Daniel	B.	Private	F	The Wilderness, May 5	5/5/64	yes
Daggett	Frederick	H.	Sergeant	G	Sharpsburg	9/17/62	no
Davis	Christopher	C.	Sergeant	D	Second Manassas	8/28/62	no
Davis	William	H.	Private	B	Second Manassas	8/28/62	yes

Last Name	First Name	MI	Rank	CO	Battle Name	Date	KIA
Dillard	James	T.	Private	G	Talley's Mill	5/10/64	no
					Bethesda Church, June 3	6/3/64	no
Donaldson	Joel	J.	Private	G	Gettysburg, July 3	7/3/63	no
Drake	Richard		Sergeant	G	Gaines Mill	6/27/62	no
Earle	Ezias	L.	Corporal	G	Spotsylvania Court House	5/12/64	no
Easterwood	George	M.	Corporal	G	Falling Waters	7/14/63	no
Eddings	Paschal	C.	Private	B	Bristoe Station	10/14/63	no
Edwards	William	A.	Private	G	The Wilderness, May 5	5/5/64	no
Elliott	John	B.	Private	D	Sharpsburg	9/17/62	no
Faris	Micajah		Private	A	Gettysburg, July 1	7/1/63	no
Fife	Samuel	T.	Private	E	Weldon Railroad, August 19	8/19/64	no
Flinn	John	C.	Private	C	The Wilderness, May 5	5/5/64	no
Freeman	John	L.	Private	I	The Wilderness, May 5	5/5/64	no
Fulton	Jeremiah		Private	D	Gettysburg, July 1	7/1/63	no
Gibson	Jarrett	W.	Private	K	Sharpsburg	9/17/62	yes
Golding	Marcus	L.	Corporal	I	Sharpsburg	9/17/62	yes
Griffin	James	T.	Private	E	Unknown		no
Griffin	Leander		Private	L	Sharpsburg	9/17/62	yes
Grisham	Jasper		Private	D	Talley's Mill	5/10/64	no
Guyton	Luther	C.	Private	B	The Wilderness, May 5	5/5/64	no
Hampton	Thomas	D.	Private	K	Seven Pines	5/31/62	no
					Gaines Mill	6/27/62	yes
Handly	William	C	Private	G	The Wilderness, May 6	5/6/64	no
			Corporal		Weldon Railroad, August 18	8/18/64	no
Harbin	John	L.	Private	F	Second Manassas	8/28/62	yes
Harris	Peter	F.	Sergeant	H	Sharpsburg	9/17/62	yes
Harris	Robert		Sergeant	C	South Mountain (Boonsboro)	9/14/62	no
Harwell	John	T.	Private	H	Talley's Mill	5/10/64	no
Helms	Robert	A.	Private	B	Spotsylvania Court House	5/12/64	no
Houston	William	B.	Private	D	South Mountain (Boonsboro)	9/14/62	no
Howard	A.	C.	Private	C	Sharpsburg	9/17/62	yes
Hughes	Dolphus	E.	Private	C	Bethesda Church, 31 May	5/31/64	yes
Humphreys	Charles	L.	Private	E	Gettysburg	7/1/63	yes
Jeter	Richard	C.	Private	L	The Wilderness, May 5	5/5/64	no
Johns	Henry	H.	Private	B	Sharpsburg	9/17/62	yes
Key	William	J.	Private	A	Gaines Mill	6/27/62	no
Key	William	J.	Private	A	Malvern Hill	7/1/62	no
Knox	Mathew		Corporal	B	Weldon Railroad, August 19	8/19/64	no
Kyle	Samuel	D.	Private	E	The Wilderness, May 6	5/6/64	no
Levett	William	F. M.	Private	E	Talley's Mill	5/10/64	no
Lewelling	John		Private	K	The Wilderness, May 6	5/6/64	no
					Talley's Mill	5/10/64	no
					Spotsylvania Court House	5/12/64	yes
Lewis	James	P.	Private	D	Gaines Mill	6/27/62	yes
Looney	William	H.	Private	A	Sharpsburg	9/17/62	yes
Luna	William	L.	Private	F	Gettysburg, July 1	7/1/63	no

Last Name	First Name	MI	Rank	CO	Battle Name	Date	KIA
Manahan	William	E.	Private	G	Seven Pines	5/31/62	no
Marrs	Albert	C.	Private	H	Gaines Mill	6/27/62	yes
McAllister	John	A.	Private	L	Seven Pines	5/31/62	no
McAnally	Thomas	J.	Private	A	Gettysburg, July 1	7/1/63	no
McCarty	Jacob		Private	L	South Mountain (Boonsboro)	9/14/62	yes
McCully	James		Sergeant	E	Seven Pines	5/31/62	no
McDole	Robert	J.	Corporal	G	Bethesda Church, June 2	6/2/64	no
McKay	Trussie	B.	Sergeant	B	South Mountain (Boonsboro)	9/14/62	no
McKeown	Isaac		Private	K	The Wilderness, May 5	5/5/64	yes
McKinney	Franklin	S.	Private	H	Seven Pines	5/31/62	yes
McNally	Patrick		Private	G	Weldon Railroad, August 19	8/19/64	no
McPherson	Henry		Private	H	Gettysburg, July 3	7/3/63	no
Middleton	James		Private	L	Second Manassas	8/28/62	yes
Milam	Wiley	F.	Private	I	Bethesda Church, 31 May	5/31/64	no
Miller	William	H.	Private	F	Falling Waters	7/14/63	no
Monk	George	W.	Private	E	South Mountain (Boonsboro)	9/14/62	no
Moore	John	M.	Private	K	Malvern Hill	7/1/62	no
Moore	William	T.	Private	D	Gettysburg, July 3	7/3/63	no
Neely	Samuel	G.	Corporal	A	The Wilderness, May 6	5/6/64	no
					Talley's Mill	5/10/64	no
					Spotsylvania Court House	5/12/64	no
					Bethesda Church, 31 May	5/31/64	no
					Weldon Railroad	8/18/64	no*
Northcross	Richard		Private	F	Gaines Mill	6/27/62	yes
Nunnalee	James	M.	Private	H	Falling Waters	7/14/63	no
Parker	Joseph	H.	Private	B	Malvern Hill	7/1/62	yes
Pegram	Amos	J.	Private	B	Gaines Mill	6/27/62	yes
Prescott	Zachariah	D.	Sergeant	D	The Wilderness, May 5	5/5/64	no
Raines	James	A.	Corporal	H	Gettysburg, July 1	7/1/63	no
Ralph	John	L.	Private	F	Malvern Hill	7/1/62	no
Ralph	William	H. H.	Private	F	Spotsylvania Court House	5/12/64	no
Rea	Andrew	M.	Private	H	Spotsylvania Court House	5/12/64	no
Roberts	Atlas	K.	Private	H	Malvern Hill	7/1/62	no
Roberts	Ruffin	A.	Sergeant	C	Seven Pines	5/31/62	no
Robinson	Thomas	J. S.	Private	L	Weldon Railroad, August 18	8/18/64	yes
Sargent	Aaron	T.	Private	C	Talley's Mill	5/10/64	no
Scott	James	M.	Private	I	Gaines Mill	6/27/62	no
Sims	Drury	F.	Private	I	Talley's Mill	5/10/64	yes
Sims	Richard	A.	Private	I	Weldon Railroad, August 19	8/19/64	no
Sims	William	J.	Private	I	Seven Pines	5/31/62	yes
Smith	Francis	M.	Private	G	Bristoe Station	10/14/63	no
Smith	Jerome	B.	Private	F	Seven Pines	5/31/62	yes
Stanley	James	T.	Private	K	Weldon Railroad, August 18	8/18/64	no
Storey	Henry	H.	Private	C	Gettysburg, July 1	7/1/63	no
Suber	David	P.	Private	I	Second Manassas	8/28/62	yes
Thomas	William	A.	Private	D	The Wilderness, May 6	5/6/64	no

Last Name	First Name	MI	Rank	CO	Battle Name	Date	KIA
Thompson	Thomas	G. N.	Private	F	South Mountain (Boonsboro)	9/14/62	no
Ticer	J.	Pinkney	Corporal	B	Gettysburg, July 3	7/3/63	no
Tigert	David	P.	Sergeant	L	Bethesda Church, 31 May	5/31/64	no
Trammell	Benjamin	F.	Private	K	Weldon Railroad, August 19	8/19/64	no
Turner	George	H.	Private	C	Weldon Railroad, August 18	8/18/64	yes
Vanzant	John	L.	Private	G	South Mountain (Boonsboro)	9/14/62	yes
Vernor	Zenas	E.	Private	B	Weldon Railroad, August 18	8/18/64	no
Vincent	Charles	S.	Corporal	C	Second Manassas	8/28/62	yes
Walding	James	A.	Corporal	D	Bristoe Station	10/14/63	no
Walker	James	H.	Private	D	Seven Pines	5/31/62	no
Ward	James	M.	Corporal	L	Malvern Hill	7/1/62	yes
Weatherington	Benton		Private	H	South Mountain (Boonsboro)	9/14/62	no
Westmoreland	Jerome	W.	Private	H	Second Manassas	8/28/62	no
White	Daniel	M.	Private	L	Gettysburg, July 1	7/1/63	yes
Wilson	John	W.	Private	D	Bethesda Church, 31 May	5/31/64	no
Woodard	Thomas	S.	Private	E	Second Manassas	8/28/62	no
Wray	John	T.	Sergeant	G	Second Manassas	8/28/62	no
Yeager	Monroe		Private	I	Gettysburg, July 3	7/3/63	yes

*Mortally Wounded

Bibliography

Bassler, J. H. *The Color Episode of the One Hundred and Forty-Ninth Regiment, Pennsylvania Volunteers*. Paper Read Before the Lebanon County Historical Society, October 18, 1907.

Blair, John A. to Rufus Dawes. Letter from John Blair to Rufus Dawes, October 23, 1893, Rufus Dawes Letters Collection, McCain Library and Archives, University of Southern Mississippi, Hattiesburg, MS.

Boatner, Mark M., III. *The Civil War Dictionary*. New York: Vintage Books, 1991.

Buchanan, John H. Diary. Transcribed by Larry J. Mardis, Ph.D. and Jo Anne Ketchum Mardis. Tippah County Historical and Genealogical Society, 1998.

Buel, Clarence Clough, and Robert Underwood Johnson, eds. *Battles and Leaders of the Civil War*. 4 vols. New York: The Century Magazine, 1884-88.

Busey, John W., and David G. Martin. *Regimental Strengths and Losses at Gettysburg*. Hightstown, NJ: Longstreet House, 1982.

Bynum, G. W. Diary Extracts. Quoted in *Confederate Veteran*, XXXIII (1925): pp. 9-10.

Clemmer, Gregg S. *Valor in Gray: The Recipients of the Confederate Medal of Honor*. Staunton, VA: Hearthside Publishing Co., 1996.

Compiled Service Records of Confederate Soldiers who served in the 2nd Mississippi, National Archives Microfilm Pub. M268, rolls 111-123. Washington, DC: National Archives and Record Service, 1959.

Cormier, Steven A. *The Siege of Suffolk: The Forgotten Campaign, April 11-May 4, 1863*. Lynchburg, VA: H. E. Howard, Inc., 1989.

Crute, Joseph H., Jr. *Units of the Confederate States Army*. Midlothian, VA: Derwent Books, 1987.

Davis, Steven R. "'...Like Leaves in an Autumn Wind': The 11th Mississippi Infantry in the Army of Northern Virginia," *Civil War Regiments: A Journal of the American Civil War* 2, no. 4 (1992): 269-312.

Davis, William C. *Battle at Bull Run*. Baton Rouge: Louisiana State University Press, 1977.

Dawes, R. R. Letter to J. M. Stone, 1 June, 1876. Quoted in John C. Rietti, *Military Annals of Mississippi*, 35-36. Jackson, MS: Published by the author, 1895.

Dawes, Rufus R. *Service with the Sixth Wisconsin Volunteers.* Dayton: Morningside Bookshop, 1996.

Dunlop, Major W. S. *Lee's Sharpshooters; or, The Forefront of Battle.* Morningside Bookshop (reprint), 1982.

Early, Jubal A., J. William Jones, Robert A. Brock, James P. Smith, Hamilton J. Eckenrode, Douglas Southall Freeman, and Frank E. Vandiver, eds. *Southern Historical Society Papers*, 52 vols., Richmond: Southern Historical Society, 1876-1910.

Foote, Shelby. *The Civil War: A Narrative.* New York: Random House, 1974.

Fox, William F. *Regimental Losses in The American Civil War, 1861-1865.* Augustus S. Brandow, 1898; reprint, Dayton: Morningside House, Inc., 1985.

Hagerty, Edward J. *Collis' Zouaves: The 114th Pennsylvania Volunteers in the Civil War.* Baton Rouge: Louisiana State University Press, 1997.

Hankins, Samuel W. *Simple Story of a Soldier*, Nashville: Confederate Veteran, 1912.

Hennessy, John J. *Return to Bull Run: The Campaign and Battle of Second Manassas.* New York: Simon & Schuster, 1993.

Herdegen, Lance J., and William J. K. Beaudot. *In the Bloody Railroad Cut at Gettysburg.* Dayton: Morningside, 1990.

Hewett, Janet B, Trudeau, Andre, and Bryce A. Suderow, eds. *Supplement to the Official Records of the Union and Confederate Armies.* 12 vols. Wilmington, NC: Broadfoot Publishing Company, 1994-Present.

Horn, Stanley F. *The Army of Tennessee.* Norman: University of Oklahoma Press (paperback reprint of Indianapolis, 1949 edition), 1993.

InfoConcepts, Inc. *The American Civil War Regimental Information System: Volume I -- the Confederates* [database available on diskette]. Albuquerque, NM: InfoConcepts, Inc., 1994-95.

Krick, Robert K. *Lee's Colonels: A Biographical Register of the Field Officers of the Army of Northern Virginia.* Dayton, OH: Morningside, 1992.

_____. "Three Confederate Disasters on Oak Ridge: Failures of Brigade Leadership on the First Day at Gettysburg." *The First Day at Gettysburg*, Kent, OH: The Kent State University Press, 1992, 102-114.

Livermore, Thomas L. *Numbers and Losses in the Civil War in America: 1861-65*. Bloomington, IN: University Press, 1957.

Long, E. B. and Barbara Long. *The Civil War Day by Day*. New York: Da Capo Press, Inc., 1971.

McFarland, Baxter. "Casualties of the Eleventh Mississippi Regiment at Gettysburg," *Confederate Veteran*, XXIV (1916): pp. 410-411.

Madaus, Howard M. Personal Telephone Conversation, May 12, 1998.

Martin, David G. *Gettysburg July 1*. Conshohocken, PA: Combined Books, Inc., 1995.

_____. *The Second Bull Run Campaign: July-August 1862*. Conshohocken, Penn.: Combined Books, Inc., 1997.

Matter, William D. *If It Takes All Summer: The Battle of Spotsylvania*. Chapel Hill, NC: The University of North Carolina Press, 1988.

Miller, Hugh R. *The Great Battle of Manassas*. The Examiner, September 13, 1861.

Murfin, James V. *The Gleam of Bayonets: The Battle of Antietam and Robert E. Lee's Maryland Campaign, September 1862*. Baton Rouge: Louisiana State University Press, 1965.

Murphy, William B. to F. A. Dearborn, 29 June 1900, State Historical Society of Wisconsin, Madison, Wisconsin.

_____. Letter fragment to R. R. Dawes, 1 August, 1892. Madison, WS: State Historical Society of Wisconsin.

_____. Letter to R. R. Dawes, 20 June, 1892. Madison, WS: State Historical Society of Wisconsin.

Priest, John Michael. *Antietam: The Soldiers' Battle*. New York: Oxford University Press, 1989.

_____. *Before Antietam: The Battle for South Mountain*. Shippensburg, Penn.: White Mane Publishing Company, Inc., 1992.

_____. *Nowhere to Run: The Wilderness, May 4th & 5th, 1864*. Shippensburg, Penn.: White Mane Publishing Company, Inc., 1995.

_____. *Victory without Triumph: The Wilderness, May 6th & 7th, 1864*. Shippensburg, Penn. White Mane Publishing Company, Inc., 1996.

Rhea, Gordon C. *The Battle of the Wilderness May 5-6, 1864.* Baton Rouge: Louisiana State University Press, 1994.

_____. *The Battles for Spotsylvania Court House and the Road to Yellow Tavern, May 7-12, 1864.* Baton Rouge: Louisiana State University Press, 1997.

Rietti, John C. *Military Annals of Mississippi.* Jackson, Miss.: Published by the author, 1895.

Rowland, Dunbar. *Military History of Mississippi, 1803-1898.* Spartanburg, SC: Reprint Company, 1978.

Scott, Robert Garth. *Into the Wilderness with the Army of the Potomac.* Bloomington, IN: Indiana University Press, 1988.

Sears, Stephen W. *Chancellorsville.* Boston: Houghton Mifflin Company, 1996.

_____. *Landscape Turned Red: The Battle of Antietam.* Boston: Houghton Mifflin Company, 1983.

_____. *To the Gates of Richmond: The Peninsula Campaign.* New York: Ticknor & Fields, 1992.

Sibley, F. Ray, Jr. *The Confederate Order of Battle: The Army of Northern Virginia*, Volume 1. Shippensburg, Penn.: White Mane Publishing Company, Inc., 1996.

Sifakis, Stewart. *Compendium of the Confederate Armies.* 10 vols. New York: Facts on File, Inc., 1992-95.

Stone, John M. Letter fragment to his mother, undated. Jackson, MS: Mississippi Department of Archives and History, Acc. No. Z26S.

Strain, J. H. "Heroic Henry McPherson," *Confederate Veteran*, XXXI (1923): p. 205.

Tucker, Glenn. *High Tide at Gettysburg.* Dayton, OH. Morningside, 1973.

U. S. War Department, *War of the Rebellion: The Official Records of the Union and Confederate Armies.* 128 vols. Washington, D. C., 1880-1901.

Vairin, A. L. P. Diary. Jackson, MS: Mississippi Department of Archives and History.

Warner, Ezra J. *Generals in Gray: Lives of the Confederate Commanders.* Baton Rouge: Louisiana State University Press, 1959.

Winschel, Terrence J. "Part I: Heavy Was Their Loss: Joe Davis's Brigade at Gettysburg." *The Gettysburg Magazine*, January 1990, 5-14.

_____. "Part II. Heavy Was Their Loss: Joe Davis's Brigade at Gettysburg." *The Gettysburg Magazine*, July 1990, 77-85.

_____. "The Colors Are Shrouded in Mystery." *The Gettysburg Magazine*, January 1992, 77-86.

Wright, Stuart, ed. *Memoirs of Alfred Horatio Belo*. A thesis submitted to the Graduate Faculty of Wake Forest University. Winston-Salem, NC: Wake Forest University, 1980.

About the Author

Why my interest in the Civil War? I suppose that would only be natural for someone who, as a kid, grew up only 30-miles from Shiloh National Military Park. In 1993 however, I discovered my maternal great-grandfather was a member of the 2nd Mississippi Infantry Regiment. That discovery is what finally "got the ball rolling" for me in a serious way. I am still working on a full regimental history by the way, so I will keep you posted on my progress.

I was born and raised in West Tennessee, near where my great- grandfather moved following the Civil War. I served 20 years in both an enlisted and officer capacity in the United States Air Force. At the present time I still work in the defense industry as a systems engineer.

I graduated from the University of Tennessee with a degree in Electrical Engineering. While still in the Air Force, I obtained an MBA from Baldwin-Wallace College. Later, after retiring (and vowing not to allow any of my GI Bill educational benefits to go unused), I obtained a MA in history (with a specialty in Civil War Studies) in 1999 from American Military University.

To see my other published books on Amazon, please go to my author page at amazon.com/author/michaelrbrasher or at my author website, mrbrasher.com. You can also contact me at my e-mail at mrbrasher@yahoo.com.

Also by Michael R. Brasher

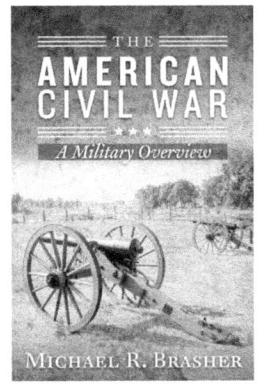 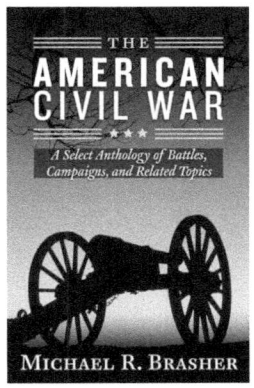 

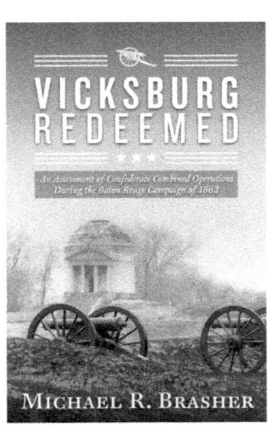  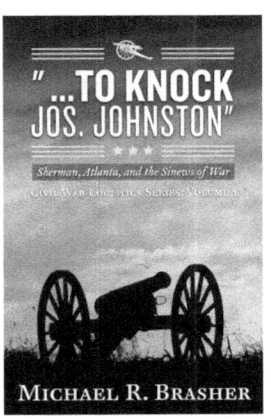